Deschutes
Public Library

P9-AFH-173

RUSSIA

ALSO BY ANTONY BEEVOR

Crete 1941: The Battle and the Resistance

Paris After the Liberation 1944–1949 (with Artemis Cooper)

Stalingrad

The Fall of Berlin 1945

The Mystery of Olga Chekhova

A Writer at War: Vasily Grossman with the
Red Army 1941–1945 (ed. with Lyuba Vinogradova)

The Battle for Spain: The Spanish Civil War 1936–1939

D-Day: The Battle for Normandy

The Second World War

Ardennes 1944: The Battle of the Bulge

The Battle of Arnhem: The Deadliest Airborne
Operation of World War II

RUSSIA

Revolution and Civil War
1917–1921

ANTONY BEEVOR

VIKING

VIKING
An imprint of Penguin Random House LLC
penguinrandomhouse.com

First published in hardcover in Great Britain by Weidenfeld & Nicolson,
an imprint of Hachette UK Limited, London, in 2022

First North American edition published by Viking, 2022

Copyright © 2022 by Ocito Ltd
Penguin Random House supports copyright. Copyright fuels creativity,
encourages diverse voices, promotes free speech, and creates a vibrant
culture. Thank you for buying an authorized edition of this book and
for complying with copyright laws by not reproducing, scanning, or
distributing any part of it in any form without permission. You are
supporting writers and allowing Penguin Random House to continue to
publish books for every reader.

Illustration credits can be found on pp. xi–xiii

LIBRARY OF CONGRESS CATALOGING-IN-PUBLICATION DATA
Names: Beevor, Antony, 1946– author.
Title: Russia : revolution and civil war, 1917–1921 / Antony Beevor.
Description: First North American edition. | New York : Viking, [2022] |
Includes bibliographical references and index.
Identifiers: LCCN 2022032111 (print) | LCCN 2022032112 (ebook) |
ISBN 9780593493878 (hardcover) | ISBN 9780593493885 (ebook)
Classification: LCC DK265 .B415 2022 (print) | LCC DK265 (ebook) |
DDC 947.084/1—dc23/eng/20220706
LC record available at https://lccn.loc.gov/2022032111
LC ebook record available at https://lccn.loc.gov/2022032112

Printed in the United States of America
3   5   7   9   10   8   6   4   2

Set in Sabon LT Std

For Lyuba Vinogradova

CONTENTS

PART FOUR: 1920

MAPS

ILLUSTRATIONS

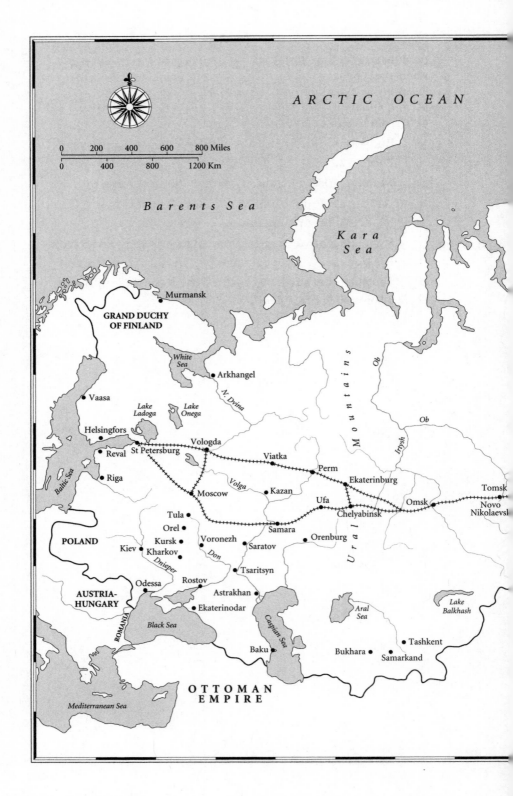

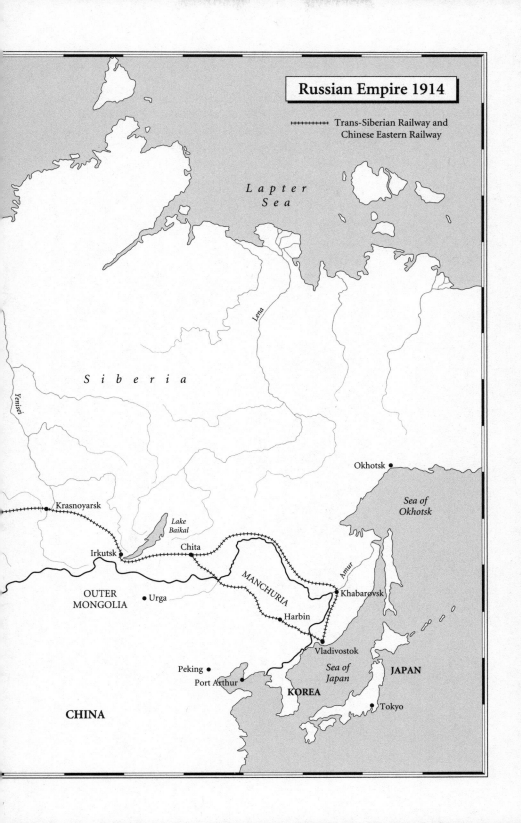

Russian Empire 1914

┼┼┼┼┼┼┼┼ Trans-Siberian Railway and
Chinese Eastern Railway

L a p t e r
S e a

Lena

S i b e r i a

Yenisei

Okhotsk ●

Sea of
Okhotsk

Krasnoyarsk ●

Lake
Baikal

Irkutsk ● Chita ●

MANCHURIA

Amur

Khabarøvsk ●

OUTER
MONGOLIA   ● Urga

Harbin ●

Vladivostok ●

Peking ●

Port Arthur ●

Sea of
Japan

JAPAN

KOREA

CHINA

● Tokyo

FOREWORD

In January 1902, the Duke of Marlborough wrote to his first cousin Winston Churchill, describing a court ball he had attended in St Petersburg. Marlborough was astonished by the anachronistic grandeur in which the Tsar of All the Russias appeared to be trapped. He described Nicholas II as a 'nice and amiable man who tries to play the proper part of an autocrat'.

The reception was worthy of Versailles in all its ostentatious glory. 'Supper was served for nearly three thousand people. The effect of this spectacle of so many people sitting down at the same time is difficult to describe. The scale on which it is carried out can only be estimated when I remind you that there were some two thousand servants in all to wait upon the guests, including Cossacks, Mamelukes and runners [footmen] like those we have heard of in eighteenth century England with huge ostrich-feather hats on their heads. A regimental band is stationed in every room, so as to play the national anthem wherever the Czar may go . . . There was another guard of honour whose duty apparently was to hold their swords at attention for five consecutive hours.'

When Marlborough's young wife, Consuelo Vanderbilt, asked the Tsar at a subsequent dinner about the possibility of introducing democratic government in Russia, he replied: 'We are two hundred years behind Europe in the development of our national political institutions. Russia is still more Asiatic than European and must therefore be governed by an autocratic government.'

Marlborough was also struck by the idiosyncrasies of the Guards regiments which dominated the military system. 'The Grand Duke Vladimir, who is the head of a portion of the army, has the recruits brought up before him. Those men who possess snub noses go into the Pavlovsky Regiment, which was created by the Emperor Paul, who possessed a snub nose.'

Like the court, the Imperial Russian Army was ossified by archaic etiquette, protocol and bureaucracy. Captain Archie Wavell, the future field marshal but then a young officer in the Black Watch, observed when on attachment there just before the First World War that even officers of field rank were afraid of showing initiative. 'An example of the conservatism of the Russian Army,' he added, 'was their custom of invariably carrying the bayonet fixed on the rifle at all times.' This dated back to an order of Marshal Suvorov in the late eighteenth century after a Russian column was surprised in an ambush and wiped out.

Russian officers regarded it as disgraceful ever to be seen out of uniform. A dragoon captain who quizzed Wavell on the customs of the British Army could not believe that their officers wore civilian clothes off duty and did not carry swords in public. He jumped to his feet, scandalised. 'But people will not be afraid of you,' he blurted out. A Tsarist officer had the right to punch any of his soldiers in the face as a summary punishment.

Wavell was not surprised that the Russian intelligentsia regarded their rulers 'as bureaucratic oppressors; they mistrusted the police and despised the army'. After the humiliating disasters of the Russo–Japanese War of 1904–5 and the massacre of Father Georgy Gapon's peaceful protest march to the Winter Palace in January 1905, respect for the regime and the armed forces had disintegrated. 'Russia swung to the left overnight,' wrote Nadezhda Lokhvitskaya, under her *nom de plume* of 'Teffi'. 'There was unrest among the students, there were strikes among the workers. Even old generals could be heard snorting about the disgraceful way the country was being run and making sharp criticisms of the Tsar himself.'

In exchange for its great privileges, the nobility was supposed to provide its sons as officers for the army and the bureaucracy in St Petersburg. The 30,000 landowners were meanwhile expected to maintain order over the countryside through local 'land captains'.

The liberation of the serfs in 1861 had done little to improve their desperate lot. 'Our peasantry lives in horrible conditions, lacking properly organised medical care,' wrote Maksim Gorky. 'Half of all peasant children die of various diseases before the age of five. Almost all the women in the village suffer from women's diseases. The villages are rotting with syphilis; the villages have sunk into destitution, ignorance and savagery.' The women also suffered from the violence of their men, usually when drunk.

Any idea of the sturdy Russian peasant forming part of an irresistible military steamroller was an illusion. Roughly three out of four young peasants were rejected in peacetime on the grounds of ill health. Officers complained of the quality of conscripts arriving during the First World War. In the Second Army, a report stated, 'It is deplorable and quite common that lower ranks inflict wounds on themselves to avoid combat. There are also a lot of cases of surrendering to the enemy.' It described them as 'just ordinary muzhiks . . . They stare in front of them in an indifferent, stupid and gloomy way. They are not in the habit of looking back cheerfully and merrily into their commander's eyes.' Evidently, the Russian peasant in uniform adopted the tactic which the British Army used to define as 'dumb insolence'.

Even enlightened members of the gentry and aristocracy feared the 'dark masses' and their occasional explosions of terrifying violence, like that of 1773 led by Yemelyan Pugachev. Aleksandr Pushkin described it as 'Russian revolt, senseless and merciless'. In the wave of unrest and manor-burnings in 1905 which followed the disasters of the Japanese war, the only hope of landowners was to appeal to the local governor to call out troops from one of the many garrison towns.

Karl Marx's notorious remark in the Communist Manifesto about 'the idiocy of rural life', with its implication of credulity, apathy and submission, was also true beyond the peasant village. Small provincial towns could be almost as stultifying. Satirists such as Saltykov-Shchedrin and Gogol peered beneath the murky surface of the stagnant pond. It was Saltykov, ironically a favourite author of Lenin, who also invoked 'the devastating effect of legalised slavery upon the human psyche', a phenomenon common to both Tsarist and Soviet eras. Leon Trotsky blamed the mental straitjacket of the Orthodox Church. He argued that revolution could never come until the people broke with 'the icons and cockroaches' of Holy Russia.

Attempts at land reform achieved results only in certain areas. Unlike that great magnate of the nineteenth century, Count Dmitry Sheremetev, who owned 1.9 million acres (763,000 hectares) with approximately 300,000 serfs, most estates were small and impoverished. Even if they had wanted to, very few landowners could afford to improve housing conditions or introduce the most basic form of mechanisation. Instead, many were compelled to sell or mortgage their properties. Relations became increasingly artificial and tense. The poorer peasants remained victims of illiteracy, which meant that they were exploited by both village elders and corn merchants, and also mistreated by many landowners, still resentful of their loss of power. As a result, obsequious tenants, bowing to their noble masters, would take any opportunity to cheat them as soon as their backs were turned.

Migration to the cities accelerated the growth of the urban working class, the proletariat which Marxists saw as the vanguard of the revolution. From little more than a million inhabitants at the turn of the century, the population of St Petersburg rose to more than 3 million by the end of 1916. Conditions in factories were appalling and dangerous. Workers were regarded as expendable by the owners since so many peasants were waiting to take their place. There was no right to strike, and no compensation for dismissal. In the case of any dispute, the police always sided with the factory owners. Many saw it as serfdom in the city. The workers slept in galleried barracks, doss-houses and tenements amid squalor and disease. 'There are no sewage systems in the cities,' wrote Gorky, 'there are no flues in factory chimneys; the open ground has been poisoned by the miasma of rotting refuse, the air – by smoke and dust.' In such overcrowded conditions, tuberculosis and venereal diseases spread alongside occasional epidemics of cholera and typhus. Life expectancy was as low as in the poorest villages. The only freedom lay in the lowest circle of hell inhabited by the lumpen proletariat of the unemployed – a subterranean world of child prostitution, petty theft and drunken fights, an existence worse than anything depicted by Dickens, Hugo or Zola. The only disaster which could make life even worse for the poor in Russia was a major European conflict.

Part One

—————

1912–1917

1

The Suicide of Europe
1912–1916

The pace of industrial growth in Russia before the First World War produced a heady over-confidence among its ruling classes. The disastrous conflict with Japan just under a decade before was forgotten. The war party in St Petersburg became more vociferous, demanding an attack on Turkey after it closed the Dardanelles in 1912. Even the formerly cautious foreign minister, Sergei Sazonov, was outraged at the way Russia had been treated by the German and Austro-Hungarian Empires over the First Balkan War. So, when Vienna issued its ultimatum to Serbia following the assassination in June 1914 of the Archduke Franz Ferdinand in Sarajevo, Sazonov asked the chief of the general staff to prepare the army for war. He told the Tsar that if Russia failed to support its fellow Slavs in Serbia, it would constitute a fatal humiliation. Nicholas II felt obliged to concede to the calls for the first stage of partial mobilisation, but then army commanders insisted that if Russia mobilised against the Austro-Hungarian armies, Russian forces would have to mobilise all along the central and northern fronts against the Germans.

The imperial family's counsellor and faith healer, Grigory Rasputin, was absent from the capital. That fateful summer, he had returned home to Siberia, where he received news of the rush to war in a telegram from the Tsarina. He set out immediately to send a reply to advise the Tsar to resist the pressure, but a peasant woman waylaid him, stabbing him in the stomach. She was a follower of Iliodor, a former priest who had turned against him, denouncing him as a lecher and a false prophet. Rasputin nearly died and was incapacitated in hospital. When he regained consciousness and heard that mobilisation had been ordered, he insisted on sending the telegram which warned that war would destroy both Russia and the Romanovs. This final chance of persuading the Tsar to stand up against the belligerents all around him arrived too late, but it would probably have made little difference.

The fear of the Russian general staff that the Central Powers could mobilise more rapidly was not the main factor in the escalation to war. That had come from the Austrian determination to crush Serbia before the major European powers could step in. Germany refused to stop them. General Helmuth von Moltke, the chief of the German general staff, even urged the Austrians to ignore any plea for moderation from his own government and push on with their attack. Diplomacy and royal connections stood little chance. War was indeed too important to be left to the generals, as the French prime minister Georges Clemenceau was soon to observe.

Once war had been declared, things could only go from bad to worse for the 'grey mass' of Russian peasant-soldiers. Altogether 15,300,000 men would be called up into the army and navy. After the defeat at the Battle of Tannenberg and then the infamous 'Great Retreat' in 1915, following the German victory of Gorlice-Tarnów (just southeast of Kraków), bitterness and suspicion of treason at court set in among officers as well as soldiers. Talk of 'the German stranglehold' soon began, partly because so many generals had names of Teutonic or Scandinavian origin. But most cursed the German Tsarina and her *camarilla* dominated by their *éminence grise*, Rasputin. The dissolute monk interfered with shameless corruption in appointments once the Tsar unwisely decided to assume the supreme command of the armies at the *Stavka*, the supreme headquarters in Mogilev.

Trench life for Russian soldiers along the whole front running through the Baltic provinces, Poland, Belarus, Galicia and Romania was an inhuman experience. 'Having dug themselves into the ground,' wrote Maksim Gorky, 'they live in rain and snow, in filth, in cramped conditions; they are being worn out by disease and eaten by vermin; they live like beasts.' Desperately short of ammunition, many lacked boots and had to resort to bast shoes made from birch bark. Casualty clearing stations at the front were almost as primitive as in the Crimean War.

Attempts to modernise failed disastrously. 'The most recent technological development has finally reached us,' Vasily Kravkov, a senior doctor on the staff, wrote bitterly in his diary. 'That is to say 25,000 gas masks for our corps. They had been tested by the supreme commission chaired by our top "pasha", the Duke of Oldenburg. I carried out a sort of test by putting gas masks on my medical orderlies. Two minutes later they started to suffocate. And we are supposed to equip everyone in the trenches with that stuff!'

Army censorship departments could have had little illusion about the state of morale at the front on reading soldiers' letters home. Many complained of being hopelessly outgunned by the German artillery and of the utterly callous attitude of officers towards them. Men were either brutalised or traumatised by what they saw. 'Corpses are still lying there,' wrote one in a letter. 'Ravens have already eaten their eyes and rats are crawling on the bodies. Oh my God, this terrible sight can neither be described or imagined.'

Another wrote about a mass grave which officers had ordered them to dig and fill with their own dead. 'We collected the bodies from the battlefield, dug a hole that was 30 fathoms long and 4 fathoms deep. We laid them in there, but as it was late, we covered half of the hole with earth and left the other half until the morning. We placed a sentry and it turned out that one of the dead clambered out of the hole at night and was found sitting on the edge of the grave, while some others had been turning, because they hadn't been killed, just wounded and shocked by explosions of heavy shells. This happens quite often.'

Intense resentment was caused by the contrast in conditions between officers and men. Many officers retired each night to the warmth and relative comfort of peasant *izbas* behind the front, while their soldiers and sergeants were left in the cold and squalor of the trenches. 'The ordinary soldier leading the attack for the Motherland is paid 75 kopecks [a month],' one conscript wrote home. 'The company commander coming on behind is paid 400 roubles, and the regimental commander who is even further back gets a thousand roubles ... Some have nice dishes and alcohol and prostitutes under the flag of the Red Cross, while the others are starving.'

The idea that Red Cross nurses were there for the sexual convenience of officers alone was almost obsessive, yet there was a basis of truth. Dr Kravkov, the head of medical services for a whole army corps, recorded how a colleague of his was dismissed. 'It was very simple. The doctor displayed too much tact and did not succumb to the demands of the headquarters clique to set up a brothel using his nurses ... This was not unfamiliar to me. I saw this at the Tenth Army and it was one of the reasons for my escape from there.'

Officers offered hard-up women students in Odessa hundreds of roubles for nude pictures of themselves: 'Please write to me if you are ready to be photographed one more time, with more details,' wrote one young officer. He then told her that if she visited the regiment she could earn up to a thousand roubles.

While officers cavorted, ordinary soldiers were not allowed to see their wives, even in areas far behind the front. Evdokiya Merkulova, the illiterate young wife of a Cossack in the 9th Independent Don Sotnia did not know the regulations and went to visit her husband in early December 1916. She had the courage to make a formal complaint afterwards about her treatment by his squadron commander. 'Commander of the *sotnia* Mikhail Rysakov soon learned about my arrival,' her dictated testimony ran. 'I don't know why, but on 5 December he ordered the *sotnia* to form up on parade and made me lie face down in front of them. Two Cossacks were ordered to roll up my skirt and undershirt and hold my arms and legs. The commander ordered my husband to whip me fifteen times on my naked body. He personally controlled the execution of the punishment and threatened my husband, saying that the strokes should be applied with full strength, and on the skin rather than clothes. My husband was afraid of his chief and administered bloody strokes that are still healing. I was then sent back across the Don with an escort.'

As cannon-fodder, the peasant-soldier hated the war, the mud, the lice, the bad food and the scurvy. Dr Kravkov despaired of their diet. 'Another delivery of foodstuffs has arrived, this time from Orenburg,' he noted in his diary. 'It consisted of 1,000 poods* of hams and sausage, all of it rotten! The whole of our mother Russia is rotting away.'

The rainy season came in October 1916 with a vengeance which disturbed Kravkov. 'Dr Tolchenov, whom I had dispatched to the positions to investigate the sanitary conditions, gave a hair-raising report on the horrible situation in which our unfortunate soldiers are living: in mud that reaches up to their waist, with no shelter from bad weather, with no warm clothes, hot food or tea.' Two weeks later he wrote: 'We received reinforcements, boys that are green behind the ears. They were sent into a bayonet attack on the following day . . . It was a stunning scene when many of them, who did not want to die, cried out in despair: "Mama!".' The military authorities suppressed news of mutinies which were ruthlessly put down.

---

* One pood was just over sixteen kilograms.

That winter in Petrograd, criticism of the government did not come just from liberals and the Left. Arch-conservatives, such as the politician Vasily Shulgin, were appalled by the irresponsibility of the rich, indifferent to the fact that Russian casualties were running at twice the rate of their German and Austro-Hungarian enemies. 'And here we are,' he wrote bitterly, 'dancing the "last tango" on the breastworks of trenches choked with corpses.' Shulgin was infuriated by the rumours and conspiracy theories which ran around the capital's salons, especially the 'chatter about treason'. He blamed the leader of the Kadet Party, Pavel Milyukov, for his sensational speech when the State Duma reconvened on 1 November.* Milyukov's savage attacks on the Tsar's ministers astonished those present because he was usually so moderate. Now, he openly denounced 'occult forces fighting for the benefit of Germany'. To great cheers, after each example of incompetence he hammered in the rhetorical question: 'And what is this? Stupidity or treason?'

The pervasive corruption in the capital shocked idealistic young officers at the front. 'Everyone knows that all kinds of swindlers at the establishment of Grand Duchess Maria Pavlovna arrange safe positions in exchange for bribes,' a young cavalry officer in the Seventh Army wrote to his fiancée, who wanted to secure a post for him in the rear. 'But I implore you to not bribe anyone. I want to live and die a nobleman.'

Even firm supporters of the monarchy despaired. The Tsar's obstinacy stemmed almost entirely from a weak nature. Against all advice, he had insisted on taking over as supreme commander from his cousin, the immensely tall Grand Duke Nikolai Nikolaevich, after the disastrous retreats of 1915. Wavell considered the Grand Duke 'the handsomest and most impressive man I have ever met. He had no great brain power or book knowledge but was full of common sense and character.' His nephew, Nicholas II, unfortunately lacked both qualities. 'Autocracy without an autocrat is a terrible thing,' observed Shulgin.

One of the main reasons the Tsar immersed himself at the *Stavka* in Mogilev was that he preferred to be surrounded by loyal officers rather

---

* The Kadet, or Constitutional Democratic (KD) Party was a liberal centrist group including both moderate monarchists and republicans. It was founded by Milyukov in 1905 and mainly supported by academics, lawyers and the more enlightened middle class, including Jews, because it believed in Jewish emancipation.

than critical politicians. He left the administration of the country to the Tsarina and Rasputin and resolutely refused to appoint a government of ministers from the Duma. Yet his presence at the Mogilev headquarters remained purely symbolic and his entourage made sure that any tours of the front were carefully managed.

'General Dolgov's chief of staff told us at dinner, without a trace of irony, about the preparations for the Tsar's visit,' Dr Kravkov noted in his diary. 'All the soldiers were brought back from the trenches, and the night was spent dressing them in brand-new uniforms and equipment. All the artillery was ordered to open fire at the moment the royal visit began, and as he put it, "a true battle scene was staged". The Tsar was happy and thanked them all, and our brave warrior was decorated with the St. George's Cross for his successful staging.'

In that winter of 1916, nobody at Mogilev dared tell the Tsar of the rumours in Petrograd. Revolutionary pamphlets about Rasputin had started to appear, such as 'The Adventures of Grishka', hinting at orgies with the Tsarina and even her daughters. These pornographic fantasies were reminiscent of those other caricatures more than a century earlier in Paris against Marie Antoinette and the Princesse de Lamballe. Inevitably, such grotesque stories turned Rasputin, the supposed peasant-debaucher of grandees, into something of a folk hero.

Rasputin's murder on 17 December by Prince Feliks Yusupov, Grand Duke Dmitry Pavlovich and Vladimir Purishkevich, the leader of the anti-Semitic Black Hundreds,* increased the impression of aristocratic corruption in the capital. The idea of Yusupov using his wife Irina, the beautiful niece of the Tsar, as bait for the lecherous monk added a salacious twist to the drama. The public's imagination was gripped above all by the difficulties the conspirators had in killing Rasputin, with poisoned cakes and several revolver shots, then finally disposing of his huge body through an ice hole below a bridge so that it was not found for two days.

The profound cynicism which developed in the rear created a dangerous apathy. An officer called Fedulenko, back from the front, was invited by his colonel to a lunch. 'Two Guards officers were sitting next to us,' he recorded. 'They began to talk about Rasputin; I was shocked by their talk.' They repeated gossip about the Tsarina and

---

* The Black Hundreds were the reactionary monarchist, nationalistic and anti-Semitic groups supported by Nicholas II.

Rasputin and the Tsar and Tsarina.

Prince and Princess Yusupov.

Rasputin and said that the Tsar was a weakling. 'As I was returning to Oranienbaum with the colonel afterwards, I asked why such a filthy thing was allowed, why these two young men who were shaming their Emperor had not been stopped. They had been talking in Russian right in front of the servants who could understand them.' The colonel made a gesture of resignation with his hand. 'Ah,' he said. 'The downfall is already beginning. A horrible time lies ahead.' Dr Kravkov had no doubts at all. 'Whatever the outcome of the war, there is going to be a revolution.'

2

The February Revolution
January–March 1917

The drift towards revolution was clear to all except the wilfully blind. The only question was whether it would come during the war or just after the end. General Mikhail Alekseev, the chief of staff, had submitted a report to the Tsar, recommending that factories and their workers should be moved from the capital. Nicholas II wrote on the report, which had been typed on the special 'Tsar's own' blue paper at the supreme headquarters: 'The current situation does not justify taking this measure, which can only cause panic and unrest in the rear.' Alekseev's simplistic solution was hardly practicable, with more than 300,000 industrial workers to be rehoused from Petrograd, but neither he nor the Tsar foresaw then that their own troops in the capital posed a similar danger.

As a result of the huge losses during the war so far, many ensigns in the reserve were anti-monarchist and had nothing in common with the pre-war army. 'Most of them were former university students,' a regular officer noted. 'There were lots of young lawyers. The brigade turned into a student hostel, with rallies, resolutions and protests. They regarded the professional officer as some kind of pre-historic animal.' In fact, the majority of the ensigns, or *praporshchiki*, were promoted from the ranks and came from *petit bourgeois* backgrounds. If anything, this would have increased their resentment towards the arrogance of the traditional officer.

The well informed in Petrograd did not dismiss the danger of a major mutiny in the capital. At a dinner given by a prince's mistress, grand dukes, senior officers and the French ambassador Maurice Paléologue discussed which Guards regiments in the capital could be counted on to remain loyal. Optimism was in short supply that evening. 'To finish we drank to the preservation of Holy Russia,' the ambassador noted in his diary.

Next day, Paléologue was dejected but unsurprised to hear how the Tsarina repulsed every attempt to make her see the existential threat to the monarchy. 'On the contrary,' she had replied to the Grand Duchess Victoria Feodorovna, 'I now have the great pleasure of knowing that the whole of Russia, the true Russia, the Russia of humble folk and peasants, is with me.' This belief was based on obsequious letters, some perhaps faked, which were passed to her daily by the Okhrana secret police on the orders of the minister of the interior, Aleksandr Protopopov. Protopopov, appointed on Rasputin's recommendation, was said to be mentally unstable as a result of advanced syphilis.

Even the Tsarina's own sister, the abbess of the Martha and Mary Convent in Moscow, was ordered to leave their presence by the imperial couple as soon as she mentioned 'the growing exasperation in Moscow'. Members of the extended Romanov family were appalled by this refusal to see what was happening. They gathered to discuss a common approach to the Tsar and Tsarina in a joint letter.

On Russian New Year's Eve, the tall and elegant British ambassador Sir George Buchanan went to see the Tsar. His Imperial Majesty evidently had a clear idea of what Buchanan intended to say. Instead of inviting him into his study to sit and smoke together according to their usual routine, he received him standing stiffly in the audience chamber.

Sir George opened by expressing how concerned King George V and the British government were at the situation in Russia. He then asked if he might speak frankly. 'I am listening,' the Tsar answered curtly. Buchanan was indeed frank. He spoke of the chaotic administration of the war which had led to such massive casualties. He urged that a politician from the Duma should head the government rather than a royal appointee. The only chance for the regime to survive was 'to break down the barrier that separates you from your people and to regain their confidence'. The Tsar stiffened. 'You say, ambassador, that I must earn the confidence of my people. Is it not up to my people to earn my confidence?'* Buchanan, albeit with exquisite politeness,

---

* Buchanan recounted his interview with the Tsar to his close colleague Paléologue immediately afterwards. It is striking that Paléologue's version, recorded in his diary, is much more frigid and ends with the Tsar dismissing Buchanan with finality: 'Adieu, Monsieur l'Ambassadeur.' Buchanan's much later account in his memoirs ends rather less convincingly with heartfelt thanks and a very warm, emotional handshake. The Tsar made no mention of the meeting in his private diary, but then

even raised the question of enemy agents and Germanophile influences around the Tsarina. He said that it was his duty to 'warn your Majesty of the abyss that lies ahead of you'. Buchanan suddenly noticed that the door to the private apartments was ajar. He sensed that the Tsarina was listening to every word.

In that frozen Petrograd January, dancing under the volcano continued. At a fashionable restaurant the next night, Paléologue saw a well-known divorcée at a nearby table surrounded by no less than three young officers of the Tsar's Chevalier Guards. She had just been released from arrest for suspected complicity in the murder of Rasputin. When asked by the police for the key to her desk, she had replied that they would find only love letters inside. 'Every evening, or rather every night,' the ambassador wrote in his diary, 'it is partying until dawn: theatre, ballet, supper, gypsies, tango, Champagne.'

While many of the rich indulged themselves in the capital as if the war did not exist, bread shortages contributed to unrest in the poorer districts of Petrograd. 'Queues began,' a naval cadet recorded. 'If there was a queue of about ten and the baker did not open the stall, bricks would start flying, and there would be the sound of broken glass. Cossack patrols that arrived in order to maintain appearances just laughed at this.'

Russia was not then short of grain. The problem was the already over-stretched railway system, struggling amid savage frosts and heavy snow falls in this harsh start to the year. Some 57,000 wagons could not be moved and many locomotives had frozen solid. Food and fuel prices had also risen much faster than wages. Yet 1917 had started with fewer strikes than the year before. Major General Konstantin Globachev, the head of the Okhrana, claimed that the regime was fortunate that industrial action had not been coordinated. 'We never faced a general strike,' he wrote. He would not have to wait long.

Globachev had to deal with the increasingly unstable minister of the interior, Aleksandr Protopopov, who was superstitious and completely under the influence of the Tsarina. Protopopov, however, had not been able to persuade Rasputin the month before to avoid the deadly ambush awaiting him in the Yusupov Palace. In Petrograd, Protopopov

he seldom bothered to record conversations with ambassadors.

was a figure of ridicule. Since the Corps of Gendarmes came under his ministry, he had a gendarmerie uniform made, although with civil service shoulder boards. When he appeared at the Duma dressed in this concoction, it provoked a roar of laughter.

Protopopov could not understand the difference between political parties and revolutionary groups in the capital, despite attempts by his subordinates to explain them. He also had to be reminded about the approaching anniversary of Bloody Sunday on 9 January, a significant event in the left-wing calendar which would be marked by a major strike. It commemorated the day when Father Georgy Gapon's peaceful march in 1905 to present a petition for reform suffered a massacre by heavy rifle fire.

The Okhrana was also concerned about the loyalty of the huge Petrograd garrison, totalling some 180,000 men. Protopopov agreed to hold a meeting with the military commanders of the Petrograd military district, General Khabalov, an officer incapable of thinking clearly, and Lieutenant General Chebykin, who had little idea of what his responsibilities were. When Globachev asked whether the troops were loyal, Chebykin, the head of reserve units, replied, 'I am certain that they are,' when evidently he had no idea at all.

Globachev was well aware of the shortage of experienced officers and NCOs. Most of the good ones had been killed or crippled at the front. The reserve battalions of the Guard in Petrograd were suffering from what the writer Viktor Shklovsky called 'the dull despair and resentment' of barrack life. The Petrograd soldier of 1917 'was either a dissatisfied peasant or a dissatisfied city-dweller'. They found themselves desperately overcrowded in barracks which were 'simply brick pens', whose trademark was 'the sour smell of servitude'.

Globachev prepared a report on the mood of soldiers in the Petrograd garrison. A copy was passed to the *Stavka*. General Alekseev agreed to replace some of the units with a Guards cavalry corps, but this was never implemented because of a German offensive on the Romanian front. To make matters worse, temperatures during February had fallen further, down to minus 20 degrees. Fuel shortages in Petrograd prompted rumours that bread rationing was about to be introduced. This produced panic buying, with many women waiting in the hard frosts in queues which were never satisfied. The shortage of fuel also meant that workers had been laid off without pay from many factories, including the giant Putilov works, which closed its gates on 21 February.

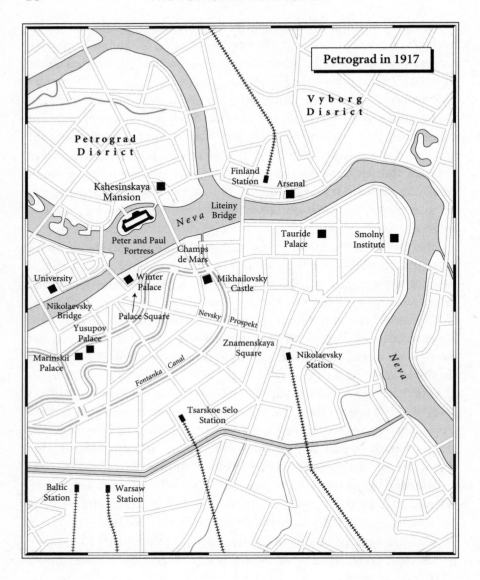

On Wednesday 22 February, having spent just over two months at the Alexander Palace in Tsarskoe Selo, Nicholas II left once again for the *Stavka* at Mogilev in Belarus. In the imperial train he read a French edition of Caesar's Gallic Wars. On several occasions over the last few weeks, he had rejected the attempts by Mikhail Rodzyanko, the chairman of the State Duma, to persuade him to appoint ministers from the Progressive Bloc to head off revolt. The preposterous Protopopov had assured him once again that the capital was in safe hands.

The very next day, 23 February, was International Women's Day, and this marked the start of the revolutionary process. A sudden change in the weather had brought sunshine, so the streets of Petrograd were even more crowded after the weeks of bitter cold and dark skies. Planned in advance, there were several different women's groups involved. Some were protesting over food shortages and chanted 'Bread! Bread! Bread!' but there was also the Russian League for Women's Equal Rights assembling in Znamenskaya Square. The struggle for women's suffrage in Russia had already been going on for nine years yet within four weeks, following a huge demonstration by nearly 40,000 women, the future Provisional Government would agree to votes for women. This was ahead of Britain and the United States and twenty-seven years before French women received the right to vote.

The two largest processions on 23 February headed for the Nevsky Prospekt from different directions. Although there were some minor disturbances with tram windows smashed, the mounted Cossack detachments and the detested police in their black uniforms seemed to have the situation under control. Yet Globachev's Okhrana noted a change of attitude among the Cossacks. They appeared to be avoiding confrontation, which was uncharacteristic. Some soldiers challenged a group of Cossacks being fed in their barracks. 'Are you going to whip and shoot workers and those soldiers that join the masses, like you did in 1905?' They were astonished by the answer. 'The answer stunned us: "No! 1905 will never happen again! We will not go against the workers. For the sake of what? For this lentil soup and rotten herring?" they said, gesturing with disgust at their bowls.'

On Friday 24 February, the mood was different. More than 150,000 men and women workers, some say close to 200,000, came out on strike and shops were boarded up. Ten thousand demonstrators from the Vyborg district assembled on the northern bank of the Neva, to find that the authorities had barricaded the bridges. Since the river was frozen, many crossed over the ice to bypass the Cossack and police pickets. The most audacious confronted the police lines. Some ducked low or scrambled through under the bellies of the Cossacks' little ponies. They had seen that the Cossacks did not have their lethal *nagaika* whips made from bull-hide.

Sergei Prokofiev, the composer, made notes in his diary that day. 'There was a certain accumulation of people on the Anichkov Bridge, mostly workers who were wearing short jackets and high boots. Cavalcades of Cossacks were passing, each group consisting of about ten Cossacks, armed with lances . . . I crossed the Anichkov Bridge and headed towards Liteiny. This was the centre of the rally. There were masses of workers there, the street was completely jammed by this crowd of people . . . As for the Cossacks, they were pushing the crowd very gently with their horses. At times they got up on to the sidewalk and chased away the onlookers if there were too many of them . . . A woman with a stupid face who completely missed the idea of the moment, urged people to "Beat up the Yids", while a worker tried to explain to her very intelligently about the objectives of his movement, evidently wasting his eloquence.'

The next day the crowds, encouraged by the hesitant reaction of the forces of law and order, were even larger and this time more aggressive. Bakeries were stormed and looted in some places. The more radical workers carried red banners with slogans attacking the 'German Woman' – the Tsarina. Workers and students sang the 'Marseillaise', a rather more lugubrious version than the lyrical violence of the French original. They also chanted 'Down with the Tsar!' and 'Down with the war!' and pelted the police with lumps of ice.

Comte Louis de Robien, one of Paléologue's young diplomats, had watched a crowd crossing the frozen river from the Vyborg district of Petrograd. He then spotted a detachment of Cossacks cantering along the embankment to head them off. 'They are very picturesque,' he noted in his diary, 'with their little horses, a bundle of hay in a net attached to the saddle and armed with a lance and a carbine.'

Robien clearly found the spectacle rather exciting and even romantic. He described the Tsarist mounted police as 'very chic with their beautiful horses, black capes with a red braid and flat astrakhan hats with a black plume'. Yet the police, known as 'pharaohs', were hated even more than the Cossacks, partly because they were exempt from service at the front. Not long afterwards, Robien saw infantry lined up in ranks in front of the Kazan Cathedral as crowds approached with red flags and banners. The police pushed back the onlookers as a mounted detachment formed up, probably from the 9th Cavalry. 'The charge was carried out with a great deal of brio,' he wrote. 'The cavalry burst out of the Kazan Square, galloping with drawn swords into the Nevsky [Prospekt] to meet the demonstrators.' Robien had no idea that the first case of mutiny had just taken place in the garrison. Soldiers of the Pavlovsky Guards Regiment had refused to obey their commander and mortally wounded him. The instigators were arrested and sent for court martial.

Although reports came in of looted bakeries, the Tsarina was unconcerned. 'The army is loyal,' she declared, 'and can be counted on.' Nobody told her about the change of heart among the supposedly loyal Cossack squadrons. Vladimir Zenzinov, a Socialist Revolutionary lawyer, recorded that 'Cossacks were riding among the crowd with rifles raised up in the air, shouting that they will not shoot at civilians, that they are on the side of the people . . . And the crowd greeted them shouting: "*Urrra!* Long live the Cossacks!".'

The first civilian deaths also occurred that afternoon when a detachment of the 9th Cavalry panicked and opened fire on the Nevsky Prospekt. 'I saw my first dead man,' the future writer Vladimir Nabokov recorded. 'He was being carried away on a stretcher, and from one dangling leg an ill-shod comrade kept trying to pull off the boot despite pushes and punches from the stretcher-men.' There were also clashes when a large crowd reached Znamensky Square, which was dominated by the massive equestrian statue of Alexander III, derided as 'the Hippopotamus'. They came up against a company of the Volynsky Guards Regiment. As darkness fell, a Cossack was said to have killed a policeman who had attacked a demonstrator. Some eyewitnesses say he cut him down with his sabre, others that he shot him. Word of this significant event spread rapidly.

Yet many people, including even some Bolsheviks, still thought they were witnessing a protest over food which would blow over as soon as sufficient bread was distributed. Protopopov and General Khabalov in their reports to the Tsar at Mogilev mentioned the scope of the unrest but claimed that the situation was under control. The Tsar, even though he did not mention it in his diary, ordered Khabalov to put an immediate stop to the disorders in the capital. Khabalov was more than uneasy. Opening fire on large crowds was virtually a declaration of war on the civil population. There would be no chance after that of the protests dwindling away. It apparently never occurred to the Tsar that his order would force his own soldiers to choose sides. Protopopov sought the advice of the dead Rasputin in a séance. That night the authorities lost the Vyborg district. Police stations were besieged and set on fire.

On the Sunday morning 26 February, another cold clear day, crowds of workers again swarmed over the Neva across the ice. They ripped down the posters signed by General Khabalov which announced that demonstrations were forbidden, troops had been authorised to open fire and bread would soon be available. Many of the upper classes in Petrograd imagined that the massive deployment of infantry and cavalry that day would end the disorder. Yet Globachev warned General Khabalov that the protests were moving towards a political stage. The workers planned to return to their factories and plants on the Monday to hold elections for a Soviet (Council) of Workers' Deputies.

Although the security forces more or less held the line on that Sunday morning, large numbers of demonstrators broke through to the centre of Petrograd. The vast majority of soldiers were not obeying orders to fire upon the crowds, but firing broke out on the Nevsky Prospekt. At first the shots came from police trying to defend themselves, but at least one NCO training company, that of the Pavlovsky Guards, was prepared to open fire when surrounded by the Moika Canal. Later a company of the Volynsky led by a drunken officer, shot down nearly forty civilians on Znamensky Square, although some accounts claimed they fired in the air. There was also a confused clash when a large group of Pavlovsky Guards, who had charged out of their barracks wanting to help the protesters, came up against a company of the Preobrazhensky Guards.

While playing dominos that evening at Mogilev, the Tsar received yet another demand from Rodzyanko, the chairman of the State Duma, that he should reform the government to avoid disaster. He did not reply, but decided to order the Duma to adjourn, which would silence liberal-conservatives like Rodzyanko. The message was to be passed on by Prince Nikolai Golitsyn, the Tsar's ancient and infirm chief minister. Rodzyanko, although both a nobleman and a former officer of the Cavalry of the Guard, was hated by the Tsarina and distrusted by the Tsar because he had been a firm opponent of Rasputin. His wife, a Golitsyn, had even written to congratulate Prince Yusupov on the murder, and Protopopov had shown her intercepted letter to the Tsarina.

In Petrograd, Protopopov summoned Globachev after dinner, not to discuss the catastrophic situation but so that he could boast of his audience with the Tsarina. That same Sunday evening, guests in evening dress made their way to Princess Radziwill's palace on the Fontanka, despite the military cordons in place. The ball was 'lugubrious', according to Robien. People had to make an effort to dance to an orchestra lacking many of its musicians. And the return home was 'sinister . . . all the streets were full of troops, and we were stopped on several occasions by soldiers standing guard by large fires. It gave the impression of crossing an armed camp.' A *sotnia* of Cossacks passed them on their shaggy ponies. 'The snow deadened the sound of their horses' hooves. One heard only the clink of weapons.'

Any hope that the Monday morning would see a return to calm and order did not last long. During the night, according to one famous account, Sergeant Kirpichnikov in the Volynsky Guards had persuaded his fellow NCOs that the regiment must refuse orders to march against the workers.* So, when the officers arrived to find them formed up for duty on the snow-covered parade ground of the Tavrichesky barracks, the sergeant gave a signal. The ranks shouted together 'We won't shoot!' As soon as the officers made threats, the men began pounding their rifle butts on the ground in rhythm. The officers, recognising a full-scale mutiny, turned and ran. A single shot killed their commander.

In Communist mythology, this was the incident which brought the Petrograd garrison round to the revolution. Their determination to help the workers was not, however, their only motive. Few wanted to be sent to the front, and everyone knew that an order to that effect was planned for a number of reserve battalions in Petrograd.

Firing could be heard from early morning onwards, first odd rifle shots then some volleys, which might have been the odd *feu de joie* in the air as soldiers discovered that their officers had lost their nerve. Rodzyanko sent yet another telegram to Mogilev addressed to '*Sa Majesté Impériale le Souverain-Empereur.*' It read: 'The situation is deteriorating. Measures must be taken immediately, because tomorrow will be too late. The last hour is upon us when the fate of the country and the dynasty will be decided.' The Tsar, after reading the message, simply remarked: 'That fat fellow Rodzyanko has again written me all kinds of nonsense which I shall not even bother to answer.'

---

* The Volynsky's service in the previous century had been largely devoted to suppressing uprisings in Poland.

The crowds of protesters that morning had headed for the State Duma in the Tavrichesky (Tauride) Palace, right next to the barracks which the Volynsky Guards had secured. The rebels had moved to the lines of the Preobrazhensky in the same huge complex and called on them to join. Both regiments then started handing out weapons from their armouries to the workers. That was the moment when people understood that a revolt had suddenly become a revolution.

Sergei Prokofiev had been at the Conservatoire for the dress rehearsal of a school performance of *Evgeny Onegin*. When he left, he found that 'a regular battle with terrifying shooting was taking place in Liteiny by the Arsenal, as some soldiers had already changed sides . . . I stopped on the bridge across the Fontanka as some vigorous rifle fire was heard from Liteiny. A worker was standing next to me. I asked him if I would be able to pass via Fontanka and he replied encouragingly: "Yes, go. This line has been taken by our men."

'"What do you mean, our men?" I asked.

'"Workers armed with rifles and soldiers that have crossed over to our side," he replied. This was news to me.'

Some groups had already set off to liberate prisoners from the Peter and Paul Fortress, the Litovsky and other Tsarist prisons. Others went to ransack ministries and destroy records. The Petrograd district court was set on fire, as were police stations and the criminal police department. Army detachments supposed to be guarding these places simply joined in. A crowd of about 3,000 people sacked the distillery in the Aleksandrovsky Prospekt and began consuming its contents.

A half-company of the 3rd Guards Rifle Regiment commanded by a lieutenant was supposed to defend the Okhrana headquarters. Globachev asked the lieutenant if he believed his men could be trusted. He shook his head, so Globachev asked him to take his men back to their barracks. It made little difference. The building was in any case ablaze before nightfall. After the writer Maksim Gorky viewed the burned-out ruins with the Menshevik Nikolai Sukhanov, he predicted that the revolution would lead to 'Asiatic savagery'. Gorky, who had lived among the poor a good deal more than Slavophile liberals or even Lenin, was under no illusion that the Russian people were the 'incarnation of spiritual beauty and kindness'. He was a striking man, physically as well as intellectually. 'Gorky was tall, with close-cropped hair,' wrote Viktor Shklovsky, 'a little stooped, blue-eyed, very strong-looking.'

*

The Tsar's younger brother, the Grand Duke Mikhail, acting on the advice of Prince Golitsyn and Rodzyanko, urged 'Nicky' that the whole Cabinet should be replaced by another one answerable to the Duma and headed by the well-known liberal Prince Lvov. More messages reached Mogilev from Petrograd, even one from the Tsarina, recommending concessions rather too late in the day. The Tsar was clearly shocked by the fact that his Guards regiments could be involved in the disorders, especially having been told by Protopopov that they were all loyal. He wrote in his diary that day, 'to my great sadness, even troops joined in'. And yet he still believed that the revolt could be crushed. He refused to imagine that he was facing a full revolution.

According to Globachev, General Khabalov's great mistake was to have used the reserve infantry battalions in Petrograd rather than the police and gendarmerie. On that Monday, although eleven protesters were shot down, fraternisation was taking place in most other places. Infantry cordons encouraged protesters to come up and talk to them. 'Cavalry patrols allowed the workers to stroke and feed the horses.' The Cossack *sotnia* in Znamenskaya Square intervened to stop the detachment of mounted police when they were about to dispel the crowd.

General Khabalov 'finally understood that he could not count on the bayonets which he had assumed were his', wrote Globachev. (This was a considerable understatement, considering that Khabalov by then had lost his head in panic and appeared hysterical.) 'Every unit sent in joined up with the rebels,' Globachev continued. 'By the evening he had nothing more than his headquarters staff. Meanwhile the rebellion kept growing. The looting of shops and private apartments had started. Officers were seized and disarmed in the street, district policemen beaten and murdered, members of the gendarmerie were arrested or killed. In short it was clear by 5 p.m. that authority had ceased to exist.'

Late that same evening, the Tsar ordered the imperial train to be made ready. The latest news from General Khabalov in Petrograd showed that Rodzyanko's warnings had not been exaggerated. At this moment of crisis, the Tsar wanted to be at Tsarskoe Selo with the Tsarina and especially his children, who were going down with measles. He summoned General N.I. Ivanov, whom he briefed during dinner, to go to Petrograd, replace Khabalov and impose martial law.

Ivanov was to take with him in another train a special battalion of soldiers who had all received the Cross of St George for bravery. In addition four regiments of infantry and four of cavalry from the front were to follow 'to crush the revolt of units in the Petrograd garrison'. General Lukomsky, the quartermaster general, warned the Tsar that it would be extremely dangerous for him and his suite to travel towards the capital when it was in open rebellion, but the sovereign was adamant. It never occurred to him that railway workers might simply decide to block his train, which would leave him stranded and completely out of touch with events.

3

The Fall of the Double-Headed Eagle
February–March 1917

Tuesday 28 February was another bright day. 'Streets were filled with crowds of people,' wrote Prokofiev. 'There were no trams or cabs, so they filled the streets from side to side. There were masses of red bows.' Street vendors, both in Petrograd and Moscow, did quick business selling red calico bows for five kopecks each. 'They sold out in a few minutes,' wrote a future Red Guard in Moscow. 'Wealthier looking people have bows which are almost napkin size. But they were told "Don't be greedy, it's equality and brotherhood now!"'

On the Fontanka, Prokofiev 'saw a big bonfire whose flames reached the first floor of a building. Window frames were being broken and thrown down into the fire. They landed with a deafening noise and were followed by all kinds of household objects and furniture . . . a green sofa, tablecloths and whole cupboards full of papers were thrown out. Homes of district police bosses were being ransacked . . . The cupboards made a particularly strong impression on me because they fell slowly over the windowsill, then precipitated downwards and fell heavily on the pavement, straight into the fire. The crowd made a gloating racket. Shouts were heard: "Bloodsucker! Our blood!"'

An attempt to assemble a loyal force from different units based at the Admiralty and the Winter Palace failed miserably. Khabalov could only confess his total inability to restore order. He admitted to a questionnaire from the *Stavka* that out of a garrison of 180,000 he could perhaps count on four companies of Guards infantry, five squadrons of cavalry and two batteries of artillery. That did not mean that all the rest had joined the revolution. Perhaps a majority, while refusing to obey orders from their officers, had avoided active rebellion. They just joined in the looting and drinking afterwards.

The myth of a 'bloodless revolution' was contradicted by the casualty figures of close to 1,500 deaths and 6,000 wounded on both sides just within the capital itself. The fighting ended with the storming of the

Astoria Hotel, where many officers and generals had sought shelter only to find themselves trapped in a massacre after police snipers on the roof provoked the crowds.

The imperial train had finally left Mogilev in the early hours of Tuesday 28 February. It avoided the most direct route to Tsarskoe Selo so as not to delay General Ivanov. The result was that when railway workers blocked the line the following night, the Tsar's train had to divert to Pskov, where the headquarters of the Northern Front, commanded by General Nikolai Ruzsky, had a Hughes apparatus to telegraph to Mogilev.

The Tsar came close to despair on hearing that the rebels had seized Gatchina and Luga to the west of Tsarskoe Selo. 'What a disgrace!' he wrote in his diary on 1 March. 'It's impossible to reach Tsarskoe, but my heart and my thoughts are there the whole time. How painful it must be for my poor Alix to be alone during all these events! May God come to our aid!' He was to receive no comfort from General Ruzsky, who had little respect for the imperial family and its hangers-on. He lectured the Tsar on the need to accept the primacy of the Duma, and then to abdicate.

The Tsar's order to Prince Golitsyn that the Duma should adjourn had produced the opposite effect on 27 February. A nervous Rodzyanko, not wanting a power vacuum in which radicals to the Left outflanked his Progressive Bloc, felt that he had no choice but to lead by defiance. The parties were summoned to a session after crowds of workers, intellectuals and soldiers overran the vast Tauride Palace, eagerly seeking news and guidance in a mood of both optimism and menace. A 'Provisional Committee of Duma Members for the Restoration of Order' was voted into being with twelve members – ten from Rodzyanko's Progressive Bloc and two socialists, Aleksandr Kerensky and the Georgian Menshevik Nikoloz Chkheidze.

Finding themselves engulfed by the populace, Rodzyanko and other liberal-conservative politicians felt nervous about their legitimacy and lacked confidence in their self-invented authority. They convinced themselves and the leading generals in the army that only they stood between the Tsar's obstinacy and total mayhem.

While the Tsar remained blocked in Pskov, early recognition of the Provisional Committee came from some military figures who called it the 'Provisional Government'. Groups of soldiers would march to the Tauride Palace to declare their loyalty, and Rodzyanko would rise to the occasion with some well-chosen booming words, to be greeted by cheers and another heavy rendering of the 'Marseillaise'. He and his colleagues felt obliged to continue playing their parts because the Petrograd Soviet, first called into being during the Revolution of 1905, was revived when workers' leaders had been released by rebel soldiers from the Peter and Paul Fortress two days before. That night, the Petrograd Soviet's Executive Committee, or *ispolnitelnyi komitet*, to be known by the acronym of Ispolkom, was also formed in the Tauride Palace. The Tsarist symbol of the double-headed eagle was being replaced by a dual form of government. 'Yes,' observed the arch-conservative Vasily Shulgin bitterly, 'we've come up with something two-headed, but it's certainly no eagle.'

In the early hours of 2 March, General Ruzsky at Pskov began negotiations on the Tsar's behalf by telegraph with Rodzyanko. They lasted four hours. Rodzyanko reminded Ruzsky of all the times he had warned the Tsar over the last two and a half years of the dangers to the throne. 'Hatred for the dynasty has reached extreme limits,' he said. The only chance of saving the country from civil war was 'abdication in favour of his son under the regency of Mikhail Aleksandrovich', the Tsar's younger brother, a rather more attractive figure who believed in a constitutional monarchy. Rodzyanko also warned that the dispatch of General Ivanov with his troops 'would only pour oil on the flames'. Fortunately Ivanov never reached Petrograd.

In an attempt to help Ruzsky persuade the Tsar, General Lukomsky, the adjutant-general at Mogilev, convinced General Alekseev to send a signal to all the other commanders-in-chief of fronts as well as the commanders of the Baltic and Black Sea Fleets to ask their opinion. Alekseev agreed. He was naturally concerned that the mutiny in Petrograd would spread to the front and the enemy would exploit it. Generals Evert, Brusilov and the Tsar's uncle, Grand Duke Nikolai Nikolaevich, all responded in a similar way, expressing their loyalty and devotion to the Tsar and his family, but begging him to abdicate immediately in favour of the Tsarevich, as Rodzyanko suggested. General Sakharov, the commander-in-chief of the Romanian front at Jassy, avoided a reply by having their Hughes apparatus disconnected. Lukomsky was furious when they discovered this. Sakharov, when forced to answer, insisted on seeing the replies of the other commanders-in-chief first.

Sakharov described Rodzyanko's behaviour as 'criminal and revolting' and the proposition of abdication as 'abominable'. 'I am certain that it is not the Russian people who have dreamed up this punishment, but a small group of criminals called the State Duma who have perfidiously profited from an opportune moment to achieve their guilty objectives.' But then he added: 'I am, as a loyal subject of His Majesty, obliged to say through my tears, that perhaps the decision to accept the conditions mentioned, could be the least painful for the country.' Sakharov may, of course, have been drunk.*

General Ruzsky was finally able to return to the Tsar in the blue and gold imperial train to inform him of the replies. After several minutes of contemplation, the Tsar, finally convinced by the opinion of his generals, as opposed to despised politicians, agreed to abdicate. The *Stavka* at Mogilev was informed and asked to send back a suggested draft to announce the abdication.

When, several hours later, the headquarters at Pskov warned that they were about to transmit the Tsar's bulletin which would announce the abdication, staff officers at Mogilev all crowded round the Hughes apparatus. Colonel Tikhobrazov took down the text word for word, but suddenly was shaken by a departure from the draft. 'Not wanting to be separated from our beloved son, we delegate the succession to our brother the Grand Duke Mikhail Aleksandrovich.'

Tikhobrazov immediately demanded verification. In 1797, Tsar Paul I had introduced a law of succession which did not allow the sovereign any such flexibility. Pskov confirmed that the sentence was correct. Tikhobrazov was about to query it again, but the Grand Duke Sergei Mikhailovich, standing just behind him, quietly told him to let them transmit exactly what they had been given. He was not surprised that his cousin could not bear to be parted from the haemophiliac Aleksei.

The Tsar gave the amended bulletin that evening to two members of the Provisional Committee of the Duma, Aleksandr Guchkov and Vasily Shulgin, who had come from Petrograd. The imperial train set

---

* Admiral Kolchak, the commander-in-chief of the Black Sea Fleet, also failed to reply, perhaps because he was in Batumi not Sevastopol. The Tsar's cousin Grand Duke Nikolai Nikolaevich had been negotiating with him there and found him 'absolutely impossible' to deal with. He replied to Alekseev as soon as he reached Tiflis.

off back to Mogilev at 1.00 a.m. on 3 March. 'I left Pskov with my soul weighed down by what I had just lived through,' the Tsar wrote. 'I am completely surrounded by treason, cowardice and deceit!' Guchkov and Shulgin, on the other hand, were appalled when they read the amended text, but there was nothing they could do.

Nicholas's change of mind about the succession caused consternation in Petrograd. Rodzyanko thought that he had convinced the socialists of the Executive Committee to accept the abdication in favour of the young Tsarevich, with the Grand Duke Mikhail Aleksandrovich as regent. But now the news that such a popular cavalry commander as the Tsar's younger brother could step straight into absolute power horrified the revolutionaries at the Tauride Palace.* They feared sudden retribution while the liberals feared chaos and even civil war. Many of the people might have softened towards the idea of the vulnerable boy as a constitutional monarch, but this change was more likely to be seen as a step back towards autocracy.

Even when a Kadet announced from the gallery of the Catherine Hall that the Tsar was abdicating in favour of his son Aleksei, a future Bolshevik leader recorded the wave of indignation that rolled through the hall. 'Instead of the enthusiastic shout of "*Urrrra!*", on which the Kadet speaker had probably counted, there broke from the throats of hundreds of soldiers a unanimous cry of protest: "Down with the Romanovs! Long live the democratic republic!".'

A panic-stricken Rodzyanko and most of his fellow members of the Provisional Committee felt they had to convince the Tsar's brother to abdicate as well – a brother who still had no idea that he had been made Tsar Mikhail II. It was typical of Nicholas's thoughtlessness about anyone outside his own immediate family that he had made no attempt to warn him. Only Pavel Milyukov still believed that the monarchy must be retained in some form.

Early on that Friday morning, as Nicholas returned in his train to Mogilev, the Provisional Committee, who had spent a sleepless night at the Duma, discovered that Grand Duke Mikhail Aleksandrovich

---

* Mikhail Aleksandrovich had commanded the Savage Division from the Caucasus, with Ingush, Chechen, Dagestani, Tatar, Circassian and other mountain people, in the Brusilov offensive of 1916.

was close by. He was staying in the apartments of Princess Putyatina at 12 Millionnaya ulitsa. It was Kerensky, the new minister of justice, who telephoned and by the middle of the morning Rodzyanko, Prince Lvov, Milyukov, the foreign minister, and Kerensky were settled in armchairs facing the Grand Duke, who regarded them quizzically. They were unshaven and nervous, if not frightened. Kerensky and Rodzyanko, half-expecting a furious mob hammering at the doors, wanted an immediate abdication. Milyukov, on the other hand, continued to argue forcefully that to abandon the Tsarist state structure would leave the Provisional Government vulnerable until elections could be held.

Eventually, Mikhail Aleksandrovich halted the heated conversation and said that he would like to confer with Rodzyanko and Prince Lvov. When they were alone in another room, the Grand Duke asked whether they could assure him of certain things. If he were to renounce the throne, could the Provisional Government restore order and continue the war? Were they confident that elections for a Constituent Assembly could go ahead without being blocked by the Petrograd Soviet? Lvov and Rodzyanko both answered positively.

When they returned to the drawing room, the atmosphere relaxed at once since it was clear from the politicians' faces that the Grand Duke had agreed to abdicate. It was now just a question of finding the right formula for the announcement, although that was not entirely straightforward since those present could not guarantee that the Grand Duke was legally Tsar Mikhail, and even he objected in the circumstances to the word 'abdicate'.

Princess Putyatina invited the assembly to join her for lunch while legal experts were summoned. They had to grapple with the Tsar's unconstitutional declaration to abdicate in favour of his brother rather than his son. By the evening, an elegant solution was concocted by Vladimir Nabokov, the father of the future novelist, working closely with the Grand Duke who knew him well. The first thing the reluctant Tsar insisted on dropping was the standard formula: 'We by God's mercy, Mikhail II, Emperor and Autocrat of all the Russias.' He insisted instead on a more informal announcement.

A heavy burden has been thrust upon me by the will of my brother who has given over to me the Imperial Throne of Russia at a time of unprecedented warfare and popular disturbances.

Inspired like the entire people by the idea that what is most important is the welfare of the country, I have taken a firm decision to assume the Supreme Power only if such be the will of our great people, whose right it is to establish the form of government and the new basic laws of the Russian state by universal suffrage through its representatives in the Constituent Assembly.

Therefore, invoking the blessing of God, I beseech all the citizens of Russia to obey the Provisional Government, which has come into being on the initiative of the Duma and is vested with all the plenitude of power until the Constituent Assembly, to be convoked with the least possible delay by universal suffrage, direct, equal and secret voting, shall express the will of the people by its decision on the form of government.

Mikhail.

After General Alekseev showed Nicholas the text that night, the ex-Tsar wrote in his diary: 'It seems that Micha has abdicated. He finishes his manifesto demanding the election within six months of the Constituent Assembly . . . God knows who gave him the idea of signing such turpitude.'

In marked contrast, the politicians and lawyers involved that day in the negotiations expressed their admiration for Mikhail Aleksandrovich, both his motives and behaviour. He may not have been any more intelligent than his older brother, but he did not suffer from that fatal obstinacy. The thought might well have crossed their minds that things could have turned out differently if he had been born before Nicholas.

4

From Autocracy to Chaos
March–April 1917

While the former Tsar was making his way from Pskov back to Mogilev on the imperial train, contradictory rumours spread in Petrograd. Some said that he had been arrested, others warned that columns of troops were on the way to crush the revolution aided by a rising of secret monarchist groups in the city. Another story even claimed that Cossacks were organising an attack on Petrograd using balloons filled with poisonous gases. The mood of anger and fear intensified. Random shots could be heard across the city. Rebels seized automobiles and charged around the streets as if on important missions. 'They were filled to the brim with soldiers and workmen, bristling with bayonets and fluttering red flags,' wrote Prokofiev in his diary.

Accounts of Tsarist police and gendarmes firing on crowds with machine guns from the tops of buildings were repeated constantly. There were many police snipers, but how many machine guns were actually used in this way is impossible to tell. A wholesale assault was made on the Astoria Hotel on St Isaac's Square where both Russian and Allied officers were quartered. This was triggered by shots fired at a revolutionary crowd from the upper floor. Any hated '*pharaons*' found hiding or in disguise risked being torn to pieces. Several were roped by their legs to the backs of commandeered vehicles and dragged through the streets. A police inspector was apparently tied to a couch, doused in petrol and set on fire. Others were shot on the Neva embankment and their bodies dropped down on to the ice. According to Dr Joseph Clare, the pastor of the American Church in Petrograd, 'thirty or forty policemen were pushed through a hole in the ice without as much as a stunning tap on the head – drowned like rats'.

The atmosphere was extremely volatile. A poor hatmaker, accompanied by his boy apprentice, spotted a brightly coloured foreign toy on a stall. He wanted to buy it for his granddaughter. Unfortunately, he did not have enough money on him because his own customers thought that the revolution would cancel debts. He asked the vendor if she could reduce the price. The woman refused angrily, and as they argued he called her an 'exploiter'. She started yelling that he was a '*pharaon*' in disguise.

Instantly, people began shouting: 'Beat the constable! Death to the "*pharaon*"!' A bloodthirsty crowd surrounded him and began tearing his clothes and hitting him. As a soldier drew his sabre the little boy apprentice screamed in horror and yelled 'People, stop! Don't kill him! He is not a *pharaon*, but just a hat-maker from Apraksin Dvor!' He then burst into tears. The crowd looked on in confusion as his boss clung to him, quivering with fear. Just as rapidly the mood switched to one of compassion. Women helped him back into his overcoat and told him to pray for his little saviour.

Army officers also had to hide in apartments and search for civilian clothes to avoid being beaten or killed, but they were still at risk. Crowds tore down any symbols of the monarchy from public buildings or double-headed eagles from shops by appointment to the imperial court. Armed groups went from building to building in the richer areas, claiming that they were searching for counter-revolutionaries. In most cases this was a cover for looting, mindless violence and in some instances an opportunity for raping any young woman found alone at home. A horrified young Grand Duke and cousin of the Tsar admitted in his diary: 'The people's hatred has been brewing for too long.' Aleksandr Kerensky referred evasively to 'the people's fury'.

The conservative politician Vasily Shulgin observed: 'Only one man could make his way in this bog, jumping from hummock to hummock – Kerensky.' A sallow-faced lawyer with extraordinary eyes, Aleksandr Kerensky seized the advantage of his unusual position with a seat on both the Provisional Committee of the Duma and on the Executive Committee of the Petrograd Soviet. This made him even more influential than Rodzyanko or any of the members of the embryo Provisional Government, which lacked the confidence to wield power on its own.

The plenary sessions of the Petrograd Soviet in the Tauride Palace were utterly chaotic with some 3,000 deputies debating, often at cross-purposes. 'Inside, the palace was boiling with energy,' wrote a Socialist Revolutionary. 'Lots of people were going in all directions,

Meeting of the Petrograd Soviet in 1917 in Prince Potemkin's Tauride (Tavrichesky) Palace.

soldiers clanked about with their rifles, non-stop sessions of revolutionary organisations and the Provisional Government were going on in the halls and rooms. Piles of rifles and boxes with cartridges were everywhere on the floor, there were masses of machine guns with belts and even a heap of dynamite sticks and hand grenades to which no one was paying attention. From time to time, arrested people were escorted through the crowd.'

Observers compared the plenary sessions to village assemblies where anyone could stand up and say what they wanted. Here, the audience was a dense mass of soldiers and workers, either rolling *makhorka* tobacco in scraps of newsprint or handbills or chewing sunflower seeds and spitting out the husks on Prince Potemkin's magnificent marble floors. Voting could go in any direction and was largely ignored. The socialist leaders on the Executive Committee simply took no notice of what was said and carried on with their own plans for power.

A soldier, fascinated by the debates, observed a group of women outside the Tauride who demanded to see Kerensky. They were told that he was not available, so the Georgian Menshevik Nikoloz Chkheidze stood in for him. The feminist delegation called out: 'We, the women, demand equality!'

'Comrade women,' Chkheidze replied in amusement. 'I will sign for your equality with both my hands. You just need your fathers, husbands and brothers to grant it to you.' The crowd roared with laughter, while the women shouted their protests.

'All of a sudden, however,' the soldier continued, 'an open car squeezed through the crowd, with several women inside. The others greet them in unison. The car reached the front row. One of the women in it stood up and started speaking. She spoke for a long time, and she spoke very well: about the lot of a Russian working woman, about that of a woman who was a mother. The crowd interrupted at times with exclamations of approval. Chkheidze soon dropped his joking tone.'

Kerensky's sense of drama became apparent as soon as leading figures of the *ancien regime* were brought as prisoners to the Duma. Shulgin described him as 'an actor to the marrow'. When the former minister of war General Sukhomlinov was led in, Kerensky made a great show of ripping off his shoulder boards. But as soon as the crowd yelled for his death, Kerensky threw out his arms in a protective gesture and shouted: 'The Duma sheds no blood!'

Altogether nearly sixty ministers and generals, as well as several women, including the Tsarina's confidante, Anna Vyrubova, were held in the pavilion attached to the State Duma. Soldiers and peasants wandered in and gazed in fascination at the former grandees as if they were rare animals in a zoo. Those held in the pavilion were at least more fortunate than those taken straight to the Peter and Paul Fortress, which like other prisons had cells to spare after the spontaneous and chaotic liberation of the victims of Tsarism.

The day after the political prisoners in the Litovsky Castle had been liberated, the fifteen-year-old Evguénia Markon, an Anarchist from a well-to-do Jewish family, found a scribbled note which had floated down from one of the top cells. It was a cry for help. The guards had disappeared, and the inmates had been left locked in with nothing to eat or drink. Appalled that only the politicals had been released, this young firebrand found some soldiers and persuaded them to smash their way in, shooting off locks with their rifles. One of the prisoners, a tall, bearded man, embraced her, sobbing and trembling with emotion.

Revolution could also reveal that the down-trodden harboured some terrifying prejudices in this time of chaos. A grandmother from an intellectual family which rejoiced over the downfall of the regime was accosted in the market by a stallholder. 'Are you a Christian?' she asked her. 'Tell me, is life going to get better?'

'Of course it is,' replied the grandmother.

'Oh, come on,' said the woman. 'Nothing's going to get better until all the yids are finished off. Because it's just the yids who are to blame for all the troubles of the simple folk.'

Vasily Kravkov, that senior military doctor at the front, could not get over the glorious news of the Tsar's downfall. 'I slept badly because of all the grandiose events that have taken place,' he wrote in his diary. 'We kept waiting until the evening for the order containing the royal announcement. The Tsar really has abdicated. My head is spinning. This phrase in the bulletin sounds so beautiful: "The Constituent Assembly will express the will of the people with its decision on the form of government." So, it is really possible that a republic will soon be announced? It is scary even to think about this.' Kravkov had to keep his thoughts to himself, however, since he was surrounded by reactionary officers who seemed to be both embittered and resigned at the same time. The fact that there was not the slightest attempt within the army to fight back against the revolution certainly indicated the extent of despair over the Tsar and Tsarina even in the most conservative circles.

Acceptance of the abdication and the Provisional Government by generals, and even some grand dukes, was prompted by fear of a total breakdown of order. That did not mean that they welcomed the turn of events. In the Caucasus at Kislovodsk, Grand Duke Andrei Vladimirovich expressed his own sense of shock in a diary entry: 'News of the Sovereign's abdication, on his own and Aleksei's behalf and in favour of Mikhail Aleksandrovich, left us dumbstruck. The second abdication is even more terrifying. It is too hard and too sad to write these lines. All of Russia's former grandeur has been destroyed in just one day.'

The sudden vacuum of power created an even greater sense of unreality at Mogilev after Nicholas returned there from Pskov. The whole staff had turned out to receive him on the platform when the imperial train arrived in the dark. 'Everyone seemed depressed, as if after the funeral of someone they had been close to,' wrote Colonel Tikhobrazov.

Next morning, Tikhobrazov happened to look out of the window from the main building to see a group of gesticulating civilians, shouting in front of the gates. The gendarmes on duty were refusing to let them through. The sentry in the hall was sent to find out what the matter was. He returned to report. 'These people are suppliers who found out about the Sovereign's abdication and came to demand the money that they are owed. They are afraid that they will no longer get paid.' The staff officer on duty went red in the face with shame. 'What a disgrace,' he said. 'I just hope that the Sovereign will not see this from the palace windows.'

When the former Tsar appeared later in the morning, Tikhobrazov could not look him in the eye because he did not know how to address him. He felt he could hardly call him 'Your Imperial Majesty' any more. The Tsar was holding a telegram message form and a piece of his own blue writing paper. He addressed General Alekseev, the chief of the general staff, and handed him the telegram which he had filled in himself and the sheet of blue paper.

'Mikhail Vasilievich,' he said. 'I have changed my mind. Please send this to Petrograd.' In the telegram he stated that he intended to pass the throne to his son after all. Alekseev explained that he could not possibly agree to send it. The former Tsar repeated his request twice more, but the general remained firm. Nicholas turned and walked slowly down the stairs.

After he had disappeared, Alekseev handed Tikhobrazov the small sheet of 'Tsar's paper'. On it was written in Nicholas's neat handwriting:

Request the Provisional Government:
    To allow me to travel without any obstacles to Tsarskoe Selo in order to be united with my family;
    To remain in Tsarskoe Selo, free, until the complete recovery of my family members;
    To return to Russia after the termination of the war and stay permanently in the Livadia Palace.*

---

* Tikhobrazov in his account wrote: 'I am quoting this text from memory but I am confident that I remember the essence of each paragraph.' The Livadia Palace was the imperial family's summer residence at Yalta in the Crimea, and the setting for the Yalta Conference in February 1945 with Stalin as host.

News of the collapse of the Romanov dynasty spread from Petrograd with different speeds. Cities and towns with telegraph and railway stations heard rapidly. Some experienced their own spontaneous revolutions. Many more remote areas knew little for several weeks.

The apprentice journalist Konstantin Paustovsky had been sent by his editor to Yefremov, a small town in the province of Tula, which Chekhov was supposed to have described as 'the incarnation of the Russian wilderness'. Newspapers from Moscow took three days to arrive. 'Dogs barked in the evenings along the main street and the night watchmen sounded their clappers as they made their rounds.'

Paustovsky described how his new friend Osipenko charged into his room. 'There's a revolution in Petersburg,' he cried. 'The government is overthrown.' His voice gave out. He collapsed into a chair and burst into tears. Paustovsky found his hands shaking as he held the piece of paper with the proclamation of the Provisional Government. As nothing was left of the police or administration, 'a people's assembly met around the clock in the hall of the town council. It was renamed the "Convention" in honour of the French Revolution.' There was another uncertain singing of the 'Marseillaise' to honour this historic moment. As word spread, peasants came into town to ask when they could take over the land and when the war would end. 'Noisy, muddleheaded days had started,' Paustovsky wrote.

One would have expected Moscow to have been better informed, yet a curator at the Historical Museum wrote in his diary, 'Lots of rumours are circulating, but what is the truth? There are no newspapers, trams are not operating, or even cabs. There are crowds of people everywhere, the atmosphere is joyful like at Easter.' He was then astonished to see a procession of Muslims in Lubyanka Square carrying a red flag and reciting a prayer.

There were public meetings in many squares, especially round Pushkin's monument or by the great equestrian statue of Skobelev, to whose outstretched sword a red banner had been attached. Orators were either cheered, or in some cases pulled down from the plinth. Soldiers with sheepskin hats and red armbands on their grey greatcoats hectored the crowds. Any dissent was greeted with retorts such as 'Go off and feed the lice in the trenches and then you can ask me questions, Tsarist good-for-nothings!' And again, wild rumours circulated – that Kerensky was a Jew, or the monks in the Donskoy monastery had gold roubles hidden in the cores of apples.

*

Russia's principal enemy was equally confused by the new situation within the country. German aircraft dropped propaganda leaflets over the front line claiming that 'the beloved Czar' had been removed by the 'brutal English'. Commander Oliver Locker-Lampson of the Royal Naval Air Service armoured car division, supporting the Russian army on the Galician front, reported drily to London that this ludicrous lie 'rendered us heroes for several days'.

German attempts were wasted. They should have remembered the Napoleonic dictum that you should not interrupt your opponent when he is making a mistake. No enemy could have hoped to achieve what the Petrograd Soviet managed for them in a single bulletin.

Even while the lynching of officers still continued at the end of February, Rodzyanko's Duma Committee saw an urgent need to have them back in their regiments to prevent a total collapse of the army. But the soldiers who had played leading roles in the uprising feared counter-revolution and a restoration of the hierarchy which might hold them to account for crimes committed during the recent events. To prevent any such possibility, a group of the most radical, both Bolsheviks and Socialist Revolutionaries, burst into a session of the Executive Committee of the Petrograd Soviet.

The chairman, N.D. Sokolov, an archetypal socialist intellectual of the period with pince-nez and beard, invited them to state their demands, which he wrote down. Soldiers would be obliged to obey their officers' orders only after they had been endorsed by the soldiers' committee. The soldiers, not officers, must keep control over weapons. So that it could continue to defend the revolution, the Petrograd garrison must not be sent to the front. The relationship between officers and soldiers had to change completely. A soldier off duty should never have to salute. Forms of address such as 'Your Excellency' must be replaced by 'Mister General' or 'Mister Colonel'. Traditional punishments, such as an officer striking one of his men in the face, must be prohibited.

The final version of the Executive Committee's *prikaz*, or Order, No. 1 on 1 March represented for right-wing officers the decisive document of the revolution and helped open the way to what came later. They blamed it for crippling the Tsarist army by destroying the authority of officers and all military discipline. The Executive Committee failed to warn the Provisional Government, with whom it was supposed to cooperate, yet there does not appear to have been a calculated plan to take the officer corps by surprise and destroy its counter-revolutionary potential in a pre-emptive strike. What it certainly did was boost the self-confidence of the Executive Committee of the Petrograd Soviet which expanded their influence to the whole country and soon became known as the All-Russian Soviet of Workers' and Soldiers' Deputies.

The wildly inaccurate warnings of counter-revolution played their part, but the real mistakes had been made by General Alekseev at the *Stavka* and by Rodzyanko and his colleagues. Despite the pleading of commanders at the front, Alekseev had refused to allow any premature announcements of the change of regime until the situation was formally announced by the Provisional Committee of the Duma. The text of *prikaz* No.1 was also held back. These delays convinced soldiers at the front that their officers were trying to keep them in the dark and it increased their anger and suspicions.

The senior army doctor Vasily Kravkov noted in his diary that most regular officers and the 'military aristocracy cannot conceal their anger when regarding the forthcoming necessity of treating soldiers like humans'. Officers unwisely made jokes about the red banners, referring to them as 'babushka's underwear'. On 5 March, General Lavr Kornilov, the commander of XXV Corps, reached Mogilev. General Lukomsky showed him what the *Stavka* called their 'Dossier of the Revolution', listing the outrages against military discipline. Kornilov exploded in anger at the state of affairs, but there was nothing he could do, even though he had been appointed commander of the Petrograd military district.

The desertion rate was so high after the issue of *prikaz* No. 1, according to Captain Wavell, that another decree followed promising that all absconders who returned to duty before a certain date would not be punished. Due to the difficulty of transport, they set the date some seven weeks hence. Soldiers at the front, who had not deserted, now saw the chance to take seven weeks' leave, so even more departed.

War-weary soldiers greeted the changes with joy, while the vast majority of officers were horrified, above all at the idea that they could not do anything without the agreement of soldiers' committees. Anti-Semites felt that their worst suspicions were justified on discovering that the committees included a significant proportion of Jews. The explanation for their election was simple. They were among the best educated, yet the Tsarist system had not allowed them to become officers.

Meetings took up much of the day and achieved little. 'The mass of soldiers had been stunned by the events and confused by them,' wrote a soldier on the Transcaucasus Front. 'Sometimes the situation became comical: one speaker would offer his slogan and the crowd approved, then another one offered the opposite slogan, and they approved of that as well, and shouted: "You are right!".'

Major General Vladimir von Dreier described his arrival as chief of staff of a division in the Siberian Corps on the Galician front. The headquarters was deserted, so he went to find the divisional commander who had been forced to attend a soldiers' rally. 'A crowd was standing all around. A skinny soldier standing on a dais was shouting at the top of his voice. "Nikolashka drank enough of our blood, comrades!" The crowd kept assuring him "That's right! That's right!" The men closest to us were grinning and looking with glee at the bosses standing nearby, while spitting out the husks of sunflower seeds. One speaker after another climbed on to the dais in turn to swear at the Tsar. I kept thinking how the hell did I end up here.'

Since cavalry, artillery and Cossack formations proved less vulnerable to the collapse in discipline, the first examples of officers suffering physical attacks and even murder occurred in the infantry and the navy. 'How could the infantry resist?' wrote Commander Oliver Locker-Lampson. 'For nearly three years they had been mowed down in millions; hurled (as they persist in stating) in unarmed masses against magnificently equipped troops, by generals whom they believed were bought with German gold. How could they be expected to want the war to go on?'

'Some officers have been shot, others beaten and most insulted,' Locker-Lampson continued in his report to London. Quite often death came from being 'lifted on bayonets' when the victim was impaled by up to a half a dozen attackers and raised off the ground. This, for example, was the fate of five officers of the Luga garrison a hundred kilometres south of Petrograd, who all had German-sounding names.

'In Kronstadt naval officers have been sweeping the streets,' Locker-Lampson added, 'and one of them was being led along by the beard by one of his men, who struck his face continually. Respect for rank has disappeared.' The Baltic Fleet sailors, who had been badly treated by many of their officers, were the most violent and radical of all, with a number of Bolsheviks and Anarchists in their ranks. The festering anger of these 'wharf-rats', pent up on ice-bound battleships was made worse by the lack of information from their officers.

On 3 March, Vice Admiral Adrian Neperin in Helsingfors (Helsinki) signalled Rodzyanko: 'Mutiny in the *Andrei*, *Pavel* and *Slava*. Admiral Nebol'sin killed. Baltic Fleet does not now exist as a fighting force.' Red lights were lit at night and red flags hoisted by day to signal revolutionary triumph. Neperin himself was shot to death the very next day by a sailor. Admiral Viren, the governor-general of Kronstadt, was stabbed to death with bayonets. Fyodor Raskolnikov, soon to be a Bolshevik leader in Kronstadt, explained that Viren had 'the reputation of a brute' throughout the Baltic Fleet. Raskolnikov justified 'these so-called "excesses" which had aroused universal indignation among the bourgeoisie but left the working class wholly indifferent' as the sailors' 'revenge for age-old humiliation and insult'. Martinets hated for their discipline had been known as 'dragons', and they were the first to be killed, or arrested and badly treated in punishment cells. Altogether 105 officers were killed at Kronstadt, Helsingfors (Helsinki) and Vyborg (Viipuri), but hardly any at the other naval bases in the Gulf of Finland.

Bolshevik poster hailing the Red Fleet as the 'Vanguard of the Revolution'.

Admiral Aleksandr Kolchak, the commander-in-chief of the Black Sea Fleet, was in a slightly less dangerous position because although his sailors were mutinous, they were not so brutalised. The conservative press seemed almost infatuated as they built him up as a possible military dictator. 'Kolchak is now commanding the Black Sea Fleet,' Yelena Lakier in Odessa wrote. 'All of the navy adore him. Newspapers write that he is full of energy and fire. One magazine published his portrait accompanied by the following verse: "Russia's heart will never forget you. Just like one's first love."'

Kolchak, who had the expression of an angry eagle, had been the youngest vice admiral in the Russian Imperial Navy. More than just a highly professional officer, he had also been an oceanographer and Arctic explorer, having taken part in several expeditions, including two years studying the archipelago of New Siberia. This would lead more than a century later to the opening of the northern route with a new generation of icebreakers.

During the Russo–Japanese War, Kolchak had been wounded and taken prisoner. Furious at the incompetence of the Tsarist government, he worked afterwards with members of the Duma to modernise the navy, introducing submarines and seaplanes. Following another Arctic expedition in 1913, he became chief of operations in the Baltic, then commander of the Black Sea Fleet shortly before the February revolution. When the sailors' soviet in Sevastopol demanded that officers give up their personal weapons, Kolchak indicated his Golden Sword of St George, presented for bravery in the Far East. 'It was not you who gave me this sword,' he told them, 'and it is not to you that I will surrender it.' Turning, he flung it into the sea.

Kolchak was fortunate to get away soon afterwards when sent on a mission to the United States. Following the Bolshevik seizure of power in the autumn, naval officers from the Black Sea Fleet, including five admirals, were bound and executed on Malakhov Hill outside Sevastopol.

5

The Pregnant Widow
March–May 1917

Aleksandr Herzen, Russia's greatest political philosopher, made a prophecy based on his study of the revolutions of 1848. 'The death of the contemporary forms of social order ought to gladden rather than trouble the soul,' he wrote. 'But what is frightening is that the departing world leaves behind it not an heir, but a pregnant widow. Between the death of one and the birth of the other, much water will flow by, a long night of chaos and desolation will pass.'

The Provisional Government in Russia in 1917 could hardly have fitted Herzen's prediction more accurately. Its self-proclaimed purpose was to act as a caretaker. All the key decisions about laws, the political system and the ownership of land could be made only after the birth of the Constituent Assembly. In the meantime, its power remained little more than a polite fiction since it could do nothing without the approval of the Executive Committee of the Petrograd Soviet. The destruction of the Tsarist administration had left no levers within its grasp attached to anything which worked. The Provisional Government found itself in a political no man's land. They were not very different from those high-minded liberals described by Herzen who 'at the same time undermine the old order and cling to it, light the fuse and try to stop the explosion'.

Prince Georgy Lvov, the prime minister, was a man of outstanding administrative qualities, yet he remained so liberal in outlook that he blindly believed in the essential goodness of the people (what Maksim Gorky called 'Karamazovian sentimentalism'). Lvov even disliked the very idea of central government authority, which was hardly a good qualification for his other role as minister of the interior. He consented to the freeing of all political prisoners, including convicted terrorists, whether or not they believed in democracy. He believed quite simply that to make Russia 'the freest country in the world' would transform the morality of its citizens.

Even Professor Pavel Milyukov, the foreign minister who had wanted to retain the monarchy, agreed to allow Vladimir Ilyich Lenin, the revolutionary leader of the Bolsheviks, to return to Petrograd from Switzerland. He also asked Britain to intercede with Canada to permit the charismatic Leon Trotsky free passage home from the United States. Yet one of the very first Bolshevik exiles to reach Petrograd to be present at 'the cradle of the revolution' was Josef Stalin. On 12 March, he and Lev Kamenev arrived from their exile near Krasnoyarsk by the Trans-Siberian Railway.

Less than two years before, at the Zimmerwald conference in the Swiss Alps, Trotsky and other delegates had joked that half a century after Karl Marx's First Socialist International it was still possible for all of Europe's internationalists to be accommodated in 'four charabancs'. Just a month before the February revolution, Lenin had doubted that he would see such an event in his lifetime. He had predicted an upheaval caused by hatred of the war, and yet even he was taken by surprise. In fact, any suggestion that Lenin, living the life of an impoverished exile in a squalid room in the Spiegelstrasse in Zurich, might soon become the absolute ruler of Russia would have seemed a fantasy. But the February revolution, unplanned by professional revolutionaries, changed everything.

Lenin, with his great bald forehead, professorial beard and penetrating, narrowed eyes, despised amateur radicals above all. He dismissed idealists as fainthearts and sentimentalists. His self-belief was such that he could not trust anyone else to have the vision or the ruthless determination to destroy the old order for ever. After lunch on 3 March 1917, while Nadezhda Krupskaya was washing up and Lenin was collecting his papers ready to return to work in the library, they heard the sound of footsteps racing up the stairs. A breathless friend burst in waving a newspaper. 'Haven't you heard the news?' he panted. 'There is revolution in Russia!'

Overjoyed by the downfall of the hated Romanov family who had executed his brother Aleksandr, Lenin sent a telegram to Aleksandra Kollontai, the Marxist and feminist theoretician, in Oslo with his instructions for the Bolshevik membership in Petrograd. He neither bothered to check on the true situation, nor consult with colleagues. Lenin burned with impatience. He was trapped in Zurich, on the wrong side of the lines in the accursed imperialists' war.

After dreaming up mad plans to get through to Russia, from disguises to aeroplanes, Lenin was saved by the idea of a Menshevik, Julius Martov. He suggested an approach to the German representative in Berne, Gisbert Freiherr von Romberg. The Wilhelmine regime would welcome any opportunity which might undermine a Russian defence of the Eastern Front before the Americans entered the war. Lenin had no qualms about accepting help from a class enemy. He was also prepared to receive secret funds from the Kaiser's government to fund propaganda. As far as he was concerned, anything that assisted a revolution which could bring the Bolsheviks to power was permissible.

So, aided by the very imperialists whom he was bent on overthrowing, Lenin and thirty-one revolutionaries were allocated a supposedly 'sealed train' to take them across Germany, escorted by two Prussian officers. The party included both Lenin's wife Krupskaya and his alleged lover Inessa Armand, as well as Karl Radek, whom Arthur Ransome described as 'a little light-haired, spectacled revolutionary goblin of incredible intelligence and vivacity'.

As they boarded the local Swiss train to take them to the German frontier, Radek asked Lenin what he felt. 'In six months' time,' he replied, 'we shall either be swinging from a gallows, or we shall be in power.' Lenin did not look the part of a future leader in his old clothes and hobnailed boots, yet an obsessive compulsion and his dictatorial instincts made him take charge of everything. He even organised a rota for the use of the train's two lavatories.

From a small port on the Baltic coast, the Bolsheviks took a steamer across to Sweden, then a train to Stockholm (where Lenin was made to buy new clothes). On 31 March, the Bolshevik group travelled in another train to Finland. There, Lenin was furious to discover from a recent copy of *Pravda* that while Stalin and Kamenev were leading the Bolshevik Central Committee, they had failed to attack the Provisional Government.

Shortly before midnight on 3 April, the train drew into Petrograd's Finland Station. Few in the waiting crowd had ever seen Lenin or heard him speak. Most of them had been called to greet him by the Bolshevik Central Committee. One uninvited guest present was Paul Dukes, a concert pianist working for the British Secret Intelligence Service, engaged by Captain Mansfield Cumming.

Inside the station, a group of sailors from the Baltic Fleet formed an improvised guard of honour. But Lenin took no pleasure in his reception and showed little courtesy to those who greeted him. He rapped out two speeches, one to the sailors and the main one to the crowd outside from the top of an armoured car. To the dismay of most of his listeners, he attacked the Provisional Government, implicitly criticising his audience for having accepted it at all, and dismissed any idea of unity between socialist parties.

A few hours later, still without sleep, Lenin shocked the Petrograd Bolsheviks in their headquarters, the expropriated mansion of the ballerina and former mistress of the Tsar, Mathilda Kshesinskaya. He berated them with elements of what later became known as his *April Theses*, which he had written during the journey from Switzerland. First, he condemned any support for the Provisional Government continuing the 'predatory imperialist war' and even called for fraternisation with the enemy at the front. Next, he argued that the revolutionary path could be shortened dramatically. The intermediate step of a bourgeois-democratic revolution as laid down by Marx was unnecessary. Soviet power could be seized immediately because the bourgeoisie, and thus also the Provisional Government, were so weak. He called for the abolition of the police, the army and the bureaucracy, as well as the nationalisation of all land and all banks. His audience was aghast at what they considered madness.

Lenin despised notions of false modesty and clearly believed himself infallible. Those Bolsheviks who disagreed with him were usually treated as either totally misguided or dishonest, but to win over others he was prepared to tread more carefully on certain questions, such as holding back in his condemnation of the war against Germany. He also realised that to talk of turning the existing conflict into a European civil war did not appeal to the pacifist mood. And in the prevailing atmosphere of unrestrained liberty, slogans like the dictatorship of the proletariat struck a jarring note.

Lenin did not, however, pull his punches later that day at the Tauride Palace when he rejected any compromise with the Mensheviks. One of them, outraged by his attack, said: 'Lenin's programme is sheer insurrectionism,' and declared that 'the banner of civil war has been unfurled in the midst of revolutionary democracy.' Ministers in the Provisional Government, from the Kadet Milyukov to the socialist Kerensky, shrugged off his attacks. Lenin's ideas seemed so extreme that he did not appear a serious threat. In any case, the Bolsheviks were numerically minuscule beside the Socialist Revolutionaries, who enjoyed enormous support in rural areas. And even Lenin recognised that 'in most of the Soviets of Workers' Deputies our Party is in a minority, in a small minority'.

In his determination to achieve total power for the Bolsheviks, Lenin did not make the mistake of revealing what Communist society would be like. All state power and private property, he claimed, would be transferred into the hands of the Soviets – or councils of workers – as if they were to be independent bodies and not merely the puppets of the Bolshevik leadership. The peasants were encouraged to believe that the land would be theirs to own and work as they saw fit. There was no mention of the need for grain seizures to feed the cities or the forced collectivisation of farms. His public speeches focused instead on hate-figures – those he could label 'parasites', such as bankers, factory bosses, warmongers and landowners. He made no attacks on all the other categories of people whom the Bolsheviks would later persecute. Lenin believed firmly in the necessity of civil war to achieve absolute power, yet there was little hint of the class genocide to come.

After an unsuccessful first attempt at addressing a mass audience, Lenin quickly came into his own as a public speaker. He hammered home his points simply and effectively. His enjoyment and unshakable self-confidence fascinated his audiences and projected an aura of powerful leadership.

Teffi, whose huge readership in the pre-war years had included both the Tsar and Lenin, described how his strength lay in an extraordinary ability to explain complex matters clearly and in a compelling way. 'As an orator, Lenin did not carry the crowd with him,' she wrote. 'He did not set a crowd on fire or whip it up into a frenzy. He was not like Kerensky, who could make a crowd fall in love with him and shed tears of ecstasy . . . Lenin simply battered away with a blunt instrument at the darkest corner of people's souls.' Above all, she was struck by his low opinion of humanity in general and the way he saw individuals as completely expendable objects. 'A man was good only insofar as he was necessary to the cause.'

In the second half of March, unrest had begun to turn to violence in many parts of the countryside, fomented by radicalised deserters returning from the front. Peasants in many areas, but especially in the Volga and central black earth regions, began to seize their landlords' implements, mow their meadows, occupy their uncultivated land, fell their timber and help themselves to their seed-grain. Their idea of revolutionary freedom was to do whatever they wanted after centuries of oppression. General Aleksei Brusilov, the commander of the great 1916 offensive who later joined the Red Army, wrote that 'the soldiers only wanted one thing – peace so that they could go home, rob the landowners and live freely without paying any taxes or recognising any authority'.

Brusilov was not exaggerating. 'Desertion in the army has increased dramatically,' Dr Kravkov observed. 'All the soldiers are keen to use the moment and seize some land from the landowners.' The military censorship department found this to be a common theme. 'Everyone here wishes for immediate peace, at any cost,' a soldier on the Western Front wrote home. 'And what do we need to fight for anyway if we are going to have a lot of land when the land of Tsar and landowners will be shared out? The *burzhuis* cannot trick us. We will go back home armed and get whatever is owed to us.'

The collapse of traditional authority in the countryside, especially the land captains who had upheld the interests of the gentry, allowed the peasants to create their own assemblies. They even made up their own unofficial laws, or decrees to provide a quasi-legal basis for their decisions. The Socialist Revolutionaries urged their followers to await the reforms which the Constituent Assembly would introduce, but patience evaporated rapidly. At a major peasant assembly in Samara, a delegate warned his audience not to trust the Party leaders. 'Will we be better off if we wait for the Constituent Assembly to resolve the land question? In the past the government decided the question for us, but their efforts led us only into bondage. Now the government says there must first be order. We are always being told "later, later, not now, not until the Constituent Assembly".'

Although some enlightened landowners were tolerated or even protected by their peasants and house servants, the vast majority had to flee during the course of the year. From the start in March, there were comparatively few examples of landowners killed, even though many manor houses were set ablaze. Yet in the charged atmosphere, a minor incident and bad timing, especially when peasants or soldiers managed to seize a store of alcohol, could lead to mindless violence. Around Mtsensk in May some 5,000 peasants and soldiers, having looted a wine cellar, went berserk and over three days set fire to estates in the area. The consummation of a desire to smash, or literally shit on, or set fire to the precious objects of the nobility and gentry only increased their bitterness. To destroy or defile the past did not make the present any better.

Liberal political views were not enough to protect an aristocratic landowner. Prince Boris Vyazemsky and his wife Lili returned to the family estate of Lotarevo in the province of Tambov. He first wished to bury his brother Dmitry, who had been killed by a stray bullet during the chaos in Petrograd. Dmitry had been hated by the peasants because of his role in suppressing local unrest during the 1905 revolution. Boris's views, on the other hand, were so liberal that they irritated his more old-fashioned relations.

A Bolshevik called Moiseev arrived in the district and encouraged the peasant committee to demand that the family hand over the bulk of their land. Boris replied that they should wait until the Constituent Assembly was elected and ruled on land reform. Some time later, Moiseev returned with a crowd several hundred-strong and surrounded the house. Boris Vyazemsky tried to reason with them, but he and Lili were seized and locked in the local school.

On the following day, Boris was taken to the local railway station to be sent to Petrograd under arrest, with the idea that he could be packed off to the front. But the station was swarming with deserters who, on hearing that Prince Vyazemsky was there, found him and beat him to death with metal rods. One account claims that his eyes were gouged out, but that was probably mutilation after his death. His wife Lili, meanwhile, had escaped with the help of her maid. Dressed in peasant clothes, she went to the station. She eventually found Boris's body in an empty railway wagon and took it to Moscow for burial. Like in many other places, their estate was completely destroyed so that the family would never return. The corpse of the hated brother, Dmitry Vyazemsky, was disinterred, broken up and scattered in the open.

Even handing over everything to the peasants seemed to do little good. In her father's absence, the young Princess Baturin addressed the local peasants who had come en masse from the village of Inozemka. She told them that the family had already declared that the whole estate and manor house were theirs. 'I implore you, don't destroy,' she said, 'don't demolish what is already yours.'

'The peasants stood there silently. They had come with poles and axes, with sacks, some brought carts. Someone in the crowd shouted out: "One landlord is gone, there will come another! Take what you can while you can." The rampage began. They broke off the huge doors of the landowner's house although no one could use them, they were too big for any *izba*. They put into the sacks everything they could lay their hands on, tore pages from leather covers of books, to use for rolling cigarettes. They tore off the padlocks from the barns and loaded and took away the grain. In less than three hours, the estate was empty.'

Even just seven years after Count Tolstoy's death, his semi-anarchist community at Yasnaya Polyana barely emerged unscathed. His peasants could not believe that he really had given them the land. The writer Ivan Nazhivin and his wife paid a visit as they were in the area in case it might be the last opportunity. 'The Countess,' he wrote, 'who was currently living in very difficult circumstances, met us with great hospitality, told us a lot, and then we went to visit the grave. When we approached we saw that some local youths were sitting behind the fence, right by the grave, playing balalaikas, spitting out husks of sunflower seeds, and screaming their repulsive songs . . . The fence was covered in filthy inscriptions . . . We didn't even dare approach the grave, just stood at a distance and went back. I was thinking that we shouldn't have come at all . . . When we came back to the estate, we saw Tatiana Lvovna [the writer's daughter] standing in the middle of a crowd of muzhiks . . . We did not go close but understood from some fragments of their conversation that the muzhiks were now demanding all of the land, and she was reasoning with them, pointing out that all of the land had already been given to them for free by her father.'

The Provisional Government 's first major crisis came in April. It was triggered from within Lvov's Cabinet by Professor Milyukov, the minister for foreign affairs. As his arguments to maintain the monarchy had shown, the intellectually rigorous, even icy Milyukov disdained the idea of bowing to political necessity. 'In those turbulent times,' wrote Paustovsky, 'he seemed to be a refugee from some other, well-ordered, academic planet.'

The whole question of continuing the war on the side of the Allies against the Central Powers was a fraught subject. The most effective German propaganda at the front claimed that Russia had been forced to stay in the conflict by Britain. Meanwhile, left-wing arguments condemned it as an 'imperialist' and 'capitalist' war. This played to the anger at the corruption in the capital over government contracts. The Soviet had even launched an 'Appeal to the Peoples of All the World' to oppose the war and called for peace without 'annexations or reparations'. The French government was particularly upset by this because one of its major war aims was to retrieve the provinces of Alsace and Lorraine which they had lost to Germany in 1871.*

When the French socialist leader Albert Thomas came to Moscow to make a speech supporting 'the sacred war alliance' a Bolshevik demonstration marched down the Tverskoi boulevard in response with placards proclaiming 'Down with the war!'; 'Peace to the peasants! War to the landowners!'; 'All power to the Soviets!'

Milyukov, however, believed firmly that Russia must stay in the war until Allied victory, and not just because of the huge French loans she was receiving. He also saw no reason why Russia should give up the promise of Constantinople and the Dardanelles once the Ottoman Empire was defeated. With the bulk of grain exports leaving Black Sea ports, he saw possession of the straits as a vital guarantee for the country's future trade.

On 27 March, to calm the Soviet's Executive Committee, Lvov's government issued a declaration of war aims as a commitment to a lasting peace and self-determination for all nations. The question of annexations was avoided. The Executive Committee insisted that it should be transmitted to the allied governments of the Entente. This was done, but Milyukov included a private explanatory note which indicated that Russia would fight on to the end.

On 20 April large-scale protests erupted when the text of Milyukov's note to the Allies finally emerged. This revealed his support for the 'secret treaties' in which Russia had been promised the Black Sea straits. Milyukov and his fellow Kadets had completely misread the mood of the country. Dr Vasily Kravkov at his corps headquarters wrote: 'To insist, as Milyukov does, on continuing the war until the victorious end, on taking the straits and Constantinople, and crushing

---

* French diplomats warned Paris of the great bitterness felt by many Russians that the western Allies were robbing them of peace by insisting on final victory and reparations. Viktor Shklovsky never forgave 'the foul ruthless policies of the Allies'. He blamed them for the Bolshevik seizure of power. 'They wouldn't go along with our peace conditions. They, no one but they, blew up Russia. Their refusal allowed the so-called Internationalists to take power.'

the Prussian autocracy, means to me that they have lost any touch with reality.'

Having failed to create a constitutional monarchy, Milyukov had hoped that the fall of the Tsar would at least revive patriotism and a determination to win the war. Most soldiers appear to have been resigned to continuing the war in March, yet that had started to change without the Provisional Government realising. Resentment against the war had intensified in April, along with the idea of defeated countries being forced to pay reparations and hand over territory.

On 20 April, Lieutenant Theodore Linde, a revolutionary officer in the Finlandsky Guards Regiment, called on his own and other reserve battalions of the Guard to march to the Mariinsky Palace, the seat of the Provisional Government, to demand Milyukov's resignation. They also called for the resignation of all 'bourgeois' ministers and their replacement by a revolutionary government. By chance, Lvov and his Cabinet happened to be meeting that afternoon at the ministry of war because Guchkov, the minister, was unwell. General Kornilov, the commander of Petrograd district, interrupted the meeting with news of the military demonstration and asked permission to bring in troops to crush this mutiny. According to Kerensky, all the ministers rejected his proposal.

The next day, the unrest was swollen by Bolsheviks and their supporters carrying banners prepared during the night proclaiming 'Down with the Provisional Government' and 'All power to the Soviets'. Lenin did not want the Bolsheviks left out of what could be another decisive moment, but the attempt to bring out the workers en masse failed. Only the most radical sailors from Kronstadt responded to their call. There were violent clashes with a number of people killed on the Nevsky Prospekt, where large crowds demonstrated their support for the Provisional Government.

General Kornilov once more demanded permission to bring in troops, this time addressing himself to the Executive Committee. His request was again refused and, humiliatingly, he was now informed that in future every such military directive had to be signed and stamped by two of their members. Sickened by what he saw as cowardice in the face of anarchy, Kornilov resigned as commander of Petrograd district and had himself transferred back to the front.

The Soviet Executive Committee, taking fright at the possibility of general disorder and even civil war, ordered Linde's followers back to barracks, to his dismay and incomprehension. The Bolsheviks, meanwhile, tried to pretend that they had had little to do with what had been a tentative coup, both in Petrograd and in Moscow. Behind closed doors, Kamenev criticised Lenin bitterly for his 'adventurism'. Lenin, however, was unrepentant. He believed that the April crisis had both weakened the Provisional Government and discredited the more moderate socialists of the Executive Committee. Lenin's little insurrection was no more than what Spanish Communists derided fifteen years later as 'revolutionary gymnastics'. Next time, he hoped, they would be better prepared and organised.

The street battles and general unrest in April deeply shocked the optimists in the Provisional Government and their supporters in the liberal intelligentsia. Lvov reached out to the Executive Committee for support, but his plea was rejected because of the reaction it might provoke on the street, with Milyukov still in place. Then, on 30 April, a depressed Aleksandr Guchkov resigned, convinced that the country was ungovernable. Milyukov also decided that his presence in government was now untenable. The departure of the two most 'bourgeois' ministers immediately changed the situation. On the following day the Executive Committee voted to allow its members to accept a position in Lvov's cabinet on the grounds that it was their duty to preserve the revolution through a coalition government. Perhaps the fact that the government was still led by Prince Lvov did not seem to matter so much in a country where the two most famous Anarchists were Prince Bakunin and Prince Kropotkin. In any case, the coalition government which resulted from this semi-merger with the Soviet did not strengthen a democratic centre, it sharpened the divide. The Kadet Party of Milyukov and Guchkov moved to the right in defence of order and private property, while the moderate socialists of the Executive Committee, tainted by cooperation with the bourgeois Provisional Government, were laid open to attack by the Bolsheviks.

Kerensky took the opportunity of the reshuffle to move from the ministry of justice to replace Guchkov at the ministry of war. This change encouraged him to transform himself in chameleon fashion. The socialist lawyer suddenly started to appear in military tunics and high boots. And ironically, after the vast unrest over Milyukov and Allied war aims, Kerensky soon set off to tour the front deploying his matchless oratorical skills, to persuade the soldiers to return to their duty and obey orders. This proved embarrassing for Irakli Tsereteli, a Menshevik from Georgia (and another prince of ancient lineage).

Tsereteli, a brilliant speaker, had invented the idea of 'revolutionary defencism', the holding of national territory without seizing anyone else's land. He managed to persuade five of his colleagues on the Executive Committee to join the Provisional Government on the grounds that they could help achieve peace more rapidly that way. But almost as soon as they had taken up their posts, they found that Kerensky's idea of 'revolutionary defencism' supported the *Stavka*'s plan for a major offensive to coincide with those of the western Allies with the argument that it would end the war more quickly. On 14 May, he published an order to the army: 'In the name of the salvation of free Russia,' it stated, 'you will go where your commanders and your Government send you. On your bayonet-points you will be bearing peace, truth and justice. You will go forward in serried ranks, kept firm by the discipline of your duty and your supreme love for the revolution and your country.'

Regrettably, discipline and duty were deteriorating rapidly, as Dr Kravkov noted later in the month. 'The scores of robberies and murders of civilians are growing the whole time in the areas held by our army. Unfortunate Jewish families suffer most of all.' As for Kerensky, Kravkov considered him 'just a grandiloquent juggler' when he claimed that 'the spirits of the soldiers were very high and victorious, and there was a "healthy growth" in the army'.

Kravkov, who had welcomed the February revolution with such enthusiasm, became utterly dejected. 'Far from joyful news is arriving from Tsaritsyn, Barnaul, Eniseisk and other places around our mother Russia: bloody jacqueries have started like those of Stepan Razin and Pugachev! The uncontrolled frenzied masses have their own ways to celebrate freedom.' Things were no better on the Galician Front. 'On the whole, less than half our troops have agreed to return to their positions,' he wrote. 'The rest of this armed horde intends to make its way to the station and demand to be put on trains, some going to Kiev, others, to Moscow. There are moments when I want to get out of this nightmarish dark pit of anarchy.'

Even those who remained in the trenches had started fraternising with the Germans or Austro-Hungarian troops opposite them. The enemy would shout to them 'Rus, don't shoot!' Both sides would then climb out of their trenches and meet up between the lines. In an attempt to stop this, Russian commanders ordered their artillery to open fire, but the infantry instead threatened the batteries involved and cut field telephone lines from forward observation officers. Starting from the unofficial truce over Easter, they frequently negotiated local agreements with the enemy troops opposite. But the German command of the Eastern Front, Oberkommando Ost, began to send agents and intelligence officers across, pretending that they too were revolutionaries and wanted to end the war. Thanks to the lack of fighting that spring, the Germans were able to transfer fifteen divisions from the Eastern Front to the Western Front, while the Austrians moved six of theirs to the Italian Front. Fraternisation even extended to prisoners of war being allowed out of their camps in Yaroslavel, Yekaterinburg and Tomsk to demonstrate against the war on 1 May alongside Russian soldiers. The Germans demanded their 'return home soon'.

'The men had fraternized long and assiduously,' wrote Viktor Shklovsky, sent as a commissar to the Galician front. 'The soldiers had been getting together in the villages situated between the lines and here they had set up a neutral exclusive brothel. Even some of the officers took part in the fraternization.' The idea of appointing commissars was copied from the *commissaires* of the Directoire after the French Revolution. Kerensky was convinced they would inspire the soldiers to fight again, but this proved excessively optimistic.

Kravkov recounted the arrival of Commissar Boris Savinkov from Petrograd. Savinkov, who had good looks and charisma, became one of the most controversial characters of the revolution and civil war. He had been a leading member of the Socialist Revolutionary combat organisation and had taken part in terrorist attacks on the Tsarist regime. After escaping from prison, he spent most of the war in the French Army. In Paris he became friends with Ilya Ehrenburg, Diego Rivera and Modigliani. But his return to Russia and the reality he encountered there disabused him of radical optimism.

Kravkov described Savinkov's attempt to persuade one of their divisions to return to the front line. 'The 45th and 46th Regiments with the 12th Siberian Artillery Brigade kindly agreed to set off after a lot of persuasion and begging by Commissar Savinkov. The 47th Regiment refused to move and declared itself autonomous, while the 48th and

49th are still thinking about it. The 51st allowed those soldiers wishing to set off to leave but took all their weapons from them. The 52nd remained where it was, having arrested all the officers including the commander.'

Two days later, Kravkov added to his diary. 'Commissar Savinkov, who turns out to be a former terrorist who had participated in the murders of Plehve and Grand Duke Sergei Aleksandrovich, tried to reason with the rebellious slaves. He admitted afterwards, sounding distressed, that the only thing that would work in such a situation is machine guns pointed at the men! He has shifted to the right considerably.'

Kerensky, infatuated with his own rhetoric, convinced himself and much of the population that he alone could inspire the Russian army to victory and to peace. He usually arrived in an open automobile and, standing up in the back, would address the troops. '"My greetings to you, comrades, soldiers of the revolutionary army!" This calculated address, expressive and spoken in a sonorous tenor voice, was followed by even more noise and shouting. Smiling, Kerensky raised his hand for silence. He then spoke about the achievements of the revolution, freedom, a cloudless future, revolutionary conscientiousness, about the Allies and loyalty to them, the steel of revolutionary discipline, and, finally, he appealed to them to make this last effort.'

'He would throw short sentences at a crowd, in his baying, petulant voice, and then choke,' Paustovsky wrote. 'He loved noisy words and believed in them. It seemed to him that they would resound like a tocsin across the desperate land and inspire people to great sacrifices and achievements. Having shouted his noisy words, Kerensky would fall back into his seat, shuddering and weeping. His adjutants would then give him a sedative.' Although hard to believe today, Kerensky's dramatics and emotional hyperbole could reduce even the most hardbitten soldiers to tears. They swore that they would storm the enemy trenches as soon as he gave the word.

During his tour, Kerensky went to Odessa and achieved a similar effect with civilians. Yelena Lakier, from a family of intellectuals, wrote in her diary: 'I am full of joy and happiness. Yesterday was one of the best days in my life. Kerensky, hope of all Russia, visited the city, and I saw him. Everyone was overcome by some sort of religious ecstasy. The crowd turned into savages. They were shouting *Urrrraa!* like mad. When his car drove up, the whole lot of them broke the line of soldiers and rushed towards him. How people love him! How they adore him!' People kissed his hands and reached out beseechingly to touch his clothes. She was convinced that 'In peasant families they regard him as a saint and even pray to him.'

6

The Kerensky Offensive and the July Days
June–July 1917

As the great offensive approached in June, attitudes veered between optimism and pessimism. Both Kerensky and General Brusilov, the new commander-in-chief, had chosen Galicia, the scene of Brusilov's famous operation the year before. Brusilov, although every inch an aristocratic cavalryman with elegant moustaches, was a professional and innovative commander, as his successes against the Austro-Hungarian armies had demonstrated. Both General Gutor, who had just taken over the Southwestern Front, and even General Kornilov, now commanding its Eighth Army, hoped that their troops there had been the least affected by the revolution.

Locker-Lampson's armoured car division was transferred to the area to support the attack. 'The nearer we approached the front,' he reported, 'the better the discipline, until in the trenches we found men even saluting their officers.' Staff officers he spoke to thought that the front-line troops would fight, at least three-quarters of them, but they had little confidence in the reserves coming from the much more politicised rear. As Locker-Lampson noted, although 'preparations were better than I had yet seen', conditions were not helped by heavy thunderstorms which turned the earth into slimy mud. His armoured car division's base was established at Kozova, which apparently made them the first British unit to occupy enemy territory on the continent in the First World War.

Locker-Lampson also witnessed the extraordinary effect of Kerensky's words. His 'fervent appeal to patriotism was read out everywhere by committed men, non-commissioned officers and officers. War-worn veterans round the camp-fires would take off their caps and cry like children. Whole audiences wept as though physically relaxed by what they heard, and I passed soldiers blubbering their way home in the dark.'

The sceptics, on the other hand, were afraid of the consequences if this huge gamble failed, especially after the way the troops had been promised that it would end the war. 'I don't think that even Kornilov clearly understood the hopelessness of the situation,' wrote Viktor Shklovsky, the commissar allocated to his Eighth Army on the Galician front. 'He was first and foremost a military man. A general charging into the fray with a revolver. He viewed the army just as a good driver views his automobile.'

Military censorship for the Southwestern Front was intercepting far more aggressive letters home than just after the February revolution. 'The officers are provocateurs and counter-revolutionaries,' one declared. 'They are trying to get their power back but that's not possible. They should all be killed, the bastards. They had been sucking our blood, but now the soldiers have become the key figures. . . I am a member of the soviet now.'

Shklovsky was dismayed that the troops refused to dig communication trenches in preparation. In a growing number of regiments motions opposing the offensive were passed at rallies. The bloody-mindedness of so-called 'trench bolshevism' was laying the ground for the real thing. Already, during May, revolutionary agitators had begun to stir up trouble. The Bolsheviks were distributing free copies of their *Soldatskaya Pravda* to soldiers at the front via the reserves arriving from Petrograd.

On 4 June, at the First All-Russian Congress of Soviets, Lenin appeared. He clashed with Tsereteli, who had just stated in defence of the broad coalition government that there was no political party in Russia prepared to take entire power on itself. Lenin shot back that the Bolsheviks were 'ready at any moment to take over the government'. The majority of non-Bolsheviks in the audience burst into derisive laughter at the idea of such a small party taking power all on its own.

This startling revelation of his intentions was carelessly overlooked by other political leaders. It proved that Lenin cynically despised the slogan 'All power to the Soviets'. Instead, he sought absolute control by using the soviets as his stalking horse to power. And because he knew very well that his plan of complete state ownership was not popular, he simply paid lip service to the idea of handing the land over to the peasants and factories to the workers. Both colleagues and opponents suffered his frequent rages, which sometimes exploded in vile obscenities. The closer Lenin came to power, the greater his contempt for any notion of morality or for the rights of others, and the greater his obsessive belief that he alone was capable of achieving the total revolution he sought. Nobody, whether Bolshevik or any other Russian politician, could hope to match his iron will and self-belief.

Six days later, the Bolsheviks pulled back at the last moment from organising a major demonstration against the coalition government. Some, like Sukhanov, the Socialist Revolutionary member of the Executive Committee, later suspected that this would have been an attempt to provoke an outright attack on the Mariinsky Palace. The Bolsheviks' own secret Military Organisation, having infiltrated even more regiments in the Petrograd garrison, was growing in confidence. At the end of April it had converted some of the worker militias guarding factories into Red Guards, who would become the intermediate step to Trotsky's Red Army in the spring of 1918.

The *Stavka* at Mogilev was determined to use the summer offensive to restore discipline in the army. So much depended on its success that Brusilov, who had taken over from General Alekseev, concentrated most of their artillery formations to support the Southwestern Front, including heavy howitzer brigades. Elite breakthrough units, called death or storm battalions, were formed with volunteers. But this innovation was double-edged since it took the best NCOs and soldiers from the line regiments, leaving them less reliable than before.

There was even a Women's Battalion of Death, led by Lieutenant 'Yashka' Bochkareva. She had been permitted by the Tsar to join the army to fight in 1915, had been wounded several times and decorated for her bravery. Commanders hoped that her rather small 'battalion' of shaven-headed women would shame the rest of the troops into advancing instead of skulking in their trenches. But the men simply saw the deployment of women as a sign of desperation.

The German and Austro-Hungarian divisions were never going to be taken by surprise. All the preparations along the front, especially the sectors of the Seventh and Eleventh Armies, could not be hidden from the enemy's reconnaissance flights and observation balloons. And their intelligence officers were well informed from all the fraternisation between the lines.

On 16 June, the artillery bombardment began. It lasted for two days, with a concentration of fire never seen before by the Russian army. Locker-Lampson was instructed by Major General Frederick

Poole, the chief British liaison officer, to position Stokes mortars in front-line trenches to increase the impression. Then, before dawn on 18 June, the assault battalions moved into the front-line trenches. At 10.00 hours, the shellfire 'walked forward' in a creeping barrage, the attackers climbed out of their trenches and, with red banners raised and spike bayonets fixed, marched into no man's land.

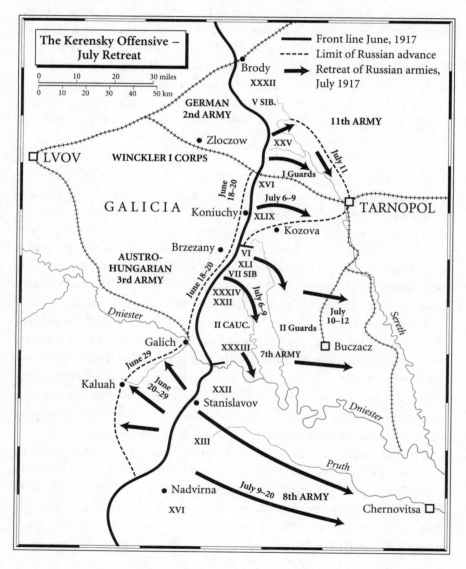

The British armoured cars of the Royal Naval Air Service had been allocated to XLI Corps in the Seventh Army, which was attacking on the main axis towards Brzezany. They faced good defensive positions manned by German troops, not Austro-Hungarians. Other British troops were spread around the corps 'to encourage and stiffen them'. Locker-Lampson's armoured cars dashed forward along the roads on both flanks and enfiladed the enemy trenches with fire. Most of the infantry was able to advance with very few casualties, watched by Kerensky. Embarrassingly, some regiments of the 74th Division refused to move. 'Their officers leapt over the parapet and advanced with mere handfuls of their soldiers following, and died to a man,' Locker-Lampson reported. 'One of our petty officers (an Australian) on duty with a Maxim in the trenches with these regiments could not watch this without protest. He ran up to a platoon and forcibly assisted a score of reluctant Russians over the parapet.'

The 3rd and 5th TransAmur Divisions had meanwhile advanced with 'magnificent dash', some even reaching the edge of Brzezany itself. They captured 500 Germans and sent these prisoners back towards their own lines. Unfortunately, reserve units coming up assumed that they were enemy columns attacking and a terrible massacre ensued. Meanwhile, the two divisions of Amur troops assumed that they had won a great victory and sat down in the woods next to the town to smoke, eat and play cards. But their flanks were completely unprotected due to the failure of neighbouring formations to advance. They were loath to occupy even abandoned German trenches, despite urging by British officers that they would support them. Order and counter-order increased the confusion, and Russian staff officers were 'distraught beyond belief'. A German bombardment and counter-attack the next day, together with the Amur troops' realisation of their vulnerable position, prompted them to pull back all the way to their start-line.

Locker-Lampson went to visit General Gutor and Kerensky in the staff train. 'Mr Kerensky seemed preoccupied. His clean-shaven, frank, ugly face brightened at the news of the damage done by the bombardment; but his prodigious efforts speaking to the troops . . . had worn him out.'

The Eleventh Army, the northern neighbour of the Seventh Army, had more success against Austro-Hungarian forces. They took 20,000 prisoners, many of them conscripted Czechs, who were only too happy to surrender and join their fellow countrymen on the other side. Kerensky was prematurely exultant in his messages to Petrograd, asking for revolutionary banners to be presented to the victorious regiments. Reports of victory provoked great celebrations in the city. 'There was noise and animation in the streets of Petrograd on 20 June,' Prokofiev wrote in his diary. 'Crowds carried banners. Russian troops had started to advance. I am happy about this. At least one won't be ashamed in front of the French and English.' In fact, this rally was an attempt to support the Provisional Government two days after a massive demonstration called by the Soviet with 400,000 participants, but largely taken over by the Bolsheviks.

The Eighth Army on the southern side was supposed to do little more than advance to protect the flank of the main attack. Shklovsky noted how the Austrian trenches were far better constructed than Russian ones. 'Our soldiers were scratching around in them looking for sugar. Fortunately, members of the committee had succeeded in destroying the wine; otherwise the soldiers would have gotten drunk.' Shklovsky found some of them 'calmly having a breakfast of Austrian rations, with the cans placed on corpses'. He went back to check on the reserves coming forward. 'While going through the woods, I kept running into stray soldiers with rifles, mostly young men. "Where are you off to?" I asked. "I'm sick." In other words, deserting from the front.'

Then, just as the rest of the Seventh Army was retreating to its start line, Kornilov's divisions unexpectedly broke through and captured the towns of Galich and Kalush. The news caused great rejoicing in Petrograd, boosting Kornilov's reputation. Unfortunately, the troops taking Kalush went wild, looting, drinking and raping. Jewish families were their main victims. Then, the 23rd Division collapsed and began to run away. Kornilov, with Savinkov's full support, ordered them to be halted with a blocking line of machine guns.

The main offensive was over a few days later. All formations had been pushed back to their start-lines by German counter-attacks and any further attempts to advance were drowned by thunderstorms. 'The trenches are streams and the roads lakes of mud,' Locker-Lampson wrote. One division which had refused all orders to advance was surrounded by Cossack cavalry and Russian armoured cars and made to disarm. Polish regiments crossed over en masse to the Germans because most of their homes were just behind their lines. The losses in good officers and NCOs with the volunteers of the so-called 'Death' and 'Storm' Battalions had been catastrophic. To make matters worse, a sudden German bombardment hit a huge shell dump by Kozova station. Massive explosions were followed by fires which destroyed most of the Seventh Army's stores, with devastating consequences both materially and for the men's morale. The station and part of the town were totally flattened. Cossack troops, convinced it must be the work of spies, started slaughtering any Jews they could find and Locker-Lampson had to send in his armoured cars to restore order.

The overall *Stavka* plan included subsequent attacks to take place on other sectors, but these encountered even less success. Part of the Fifth Army in the north near Dvinsk failed to attack. Around midday, headquarters received a report of a mutiny in one of the first line regiments. Soldiers had left the trenches but refused to advance. They were threatening the artillery, demanding that they stop the bombardment as it was making the Germans fire back. The gunners, however, were not intimidated: they threatened to fire case-shot at the rebellious infantry and carried on with the bombardment.

'Those who had doubts were proved right,' wrote Maksim Kulik, a Cossack officer working with the army commissar. 'The infantry was sent forward on the second day, by which time our artillery had to a large extent destroyed the German obstacles. The first line advanced successfully and took the German trenches, but when it was time for the reserves to support them, they stayed in their trenches. Neither orders from their officers, nor remonstrances, nor threats succeeded in pushing them forward. Meanwhile the German artillery ranged in accurately and started hitting the crowded trenches, causing a fearful massacre.'

The great June offensive had achieved the worst of all possible outcomes. It had not merely failed to impress Russia's Allies, it confirmed the belief of most soldiers that their suffering at the front was futile. This immeasurably strengthened Lenin's anti-war position, which would destroy the Provisional Government and open the way for the Bolshevik coup d'état four months later.

Kerensky, blind to the danger, returned to Petrograd determined to restore the death penalty in the army. 'Without it wholesale desertion must continue and disobedience reign supreme,' Locker-Lampson wrote. He expected a counter-revolution to develop based on 'the Cossacks, some of the cavalry, the Artillery and the elite of the Army'. The obvious person to lead such an attempt was the intensely proud yet diminutive General Lavr Kornilov. Even more than Kerensky,

Kornilov would soon be seen as the Bonaparte-in-waiting of the Russian Revolution but, as is so often the case, the historical parallels proved wholly misleading.

To read the accounts of socialist politicians in Petrograd, the failure of the offensive sounds like a distant echo in the background as they squabbled over the coalition government. On Monday 3 July, the Soviet Executive Committee in the Tauride Palace was in mid-debate when a telephone call from a factory warned Sukhanov that the Bolsheviks, without prior warning, were calling out factory workers and soldiers for a massive armed demonstration.

Lenin was taking a badly needed rest in a dacha outside the Finnish village of Neivola, some two hours by train from Petrograd. He had no idea that the Party's ill-disciplined Military Organisation had presumed to act on its own. On the other hand, it has been suggested that Lenin had left for Finland because he had been tipped off by a sympathiser within the security apparatus that Colonel Nikitin of army counter-intelligence was planning a mass arrest of Bolsheviks on 7 July. The charge would be one of treason for accepting financial support from Germany.

The 1st Machine Gun Regiment, which had become almost a praetorian guard for the Party, was on the march, although nobody was sure why or where they were headed. The machine gunners were in revolt against orders to reinforce the front, which was in danger of collapse after the failed offensive. The Bolsheviks' Military Organisation was summoning soldiers from other barracks and workers from all the most militant factories to support them. They distributed banners declaring 'All Power to the Soviets!' and 'Down with the ten bourgeois ministers!' Soldiers, assembling with their weapons, began firing in the air.

Word then reached the Executive Committee that the Machine Gun Regiment and the Guards Grenadier Regiment were marching on the Tauride Palace. The news caused consternation in the hall. Suddenly, Kamenev jumped up onto the speaker's platform. 'We never called for a demonstration,' he shouted, which must have sounded disingenuous, 'but the popular masses have come out into the streets to show their will. And once the masses have come out, our place is with them.'

A Bolshevik lieutenant led one of the rebel regiments along the Nevsky Prospekt, but the sound of firing some way off had a startling effect. The regiment panicked and fled. The Military Organisation's ill-considered attempt was not going well, although Bolshevik propaganda attacking the more moderate socialists of the Executive Committee had clearly had its effect. A threatening crowd around the Tauride Palace that night shouted: 'Arrest the Executive Committee, they've surrendered to the landlords and the bourgeoisie!' The impatient instigators had thought they could force the Executive Committee to push aside the Provisional Government, which would fall of its own accord due to lack of support. Even though Lvov and his ministers had so little control, they were inevitably blamed for food shortages, deteriorating transport and painful price rises for the poor.

The Provisional Government had inherited and increased its huge debts to the Allies for war matériel. It began printing money with the introduction of *kerenki* roubles, named after the new prime minister, but the *kerenki* inspired so little confidence that people began to hoard Tsarist banknotes. Inflation simply accelerated. In six months from the February revolution, the Provisional Government issued 5.3 billion roubles in notes. In the summer and early autumn prices increased fourfold.

The evening the unrest started, Prokofiev enjoyed a good dinner at the Kontan restaurant. 'The prices are crazy, of course, but money gets cheaper every day, so why save it?' He then added: 'We witnessed something we hadn't expected while we walked in the streets in the evening. The streets were busy, soldiers marched with rifles, crowds carried posters: "Get Rid of Capitalist Ministers!" Private cars were stopped in front of our eyes and their owners were asked to get out. Machine guns were immediately installed in the cars.'

The debates in the Tauride Palace went on all through that night until an early summer's dawn on Tuesday, 4 July. Sukhanov noted that after Kamenev's departure, no Bolsheviks were present. Lenin had known nothing about the chaos in Petrograd until early that morning, when a messenger from the Central Committee reached the dacha in Finland to warn him that they were either facing a bloody fiasco or the overthrow of the Provisional Government. Lenin was impatient for power, but he also feared another Paris Commune, when revolutionaries seized the capital, but then were crushed by a counter-revolution from outside.

Lenin and his companions packed hurriedly. They took the next train back to Petrograd, arriving at the Finland Station in rather less optimistic circumstances than his arrival from Switzerland three months earlier. If Lenin really had hidden himself in Finland to escape Colonel Nikitin's round-up, then his decision to return meant taking an uncharacteristic risk. Lenin, who could not face being locked up, was not noted for his courage when he risked imprisonment. His monomania did not allow him to trust anyone else to run the revolution. So, why would he return if he knew already that Colonel Nikitin was preparing to arrest him?

On the other hand, he was furious with the extremists in the Military Organisation for taking such a gamble. Worst of all, the 1st Machine Gun Regiment had appealed the day before to Kronstadt to send a large crowd of sailors to join in. Lenin knew how uncontrollable the Baltic Fleet sailors were, with their influential Anarchist minority.

At roughly the same time as Lenin reached Petrograd on that morning of 4 July, a large force of some 8,000 armed sailors assembled in Kronstadt's great Anchor Square to embark. Their leader was the twenty-five-year old Fyodor Ilyin, a midshipman who was the illegitimate son of a priest and a general's daughter. Now a Bolshevik, he had taken the name of Dostoevsky's murderer Raskolnikov as his *nom de guerre*. Fyodor Raskolnikov later insisted that the intentions of his large force were entirely peaceful even though every sailor had been told to come with a weapon. Trying to avoid Bolshevik responsibility for the resulting disaster, he added that the machine gunners who had asked them to come were 'apparently under Anarchist influence', when in fact they were led by the Bolshevik organiser Ensign A.Y. Semashko.

Raskolnikov had first checked by telephone with Grigory Zinoviev on the position of the Bolshevik Central Committee. Should the Kronstadt sailors come out too in support? Zinoviev went off to find out and returned to insist that it must be 'a peaceful and organised armed demonstration'. This bizarre combination of peaceful and armed contradicted itself further when Raskolnikov let slip, 'the Party always kept in hand the possibility of transforming this armed demonstration into an armed uprising'.

The mass of militant sailors arrived in a flotilla of different vessels and disembarked beyond the Nikolaevsky Bridge. With Raskolnikov at their head, they marched to the Kshesinskaya mansion, red banners flying and band playing. Raskolnikov clearly revelled in the fear that his sailors inspired among the bourgeoisie of Petrograd, who saw 'Kronstadt as a symbol of savage horror'.

He continued: 'The sailors,' he wrote, 'formed up in front of Kshesinkaya's two-storeyed mansion where not so long before the well-known ballerina and favourite of the Tsar had held luxurious banquets and evening receptions, but where now was housed the general staff of our Party.' But there was no sign of Lenin. Raskolnikov went in and found him almost ill with anxiety. Left with no choice, he emerged on to the balcony to address the sailors. To their confusion, he urged them to protest without any violence and scuttled back inside.

Raskolnikov's force marched off towards the Tauride Palace but clashes took place in the centre of the city with troops loyal to the Provisional Government. It is impossible to know who fired first, but the exchange was chaotic, with sailors angrily shooting in all directions. Even when the firing ended, the furious sailors began to smash shop windows and loot or beat up well-dressed civilians deemed to be *burzhui*. Gorky, an eye-witness, was scathing. 'The frightening sortie into the "social revolution" was undertaken by somebody hastily, unthinkingly, and that stupidity is the name of the force which pushed people, armed to the teeth, into the streets. Suddenly a shot cracks out somewhere, and hundreds of people fly convulsively in all directions driven by fear . . . They fall to the ground, tripping over one another, screaming and shouting: "The bourgeois are shooting!"' In fact, Gorky found that different groups of rebels were firing at each other.

When they reached the Tauride Palace and joined the vast crowds who wanted to force the Soviet to seize power, Raskolnikov went in to report. He saw Trotsky, who had not yet joined the Bolsheviks, and they began to talk. Suddenly, a Menshevik rushed up to them and announced: 'The Kronstadters have arrested Chernov, put him in a car and want to take him off somewhere.' Viktor Chernov was both the leader of the Socialist Revolutionaries and the minister of agriculture, who refused to agree to the seizure of land by peasants until the Constituent Assembly was formed. Some sailors had started to shoot at the palace while others began to climb into it through windows. If there had not been an immense downpour which prompted most of the crowd to disperse, the bloodshed might have been much greater. Trotsky and Raskolnikov managed to stop the sailors who had seized a very shaken Chernov, whom they were about to drive off in an automobile.

Trotsky climbed up onto the car and addressed the sailors who fell silent on recognising him. Trotsky, to the irritation of the sailors, told them to let Chernov go. The battered and confused Chernov, with his grey hair dishevelled, had to be helped out and up the steps back into the palace. Order was soon restored when the Ismailovsky Guards Regiment arrived. The sailors had no alternative but to wander off in groups. They caused much trouble in the city that night. Some 2,000 of them seized the Peter and Paul Fortress as a futile gesture, but also to shelter from the rain in the unlocked cells. Since the Executive Committee could not be forced to take over the government, the uprising had failed, and yet there were still Bolsheviks who believed that they must continue.

In the early hours of 5 July, after arguments which lasted through the night, Lenin finally persuaded the Central Committee to call off the demonstrations. But that very morning, the right-wing 'reptile press' enjoyed its revenge. The army's counter-intelligence department had been gathering evidence for the Provisional Government on Bolshevik sources of finance. Without permission, they had passed their most sensational findings to the newspapers, which published accusations that Lenin had received 'German gold'. Lenin was never a German agent as the papers claimed, on the other hand, he would have had no scruples about accepting large sums of German money to develop the increasingly powerful Bolshevik press empire.*

Police and groups of *'junker'* officer cadets raided the offices of *Pravda* that morning and the Party's headquarters in the Kshesinskaya mansion on the following day. Raskolnikov, Lunacharsky, Kamenev and Trotsky were soon arrested, but Lenin and Zinoviev slipped away. Ironically, Konstantin Globachev, the former head of the Okhrana and now a prisoner of the Provisional Government, noted that some arrested Bolsheviks brought to his prison were locked in a separate cell. This was because the head warder suspected that some of the guards were Bolsheviks themselves. When the arrested Bolsheviks were searched, several were found to possess forged ten-rouble notes, which allegedly had been provided to the Party by the German government.

Lenin, whose face was surprisingly little known, had escaped in good time. He hid in an apartment rented by Boris Alliluev and moved

---

* The Provisional Government's accusations do not amount to hard proof that the Bolsheviks accepted 'German gold', and yet it is hard to see how the Bolsheviks could have afforded all their newspapers without outside help.

into the bedroom reserved for the family's usual lodger, Josef Stalin, who later married their daughter Nadhezda. Stalin arrived shortly afterwards and agreed to shave off Lenin's moustache and beard. This altered the Central Asian cast of his appearance, which came from a Kalmyk grandmother to add to the rich mixture of his Russian, German, Jewish and Swedish ancestry. Without the facial hair, Lenin now thought with satisfaction that he looked like a Finnish peasant.

The image of Stalin shaving his leader is an intriguing one. The autodidact Stalin was acutely aware that other leading revolutionaries despised him intellectually. Trotsky never bothered to conceal his contempt for somebody he considered little more than a pock-marked Georgian gangster. His under-estimation of Stalin's conspiratorial abilities would eventually cost him his life.

Fearful of arrest for high treason, Lenin was to spend the next three months before the Bolshevik coup d'état as a fugitive in disguise, moving from safe house to safe house. He might well have thought back to the start of their return journey to Russia, when he had predicted to Karl Radek that within six months they would either be in power or swinging from a gallows. Lenin scorned half-measures as much as he abhorred compromise.

7

Kornilov
July–September 1917

On 7 July, while the unsuccessful hunt for fugitive Bolsheviks continued, Prince Lvov resigned as leader of the Provisional Government. He was replaced by Kerensky. This had nothing to do with either the July uprising or the failed offensive. Five days earlier, Kadet ministers had resigned in protest at a decision to allow Ukraine a degree of autonomy.

Both liberals and socialists in the reconstituted Provisional Government wanted to keep the Russian empire together. They had accepted in March that after the war Poland, now behind German lines, would break away to become fully independent, but they were determined to hold on to the Grand Duchy of Finland, the Baltic provinces and Ukraine. Their view was that the grievances and aspirations of national minorities were purely the product of Tsarist oppression, above all the 'russification' programmes introduced under Nicholas II which had discouraged any diversity of culture or language. A few limited concessions to autonomy were thought to be sufficient.

On 12 April, for example, the Russian Provisional Government had accorded a measure of self-government to Estonia and twelve days later the *Stavka* allowed Estonians to transfer to the new 1st Estonian Rifle Regiment. Nobody in Petrograd or Mogilev then imagined how soon it would provide the basis for the very effective army of an independent state.

Finland had been part of Sweden until 1809, when Tsar Alexander I occupied it as a personal fiefdom, making it a Grand Duchy. The country was permitted a very limited degree of autonomy, supervised by the Tsar's governor general. But in 1899, Nicholas II agreed to a policy of 'russification' of its educational system and culture. This proved deeply unpopular and gave rise to a sense of Finnish patriotism. During the First World War, Finns were not called up for military service as they were not trusted, and some 2,000 nationalistic students escaped to Germany to join the Royal Prussian 27th Jäger Battalion of light infantry.

The Tsarist regime was so concerned that the Germans might use Finland as a base of operations to attack Petrograd that it had increased the XLII Independent Corps and personnel of the Baltic Fleet to a total of 125,000 men. For a population of only 3.25 million, this was a huge presence. After the February revolution, Russian troops in the country had confused feelings towards the Finns, whose language they did not speak or understand. Yet many on the Left began to sympathise with Finnish hopes for independence. By the early summer of 1917, Finnish workers in the more industrialised south of the country began to fraternise with Russian soldiers and sailors who supported their demands for an eight-hour working day.

The abdication of the Tsar, the Grand Duke of Finland, and his replacement by the Provisional Government encouraged Finnish nationalists to believe that their time had come. The Senate set up a constitutional committee to prepare the ground for full independence. But the Russian Provisional Government, especially Kerensky when minister of war, feared that Germany might exploit the situation. Finland could not be granted independence, he insisted, until it was approved by the future Constituent Assembly. The Finnish parliament, the Eduskunta, then took advantage of the July Days of chaos in Petrograd to assume supreme power. But on 18 July, the Provisional Government retaliated by dismissing the Eduskunta.

Finnish socialists, who had been the most outspoken advocates of independence, appealed to their Russian comrades in the garrison to help them against the 'reactionary' policy of the government in Petrograd. This they agreed to do, but the Eduskunta was closed instead by Cossacks, whom Kerensky had ordered to Helsingfors. He ordered the Russian forces in Finland to supervise fresh elections. This was done, but to the frustration of the Finnish Left the conservative parties emerged in a much stronger position, controlling the Senate.

On 13 September, the Helsingfors Soviet and the representatives of the Russian army and navy overwhelmingly supported the motion of the Bolshevik Vladimir Antonov-Ovseenko, which condemned the Provisional Government and supported the Finnish drive for independence. Ironically, as things were to turn out, this attempt to show that Russian national chauvinism died with Tsarism would enable Finland to escape Communist rule from Moscow shortly afterwards.

*

The immediate crisis for the Provisional Government in June and July had been triggered by the Ukrainian Central Rada in Kiev declaring independence. The leading Ukrainian nationalists, Symon Petliura, Volodimir Vinnichenko and the historian Mykhailo Hrushevsky, who presided over the Rada, had attempted to negotiate a degree of autonomy in May with Lvov's government, but their delegation had been virtually ignored. Every point they made was dealt with by the insistence that nothing could be decided except by the Constituent Assembly. Not surprisingly, this obfuscation had only increased their determination to go for full independence. They chose the pale blue and yellow flag, and a 'Universal' declaration, based on a seventeenth-century charter from the Hetman of the Zaporozhian Cossack Host, which Hrushevsky had defined as their ancestral right. Petliura, a pro-lific journalist, would later become the notional president and chief ataman of a Ukrainian People's Republic.

The Provisional Government, agreeing to compromise rather late in the day, sent a delegation led by Kerensky and Tsereteli to Kiev. They offered a partial recognition of Ukrainian demands to calm things down. But this provoked outrage among Russian nationalists in Kiev and disorder broke out. Three increasingly right-wing Kadets still in the government demanded that the Russians in Ukraine, which they preferred to call 'Little Russia', should be supported. They refused to accept the compromise agreement which Tsereteli and Kerensky had brought back, and resigned on 4 July, the very day the Bolshevik insurgents had wanted the Petrograd Soviet to replace the Provisional Government. With representatives joining from elsewhere, it had already started to call itself the All-Russian Soviet of Soldiers' and Workers' Deputies.

Kerensky saw himself as above the fray between socialists and liberals, but he failed to see how dangerous the gulf between them had become. Most socialists, appalled by the extreme attacks of the right-wing press on the Bolsheviks, began to side with them out of an exagger-ated fear of counter-revolution. Yet at the same time, the disorders across the country were such that not only officers and the middle class yearned for a strong leader. It was perhaps no coincidence that on 7 July Kerensky made the fateful decision to dispatch the impe-rial family from Tsarskoe Selo to Tobolsk in Siberia. He feared that the extreme Left uprising of the last few days might well provoke a monarchist backlash.

Many of those who had welcomed the February Revolution with joy and hope were now utterly disillusioned by the chaos and crime which had followed. 'Very few people are conscientious now,' wrote Lakier. 'They fail to understand that freedom is not outrage and the usurpation of power. For the majority, however, freedom and highway robbery have become synonymous. Russian people are like children run wild; they know no restraint.' And Dr Kravkov recorded his belief that 'Only a major take-over can bring relief to a suffering Russia, many of whose people after centuries of slavery are still inert, ignorant and only suited to be a blind weapon in the hands of a random hypnotist . . . Robberies and plunder are increasing on a colossal scale. It is going from bad to worse: the corps commander was burgled in the morning, and in the evening the chief of staff was stripped of everything that he had on him, and this happened in front of the sentry. The extreme brazenness of Bolshevism!'

On 6 July, just after the Russian offensive petered out on the Galician front, a German strike-force under General Arnold von Winckler suddenly smashed through the battered Eleventh Army. It headed towards Tarnopol, which fell five days later. The vast Ukrainian steppe lay open. Lakier wrote anxiously in Odessa, 'The army is bolting. There is a colossal breach. 120 kilometres.' Kerensky's re-introduction of capital punishment seemed to make no difference to discipline. 'It is a terrible feeling when your favourite idol turns out to have feet of clay and falls,' Lakier wrote. 'I believed blindly in Kerensky, but now he is making one mistake after another.' Word even began to spread that Odessa would have to be evacuated and the banks there were already packing up.

A German advance towards Riga on the Baltic coast also prompted rumours that the capital itself would have to be abandoned. 'A mailed fist was raised over Petrograd,' Prokofiev wrote in his diary. '[Riga] was still far away but were the revolutionary troops strong enough, and what would happen if three million inhabitants fled from Petrograd? And the Zeppelins can visit any day. There were crowds in the station, and packed trains were taking scared residents to the south.'

*

The lynching of officers increased, with obscene mutilation while they were still alive, as did the number committing suicide. The soldiers' attitude of 'we are the masters now' appeared to give them an urge to exact revenge for every past humiliation and injustice, both imagined and real. 'Everything is crashing down and officers are at the very bottom of society,' wrote a young officer in the Guards Artillery. 'We are class enemies. The non-commissioned officers are treating us like shit. We have to be careful because thousands of eyes are watching us.' He then added, 'Our generation is doomed . . . All that is left to us is exile or death.' The demoralisation of the officer corps was clearly a contributory factor in the collapse of the Southwestern Front in July, but not all lost their nerve.

Vladimir von Dreier managed to transfer to the 7th Cavalry Division, of which Major General Pyotr Wrangel, from a family of Baltic barons, took command during the retreat. The immensely tall and slim Wrangel, with his sunken eyes and piercing gaze, intimidated many, but also won intense loyalty. He was not merely energetic. 'He always forced everyone to be active even when there was nothing to do,' Dreier noted. He would gallop from regiment to regiment in his division to check on things for himself. Like other mounted divisions, Wrangel's 7th Cavalry had to act as a rearguard after the German breakthrough. The adjacent cavalry division was commanded by Major General Baron Gustaf Mannerheim, a Finn of German Swedish ancestry and a former officer of the Chevalier Guards.

'The infantry at first retreated in reasonable order with a show of resistance from time to time,' Dreier recorded, 'but then simply abandoned their weapons and fled. On some days they marched sixty kilometres in a day, so keen were they to get back to the Russian border. During their retreat the soldiers looted and set on fire everything they could find: depots, villages, haystacks and houses in towns. One night the division headquarters stopped for a night in the town of Stanislavov through which the last infantry groups were passing. I was standing in the street with Wrangel watching them. Suddenly we saw several soldiers break away from the crowd and smash a shop window on the ground floor of a five-storey building. They entered and tried to set the goods on fire. Wrangel and [Colonel] Zykov immediately ran over there and began beating this riff-raff, Wrangel with his horsewhip and Zykov with his fists.' The supposedly more disciplined Cossacks could be just as bad as the infantry. 'Who robs the civilians?' a foot soldier wrote home. 'Cossacks. Who rapes and kills civilians? Cossacks.'

Viktor Shklovsky, Kornilov's commissar from the Eighth Army, described the savage punishment inflicted on deserters and looters by ordinary soldiers. '*Ad hoc* committees from the units that had stood fast caught the deserters. Infuriated that this had happened on Russian land, where the Volhynian villages were burning, they flogged the men . . . The deserter was offered a choice of being shot or flogged. A monstrous sort of oath was invented by which he renounced his rights as a citizen and testified that what was being done to him was being done with his consent.' The floggings were carried out with rifle-cleaning rods, as had been the custom in the old Tsarist army.

Shklovsky was wounded in the stomach and moved to an improvised field hospital in Nadvirna. Soon after Kornilov had presented him with the Cross of St George, Shklovsky heard that the Germans were approaching. Three Russian regiments had left the line open and German cavalry had just streamed through. 'The supply depots were burning. Almost by force of arms, the wounded were fighting for places in the very last train . . . The infantry was on the move. The artillery too . . . The front had fallen apart; only our armoured cars were holding back the Germans.'

On 16 July, Kerensky called a conference at the *Stavka* to discuss the disaster. It was held in the neo-classical Governor's Mansion, which had been Nicholas II's residence when at Mogilev. As well as Brusilov and General Ruzsky, Anton Denikin, a future commander-in-chief of the White armies in the south of Russia, attended and proved to be the key participant. Also present were the two leading commissars, Boris Savinkov and Maksimilian Filonenko, both Right Socialist Revolutionaries. When Kerensky, accompanied by the foreign minister Mikhail Tereshchenko, arrived at Mogilev station, he was outraged not to be met by the commander-in-chief, but by an aide. He refused to move until Brusilov arrived in person.

Once the meeting started, Brusilov said little and, for once, so did Kerensky. He was clearly shaken by the other generals' denunciations of the way revolutionary politics had destroyed the army. Led by Denikin, they demanded the cancellation of *prikaz* No. 1, which in their view had turned military authority upside down. As they listened to accounts of the retreat, Kerensky sat bowed in silent horror, his head in his hands, while Tereshchenko was reduced to tears.

Kornilov, who could not leave his headquarters, congratulated Denikin afterwards when he heard what he had said. While Savinkov and Filonenko returned by train to Petrograd with the two ministers they took the opportunity to promote Kornilov as the exhausted Brusilov's successor, since he was one of the few generals to support the role of commissars at the front. Kerensky agreed. With his easily injured vanity, he was also unlikely to have forgotten the perceived slight at the station. On that same day he appointed Savinkov to be the deputy minister of war.

The *Stavka* report on the collapse of the Southwestern Front played into the hands of the right-wing press, which immediately linked army ill-discipline to the July Days. Calls increased for a strong leader to put an end to disorder. Kornilov, with his Siberian and Kazakh, or perhaps Buryat ancestry, seemed the obvious candidate. He could not have appeared less like the archetypal Tsarist general of the imperial guard, yet Kornilov failed to live up to his modest claim of being the 'son of a peasant Cossack'. He had formed a personal bodyguard of 300 Tekintsy lancers in scarlet cloaks, rather reminiscent of Napoleon's Mamelukes. He certainly had his admirers in the army, yet there were many senior officers who thought that Kornilov had rather more courage than intelligence.

Kerensky, meanwhile, still fancied himself as the Bonaparte of the Russian Revolution. Despite the terrible setback of the offensive, he took over the Winter Palace as his headquarters, and Tsar Alexander III's suite as his residence, which led to his nickname of 'Alexander IV'. Such a *folie de grandeur* certainly suggested that he was losing his judgement at a moment when counter-revolutionary sympathies were hardening. Even though nobody had lifted a finger to defend the old Tsarist order in February, officers, landowners and capitalists were now so appalled at the collapse of law and order that they believed that the time to act had come, with the Bolsheviks suppressed after the fiasco of the July Days. Yet while the Bolsheviks stayed out of sight, they continued to prepare. Their Sixth Congress was held in secret from 26 July to 2 August. Lenin, still in hiding in Finland, was starting to write *The State and Revolution*, as well as his bitter denunciations of the Socialist Revolutionaries and Mensheviks for supporting Kerensky's Provisional Government. As Shklovsky observed, the Bolsheviks might have been 'utterly crushed. But that did not mean anything – they were building up again.'

Early in August, Kerensky began to wonder whether it had been a wise move to appoint Kornilov, who was behaving in an increasingly authoritarian way. As well as demanding reforms to strengthen discipline in the field army, he wanted the death penalty extended to garrisons in the rear, which was clearly aimed at the reserve regiments infiltrated by the Bolsheviks in Petrograd. Kornilov even wanted martial law applied to the whole country and the militarisation of transport and the defence industries to prevent strikes.

The evidence today indicates that Kornilov himself was not planning a *coup d'état*, as Soviet historians always maintained. His main objective was to strengthen the Provisional Government so it could break free of the Petrograd Soviet and restore order. But there were many of his supporters, both in the army and outside, who were convinced that he should seize power himself and oust the increasingly volatile Kerensky. The British ambassador was approached by a banker, who asked him to 'assist them by placing the British armoured cars at their disposal and by helping them to escape should their enterprise fail'. Buchanan refused politely but firmly, replying that it was very naïve 'to ask an ambassador to conspire against the Government to which he was accredited'.

General Lavr Kornilov and Boris Savinkov.

Kerensky, hoping to gather support, called a State Conference in Moscow at the Bolshoi Theatre. His objective was to position himself as the one figure who could keep the country together. But when it opened on 12 August, the political divide between the opposing sides, reflected in their choice of seating, did not look encouraging amid the pillars and gilt of the lingering imperial decor.

Kornilov did not bother to attend on the first day, yet his arrival in Moscow turned out to be both a triumphal progress and a provocation. From the moment he reached the Aleksandrovsky Station, Kornilov was showered with flowers by adoring ladies beseeching him to 'Save Russia!'. He was carried on the shoulders of officers out of the station to an open touring automobile. Followed by scores of other motor cars filled with his admirers, he paid a visit to the Iversky shrine, where the tsars had usually prayed on arrival in Moscow.

General Kornilov hailed by officers and right-wingers as a hero on his arrival in Moscow for Kerensky's State Conference on 12 August 1917.

When General Kornilov finally joined the conference on the second day, right-wingers, many of them industrialists dressed in frock coats, leaped to their feet to give him a standing ovation and cheer. All those on the Left had faces like thunder and did not move. The Right, joyful at the prospect of turning back the clock, was as blind as the moderate Left to the danger that this political polarisation could only benefit the Bolsheviks. Kornilov's speech to the conference was short and unimpressive, but that did not seem to matter to his large and vociferous claque in the auditorium. Sukhanov referred to 'upstarts on the Right, who were shouting too immoderately about General "Fist" as the sole recourse'. Kerensky's closing speech, on the other hand, seemed interminable, meandering and increasingly incoherent. The mounting embarrassment of the audience ended only when people started clapping to signal they had had enough. Kerensky, emotional as ever, fainted away. The moment demonstrated his declining power to control events.

On 20 August, an election was held for the Petrograd city council. The results were surprising. 'Who was the only victor?' Sukhanov demanded rhetorically. 'It was the Bolsheviks, so recently trampled into the mud, accused of treason and venality, utterly routed morally and materially and filling till that very day the prisons of the capital.' They attracted nearly a third of the votes, just behind the Socialist Revolutionaries. But the moderate socialist leaders, the true democrats who had defended the Bolsheviks against the attacks of Kerensky's Coalition and the right-wing press, still failed to see the danger. Sukhanov, the Menshevik-internationalist, was exasperated by their failure to see the threats from both extremes. 'Now do you see the Bolsheviks? *Now* do you understand?' he emphasised. Sukhanov believed that the Right had a much better idea of the implications and would make a pre-emptive strike.

Kornilov, who despised politics, barely took any notice of these results. With the editorial help of Kerensky's deputy war minister, Boris Savinkov, he had submitted his demands for martial law to be applied to rail transport and the defence industries, the restoration of discipline and the chain of command in the army. Kornilov had understood that Kerensky had agreed to all these points. But after several frustrated attempts to secure his signature, he heard that the prime minister refused to agree to the death penalty being extended to troops in the rear. Meanwhile, in some of the armies at the front, commanders had started to reassert discipline and arrest Bolshevik agitators. In the Fifth Army, which had performed so abysmally in the offensive, 'no less than 12,275 soldiers and 37 officers were taken into custody'.

Kerensky became alarmed that Kornilov's demands and growing influence could wreck his balancing act between Left and Right, especially since the Soviet remained opposed to the death penalty in any form. Kornilov, on the other hand, had not been reassured by Kerensky's failure to hunt down the Bolsheviks after the July Days. He also suspected other ministers on the Left of collaborating secretly with the Bolsheviks. Kornilov felt that he must force Kerensky into making a stand. And just in case the Bolsheviks attempted another uprising with support from the Kronstadt sailors, he wanted to be ready.

According to Savinkov, Kerensky had been informed by the chief commissar Filonenko of an officers' plot against him at the *Stavka*. Kerensky wanted Savinkov to go to Mogilev to investigate, but also to obtain Kornilov's agreement to transfer the Petrograd military district from his command to that of the government. And to protect the government against another insurrection like the July Days, Kerensky told Savinkov to ask Kornilov to transfer a cavalry corps to the capital, which he agreed to do. Unfortunately, none of this was recorded.

Another version has Kornilov telling Savinkov that he was ordering General Krymov's III Cavalry Corps to move north from the Romanian front to Velikie Luki, which was much closer to Petrograd and Moscow. The corps included two Cossack Divisions and the Caucasian 'Savage' Division, which the Tsar's brother Mikhail had commanded. When General Lukomsky questioned the reason for this move, Kornilov explained. He added that he had no intention of reviving the old regime, which he had always hated. But he was determined to restore government authority to save Russia and ensure the installation of the Constituent Assembly. His feelings were made more urgent by the German capture of Riga on 21 August.

Kerensky, however, haunted by the raucous cheers for Kornilov at the State Conference, was aggrieved by the calls of the right-wing press to give the commander-in-chief full powers. The distrust and rivalry between the two men then led to a series of disastrous misunderstandings, all brought on by a fantasist who put himself forward as an emissary between them. No relation of Prince Lvov, a former Duma deputy named V.N. Lvov approached Kerensky with his own version of the story of a *Stavka* plot, adding that generals wanted to kill him. Kerensky, who was developing a persecution complex, listened to him. He probably did not authorise Lvov to negotiate with Kornilov, but he may well have asked him to find out more. Lvov seems to have taken it into his head that he should be the one to force the commander-in-chief to seize power. He went to Mogilev on 24 August and managed to see Kornilov, who naïvely did not ask him for proof that he was acting as Kerensky's representative.

Lvov proposed three alternatives, which he implied came from the Minister-President, as Kerensky now styled himself. They were a Kerensky dictatorship; a joint dictatorship, similar to the French *Consulat*; or a Kornilov dictatorship, with Kerensky and Savinkov as key ministers. Assuming still that Lvov was authorised to say all this, Kornilov thought that Kerensky was inviting him to take power in an indirect fashion. After some reflection, he said that on balance he would prefer the third option, but he was perfectly happy to serve as Kerensky's subordinate. He suggested that if Kerensky came to Mogilev they could discuss the details.

Two days later, when Lvov had returned to Petrograd, he visited Kerensky in the Winter Palace in a state of great agitation. He told the Minister-President that he was doomed. There was to be a Bolshevik coup and General Kornilov demanded supreme power for himself. The already nervous Kerensky became even more paranoid when he heard that Kornilov wanted him to travel to Mogilev. He became convinced that Kornilov was preparing a coup assisted by the Union of Officers, an unofficial organisation linking serving and retired members opposed to the democratisation of the army. As a result, Kerensky could see only the danger from the Right and felt he needed a rapprochement with the Left. He decided that to defeat his rival, he would pose as the saviour of the revolution.

The whole imbroglio of misunderstandings caused by Lvov might have been comical if it had not produced such tragic consequences. During that night of 26 August, while Kornilov discussed Cabinet appointments with General Lukomsky, Kerensky summoned an emergency meeting of the Council of Ministers at midnight. He denounced

Kornilov as a traitor and demanded dictatorial powers to confront the conspiracy, which meant that all ministers were to resign.

Savinkov guessed immediately that a terrible mistake had arisen and spoke up. He had discussed the move of the III Cavalry Corps with Kornilov at the *Stavka* on 23 August and he had spoken to Kerensky about it on his return. Savinkov urged Kerensky to contact Kornilov directly but he resolutely refused, saying it was too late, which was simply not true. Kornilov was not trying to overthrow the government. At 02.40 hours on 27 August, to confirm what he understood to have been agreed, he sent Telegram No 6394 to Kerensky as minister of war. 'The Corps will concentrate in the area of Petrograd in the evening of 28th August. I request that martial law is declared in Petrograd on 29 August. General Kornilov.'

Kerensky, tense with suspicion, sent his own signal to Kornilov to inform him that he had been removed from the command of the armies. It did not reach the *Stavka* until 07.00 hours. Since the commander-in-chief could not be dismissed without the involvement of the whole cabinet, and because he had heard nothing from Savinkov, Kornilov assumed at first that a Bolshevik coup had taken place and they were prisoners. When it became clear that Kerensky was not a prisoner, Kornilov believed he had been deliberately tricked. Later that day, he made a proclamation to the nation in answer to Kerensky's accusation of treason. It began: 'Russian citizens! The telegram from the Chairman of Ministers contained false information . . . A great provocation has taken place which puts at stake the fate of the Motherland.' Carried away by his fury, Kornilov even accused 'the Provisional Government, under pressure from the majority of the Soviets, is operating in full coordination with the plan of the German General Staff'.

Kornilov was by now stung into outright revolt. He called for support by telegram to the army commanders and even asked for the British armoured car squadrons to be deployed. 'His staff subsequently attributed their failure to our refusal to cooperate,' Commander Locker-Lampson reported to the First Lord of the Admiralty, Sir Edward Carson. 'Within seven days Mr Kerensky expressed much the same opinion,' he added. Yet the presence of British armoured cars in Kiev were thought to have prevented a Bolshevik rising there in response to the Kornilov démarche.

When Kornilov's telegrams arrived from Mogilev, army commanders faced a quandary, not really knowing what was happening or whom to believe. Wrangel and Mannerheim, now both corps commanders and strong supporters of Kornilov, fell out over which faint-hearted army commanders they should arrest. Wrangel said he would deal with Sokovnin, the new commander of the Eighth Army who was hesitating, but when he urged Mannerheim to arrest General Kelchevsky of the Ninth Army, 'Mannerheim reacted coldly to this suggestion like a proper Finn.'

While General Krymov's corps, led by the Savage Division, advanced on Petrograd, Kerensky summoned General Alekseev, who accepted his emergency reinstatement as commander-in-chief purely in the hope of sorting out the mess. Despite two meetings and the night of 28 August spent in the Winter Palace, he was not reassured by Kerensky's 'evasiveness'. As he subsequently discovered, Kerensky was well aware of the plan to move the III Cavalry Corps to Petrograd to forestall an attack on the government.

Kerensky's denunciation of Kornilov as a traitor to the revolution meant that the All-Russia Soviet, as it was now called, would support him. In fact Tsentrobalt, the Baltic Fleet Soviet, reported that 'Minister Kerensky . . . works in close contact with the Executive Committee' of the All-Russian Soviet of Workers' and Soldiers' Deputies. So did Tsentroflot, representing the whole navy. Signals back and forth show how close the collaboration was. 'Urgent. To Naval Minister Kerensky. Tsentroflot thinks it necessary to immediately summon two destroyers to Petrograd to defend the revolution. Please reply.' Kerensky answered asking for four and instructed them to enter the Neva and tie up by the Nikolaevsky Bridge.

Tsentrobalt also informed Kerensky that 'the 2nd Baltic Guards has a company of sailors who had served for two and a half years as part of the Savage Division. This long period of joint service has bonded them, and some of them have good friends there. Considering this bond between sailors and the Savage Division, Tsentroflot requests urgent instructions for the meeting of the two units. In the opinion of Tsentroflot, this could prove extremely useful.'

Even the Black Sea Fleet sent signals to Kerensky declaring that they 'would rather die than allow the pitiful Tsarist mercenaries to drown our beloved liberty in blood'. The outburst of moral outrage from the hard Left in support of Kerensky was remarkable. Their own comrades had tried to overthrow him and the Provisional

Government just the month before and Kerensky had tried to disband Tsentrobalt on 7 July.

Kerensky seemed to have no idea how far he was handing power to the Bolsheviks on a plate. The Red Guards, banned after the July Days, were rearmed and redeployed. Tsentrobalt ordered up to 5,000 sailors from Kronstadt to deploy in Petrograd in defence of the Soviet. Kerensky even agreed that Tsentroflot should send its own post and telegraph specialists, fully armed, 'to occupy and hold the Main Post Office, for the sake of more efficient work for the cause of the Revolution'.

Seeing that Kerensky was being so obliging to the Left, the Kronstadt Soviet demanded 'for the sake of achieving a greater trust towards the central organ of the revolution, the release of our comrades who are the best fighters and sons of the revolution. Currently, at this very moment, they are suffering in prisons while they could be useful as the best defenders of the Revolution.'

Railway workers had already mobilised to halt the troop trains, just as they had blocked the Tsar. Kerensky was informed that 'railway tracks have been disassembled on the Baltic, Vinava and Rybinsk lines in the path of Kornilov's advance. All measures are being taken to stop his troops.' Commissar Onipko of the Baltic Fleet reported that 'seven trains of Don Cossacks, supporters of Kornilov, were stopped between Narva and Tamburg, a total of 2,000 men with machine gun teams'. They were stopped by removing lengths of tracks. 'The Cossacks are trying to fix this in order to move forward.'

Kerensky's denunciation of Kornilov triggered more attacks on officers by their soldiers, convinced that they were all secret counter-revolutionaries. In Finland, the commander of the XLII Corps, General Oganovsky and most of his staff were seized, as the Cossack officer Maksim Kulik witnessed. 'The agitated crowd of soldiers assembled, for some reason, on the bridge that connected the two parts of Vyborg. They dragged over the corps commander and other officers, allegedly to have them declare to the gathering whether they supported Kerensky's government, or "traitor" Kornilov. After that the soldiers started throwing their captives into the gulf. When the officers tried to swim they were shot with rifles. The brutalized crowd accompanied these atrocities with jeers and roaring laugh-ter. They were probably shocked by their own brutality, because soon after the execution the crowd went back to their barracks, and the bridge emptied.'*

As part of this 'spree of violence', four officers from the battleship *Petropavlovsk*, who were sent ashore 'to be at the disposal of the Revolutionary Committee of Finland, were killed by their guards on the dockside'. Their crime was to have answered 'No', when asked whether they would obey the Executive Committee of the Soviet of Workers' and Soldiers' Deputies.

On 1 September, Tsentroflot reported that 'Generals Kornilov, Lukomsky, Romanovsky and Colonel Plyushchevsky were arrested by the Mogilev Soviet of Workers' and Soldiers' Deputies.' They would be handed over to the Special Investigative Commission, and 'other arrests linked to the Kornilov plot will be carried out on its orders'. General Krymov, after surrendering, was taken to the Winter Palace to be interrogated by an Extraordinary Commission. Kerensky refused to speak to him. 'The last card for saving the Motherland has been played and lost,' Krymov wrote on a scrap of paper. 'It is not worth living any longer.' He then shot himself through the heart.

General Alekseev, widely regarded as the most honest of men, resigned in disgust at Kerensky's bad faith in the whole affair. In a letter of 12 September to Pavel Milyukov, he wrote: 'Greatly respected Pavel Nikolaevich! I was unable to see you before my departure from Petrograd on 31 August. Now I have given up my position and cannot come to Petrograd, therefore I have no choice but to bother you with a letter. Urgent, broad, and active help is needed from you and other public figures, in fact from everyone able to help. The reason for my resignation was my fundamental rejection of the line that was taken on the Kornilov affair.

'Members of the government are making a great effort to convince all of Russia that the events of 27-31 August were nothing but a mutiny initiated by a handful of generals and officers whose aim is overthrowing the existing regime and becoming the rulers themselves. These people are trying to prove that the small group of rebels that

* Tsentroflot's version of events was brief. 'The corps commander, as well as General Aranovsky, commandant of the Vyborg Fortress, and Colonel Tyurenius and some others were arrested for supporting Kornilov. The first three were killed by the excited crowd when they were being moved to the fortress.'

betrayed their country was not supported by any group within society. Therefore, they should be tried by the most primitive of trials, i.e., the revolutionary court martial, and sentenced to capital punishment. The aim of the trial's great speed is to conceal the whole TRUTH and the true goals of the movement, as well as the participation of government figures in it.

'Kornilov's action was not a secret from members of the government, it had been discussed with Savinkov, Filonenko and, via them, with Kerensky. Only a primitive court martial would be able to conceal participation of the above officials in the preliminary negotiations and in concluding the agreement. Kerensky's participation is undoubted. I cannot say why all these people stepped back when the movement began, why they went back on their word.

Fortunately, Kerensky did at least step back from a revolutionary tribunal. His Extraordinary Commission, which reached Mogilev on 2 September, arranged for Kornilov and some thirty other arrested generals and officers to be imprisoned in the nearby monastery of Bykhov. Generals Denikin and Markov were to be taken there, guarded by two companies of cadets from the School of Lieutenants of the Southwestern Front. 'The prisoners were brought out,' one of the escort wrote, 'Generals Denikin and Markov in front, followed by a group of general staff officers. Our company commanders ordered: "Present arms!" The group entered the space between the companies that were standing to attention. There was a new command: "Shoulder arms!" A disgusting scene followed. This was a true Via Dolorosa for the Generals and their staff officers. The unbridled crowd of soldiers were jeering, swearing and whistling. Small stones started flying; one of them hit General Markov on his cheekbone, and blood appeared. The company commanders ordered: "At the ready!".' The cadet lieutenants raised their rifles to their shoulders. 'The crowd immediately recoiled.' Kornilov never faced such insults. He was permitted to ride to the improvised prison, surrounded by his Tekintsy cavalry escort.

General Wrangel's support for Kornilov soon became common knowledge and he was sacked as corps commander. Seeing the way things were going after Kornilov's arrest, he disappeared down to the Crimea to join his wife on her family estate. And when the Bolsheviks came to power two months later, he went into hiding with Crimean Tatar friends.

Exile in one form or another suddenly became a question for many. After the Kornilov fiasco the future looked deeply threatening. Russia could become a prison. The Central Committee of what was now known as the All-Russia Congress of Soldiers' and Workers' Deputies, wanted to come to an urgent decision 'about the unacceptability of allowing the traitors of the people to leave Russia'.

Any illusions Kerensky might have held about being seen as the saviour of the revolution evaporated rapidly. He received no thanks from the leading Bolsheviks as they were released from prison. Having turned against the Right he had played to the Left, but the Left had no further use for him and his days were numbered. Lenin was in no doubt about this, even though he still felt obliged to remain hidden in Finland. On 14 September he wrote to the Party's Central Committee: 'All the objective conditions exist for a successful insurrection.'

8

The October Coup
September–November 1917

The defeat of Kornilov was far worse than a Pyrrhic victory for Kerensky. Early in September he abolished the Department of Political Counter-Intelligence. It was obviously a key target for the Bolsheviks, and Kerensky either made the decision as a sop to the extreme Left, or because it had been infiltrated already. During the Kornilov crisis Tsentrobalt reported: 'On the subject of counter-intelligence: the branch in Helsingfors is under the strict control of the newly established Revolutionary Committee.'

On 4 September, just three days after General Kornilov's arrest, Leon Trotsky was released on bail from prison. In Lenin's absence, Trotsky, who had only just joined the Bolshevik Party, assumed the role of leader even though Stalin was in a stronger position at that moment. Trotsky's high-handed manner did not endear him to his colleagues, especially the less charismatic Stalin. A natural stage performer, Trotsky was soon in his element, rousing packed audiences in Petrograd halls such as the vast Cirque Moderne with his barbed wit. He enjoyed taunting any obvious bourgeois, or *burzhui*, that he spotted from their clothes in the crowd. 'His thin pointed face was positively Mephistophelian in its expression of malicious irony,' wrote the American journalist John Reed.

Like Lenin, Trotsky had no time for democracy and derided the 'pre-parliament' of party representatives who were preparing the ground for the Constituent Assembly. Their slowness, due to long debates, played into Bolshevik hands since there could be no decision on land reform until they were done. Trotsky scorned democrats with their 'intellectual, pseudo-aristocratic, squeamish attitude toward the people', and despised their distrust 'in those dark masses'. Yet it was hardly as if Lenin had the slightest intention of placing trust in any non-Bolsheviks, least of all in the 'dark masses', who had blindly bulldozed the opening he needed. Strikes in city factories and the mindless destruction of the gentry's manor houses and farms revealed day after day the impotence of the Kerensky regime.

This was indeed a promising moment for the Bolsheviks. Lenin agreed to revive the slogan 'All power to the Soviets!' now that he saw the chance of infiltrating and dominating their committees to obtain control. The Kornilov affair and Kerensky's murky part in it had undermined trust in parliamentary democracy. Mensheviks and Socialist Revolutionary leaders, mostly members of the high-minded intelligentsia, seemed increasingly out of touch. They had taken part in coalitions with the Kadets, who had supported Kornilov, and they had refused to take power from the Provisional Government in July when offered the opportunity.

The 'grey mass' of soldiers, who tended to see all officers as counter-revolutionaries, now suspected Kerensky and his ministers of wanting to prolong the war to increase their power. Large numbers joined the Bolsheviks simply because of their opposition to the 'imperialist war'. The Socialist Revolutionaries, who had tried to justify it, lost credibility, as did Menshevik supporters of that feeble compromise, 'defencism'.

'The Bolsheviks were a lot more logical,' Ivan Serebrennikov argued. 'In their opinion, since the war served the interests of capitalists, then away with the war. Stick your bayonets into the ground and go home. This was clear, simple, and very attractive to the peasants in grey greatcoats . . . The front, collapsing further and further, was preparing armies of millions of active Bolshevik agitators, those *frontovik* soldiers, who would soon swarm all over Russia.'

One of the Bolsheviks' great strengths at a time when the masses had little political sophistication was to make their orators repeat slogans, not to try to convince their audience through argument (a technique which still seems to work). On a train to Orel, a right-wing relative of the composer Rimsky-Korsakov found himself in a carriage with a group of apprentice agitators. One or two had little Bolshevik-fashion goatees. 'They repeated slogans aloud in order to memorize them: "Peace to the huts and war to the palaces!" "Peace without annexations or reparations!" "Land to the working people!" "Nationalization of plants and factories!" "Death to the *burzhui*!", etc., etc. They were delegates going to some congress in Moscow.'

During September, support for the Bolsheviks increased sharply among factory workers in Petrograd and garrison troops. The Party now controlled a majority on both the Petrograd and Moscow Soviets. Lenin felt that the Bolsheviks were now in a position to launch their bid for power. In the second week of September he wrote from his hideout in Finland two letters to the Central Committee. With the over-optimistic claim that 'the majority of the people are on our side', he demanded that the Bolsheviks 'can and *must* take state power into their own hands . . . The present task must be an armed uprising in Petrograd and Moscow (plus their regions), the seizing of power and the overthrow of the government. We must consider how to agitate for this without expressly saying as much in the press.'

The Central Committee, however, was deeply alarmed. A premature attempt could allow Kerensky to suppress the Party entirely. Lenin turned that argument around, insisting that the threat of being crushed was a reason to move immediately. His real concern was that if they waited until the Soviet Congress in October, the Bolsheviks might have to share power with the Mensheviks and Socialist Revolutionaries, whom he despised as 'compromisers'. More than ever, Lenin wanted sole control.

Even Trotsky was unsettled by Lenin's raging impatience to mount a coup straight away. 'Distrust of the Bolshevik had been replaced by sympathy,' Trotsky wrote, 'or at the worst by a watchful neutrality. But the sympathy was not active. The garrison remained in a political sense extremely shaky and – as *muzhiks* are – suspicious.' He estimated that not more than 1,000 soldiers were 'ready to fight on the side of the revolution . . . among the more passive units'. His hopes lay much more with the Red Guards – 'no longer a militia of the factories and workers' districts, but the cadres of a future army of insurrection'.*

The disintegration of the army accelerated, as officers deserted to save their lives. Colonel Count Dmitry Heiden, coming from the *Stavka* at Mogilev, was shaken when changing trains at Zhmerinka to see the way soldiers treated officers, pushing them around and insulting them. 'It was clear,' he wrote revealingly, 'that the beast had broken free of its chain. After three years they were used to blood and were talking about murders as if they were the most ordinary thing, that

---

* Uritsky estimated the Petrograd Red Guard to have reached 40,000 men by mid-October, but even Trotsky admitted that the figure was probably exaggerated, and later suggested it was less than 20,000.

was necessary just like air and food.' All that local authorities could do to mitigate the destruction was to destroy stocks of alcohol. 'A wave of returning soldiers stopped in Brailov, seventeen versts from us and stormed the alcohol factory. Many people died in the tanks with spirits.'

The continued German advance up the Baltic coast in the direction of Petrograd caused great alarm. Kerensky's government began to take precautions in case they needed to abandon the capital. 'Boxes with the Hermitage collections have started arriving at our museum,' wrote Oreshnikov, the curator at the Historical Museum in Moscow on 1 October. Yet the government waited until 6 October before ordering a large part of the Petrograd garrison to defend the western approaches. Trotsky and the Bolsheviks presented this in the Soviet as a plot to denude the capital of its revolutionary defenders. Reversing the true situation with their own plans for a coup, the Bolsheviks pretended that the February revolution was still in danger from 'the openly prepared assault of military and civilian Kornilovites'. This was a deliberate strategy. 'Although an insurrection can win on the offensive,' Trotsky admitted, 'it develops better the more it looks like self-defence.'

Lenin had meanwhile moved from Helsingfors to Vyborg on the Finnish side of the border. He shaved off his beard again, and from there, disguised in a grey wig and the costume of a Lutheran pastor, he moved back secretly to Petrograd. He wanted to confront the Bolshevik Central Committee in person to force them to agree to his demands as quickly as possible.

On the night of 10 October, Lenin, still in his ecclesiastical outfit and wig, joined a dozen members of the Central Committee in an apartment. It belonged to the Menshevik Nikolai Sukhanov and his wife, who was a Bolshevik. She had persuaded him to spend the night close to his work to avoid an exhausting journey home, so he remained ignorant of the meeting. Those assembled included Trotsky, Stalin, Feliks Dzerzhinsky, Moisei Uritsky (another future Chekist), Sverdlov, Aleksandra Kollontai, Kamenev and Zinoviev.

The amusement caused by Lenin's improbable disguise did not last long. His determination to launch an armed coup had not abated. The time for words was over, he argued. He was also convinced that revolutions would ignite right across Europe, if not the world. After he had spoken for an hour, the debate began and lasted through most of the night. In the end, a majority of the Central Committee present voted for insurrection as he demanded, but Kamenev and Zinoviev opposed it. They argued that he was putting at risk the whole future of the Party. Zinoviev observed quietly that if they failed, they would all be shot. Lenin's impatience for action was also prompted by forthcoming negotiations between the major parties over elections in November for the future Constituent Assembly. He suspected that the Bolsheviks would not win a majority in the whole country. The peasantry would still vote for the Socialist Revolutionaries.

Three days later, the All-Russia Soviet, at Trotsky's urging, formed a Military Revolutionary Committee, soon to receive the acronym of Milrevkom. It was given wide-ranging tasks to conceal its principal purpose of preparing for the uprising. 'With this same purpose of camouflage,' wrote Trotsky, 'a Socialist Revolutionary and not a Bolshevik was placed at the head.' Pavel Evgenevich Lazimir, he explained, was 'one of those Left Socialist Revolutionaries who were already traveling with the Bolsheviks'. To the alarm of Mensheviks and Right Socialist Revolutionaries, the Military Revolutionary Committee was little more than a veiled version of the Bolsheviks' own organisation. Yet they were still more frightened of a non-existent counter-revolutionary coup than the very real Bolshevik plan to seize power.

On 16 October, another Bolshevik Central Committee meeting took place on the edge of Petrograd. This too lasted through most of the night and proved even more fractious than the first. An exasperated Lenin hammered away with his argument that the people were behind them and that the working class in Europe would follow. Although he had started with most of the audience against him, he wore down, through sheer force of personality, those critics who had argued that the majority of Russian workers and soldiers did not yet want to take part in an insurrection. His resolution was approved. It gave him the freedom of action that he needed, yet Lenin remained in a foul mood, convinced that he was surrounded by incompetence and faint-heartedness.

Lenin was extremely fortunate to have Trotsky preparing the coup with shameless dexterity. Having taken over the Petrograd Soviet, Trotsky created the Milrevkom, which he furnished with spurious credentials to control the actions of the garrison. Bolshevik planning for an armed uprising had begun, even if not in the way Lenin wanted. Most of his colleagues supported Trotsky's initiative of working through the Milrevkom. Using his position as its president, Trotsky signed an order to a Petrograd arms factory for 5,000 rifles to be distributed to the Red Guard.

Kerensky was well aware of the Bolsheviks' preparations, but even they could not shake his complacency. He told the British ambassador, Sir George Buchanan, 'I only wish that they would come out, and I will then put them down.' On 20 October, he boasted to Vladimir Nabokov that he welcomed a Bolshevik revolt, because they would be utterly defeated. The same day the minister for war, General Aleksandr Verkhovsky, warned Kerensky that the army was incapable of fighting, so the best policy would be to open negotiations with the Germans and steal the Bolsheviks' thunder. Kerensky angrily rejected the idea and sacked him. Military commanders also did not take the threat seriously enough on the grounds that a large majority of the garrison was opposed to a coup. But that did not in any way mean that they were prepared to act to save the government. On hearing that Kerensky refused to declare the Bolshevik organisation illegal, the Cossacks saw no point in risking their lives for this government. They decided to remain neutral.

On the basis of faulty information whipped up by the more right-wing press, the government prepared for an uprising, first on 17 October, then on 20 October, and once more two days later. 'Rumours are more and more persistently being spread,' wrote Gorky on 18 October, 'that some "action by the Bolsheviks" will take place on 20 October; in other words, the disgusting scenes of 3–5 July may be repeated.' The cries of 'Wolf!' worked in their favour. On 22 October, the ministry of war issued an ultimatum to the Military Revolutionary Committee to withdraw Trotsky's order to garrison regiments and not to obey anyone but the Milrevkom. To avoid arrest, the Bolsheviks offered to negotiate purely to spin things out. The tactic worked. Kerensky preferred to think that the Bolsheviks' nerve would again fail as it had in July.

Tension increased in other Russian cities as the storm clouds gathered. In Moscow, the Historical Museum again began to receive national treasures for safekeeping. The Academy of Sciences sent over their most valuable Lermontov and Pushkin manuscripts, as well as Pushkin's emerald ring. Yelena Lakier in Odessa wrote in her diary: 'None of us went out today as there was an armed demonstration by the Bolsheviks. There are more and more of them. They agitate without rest and achieve brilliant results. They stir up the population and incite them to take part in raids and riots. This is not going to end well. There are robberies in the streets. They take people's hats, coats and even clothes. Citizens are forced to stay at home after dark.'

Descriptions in Trotsky's account of nightly Cossack mounted patrols in the proletarian districts of Petrograd and the reinforcement of the Winter Palace were grossly exaggerated. This was part of the Bolsheviks' false narrative that the Military Revolutionary Committee was not the instigator, but reacting to a threat from the Right. It ran with their false rumour that Kerensky was planning to surrender Petrograd to the Germans to smash the revolution.

Trotsky talked of cold and raw Baltic winds from the direction of Kronstadt blowing through the squares and along the quays of Petrograd. This was his way of threatening the bourgeoisie with the much-feared sailors of the Baltic Fleet. In this period of autumn rain streets had turned to mud. Mass meetings were permeated by the smell of damp wool from the sodden sheepskin caps and grey greatcoats of the soldiers, as well as the woollen shawls covering the heads of women. Meanwhile, according to General Alekseev, the large number of demoralised officers, of whom there would have been enough in Petrograd to resist the coup if they had been organised, relapsed into drunken despair.*

Glittering Petrograd was a caricature that had worn very thin since February, but Trotsky still found it useful. 'Guards officers still click their spurs and go after adventures,' he wrote. 'Wild parties are in progress in the private dining rooms of expensive restaurants. The shutting off of the electric lights at midnight does not prevent the flourishing of gambling clubs where Champagne sparkles by candlelight, where illustrious speculators swindle no less illustrious German spies, where monarchist conspirators call the bets of Semitic smugglers, and where the astronomical figures of the stakes played for indicate both the scale of debauchery and the scale of inflation.'

Like most successful coups, the outcome in Petrograd would depend mostly on the apathy of the majority and the existing government's loss of faith in itself. The aristocracy and middle classes, having no

---

* Alekseev believed that there must have been around 15,000 officers in Petrograd of whom a third might have been prepared to fight.

confidence in Kerensky, awaited their fate with resignation or helpless despair. Kerensky, still cocooned from reality, revealed that he was no Bonaparte.

Trotsky, meanwhile, was paying particular attention to the armoured car division and the Peter and Paul Fortress. On the afternoon of Monday 23 October he went to the fortress where a meeting of the garrison was taking place in the courtyard. He claimed that most of the soldiers were ready to support them and promised to take orders only from the Milrevkom. It was not just the fortress as a symbol – the Tsarist Bastille – which interested him. The adjoining Kronverksky arsenal was supposed to contain 100,000 rifles. Attempts were also made to win over the Cossack regiments in Petrograd as they were the most likely to oppose a coup, but in the absence of any leadership they remained neutral. Apart from the Pavlovsky Guards, the 1st Machine Gun Regiment and a few detachments from other reserve battalions, far fewer troops from the garrison turned out to support the Bolshevik coup than has often been claimed.

Early the next morning, Tuesday 24 October, the Military Staff in Petrograd sent a company of young 'junker' officer cadets to close the Bolshevik Party's printing presses. An order was also issued to arrest the members of Trotsky's Military Revolutionary Committee, but by then it was far too late. All the government managed to achieve was to raise the bridges over the Neva to impede mass demonstrations from flooding the centre of Petrograd. Other junker detachments from the Ivanovsky Military Academy were sent to defend the Winter Palace. They were reinforced by a bicycle company, a few Cossacks and two reinforced companies from the Women's Death Battalion, making a force of less than 1,500.

At 3 a.m. on Wednesday 25 October, the light cruiser *Aurora* arrived from Kronstadt, entered the Neva and anchored just below the Nikolaevsky Bridge. Still before dawn, Red Guards began occupying key buildings, railway stations and disarming junker pickets on the bridges. Trotsky claimed that the central telephone exchange was captured by an infantry company without a battle, while a detachment of sailors occupied the state bank.* In fact, a group of junkers had

---

* Trotsky's account tries to give the impression that there was hardly any resistance during the coup and afterwards, and that almost every regiment in Petrograd had gone over to the Bolsheviks.

arrived first to seize the telephone exchange on Gorokhovaya ulitsa, running up towards the Admiralty.

Several trucks pulled up outside containing soldiers from the Latvian Rifle Regiment, commanded by the Bolshevik Mikhail Lashevich. The first Latvians out of the vehicles shot down the sentries. The detachment charged into the building and opened fire on the *junkers* upstairs. The women telephone operators there screamed in terror.

A young onlooker, an apprentice hatter, sheltering in an adjoining alley, recorded that 'Latvians and *junkers*, both killed and wounded, were being thrown from the windows. I heard their bones breaking. Women standing next to me were praying to the Mother of God and crying. A Latvian soldier who could speak Russian explained to me that an uprising had started in the city. Workers and soldiers had rebelled against the bourgeois Russian government. When everything was over, we emerged to see the bodies. They lay with bloodied faces and split heads. We saw how they were loaded on to trucks and heard Lashevich's order to take them to the Neva and throw them in.'

Disguised as a Serbian officer, Kerensky had slipped away soon after 9 a.m., leaving his ministers in the Malachite Room of the Winter Palace. He was driven out of the city in an American Embassy car flying the stars and stripes, on his way to the headquarters of the Northern Front at Pskov to seek reinforcements. It is ironic that the only troops Kerensky could find to move against the Bolsheviks were Don Cossacks from III Cavalry Corps now commanded by Lieutenant General Pyotr Krasnov.

On this momentous day, Lenin had been unable to stay cooped up any longer in the Petrograd apartment where he had been lying low. Taking a companion with him and disguised with the wig, spectacles and a bandage round his head for good measure, he set off by tram to the headquarters of the Military Revolutionary Committee. It was based in the Smolny Institute, a huge Palladian palace in which the daughters of the aristocracy had been educated. Now, it was like a fortress with Maxim machine guns mounted on the roof and pieces of light artillery by the entrance.

Having replaced the Tauride Palace as the home of the Soviet and its Executive Committee, the Smolny was also occupied by Socialist Revolutionaries and Mensheviks. So Lenin entered with great caution, maintaining his disguise. Nobody recognised him at first as he sat on the edge of a table. One account describes how the Menshevik leader, Fyodor Dan, entered the room with a couple of friends to retrieve his coat. Dan immediately recognised him in spite of his appearance and beat a rapid retreat from the room. Lenin exploded in contemptuous laughter.

He wasted little time in writing the proclamation 'To the Citizens of Russia!' It began with a typically premature announcement: 'The Provisional Government has been deposed. State power has passed into the hands of the organ of the Petrograd Soviet of Workers' and Soldiers' Deputies – the Military Revolutionary Committee, which heads the Petrograd proletariat and the garrison.' In spite of this statement of unshakable confidence, Lenin still did not relax, even when lying on the floor, pretending to sleep.

Kerensky's ministers waited in the Malachite Room of the Winter Palace for their leader to appear at any moment at the head of a relief column of cavalry. Yet the famous storming of the Winter Palace of Bolshevik myth, perpetuated to this day by Sergei Eisenstein's propaganda film, was far from heroic.

Palace Square was defended by *junker* cadets with machine guns and light artillery. These were positioned in small redoubts made from logs and sandbags. At the first volley of fire from the defenders, the timid attack by Red Guards collapsed. Lenin's claims of strong support from the garrison proved to be false. In the early afternoon a large body of sailors from the Baltic Fleet, some say as many as 5,000 strong, were landed by an assortment of vessels from Kronstadt to attack the Winter Palace. But they too quailed before the fire of the *junkers* and the Women's Battalion.

Since the Kronstadt sailors were not prepared to attack across the open space of Palace Square, the light cruiser *Aurora* moored at the quay opposite the Winter Palace traversed its 6-inch gun turret to bear. At 6.30 p.m. Trotsky and the Milrevkom issued an ultimatum to the members of the Provisional Government. They warned that unless they surrendered, the guns of the Peter and Paul Fortress and the *Aurora* would open fire. The ministers inside the palace could only hope that Kerensky would appear at the head of loyal troops. The cruiser had in fact arrived without any live shells, so when the order came at 9 p.m., it could fire only a single blank round. The guns of the fortress did have live ammunition, but the standard of gunnery was pathetic considering how large their target was. Only two shells out of more than thirty struck the façade of the Winter Palace on the Neva side. Colt machine guns on the fortress walls also fired across the Neva with little effect.

Soon afterwards, some Red Guards discovered an unmanned entrance to the Winter Palace and entered, but they surrendered as soon as they encountered some *junker* cadets inside. The defenders, however, depressed at the lack of reinforcements which they had been promised, began to slide away. When it became clear that the defence was evaporating, some sailors and soldiers approached. Emboldened by the lack of reaction, they climbed in through some other windows. In no time at all a mob was ransacking the palace cellars for wine and vodka, ripping leather from chairs and sofas to repair their boots, and smashing mirrors. Vladimir Antonov-Ovseenko, who was theoretically in command, described how the sentries from first the Preobrazhensky, and then the Pavlovsky Guards, stationed to prevent entry to the wine cellars joined in the drinking and also became utterly drunk. 'When evening came, a violent bacchanalia overflowed. "Let's drink the Romanovs' remains."' They even tried flooding the cellars, 'but the firemen sent to do the job got drunk instead'.

After surrendering to Antonov-Ovseenko, the ministers were escorted to the Peter and Paul Fortress. A few members of the Women's Battalion were said to have been raped after the orgy of destruction when they were taken to the barracks of the Grenadier Regiment. But the senior British liaison officer, Major General Knox, who persuaded Antonov-Ovseenko to release them, reported: 'As far as could be ascertained, though they had been beaten and insulted in every way in the Pavlovsky barracks and on their way to the Grenadersky Regiment, they were not actually hurt.'

The leading Bolsheviks at the Smolny Institute waited impatiently for news of the surrender. The Second Congress of Soviets had gathered in the grandiose ballroom with its white-pillared colonnade. Calls for a coalition of socialist parties proved popular, but the Bolshevik assault on the Provisional Government prompted condemnations that it represented a declaration of civil war. 'One party after another,' wrote Vladimir Zenzinov, a Socialist Revolutionary, 'declared their protest against the actions of the Bolsheviks, their double-dealing tactics. Representatives of revolutionary movements went up to the tribune one after another, declared their protest in outraged terms and walked out of the congress to show that they wanted to have nothing in common with the Bolsheviks.'

The Menshevik leader Martov warned the Bolsheviks of the consequences of their actions. They would bring about 'the inevitable hunger and degeneration of the masses'. Trotsky simply dismissed him as a 'frightened petty bourgeois confronted by great events'. And as Martov walked out in protest, Trotsky shouted his famous insult: 'You are miserable bankrupts. Your role is played out. Go where you belong from now on: into the dustbin of history!'

Walking out in protest abandoned the field to Lenin, who wanted civil war to destroy all opponents and rivals. Although Maksim Gorky had been quite a close friend of Lenin, he had no illusions about his character and was not afraid to speak his mind. In his 'Untimely Thoughts' column in *Novaya Zhizn* on 7 November following the Bolshevik coup, Gorky wrote: 'The working class should know that miracles do not occur in real life, that they are to expect hunger, complete disorder in industry, disruption of transport, and protracted bloody anarchy followed by a no less bloody and dire reaction. This is where the proletariat is being led by its present leader, and it must be understood that Lenin is not an omnipotent magician but a cold-blooded trickster who spares neither the honour nor the life of the proletariat.'

9

The Boys' Crusade
Revolt of the *Junkers*
October–November 1917

During the night of 26–27 October, Lenin addressed a packed assembly in the former Smolny Institute for Noble Maidens. This was the closing session of the Second All-Russia Congress of Soviets. The air was almost unbreathable from the *makhorka* tobacco smoke, sweating bodies and lack of oxygen, but people were too keyed up to fall asleep. When he declared 'We shall now proceed to construct the Socialist order!' there was a truly deafening roar of triumph. For Lenin there was no paradox when he called on the peoples of all belligerent countries to make peace immediately, and then added: 'But we hope that revolution will soon break out.'

A few hours later, at 2.30 a.m. on the morning of 27 October, Kamenev told the vast audience that until the Constituent Assembly could take over, a 'provisional workers' and peasants' government', the Council of People's Commissars, would run the country. He read out their names. They included Vladimir Ilyich Ulyanov (Lenin), the chairman of the council, Lev Davidovich Bronstein (Trotsky), the People's Commissar for Foreign Affairs, Vladimir Antonov-Ovseenko for War, Aleksandra Mikhailovna Kollontai for Social Welfare, Anatoly Vasilyevich Lunacharsky for Popular Education and Enlightenment, and Josef Vissarionovich Dzhugashvili (Stalin) as People's Commissar for Nationalities. This government, however, would prove to be permanent, not provisional, and the Constituent Assembly would never be allowed to sit. The congress delegates finally dispersed exhausted at 4 a.m.

Later that same morning, a biplane appeared over central Petrograd and followed the Nevsky Prospekt, dropping copies of a proclamation by Kerensky. It claimed that his troops had taken Tsarskoe Selo and would be in the capital the next day. General Krasnov, although he despised Kerensky after the Kornilov affair, had advanced towards the capital from Pskov with little more than 1,000 men, mainly his Don Cossacks from the III Cavalry Corps, with one armoured car and an armoured train. They put a force of Red Guards to flight and occupied Gatchina before dawn, before pushing on to Tsarskoe Selo the next morning. Altogether they disarmed 16,000 troops and sent them away. The Cossacks lacked the men to guard them as prisoners.

Trotsky called on the Red Guards to march out of the city to defend the revolution. Those who had no weapons took spades to dig trenches. A large procession with women volunteering as nurses marched southwest out of Petrograd. They were commanded by Nikolai Podvoisky of the Bolsheviks' Military Revolutionary Committee. He was overwhelmed with the task, and the situation was not helped by Lenin's attempts to run things from the Smolny. When Podvoisky threatened to resign, 'Lenin ordered him to stay at his post or be turned over to a party tribunal and shot.'

Lenin was in constant touch with Tsentrobalt, demanding more sailors from Helsingfors and Kronstadt, as well as warships. Raskolnikov dispatched the cruiser *Oleg* and the destroyer *Pobeditel*. Reinforcements were also sent forward from the Petrograd garrison to the defence line on the Pulkovo Heights. The Volynsky Guards Regiment did not distinguish itself. A lieutenant ordered to reconnoitre failed in his duty, and the whole advance was chaotic. The Red Guards at the Pulkovo Heights accused the commanding officer of being a former monarchist and forced the regimental commissar to resign. Altogether some 5,000 sailors from the Baltic Fleet and 10,000 Red Guards assembled at Pulkovo.

Krasnov was sending telegrams to front commanders at every opportunity begging for reinforcements, but without success. He was frustrated by bad communications and uncooperative senior officers, particularly General Cheremisov at Pskov, who had refused to help Kerensky on his escape from Petrograd. Generals were afraid either of provoking the Bolsheviks or of being responsible for the first step towards civil war. The leadership of the railwaymen's union Vikzhel, which consisted of both Mensheviks and Socialist Revolutionaries, blocked lines again to prevent reinforcements arriving on both sides. They were demanding a truce and a coalition government representing all socialist parties.

Heavy rain made an uphill cavalry charge against the Pulkovo Heights a desperate affair, despite the poor marksmanship of Red Guards firing at them. Through his binoculars, Krasnov could see the Baltic Fleet sailors in their black jackets and peakless naval caps holding the flanks. A *sotnia* of Cossacks of the Guard attempted an attack, but they became bogged down and lost many of their horses.

On Monday 30 October, facing odds of nearly twenty to one, Krasnov had to abandon any further idea of attacking the Pulkovo Heights. His men, whose determination had been undermined by contacts with Bolsheviks, were short of ammunition, rations and hay for their horses. Krasnov could do little when his Cossacks sent across a delegation to the sailors to arrange a ceasefire. They returned accompanied by a number of sailors and their black-bearded leader Pavel Dybenko, a Ukrainian Bolshevik and the young lover of Aleksandra Kollontai, the People's Commissar for Social Welfare. Dybenko, exercising great charm and subterfuge, pretended that the Bolshevik leadership was going to agree to the Vikzhel union's proposal for a coalition, so that there was no need to fight.

All the Cossack soldiers wanted was to return home to the Quiet Don. To achieve that they were even prepared to hand Kerensky over to the Bolsheviks, but the former leader of Russia managed to escape just in time, disguised as a rather unconvincing sailor. Having lost support on all sides, the hero of the February revolution left Russia for Paris. In that respect he was more fortunate than the imperial family, whom he had sent to Tobolsk.

To coincide with Krasnov's advance, the so-called 'Committee for the Salvation of the Country and the Revolution' (a mainly Right Socialist Revolutionary organisation) called on supporters to rise up against the Bolshevik dictatorship. Remarkably few Tsarist officers joined the revolt, so it turned into a boy's crusade, with *junker* cadets from a number of military academies led into battle by their instructors. Some were little more than fourteen, handling rifles almost as tall as themselves. Their eagerness to prove themselves and sacrifice their young lives in a cause was reminiscent of Stendahl's fictional hero Fabrice del Dongo in the *Chartreuse de Parme*.

Central Petrograd awoke on Sunday, 29 October to the sound of machine-gun fire. Young *junker* cadets from several of the military academies in and around Petrograd had been preparing all night. The

Military School of Engineers fortified their academy, the Mikhailovsky Castle on the confluence of the Fontanka and Moika Rivers. Built by Tsar Paul I, who was murdered there, this immense architectural curiosity had then become an academy for engineer cadets. Fyodor Dostoevsky had been trained there in the late 1830s, before becoming a lieutenant and writing his first novel.

The night before the revolt, the *junkers* arrested two of their number, one a Bolshevik and the other a Left Socialist Revolutionary to prevent them warning the Milrevkom in the Smolny. Then, in the early hours, some of their number raided the Mikhailovsky manège which housed the armoured car detachment. 'Before dawn a group of *junkers* suddenly approached the back gate and took the sentries without resistance,' Commissar Zybin reported the next day, criticising the lax discipline. 'The machine gunner on duty was not there and there was no resistance . . . The attitude of the soldiers was unreliable. Only a minority had strong revolutionary views.' As a result the *junkers* were able to make off with a number of vehicles, including three armoured cars, which they brought back in triumph to the Mikhailovsky Castle next door.

Shortly before dawn, officer instructors issued the cadets with ammunition. Soon a group of Red Guards with red arm bands from the Putilov works arrived with some Kronstadt sailors and a light field gun. They were reinforced by troops with red cockades. Other groups of cadets meanwhile had seized the telephone exchange and the Astoria Hotel, where both Bolshevik functionaries and foreign journalists were staying. 'Suddenly a boy officer,' an American woman correspondent reported, 'a cigarette hanging nonchalantly from the corner of his mouth and a revolver in his hand, lined the Bolshevik guards up against the wall and disarmed them.' The plan in each case was to hold the building until Kerensky arrived with the cavalry.

One group of youngsters at the telephone exchange captured the myopic Antonov-Ovseenko, the new People's Commissar for War, out on the street. 'Officers supporting the committee arrived secretly,' a Bolshevik report into the revolt stated. These officers told the cadets that 'some units of the garrison, such as the Ismailovsky Guards, the Semenovsky Guards, the Volynsky Regiment, Cossacks and others' supported the insurrection, 'however this information turned out to be false and a gross provocation. *Junkers* who did not know much about politics believed these dirty lies.'

Major General Knox, the well-established British military attaché, was unimpressed by the reluctance of former officers to support the cadets. 'While the firing was in progress I met an officer I knew walking in the next street arm-in-arm with a lady friend. I expressed my astonishment that he took no interest in the fighting, and he said that it had nothing to do with him!'

Bolshevik sailors surrounding the telephone exchange were enraged when they heard that the cadets had taken Antonov prisoner. They already knew that the *junker* cadets were listening in to Bolshevik communications, as Raskolnikov had found out. Eventually, the officer instructors admitted to the cadets that Kerensky's troops were nowhere near Petrograd and there was not a single unit among the Petrograd garrison that supported the committee. These academy officers who had led the cadets out to fight were the first to disappear, cutting off their shoulder boards and abandoning their charges.

Surrounded by an overwhelming force of Kronstadt sailors, and with no hope of relief arriving, the boys started to panic. The sailors wanted to kill them all, because some of them had been captured at the Winter Palace and on their surrender had given their parole not to take up arms again. The boys offered their hostage his freedom if he would save their lives. To the disgust of the sailors, Antonov kept his word and prevented any harm coming to the cadets.

The young cadets' revolt came to an end at five that evening at the Mikhailovsky Castle. 'The *junkers* capitulated and were marched off to the Peter and Paul Fortress,' Morgan Philips Price of the *Manchester Guardian* reported. 'But not before a number of them were selected from the rest and done to death with the butt-ends of rifles.'

The Bolshevik coup did not go nearly so well in Moscow. This was mainly because their leaders there had opposed the idea of seizing power by force, as Kamenev and Zinoviev had in Petrograd. There was also considerable confusion. 'Editorial offices of "bourgeois" newspapers have been seized by the Bolsheviks,' wrote Oreshnikov on Friday 26 October in his diary at the Historical Museum, 'therefore there is no news on the Petrograd events.' But then he revealed that a detachment of young *junkers* from one of the Moscow military academies had secretly spent the night in the Historical Museum, which was next to the Kremlin.

Later that morning, two representatives of the Moscow Revolutionary Committee came to the Kremlin to ask the 56th Regiment to hand over the weapons held there, but found they were too late. The cadets hidden in the Historical Museum had surrounded the Kremlin and seized it. Bolshevik sources insist that the cadets persuaded the soldiers to come out to surrender and then shot them down. This clash, in which supporters of the Provisional Government occupied the Kremlin and the centre of Moscow, marked the start of several days of street fighting. The Soviet of Workers and Soldiers in the former governor-general's residence on Tverskaya, the great thoroughfare running northwest from the Kremlin, found themselves besieged. Wild fusillades forced the inhabitants of apartments overlooking the boulevard to shelter on back staircases.

Trenches were dug and barricades were erected in many places, including one on the corner of Lubyanka Square consisting of 'firewood, furniture and all sorts of rubbish' where the *junker* cadets installed two machine guns. Many university students in Moscow joined the *junkers* as volunteers but, as had been the case in Petrograd, there were few former officers prepared to risk their necks.

Both sides, *junkers* and Red Guards, mounted constant patrols at night. They clashed in what seemed like an eerily empty city. The main railways stations, although deserted, were all lit up. 'The shots keep echoing,' one young Bolshevik worker wrote, 'and it seems as if the shooting carries on all around us.' At first they just fired at shadows from behind street lamps. 'Our eyes got used to the dark and we tried to make out what was ahead of us.'

On the night of 28 October artillery fire was heard for the first time, and intensified dramatically the following day. The *junkers* were firing from the Kremlin at the Einem Factory, a Bolshevik stronghold, while the Bolsheviks fired back at the Kremlin from the Sparrow Hills, inflicting more damage on the ancient monuments than the Germans managed in the Second World War. The writer Ivan Bunin was trapped in his mother-in-law's apartment just off the Arbat. 'There were very many artillery rounds during the day,' he wrote, 'constant explosions of grenades and shrapnel, constant cracking of rifle shots. A heavy hail was thundering on the roofs just now, I don't know from what sort of weapon . . . It is almost midnight. It is scary to go to bed. I barricaded my bedroom with the wardrobe.' With no newspapers wild rumours spread, often ridiculously optimistic. An engineer who had arrived from Petrograd even told Oreshnikov on 1 November that troops loyal to Kerensky had now occupied the capital and that 'Lenin and company escaped to Kronstadt on the *Aurora*'.

There were thought to be 300 *junker* cadets defending the Moscow telephone exchange. The Red Guards and some soldiers brought up a mortar so that they could charge the barricades outside when the mortar bomb exploded. After a second bomb hit the roof, the Red Guards managed to get into the telephone exchange. They shouted at the defenders to surrender and hammered on doors with rifle butts. Eventually, a white flag appeared from a third-floor window. Some firing continued, but then the boys emerged to surrender. There were less than 200 of them. 'We had been told that they were all cadets, but now we saw a lot of civilians among them including people wearing students' peaked caps. They looked very frightened.' As they emerged the soldiers tried to beat them and shouted threats and swore. They had heard the stories of the 56th Regiment from the Kremlin being mown down with machine guns when they surrendered. The Red Guards felt sorry for the young officer cadets, but the soldiers retorted: 'So what if they're children. They still want to be "Your Excellencies".'

'The *junkers* were standing in rows around the flag next to the wall of the building,' wrote Paustovsky about their surrender on 2 November. 'Their caps were crumpled, and their coats were grey with plaster dust. Many of them were half asleep leaning on their rifles.' An unarmed man in a black leather coat and escorted by several Red Guards approached. The officer commanding the *junkers* stepped forward and threw down cap and revolver. The *junkers* followed his example, making a pile of their rifles and cartridge belts, then they too walked slowly away . . . The linden trees with their shattered branches stood in the hoar-frost and the smoke. The torches of broken street-lamps blazed along the boulevard all the way to the Pushkin monument. The street was piled high with broken wires. They jingled complainingly as they swung against the pavement. A dead horse, showing its yellow teeth, lay across the streetcar tracks . . . There was as yet none of the bitterness which came later, during the civil war.'

The first uprising against the Bolshevik coup took place far from Petrograd. On 26 October, the day after the capture of the Winter Palace, Colonel Aleksandr Dutov led a small group to take the city of Orenburg at the southern end of the Urals. This was the home of the

Orenburg Cossack Host, a population half a million strong. Dutov declared martial law in the city and war against the Bolsheviks. Even with only 2,000 men, mostly officers, he was in a position to threaten communications with Siberia. Yet Dutov, who was about the only reasonable Cossack ataman east of the Urals, conscientiously organised elections for the Constituent Assembly.

Further east in Siberia at Verkhneudinsk, Colonel Grigory Semenov rose against the Bolsheviks on 18 November. He was backed by some of his Transbaikal Cossacks and a Buryat cavalry regiment, which he had been training with the even more murderous Baron Roman von Ungern Sternberg. Semenov, a thick-set character with moustaches shaped like a water buffalo's horns, was uneducated and brutal but his suspicious eyes indicated great peasant cunning. Ungern Sternberg, from a family of Baltic barons, on the other hand, was an intelligent psychopath.

In 1913, a Russian traveller in Mongolia called Burdukov had encountered the baron. He described him as an ascetic, obsessive warrior. 'He was lean, shabby and untidy, with yellowish stubble and the faded, frozen eyes of a maniac. His uniform was extremely dirty, trousers threadbare, boots with holes in them . . . A Russian officer travelling on horseback from the Amur all across Mongolia with no bedding or spare clothes, or foodstuffs, was something extraordinary.' Everyone seemed to remember his eyes, which were often described as cold as ice, with the impression that they could see straight through you. He also had an unusually small head on his broad shoulders, from which extended long arms.

A report on his military qualities was in many ways more favourable, although it attributed all deficiencies to one major fault. 'His only serious vice is constant drinking,' it recorded. 'When inebriated he is capable of conduct that is incompatible with the honour of an officer.' Ungern Sternberg also despised regulations and bureaucracy. He so hated paperwork that he simply threw all official correspondence straight into the stove.

On 31 December, a train of the Trans-Siberian Railway was approaching Chita. Several Bolsheviks, confident that they controlled the line, continued carousing in a reserved first-class compartment to celebrate the new year of 1918. Their leader, a Bolshevik commissar from the navy was a sailor called Kudryashev on his way to Vladivostok with 200,000 roubles for the local organisation. He was so drunk that he forgot to change trains to the Amur Railway. He did not realise the danger he was in until after they halted at Dauria. A lean, fair-haired officer, followed by subordinates, entered the compartment. He fixed his pale eyes on Kudryashev. 'Deputy Naval Commissar, that's you?' Kudryashev quailed in terror as he admitted that he was. Baron Ungern looked through his papers, then made a cutting gesture with his hand to his companions. 'As for these shits,' he added, pointing to the others from Kudryashev's party, 'whip them and throw them out.' According to an eye-witness, Kudryashev grovelled, begging for his life, as he was hauled out into the snow, where Ungern gave the order to fire. The large sum of money they found on him was used to pay Ungern's men. All goods travelling to European Russia were seized on Ungern's orders to be auctioned. He never spent anything on himself and avoided the company of women. Instead, he kept wolves in his house in Dauria.

In what became known as the *atamanshchina*, the rule of terror of the Cossack atamans, Siberia beyond Lake Baikal would suffer more than anywhere else in Russia from the unbelievable cruelty of warlords such as Semenov, Ungern and Boris Annenkov.

Of all the regions of Russia, the most likely to become a centre of resistance to Bolshevik rule was the Don. In 1812, during the Patriotic War against Napoleon, the Don Cossacks alone had provided twenty-six regiments of cavalry, amounting to nearly 50,000 sabres. General of Cavalry Aleksei Kaledin had been elected Ataman of the Don Cossacks in June. Several weeks afterwards he formed an alliance with the right-of-centre Kadet Party, but regretted this as soon as their leaders flocked to the Don capital of Novocherkassk, along with officers from Moscow and Petrograd who no longer received any pay. The Bolsheviks were furious to hear that the Ukrainian Rada was disarming Soviet troops, while allowing officers and armed Cossack detachments from the Romanian Front back through their territory to join Kaledin.

Kaledin naturally welcomed the return of Cossacks complaining about their treatment under the new Bolshevik regime. The commissariat of Cossack troops at the *Stavka* reported: 'Cossacks, especially the front Cossacks who don't recognise the Sovnarkom government, have found themselves outlaws. The mass of the soldiers, influenced by the Bolsheviks, insult and hate Cossacks. Cossack units are the last to receive vital supplies, sometimes none at all. And due to the lack of forage, the Cossacks have lost most of their horses. Cossack regiments based in Finland and Petrograd are forced to stay there. Trotsky declared to their delegates that they are regarded as hostages. The new authorities, using the tactic of divide and rule, are taking all measures to prevent any concentrations of Cossack units.'

Unity was fragile, even within the Don Cossack Host. There were tensions between officers and soldiers, and when younger Cossacks returned home from the front, a generational split appeared between traditionalist 'fathers' and those 'sons' who supported much of what the revolution stood for. There was also hostility between the Cossacks and non-Cossack peasant migrants, known as the *inogorodnye,* who lacked land and were treated as second-class citizens. And not surprisingly, the industrial workers of Taganrog and Rostov-on-Don, as well as the miners of the Donbas, regarded the Cossacks as Tsarist reactionaries.

After the Don *Krug* assembly in Novocherkassk declared its independence on 20 November, Red Guards from the local proletariat took over Rostov, proclaiming instead a Soviet Republic of the Don. Industrial workers in nearby Taganrog surrounded fifty *junker* cadets, who surrendered on the understanding that their lives would be spared. But they were marched off to a metal factory, where their arms and legs were bound and they were thrown one at a time into a blast furnace.

On 2 December, Kaledin and his followers seized back Rostov-on-Don, the gateway to the Caucasus. The Bolshevik reaction was immediate. The Naval School of Air Battle signalled the Naval Revolutionary Committee that 'Due to Kaledin's uprising, the Committee of the Naval School of Air Battle requests . . . the urgent allocation of 20 one-pood bombs [16.38 kilos] and 40 half-pood bombs.' The 'Quiet Don' was to become one of the key battlefields of the civil war.

There were many other insurrections against the Bolsheviks' seizure of power, but they rose in revolt without any co-ordination like independent city states and were crushed individually. On 14 November, the Finlandsky Guards were sent by train from Petrograd to Nizhny Novgorod to suppress a counter-revolutionary uprising there. Finlandsky soldiers wanted to abolish rank altogether and even opposed their commissar's attempts to promote them. They also voted in a meeting that all the silver from the officers' mess should be given to the state bank and appealed to other Guards units to do the same. This was to help raise the value of the rouble abroad, which in just ten days had halved in value against the dollar on news of the Bolshevik coup.

In Siberia, the Bolshevik takeover of Irkutsk did not take place until 8 December, when the inhabitants woke up to find armed groups of pro-Bolshevik soldiers patrolling the streets. To remove any doubts about who was in charge, they installed some machine guns on the Jerusalem Hill just outside the city and some artillery pieces were pointed at the centre from behind the railway station. 'And so, the Bolsheviks would have come to rule Irkutsk without a single drop of blood shed,' wrote the lawyer and ethnographer Moisei Krol, 'if it wasn't for several dozen *junker* cadets, Cossacks, officers and politicians who decided to defend the new regime with weapons in their hands.'

'I saw a small *junker* detachment with an officer,' wrote Serebrennikov. 'They were standing in full battle gear. They were wearing Siberian *valenki* felt boots, sheepskin coats over the greatcoats, rifles over the shoulder, and hand grenades were hanging at the belt.' They installed themselves at their military academy. At first they seized the initiative and besieged the Red Guards in the governor-general's house. The Bolshevik force 'had not counted on prolonged battles and did not have any serious supplies so soon began to starve. They had no drinking water, either. When a brave one dared to run to the Angara with a bucket to get some water, or even some snow from the courtyard, he would fall under well-aimed bullets from the *junkers*. The windows had been smashed on the very first day, and it was severely cold in the building. The Reds were using whatever they could for heating: boards from the parquet floor, palace furniture and paintings. Finally they had no choice but to surrender.'

There were many civilian casualties as the machine guns fired down streets. 'Occasionally we were able to see, from our window, a sledge passing, which had a Red Cross flag flying on it. Some brave people were driving around the streets picking up the dead and the wounded.' These battles went on for almost ten days, until the Bolsheviks in Krasnoyarsk sent large reinforcements to Irkutsk and they in turn surrounded the *junkers*, forcing their surrender.

'The victors guaranteed the defeated complete personal freedom; they could stay in Irkutsk or leave the city without any reprisal. The agreement was signed by representatives of both sides and I must say

Irkutsk Bolsheviks adhered to it.' But those anti-Bolsheviks who left in the hope of joining Ataman Semenov further east, did not know that other Red groups further along the Round-Baikal Railway had set up 'a control post for catching counter-revolutionaries, where many lives were lost'.

There were reports of disturbances and looting almost everywhere. 'Something mad is going on in Belets and Kharkov,' Lakier wrote, 'but the worst riots are in Bessarabia. The wave of pogroms has not reached Odessa so far, but riots are expected here too.'

In Irbit in the Urals, the looting did not begin until towards the end of November. Predictably, the first target was a distillery called The Siberian Inn, which happened to be opposite the Mosque. Soldiers came staggering out holding three-litre bottles of vodka in each hand. Soon, a shop by the market area was ablaze, a student recorded. 'Local women set it on fire to get some light and became very busy seizing things. Not more than ten soldiers were looting, most were just watching from the side, and from time to time fired their rifles in the air. They were all drunk. Diagonally across the street there was another shop with hams, sausage, brandy and different wines. That is where the soldiers went and I followed. In the crowd standing there was a middle-aged woman who kept saying: "Here, take the keys. Don't smash it up." She was the owner of the shop. Of course, they did the opposite. They smashed the windows and doors to get in. The woman threw the keys on the ground and left.'

Nobody had a more thankless task at this moment than General Nikolai Dukhonin, the last commander-in-chief of the old army, who had been rapidly promoted in the wake of the Kornilov affair. Wavell, who had come to know him quite well, described him as 'a nice, quiet capable but not very impressive man'.

On 8 November, Lenin ordered Dukhonin to contact the German military authorities to cease hostilities and enter into peace negotiations. Dukhonin played for time, saying that he needed to contact the Allies first, but he was cornered into admitting that he did not recognise the Sovnarkom as the authoritative central government of Russia. Lenin promptly removed him from his post and sent a signal to all formations to announce that Ensign Krylenko was replacing General Dukhonin.

On 20 November, the Bolshevik Krylenko, backed by a force 3,000 strong of Baltic Fleet sailors and soldiers from the reserve battalion of the Findlandsky and Litovsky Guards, reached Mogilev. The railwaymen of Vikzhel were no longer blocking Bolshevik forces. Dukhonin, who had turned down an offer to escape by car, went to the station to surrender himself to Krylenko. This was most unwise as he should have guessed that the sailors would be enraged to hear that he had allowed Kornilov, Alekseev, Denikin, Lukomsky and the other generals held in the Bykhov monastery prison to escape.

Krylenko tried to shelter Dukhonin in his carriage, but the Kronstadt sailors were out for blood and stormed it. They dragged Dukhonin onto the platform, beat him, stripped him, 'lifted him on their bayonets' and then mutilated his naked corpse. Bolsheviks turned his death into a knowing joke. 'Checking someone's papers at Dukhonin's headquarters' became a slang term for executing an officer.

A week later, the new *Stavka* sent out a stark warning to all senior officers who might sympathise with 'Generals Kaledin, Kornilov, Dutov and others . . . We are warning commanders that any counterrevolutionary activities on their part and by those sympathising with them will be punished without mercy. Anyone guilty will be dismissed from their position and handed over to a military revolutionary tribunal.' Krylenko also ordered all officers to remove their shoulder boards, which had become hated symbols of oppression in the eyes of angry soldiers.

As the hungry winter approached, it brought a marked change in mood. The young journalist Konstantin Paustovsky wrote that 'the misty romanticism' of the February Revolution and the 'belief in universal happiness' had evaporated. He described how the veteran writer Vladimir Gilyarovsky, with his sheepskin cap, extravagant Cossack moustache and hoarse voice, entered the newsroom. 'You suckling babes!' he growled at all those present. 'Socialists! Mouldering liberals! You don't know any more about the Russian people than that old fool Madame Kurdyukova.* I know the Russian people. And they'll show you yet where lobsters spend the winters!'

---

* Madame Kurdyukova, a sort of Russian Mrs Malaprop, was the protagonist in the comic novel by Ivan Myatlev, *Sensations and Observations of Madame Kurdyukova Abroad, Dans l'étranger* (1840–44).

10

The Infanticide of Democracy
November–December 1917

Lenin's order to General Dukhonin to start negotiations with the Germans had an immediate consequence. Another rush of soldiers abandoned the front to go home. If peace were coming, no peasant wanted to lose out on the distribution of land seized from landowners and the Church.

'The army of departing soldiers poured along the railway tracks of Russia, recklessly destroying everything in its way. Anything in the trains themselves that could be taken or destroyed had been taken or destroyed. Sheets of metal had been prised off the roofs of the cars. There was an active trade at the Sukharevsky market in washstands, mirrors, and pieces of red velvet ripped off the seats.' Station masters would run away whenever a mass of them 'pulled in with bandit yells, accordion music and machine gun fire'.

Trotsky justified the way they ripped the velvet from former first-class seats for foot bandages, saying that they deserved a little luxury in their lives. Lenin, on the other hand, welcomed destruction for its own sake. He had long been conscious of the fact that the Bolsheviks' only chance of seizing power across the Russian land-mass and retaining it would be to achieve *tabula rasa* through violence, so that there could be no possibility of a return to the past.

In September Lenin had written that 'civil war is the sharpest form of the class struggle'. He then argued that 'the proletariat came very close to starting a civil war' during the July Days, but that the Kornilov revolt was 'a conspiracy by which the bourgeoisie has actually begun a civil war'. Bolshevik propaganda of course needed to claim that the reactionaries started the conflict. The essential point, as he recognised very clearly, was that 'the revolutionary proletariat is incomparably stronger in the extra-parliamentary than in the parliamentary struggle, as far as influencing the masses and drawing them into the struggle is concerned. This is a very important observation in respect of civil war.' Thus, aware that the Bolsheviks might not win outright power in elections for the Constituent Assembly, Lenin knew that 'the strength they can develop in civil war' would be far greater. Right from the start, civil war quite clearly constituted his extension of politics by other means. Yet he did not dare cancel the elections for the Constituent Assembly since that would have united all the socialist parties against the Bolsheviks. It would be easier to dismantle the Constituent Assembly later, once they were firmly in the saddle.

In November, just after the Bolshevik seizure of power in Petrograd, Lenin began directing hatred and violence against 'class enemies', already defined as 'enemies of the people'. This was the start of his deliberate strategy of 'mass terror'. 'Far more than simply channelling social violence,' as one French study put it, '"mass terror" spread and developed as a determined, theorized and asserted policy, without any inhibition whatsoever, as an act of regeneration of the entire social body.'

Lenin flew into a rage whenever he was opposed, seeing it as treason or sabotage. On 29 October, he was infuriated to find that civil servants had called a general strike in protest at the Bolshevik takeover. Files in every ministry were locked away and the keys removed from the premises. Worst of all, the State Bank and State Treasury, as well as private banks, refused to issue any money or recognise the authority of the Sovnarkom. The Bolsheviks were thwarted for a month and a half. Eventually, Red Guards were sent in to occupy the premises of all banks. Their nationalisation was announced that afternoon. The next day the Supreme Council of National Economy was established.

Trotsky did not pay a visit to his ministry as People's Commissar for Foreign Affairs until 9 November, when he summoned all the officials. 'I am the new Minister of Foreign Affairs, Trotsky,' he announced. This was greeted with ironic laughter. He told them to go back to work, but they all went home. As in other ministries, only porters, couriers and some secretaries reappeared.

Trotsky subsequently sent a signal in French to all Russian embassies abroad ordering personnel to reply immediately if they consented to follow the orders of the new regime. 'All of those refusing to serve these policies must leave their employment and hand over documents and materiel to juniors who agree to carry out the instructions of the Sovnarkom.' It was signed 'Commissaire du peuple pour affaires étrangères, Trotzky'. Few senior diplomats chose to remain at their post.

Eventually, the Bolsheviks felt obliged to impose their own commissars on every ministry and major government office. Civil service personnel had to resume work, signing a declaration of loyalty to Sovnarkom, or face a revolutionary tribunal. Senior officials who had served the Tsarist regime were replaced by younger careerists or by ambitious outsiders who were frequently ignorant and uneducated. Lenin had expected this problem, but even he was shaken by the chaos and corruption which resulted. Opportunists were often the most effective administrators, but they were hardly loyal to the regime they served. 'You know,' Radek admitted to one of them who secretly opposed the regime, 'all my people are unreliable. All of them are right-wing, but I am gripping them in my fist.'

Lenin had firmly resisted all calls, even from members of the Party's Central Committee, to compromise with the sort of coalition government demanded by the Vikzhel railway union. He completely dominated all meetings of the Sovnarkom Cabinet and made no bones about side-lining the Executive Committee of the Soviet, despite having carried out the coup under the slogan 'All Power to the Soviets'. Kamenev, as its chairman, resigned in protest but it made no difference. Lenin rammed ahead like an icebreaker. He simply replaced Kamenev with Yakov Sverdlov, who ensured that the Soviet remained little more than a rubber stamp for the Sovnarkom.

All non-Bolshevik newspapers were banned, which made them pop up again under a new masthead the next week until they were banned again. The only exception was *Novaya zhizn* which, despite Gorky's outspoken attacks on Lenin and the Bolshevik dictatorship, somehow survived until the following July. Lenin closed it then on the grounds that they could not allow any more 'intelligentsia pessimism' during the civil war.

On 12 November, voting began in the elections for the Constituent Assembly, to which even Lenin had been obliged to pay lip service. The Bolsheviks had frequently attacked the Provisional Government over delays in bringing the Constituent Assembly to reality, and a number of their more moderate members genuinely believed in it. For the opposition, the election was the last chance to halt the development of what would become the first one-party state, presided over by a leader even more autocratic than Nicholas II. It was Marx's opponent, Mikhail Bakunin, who had warned that 'If you took the most ardent revolutionary, vested him in absolute power, within a year he would be worse than the Tsar himself.'

Polling took a long time because of the vast distances involved between European Russia and eastern Siberia. The event was also unprecedented because women were allowed to vote for the first time. In some areas, however, reactionary priests as well as the extreme Left still tried to manipulate the election. In Don country, Filipp Mironov, a Cossack lieutenant colonel, but also a Left Socialist Revolutionary, went on 15 November to his local polling station. 'Of course, a priest was appointed the chairman,' he wrote. 'He was sitting, his long hair loose, next to the ballot box, saying to everyone: put it in for the 4th list (which of course was organised by General Kaledin and his assistants). I said: "Put it in for the 2nd list, where there are socialist revolutionaries", and they started roaring at me like beasts. That's how intimidated they had been by those hairy idlers [the priests]. And now they think that I am a Bolshevik!'

This unprecedented election was bound to have its irregularities and distortions, although there were not many. Yet the results have always been a matter for debate. The Bolsheviks, although their support had been rapidly increasing, were dismayed to find themselves with only 10 million votes, just under a quarter of the total. The largest party, the Socialist Revolutionaries, received some 16 million votes, which represented 38 per cent of the total cast. This was misleading, however, since it did not take into account the irreconcilable split between Left and Right SRs into virtually separate parties, an event too recent to be reflected on most ballot papers. And since many of the Left SRs were prepared to work with the Bolsheviks at that time, it was not an accurate snapshot of political strength. The one thing it revealed clearly, however, was that the Bolsheviks did not enjoy anything like the support they claimed, above all away from the cities of northern Russia.

To Lenin's irritation, the Kadets did better than expected, particularly in Petrograd and Moscow. Their support came not only from the middle classes but also from many of the poorer voters appalled by the chaos and rise in crime. 'Many people, even the common people, are nostalgic for the Tsar and order,' wrote Yelena Lakier in Odessa three days before polling started. 'Every night there are gunshots, but we are so used to this that we just roll over and go back to sleep . . . I am shifting further and further to the right. I might soon become a monarchist. Right now I am a pure-bred Kadet and only a short time ago I used to be an SR. Our maid and cook signed the election list for the Kadets. They are sure that this is the only way to re-establish order.'

The political polarisation meant that support for the Mensheviks and other moderate left-wing parties dropped drastically, but this was also due to the vagueness of their electoral message. 'Almost nobody had any clear idea of what the different socialist parties intended to do,' wrote Globachev, the former head of the Okhrana. 'The Russian masses were absolutely ignorant.'

The Bolsheviks wasted no time in questioning the results and demanding fresh elections. They claimed the right to recall individual deputies, but even clearer signs emerged that they intended to sabotage the Constituent Assembly itself. On 20 November, the Sovnarkom announced a delay to its official opening. Then, on 23 November, Bolshevik members of the Military Revolutionary Committee arrested the three electoral commissioners during a meeting in the Tauride Palace. They were taken to the Smolny and the Sovnarkom appointed the Bolshevik Moisei Uritsky, the future head of the Cheka secret police in Petrograd, to take over the role.

Such shameless interventions provoked opposition parties to organise demonstrations outside the Tauride Palace, which the Bolsheviks described as counter-revolutionary. Accusing the Kadet Party, they outlawed it and imprisoned its leaders as 'enemies of the people' in the Peter and Paul Fortress. Lenin also tried to blame bourgeois speculators for the severe bread shortages in most cities, where the ration had shrunk to a quarter of a pound. Many did not consider it proper bread. 'They have started making dreadful bread with straw and bran,' wrote Lakier. 'The crust is so hard that it is difficult to cut it with a knife. Then pieces of straw get stuck in your teeth.' Lenin knew that a new government which could not feed the cities would not survive, especially one which relied on urban workers for its support.

On 4 December, barricaded in his office in the Smolny and closely guarded by Latvian riflemen, Lenin complained bitterly to Feliks Dzerzhinsky about the problem of sabotage by the bourgeoisie. The very next day, the Bolshevik secret police, the Cheka – The All-Russia Extraordinary Commission for Combatting Counter-Revolution, Profiteering and Sabotage – was established to replace the Military

Revolutionary Committee. Lenin's instruction to Dzerzhinsky, appointed to head it, began:

> The bourgeoisie are prepared to commit the most heinous crimes; they are bribing the outcast and degraded elements of society and plying them with drink to use them in riots. The supporters of the bourgeoisie, particularly among the higher clerical staff, bank officials, and so on, are sabotaging their work, and organising strikes to thwart the government's measures for the realisation of socialist reforms. They have even gone so far as to sabotage food distribution, thereby menacing millions of people with famine.

It was not explained exactly how the bourgeoisie were managing to sabotage food distribution, yet Lenin's own declaration of war later that same month could hardly have been clearer. 'War to the death against the rich and their hangers-on, the bourgeois intellectuals.' His dehumanisation of them as 'lice', 'fleas', 'vermin' and 'parasites' was tantamount to a call for class genocide.

Feliks Dzerzhinsky, a tall, emaciated Pole from a background of impoverished nobility, had a pale, ascetic, El Greco face, a wispy wizard's beard and hooded eyes. He was a true fanatic, devoted to a belief for which he would sacrifice everything, even his own health and sanity. Senior Bolsheviks remarked with a mixture of pride, fear and admiration that 'Feliks would not spare even his own mother in the name of the Revolution.' Like his subsequent ally Stalin, Dzerzhinsky had trained for the priesthood before turning savagely against the Christian religion. His determination to unmask every enemy and traitor was both pitiless and obsessive, and yet he was not addicted to bloodlust like some of his successors. The killings and torture he left to others. Utterly incorruptible, he mortified the flesh with the purity of his stance against any form of privilege. He would not touch any food beyond the most basic ration, and his office, where he slept on the floor wrapped in a greatcoat, was unheated at his insistence.

Apart from smoking, Dzerzhinsky's one *faiblesse* was for poetry. Although it was the highest form of art in the Slavic imagination, the mutual fascination which rapidly emerged between Chekists and poets, such as Sergei Esenin, Vladimir Mayakovsky and Aleksandr Blok, was indeed striking, as Donald Rayfield has emphasised. Chekists found the romanticisation of violence combined with self-sacrifice intoxicating.

In an anthology published by the Cheka, one of their executioners produced these verses:

> There is no greater joy, nor better music
> Than the crunch of broken lives and bones.
> This is why, when our eyes are languid
> And passion begins to seethe stormily in the breast,
> I want to write on your sentence
> One unquavering thing: 'Up against a wall! Shoot!'

The Cheka called itself 'The Sword and Flame of the Revolution'. This summed up the Bolsheviks' idealised ruthlessness, elevating their cause above any humane concern such as natural justice or respect for life. Dzerzhinsky had hoped to recruit men with his own spiritual purity and create a Bolshevik elite. He even issued his men with the black leather aviator jackets which had been provided by the British for the fledgling Tsarist air force. The advantage of leather was that, unlike wool, it resisted the infestation of typhus-bearing lice.

Dzerzhinsky claimed that the ideal Chekist had a 'burning heart, a cool head and clean hands'. But Lenin knew only too well that the Cheka was also bound to attract criminals, killers and psychopaths. Some had been brutalised in the trenches, others were released from prison during the revolution, yet the majority were not ethnically Russian. There were Trans-caucasians – Azeris, Armenians and Georgians – as well as Poles, Latvians and Jews. Dzerzhinsky's two principal lieutenants were both Latvian, Yakov Peters (Jēkabs Peterss) and Martin Latsis (Mārtiņš Lācis). Peters, who had sought refuge in London before the First World War, had first attracted attention in 1911 following the murder of three policemen and the siege of Sidney Street.

During the crucial post-coup period, Latvians played a vital role as Lenin's praetorian guard. In August 1915, during the war with Germany, the Tsarist *Stavka* had formed eight rifle battalions with Latvian evacuees from Courland. They had been used to defend Riga and the line of the River Daugava, which they did with great bravery despite heavy losses. But their treatment at the hands of their Russian commanders prompted the majority of their soldiers, and even a number of officers, to support the Bolsheviks during the late summer of 1917 as the Tsarist army disintegrated. The advance of the German Eighth Army that autumn, occupying Latvia and then Estonia, had forced them back to Petrograd, where they were just what the Bolsheviks needed. Anti-Bolsheviks soon claimed that 'Lenin made the revolution with Jewish brains, Russian stupidity and Latvian bayonets.'

Anti-Semitism was deeply ingrained across most classes and parts of the country and infected even Bolshevik ranks. Yet it was hardly surprising that Tsarist anti-Semitism, whose most extreme form consisted of murderous pogroms launched by the Black Hundreds, should have pushed angry young Jews into the arms of the Bolsheviks. This in turn created a vicious circle of hatred in the civil war, with more pogroms by right-wing officers, Cossacks and Ukrainian nationalists.

The widespread belief on the Right that almost all Jews were Bolsheviks was gravely mistaken. In Smolensk, for example, Jewish socialist parties worked with Socialist Revolutionaries and Mensheviks to form an electoral bloc against the Bolsheviks. Jews were twice as likely to be robbed as gentiles, often by soldiers of the local garrison as well as deserters passing through who professed Bolshevik beliefs. Not just merchants, but even impoverished Jewish market traders were insulted and attacked as 'burzhui'.

Despite the Provisional Government's emancipation of the Jews in March, many peasants in Belarus had retained their prejudices. They blamed shortages of flour and rising prices on Jewish hoarding and speculation. It appeared that 'Soviet authorities tacitly condoned violence against Jews.' In late November and early December, soldiers attacked the Jewish socialist parties' offices and smashed them up, broke up a meeting, and forced those present 'through a gauntlet of blows from rifle butts while calling them "burzhui" and "yids".' As food shortages became worse and popular anger intensified, Bolshevik authorities often deflected blame onto the Jews.

Although Lenin had blocked the Vikzhel plan of a coalition government, he came round in December to the idea of using Left Socialist Revolutionaries as fellow travellers. This spread responsibility for harsh decisions, and Lenin did not want to alienate the peasantry entirely, 'the infantry of the revolution' as the Left SRs called them.

Left SRs viewed the idea of a pact as their duty to support the 'spontaneity of the masses', after their recent split with the Right of the party. They were encouraged by the way Lenin had shamelessly copied their own policies on land reform. On 12 December, Left SRs joined the Bolsheviks in the Sovnarkom, where they were given minor posts. When faced with intense criticism from other left-wing parties, they justified their collaboration as the only way to temper Bolshevik authoritarianism while pushing forward parts of their own programme. They could not believe that the Bolsheviks would always insist on governing alone and hence utterly failed to understand the dynamics of dictatorship.

In most cases the few Left SR commissars which the Sovnarkom agreed to appoint were ignored. In Ukraine, the Left SR Mikhail Muraviev complained bitterly at the way Lenin encouraged Antonov-Ovseenko in the mass arrests of 'Kaledinites' and 'capitalist-saboteurs' without any consultation. Leading Left SRs also fought for the distribution of land to peasants against what they now suspected was the Bolshevik plan of outright nationalisation. Above all, they tried to control Dzerzhinsky's mass arrests of 'class enemies'. Their most senior appointment was the People's Commissar for Justice, Isaac Steinberg.

After the Cheka arrested opposition politicians campaigning in support of the Constituent Assembly, Steinberg had them released. The next morning, 19 December, Dzerzhinsky attacked Steinberg at a meeting of the Sovnarkom in the Smolny. He claimed that this action had 'humiliated and demoralised' the Cheka. Steinberg was reprimanded for contravening a Sovnarkom decision and told that only the Sovnarkom could overturn a Cheka order.

Steinberg fought on bravely and even demanded that Left SRs should be appointed to the Cheka. This Dzerzhinsky rejected, but the Sovnarkom finally permitted four members of the party to join, with one of them, Petr 'Viacheslav' Aleksandrovich, as Dzerzhinsky's deputy. To Dzerzhinsky's surprise, he became rather fond of Aleksandrovich. But when the Left SRs finally rebelled against the Bolsheviks the following year, Dzerzhinsky took on the responsibility of shooting him with his own hand, rather as if he were a favourite dog who had suddenly become dangerous.

December 1917 was also notable for the way the focus of the nascent civil war suddenly switched towards the south, with the Sovnarkom declaring war on the Ukrainian Rada and Ataman Kaledin's revolt on the Don. The generals who had escaped the monastery prison of Bykhov just in time also headed for the Don capital of Novocherkassk. Kornilov, the proudly proclaimed Cossack peasant, disdained any disguise. He also refused to travel by train. Incredibly, he set off on his grey charger in Tsarist uniform with shoulder boards, surrounded by his full Tekintsy cavalry escort, instantly recognisable from their huge fur *papakhas*.

The other generals had no qualms about disguising themselves. Lukomsky shaved off his luxuriant moustache and imperial beard and affected a German accent. Romanovsky, despite his age, dressed as an ensign; Markov played the part of a cheeky orderly; and the portly General Denikin, the future commander-in-chief of White forces in the south, pretended to be a Polish nobleman, despite travelling in third class.

With a journey of 1,400 kilometres in front of them, Kornilov and his Tekintsy cavalry faced many battles and ambushes ahead in a journey almost worthy of Xenephon's escape to the other side of the Black Sea. Red Guards who engaged them with little success telegraphed on to the next garrison. After innumerable skirmishes, Kornilov's Tekintsy eventually met their match in the form of an armoured train. The general's charger was killed and the survivors of his escort were so demoralised that Kornilov told them to make their way individually to their homes beyond the Caspian. He had no choice but to follow the example of his colleagues and take trains on to Novocherkassk, disguised as a peasant. He was the last of the Bykhov prisoners to reach the Don capital.

Another traveller in the region was heading well beyond Novocherkassk. Viktor Shklovsky, Kornilov's commissar in the Eighth Army, had been sent to the Transcaucasian front in Persia to supervise their withdrawal and demobilisation. 'Near Baku,' he wrote, 'I saw the Caspian Sea, a cold green not like any other sea. And camels walking with their easy gait.'

He carried on to Tiflis (Tbilisi). 'I arrived in Tiflis. A nice town, a poor man's Moscow. There was shooting in the streets; wildly enthusiastic Georgian troops were shooting in the air. They couldn't not shoot – [it was] the national character. I spent one night with the Georgian Futurists. Nice kids, more homesick for Moscow than Chekhov's sisters.' From Tiflis the train took another two days to Tabriz, and from there he travelled on to the headquarters of VII Detached Cavalry Corps at Urmia amid desert and salt marshes.

The corps and its support personnel amounted to some 60,000 men, who had not received any rations for some time. Instead, they seized all the sheep and grain they needed, reducing the locals to starvation. One third of the population of Persia died from famine and disease during the First World War, a higher percentage than any country even in the Second World War.

Shklovsky was horrified as he learned what ten years of Russian occupation had done to this region, which was part Kurdistan and part Azerbaijan. The population was even more mixed, with Persians, Armenians, Tatars, Kurds, Nestorian Aissors (Assyrians) and Jews. 'None of these tribes had got along together since time immemorial. When the Russians came, this changed; it got still worse.' Shklovsky saw with his own eyes the crimes that their regiments committed without any fear of disciplinary retribution. The Transbaikal Cossacks were the worst. 'In the army committee, they were referred to as the "yellow peril", and not just because of the colour of the stripes down their pantaloons. Broad-faced, very swarthy, they rode ponies that could live literally on roots; the Transbaikal Cossacks were valiant and cruel, like the Huns . . . however, I think that the cruelty of the Transbaikal Cossacks was more absent-minded. One Persian told me, "When they slash with their sabres, they probably don't realize they're using sabres. They think they're using whips."'

The greatest hatred and thus cruelty of the Russian troops was directed against the Kurds, who set up train wrecks and then attacked the carriages. A terrible revenge was exacted. 'Men I knew,' Shklovsky recorded, 'told me that when our troops burst into a village the women would smear their faces, breasts, and body from knees to waist with excrement to save themselves from rape. The soldiers wiped them off with rags and raped them.'

'I kept seeing the same thing on the road: ravaged villages and dead people. I've seen a lot of corpses in my lifetime, but these struck me by their everyday appearance. They hadn't been killed in the war. No, they had been killed like dogs by someone wanting to test his rifle . . . On the face of one corpse, a cat was sitting, all bristled up, awkwardly gnawing at the cheeks with its small mouth.'

Shklovsky's task of demobilising Russian forces in Persia to send them home was complicated by the soldiers' refusal to surrender their guns. They had found out what they could buy with them in a culture of total inhumanity towards women. 'A rifle – especially a Russian one – is a treasure in the East,' an appalled Shklovsky explained. 'At the beginning of our retreat, the Persians gave two to three thousand roubles for a rifle; for a cartridge, they paid three roubles in the bazaar . . . For the sake of comparison, consider the price of the women abducted from Persia and from the Caucasus by our soldiers. In Feodosia, for example, a woman cost fifteen roubles used, and forty roubles unused, and she was yours forever. So why not sell a rifle!' Gorky also described this barbaric slave trade. According to him, in Theodosia the Transcaucasian women were sold for just twenty-five roubles each.

Corruption in military circles even extended to the Russian flotilla on the Caspian, which was needed for the withdrawal. A Bolshevik officer named Khatchikov, through various intrigues, won sufficient support among his colleagues to become the commander. He then managed to take over the ships owned by the railway along with the military vessels and began trading dried fruit. Shklovsky later heard from the commissar of the Baltic Fleet that 'Khatchikov eventually helped hand over our Caspian flotilla to the English.'

British interest in the region was considerable, with the Baku oilfields and their own forces in Persia and the Mesopotamian front against Turkey. Now, the withdrawal of General Nikolai Yudenich's Russian armies from the area posed a strategic threat. The British and Indian divisions facing the Turks found their right flank to the north exposed. The Turkish armies, no longer blocked by Yudenich's 200,000 Russians, could push through south of the Caspian into Central Asia and outflank them, possibly threatening British India.

Without consulting GHQ in Baghdad, the War Office in London and Indian Army headquarters in Simla agreed to raise three special forces to train and command local levies to block the Turkish advance. But to achieve this, they would need to bring together Armenians, Azerbaijanis, Aissors, Kurds, Georgians, Turkmen and Russians, who hated each other. Major General Lionel Dunsterville's force would advance from Basra across eastern Persia to Enzeli and then secure Baku on the western shore of the Caspian. Major General Wilfred Malleson's force was to secure the eastern side of the Caspian, especially the Central Asian Railway to Bukhara and Samarkand, in order to protect the Persian city of Meshed. And Major General Macartney's force, the smallest of the three, would head for Tashkent itself, deep inside Russian Central Asia.

Lionel Dunsterville, although he looked like a typical English major general of the period with a regulation military moustache, was much more original than most of his contemporaries. A schoolfriend of Rudyard Kipling and the original for Kipling's character 'Stalky', Dunsterville was an adventurous type and a good linguist. He insisted on recruiting as many Australian, New Zealand, South African and Canadian officers and NCOs as possible, because he found them rather more self-reliant and enterprising than regulars from the British Army. Unfortunately, the process of selection and extracting them from the Western Front, then transporting them from London to Basra, took far longer than predicted. General Dunsterville and his men would not be able to reach Baku until the early summer of 1918. There, as part of a most improbable alliance of Bolsheviks, Cossacks and Armenians who had fled the Turkish massacres, Dunsterforce would fight to defend the city from a far larger Ottoman formation.

Part Two

1918

11

Breaking the Mould
January–February 1918

Lenin became increasingly nervous in the first few days of the new year. He had just survived the first attempt on his life when, on the evening of 1 January, two would-be assassins had fired revolvers at his limousine. Yet his greatest preoccupation was how to sabotage the Constituent Assembly, due to open on 5 January. To ban it before it met seemed too great a risk. He was still unsure how to handle the inaugural event at the Tauride Palace, which had been badly redecorated for the occasion with reds and browns. Lenin kept asking for advice, which was unusual, so Uritsky and Sergei Gusev put forward their ideas for disrupting the opening session. His first reaction was to dismiss them angrily, but then he came round to what they suggested.

Although very cold, with snow piled high beside the roads, 5 January proved to be a beautiful day. The sky was clear because the factories were all idle due to the lack of fuel. Patrols of Red Guards and sailors from the Baltic Fleet, armed with cutlasses and rifles with bayonets, blocked any demonstrations in support of the Constituent Assembly. 'Anyone who took part that day . . . will never forget it,' wrote the Socialist Revolutionary deputy Vladimir Zenzinov. 'To begin with, the city turned into a military camp.' The Latvian riflemen guarding the Smolny were reinforced in case of an attack, but troops from the garrison were not deployed because the vast majority supported the Constituent Assembly. Only Red Guards and sailors were used to break any demonstrations. The slogan 'All Power to the Constituent Assembly' was now declared by the Sovnarkom to be counter-revolutionary.

There were clashes on the Liteiny Prospekt. The writer and journalist Arthur Ransome estimated that some fifteen people were killed there and another hundred wounded. One of the dead was an elected deputy. An outraged Gorky compared the killings to Tsarist troops opening fire on Father Gapon's march in 1905. The Tauride

Palace was ringed with barricades, and at its entrance machine guns and two artillery pieces threatened the members even before they entered. One or two foreign journalists, including Ransome, could not understand why the fifteen Kadets elected had not appeared. It never occurred to them that they had all been arrested, along with a few Right SRs.

A young Bolshevik described her part in Gusev's plan. 'Gusev assembled young people like myself – secretaries, typists, couriers, and cleaners – and gave us all whistles and rattles. He installed us on the diplomatic balcony of the Tauride Palace and sat himself down behind the curtain. When the deputies started arriving, they were received by sailors. These bluejackets were all armed and had machine-gun belts wrapped around them. Replacing doormen, they welcomed everyone. The delegates then went to the cloak room, and once again it was sailors who offered to take their coats. So, the delegates went into the hall with their coats on, already feeling scared. They sat down and kept looking around.'

Lenin sat on one side of the speaker's tribune, his bald head clearly visible to all. He had no intention of taking part himself. He had designated Sverdlov to speak in his stead to open the proceedings with the demand that the assembly recognise the All-Russian Soviet as the supreme power. All the Bolsheviks present as well as the sailors and Red Guards applauded and cheered while the Right SRs remained stonily silent. But even they could not refuse to stand and join in singing 'The Internationale'.

After an interminable wait while votes were counted, the Right SR leader leader Chernov was elected chairman of the Constituent Assembly. By that time it was close to midnight. Lenin stretched out conspicuously, pretending to fall asleep. Chernov's speech was over-cautious and over-long, as he carefully avoided any acknowledgement of Sverdlov's insistence on the primacy of the All-Russian Soviet over the Constituent Assembly. He was followed by the Menshevik leader Tsereteli, who was once again the most impressive speaker of all.

Gusev gave the signal. His recruits as well as the sailors started to create pandemonium. 'The night session,' wrote Zenzinov, 'was conducted in an unbearable atmosphere. We, the deputies, were surrounded by a raging crowd.' Gusev's mob in the gallery started their 'whistling, rattling and shouting: They yelled at the delegates: "How much is Antanta paying you?"* or "Away with the war!".' Chernov, in an attempt to quieten them, shouted back: 'Comrades on the diplomatic balcony! If you don't stop the noise, I will give orders for you to be removed!' They just laughed at him. 'To whom could he give the order? The sailors?'

One of the Bolshevik deputies announced that the Constituent Assembly, by refusing to acknowledge the supremacy of the All-Russian Soviet, was a counter-revolutionary organisation. This was the sign for all the Bolsheviks to leave the hall. They were followed soon afterwards by the Left Socialist Revolutionaries. Sailors began to yawn openly, then they surrounded the deputies with rifles raised, cursing them as counter-revolutionaries. A deputy hurriedly proposed a motion that they should adjourn until 5 p.m. It was passed and they filed out of the Tauride Palace. The Constituent Assembly was closed. What Lenin contemptuously called 'bourgeois democracy' had not even been allowed to last twelve hours, signifying the death of the liberal and socialist intelligentsia. Open minds never stood a chance against the ruthless single-mindedness of the Bolsheviks.

Later that day, 6 January, ministers of the Provisional Government were transferred to the Peter and Paul Fortress. Two of the Kadet deputies already there, Shingaryov and Kokoshkin, were moved to the prison department of the Mariinsky Hospital because they were ill. The following night, ten sailors arrived and apparently shouted: 'Let's butcher them and free up a couple of bread rations!' They claimed afterwards that they were taking revenge for the repression following the 1905 revolt.

As in war, good luck or bad luck could turn in a matter of seconds. Among the arrested members of the Constituent Assembly was Vladimir Dmitrievich Nabokov, the executive secretary of the Provisional Government's council of ministers and the lawyer who had drawn up Grand Duke Mikhail's abdication statement. In those chaotic times, the Red Guard escorting Nabokov left him for a moment in a corridor and he managed to escape into the street through an unlocked door. The elegant Nabokov had everything organised in a very short time. His clothes were packed by his valet Osip while the family cook prepared caviar sandwiches. Nabokov had already sent his family, including his eldest son the writer, ahead to the Crimea to

---

* 'Antanta' was what Russians called the Triple Entente of Allies.

save the boys from being called up into the Red Guards. He followed them by train.

On 8 January the Bolsheviks, having protested bitterly against Kerensky's reintroduction of capital punishment in the summer, insisted on the death penalty for counter-revolutionary agitators and any bourgeois who resisted or avoided compulsory labour. Grounds for execution soon included flyposting, the non-payment of taxes, breaking the curfew, and traders resisting arrest. The Bolshevik tactic was to claim that proletarian anger was so intense that they could not resist the demands for 'popular justice'.

The following month, Lenin granted the Cheka the right to torture and kill, without trial or any judicial supervision. With a mountain of caseloads, it became quicker and easier for Chekists to condemn each prisoner to death rather than investigate. Long working hours, however, did not deter applicants attracted by the unlimited power to torture and kill. Within two years Dzerzhinsky had 20,000 men and women under his command.

Those escaping starvation and fear of arrest in Petrograd, in the hope of finding life easier in distant provinces, could be sorely disappointed. On finally reaching Saratov, members of the Borel family found that the local revolutionary committee was imposing huge fines or 'contributions' on the bourgeoisie. Non-payment meant that they could all be rounded up by the local Cheka.

'They were inventing all kinds of torture and executions. Hundreds of people were imprisoned every day in Saratov, which was not a big city at the time. City jails were overcrowded, so several large private buildings were requisitioned and also converted into prisons. The methods that they used for torturing could only be compared to medieval ones. They pulled "gloves" off people's hands, i.e., the skin, after soaking the hands in boiling water; they made belts from the skin off people's backs, broke bones and tortured with fire. A barge with a large leak was anchored in the middle of the Volga especially for the *burzhuis*. The doomed people were brought there and not given any food. They had to bail out the water, but people could not survive for more than a few days. Some went mad and killed themselves while others continued, but as they were losing their strength the barge was sinking lower and lower and finally sunk with several hundred people on board.' Sinking barges – the *noyades* – of the French Revolution were copied in many places. Kronstadt sailors tied up their victims with barbed wire before they scuttled their prison barges. The bodies were washed up later on Finnish beaches.

There was virtually no control over the application of Red Terror by sailors, from both the Baltic and Black Sea Fleets. Assembled into anti-profiteer detachments, they based themselves at railway stations and seized any articles at random. There was no appeal. One man whose goods had been impounded described the head of one these groups: 'a sailor with high cheekbones, a Mauser on his belt, and a pewter earring in one ear. He was eating salt fish with a wooden spoon, like porridge, and he was not at all eager to talk.' Their favourite task was spotting disguised *burzhui* and taking revenge. A group searching a train seized General Abaleshev, who could hardly pass himself off as a worker. He was forced to open his suitcase. Right at the top were his shoulder boards with Tsarist insignia. They shot him beside the track.

Indiscriminate class revenge was the mission of many sailors. In mid-January Bolsheviks from the Black Sea Fleet took part in the confused fighting in Odessa against *junker* cadets, officers and Ukrainian nationalists. There were estimated to be 11,000 unemployed officers in Odessa alone. 'An arrested officer has just been led past,' Yelena Lakier noted in her diary. 'He was tall and very young. Poor man. Are they taking him to the *Almaz*, a cruiser anchored in the port? They take officers there, torture them and then dump the bodies in the sea.' The next day, when their apartment was searched by sailors, one of them poked around under beds and cupboards with a sword. He boasted to Yelena Lakier 'I took this sword from an officer on the Chumnaya Hill, then I finished him off.'

'Didn't you feel sorry for killing him? He was a fellow Russian.'

'Who should feel sorry for killing a counter-revolutionary? We "bathed" a lot of them from the *Almaz*.'

Echoes of the atrocities in the south soon reached Moscow. A friend of the writer Ivan Bunin who had just returned from Simferopol in the Crimea reported that 'indescribable horror' was taking place there. 'Soldiers and workers are "walking up to their knees in blood". An old colonel was roasted alive in the furnace of a locomotive.' On 14 January, Bolshevik sailors from the Black Sea Fleet killed some 300 victims at Evpatoria by throwing them in the sea from the steamship *Romania*, having first broken their arms and legs. 'The most senior officer, who had been wounded, was picked up and thrown headfirst into the ship's furnace. On the transport *Truevor*, the officers were brought up from the hold one by one, and their bodies were mutilated while they were still alive before being thrown overboard.' Similar events took place at Theodosia and Sevastopol. At Yalta they were shooting *burzhui* victims off the pier where Chekhov's most famous short story, 'The Lady with the Little Dog', had been set.

In Petrograd and Moscow, searches of apartments for weapons or officers soon turned into officially permitted looting. In Petrograd, the Chekist leader Peters claimed that when he called for volunteers to search the homes of the bourgeoisie, 'up to 20,000 workers, sailors and Red Army men took part'. Red Guards, sailors and soldiers did not hesitate to stop well-dressed citizens in the street and demand their clothes. Men wearing starched collars and women wearing hats were automatically defined as *burzhui*. In all major cities it was becoming dangerous even to wear spectacles in the street if you did not wish to be insulted and robbed as a bourgeois. 'Everyone treated people in glasses suspiciously in those violent times,' wrote Paustovsky in Moscow. Members of middle-class families used to go out bundled in old clothes in an attempt to conceal their origins, with the *papa de famille* letting his beard grow to look like a peasant. Robbers, many of them demobilised soldiers, made it far too dangerous to venture out at night. Even Uritsky, the head of the Petrograd Cheka, was stripped at gunpoint.

The Bolshevik authorities ordered the confiscation of wine. Sometimes whole detachments of soldiers broke into houses looking for cellars. Once they discovered a source of alcohol, they wasted no time becoming dead drunk. At times it was necessary to call firefighters, who used cold water to wake them up or stop them fighting with each other. To halt the drunken riot, they smashed the remaining bottles.

At first officers, although unpaid, were allowed to queue for food at military canteens. These offered a soup with herring heads and bones, or horse-meat stew and potatoes rotten from frost. But even that privilege was withdrawn. Some officers were obliged to work as porters in railway stations because any government employment was barred to them. Then the Bolshevik regime heard that Boris Savinkov was setting up an underground organisation. On the assumption that the vast majority of officers were hostile, the Bolsheviks decided to deal with them in a double operation. They were ordered to register with the local Cheka on pain of execution if they failed to do so, but were arrested as soon as they turned up. The prisons overflowed, so some were executed. District by district, a register of buildings and tenants, porters and janitors was established. Then each block was surrounded by Red Guards so that Chekists could charge in to search and seize all officers and suspicious *burzhuis*. 'One often heard sinister salvos from the Peter and Paul Fortress,' wrote a lawyer planning to escape. 'Inhabitants of the capital dreaded tomorrow. Hunger was coming, together with Death with its long scythe.'

Economic catastrophe led to some 30,000 prostitutes working the streets, of whom between a third and a half came from respectable families. The American Anarchist Emma Goldman was shaken by the number of well-brought-up young girls along the Nevsky Prospekt 'selling themselves for a loaf of bread or a piece of soap or chocolate'. Others joined the harem of young commissars, who held cocaine orgies in the great gilded palaces of St Petersburg, where huge stuffed bears in the hall holding trays for visiting cards contrasted with Louis XVI furniture.

Unlike the reluctant amateurs, professional prostitutes were instantly recognisable by their triumphant, 'revolutionary' manner. In Odessa on 22 January, Yelena Lakier wrote: 'In the very centre of the city, three prostitutes were walking in front of me, heavily made-up, dreadful and brazen. A well-dressed lady, young and very attractive, was coming towards them in a seal fur coat. One of the prostitutes spat in her face. The three continued on laughing at the top of their voices.'

The Bolshevik term of 'former people' to describe the dispossessed middle and upper classes was a dehumanised version of the '*ci-devant*' used during the French Revolution. Almost all had to sell or barter possessions in the flea markets, anything from jewels and Tsarist medals or dress uniforms for a minuscule fraction of their cost simply to buy food. In Moscow, Ivan Bunin noted: 'On Tverskaya a poor old general wearing silver glasses and a black fur cap was selling something. He stood timidly, meekly like a beggar.' A number of aristocratic families were fortunate to be saved by servants smuggling them food from their estate in the countryside, or a former chef who had been given work in a public canteen. Tea, that vital Russian commodity, was unobtainable, so people resorted to carrot peelings. Even those who had been able to extract some of their own money from a bank before it was nationalised had to queue endlessly like the rest of the population. By the spring, a worker's ration produced little more than 300 calories a day. Petrograd was literally starving.

Women of the 'former classes' sell their last possessions on the streets of Moscow.

Few could escape selection for forced labour when named by the all-powerful building representative, usually a former porter or concierge. They 'were given a spade or a hoe and their names were called out at the start and the end of the shift'. The sight of them in the streets clumsily clearing snow and ice or rubbish was a humiliation greatly enjoyed by their Red Guard escorts and other onlookers. For the former gentry, this was a harsh glimpse of their future under Leninist class warfare, as was the loss of privacy in their own homes. The Bolshevik policy of moving poor families into apartments in residential areas was not just a way to share out housing more fairly. It was also a popular form of revenge and a way of introducing eyes and ears among the *burzhui* enemy.

Many members of the aristocracy and bourgeoisie in Petrograd had stayed on in the belief that the Bolshevik regime was bound to collapse amid the anarchy it had encouraged. But the closure of the Constituent Assembly, and especially the brutal murder of the two Kadet members in their hospital beds just afterwards, convinced many that they had to escape. Those who had left rapidly, just before or after the Bolshevik coup in October, had the easiest journey to Finland, then Sweden, and eventually Berlin or Paris when the war in the west was over. But most of those fleeing Petrograd and Moscow, unaware of the exact situation in the south, hoped that they would survive there, either in the Crimea, or Kiev, or in Novocherkassk. Word had spread of a 'Volunteer Army' assembling on the Don under Generals Kornilov and Alekseev. This, they told themselves, was where anarchic Russia would be saved from itself.

The Bolsheviks were well aware of the dangers if they failed to hold Ukraine and southern Russia. Antonov-Ovseenko was appointed commander of a newly created Southern Front. It was based at Kharkov along with a rapidly manufactured 'Ukrainian People's Republic' ready to take the place of the Rada. While Antonov intended to concentrate against General Kaledin, he sent a force of Red Guard units mixed with Baltic Fleet sailors and some conscript infantry from the old army to advance on Kiev. They were commanded by a Left Socialist Revolutionary and professional officer, Lieutenant Colonel Mikhail Muraviev. He first took Poltava, where he executed all the officers and *junker* cadets captured. He then advanced on Kiev, defeating a small Ukrainian force little more than 500 strong at Kruty on the way.

Russians in Kiev never expected the Ukrainian forces to put up much of a fight. Deliberately ignoring the reality of Ukrainian culture and history, they had taken Ukrainian patriotism as little more than a joke. General Count Dmitry Heiden wrote: 'The same circus went on even in the smallest details. They dressed the army in some fantastical uniforms. For the first parade that Hrushevsky organized in the Sophia Square, they had taken costumes from the Ukrainian Theatre which had once staged a historic play called "Zaporozhie Cossacks at the Danube".' The writer Ivan Nazhivin was equally amused and irritated at the same time with 'the history-themed operetta in fancy dress, which Professor Hrushevsky, the writer Vinnichenko, and Austrian agents were trying to stage here. One could catch glimpses of a Zaporozhie Cossack, straight from Gogol's book, or a brave warrior with a scalp-lock that he had just started to grow. Everyone was making fun.'

On 15 January Muraviev's so-called 1st and 2nd Revolutionary Armies, totalling just 4,000 men, reached the east bank of the Dnieper and began to bombard the city for ten days. Muraviev boasted in a signal to Lenin of the destruction of palaces and churches, and especially Hrushevsky's own house. Ukrainian resistance was reduced to a tiny pocket. On the morning of 27 January, the war minister of the Ukrainian Republic swore 'Kiev's situation is stable and there is nothing to fear', while the Central Rada led by Hrushevsky fled west to Zhitomir.

Russian officers in Kiev had refused to take part in the fighting. However much they hated the Reds, they would not fight under the yellow-and-blue Ukrainian flag due to the fact that the Rada was pro-German. This neutrality did not save them. Muraviev's Red Guards 'started dragging the unfortunate officers from hotels and apartments', wrote an eye-witness, 'literally to their death at "Dukhonin's headquarters", which was the ironic nickname given to the Mariinsky Park. That was the favourite spot for executions.'

In breaks from the killing, Muraviev's Red Guards embarked on a spree of robbery blessed by Lenin's slogan of 'loot the looters', which all too often also led to murder and rape. There were rich pickings with so many distinguished refugees from Petrograd and Moscow. The geographer Nikolai Mogilyansky described the pair who robbed his apartment. One was an earnest and well-behaved boy, clearly under the thumb of an older man, a Red Guard from the Putilov works in Petrograd who boasted of the executions. 'Machine-gun belts were hanging criss-cross on him, and he was full of hatred and revenge. Threats poured from his mouth that stank of alcohol. "Oh, I am going to find them all, I know them well, these counter-revolutionary officers", he would say and lift up his revolver and aim it as if at an imaginary victim.'

'Mass executions were being conducted in a most brutal manner,' a senior member of the Russian Geographical Society recorded. 'Victims, who had to undress before the execution, were shot in the back of the head, or bayonetted, to say nothing of torture beforehand. Most executions took place in the square in front of the palace where Muraviev's headquarters were located, as well as in the Mariinsky Park behind it . . . The sight was dreadful. The undressed bodies scattered about the square and paths in the park; dogs wandering among them. Everywhere there was blood on the snow. Many lay with the "Red ticket" stuck in their mouth, and a number of corpses had their fingers folded to make the sign of the cross.' According to the Ukrainian

Red Cross, of the 5,000 victims killed by Muraviev's men, two thirds were officers.

General Heiden, who managed to escape the massacre, wrote that 'The anatomy theatre of the University was packed with the corpses of killed officers, piled like logs. People found their relatives and secretly took the bodies away to the cemetery. Of those that I knew personally, General Viktor Ivanovich and his son were killed, also General Guslevsky, for whom his daughters managed to get a pardon from the commander Muraviev, but it was already too late, the young Colonel Domantovich, and the 80-year-old retired General Rydaevsky, who was taken from his apartment and shot in the street.'

The whole population of Kiev was terrorised. 'At night it is dark, empty and terrifying,' one citizen wrote. 'Soldiers are wandering everywhere, sloppy, dishevelled, yelling out songs. Once in a long while, an armed patrol passes. There are rifle shots here and there, or short machine gun bursts. Frightened civilians are at home, listening tensely.'

12

Brest-Litovsk
December 1917–March 1918

After Lenin's first approach in November to the Germans to request an armistice, the conventions of traditional diplomacy were soon turned inside out. The Soviet delegation departing for the citadel of Brest-Litovsk, the German headquarters in the east known as *Ober Ost*, was unusual, to say the least.

The party included an ordinary soldier who glared at everyone and barely opened his mouth; a lower-deck sailor of the Baltic Fleet; a cheekily self-confident young worker called Obukhov; and Anastasia Bitsenko, a Left Socialist Revolutionary former terrorist, who in 1905 had assassinated a Tsarist general. The leaders who were to negotiate with Prussian officers consisted of three Jews: Adolf Yoffe, a sophisticated revolutionary intellectual: Lev Kamenev, who was Trotsky's brother-in-law; and Grigory Sokolnikov, who had been on the 'sealed train' from Switzerland with Lenin.

As they headed towards the Warsaw station, Yoffe and Kamenev suddenly realised that they had forgotten to include a peasant in their delegation. They stopped their expropriated automobile at a corner and waylaid a suitably shaggy old man called Roman Stashkov. He was going to the station, so they offered to give him a lift. Because Stashkov had to correct himself when he called them *barin* (master), instead of *tovarishch* (comrade), Yoffe thought they had better ask about his political sympathies. Stashkov replied that he was a Socialist Revolutionary, like everyone in his village.

'A left one or a right one?'

Stashkov paused to make sure he came up with the correct answer. 'Left, Comrades, of course. The very leftist.' Stashkov then became flustered when he found that they were not headed for the Nikolaevsky station, which was the one he needed to return home. But once he was persuaded with numerous inducements to accompany them to

Brest-Litovsk to make peace, he settled back to enjoy this strange stroke of fortune.

The Bolsheviks had taken a reckless gamble in demolishing the remains of the Tsarist army while the country was still at war with the Central Powers. Yet Lenin had known that he could win the political battle only by putting an end to the fighting. Now, to achieve a breathing space and consolidate Bolshevik power, they had to keep that promise. Bolshevik strategy was also based on a fervent belief that a European-wide upheaval would instantly follow their own revolution and declaration of peace.

Lenin and Trotsky had called on the governments of France and Britain to join them in negotiations with Germany to end the war. Predictably, this proposal was greeted with a stony silence. Lenin then published a 'Decree on Peace' designed for an international audience, hoping it would embarrass the Allies and provoke strikes and mutinies in Britain and France.

Because of the state of the railways, it took the Russian delegation two days to reach Brest-Litovsk. The titular commander-in-chief on the Eastern Front was Field Marshal HRH Prince Leopold of Bavaria, but the real power at *Ober Ost* headquarters lay with his brilliant chief of staff, Major General Max Hoffman, large, gluttonous and smooth-skinned with a pince-nez. The leader of the German delegation was Baron Richard von Kühlmann, the secretary of state for foreign affairs, a man of great charm and intelligence. He was genuinely interested in a lasting peace, and much more enlightened than those victory-obsessed generals in Berlin.

More days went by as the delegations arrived from the other Central Powers of Austria-Hungary, Bulgaria and the Ottoman Empire. Now that an armistice had been agreed, this hiatus seemed to be an advantage for the Bolsheviks as they waited for the revolution to break out across Europe and save them. They distributed revolutionary pamphlets to the German troops across no man's land, and even at Brest-Litovsk to Hoffman's initial amusement, then anger.

On the evening of 7 December, Prince Leopold gave a dinner for the delegates. With perfect good manners, he placed Yoffe on his right, 'a Jew recently released from a Siberian prison'. On Yoffe's other side was Emperor Karl's foreign minister, Ottokar Graf Czernin von und zu Chudenitz. Yoffe, in a 'kindly tone', confided to him: 'I hope we may be able to raise the revolution in your country too.' Czernin, all too aware of the desperate state of the Austro-Hungarian Empire, commented in his diary that night: 'We shall hardly need any assistance from the good Yoffe.'

The old peasant Stashkov, with straggling grey hair and a long beard, through which he shovelled large amounts of food, was having the time of his life. When the German orderly enquired whether he wanted red wine or white wine, Stashkov turned to his neighbour, Prince Ernst von Hohenlohe. 'Which is the stronger? Red or white? It makes no difference to me which I drink, I'm only interested in the strength.' On Prince Hohenlohe's other side at this extraordinary dinner was Anastasia Bitsenko, the 'quiet and reserved little grey-haired assassin'.

Soon after negotiations began, Yoffe thought he had secured a major success. The Central Powers appeared to agree to his proposals of peace without annexations, but then it became clear that the Germans had no intention of giving up their occupation of the Baltic states and Poland. They cited the Bolshevik declaration on self-determination, confident that the promise of local elections at a later date would allow the German army to hold on to their present positions.

With little hint of the anticipated revolution in western Europe, Lenin was now very uneasy at their prospects. Trotsky even made rather more genuine overtures to the British and French in an attempt to bring them into the negotiations. The Bolsheviks had to buy time at any cost and this is why Lenin chose Trotsky to take over the negotiations. Trotsky reached Brest-Litovsk by train, accompanied by the 'spectacled revolutionary goblin' Karl Radek, who announced their arrival by throwing insurrectionary appeals out of the carriage window to bemused German soldiers.

Trotsky was a brilliant speaker who could argue any issue inside out and back to front, in German and several other languages. For days he managed to engage Kühlmann in abstract and philosophical theory as part of his delaying tactics. Kühlmann's longer-term plan was to secure the Baltic provinces, Poland and Ukraine as German satellite states under the guise of self-determination. But then the supreme command in the form of Field Marshals Paul von Hindenburg and Erich Ludendorff stamped their boots. They wanted the transfer of German divisions to the Western Front to be speeded up ready for their spring offensive, the aim being to knock out the British and French before the Americans came to save them. Poor Count Czernin, on the other hand, wanted only peace for the tottering Austro-Hungarian Empire, which suffered even worse starvation than Germany.

The Bolshevik position deteriorated further when a Ukrainian delegation sent by the Rada turned up unexpectedly. At that moment Muraviev's offensive against Kiev was imminent, and the Ukrainian nationalists decided that life would be better under a German occupation than Bolshevik rule from Petrograd. A 'Treaty of Peace Between Ukraine and the Central Powers' was signed on 11 January. This meant that Ukraine would become a German protectorate, and its loss was seen as a disastrous development for the Bolsheviks. The German position was greatly strengthened, both in negotiation and vital resources. A million tons of foodstuffs were immediately available. This would shore up the German and Austro-Hungarian governments' internal position and make a revolution far less likely.

On 5 January, just as the Bolsheviks were about to crush the Constituent Assembly in Petrograd, Major General Hoffmann presented the map with the future borders which the German supreme command demanded. It represented a major humiliation for Russia, with its evacuation of the Baltic states, Poland, Finland and Ukraine. It was a far more ferocious *Diktat* than what the Germans themselves were forced to accept at Versailles later, to their lasting bitterness. Trotsky tried to argue that newly formed nations needed a referendum to express the will of the people, which was a bit rich considering the destruction of democracy planned for the Tauride Palace that very evening.

Trotsky returned to Petrograd with the map showing the borders. It was a sickening shock for the Central Committee. Lenin was prepared to accept almost any terms, however humiliating, simply to ensure the survival of Bolshevik power. His opponents on the Central Committee led by Bukharin believed that to concede would undermine any hope of an international revolution. They argued instead for a guerrilla resistance against a German occupation which would surely inspire their sympathisers across Europe to rise up in support. Left Socialist Revolutionaries and their firebrand leader Maria Spiridonova believed the same, but they were wrong.

Lenin, on the other hand, had suspected that they could not count on any help from outside, at least not for some time. Resistance to the German war machine was out of the question. Not only would they lose the Baltic, but Petrograd too and most of central Russia if they tried to resist. The Central Committee met as soon as Trotsky returned. Bukharin and the advocates of revolutionary warfare were the largest faction. Trotsky, who had been forced to recognise the strength of Lenin's arguments, still could not abandon the hope of international revolution, so he adopted the unprecedented position and slogan of 'Neither war nor peace'. His tactic would be to return to Brest and declare that the war was at an end, refuse to sign the German document, then walk out and return to Petrograd. This, he argued, would make Germany the blatant aggressor against a peaceful country.

Lenin knew that such a theatrical performance would achieve nothing. Their duty was to save the one revolution which had succeeded, and keep it alive by winning the civil war which they had started. In Lenin's inimitable phrase: 'The bourgeoisie has to be throttled and for that we need both hands free.' But to prevent Bukharin's majority triumphing, Lenin and his handful of supporters had no choice but to support Trotsky and his faction.

Trotsky returned to Brest-Litovsk on 15 January to find the Germans in a much more resolute mood. He countered by arguing that the Bolshevik conquest of Kiev rendered the treaty with the Ukrainian Rada null and void. The representatives of the Central Powers rejected this out of hand. Their forces could sweep Muraviev's Red Guards and sailors aside in a moment. General Hoffmann became increasingly impatient with the puckish Karl Radek, who argued that all Poles in the German and Austrian armies should be allowed to agitate for their country's independence. He also kept leaning across the table and puffing smoke in Hoffman's face. Such childish games were even more pointless than Trotsky's refusal to recognise the Central Powers' treaty with the Ukrainian Rada.

Trotsky also did not know that wildly optimistic Bolsheviks back in Petrograd had started to broadcast to Germany over the radio station in Tsarskoe Selo. The German radio station at Königsberg intercepted messages 'inciting the German troops to mutiny, to murder the Emperor Wilhelm, the Generals of the High Command and their own regimental officers, and to conclude an independent peace with the Bolsheviks'. The outraged Kaiser was no longer prepared to listen to the moderate arguments of Kühlmann. Informed that without the Latvian rifle regiments Lenin's regime would collapse, he now swung entirely behind the hard line of Hindenburg and Ludendorff.

On 9 February, the Kaiser ordered Kühlmann to present the German terms to Trotsky as a straight ultimatum to be answered within twenty-four hours. Failure to reply would end the armistice. The fact that a wave of strikes had broken out both in Berlin and Vienna strengthened rather than weakened the German determination. The next day, Trotsky played what he thought would be his brilliant wild card of 'neither peace nor war'. He launched first into a bitter diatribe against all those who opposed the Bolshevik revolution. Then he announced that Russia declared that the war against the Central Powers was over yet refused to sign a peace of annexation.

The delegates sat there speechless with disbelief, until Hoffmann exploded: 'Unheard of!' Trotsky led his team from the room, savouring the shock effect of what they had just done. But he was about to discover quite how wrong he had been in his confident declaration to Lenin that 'the Germans will be unable to attack us after we declare the war ended'. Hindenburg and Ludendorff ordered Hoffmann to prepare the armies of *Ober Ost* to advance.

Trotsky and the members of his delegation returned to a heroic welcome back in Petrograd. But on 16 February, Kühlmann was forced to announce that hostilities would resume in two days' time at noon. As soon as he heard, Lenin wanted to sign the German terms immediately, if that were still possible, but Trotsky insisted on waiting at least until *Ober Ost* started its advance so that they could condemn German imperialist aggression to the world. He still hoped that this might be enough to trigger the revolution in Germany. Lenin, quite rightly, was unconvinced but remained in a minority.

All the next day, German aircraft reconnoitred east of the cease-fire line. Then, on the morning of 18 February, divisions of infantry in *Feldgrau* and mounted regiments of uhlans, in their distinctive *czapka* helmets like miniature mortar boards, their pennons fluttering on their lances, advanced east from the front line, which ran all the way from the Gulf of Riga on the Baltic to the Danube delta on the Black Sea. Both German and Austro-Hungarian troops advanced into Ukraine.

Dvinsk was the first city to fall. It took just a few hours on that first day. German jackboots echoed in empty streets. The collapse of resistance was total. Six hundred Cossacks surrendered to a lieutenant and six men.

The next day in the citadel of Brest-Litovsk, Hoffmann received a telegram from Lenin and Trotsky accepting the conditions which they had refused earlier. On reporting this to supreme headquarters, Hoffmann was told by Ludendorff to react as slowly as possible to allow the advance to continue. The big major general was in a fine mood of *Schadenfreude* after all the irritating Bolshevik games and insults of the last few weeks. 'It is the most comical war I have ever known,' he famously recorded. 'We put a handful of infantrymen with machine guns and one gun onto a train and push them off to the next station; they take it, make prisoners of the Bolsheviks, pick up a few more troops, and go on. This proceeding has, at any rate, the charm of novelty.'

The Sovnarkom's formal acceptance of German conditions was delivered in Berlin on 21 February. But two days later, as the German army marched on up the Baltic coast towards Petrograd and deep into Ukraine, even harsher terms reached the Smolny. The Germans now wanted all the territory they had covered up until that moment. It was little consolation to Lenin that he had been right all along to argue for immediate acceptance of the original terms. He argued that they should request military support from Britain and France. Since the Sovnarkom was repudiating all treaties and cancelling all foreign debts, the request was badly timed to say the least. Bukharin and his followers condemned Lenin and resigned, while the Left Socialist Revolutionaries called him a 'Judas'. Lenin invoked martial law, called up labour battalions to dig trenches and gave orders to prepare to evacuate Petrograd. This triggered a panic-stricken rush to leave and a bout of last-minute looting.

Finally, on 3 March, the Treaty of Brest-Litovsk was signed. In Russia, it was seen as a humiliation, but this brilliant stroke of *realpolitik* by Lenin preserved Bolshevik power. In Germany it represented the greatest and cheapest victory of the war, saving the country from starvation and enabling it to fight on. It tripled the size of German territory. Tragically for both countries, however, it gave German nationalists the idea that European Russia and Ukraine should become their colonial possessions in the next war.

The civil war in the former Grand Duchy of Finland had been brewing since the October elections ordered by Kerensky in which the Left lost control. The Bolshevik coup d'état in Petrograd soon afterwards accelerated the whole process. On 2 November 1917, Lenin had declared a right of self-determination for the peoples of Russia. He justified it to fellow Bolsheviks on the grounds that they would otherwise be accused of 'Great Russian chauvinism masked under the name of communism'. In fact, he believed that frontiers and national identity were irrelevant with the oncoming world revolution. On 15 November (NS), led by the conservative Senate, the Finnish parliament declared independence. The nationalists of the Right were to seize the opportunity created by the Bolsheviks.

Clashes soon began between the Civil Guard supporters of the Senate and the Red Guards. On 27 January 1918 (NS), local Communists proclaimed the Finnish Socialist Workers' Republic in Helsingfors. The capital and the more industrialised towns of southern Finland provided most of the 70,000 Red Guards, of whom some 2,000 were young women. Groups of Red Guards raided middle-class houses to confiscate their owners' rifles for hunting deer and elk, but most of their weapons came from Russian soldiers or over the border from Petrograd.

Conservative leaders fled north from Helsingfors and a White Provisional Government, headed by the chairman of the Senate, Pehr Evind Svinhufvud, was set up in Vaasa on the west coast of Ostrobothnia. It could count on the loyalty of the old Swedish-speaking ruling caste, those afraid of revolutionary chaos, and farmers and independent peasants from central and northern Finland. As military commander, Svinhufvud's administration appointed Lieutenant General Baron Carl Gustaf Mannerheim, the officer who had served in the Tsar's Chevalier Guards and risen to a corps commander in the war. Mannerheim ordered the Civil Guard to start disarming Russian troops in the west and introduced conscription.

Although the Swedish government intended to remain firmly neutral, White sympathisers in the country raised a brigade of inexperienced volunteers nearly 1,000 strong to support the Whites. And in February the 27th Jäger Battalion crossed the frozen Baltic by icebreaker from Germany, reaching the Gulf of Bothnia. Other Finnish Jägers, who had served in the German army, would reinforce Mannerheim's White Army and provide experienced leadership. In southern Karelia, two former Jäger officers raised a force to fight back Russian Bolsheviks arriving to help the Finnish Reds. While the Whites had a core of experienced troops to train their men, the Reds were at a disadvantage because Finns had not been conscripted for the European war.

Six days after the signing at Brest, the Royal Navy landed a small contingent of Royal Marines at Murmansk in the far north to guard the depots and dumps of war materiel shipped to the Tsarist army during the war. The Murmansk Soviet had made the request, fearing attack from White Finnish forces just across the border. The British for their part were concerned about the build-up of German forces in Finland. This marked the first step of what would become Allied intervention in the Russian Civil War.

In the second week of February, the British Military Mission to the Tsarist army was finally allowed to leave Petrograd for home. They departed from the Finland Station, where Lenin had arrived less than a year before, only to find themselves facing the battle lines between the Red and White Finns in their civil war. The British then endured the 'somewhat embarrassing' situation of depending on German officers supporting the White Finns to manage their onward journey by train to Stockholm. Finally, taking ship from Norway, they reached Aberdeen.

The White Finns managed to hold off an ill-planned offensive launched by the Red Guards in February. Then, in early March, Mannerheim's White Guards, now some 17,000-strong, counter-attacked to the south of Vaasa towards the capital of Helsingfors. The key battle was for the industrial city of Tampere, a stronghold which the Reds were determined to defend. By the end of the month Mannerheim had encircled the city and the savage battle continued. Despite heavy losses among the Jägers and the Swedish volunteers, the Whites broke into the town on Thursday, 28 March. Mannerheim ordered a pause to regroup, while his artillery bombarded the city centre which was packed with refugees. Then, on 5 April, the final offensive began. A last stand was made in the town hall by a mixed force of men and women Red Guards while many of their leaders escaped across a frozen lake.

Despite a promise by General Mannerheim that the Whites would not shoot prisoners, a brutal retribution was exacted. Both sides suffered around 800 casualties in the fighting, but Mannerheim's men shot another 1,000 Finnish and 200 Russian prisoners after they surrendered. Some 10,000 were marched off to a rudimentary prison camp where a further 1,228 died of exposure, disease and malnutrition.

Against the wishes of Mannerheim, Senator Svinhufvud had already appealed to Berlin for help. The former Tsarist general, however, had to swallow his pride and acknowledge the assistance of his recent enemy. 'In accordance with the request of the Finnish government,' he felt obliged to declare, 'detachments of the victorious German army landed on Finnish territory to help us in the fight against the Bolshevik scoundrels. I am convinced that the companionship in arms, which will be signed in blood in this fight, will still more strengthen the friendship and faith that Finland always showed for the Kaiser and the German people.'

The 13,000 German troops who would ensure a rapid White victory were Lieutenant General Rüdiger Count von der Goltz's *Ostsee* Division and Colonel Otto von Brandenstein's detachment. Goltz claimed that their mission was simply to liberate Finland 'from the Red Terror'. General Erich Ludendorff, however, having declared that he had made the decision to intervene in Finland with 'both my head and my heart', had a dual plan. He wanted to be able to threaten Petrograd from the Finnish side to the north as well as from the Estonian flank to the southwest. It would certainly prevent any unpleasant surprises on Germany's Eastern Front as Ludendorff prepared his great *Kaiserschlacht* offensive against the British and French armies in the west. He hoped that it would also provide Germany with permanent bases on both the northern and southern shores of the Gulf of Finland.

Goltz and Brandenstein's forces landed on the Finnish coast west of Helsingfors and advanced on the capital, which they took on 13 April. White victory was completed in the battle for Vyborg on the Karelian Isthmus north of Petrograd. Vyborg, which had become the capital of Red Finland after the loss of Helsingfors, was also packed with left-wing refugees who now lacked an escape route. The Whites encircled the city on 23 April to prevent Bolshevik reinforcements and weapons coming from Petrograd. Only the Red leaders managed to get away in time by sea. Following a similar pattern to the battle at Tampere, the Whites suffered heavy losses, especially among their untrained conscripts.

Shortly before the Whites took the town on 29 April, drunken Red Guards shot a group of thirty prisoners held in the jail, including two conservative members of the Eduskunta. Many other middle-class victims were found slaughtered in their houses. The White vengeance which ensued was as bad as it had been at Tampere, with some 1,200 Russian and Finnish prisoners executed, and another 800 dead from the appalling conditions in the prison camp outside the city later.

There appear on balance to have been rather fewer atrocities committed by the Reds, although according to General von der Goltz, at Kouvola, northeast of Helsingfors, right-wingers were bound and buried in the ground up to their necks. Straw was then piled on top of their heads and set on fire. But, as the Finnish conflict demonstrated, the winning side in a civil war usually ends up executing the greater number of victims. Altogether, the four-month struggle led to just under 40,000 deaths, of whom some 12,500 were Red prisoners of war.

The combination of Brest-Litovsk and the Finnish Civil War led to the most brilliant action of the Baltic Fleet, and one of the most grotesque examples of Bolshevik justice. In early April, part of the Imperial German Fleet was heading towards Helsingfors to secure the Finnish capital, but also to capture a Russian squadron of the Baltic Fleet iced in there. The British naval attaché in Petrograd, Captain Francis Cromie, reported on the corruption and apathy of the Russian crews as observed by British submariners who were trapped there too. 'There was no pretence of morals anywhere: the ships were full of girls day and night, officers embezzled public money and organized the sale of Government stores, which were eagerly sought ashore, where famine prices reigned. Our sailors got their pleasure for ten lumps of sugar.'

Captain Aleksei Shchastny, the local commander, faced the decision whether to scuttle the warships or attempt to rescue them by taking them across the frozen Gulf of Finland to Kronstadt. He smartened up the demoralised crews by suggesting that the Germans would hang them when they arrived. Using the fleet's icebreakers, he extricated the six battleships on the night of 12 March. Five cruisers followed, then fifty-nine destroyers and twelve submarines.

Shchastny was hailed as the 'Saviour of the Navy' for what became known as the exploit of the 'Ice Cruise', but then on 27 May he was arrested on Trotsky's orders, having crossed swords with the arrogant new People's Commissar for War. Trotsky accused him of treason and prosecuted him personally, claiming that Shchastny had tried to drive a wedge between the Baltic Fleet and the Sovnarkom purely for his own glory. 'The Brest Treaty has been printed and anyone can read it,' Trotsky stated. 'All statements about some kind of a secret agreement concerning the Navy are brazen inventions by the Whites. The Brest Treaty stipulates that our fleet has to remain in its ports.'

Shchastny was found guilty. The indictment of the revolutionary tribunal read: 'Shchastny, acting heroically, made himself popular with the intent to use that against the Soviet government.' He was shot on 22 June. The Menshevik leader Martov called it 'a bloody comedy of cold-blooded manslaughter'. The new commander-in-chief of the Baltic Fleet, informed Trotsky: 'The execution of Shchastny has had a depressing effect on the commanders, but this low morale has not yet taken any particular shape. The crews are calm, they only want an explanation.'

By the first week in March, when the treaty was signed at Brest-Litovsk, the German armies on the southern side of the Baltic had progressed some 200 kilometres to Narva on the Estonian border, just 150 kilometres from Petrograd. A week later, the Bolshevik leadership moved their seat of government from Petrograd to the Kremlin in Moscow. Lenin had never liked the city, but Moscow offered better communications with the rest of the former empire while Petrograd was now threatened on two sides as Ludendorff had planned.

Two other changes came more or less together. The description of Bolshevik was dropped at the Seventh Party Congress that month, which also signalled the abandonment of the socialist Second International and the first step towards the Communist International, or Comintern. From henceforth the Bolsheviks were to be the Communist Party, although the description 'Bolshevik' remained in common currency. Meanwhile, the Sovnarkom stopped using the old-style Gregorian calendar. The country jumped forward thirteen days to be in line with the Julian calendar of the western world.

Starving, darkened Petrograd, abandoned by its leaders, was in a pitiful state. 'Ration cards could only provide minimum amounts of the poorest quality bread, the worst type of oil and rotten, frost-bitten potatoes,' wrote a Pole trapped there. 'Starving and poor people rummage through refuse in search of food. Dustbins were infested with rats which had multiplied madly, while cats and dogs had disappeared. Horses were dropping dead of starvation and exhaustion in the streets, squares and on bridges.'

'We live in a dead city,' wrote Teffi. 'On the streets are corpses of horses, and quite frequently of people ... At night, frightened figures steal up to the horse carcasses and carve out a piece of meat.' Petrograd was completely transformed after just a couple of months of Soviet power. All private shops were closed. Their windows were partly broken, partly covered in chalk. Streets were empty and dead. The authorities started removing statues in squares. In their place 'they

The German Advance
and Occupation
March–November 1918

⌐⌐⌐⌐⌐⌐ Front line at the beginning of armistice
        talks at Brest-Litovsk, December 1917
━━━━━ Furthest line of German advance, August 1918

put ugly gypsum sculptures of new revolutionary stars and various emblems on the old pedestals. Houses were full of dirt, streets filled with rubbish, cobbled roads were full of holes and the few cabs and commissar's cars moved in them with great difficulty.'

Factories were at a standstill without fuel, but also because starving workers stole their raw materials to sell. There was no electricity, gas or oil for lamps. In the harsh frosts which penetrated buildings through broken panes, the only glimmer came from starlight reflected off the less than pristine snow. Victor Serge called it a 'prehistoric gloom'. 'People slept in frozen dwellings where each habitable corner was like a corner in an animal's lair. The ancestral stench clung even to their fur-lined cloaks which were never taken off.' Often the only sources of fuel for a small cast-iron stove, known as a *burzhui* because of its pot-bellied shape, were books, broken furniture or torn-up floorboards. Almost everyone was reduced to stealing wood, whether from fences or abandoned houses stripped bare. 'Fire is life. Like bread,' wrote Victor Serge.

In that unheated granite city, water pipes and lavatories were frozen solid. Some sailors from Kronstadt who had seized an apartment on the *piano nobile* of a former palace simply smashed open a round hole in the floor which they used as a latrine down to the living space below. The thaw, when it came, would not just release an appalling stench of sewage, but disease.

Victor Serge memorably described an anarchic underclass taking over empty embassies and grand buildings. 'Bandits get in through the courtyards and live there, careful that no light can be seen from outside to betray their presence. They play cards, drinking old cognac swiped from the cellars of great houses. Girls with lips painted fiery red, with names like Katka-Little-Apple, Dunya-the-Snake, and Pug-Nose-Marfa-Little-Cossack, who wear luxurious dirty underwear and dresses by the great couturiers, taken from empty apartments, sometimes peer out, invisible from behind the dark windows.' The capital of the empire was dead and Peter the Great's 'window on the west' was closed. It would be nailed shut by the end of the summer, once the Cheka had done its work.

13

The Volunteer Army's Ice March
January–March 1918

General Alekseev, the Tsar's last chief of staff, was a modest man respected by all for his honesty. Unlike more dashing generals, such as Wrangel, he was an infantryman who hated horses. He was famous within the army from his time as a captain instructor at an academy for cavalry cadets. When offered a horse on an exercise he replied, 'No thank you, I am in a hurry,' and set off on foot.

Since the Kornilov affair, Alekseev had been doing all that he could to help arrested officers and their families. His standing and contacts among politicians and industrialists enabled him to raise funds at a time when most people were thinking only of themselves. He managed to convince some of them that an army must be formed to combat the Bolshevik dictatorship.

After the apathy which almost all officers had shown both in the February revolution and during the Bolshevik coup in October, the realities of the new regime's class warfare started to change attitudes. Young officers in Petrograd and Moscow soon heard on their own grapevine of a counter-revolutionary army forming on the Don. They also heard of the help which Alekseev's organisation and others could offer in the way of false identity papers, money and tickets to reach the south. There was an extraordinarily brave and resourceful nurse who took groups of them by train, heavily bandaged as if they were seriously wounded soldiers sent on doctors' orders for recuperation in the south.

Alekseev assembled just forty officers soon after his arrival in Novocherkassk in mid-November, well before Kornilov and the other generals imprisoned at Bykhov turned up. Even by the end of November the 'Volunteer Army' numbered little more than 300 men. At first, Alekseev could not offer them any salary, just food. Every spare rouble was spent on weapons, ammunition and equipment.

Initially, General Kaledin as ataman had welcomed the idea of Alekseev's Volunteer Army. Yet most ordinary Cossacks, sick of the fighting, resented its presence because it would attract war to the Don. When Red Guards took Rostov and threatened Novocherkassk, Alekseev had immediately offered Kaledin his small force to help. On 9 December, with few Cossacks then willing to fight, Alekseev's officers succeeded in taking the city. Many regarded this as the opening action of the civil war.

General M.V. Alekseev.

Despite his reputation as a reactionary, Kaledin introduced reforms in the *krug* to allow the non-Cossack *inogorodnye* to participate in Don politics and the government. He felt that the Don's declaration of independence had disenfranchised them and that the injustice must be corrected. But this was not enough to deflect the hostility of the non-Cossacks, nor the leftist sympathies of the younger Cossacks still returning from the front.

The fighting out in the Don steppe took on a strange pattern as Antonov-Ovseenko's two Red 'armies' advanced on Rostov and Novocherkassk. The 1st Army, commanded by the Left Socialist Revolutionary Yuri Sablin, consisted mainly of Red Guards sent down from Moscow and strengthened with some sailors from the Black Sea Fleet. Their task was to block the Don steppe from the north and push down on Novocherkassk. Meanwhile the 2nd Army of Rudolf Sivers advanced from the Donbas to retake Rostov from the west along the coast of the Sea of Azov.

The Red Guards, who had experienced no warfare apart from the clashes with the *junker* cadets in Moscow, were naturally nervous about facing *frontovik* Cossacks, but 'many workers had scores to settle with them after the punitive expeditions of 1906 and 1907', wrote the Latvian Eduard Dune. Their commander was a naïve lieutenant – 'he was not a Bolshevik at all' – who astonished them by turning up with shiny boots and shoulder boards on his uniform tunic. They had to advise him very firmly that he must never appear with shoulder boards again. But he proved brave in battle and they came round to him.

The initial task for Dune and his 300 comrades was to disarm Cossacks returning from the Romanian Front. Since Cossacks provided and owned their own horses and weapons this was a potentially explosive activity, but with some basic diplomacy and the support of the railwaymen, who could isolate the Cossacks in a siding, it was usually successful. Miners from the Donbas would volunteer as replacements, while the *inogorodnye* peasants were sympathetic, sometimes bringing food, but reluctant to commit themselves because they assumed that the experienced officers and Cossacks were bound to win.

*The 'Railway War'. Red Guards (armed workers) and de-mobilised
soldiers helped the Bolsheviks to take control of most of central Russia
in the winter of 1917–18.*

The great distances over the ice-bound Don steppe, and the
Reds' lack of cavalry, meant that the fighting followed railway lines.
Engagements were little more than skirmishes. A train with Reds proceeded until a White train was spotted. The men dismounted from
the livestock wagons, and as the steppe was flat the riflemen lay down
in an extended line on the frozen ground. Dune recorded his first

encounter with the Whites. He and his comrades tensed as the figures approached. Somebody shouted 'They're officers. Their shoulder boards are gleaming.' Dune, however, had guessed they were officers simply because they had the confidence to advance without firing and did not throw themselves down when the Red Guards began shooting wildly with their rifles. Their machine guns had jammed after just a few bursts. 'It was the first time I saw the enemy so close,' wrote Dune. 'I shivered from the sound of bullets flying past.' But then they heard three toots from their train's whistle and saw it backing away. Terrified of being abandoned out in the steppe, they raced back to the wagons despite the curses of their furious commander.

Dune recounted how, soon afterwards, they captured two young officers and a nurse who had arrived on a sledge, unaware of the Red advance. It was all very civilised. After they surrendered their pistols, Dune let them leave. 'Would they have treated me in the same way?' he wondered afterwards. 'I remember the battle at Likhaya and what happened to our wounded.' Locals pointed to a hillock in the distance. 'There is a communal grave of your people over there.' There were no wounded and no prisoners. Only the dead. 'Officers don't take prisoners,' they reminded themselves, and they were right. General Kornilov had expressly ordered that no prisoners should be spared.

'On one occasion,' Dune recorded, 'the train halted between two stations when we spotted the corpses of three people tied to telegraph poles. The bodies were covered in blood and dressed only in their underwear and striped naval undershirts. No boots. One had a sailor's cap propped on his drooping head, covered in blood. The same caps were lying next to the two other bodies.' They untied them and buried them by the railway embankment.

'Of course, we felt class hatred,' Dune wrote, 'but it was not the same feeling as the wild personal anger that turns a human being into a brutal savage and butcher . . . Compared to the enemy, we had a great advantage. We believed in the cause of universal justice as opposed to personal class privileges.' Dune was certainly telling the truth, as far as he was concerned, but the pattern of killing was hardly one-sided.

On 14 January, workers in Taganrog rose in revolt behind Volunteer Army lines. Savage street fighting ensued, with the barely armed workers vastly outnumbering the Volunteers. Some enraged *junker* cadets captured a dozen workers. It was said that they cut off their noses, put out their eyes and buried them alive with dead dogs. Sivers's Red

Guards and sailors retook Taganrog on 20 January and exacted vengeance. The officers and cadet defenders surrendered on condition they would be allowed safe passage out of the city, but then their wounded and sick were hauled out of the hospitals and killed in the streets. Apparently around fifty officers were tied and then thrown into the furnace at the Baltic ironworks. Many of the victims were hacked to death with sabres, either to save ammunition or to satisfy the rage of the Red troops.

By the end of January, Alekseev's Volunteer Army was still disappointingly small. No more than 3,000 officers, cadets and students had signed up, while many thousands of officers who had sought safety in the south refused to join. The volunteers tended to be young and vengeful after their family's estates had been destroyed. Many were reactionary monarchists and wanted the return of Tsarist autocracy. They viewed the minority who believed in the Constituent Assembly almost as 'Reds'.

A bitter row also broke out over the leadership. Even though Alekseev had set the Volunteer Army in motion, Kornilov insisted on becoming its commander-in-chief, otherwise he would leave for Siberia. He still could not forgive Alekseev for his arrest on Kerensky's orders, when all Alekseev had been trying to do was to sort out the tragic muddle and protect the senior officers involved from a revolutionary tribunal. Eventually it was agreed that Kornilov would be the Volunteer Army's field commander while Alekseev, already suffering from the cancer which would kill him, would be the political, financial and administrative head. Alekseev gave Boris Savinkov responsibility for relations with foreign governments, despite the lack of contact with anyone outside Russia.

Relations between Kornilov and Alekseev never improved. Kornilov's arrogance was deliberately provocative, not only towards Alekseev, but also towards the Kadet politicians, especially Milyukov, whom he loathed. The great mistake of almost all White generals was their obstinate belief that they must continue the long war against Germany, as well as against the Reds. This turned almost all peasants and former soldiers against them, including Cossacks.

Ataman Kaledin was equally depressed by how few Cossacks were prepared to resist the advance of Sablin's and Sivers's forces. The overwhelming majority simply wanted to cultivate their own fields in peace. On 28 January, Alekseev wrote to Kaledin to warn him that his men could not continue to protect the Don more or less on their own. 'The complete unwillingness on the part of Don Cossacks to defend their legacy puts an unbearable burden on the shoulders of the Volunteer Army and makes it very hard to prolong the struggle.' The move north of the Bolshevik 39th Division from the Kuban threatened the Volunteer Army's line of escape. Kaledin begged Alekseev to stay, but both Kornilov and Alekseev agreed that they must save the Volunteer Army to keep the anti-Bolshevik cause alive.

Kaledin's task was not helped by Cossack officers speaking out against resistance to the Bolsheviks. Lieutenant Colonel Filipp Mironov, a Left Socialist Revolutionary, wrote on 25 January, 'The ground is wobbly under the feet of General Kaledin, his assistant Bogaevsky and the Military Government. They have failed to trick the *frontoviki*! There are already military-revolutionary committees in the Cossack villages of Ust-Medveditskaya, Kamenskaya and Uryupinskaya that don't recognize the rule of General Kaledin and his military government and demand their resignation.'

By the end of January both Rostov, the headquarters of the Volunteer Army, and the Don capital of Novocherkassk were under threat. The Cossack partisan leader Chernetsov was hacked to death and his detachment almost completely destroyed after another Red Cossack officer, Lieutenant Colonel Golubov, crossed over to the Reds with several hundred men. Novocherkassk was left defenceless. Kaledin lost his courage. On 29 January (O.S.), he announced to the Don government: 'There's been enough talking.' He went into the next room and shot himself through the heart. A new ataman, General Anatoly Nazarov, was elected, but stood little chance of defending the Don.

General Mikhail Svechin knew Nazarov from the general staff academy. 'I congratulated him on his courage at accepting the post. He smiled bitterly and replied: "I could not say no. For as long as a tiny part of Cossack lands remains, somebody has to take over and hold the ataman's mace."' Svechin asked what he was planning to do. 'I have ordered the field ataman General Popov to assemble small groups of Cossacks and to be on the move towards Zimovniki beyond the Don.' Svechin volunteered to join Popov, who was about to leave with 1,500 men, but Nazarov warned him of the most spartan conditions. 'No supply carts, no couriers, you will just have a horse and a Cossack saddle, with all your kit in the saddle-bags.' Nazarov then warned the

Volunteer Army that resistance was at an end. It was time for them to leave.

On 23 February (N.S.), Sivers's troops entered Rostov, and two days later, Sablin's Red Guards made their final advance on Novocherkassk. They dismounted from their trains and even offloaded their field kitchens. Marching across the snow-covered steppe in a long column, they looked around. 'The enemy was nowhere to be seen,' Dune wrote. 'In the distance we could see Cossack hamlets. Men and women were watching us carefully. We could see the golden cupola of Novocherkassk Cathedral and then the town itself. There was an air of expectancy in the silence.' Ahead, their reconnaissance section had reached the outskirts and was waving them on.

The streets were empty when General Svechin emerged that morning to find out what was happening. Towards the cathedral, he saw a cavalry detachment moving up the hill. It turned out to be that of Lieutenant Colonel Golubov, who had joined the Bolsheviks. Svechin rushed home to hide his uniform, while his wife hid her jewellery. Ataman Nazarov, who had refused to abandon the city, went to the assembly of the Don *Krug*. Golubov burst into the hall with a crowd of followers and shouted at Nazarov, who remained seated.

'Stand up when the state authority enters the room!'

'I am the Don ataman elected by all the Don Cossacks,' Nazarov replied. Golubov strode over, ripped off his shoulder boards and arrested him. Two days later Golubov had him shot.

Svechin described how, over the following days, bands of Reds began looting apartments. Many Cossack generals, officers and regional officials had remained in the city, and there were a number of executions. The elderly General Ivan Orlov was stopped in the street even though he was wearing a sheepskin coat and no shoulder boards. 'They did not ask who he was but shot him on the spot. Constant gunfire could be heard around the city. They seized the wounded from the hospitals, threw them in trucks like logs, drove them to the rubbish dump and left them there, shooting some, while the others were left to die.'

With the loss of Novocherkassk, the Volunteer Army had no alternative but to leave Rostov and pull back south of the Don, in the hope of support from the Kuban Cossacks. They knew that in the Caucasus they faced starvation, ferocious winter conditions and vastly superior Red forces, including the 39th Division, but there was no other escape route.

General Alekseev wrote to his wife from Rostov just before they pulled out. 'My dear, beloved Nyuta! It seems as if our handful of men, who have no support whatsoever from the Cossacks, are abandoned by everyone . . . We will be in an extremely difficult situation when leaving the Don. We will be faced, most likely, with a long move on foot, only God can decide where to. You can understand what state I am in, although I am having to hide it here and appear calm amidst considerable chaos. It is especially hard since I have no news about you and the girls. I have to go off into the unknown without being able to see you all before departure, to bless and to kiss you. But there is nothing to be done. If it is my fate not to return and never to see my nearest and dearest, you should know that the thoughts of you and my children are always with me, and it is with the thoughts of you that I will live my last minute if I am now destined to die.'

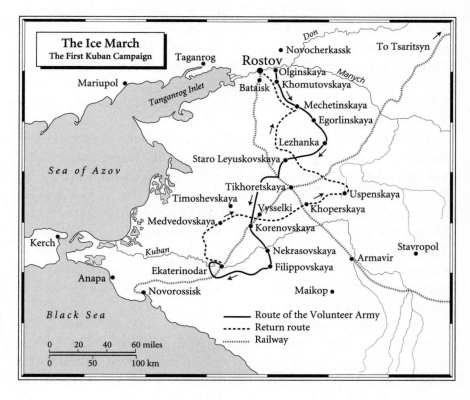

On 23 February (N.S.), as Sivers's Red Guards entered Novocherkassk, the Volunteer Army crossed the frozen Don without mishap

despite an ineffectual attack by two Red aircraft. They were out of immediate danger on reaching the Cossack *stanitsa*, or settlement, of Olginskaya. Their presence in the area caused great alarm among the neighbouring settlements who naturally feared Red retribution.

Kornilov commanded what was probably the most unbalanced formation in the history of warfare. The Volunteer Army of some 3,700 men numbered 36 generals including Kornilov, Alekseev, Denikin, Romanovsky, Lukomsky and Markov; 199 colonels; 50 lieutenant colonels, 2,083 captains, lieutenants and ensigns; and 437 *junkers*. Only 880 were not officers or officer cadets. Kornilov reorganised what had been a mass of small groups into an Officer Regiment, commanded by Markov, the 'Kornilov' Regiment, the Partisan Regiment of mainly Don Cossacks under General Bogaevsky, and a *Junker* Battalion. There was also an artillery battery of eight guns, a couple of which had been bought off Red Guards in exchange for vodka. They were severely hampered, however, by almost 1,000 camp-followers, mainly politicians and wives who could not be left behind in Rostov. This meant that their long column on foot could never make more than 30 kilometres a day, and usually during that winter much less. Only the wounded and gravely ill were allowed to travel in the convoy of two-wheeled *arba* carts.

The Volunteer Army's gravest deficit was in cavalry. General Popov appeared at Olginskaya on 26 February with his Don Cossacks. The Volunteer Army generals begged him to join forces with them, but he knew that he could not keep his men together if they strayed too far from Don territory. On the next day, the Volunteer Army set off from Olginskaya towards the region of Stavropol deep in the Caucasus. This was a compromise since the generals could not agree on where they should go or what they should do. Denikin, Alekseev and others hoped to take the Kuban capital of Ekaterinodar as a base and a focal point for anti-Bolshevik forces.

The Volunteers saw their journey into the unknown as a heroic enterprise, but if they had known the degree of suffering ahead, their hearts would have quailed. In any case, their survival represented a huge blunder on the part of the Bolsheviks, who had allowed both the Volunteer Army and Popov's Cossack force to escape into the hostile wilderness. Despite their slow speed, the Reds did not manage to intercept the long winding column of the Volunteers until 6 March (N.S.) at Lezhanka. The mixture of Red Guards and soldiers from the 39th

Division were surprised when Markov's Officer Regiment crossed a small river and outflanked them. They fled but a number of the division's officers were captured. Kornilov ordered their court martial but was persuaded to spare them if they joined the Volunteer Army, and yet young officers in a vicious mood whipped and slaughtered some sixty peasants. Three days later the Volunteer Army, turning west, entered the Kuban and found the local Cossacks much more supportive despite the presence in the region of Red forces. They even gained recruits from some of the *stanitsas* in the area, although they were sometimes obliged to fight off groups of poor Cossacks and *inogorodnye*.

The biggest battle was at Korenovskaya when, instead of the small force of Reds they expected, the Volunteer Army faced a total of 10,000 Red Guards and sailors. Instead of withdrawing, Kornilov, whose forces were low on ammunition, took the risky decision to fight in the hope of capturing enemy reserves. The battle lasted for four days and cost the Volunteers 400 men, but they prevailed despite the odds and on 17 March captured the station at Korenovskaya with all the supplies they needed. Even a few casualties meant that more of their precious carts had to be given over to the wounded, but the casualty rate they had just suffered meant packing the badly wounded on top of each other. The unsprung *arbas* lurching in and out of potholes added to the pain of their wounds.

The Kuban had lacked good leadership in the crucial period after the Bolshevik coup in Petrograd. It also suffered from the tens of thousands of bolshevised troops retreating through it from the Persian and Turkish fronts, those that Viktor Shklovsky had been sent to demobilise. When the Volunteer Army generals heard that Red troops had forced the Kuban Cossacks to abandon their capital of Ekaterinodar, there was no consensus on what to do next. Alekseev and Denikin still wanted to attack the city, but Kornilov insisted they were not strong enough.

Kornilov gave the order to head south towards Maikop, not knowing the strength of Red forces in the area. Instead of having a chance to recover and reorganise, the Volunteer Army found itself fighting one engagement after another. Physically exhausted, starving and with an increasing number of sick and wounded, the soldiers and the civilians suffered terribly. Their boots and footwear were rotting, and too many lacked sheepskins against the ferocious cold in the hills. Many suffered from frostbite after fording swollen rivers with no chance to dry their clothes or foot bandages.

They were close to despair, but finally on 22 March (N.S.), they heard the unmistakable sound of cannon in the distance. In their circuitous route, they had stumbled by chance on the Army of the Kuban led by the remarkable Colonel Viktor Pokrovsky, who had been a pilot in the war against Germany and was now proving one of the great cavalry leaders of the White cause. His recent successes had acted as the best recruiting sergeant imaginable. After the outrages and robberies committed by the Reds and demobilised soldiers passing through their territory, more and more Kuban Cossacks had brought out their rifles from hiding places in barns and byres, saddled their chargers and ridden off to join him.

The Volunteer Army and Pokrovsky's Kuban Cossacks were of roughly equal size when they met up. At last, Kornilov had the cavalry he needed, but so convinced was he of his position as the future leader of Russia that he treated Pokrovsky and the members of the Kuban Rada with an arrogance bordering on contempt. The Cossack leaders very nearly refused to serve under him. Only frantic background diplomacy managed to arrange another meeting and an agreement.

With these combined forces, Kornilov advanced rapidly on Ekaterinodar, where the Reds had many more men than the 18,000 which the Whites had estimated. This time the sailors and industrial workers of the Red Guard were defending fixed positions, so they did not feel as vulnerable as they usually did out in open countryside. On 11 April, the morning of their attack, Kornilov did not wait for Markov's brigade to cross the river, which was a mistake made worse by bad communications and confusion. In the furious fighting casualties were very heavy on both sides, mainly because the Reds held their ground bravely. The exhausted Volunteers were given a day to rest after the onslaught, before another assault was planned by Kornilov. He rejected the pleas of Alekseev and Denikin to pull the army back to recover properly after such a bloodbath. His argument was that they had to win and take the city, having expended so much ammunition. Kornilov was adamant.

His personal courage was a form of arrogance, as if no enemy would dare to kill him. Alekseev had once said that Kornilov had the bravery of a lion and the brains of a sheep, and this became his epitaph. Ignoring advice to the contrary, Kornilov had established his command post in a whitewashed farmhouse in full view of the Red artillery. That next morning, 13 April, just before the attack was renewed, a shell scored a direct hit. Kornilov died under the rubble with members of his staff. Denikin kept the news from the troops, but when word slipped out later that day, the Volunteer Army nearly went to pieces.

Alekseev promptly named Denikin as Kornilov's replacement. He wrote to a friend that things were much better as a result. 'I act in complete concordance with Denikin, we are solving issues together to everyone's benefit.' He added that if Kornilov had carried on commanding, 'this would have put at risk all that we still had and threatened to ruin the entire cause.' The two men indeed worked well together, but the large and avuncular Anton Denikin could never match Kornilov's dangerous charisma.

Denikin, knowing that the army needed to recover from the shock to their morale, ordered a rapid withdrawal towards the north. The Reds celebrated their victory with a public burning in Ekaterinodar of Kornilov's exhumed corpse and failed to follow up their advantage. 'The half-destroyed army,' wrote one of Kornilov's devoted officers, 'spent a long time wandering constantly in danger, persecuted and surrounded by enemies. Everywhere it dragged behind it its frightening, bloody tail, the train of carts with the wounded that was several kilometres long. It was not possible to leave the wounded behind. The war had been equally brutal on both sides. The Volunteers had been shooting their prisoners and finishing off the wounded with such brutality that they could not possibly hope for mercy. And yet the situation was so bad, and this terrible train of carts was such a burden for the exhausted army, that several hundred of the gravely wounded were finally abandoned in different places. Most of them died and only a few survived. It was only this horrifying sacrifice as well as unbelievable efforts that allowed the Army to break out of the encirclement and reach the Don.'

The Volunteer Army's failure to secure the Kuban was not nearly as important as its ability to survive until the Don and Kuban Cossacks were roused to resistance. The revenge of the Reds in what they thought was the moment of victory, proved worse than counter-productive. A Red detachment reached the Cossack *stanitsa* of Gundarovskaya and thought that they could act with impunity, looting, raping girls and women, and setting the larger houses and shops on fire. A group of Cossacks with some students and officers planned a reprisal attack, and this turned into the so-called Gundarovsky Revolt, which also led to them setting up their own Gundarovsky Regiment.

Inevitably, a vicious circle of violence established itself. 'Neither side took prisoners,' a new arrival with the Volunteer Army soon discovered. 'We were forbidden to shoot prisoners. They were to be killed with a sabre or the bayonet. Ammunition was too precious and had to be kept for combat.' And in Odessa Yelena Lakier heard from a friend with the Volunteer Army that: 'The Bolsheviks are burying captured officers alive, while officers in turn burn captured Bolsheviks alive.'

The writer Ivan Nazhivin, who had been a close friend of Tolstoy, spoke to senior officers in the Volunteer Army about the fighting in the south of Russia. 'On the other side, sailors are the best fighters, they are desperate,' the White commanders told him. 'The Chinese fight furiously, Red Army soldiers are weak.' Chinese 'internationalists' fighting for the Reds were recruited from those used by the Tsarist government in digging trenches and transport during the war. In southern Russia, the Bolshevik Iona Yakir led a battalion of Chinese 600-strong.

'On both sides,' Nazhivin continued, 'bitterness has reached an extreme, inhuman scale. The Reds, once they have taken a *stanitsa*, plunder everything they can, rape women regardless of their age, and don't spare bullets . . . The Cossacks, too, are extremely embittered towards the Reds, especially sailors and the Chinese. They whip them to death with metal ramrods, bury them in the ground up to their neck and then cut off the head with their sabre, or castrate them, and hang them on trees in their dozens . . . Even those who would like to surrender are not surrendering. By exterminating the Reds in this manner, the Whites are often killing friends and potential helpers who were forced to join the ranks of the Reds.'

General Alekseev, in a letter to his wife, wrote: 'A civil war is always a cruel thing, especially so with a nation like ours. Bolsheviks are destroying everything that is above a worker or a peasant. Hostility to everyone who is above this low level is striking. It is hard to prevent our people from taking revenge, from paying back. And this cruel kind of war brings more horrors than an external war. It is hard, but inevitable.'

Attitudes among the younger Cossacks also changed for other reasons. Many of those returning from the front to their *stanitsas* had been susceptible to Bolshevik propaganda, but once they were home, the older generation started to reassert patriarchal values. Any lingering Bolshevik sympathies were shaken by Red food detachments coming from the larger cities to seize grain and livestock. Villages closest to the cities suffered most because it was too much trouble and too expensive to send the detachments a great distance away. The Cossacks stopped taking produce to market in case it was taken from them. *Stanitsas* were also harassed by gangs pretending to work for the authorities.

While in Sevastopol, awaiting his chance to join the Volunteer Army, the former artillery officer Aleksandr Makhonin received a letter from his faithful orderly who had returned home. He recounted how a group of Bolsheviks had turned up and demanded that he surrender his cow. 'I told them,' he wrote, 'that the cow was all I had left and that my youngest child needed milk, so that I could not give her to them. "Very well," they answered, "we will see to it that your brat does not need milk any more." And in spite of my struggles, they tore my youngest child out of my arms and bashed her head in against a wall, then they took my cow and left me with my dead baby.'

Cossack resentment over the seizures became intense. The village of Krivyanskaya, just five kilometres from Novocherkassk, exploded in revolt like Gundarovskaya. In late March, the Cossacks threw out those who came to requisition food. Cossack Captain Fetistov gathered 300 or 400 Cossacks and led them on Novocherkassk, taking the city by surprise. The Communist leaders and all their Red Guards fled.

'There was great joy in the city, but it was necessary to defend it,' wrote General Svechin, who met up with some Cossack commanders and officers who had also survived in hiding. The Ataman's Palace became their defence headquarters, and posters calling for volunteers to defend the city were plastered up in the streets. 'We had 5,000 Cossacks on foot and a few hundred mounted, so we were stronger that General Popov's force, who had only 1,500, but Popov as field ataman took precedence.' Soon afterwards, the Don *krug* assembled to elect a new ataman and they chose General Pyotr Krasnov, the commander of III Cavalry Corps at Gatchina. Krasnov's self-importance and opportunism provoked the leaders of the Volunteer Army, especially when he started making overtures to the Germans occupying Ukraine.

*

While the Volunteers were suffering on the Ice March in the northern Caucasus, another heroic tale was created around General Mikhail Drozdovsky. On the Romanian Front, Drozdovsky had heard in December of Alekseev's plan to raise an army. He sent a message offering to recruit as many officers and men as possible and bring them across Ukraine to join him. On 26 February, Drozdovsky had set off with 1,100 men, mostly officers, and brushed aside the attempts of Romanian troops to disarm them. On 21 April, after a 1,200-kilometre march, Drozdovsky's men reached Rostov and captured it. His timing was perfect. Drozdovsky's force then joined the Don Cossacks of Krivyanskaya to defend their capital of Novocherkassk. The Ice March of the Volunteer Army and Drozdovsky's journey together formed the foundation myths of the White armies in the south of Russia.

Colonel V.G. Buizin, commander of the regiment named after General Alekseev, with his wife, V.I. Buizina, who served as his adjutant.

14

The Germans March In
March–April 1918

Following the signature of the Treaty of Brest-Litovsk on 3 March, the German and Austro-Hungarian armies began to advance east to secure the food supplies their countries needed so badly. On 7 March, when the Germans were only 18 kilometres from Odessa, the population dreaded savage reprisals from Muraviev's Red Guards and sailors before they were forced to leave.

'We haven't slept since Saturday,' wrote Yelena Lakier. '*Burzhuis* who cannot pay "revolutionary taxes" are being arrested.' Officers and other suspects were still being murdered on the cruiser *Almaz* in the port. The Reds threatened to bombard the city with their warships. Down by the harbour, the crowd started to shout at Red Guards demanding that they release an old railway worker with a white beard and a terrified young soldier who were being taken to the *Almaz*. 'Suddenly, there were some deafening volleys. A truck full of sailors arrived and they started firing at the crowd. I could see people falling. One gentleman stepped on a girl who had fallen to the ground and she screamed hysterically.'

On 12 March, a group of German officers entered the city to warn the Communist central executive committee that all Red forces must leave. When the officers in their Pickelhaube helmets emerged from the meeting, a large number of people who had gathered began to cheer. 'They came down the steps, straight as ramrods. Suddenly the crowd started yelling "*Urrraaa!*" without any restraint, and threw their hats in the air and applauded. The Germans, rather surprised, turned to bow, and their automobile departed . . . Suddenly, several Bolsheviks came out on to the balcony, and one of them brandished his revolver and shouted: "If you don't disperse this very minute I am going to shoot!" The crowd, seized with panic, started scattering in all directions.' Two days later the Germans marched in. 'The Germans are in Odessa. They entered calmly, as if coming home, and set up their field guns in the boulevard.'

March 1918, German divisions of Ober Ost march into Kiev as part of their occupation of the Baltic provinces, Belarus and Ukraine following the Treaty of Brest-Litovsk.

In Kiev, Dmitry Heiden was in the crowds to see 'the well-organized, metal-like mass of Germans who were wearing helmets and the proud expression of victors. Of course, it was nice to be rid of Bolshevik authority; however, the sight of German troops against whom we had fought for three years and who now made themselves at home in the Sophia Square, near the State Duma, horrified me.' The young Vladimir Nabokov also expressed the mixed feelings of many. 'The Bolsheviks vanished, and a singularly silent army of Germans replaced them. Patriotic Russians were torn between the animal relief of escaping native executioners and the necessity of owing their reprieve to a foreign invader – especially to the Germans.'

For those who had escaped from Communist territory and evaded the searches, the moment of crossing the frontier at Orsha into German-occupied Ukraine was an emotional moment. 'As soon as the train crossed the barrier, a loud *"Urraaa!"* sounded in all the wagons,' wrote Major General Vladimir von Dreier. Many people cried and hugged each other and waved their handkerchiefs at the German soldiers who gazed back impassively from under their coal-scuttle helmets. 'They saw the soldiers as their saviours.'

After the impoverishment and lawlessness of Moscow and Petrograd, the impression of calm prosperity acted like a heady elixir for the refugees from the north. Teffi saw the bustling streets of Kiev as 'a wonderful and unprecedented scene, like a dream from a life forgotten, something improbable, exhilarating and even awe-inspiring – in the door of a bakery stands an officer with epaulettes, eating a cake!'

The city was so over-populated by the middle and upper classes that finding a room at any price was virtually impossible. Former members of the Tsarist court would be grateful for an armchair to sleep in. 'In those days life in Kiev was like a banquet in the middle of a plague,' wrote Paustovsky. 'A lot of coffee houses and restaurants were opened. In its external appearance, the city gave an impression of shabby wealth . . . The ox-eyed beauties of Kiev roller-skated on the city's rinks with officers. Gambling dens and houses of assignation sprang up overnight. Cocaine was sold openly on the Bessarabka, where ten-year-old prostitutes offered themselves to passers-by.'

Once again, more officers preferred to indulge themselves in a louche existence of drinking and gambling than attempt to join the Volunteer Army. Borrowing money quite shamelessly, they lived parallel but separate lives with the intelligentsia of poets, writers, singers and actresses who could enjoy the night life of clubs and cafés without fear of robbery.

Meanwhile, each morning, the geographer Mogilyansky noted how their saviours, the German soldiery, 'gathered in front of the windows of food shops which exhibited fried piglets, geese, ducks, chickens, bacon fat, butter, sugar and various sweet things that one could buy cheaply and without any rations cards. The Germans were particularly keen in the mornings to buy bacon fat in the markets. They chewed greedily on huge slices of delicious Ukrainian bacon. Their bodies must have been starved of fat.'

The German military authorities decided to ignore their treaty with the Ukrainian Rada because it had proved incapable of providing the supplies promised. On 18 April, in a manufactured coup aided by Prince Kochubei of the grain-producers' association, they picked their own Ruritanian figurehead in the form of the Hetman Skoropadsky. 'This whole comedy, prepared in advance, went very smoothly,' wrote Count Dmitry Heiden, one of the grain producers. Skoropadsky, dressed in Cossack regalia, was acclaimed just as the Germans were arresting the Ukrainian leaders Petliura, Vinnichenko and Golubovich.

Pavlo Skoropadsky was a descendant of the Skoropadsky who had replaced Ivan Mazepa as the hetman of the Zaporozhian Cossack Host in 1708. Acutely conscious of his ancestry, 'little Pavel had been referred to as "the Hetman", even while still sitting in his nanny's lap'. Following the fairly typical career of the higher nobility, he been in the Corps of Pages in St Petersburg, then an officer in the Tsar's Chevalier Guards like Generals Svechin and Mannerheim. Skoropadsky was elegant and extremely polite, but not very intelligent, and thus an ideal candidate as a German puppet. His very rich wife, a Durnova, was trapped in Soviet territory, and the Germans were able to pressure the Sovnarkom into releasing her. Skoropadsky refused to live in the royal palace on the Dnieper and chose instead the residence of the former governor-general of Ukraine, but he was still addressed by his entourage as 'Most Illustrious Hetman'.

General Svechin, acting as an informal ambassador for the Volunteer Army, went to visit his former brother officer. Svechin could sense that Skoropadsky was uneasy when the German sentries presented arms. 'I can see that they are guarding you well,' he remarked.

'I am just a prisoner,' Skoropadsky said sadly. 'I was elected by the so-called "Grain Producers Association" of rich peasants and land-owners, but I cannot deny that I was also chosen by the Germans who preferred a state with a hetman to Petliura's socialist experiment. However, we have to put up with the heavy hand of the Germans. It is the Bolsheviks who have allowed them to rule over us. I personally think that the war is going to end with the complete victory of the Germans.' He believed that it would take the Americans far too long to bring their men and weapons across the Atlantic.

As an old friend, Svechin was able to mention the accusations of treachery against him by many of the Russian officers in Kiev. 'They are guarded by the same German jackboot, for which they are condemning me,' he replied. 'Haven't they sold themselves to the Germans just by being here? And why doesn't their conscience tell them to go to fight for Russia?'

They discussed the German demands for grain and fats. 'They do pay for everything,' Skoropadsky said, 'but now money has less value than grain. The Germans have allowed each soldier to send home a weekly parcel of three kilos to feed their families. The peasants accept their marks more willingly than our money.'

Skoropadsky clearly had little idea of the true situation in the countryside, but Major General Hoffmann, the chief of staff at Brest-Litovsk, had no illusions. 'Ukraine interests us only until the next harvest,' he said. 'Then you can do with Ukraine whatever you want.' The trouble was that German seizures of grain to feed the Reich were made far worse by their own troops looting for themselves and their own families. 'There were many cases,' reported the geographer Mogilyansky, 'when landowners used German troops to restore their looted estates. At times this led to such serious clashes that the Germans were forced to use artillery.' In most cases the peasants obeyed, realising that they were helpless. 'What can we do, master?' a peasant had said to him. 'The Germans are demanding hay from us at a price of 1 rouble per pood, while it costs 8 roubles. They take bacon fat and pay 1 rouble per pound, while it costs 5 roubles in Chernigov.' Mogilyansky heard that Austro-Hungarian troops were even worse than the Germans when resorting to violence.

The air of normality and good living in Kiev was bound to be short-lived since Skoropadsky's regime depended entirely on foreign bayonets. 'As soon as the Germans depart, his administration is bound to collapse like a house of cards,' Globachev, the former head of the *Okhrana*, observed. Having finally escaped to Kiev, he was back working with some of his former agents. He knew that underground Bolsheviks in the city were preparing for that day. Ukraine would then be engulfed in civil war too. There was little chance of any permanence in areas controlled by the Whites.

The unreal atmosphere of the German protectorate encouraged extraordinary dreams of empire-building within southern Russia. Svechin was astonished to see in the hetman's palace a floor-map in marble of Ukraine, which included both the Don and the Kuban. He expressed his surprise. Skoropadsky tried to claim that they spoke Ukrainian in the Kuban. Svechin pointed out that Ukrainian speakers were a tiny minority there. Meanwhile, in Novocherkassk, Ataman Krasnov fantasised about bringing the Cossack Hosts together in a federation to be led by the Don Cossacks.

To the outrage of Rodzyanko, the former chairman of the State Duma, as well as the leaders of the Volunteer Army, Krasnov fawned on the Germans. Their advance across Ukraine towards Rostov-on-Don pushed Antonov-Ovseenko's Red forces from eastern Ukraine and the Donbas on to Cossack territory. To resist the Reds, Krasnov wanted to take the contents of the Russian arsenals established in Ukraine during the war for the Romanian and Southwestern fronts. He was perfectly prepared to share the proceeds with the Volunteer Army and claimed with amusement that he had saved Denikin from contamination, as the weapons he received had been purified by the waters of the Don. Krasnov then wrote to Kaiser Wilhelm II asking for help in his struggle with the Bolsheviks, almost as if he were a fellow sovereign.

YOUR IMPERIAL AND ROYAL EXCELLENCY,

Today, nine tenths of the land of the Great Don Army is free from the Red gangs . . . We have made an alliance with the Astrakhan and the Kuban armies . . . Once they have cleared the Bolsheviks from their land, we will be able to form a stable federative state of the Great Don Army, the Astrakhan Army with the Stavropol Kalmyks, the Kuban Army, and later, upon clearing up their territories, also the Terek Army as well as the peoples of the Northern Caucasus. Ataman Zimovoi has been authorized by me to ask Your Excellency to recognize the Great Don Army as an independent state, and to do the same for the Astrakhan, Kuban and Terek Armies as well as the North Caucasian territories as soon as they are liberated. The name of this state will be the Union of the Don and the Caucasus.

We would like to ask Your Majesty to join Kamyshin and Tsaritsyn of the Saratov region to that of the Great Don Army, as well as Voronezh. This is necessary for strategic reasons . . . The Great Don Army will grant Germany priority in removing the excess of bread, grain and flour upon satisfying the local demand in those, as well as leather, fish products, wool, plant and animal fats, tobacco, livestock, and wine, in return for which Germany will supply agricultural machinery, chemicals, extracts for leather production, and equipment for chemical and other plants including those producing banknotes etc.

This was too much for Rodzyanko, whose self-regard matched his formidable, bearded bulk. He wrote: 'To the Ataman of the Great Don Army. I have received the copy of your letter to the German Emperor. The anonymous person who had forwarded this copy assured me that the original had been sent to Berlin with the Duke of Lichtenstein. If this letter to the German Emperor really was written and sent by you, then you, just like Hetman Skoropadsky, have put yourself into the situation of a vassal towards Germany, and by no means are you serving the Russian cause.'

The reply came back two days later. 'To the Citizen of the Russian Democratic Republic Mikhail Vladimirovich Rodzyanko. In accordance with the orders of the Ataman of the Don Cossacks, I would like to ask you, dear Sir, to leave the territory of the Great Don Army within three days.'*

The British agent in Moscow, Robert Bruce Lockhart, was rather more realistic in his assessment of Krasnov. 'Like most of the well-to-do class in Russia, he is an opportunist: pro-German today, pro-Ally tomorrow.' In Kiev, Field Marshal Hermann von Eichhorn, the German commander-in-chief in Ukraine, did not object to Skoropadsky allowing Krasnov to have the weaponry from Russian arsenals, but he objected strongly to them being passed to the Volunteer Army 'because they rejected any idea of peace with Germany'.

Lenin's former allies, the Left Socialist Revolutionaries, also opposed any dealings with the Germans. 'All the Red Army detachments obeyed the orders of the Soviet authority, except for the Left Socialist Revolutionaries,' wrote Eduard Dune, with Sablin's army. 'They did not agree. Our army commander Yury Sablin was one of them.' But whenever Left SRs clashed with the Germans, they were of course defeated.

The Left SR and Red Cossack Colonel Mironov, denounced Krasnov as roundly as Rodzyanko. 'Our eternal enemies of yesterday, the Austrians and Germans, have entered Don territory . . . The General's baton and German discipline are now hanging over Cossack heads, together with serfdom.' But Mironov also warned the Red Army leaders against the 'actions of revolutionary troops directed against property and people's homes, and, consequently, against women and children. Hamlets are often in flames due to the whim of some emotionally ignorant comrade.' This, he felt, was simply playing into the hands of the reactionaries.

---

* It is very tempting to include the whole correspondence between Krasnov and Rodzyanko, which is most amusing, but it goes on for pages and pages.

Mironov then contacted the North Caucasus Military District in Tsaritsyn, demanding that his questions be passed to Comrade Trotsky. 'I need to know how the Military Commissariat sees the Don Region, in the political sense. The thing is, Moscow keeps sending commissars that have no idea whatsoever about either the everyday life or the mentality in the Don Oblast ... it is perhaps thanks to these commissars that half of the Don Oblast is now in the hands of counter-revolutionaries. That is why I would like to ask Comrade Trotsky for a definitive answer, what are you planning to do in the Don Oblast, are you going to grant the Cossacks the right to create their own forces and to chase away counter-revolution with support from the central authority? If that is what the Sovnarkom has decided, I insist that you recall all of these "extraordinary commissars" and give our Central Executive Committee the right to work independently.'

In Moscow, the Left SRs had resigned from the Sovnarkom in protest at the Treaty of Brest-Litovsk and Lenin's rejection of 'revolutionary war' against the Germans. Yet a number of their members retained their positions within the Cheka and other institutions. As well as their implacable hatred towards the German occupation, Left SRs were also unhappy about the increasing use of food detachments raiding villages to seize supposedly 'surplus' grain from the peasants. As the representatives of the peasants, the Left SRs had greeted Lenin's adoption of their takeover of the land with enthusiasm. They had no idea that this was a purely tactical ruse before bringing it under complete state control later. But they knew that the Communist idea of class warfare within the villages, between poor peasants and rich 'kulaks' was much too schematic for the more complex reality. And as they heard of more and more lethal clashes between Red Guards and villagers, they became increasingly wary of the Leninist rhetoric of merciless struggle and pitiless punishment.

Moving the capital from Petrograd to Moscow, under threat of further German advances, brought out the contrasts between the two cities. Lenin did not like the old Russian Orthodox, almost Slavophile aspect of Moscow. He was a ruthless moderniser and dreaded the prospect of living and working in the Kremlin, with its gilded onion domes and ancient battlements. Trotsky too saw it as a paradoxical choice for a revolutionary dictatorship.

After a year of total neglect and the fighting there the previous autumn, the Kremlin was in a terrible state, so for a short time Lenin lived and worked in the nearby Hotel Nationale. Once the Kremlin's Senate Building was ready for the Sovnarkom, with an adjacent apartment for Lenin, his sister and Krupskaya, they moved in, again guarded by Latvian riflemen. This did not prevent Lenin from meeting up with Inessa Armand, either in the Kremlin or at her apartment off the Arbat where they could talk uninterrupted. Armand, like the Left Communists of Bukharin, had bitterly opposed the Treaty of Brest-Litovsk, but Lenin never held that against her. He had far too much respect for her mind and judgement.

Back in the Kremlin apartment, Lenin found it mildly amusing when the old-regime retainer served his vegetable soup and *kasha* on a Romanov dinner service with double-headed eagles carefully aligned, but he did draw the line musically. He insisted that the chiming bells in the Spassky Gate clock play 'The Internationale' rather than 'God Save the Tsar'.

Both Lenin and Trotsky were pragmatists as well as ideologues. They had already recognised the need to recruit 'experts' of doubtful loyalties rather than incompetent fanatics. Many other commissars also believed that to choose the brightest and the best was the only chance of the regime surviving. One of the recruits to the higher levels of the Communist bureaucracy was a secret supporter of the Whites called Borman. He worked with Manuilsky, Rakovsky, Radek and others from March 1918.

Manuilsky, like many in the hierarchy, did not believe that Bolshevik rule would last very long. He apparently told Borman on several occasions: 'They are going to slaughter us all, but before leaving we are going to slam the door properly and give the *burzhuis* a tough time.' When Borman asked why they needed to be exterminated, he replied: 'So that it will be easier to seize power again in the future, and in any case, the fewer *burzhuis* there are in the world, the better.'

Borman observed the 'completely new class of bureaucrats' who had installed themselves in the Metropole Hotel close to the Kremlin. 'They were attracted by the cheap rooms and the cheap canteen downstairs in which the food was bad, but still better than elsewhere in the city.' In the frenetic atmosphere of meetings in the Kremlin that could last half the night, most of the commissars lived fairly frugally, but the economist Yuri Larin apparently lived well in Room 305. 'Larin was completely different,' Borman noted. 'His food was abundant and refined. Two black-eyed ladies cared beautifully and devotedly for this repulsive man who had the hands of a paralytic and a terribly distorted mouth.' (Perhaps it was Larin whom Kurt Riezler, the deputy of the newly arrived German ambassador, was thinking of when he noted 'the pervasive corruption of Communist officials and their loose habits, especially their insatiable demand for women'.)

Borman was struck by the fact that most of the Communists he met in the Metropole were not Russian. 'They had come to a foreign country, or at any rate to a country for which they had no feelings, in order to make their experiment. They treated people like material, like rabbits in a laboratory. One could sense that they were completely detached from real life. At that time, the main Communist figures did not expect that their experiments would survive for long. On numerous occasions I heard them let slip "we should try this and that while we are still sitting here".'

On at least a couple of occasions, Borman was admitted to the presence of the Sovnarkom in session. 'The tables were arranged in an open square covered in green baize. Sixteen to twenty people were seated at them. Others were sitting on chairs and benches along the walls. Lenin was sitting alone at the head of the table. Trotsky was standing behind him by the wall. Chicherin was reclining on the window-sill gazing absent-mindedly at the domes of the churches lit by the evening sun . . . Lenin had the look of a person who definitely knows what he is doing and what he wants. His eyes are cunning and smiling. Somehow, he reminded me of a trader from the Russian north. He conducted sessions with confidence, explained the issues, questioned those present and then dictated his version of the resolution to the secretary.'

While the Bolsheviks were the only disciplined political party in Russia, they could also be spontaneous improvisers. In mid-March, Borman ran into the Bulgarian Khristian Rakovsky in the Hotel Metropole. Rakovsky asked him if he would like to join a delegation with Manuilsky and Stalin, the People's Commissar for Nationalities, going 'to Kursk in order to negotiate peace with the Ukrainians'. This was just after the German occupation when the Rada was still recognised.

Borman turned up as instructed at the Kursk Station ready for their departure. 'Stalin's face was unremarkable,' he wrote. 'His eyes are unpleasant and angry. His cheeks are covered in pockmarks. He was wearing a dark-blue velvet shirt under his jacket. He sat in silence without moving. Manuilsky is a dark and agile small man. He is Russian, he kept trying to convince me that he was a peasant from the Kiev guberniya . . . The "experts" are looking rather confused. They do not know how to behave. A lot of middle-aged faces. A young Jew is hanging around Rakovsky. He is wearing a tunic and breeches and high boots. He was the Chekist Zaitsev, secretary of the delegation.'

They sat there waiting, then it transpired that nobody had warned the railway administration, so no special train had been prepared. 'Finally, Stalin rang the Kremlin. For some reason he spoke to the commander of the Latvian rifles. Despite pressure from the Kremlin, we still had to wait two more hours. Podvoisky [the former head of the Bolshevik Military Organisation] came to our train at the Kursk station and climbed on board. He was the commander of the local sector of the front against Germans and Haidemaks.* He told us how he had to revert to shooting men in order to restore discipline in the units. But he was accompanied by a huge red-haired sailor with a terrifying appearance. We were seated in the restaurant car which had still its past neat appearance. The sailor immediately reprimanded us for the white tablecloth. He declared to us: "It is time to abandon these bourgeois manners. For example Comrade Podvoisky and I are living like proletarians. If you are serving the Soviet authority, you have no business eating off a tablecloth." This was my first encounter with sailors. Soon however, matters became more serious. The sailors' detachments, or rather independent gangs, did not recognise any authority and were greatly upset by our arrival. "What kind of peace do you want to sign?" they demanded. "We are fighting here killing *burzhuis* and Haidemaks and you are trying to get in the way. We need to check who you are."'

The sailors' resentment and suspicions did not abate. 'On the very first day after our arrival, it was reported to Manuilsky that some naval detachments were going to attack the delegation. The fact that there were several hundred sailors in the city did not stop Manuilsky.

---

* Haidemaks were Ukrainian soldiers. Originally they had been peasants who had revolted in the eighteenth century against their Polish overlords. Their heads were semi-shaved with a long top-knot in traditional Ukrainian style escaping from their sheepskin caps.

Immediately he took twenty Latvians from our escort and set off for their headquarters. Probably he treated them quite harshly. There were rumours that several sailors were shot on the spot . . . Indeed, after this incident no sailor detachment tried to interfere with the work of the delegation.'

In the end, the delegation did not stay long in Kursk because they heard that the Germans had arrested Petliura and the Rada and replaced them with their puppet Skoropadsky. On their return to the Kursk station in Moscow, the delegation was blocked by a Red Army food detachment, insisting on a full search of their luggage. The Latvian escort closed ranks and shouted back: 'What permission do we need? We were the ones who started the Revolution!' The soldiers called for support from their commander, but 'the Latvians behaved like overlords', Borman recorded with amusement. 'You're welcome to complain to the Kremlin!' they said as they pushed the commander of the food detachment aside.

Enemies on the Periphery
Spring and Summer 1918

After the disastrous loss of territory to the Central Powers, to say nothing of the opposition growing elsewhere, it was hardly surprising that Communist cadres in Moscow were nervous. Desperate food shortages, especially in the cities, began to undermine support even within the proletariat. But the attempt to attribute their problems entirely to 'hunger and the ignorance of the masses' came from a refusal to recognise their own mistakes.

Well before the countries of the Entente had even considered their future policy, Lenin had no illusions about what the renamed Russian Socialist Soviet Republic should expect once the war in the West ended. He was convinced that their capitalist and imperialist nature must propel them to strangle the Communist infant before it developed the strength to defend itself. But apart from the 20,000 in the Latvian Rifle Division, the Sovnarkom had no trained troops to face a potential foreign enemy, let alone enough to deal with revolts at any number of points around the country's huge periphery.

As already mentioned, the Royal Navy had landed Royal Marines at Murmansk to guard military stores previously delivered to the Tsarist armies. But when this small garrison was strengthened in May with another 370 marines and then 600 infantry, Lenin and Trotsky reacted against the idea of foreign forces on Soviet territory. Ironically, the marines' first action was in support of Red Guards fighting off a force of White Finns who had seized some territory between Murmansk and the border.

The British force in North Russia covering both Murmansk and Arkhangel eventually grew to some 18,400 men. During the course of the year they were joined by detachments from other Allied nations, including Americans, Canadians, French, Serbs and Italians. President Woodrow Wilson had been firmly against meddling in Russia at the start of 1918 but, influenced by his Secretary of State Robert Lansing, he came round to the idea of defending Murmansk. The dangers of intervention were clearly spelled out in advance by the British chief of the general staff, Field Marshal Sir Henry Wilson. 'Once a military force is involved in operations on land,' Wilson wrote in an assessment, 'it is almost impossible to limit the magnitude of its commitments.' Then, more than a year after they had intervened, he justified the delay in pulling out troops on the grounds that they could not abandon their local Russian allies to the tender mercies of the Bolsheviks. Little has changed with military expeditions since then. Wilson, although an Ulsterman, adopted an Irish accent in London, as a matter of pride. He refused to call himself British. Known as the ugliest officer in the army because of a facial wound received in Burma, Wilson cared as little for vanity as for fawning to politicians.

The original landings at Murmansk were completely defensive in intention, even when reinforced by more troops commanded by Major General Maynard. But the capture of Arkhangel in August, combined with an anti-Communist coup, led to a much more aggressive strategy. Major General Poole, the British commander, interpreted his orders in a very cavalier fashion. He declared martial law, treated the heads of the independent government of the Northern Region in an off-hand manner, and prepared to invade south towards Vologda. A plan based on a map fantasy developed later with the idea that anti-Bolshevik forces attacking west out of the Urals could join up at Vologda with Allied troops from Arkhangel.

The local authorities in both Murmansk and Arkhangel had received no support at all from Moscow and had no money to pay any salaries. The Murman region, with just some mines and fisheries, informed the Kremlin that it needed 50 million roubles to survive. The Sovnarkom ignored the request and simply ordered them to resist the Allies, even though they had no weapons or troops. 'If we receive no help,' they told Moscow, 'then we must apply for help to the Allies.'

The weakness of Lenin's regime was underlined in April by the reports of the German ambassador in Moscow, Count Wilhelm von Mirbach-Harff. He told Berlin that Bolshevik control of the capital depended entirely on the Latvian rifle regiments. Meanwhile Yoffe, who had led the Bolshevik delegation at Brest-Litovsk, moved as 'ambassador' into the old Tsarist embassy on Unter den Linden, where, as a Jewish

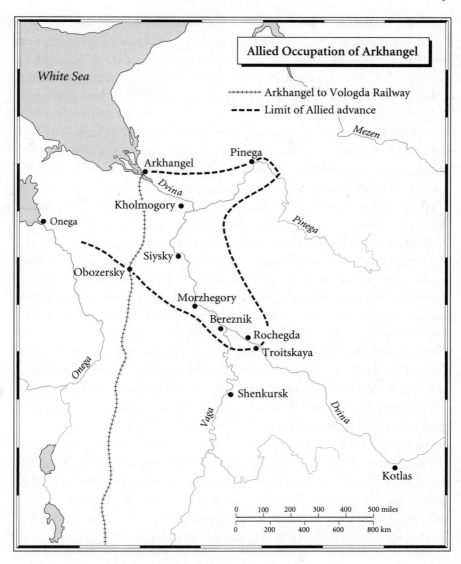

Bolshevik hoping to overthrow the traditional order, he was treated as something of a joke.

Lenin was fascinated by Germany, and not just because he saw it as the key country in the spread of universal revolution. Less predictably, he envied and even praised the state capitalism which Wilhelmine Germany had adopted during the First World War. (The British, on the other hand, saw it as 'war socialism' because they heard it was forbidden to own more than two pairs of boots.) Lenin viewed the

German system as a good model for state socialism. He lauded their 'principles of discipline and organisation, of solid working together on the basis of the most modern machine industry, of strict accounting and control'. These were all qualities of which he could only dream in chaotic Russia, but he was determined to impose them by force.

The year before, the Provisional Government under Prince Lvov had allowed Estonians to make their first step towards nationhood, with borders and a provincial assembly, the Maapäev. Yet the Bolsheviks in Estonia retained a *de facto* power, due to the number of Russian soldiers still stationed there. Support for Bolshevism had nevertheless started to decline at the end of 1917. When it came to elections, the Bolsheviks simply cancelled the result as it did not accord with the 'interests of the working masses'. Their excuse was also cloaked with hints of a supposed conspiracy between German landowners and Estonian *burzhui*. A wave of arrests followed, but then Red forces had to withdraw as the Germans advanced from Latvia into Estonia, eventually heading for the Russian border at Narva.

The German military occupation of Estonia was naturally welcomed by the Baltic barons, but under the surface it aroused Estonian patriotism as well as resentment. The 'Baltic barons', with ancestries often going back to the Teutonic Knights of the Middle Ages, owned almost half of all the agricultural land.

In a great symbolic gesture, Estonian independence was declared on 23 February 1918 and a provisional government took power. This was backed by the Estonian National Division, which had been formed in secret to take on the Bolsheviks. When the German Eighth Army occupied most of Estonia at the end of the month, the Estonian units, together with a Self-Defence Force for the capital Tallinn (formerly Reval), were at first permitted to remain in place provided they stayed neutral, but then were disarmed in April. The Estonian provisional government, meanwhile, was replaced by an administration of 'Baltic barons' who dreamed of creating a German Baltic duchy out of the three provinces. But this fantasy, encouraged by General von der Goltz and Ludendorff, would soon founder on the defeat of the German armies in the west, as did their dreams of a Germanic monarchy in Finland.

On 5 April, more than 9,000 kilometres to the east, at the other end of the former Tsarist Empire, the Imperial Japanese Navy landed a battalion of marine infantry in Vladivostok. Officially, this was in response to the killing of three Japanese civilians. In fact, the deaths provided a pretext for the first step in Japanese ambitions in the region. Two infantry divisions had already been sent to Korea and two cruisers crammed with more marine infantry had been waiting in Vladivostok harbour. The Royal Navy cruiser HMS *Suffolk* landed fifty Royal Marines and bluejackets in support of her then ally. United States Marines were also landed from the USS *Brooklyn*. The United States, Japan's great rival in the Pacific, had already established a Russian presence by offering technical help to Prince Lvov's Provisional Government, improving the Trans-Siberian Railway with engineers of the Railway Service Corps.

The Trans-Siberian Railway became important in the next and most unexpected development of what was fast becoming an international civil war. The Tsarist Empire had been as multi-national as its Austro-Hungarian counterpart. In 1914, Czechs in Russia had volunteered to fight alongside their fellow Slavs against the Austrian army which included large numbers of reluctant Czech conscripts who took every opportunity to surrender. Once captured, they then volunteered to join the Czech formations in Russian uniform based in Ukraine.

In the autumn of 1917, while the old Tsarist army disintegrated, the Czechs maintained their cohesion and discipline. The imminent collapse of the Austro-Hungarian Empire encouraged great hopes of Czech independence once the war ended in an Allied victory. The Allies, however, could not agree on what to do with a whole Czech corps some 40,000 strong. The French wanted them brought back to reinforce the Western Front in France, while the British preferred to keep them in Russia in case there was a chance of reviving an Eastern Front against Germany. The American consul-general in Irkutsk entirely agreed with the British position. 'It is absolutely necessary that the Czechoslovak troops should remain in Russia,' he reported to Washington, 'and not be sent to France as was originally intended . . . They all speak Russian and if their units are left unimpaired they will form the backbone of Allied intervention, and succeed in once more re-establishing a front against Germany in Russia.'

General Pierre Janin, the future head of the French Military Mission in Siberia, was told later by the Czech leader Tomáš Masaryk that General Alekseev had asked for the Czech forces to be transferred to Don territory. But Masaryk, 'not wanting to cooperate in any way with a Tsarist restoration', had refused. He in any case feared that it might be very hard to extricate them from the Black Sea while the Ottoman Empire remained in the war.

In March, following the unopposed German advance, Lenin and the Sovnarkom were acutely conscious of their own military weakness. They wanted the Czechs out of the country, and so agreed to allow them to travel via the Trans-Siberian Railway to Vladivostok, from where Allied ships would take them to western Europe. A shuttle commenced moving them east, with Czech formations spread out along the route. But then the Czechs found their trains were being held up deliberately by local Soviets. They seemed to be backing the German and Austrian prisoners of war, hoping to win them over to Communism. According to Consul-General Harris in Irkutsk, Georgy Chicherin, the new People's Commissar for Foreign Affairs, had sent a message on 20 April saying: 'Transport German prisoners as rapidly as possible towards the west. Hold back the Czechoslovak echelons.'

The Soviet authorities wanted them disarmed, but the Czechs were suspicious of Bolshevik relations with the Central Powers. They feared that they might be handed over to the Austrians and treated as traitors. Trotsky, now the People's Commissar for War, then made the extraordinary blunder of ordering the arrest of any Czech soldier who did not surrender his weapon. This would transform the whole conflict, extending it right across the whole Eurasian land-mass.

Further south in the Don and the northern Caucasus, the Reds were under pressure. As Mironov had tried to warn Trotsky, the looting of Cossack *stanitsas* by Red Guards and naval infantry detachments had aroused the fury of the Don and Kuban Hosts.

Ataman Krasnov, with his dream of an enlarged Cossack federation, assembled an army of 40,000 men. Knowing that his western flank right up to Rostov-on-Don was guarded by the Germans, his forces rode north towards Voronezh while a strong detachment under General Konstantin Mamontov rode northeast across the steppe to the Volga to attack Tsaritsyn. Mamontov was a great leader (and after Yudenich possessed the largest Victorian moustaches of any White commander), but since light cavalry is not usually the best force for seizing a city, his men received a bloody nose. The British Military Mission reported on him with the highest praise of an English gentleman: 'He is a great sportsman and used to keep a pack of hounds at

Moscow.' More attempts to seize the city were made later, and with Josef Stalin acting as the chief commissar, the 'siege of Tsaritsyn', the future Stalingrad, later became a heroic myth for Soviet propagandists.

Josef Stalin as commissar of the 10th Army in Tsaritsyn.

On 22 June, the Volunteer Army under General Denikin, still no more than 9,000 strong, marched back into the Kuban for a second attempt to capture its capital Ekaterinodar, where Kornilov had been killed. General Alekseev and others had tried to persuade Denikin to march north up the Volga towards Samara to link up with the Czechs, but Denikin was resolute. He wanted to establish a solid base for the Volunteer Army in the Kuban and bring its Cossack regiments into a close association. Perhaps he was also determined to reverse the outcome of 'the brutal five-day battle on the approaches to the city when the Volunteer Army left three-quarters of their strength behind as well as the body of their leader and hero General Kornilov'. In any case, many believe that Denikin's failure to concentrate forces on the middle

Volga in 1918, as Alekseev urged, was the great lost opportunity for the White cause.

In the industrial city of Armavir, the Communists slaughtered not just Whites, but also Armenian and Persian refugees. Denikin was not an adventurous general and the 80,000 Red Guards and sailors remaining in the north Caucasus clearly preoccupied him. Although heavily outnumbered, the Volunteer Army was reinforced by Kuban Cossacks as Denikin had hoped, and by mid-August they were in striking distance of Ekaterinodar. 'This time,' as one of his officers observed, 'the Army was supported by the local population, whose attitude towards the Volunteers had changed radically after close acquaintance with the Bolsheviks.'

After a succession of defeats, the ill-disciplined Red forces retreated in complete confusion from Ekaterinodar. Six White officers held prisoner in the jail near the bridge over the River Kuban watched them flee with nervous excitement. They had been among the wounded left behind during the Ice March. Miraculously they had been well-treated, considering that their own side had been killing all captured and wounded Reds. But now some sailors had discovered their presence in the prison. 'Everything was mixed up in that endless train of carts,' wrote Pavel Konstantinov, who was one of them. 'There were field guns, carts with feather beds and samovars, field kitchens, luxury motor cars, boxes of shells and bundles of goods. Everywhere there was chaos and despair. The sole driving force of this mass was the complete certainty that the Volunteers were going to be ruthless. Of course, those who supported the Whites watched this agony of growing panic with malicious pleasure and held their breath awaiting the moment . . . With desperate hope, we listened to the sound of artillery which was now very close.'

As the end of the retreating column came in sight, the six officers at last dared to think that they really were safe after all. But then the sailors reappeared. They had not forgotten about them. They hauled them out, escorted them over the bridge and, as darkness fell, led them off the side of the road to execute them. Konstantinov fell with a bullet through the shoulder. Paralysed by the pain, he managed to remain still when the sailors went round giving their victims the odd stab in the buttocks with a bayonet to check they were dead. He lay there until the sailors departed, then crawled to a peasant's hut in the early hours just as Denikin's forces entered the city. His fellow officers and commander from the Ice March could not recognise him after what he had been through.

Denikin's victory, forcing the Reds back to Stavropol and Pyatigorsk deep in the Caucasus, was helped by the cavalry guerrilla force of Colonel Andrei Shkuro operating behind Red lines. Cunning as well as cruel, the thirty-one-year-old Shkuro had a devoted following. His personal escort was known as the Wolf Sotnia because of the wolf-skin *papakhas* they wore, and his personal guidon bore the image of a wolf's head. Shkuro was an effective recruiter. 'He would take five or six reliable Cossacks and a trumpeter, turn up in a *stanitsa* and assemble the locals. He announced: "Cossacks, I am declaring a call-up in your *stanitsa*. In two hours all Cossacks should be on their horses by the church."'

Colonel Andrei Shkuro with his wolfskin papaha.

To those who criticised his strategy, Denikin's response was that by the end of the Second Kuban Campaign in September, the Volunteer Army had increased fourfold in size and the Reds had lost control of the Caucasus. Whether he could have changed the outcome of the war by heading north instead of south is of course impossible to tell for certain, but it is unlikely.

*

While the final stages of the First World War produced complex ramifications around the periphery of the Russian Empire, the consequences were also far-reaching in the Middle East with the collapse of the Ottoman Empire. The focus on trench warfare in western Europe tends to obscure the fighting in Iraq on the Mesopotamian Front and the occupation of Persia by Turks, Russians and British.

Major General Lionel Dunsterville, leader of one of the three special forces deployed by the British to the southern Caucasus and Transcaspia, had gone on ahead of his troops during the winter. He had assembled a small advance party from the Mesopotamian Expeditionary Force and set out across the snow-bound mountains of eastern Persia in Ford motor cars and vans. Less than sixty strong, they reached Enzeli on the Caspian in the second half of February 1918. They faced a hostile reception. Although a Persian town, the Bolshevik commander there with 4,000 men insisted that after the Treaty of Brest-Litovsk, the Soviet state was no longer at war with Turkey and Germany. British imperialists were not welcome. Dunsterville had no option but to withdraw to Hamadan and await reinforcements. Generously supplied with British gold and Persian silver, he did much to alleviate famine in the region and rebuild roads during this period of enforced idleness.

It took more than three months for the main body of Dunsterforce to arrive from Basra so they were not able to occupy Enzeli until 27 June. By then the Turkish vanguard was only 60 kilometres from Baku, which was defended mainly by ill-trained Armenian Red Guards.

Although the Bolsheviks were still in charge in Baku, Dunsterville sent an advance group to the city in mid-July. The threat from the Turkish advance was so great that the Bolsheviks were prepared to cooperate reluctantly in its defence with both British imperialists and with a local Cossack ataman called Colonel Lazar Bicherakhov. Dunsterforce had been equipped with a squadron of Rolls-Royce armoured cars, so four of them were detached to strengthen the Cossacks.

Led by Stepan Shahumyan, Soviet rule in Baku was not nearly as brutal as in other places. Even the Cheka was remarkably restrained, executing only two men, both embezzlers. Among the military commissars in Baku was the young Anastas Mikoyan, one of the very few Communist leaders to survive all the changes in leadership over the next sixty years and die peacefully in his bed.

The Baku Commune could not improve the meagre food supplies, nor prevent their Armenian troops from drinking and mistreating local Muslims. Eventually on 25 July a group of Right Socialist Revolutionaries, Mensheviks and Armenian Dashnaks, calling themselves the Centro-Caspian Dictatorship, mounted a bloodless coup against the Bolsheviks. This was supported by Bicherakhov and the armoured cars. The Bolsheviks were removed from power but remained at liberty.

Around this time on the eastern shore of the Caspian, the Germans, in cooperation with the Bolsheviks, were buying up the whole of Turkestan's cotton production in the port of Krasnovodsk. But a British intelligence officer, Captain Reginald Teague-Jones, managed to prevent its removal with the assistance of some local sympathisers. They faked a signal in cypher, instructing the ships to offload the cotton bales and return empty to Astrakhan. They then promptly sabotaged the transmitter so the order could not be countermanded.

Further to the east beyond the Aral Sea, the Uzbeks and Kirghiz, cut off by the fighting south of the Urals, were suffering greatly. 'The poor native people are reduced to eating cats and dogs to keep alive,' Consul-General Harris in Irkutsk heard from one of his assistants. 'After the Treaty of Brest-Litovsk, the Bolsheviks turned the German and Austrian prisoners of war loose so they too starved. So great is the scarcity of food that the nomad Kirghiz of the Syr-Daraya deserts have started a slave market in Tashkent. I saw as many as fifteen young girls exhibited for sale. One was sold for 1,500 roubles.' It seems that they were being sold by their own families to reduce the number of mouths to feed.

As British forces began to concentrate on the Caspian's western shore, GHQ Baghdad wondered whether the Royal Navy should become involved on the inland sea as well. They asked whether the Navy could take a 'Fly' class gunboat armed with a 4-inch gun to pieces and transport it overland. That idea was dropped, but instead they considered taking just the guns and mounting them on local vessels. Ammunition resupply by camel train would, however, be limited since each camel could carry only eight 4.7-inch shells. In July, it was decided to create armed merchant cruisers and to set up a seaplane base at Enzeli. The objective was 'to deny sea-power to others', as part of Dunsterforce's defence of the Baku oil fields from the Turks and Germans.

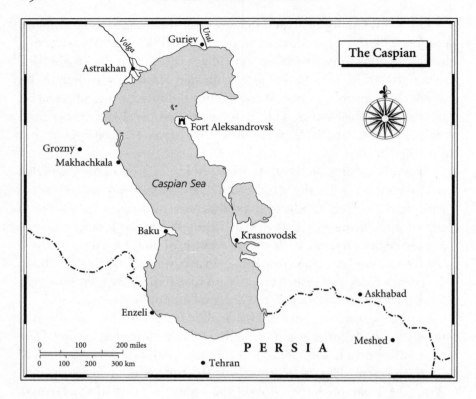

By the end of the month, Commodore David Norris left Baghdad with a party of officers and ratings from the Royal Navy flotilla on the River Tigris. His Coxswain Petty Officer Dickason had been on Scott's Antarctic Expedition. The guns shipped from Bombay to Basra were to follow in trucks. Norris met up with General Dunsterville in Kasvin and also Gertrude Bell, the explorer.

On 26 July, Turkish troops, reinforced with Tatar tribesmen to make a force some 14,000-strong, encircled the Baku peninsula. Five days later panic broke out in the town as the Turks advanced again. The mainly Armenian troops fled, leaving the Cossacks to hold the line. As thousands of Armenian civilians in Baku fought to get onto steamers to escape Turkish vengeance, Bicherakhov knew his men did not stand a chance on their own. He prepared to pull out as well, but the situation was saved unexpectedly.

The Bolsheviks had withdrawn their field guns to the port ready to evacuate them to Astrakhan, when one of their commissars, Grigory Petrov, was alerted to enemy troops advancing on foot towards the town. Petrov, a volatile character, changed his mind. Instead of embarking the field guns, he told his men to open fire. The effect was astonishing. The Turks turned and fled. Bicherakhov rallied his Cossacks and chased the retreating enemy.

Within a week Dunsterville's advance party reached Baku. Dominion and British officers and NCOs worked hard trying to turn the mainly Armenian Red Guards into a fighting force to hold an enemy of twice their strength. To their surprise, they discovered Armenian women in the trenches. 'They preferred to take their chances with their own men rather than stay behind unprotected,' noted Captain William Leith-Ross of the Frontier Force Rifles. On a number of occasions these women proved a good deal more courageous than their menfolk. 'The town is a queer mixture, reflecting the population of Russians, Tatars and Armenians,' wrote a naval officer. 'The place is half finished; one can see a building that would not disgrace the Strand, and next to it a row of hovels.'

British reinforcements from the 39th Infantry Brigade arrived, bringing Dunsterforce up to nearly 1,000 men. They were used as stiffeners for the Armenian units. Stepan Shahumyan, Petrov and the other Bolshevik leaders tried to escape to Astrakhan one night in a variety of vessels, but the armed steamer *Astarabad* cut them off and issued an ultimatum. There was no reply, so the *Astarabad* fired and hit one of their ships. The convoy returned to Baku. Their ships were searched at the dockside and were found to be stacked with loot, as well as badly needed guns and ammunition. Most of the Bolshevik leaders were imprisoned this time, but for some reason not Mikoyan.

On 17 August, Major General Dunsterville sailed into the port at Baku aboard the armed steamer *Kruger*, which a month later became the flagship of the British Caspian flotilla. Dunsterville had hoisted the traditional Russian tricolour of white, blue and red. But when somebody pointed out that it might now be seen as a counter-revolutionary flag, since General Denikin's Whites used it, he had it flown upside down so that the red stripe was on top. He did not tell anyone at the time that this transformed it into the Serbian national flag. Dunsterville relished the paradoxes of his situation. 'A British General on the Caspian,' he wrote, 'the only sea unploughed before by British keels, on board a ship named after a South African president and [former] enemy, sailing from a Persian port, under the Serbian flag, to relieve from the Turks a body of Armenians in a revolutionary Russian town.'

On Sunday 1 September, the British had to tell the Centro-Caspian Committee which ruled Baku 'that unless the Armenians did more and showed more courage the Turks could walk into the town when they liked. . . and if the inhabitants would not, or could not, defend the town, then they had best make terms, and the British would evacuate.' The committee took the criticism badly. They tried to argue that it must be the fault of the British, because 'the Armenians were the bravest of the brave'.

On 14 September, after just over six weeks of fighting, the Turkish-Tartar force finally broke the Baku defence line, despite all the efforts of Dunsterforce to hold their scratch battalions together. Altogether 180 of their men had fallen in the fighting, a fifth of their strength. General Dunsterville had received orders to extricate his men once the port came under direct artillery fire. So, behind a rearguard from the 7th Battalion of the North Staffordshires, his staff directed the withdrawal into the town and their evacuation back to Enzeli by boat, along with several thousand Armenian refugees.

In the chaos, the Bolshevik commissars held prisoner in Baku were apparently liberated just in time by Armenian soldiers led by Mikoyan. They boarded the steamer *Turkmen* and told the captain to head north for the Communist stronghold of Astrakhan, but he feared arrest there, so he quietly set a course east instead to Krasnovodsk in Transcaspia. This decision was to lead to the notorious massacre of the 'twenty-six commissars', two of whom were friends of Lenin. Moscow's accusation that this was 'a British war crime' was off the mark, but the incident became an article of Communist faith for years afterwards.

The scenes of rape and murder during the sack of Baku were atrocious. 'The Turks and Tatars entered the helpless town,' Captain Teague-Jones wrote in his diary, 'and worked their savage will on the wretched Armenian population . . . sparing neither man, woman, nor child.' Estimates of the numbers massacred vary between 5,000 and 20,000, but the true figure is probably closer to 7,000. The Tatars had much to avenge. Earlier in the year, Armenian troops in Baku had massacred most of the Muslim Tatars living there, and the Turks told them that they could exact a revenge of three to one. Bicherakhov and his Cossacks, meanwhile, had escaped north up the coast to Petrovsk (now Makhachkala, the capital of Dagestan), where they managed to gather most of the shipping.

Despite the defeat at Baku, Captain Teague-Jones, who had little time for most senior officers, expressed the highest praise for Dunsterville and his men for managing to hold off the vastly superior forces for as long as they did. Their task had simply proved far too great for their numbers.

The Turkish triumph at Baku was in any case short-lived. The great victory of General Allenby's army at Megiddo in Palestine a week later prevented the Turks from exploiting the oilfields, and a month after that the Middle Eastern war ended in an armistice. The departure of the Turks from Baku prompted the local leaders to ask for British help once again. The 27th Indian Division was soon based there to guard the oilfields, while the Royal Navy's White Ensign was hoisted as its improvised warships set off to fight the Red flotilla based at the mouth of the Volga near Astrakhan.

16

The Czechs and Left Socialist Revolutionaries Revolt May–July 1918

After the Bolsheviks in Petrograd closed down the Constituent Assembly in January, Right Socialist Revolutionaries escaped to their heartlands further east – especially to the Volga region. They were disappointed to find that although the peasants may have voted for them, they showed little appetite for revolt. The balance of power only started to swing against the Communists in May with the movement of the Czech corps along the Trans-Siberian Railway.

On 14 May, in Chelyabinsk on the edge of the Urals, there was an ugly clash between Hungarian prisoners of war and Czechs, leaving several dead. The German and Austro-Hungarian prisoners of war were angry because, following the Treaty of Brest-Litovsk, they thought that they should be going home. And the Czechs sitting in trains all along the Trans-Siberian Railway appeared to be blocking it. The Chelyabinsk Soviet arrested some of the Czechs, but their comrades released them at gunpoint and took over the town.

Trotsky was outraged. He first ordered the arrest of the representatives of the Czech National Council in Moscow, and then instructed that the Czech Legion be halted in its trains. Its members must either join the Red Army or be drafted into labour battalions. On 22 May, the Czechs refused to disarm. Trotsky sent his fatal signal on 25 May. 'All Soviets on the railways are obliged, on pain of grave responsibility, to disarm the Czechs. Each Czech found with arms on the railway line is to be shot on the spot. Each echelon in which a single armed man is found, must be thrown off the wagons, and the men confined in a prisoner-of-war camp. Local military commissariats are to execute this order at once ... Reliable troops are being sent against the rear of the Czech echelons to teach the mutineers a lesson. Those Czechs who lay down their arms will be treated as brothers. Trotsky.' For the

Czechs, there was now no going back. They did not trust Trotsky's idea of brotherhood.*

One city after another fell to the Czechs all along the Trans-Siberian Railway, starting with Novo-Nikolaevsk (Novosibirsk) in central Siberia on the day after Trotsky's signal. The last few days of May saw the Communists chased from Penza west of the Volga, Syrzan on the Volga and Tomsk in western Siberia.

Thanks to the railway telegraph, word spread like wildfire and both Right Socialist Revolutionaries and groups of officers began contacting the Czechs to coordinate their actions. News of the Czech revolt also encouraged even more Right SRs and other anti-Bolsheviks in Moscow and Petrograd to head for the Volga and the Urals, to take part in any government which might emerge.

In the quiet town of Kurgan between Chelyabinsk and Omsk, two trains with Czechs arrived from the west. 'Tall, young and handsome soldiers appeared in the streets,' wrote an anti-Bolshevik, 'dressed neatly in grey greatcoats with red-and-white ribbons on their caps. They presented a sharp contrast with the Soviet security troops, who were dressed in shabby and dirty uniforms.' A local group of 120 men who wanted to overthrow the Communists immediately made contact. The Czechs gave them weapons. 'We split into groups of 15–20 men and started a fast advance towards the positions of the Reds. They were caught unawares and did not put up much resistance, except for the defenders of the railway bridge across the River Tobol and the jail, where the Reds had already amassed quite a lot of those who did not favour them.'

The most important city on the Volga to be liberated was Samara. 'News of the Czech intervention in Penza and Syzran spread like lightning,' wrote Yakov Dvorzhets, a prominent Socialist Revolutionary. The Czechs marched in at 5 a.m. on the morning of 8 June. They were soon shooting any Communists pointed out to them. 'Corpses were scattered across the city,' Dvorzhets wrote. 'The bodies of well-known Bolshevik figures lay around in the cathedral garden . . . Someone had to put an end to this outrage. Exhausted, I went to the headquarters

---

* The American 'consul on special detail' reported more than a year later to Lansing in Washington that 'The German government, through its ambassador von Mirbach, urged Trotsky to disarm the Czechoslovaks and thus precipitated the crisis earlier than had been designed.'

where I found that communications had been established with the Czech leadership.' From that first day a deep divide became apparent between reactionary officers and the anti-monarchist Right SRs who had the full support of the railway workers. Their slogan was 'Away with the Bolsheviks in the name of Constituent Assembly!'. The more reactionary officers did not believe in democracy at all and simply wanted a military dictatorship.

Outside the Samara Duma, Dvorzhets found officers and wealthy citizens celebrating their liberation by tearing down the boards with which the Reds had boxed in the statue of Tsar Alexander II. The crowd shouted '*Urrrah!*'. When Bolshevik prisoners were led to the Duma, the threats and curses prompted Dvorzhets to fear that they might be lynched. 'I opened the door and ordered the Czech soldiers escorting them to take the prisoners inside, while I stood on the top step and addressed the crowd with a speech saying that excesses were not acceptable at this moment when we were establishing law and order. They must be handed over to the courts.' This did not go down well with the reactionaries, partly because Dvorzhets was Jewish.

'A crowd of officers led by Lieutenant Zybin surrounded me in the hall. I learned that somebody for some reason had appointed him the commandant. Loudly and threateningly, Zybin demanded an explanation why I had been allowed to speak. He hinted that now this was no longer a place for Yids. I was shocked and infuriated and I declared loudly that I would not allow him to interfere. I spoke as a senior member of the Right SRs and part of the committee. He should know that I, and not them, had the right to make statements . . . For me this confirmed that we could not trust the officers.'

The Right Socialist Revolutionaries set up a government based in Samara called the Committee of Members of the Constituent Assembly – or Komuch in its abbreviated form. But as Dvorzhets feared, the military faction would soon take control. He found the contrast between the glittering uniforms and 'the shabby jackets and the baggy-kneed trousers' of the Komuch representatives revealing. 'On the very day after the coup officers appeared in the streets in full uniform of the old regime, with all their medals, uniform caps and shoulder boards.'

On 10 June, another group of officers appeared and began to set up an embryo People's Army, with just 350 men. There was a dubious schemer called Colonel Galkin who refused to let the committee know what was planned, but also one of the most impressive leaders of the whole war, Colonel Vladimir Kappel. According to Dvorzhets, in the People's Army 'the lower ranks clearly resented their commanders. This was true not only of the conscripts but even many of the volunteers. A lot of them sympathised with the Red Army and the Bolsheviks, because their own officers reintroduced corporal punishment.'

Kappel could not have been more different. He was one of the very few White commanders genuinely loved by his own men for his modesty and his determination to share their dangers. As an impoverished young cavalry officer he had eloped with Olga, the daughter of a state councillor who refused to consider him as suitable for a son-in-law. Kappel's father-in-law soon recognised his mistake during the First World War when the young officer was rapidly promoted, having learned a great deal about strategy as a staff captain and managed to put it to good effect when back in the front line. Kappel believed in psychological warfare, which became known as *Kappelevtsy* after him. For example, he believed in advancing silently on the enemy without firing because that unsettled them much more. Even when he became a general in Siberia in 1919, Kappel still armed himself with just a rifle and lived off the same rations as his men.

The Komuch was naturally keen to learn about and link up with other anti-Bolshevik groups across Russia. Ataman Dutov of the Orenburg Cossacks was welcomed by the military faction on a visit, with a parade at the railway station and a gala dinner at their headquarters. 'The People's Army headquarters regarded this as their sacred duty for a "brave fighter against the Bolsheviks",' but Dvorzhets suspected that they were dreaming of Dutov as 'a future Napoleonic dictator'. In fact this elected chairman of the Orenburg government was probably the least murderous of all the Cossack leaders. He turned out to be 'a small plump figure in a blue *chokha* with a colonel's silver shoulder-boards, carrying a Cossack sabre, with lowered head and angry eyes looking up from under his brows'. Dutov's first request was for money and weapons. 'He claimed that everything they and their fellow Cossacks did was for the Constituent Assembly. That the Cossacks were the true guardians of the revolution.'

The first 12,000 Czechs to reach Vladivostok placed themselves under the command of the Russian General Mikhail Diterikhs. They claimed that the artillery ammunition being used against General Radola Gajda's formation of Czechs had been taken by the Reds from Allied dumps outside Vladivostok.

The Allied build-up also gathered pace. Altogether three Japanese divisions landed, as well as two American infantry regiments from Manila, a French colonial battalion from Indochina, and two British units: the 25th Battalion of the Middlesex Regiment from Hong Kong and the 9th Battalion of the Hampshire Regiment from Quetta. A Canadian brigade followed later. All this anti-Bolshevik strength in the Far East encouraged General Dmitry Horvat in Harbin, who was in charge of the Chinese Railway. He declared himself head of yet another 'Provisional All-Russia Government', with the support of Ataman Ivan Kalmykov's Ussuri Cossacks. This rivalled a so-called 'Provisional Siberian Government' led by a Socialist Revolutionary called Pyotr Derber.

Vladivostok itself was taken over by the Allies in an underhand coup. The concentration of Czech troops in the city and the Czech action against the Bolsheviks along the Trans-Siberian Railway prompted Allied representatives to get rid of the Soviet administration in the city. On 29 June, in a battle lasting just a few hours, 'the Czechs stormed the fortress headquarters, the hiding place of the Soviet leaders who had failed to flee from the city'. A week later, 'the Allies announced that they had taken Vladivostok under their protection due to a threat to Vladivostok and the Allied forces concentrated within, from Austrian and German prisoners of war, spies and emissaries'. This was plainly nonsense as there were none. The proclamation made no mention at all of the Bolsheviks who were the true target of the Allied operation.

Kalmykov's Cossacks joined the Czechs under General Diterikhs. Together, they cleared the rest of the Vladivostok region of Red forces before pushing westwards to join up with Gajda's force approaching Irkutsk. Diterikhs, who had adopted Czech uniform, was deeply religious and had his own chapel with icons and candles on his headquarters train. A British liaison officer, Major Leo Steveni, was attached to him in both senses of the term, by hitching his own carriage to the general's.

Communists in Irkutsk, the great Siberian city close to the southwestern edge of Lake Baikal, became very nervous as Czech forces approached from both directions. Their only reliable unit was a battalion recruited from Magyar prisoners of war. 'Its presence greatly annoyed the locals, who could not put up with the fact that former prisoners of war were now almost the masters of the city.'

Irkutsk was also the Red base, from which to fight back against Ataman Semenov based at Chita. 'The Irkutsk Bolsheviks were alarmed when the Ataman started a successful offensive from Manchuria and took Borzya station on the Trans-Baikal Railway. Their newspapers at the time were filled with articles about the "hydra of counter-revolution that is raising its head". They panicked easily . . . and started searching all the trains coming from the west, checking all passengers. A rumour had spread that the Tsar and the Tsarevich had escaped from their prison in Tobolsk, and were on their way to the Far East.'

The local underground organisation of officers in Irkutsk had attempted a coup on 14 June. They made a feint attack on the railway bridge on the southern edge of the city, while another group seized the prison in the north and released 100 Russian officers as well as political prisoners. 'Factory whistles sounded to call the workers to arms, but groups of Whites disarmed them as they emerged.' The rising failed, however, when the Magyar and German prisoners of war who had joined the Bolsheviks counter-attacked using motor cars with machine guns mounted in them. After defeating this threat, the Bolsheviks began seizing the food supplies, including those provided by the Danes for German and Austrian prisoners of war. The Danish vice-consul protested bitterly, but the only prisoners left in the camps now were those who had refused to join the Bolshevik Red Guard and been left to starve.

On 11 July, Gajda's Czech and Cossack troops captured Irkutsk practically without resistance. The Red Guard, 'consisting chiefly of armed prisoners of war in German and Austrian uniform', had retired from the city the day before having first looted the city and blown up the bridge over the River Irkut. Radola Gajda, behind the fresh Czech façade, was a complex national mixture from the Austro-Hungarian Empire. Born Rudolf Geidl in the Kingdom of Dalmatia, the son of an officer in Emperor Franz Josef's *Kaiserlich und Königlich* Army, he had followed in his father's footsteps until captured in Bosnia in 1915. He had promptly switched sides and joined the army of Montenegro as a captain. A year later, when the Montenegran army collapsed, he escaped to Russia and joined a Serbian battalion. That too was destroyed, so he became an officer in the Czech Legion, his fourth army in three years. Rapidly promoted, Gajda proved an able commander but no democrat, as his post-war admiration for fascism would reveal.

General Radola Gajda.

For the anti-Bolshevik forces, the greatest disaster at that time was the rising of 6 July organised by Boris Savinkov in Yaroslavl on the upper Volga, northeast of Moscow. The city had already shown resistance to the Bolsheviks the year before and had recently attracted a large number of officers from Moscow. They could also join up with other revolts at the nearby towns of Rybinsk and Kostroma, but they were too far north to receive any help from the Czechs. Savinkov's Union for the Defence of the Motherland and Freedom was also hoping that they would receive support from a French force due to land at Arkhangel. He had been in touch secretly with Robert Bruce Lockhart to say that his organisation was ready to kill Bolshevik leaders as soon as an Allied intervention began, but the French wanted him to take the first move. Bruce Lockhart reported all this to London. '[Savinkov] bases his hopes for success mainly on discontent of the population with famine conditions. He proposes to win peasant sympathies by declaring free trade between all Governments and removing unpopular bread monopoly. His agrarian policy is to leave land to peasants and compensate landowners.'

Although some 6,000 men volunteered to join the July revolt led by Colonel Aleksandr Perkhurov, there were weapons for little more than 1,000 of them. Railwaymen manufactured an armoured train in the workshops there, but the Latvian Chekist Martin Latsis brought in a far more powerful armoured train to bombard the city and set it aflame. The destruction inflicted in just over two weeks of fighting was terrifying. Water supplies were cut off and the defenders became desperate. The Communist leadership wanted it to serve as a conspicuous warning to others. On 21 July, the rebels surrendered to Lieutenant Balk of the German Prisoner of War Commission, on receiving an assurance that there would be no reprisals, but as the Cheka boasted later, few escaped with their lives.

Another revolt, this time much closer to home, also took the Kremlin by surprise.

After the Left Socialist Revolutionaries had left the Sovnarkom in protest at the Treaty of Brest-Litovsk, Lenin had remained remarkably unperturbed. He felt that it had been little more than a gesture, and a number of their members remained in key positions. Muraviev, who had captured Kiev in January and then Odessa before the Germans marched in, became commander-in-chief of the Eastern Army Group on the Volga. Petr 'Viacheslav' Aleksandrovich, the thirty-three-year-old peasant from Riazan who had become Dzerzhinsky's deputy, gave no hint of resentment and there were quite a number of Left SRs remaining in the Cheka, especially in its paramilitary combat department.

Yet many Left SRs were increasingly angry, and not just with the German occupation. They loathed the arrogance of Lenin's dictatorship, the executions of opponents and the brutality with which Communist food detachments seized the peasants' grain. Maria Spiridonova, the leader of the Left SRs, may have been small and delicate, but she had an iron will. She now regarded the regime they had helped to put in power the previous October as worse than the Kerensky government they had overthrown. The Left SRs sought a spectacular provocation to shatter the Sovnarkom's cooperation with the German imperialists, if necessary triggering war. They did not seek power for themselves, in fact they were now closer to the Anarchists than to Bukharin's Left Opposition. This was a reversion to their political ancestors, the nineteenth-century Narodnik assassins of Tsarist officials. Their target would be Count von Mirbach, the German ambassador in Moscow.

Russian revolutionary women. Maria Spriridonova, later the fearless leader of the Left Socialist Revolutionaries, is seen here on the left in the Tsarist Nerchinsk prison in 1907, with five comrades.

The Cheka had no inkling of the plot, because the three men chosen to carry out the act were Left SRs within their own organisation. When the Fifth Congress of Soviets opened in the great Bolshoi Theatre, the stage was still set with a scene from *Boris Godunov*. The journalists were all packed into the orchestra pit, from where they watched Lenin pace up and down along the footlights as he spoke, 'sometimes pushing his hands deep in his trouser pockets, sometimes holding with both hands the armholes of his black waistcoat'.

Count von Mirbach was seated as an observer in a box at the side. He was tall and balding, with a moustache and an unusually high stiff white collar which gave him a haughty look. When the Left SR Kamkov started to denounce the German army's repression of peasant revolts in Ukraine, Mirbach picked up his newspaper and pretended to read it. Kamkov walked towards Mirbach's box and demanded war against the German occupation. 'Long live the rebellion in the Ukraine! Down with the German occupation! Down with Mirbach!' All the Left SRs present rose to their feet, yelling and cheering and brandishing their fists in the air. Amid the pandemonium, Mirbach stood up, left his newspaper on the brass rail at the front of the box and departed in a conspicuously unhurried fashion.

Trotsky firmly rejected the Left SR calls to help workers in Ukraine resist the German occupation. He declared that if any Left Social Revolutionaries attempted this, they would be denounced 'as *agents provocateurs*'. With Bolshevik delegates in an artificially inflated majority, the Congress voted for a motion stating that 'all questions of peace and war are to be decided exclusively by the Council of People's Commissars and the central executive of the Soviets'. The Left SRs claimed that this was what forced them into action.

The next day, 6 July, the Bolshoi filled early. There was an air of excitement among the journalists in the orchestra pit. Some form of explosion was expected but, surprisingly, nobody outside the conspiracy guessed what it would be. The start of the congress was delayed and delayed again. Nobody knew what was going on. Left SR delegates noticed the absence of their leader Spiridonova and her close associates.

Soon after 2.15 p.m., an automobile of the Cheka drew up outside the German embassy. Two young Chekists who were both Left Socialist Revolutionaries, Yakov Bliumkin and Nikolai Andreev, got out. Just inside the front door they announced that they needed to see the ambassador urgently and produced a pass written by Aleksandrovich, the Left SR deputy head of the Cheka, with a forged version of Dzerzhinsky's signature. Riezler, Mirbach's deputy, spoke to them in the hall saying that he could deal with anything they needed, but they insisted on seeing the ambassador with some story of the arrest of a relative of his. Mirbach came down the stairs, and the two assassins produced their pistols and began shooting. They were so tense that they missed both Mirbach and Riezler at close range. Even the improvised bomb which they threw did little damage. Mirbach began to run back upstairs but Andreev chased him and shot him through the back of the head. Then he and Bliumkin jumped from an open window into the garden. They managed to scale a security fence, found their driver waiting and got clean away.

Before Mirbach died, less than an hour after being shot, the German military attaché rushed round to the Hotel Metropole to inform Chicherin, the People's Commissar for Foreign Affairs. Lenin received the telephone call in the Kremlin. According to his secretary Vladimir Bonch-Bruevich, 'Lenin did not turn pale – he turned white'.

Communist leaders, shaken by the assassination, made their way to the embassy to present their condolences. Radek went first, then Chicherin and Dzerzhinsky. Lenin did not want to leave the Kremlin, even well-guarded with a Latvian escort, but Riezler insisted, and in the circumstances he could not refuse. On discovering from Riezler that Left SR members of the Cheka were involved, Dzerzhinsky went straight round to the Pokrovsky Barracks, the base of the Cheka combat section. This was where the Central Committee of the Left Socialist Revolutionaries had gathered. Dzerzhinsky's sudden appearance was a rash move considering the odds he faced, but that did not stop him from threatening to shoot the lot of them if they did not hand over the assassins immediately. Instead, he was held hostage as a guarantee that Spiridonova, who had set off for the Bolshoi, would not be harmed.

On reaching the theatre Spiridonova rushed onto the stage, waving a pistol above her head, shouting 'Long live the revolt!' This and the discursive speech which followed had no effect because the Bolshoi was soon surrounded by Latvian riflemen, trapping the Left SRs inside. All they had achieved was to seize the telegraph office, to broadcast to the world their opposition to the German occupation.

Spiridonova's rebellion, which was never intended to seize power, represented the most useless form of gesture politics, with many killed and sacrificed for nothing. As Ioakim Vatsetis, the commander of the Latvian rifle regiments, argued, the Left SRs could easily have seized the capital. They had secretly assembled a force some 2,000 strong, mainly Baltic Fleet sailors armed with 'eight artillery guns, sixty-four machine guns, and four to six armoured cars'. Vatsetis, on the other hand, had less than half of his battalions in the city, as well as an under-strength unit of Hungarian prisoners of war commanded by Béla Kun. The Moscow garrison troops, meanwhile, were reluctant to move against the Left SRs. According to Steinberg, the former People's Commissar for Justice, Lenin was very nervous that the Latvians might not be able to hold Moscow. He summoned Vatsetis and asked him straight off: 'Comrade, will we hold out until the morning?' Lenin now was suspicious even of Vatsetis and insisted that more commissars be detailed to watch him. Vatsetis, an immensely tough character with a round bald head, was no politician and no traitor, yet he somehow inspired the distrust of both Lenin and Stalin.

The next morning, 7 July, was foggy as Latvian rifle companies took up position around the Pokrovsky barracks. They dragged a field gun from the nearby artillery training school into position at a range of no more than 300 metres. The gun crew fired seventeen rounds. One exploded in the room next to where the Left Social Revolutionary Central Committee was meeting. Having withstood the shelling, their leaders decided that they could surrender with their honour satisfied.

The two assassins could not be found in the wave of arrests which followed. A dozen executions were carried out, including Dzerzhinsky shooting his trusted deputy Aleksandrovich with his own hand. Lenin even started to harbour suspicions that Dzerzhinsky himself had been secretly involved in the Left SR plot. Some of the arrested were taken to the Cheka's Lubyanka. Its ill-lit corridors and the clang of metal cell doors made it seem like the bowels of a great vessel. Prisoners called it the 'Death Ship'. There was even an iron ladder down to the cellars known as the 'engine rooms' where executions took place, with a shot to the back of the head of each kneeling victim. But on the whole the reprisals were far less savage than might have been expected. This was because the Communists feared provoking the Left SR rank and file at a time when they faced so many other revolts.

Muraviev, the Red Army commander on the Volga Front, immediately resigned from the Left Socialist Revolutionaries. Despite his general suspicions, this seemed enough to satisfy Lenin. He simply told the commissars to keep a close eye on Muraviev so that the Red Army could continue 'to make use of his excellent fighting qualities'. But on 10 July, just three days after the suppression of the Spiridonova revolt in Moscow, Muraviev and 1,000 of his loyal men followed her doomed example. They sailed downstream from Kazan to Simbirsk, Lenin's birthplace. Muraviev demanded the renewal of the war against Germany and called on the Czechs to join the fight. But he was tricked into an ambush and was shot down before he could draw his own pistol. 'It was reported that Muraviev committed suicide,' Evan Mawdsley noted, 'but since his body had five bullet holes and several bayonet wounds this seems a little unlikely.' Lenin and Trotsky immediately agreed on Muraviev's replacement as commander on the Volga. They chose Vatsetis, whose Latvians had saved the regime.

Despite the failure of Spiridonova's Moscow revolt, the Left Socialist Revolutionaries had not abandoned their campaign to provoke a German reaction. On 30 July in Kiev, the Left SR Boris Donskoy assassinated the old Prussian Field Marshal Hermann von Eichhorn, the commander-in-chief in Ukraine, with a bomb. Eichhorn was hardly an aggressive general. He liked smoking a cigar in his office and talking about the past. 'Isn't it a shame that war has changed so much,' he had lamented to Svechin. 'In the old days troops went into battle in their dress uniforms.'

Eichhorn's death did not mark the last terrorist act of the old Narodnik tradition, although the Left SRs began to fragment. Most joined the Communists, but that would be no guarantee of safety in the future under the paranoid regime of Stalin.

Far more famous murders than those of Mirbach and Eichhorn took place that month. On the last day of April, the former Tsar and Tsarina had reached Ekaterinburg in the Urals, the symbolic border between Europe and Asia. It had also been one of the stops along the *via dolorosa* for prisoners condemned to trudge all the way to their Siberian exile under the Romanov regime. On their way from Tobolsk to Ekaterinburg, the imperial family had passed through Rasputin's village of Pokrovskoe. The former Tsarina, while closely guarded, had insisted on halting for a long time to gaze at his house. Members of his family watched her from its windows, not daring to go out.

The Bolsheviks' plan had been to bring Nicholas and Alexandra back from Tobolsk to Moscow for a show trial presided over by Trotsky, but the internal threats to the regime had grown suddenly during the spring, as had rumours of rescue plots planned by monarchist groups. The biggest danger had arisen with the revolt of the Czech corps at the end of May starting at Chelyabinsk, little more than 200 kilometres south of Ekaterinburg.

The royal couple and their five children were held in the Ipatiev House, the rather gloomy residence of a railway engineer. Now renamed the 'House of Special Purpose', a sinisterly unspecified designation, it had been converted into an improvised prison with a wooden palisade all around to block the view in both directions. In comparison to the house arrest they had endured at Tobolsk, the former Tsar was soon moved to write in his diary: 'It is certainly a prison regime!' Yet it was still far more comfortable than a real Cheka prison. They had their own rooms and after dinner the ex-Tsar would read to his wife and their daughters or they played bezique. In the Ipatiev House, the Tsar discovered the satirical novels of Saltykov-Shchedrin. He read eight of them in a row and was surprised by how much he enjoyed them. It was a pity that he had not encountered them when much younger.

From the sunshine and snow showers of spring, they were soon experiencing the rising heat of the Siberian summer with humid nights. The shortages of water contributed to a growing typhus epidemic in the city. The royal family had sensed the hostile atmosphere, but they were not told of the Kronstadt sailors who had arrived in late May and killed forty-five members of the local Orthodox clergy. They also 'assaulted and raped women, attacked and murdered members of the bourgeoisie and raided the local distillery for vodka, distributing it to the mob'. Nor did the former Tsar know that his younger brother, the Grand Duke Mikhail, for whom he had in theory abdicated, had been taken from his prison in Perm on 12 June by the Cheka and shot in the woods outside. His body was disposed of in a smelting furnace. The Cheka spread the story that he had been spirited away by 'White Guardists'.

By the end of June gunfire could be heard in the distance as the Czechs advanced in their direction. On 29 June, the former Tsar noted that in recent days 'we received two letters, one after the other, in which we were warned to prepare ourselves for a rescue by persons devoted to us. But several days have passed without anything happening, it was torture to wait in an atmosphere of uncertainty.'*

The advance of the Czechs caused panic in the whole region. In Irbit, less than 200 kilometres to the northeast, the Military Revolutionary Committee announced on 6 July that a number of wealthy residents would be taken hostage and shot if there was any attempt at an uprising. One of their posters announced: 'The counter-revolution is advancing on all fronts, while factory owners, landowners, merchants and other parasites are walking around freely in our cities. Traitors should remember that 100 of their people will die for every one of us.'

The last entry made in Nicholas's diary was on 13 July. It was about his son, who had been in such pain. 'Alexis has had his first bath since Tobolsk; his knee is better, but he cannot yet bend it completely. The

---

* Nicholas, deliberately ignoring the recent Bolshevik switch to the Gregorian calendar, stayed with the Julian calendar of his ancestors by giving the date as 16 June.

weather is gentle and pleasant. No news from outside.'

Their fate, together with that of other relatives imprisoned in the region, was already decided. Lenin, Dzerzhinsky and Sverdlov had agreed at a meeting in the Kremlin that with the Czech advance, they did not want the Whites to have a 'banner'. They entirely failed to see that the Romanovs, once dead, were far more useful to their enemies as martyrs. Lenin did not want to take any responsibility for the decision, especially the murder of the children, so it was to be blamed on the Ural Soviet. In the early hours of 17 July, the family was woken in the Ipatiev House and shepherded down to the basement by the guards, half of whom were Hungarian internationalists, and their commander Vasily Yurovsky. The former Tsar had to carry his son in his arms as the boy could not manage the stairs. Yurovsky read out the sentence of death and the shooting started. The boy Aleksei, the former Tsarevich, was still alive despite lying in a pool of blood, so Yurovsky fired two more bullets from his Colt into his head.

The following night in Alapaevsk, 130 kilometres north of Ekaterinburg, other Romanov prisoners as well as the Tsarina's sister, Grand Duchess Elizaveta Fedorovna, were taken from their improvised prison. The guards, half of whom this time were Austrian internationalists, escorted them to a flooded mine. The Grand Duke Sergei was shot at this point because he resisted. All his companions were thrown down the shaft. But a short time later they heard splashing and the singing of hymns. They dropped grenades to finish them off. Once again, the ludicrous story of them being spirited away by 'White Guardists' was given out. The murders of all these Romanovs, together with other relatives and friends, represented a declaration of total war in which 'the sanctity of human life', as well as notions of guilt and innocence, counted for nothing.

17

Red Terror
Summer 1918

In the inescapable argument over the origins of the civil war and responsibility for its cruelty, the Communists claimed they had no choice. Red Terror was forced upon them. They variously blamed it on counter-revolution, which by their own definition meant anybody who did not support them, attempts on the lives of their leaders, and foreign intervention. Yet in civil wars, a policy of terror is almost always the response of those most conscious of the fact that they are in a minority. It starts as a knee-jerk reaction, yet the regime holds on to it long after the threat has been defeated. In Lenin's case, the mind-set was there from the start, with the foundation of the Cheka in December 1917 well before the civil war began in an overt and recognisable form. Communist coercion through terror was thus a pre-emptive measure, but at the end of August 1918 two attacks on Communist leaders on the same day triggered an explosive escalation of violence.

On the morning of Friday 30 August Leonid Kannegiser, a twenty-two-year-old former cadet of the Mikhailovsky Artillery School, shot Moisei Uritsky, the head of the Petrograd Cheka. Kannegiser had gone to the waiting room of Cheka headquarters on the day reserved for Uritsky to receive denunciations. Uritsky arrived half an hour later and, as he entered the room, Kannegiser shot him through the back of the head at point-blank range with his Colt revolver. According to his father, the young man simply wanted to take revenge for the killing of his best friend Perelstveyg, on Uritsky's order. Soviet authorities, however, were convinced that the attack must have been part of a conspiracy.

Kannegiser dashed out of the building, jumped on his bicycle and pedalled away, with Chekists in furious pursuit. He reached Millionnaya ulitsa, dumped his bicycle and ran into the courtyard of No. 17 and up the stairs. Choosing the first door he opened, he forced his way into the former apartment of Prince Melikhov, grabbed a coat off a peg in an attempt to change his appearance and went back onto the landing. There he saw his pursuers on the ground floor and opened fire. Sangaylo, the senior Chekist present, wanted to take him alive in order to discover who else was involved in the plot. He put a dummy in the lift wearing his overcoat and sent it up to the first floor. The idea was that assassin should expend his bullets firing at it. But the young man took the coat off the dummy, put it on and went downstairs, claiming that the man they were chasing had continued upstairs. Recognising his own coat, Sangaylo seized him and took him off for interrogation.

Lenin had been rattled by the Left SR revolt in July, which showed how vulnerable the Communists were even in their own capital. Considering how concerned he usually was for his own safety, his decision to carry on with a factory visit in Moscow was out of character, especially since he had just heard of Uritsky's assassination in Petrograd. Krupskaya and his sister begged him not to go.

After a rally at the Grain Commodity Exchange, Lenin was driven on to the Mikhelson factory in south Moscow. While he gave his usual talk inside, a young woman approached his driver to ask if Lenin really was there. This was Fanya Kaplan, the daughter of a teacher of Hebrew. She had joined the Left SRs after being in prison with Spiridonova. Kaplan had been an Anarchist, sentenced to hard labour for life at the age of sixteen for a terrorist explosion. After the Bolshevik coup and the suppression of the Constituent Assembly, she decided to shoot Lenin and volunteered for the Socialist Revolutionary combat organisation.

As the audience emerged at the end, Kaplan followed close behind Lenin, who paused just before climbing into his car when a woman asked him about food confiscations at railway stations. Kaplan fired three shots with her Browning pistol. Two bullets hit Lenin, one in the arm and the second in the neck by his jaw. The third hit the woman who had addressed him. Kaplan ran off, then stopped by some trees where she was arrested.

While an unconscious Lenin was driven at top speed back to the Kremlin, Kaplan was taken straight to the Lubyanka for interrogation by the Latvian Chekist Iakov Péters. She admitted shooting Lenin, but refused to say who had given her the gun and denied having any fellow conspirators. The Cheka, convinced that this was an English plot, arrested the British representative Robert Bruce Lockhart that night and took him to a cell in the Lubyanka. They then put Kaplan in the same cell to see if the two knew each other. Clearly there was no sign of recognition, so Kaplan was taken away soon afterwards and locked in the basement of the Kremlin. She was shot in a side courtyard on 3 September. The noise of the execution was concealed by the revving of automobile engines.

In Petrograd, while Kannegiser was still being interrogated on Saturday 31 August, a strong contingent of the Cheka stormed the British Embassy. Their target was Captain Francis Cromie of the Royal Navy's intelligence department, who was indeed plotting to overthrow Lenin's government. Cromie, in an attempt to cover the escape of two of his Russian agents (one of whom may have been a Cheka spy), fought back until his revolver ran out of bullets and he was shot down on the grand marble staircase. Other officers and staff at the embassy were arrested and taken away, to be released in an exchange of prisoners much later.

That same day, Dzerzhinsky arrived in Petrograd to interrogate Kannegiser in person. The young man still refused to say whether he had accomplices, or how he had obtained the revolver. The Cheka claimed to have found in his apartment 467 addresses of members of Kerensky's Provisional Government, Tsarist generals and Right Socialist Revolutionaries, and yet he had been a member of the tiny Popular Socialist Party. Kannegiser did not finally receive his 'nine grams of lead' until 21 December. One can only imagine the tortures he must have suffered during the intervening period.

Lenin survived his wounds, despite the fears of his doctors, and this 'miracle' marked the start of the cult of personality that grew around him. He was elevated to a secular sainthood, even to Christ-like comparisons, while Kaplan was derided as a failed Charlotte Corday. The moral outrage of the regime and its followers became quite hysterical. 'We need to take revenge for the wounds inflicted on the dear leader of the World proletariat, Comrade Lenin.'

Even the sinister secret policeman Uritsky was treated as a martyr. 'Uritsky's funeral was very pompous,' wrote a witness. 'The body was carried around the streets for several hours under a luxurious balda-chin.' The Bolsheviks in the procession were dressed in various uniforms and carried a great number of threatening posters. 'Thousands of your heads for each one of our leaders'; 'A bullet through the chest of each enemy of the working class'; 'Death to the mercenaries of Anglo-French capital'. Party newspapers all expressed the same mood of vengeance.

The threats were not idle. In Petrograd, 500 hostages were shot straight off by the Cheka in blind vengeance for their chief's murder. Hostages were packed onto two barges which were towed out into the Gulf of Finland and sunk. Some of the bodies that washed up on the shore revealed that their hands had been bound with barbed wire. Some claim that with the killings carried out at Kronstadt and in the Peter and Paul Fortress, the reprisals accounted for 1,300 lives, with another 6,229 arrested as hostages. Provincial Chekas boasted of their own reprisals in Yaroslavl, in Sumy, Pyatigorsk, in Pskov, in Smolensk. They shot not just Socialist Revolutionaries, but anyone who might be considered anti-Bolshevik. In Nizhny Novgorod they claimed 41 shot, and another 700 hostages rounded up.

The Cheka seemed to revel in its reputation for nocturnal terror. 'Dzerzhinsky only works at night,' wrote the Jewish historian Grigory Aronson. 'So does Péters. Ordinary investigators imitate their bosses. So do, as we know, the executioners. They call people at night for interrogations. The Collegium sits at night. Final sentences are announced at night. They are shooting people at night in different parts of Moscow and in Cheka basements and sheds.' Those already in prison used to refer to 'Commissar Death coming in the night'.

In a foretaste of the Nazi death squads in Russia less than a quarter century later, the Cheka's prisoners were forced to undress completely so that their clothes could be reused. They were then made to kneel in cellars, or by open graves, so that their executioners only had to raise their heavy Mauser pistols with wooden stocks and shoot them in the back of the head. Some gloried in the bloodshed, while other executioners were driven mad by the relentless slaughter, just as Himmler discovered later with his own *Einsatzgruppen*.

Red Terror was not, of course, restricted to arrests and Cheka buildings in cities. Fear and hatred of counter-revolutionary Cossacks in the Don regions took on an even more indiscriminate and almost genocidal form. A former member of the Cheka reported on events in the Morozovsky district, 220 kilometres west of Tsaritsyn. 'The district's population went through an incredibly bloody period, which in general simply consisted of the extermination of Cossacks aged from 45 years onwards, without an upper limit age. "Exterminate completely!". That was the resolution by members of the revolutionary committee of Morozovskaya Cossack Village chaired by a certain Boguslavsky ... After finishing their day at the institutions, some members of the Revolutionary Committee ... gathered in the evening in Boguslavsky's place, got themselves completely drunk, had unbelievable orgies, and after that would bring individual Cossacks from the local jail in order to practise on them. They enjoyed target practice shooting at them, striking them with swords, stabbing with daggers, etc. ... It was revealed later that no trials had taken place. Later sixty-seven corpses were found buried in Boguslavsky's garden.'

A Communist Party member from Moscow reported: 'Sometimes they shot 50–60 people daily. The guiding principle was the more Cossack seed we shoot, the stronger the Soviet authority on the Don will become. Not a single attempt was made to find agreement with Cossacks ... Almost every day one could witness the mad scene when yet another party of prisoners were being led off for execution. Healthy people were made to carry the sick. The guards, armed with rifles, chased away passers-by, clearing the way. Everyone knew that these people were condemned to death. Often I would see Cossacks that supported the Soviet regime cry when they witnessed such scenes. They grew indignant and asked: "Can this be true, that the Soviet regime brings such horrors with it? We cannot believe this." ... When carrying out searches, officials from the Revolutionary tribunal confiscated glasses, spoons, dishes, often for themselves ... Some people were hoping that there would be an inspection from Moscow, while others, of course, were waiting for Cossacks to rebel.'

The truth was that Dzerzhinsky had little control over the local Chekas, many of which were virtually self-appointed. A Cheka report of August 1918 revealed the chaos and corruption in Kursk. 'In Kursk, the population has not received its bread ration for about three weeks. Clashes occur between provision patrols engaged in requisitioning grain. This can lead to one patrol disarming another, with exchanges of fire and deaths. Groups from particular patrols and entire grain requisition patrols sell the grain on the spot at the railway station, thereby provoking discontent among the masses. The standard of discipline of Red Army units in Kursk is poor. They fraternise with the local population, and engage in drunkenness and debauchery. They have taken all the best houses in town and drive around in motorcars.' Many other reports from Kursk confirmed that both Cheka members and provision patrols used their power to steal grain, either for personal consumption or resale.

In Kiev Péters created a fake Brazilian consulate, where his Cheka operatives sold visas for large sums of money to refugees desperate to escape, and then arrested them. When the Whites captured Kiev, they claimed to find 5,000 corpses and estimated that another 7,000 people were missing. The Cheka had two key priorities: seizing money and valuables from their victims to finance the Red cause and crushing all potential opposition by pitiless class warfare. Latsis, in his instructions to Chekists, made this perfectly clear. 'When interrogating, do not seek material evidence or proof of the accused's words or deeds against Soviet power. The first question you must ask is: what class does he belong to, what education, upbringing, origin or profession does he have? These questions must determine the accused's fate. This is the sense and essence of Red terror.' Evidence found in searches was used to establish guilt, never innocence.

Most widespread of all, the Red Terror was used to reduce the countryside into submission because the cities were starving. A differential ration system was introduced in Petrograd and Moscow in the summer of 1918, with manual workers, other workers and members of the bourgeoisie based on a ratio of 4:3:1. The 'iron-clad' top level of ration was for Red Army soldiers and industrial workers. The ration set for *burzhui* non-workers was, whether deliberately or not, insufficient to stay alive. Their only hope was to bargain away their most treasured possessions on Sukharevskaya Square in exchange for food, and the black market became known as the *Sukharevka*. Senior Party members, cadres and especially commissars soon had their own privileged canteens. The stratification became far more complex, with 'intellectual workers' receiving priority, as well as 'bourgeois specialists'.

In May 1918 a delegation of Putilov workers went to see Lenin about the disastrous food situation in Petrograd. He responded by calling on them to serve in the food detachments to save the revolution. He said that the revolution needed ten times as many food detachments if they were to conquer hunger, yet it was the food detachments which were making the problem far worse. They began seizing seed grain for the next harvest, terrifying the peasantry into hiding or consuming their grain before it was taken from them.

The peasants may not have benefited from much education, but they soon suspected that the Bolsheviks were turning them into the serfs of the industrial proletariat. 'Markets were banned and those buying from them persecuted. As a result, city populations starved while peasants disposed of the excess grain as best they knew how, feeding it to livestock and making alcohol.'

This deliberate defiance of all economic forces produced its own vicious circle. One pood of flour cost twenty-five to thirty roubles in the Volga region in 1918, while in Petrograd it could reach 1,000 roubles. The Communist food detachments started to confiscate all grain, not just the ill-defined 'surplus' produce. Lenin refused to accept that the forced requisitions reduced food production disastrously. Outraged at the resistance, his reaction was to intensify the repression. Food detachments were told to recruit poor peasants as informers against the rich peasants, the 'kulaks'. The food detachments, made up mainly of Communists from cities and towns, could not tell the difference between a poor peasant, a 'middle peasant' and a supposedly rich 'class enemy'. They paid no attention to the need to hold back seed corn for the next year's harvest. All they were interested in was extracting the estimate they had been given. As a result, peasants decided to grow no more than their own needs for the following year. They hid their grain by sealing it in large earthenware jars which they buried. Food detachments then resorted to torturing family members, to force them to reveal their hiding places. In a cycle of violence, peasants attacked members of the detachments, in some cases even killing them and slitting open their stomachs which they stuffed with grain as a warning.

Europe had not seen such conspicuous cruelty used as a weapon of terror since the wars of religion. This raises the question whether the modern equivalent, the political civil war, was a predictable development. On 23 August, even before Kaplan's attack on Lenin, the Chekist Latsis published an article in *Izvestia* stating that the 'established customs of war' were irrelevant. 'Massacring all the wounded who fought against you – that is a law of civil war.' Yet where did the extremes of sadism come from – the hacking with sabres, the cutting with knives, the boiling and burning, the scalping alive, the nailing of epaulettes to shoulders, the gouging of eyes, the soaking of victims in winter to freeze them to death, castration, evisceration, amputation? Was all this just an atavistic part of Pushkin's 'senseless and merciless'* depiction of Russian revolt? Or had the frenzy of vengeance been intensified to another level by the rhetoric of political hatred?

---

* 'God save us from seeing a Russian revolt, senseless and merciless. Those who plot impossible upheavals among us, are either young and do not know our people, or are hard-hearted men who do not care a straw either about their own lives or those of others.' Pushkin's observation on the unbelievably violent rebellion by Emelian Pugachev (1773–4) comes in *The Captain's Daughter*, London, 2009, p. 203.

18

Fighting on the Volga and the Red Army Summer 1918

July was a bad month for the Red Army. Apart from the crushing of Savinkov's rising at Yaroslavl, it faced one defeat after another. On 21 July the Czechs took Ekaterinburg, four days after the massacre of the imperial family. Then, the next day Colonel Kappel reported the occupation of Lenin's birthplace of Simbirsk (Ulyanovsk) by his men and a Czech regiment. This was made possible by an approach march of 140 kilometres which enabled them to take the Red troops by surprise. Kappel's telegram on 22 July announced: 'At 08.00, after a battle in the area, the units of the 1st Samara Detachment entered Simbirsk. A great amount of military and artillery equipment has been captured, and many steam locomotives, an armoured train and various items which cannot yet be counted.'

There was another frenzy of panic in Moscow. The morale of the Red Army on the Volga had collapsed and there was little that Vatsetis could do in his new command. Fyodor Raskolnikov, now deputy commissar for the Navy, was ordered to take gunboats and light warships down the Volga from Nizhny Novgorod to help the beleaguered Red forces facing the Czechs. He was accompanied by his wife of just a few days, Larisa Reisner, his 'warrior Diana'. This beautiful twenty-two-year-old poet became the first woman front-line commissar. Armed with no more than a small Browning pistol, Reisner was to act with reckless bravery as a scout and spy, to say nothing of her role as political instructor to the roughest of Baltic sailors. On her death from typhus less than a dozen years later, Trotsky also hailed this heroic legend as 'an Olympian goddess who combined a subtle, ironical wit with the courage of a warrior'.

Raskolnikov's Volga flotilla headed south for Kazan with only an inkling of what they were about to sail into. They found the Red Guards utterly demoralised. 'The town isn't taken yet,' Reisner noted, 'but its defeat is certain. The doors of abandoned rooms are

The Red Volga flotilla commanded by Fyodor Raskolnikov with his wife the writer Larisa Reisner as commissar.

slamming. The floors are littered with papers and scattered possessions. Nothing is worse than retreat.' On 5 August, Vladimir Zenzinov was just about to leave the city when he heard artillery salvos coming from the Volga. 'Suddenly the rumour spread, that anti-Bolshevik troops and Czechs had arrived on steamers from Samara . . . The Bolsheviks were taken aback by the suddenness of the attack. No one had any doubts left when the first shrapnel started exploding over the city. One could already hear rifles and the chattering of machine-guns.' The city was defended by the 5th Latvian Rifle Regiment while 'the Serbian International Battalion which was occupying the Kazan fortress went over to the enemy', the Red *Stavka* reported. In the chaotic flight the Red commander-in-chief Vatsetis was nearly captured. He escaped only because a group of his men forced a way through the crowd of refugees for him.

Colonel Kappel was again in the vanguard with his Samara Detachment of the anti-Bolshevik People's Army on six armed steamboats. 'Our leading units entered the city at noon. There was a battle in the main street of the city against infantry and armoured vehicles of the enemy. We had no armour-piercing bullets and no artillery support.' Because of the heat and the exhaustion of his men, who had not eaten as their supplies were still on the river steamers which had landed them, Kappel pulled them back to the edge of the town. The next morning at 4 a.m., they went back in. 'Elimination of Bolsheviks in the city,' he reported to the Komuch by the end of the day. 'Seizure by our detachment of the whole gold reserves – 645 million, as well as a large amount of cash in money boxes belonging to Soviet units.'*

Kerensky's former minister of marine, Vladimir Lebedev, whom Dvorzhets described as 'the Komuch's evil genius', took the gold reserves down the Volga the next night by steamer to Samara. Prokofiev was another who disliked Lebedev. Some months later, after being taken off by some friends 'to visit some expensive tarts', Prokofiev met Lebedev at a musical soirée. 'I asked him if he had hanged any people after taking Kazan,' Prokofiev noted in his diary. 'He replied: "I shot two hundred." I exclaimed: "Two hundred?!" and he added: "Scoundrels." He then asked Shindler [their host] to play something by Kalinnikov. He likes tender music.'

The humiliation of the Treaty of Brest-Litovsk, compounded by the military superiority of the Czechs, had provided a bitter lesson to the Communist leadership. The followers of Bukharin in the 'Left Opposition', and the Left SRs who had advocated revolutionary warfare to resist the Germans, remained viscerally opposed to any idea of a professional army. Ideologically, they could accept nothing more than a citizen's militia based on the armed factory workers of the Red Guards.

To start with, the Communists promoted talented NCOs. Several went on to the highest command in the Second World War, especially those associated with Stalin and Kliment Voroshilov in Tsaritsyn. They included Georgy Zhukov and Semyon Budyonny, both dragoon sergeants, Semyon Timoshenko and Ivan Konev, an artilleryman.[†] But both Lenin and Trotsky knew that if Communism was to survive

---

* Many assume it was the Czechs who captured the gold reserves, but in fact it appears to have been Kappel's men. In any case it was a massive blow for the Sovnarkom at a moment when the rouble was now worth only a fifth of its value just prior to Kerensky's downfall.

† Budyonny was famous for his vanity. His cavalry moustache grew larger and larger as he progressed up the ranks, and he wore red breeches with silver stripes. Timoshenko was the original for Savitsky in Isaac Babel's short story 'My First Goose'.

they needed not just discipline and organisation but experts to train an effective Red Army, able to defeat more than rebellious peasants. They therefore recruited members of the Tsarist officer corps, despite all their rhetoric about never trusting class enemies. An initial step in this direction had been taken with the hiring of economic and other commercial experts, but the very word 'officer' was anathema to their followers, so they were given the euphemistic title of 'military special- ists'. This was a policy which Stalin, supported by Dzerzhinsky, fought against with all his might.

Trotsky bitterly resented Stalin's encroachment into military affairs. Lenin had sent Stalin down to Tsaritsyn to increase grain requisitions in the lower Volga region, yet Stalin, taking on the role of commissar, proceeded to act as if he were Front commander. He also increased the Cheka in Tsaritsyn and impelled them into carrying out terrifying massacres.

Some Red Army commanders appointed at this time had been junior or middle-ranking officers in the war, such as Mikhail Tukhachevsky and Aleksandr Vasilevsky. A number were already generals. For exam- ple, General Mikhail Svechin's younger brother, Aleksandr, had also been a Tsarist general. He later became the chief military theorist of the Red Army in the 1920s and the father of Soviet 'operational art', until executed in Stalin's purges nearly twenty years later along with Tukhachevsky.* By the end of the civil war no less than 75,000 Tsarist officers had served with the Red Army. Many had been forced to join up either because no other work was available or through coercion, with their families taken hostage, yet a large number proved loyal and worked well with their commissars.

The Red Army of Workers and Peasants failed to recruit more than a third of the volunteers Trotsky had counted on. Conscription had to be introduced as the number of fronts to be manned multiplied as the civil war developed. But even conscripts needed encouragement, other- wise they would desert at the first opportunity. One method, which the authorities tried, was to provide more perks than just rations and clothing, especially if they were to recruit peasants as well as

---

* Wavell did not like Tukhachevsky. 'Tukhachevsky, with whom I lunched one day, was rather a nasty piece of work, to whom I took an instant dislike, but he was un- doubtedly able, ambitious and energetic.'

*M.N. Tukhachevsky, an army commander at the age of 25,
a Marshal later and executed on Stalin's orders in 1937 in his purge
of the Red Army.*

proletarians. Accordingly, they produced a 'protection document' for families of Red Army soldiers, which stipulated that 'neither their land, nor livestock, nor seeds can be confiscated' by the food detachments. It was probably not worth the paper it was printed on.

The Reds needed cavalry to match the Whites, especially across the huge steppe of southern Russia and western Siberia. Trotsky regarded regiments of horse as the old-fashioned plaything of the aristocracy, but he came round to the idea out of necessity. Posters would be plastered all over the place depicting a Soviet worker galloping on horseback with a drawn sword in his hand and a red star on his hat. Across it was written in large letters: 'Proletarians, to Horse!' Not many industrial workers followed this exhortation. The Red cavalry had better luck recruiting poor Cossacks or *ingorodnie*.

Uniforms hardly existed at the time, so soldiers invented their own. They were obsessed by the colour red. Even experienced commanders were not embarrassed to be seen wearing a woman's red coat. Soldiers sought out red fabric to make shirts or tunics. Apparently there were some units where soldiers dressed entirely in red.

Trotsky had also realised early on that the roughly 2 million German, Austro-Hungarian and Bulgarian prisoners of war still in Russian camps could provide a good source of recruits for his Red Army. They were already trained soldiers, many of them could be won over to the Communist cause and they could spread the revolutionary word when they went home afterwards. Some emerged later as commanders or organisers of the International Brigades in the Spanish Civil War, such as Gall, Kléber, Lukács and Josip Broz Tito. Prisoners of war repatriated in 1918 were given Communist propaganda leaflets in German to distribute. In Vienna, the high command of the *Kaiserlich und Königlich* Army was alarmed. 'A "moral quarantine" is deemed to be imperative, so that the "bolshevik poison" which the men may have absorbed in Russia is not imported to Austria.'

Rudolf Rothkegel, a German Communist prisoner of war, had been summoned to Moscow at the end of January 1918. He was instructed to visit prison camps in order to persuade German prisoners of war to join the Red Guard. He and others like him used the slogans: 'The socialist Fatherland is in danger!' and 'The Russian Revolution is also our revolution and our hope!' The efforts to brainwash prisoners of war were relentless. 'In the [Khabarovsk] camp,' an Austrian major reported, 'the agitation and propaganda speeches in aid of communism, and the conversion to Bolshevism were, despite energetic protests, the order of the day. The men were vulnerable, because many officers dared not speak out against the agitators for fear of persecution.'

The Communist recruiters did all they could to persuade the prisoners to stay on in Russia and not return home. The war ministry in Vienna heard that 'propaganda is being spread among the prisoners-of-war in Russia, that all returnees will be called up to active military service immediately. Hence, there is depression among the men and not much motivation to come home.' Pressure could also be exerted by offering Red Army rations since those left in the prison camps were starving, as had been the case in Irkutsk and Turkestan. In the camp at Tsaritsyn some 4,000 Austro-Hungarian prisoners died of starvation in a few weeks, because the Red Guards holding them did not even allow them to buy any food.

Even before the Communists came to power, the conditions had been terrible. In the prisoner-of-war camp near Krasnoyarsk, 54 per cent of the inmates had died. In Novo-Nikolaevsk 80 per cent of the prisoners succumbed to typhus in the winter of 1915, and in Omsk 16,000 had died in the first ten months of the war. It was not surprising that so many prisoners from the Central Powers greeted the revolution with relief, and hated the Tsarist regime. It must also be remembered that the Kaiser had been tempted by the idea of starving Russian prisoners to death, a precursor to the cruelty of Operation Barbarossa.

The Whites and several historians have nevertheless tried to argue either that the Internationalists were mercenaries, or that the Soviet regime was essentially a 'foreign invasion' or an 'internationalist occupation'. Already in the spring of 1918 before the push to convert them there were groups of German and Austro-Hungarian prisoners in improvised units in Siberia, on the Volga and in the south. There had even been 160 German Communists attached to the Cheka in Kazan. Estimates of how many prisoners became 'Internationalisten' in the Red Army vary wildly between 40,000 and 250,000. In addition, there were of course also the 25,000 Latvian riflemen, to say nothing of the Chinese who served in the Red Army and Cheka.

After the outbreak of the Great War in 1914, the Tsarist government had recruited or conscripted more than 150,000 Chinese labourers to assist their armies at the front and in the rear. Nearly 10,000 Chinese worked on the Murmansk Railway up to the Arctic Circle. Many more were living in the country illegally, especially in the far east. Since the Chinese had suffered ill treatment and appalling conditions at the hands of the Tsarist military authorities, the Bolsheviks spotted the opportunity and began to recruit them. Few spoke any Russian or understood Bolshevik ideology, but many were prepared to fight in the ranks of the Red Army simply to receive food and clothing. In Siberia, however, the Chinese settled there did not support the Bolsheviks. 'Soviet authority needed, once it arrived in the region, to start the political and propaganda work in order to win the migrants over.'

After the Bolshevik coup, the majority found themselves without work. In May 1918, a recruitment centre was established in Moscow and led by the Bolshevik commissar Shen Chenho. It had also been Trotsky's idea to involve the Chinese in the Red Army. The execution squad which shot Trotsky's victim Captain Aleksei Schastny was entirely Chinese. They soon proved to be 'not only reliable soldiers in the front line but were used on a mass scale to perform punitive functions suppressing rebellious Red Units, executing hostages, suppressing peasant uprisings in the rear, and forcefully taking foodstuffs from peasants'. They also manned blocking detachments, to arrest or shoot down any Red Army soldiers retreating without orders.

Russian sources state that some 30,000–40,000 Chinese served in Bolshevik ranks during the civil war, yet the estimate of Chinese diplomats pointed to double that figure. Shen Chenho claimed the true number was close to 100,000. There were even some units formed entirely by 'Chinese internationalists'. And by the height of the civil war, the Kiev Cheka had a purely Chinese 'special detachment' commanded by Li Xu-Liang. A number were recruited by the Cheka because they seemed to have no qualms about killing or torturing White prisoners when Russian personnel could not stomach any more blood. It is said that it was the Chinese torturers who invented such ideas as nailing a captured officer's epaulettes to his shoulders. Whether entirely true or not, a terrible vicious circle of cruelty developed with the vengeance of Cossacks and Whites on any Chinese unfortunate enough to be taken alive. 'I feared capture more than death,' recounted the machine gunner Yao Sin-Cheng, 'because the White bandits had a particular hatred for Chinese soldiers. As soon as a Chinaman fell into their hands they would torture them: cut off his ears and nose, poke out the eyes, and only after that they killed them.' In April 1918, the Chinese Embassy reported to Peking (Beijing): 'In the area controlled by the Don Army, the Cossacks arrest all Chinese without exception and send them off we know not where. The same happens in areas controlled by the Volunteer Army.'

Iona Yakir, a Bolshevik commander, raised a Chinese battalion of nearly 500 men. He admired their discipline and bravery, saying that only a cavalry charge with drawn sabres could throw them off balance. He also observed: 'The Chinese were very serious about their salary. They parted easily with their lives but wanted to be paid on time and fed well.' They demanded in addition that the whole battalion should be paid regardless of losses, so that the salaries of those killed could be sent to their families. Yakir agreed to this, but they did not know that he was paying his Russian soldiers at least thirty times more.

*

The weakness of the Soviet government was so great that summer that the Germans felt obliged to support the regime to prevent its collapse. They feared that the Allies would otherwise reactivate the Eastern Front. In France they faced the deployment of fresh American troops and on 8 August the massive Allied general offensive known as the Hundred Days began. As well as making remarkably little fuss about the assassinations of Mirbach and Eichhorn, the German government gave an assurance that they would not attack Russia. This enabled Trotsky to move the remaining Latvian battalions from the west to the Volga, and specifically to the battle to retake Kazan.

Just after Kazan fell to the Whites on 7 August, the Red forces, including Larisa Reisner, fell back some 20 kilometres to the west of the village and railway station of Sviazhsk. Raskolnikov had been captured, but then escaped. Trotsky, on receiving news of Kazan's loss, reacted with manic activity. Within forty-eight hours of the fall of the city, he had organised his armoured train, which he took to the front. It was much more than a command post on wheels, bringing 200 Communist volunteers from Petrograd, and in other rolling stock a radio station, electrical generators, printing press, and five automobiles with large reserves of fuel. Other wagons carried spare weapons, ammunition, boots and uniforms. One carriage was set aside as a revolutionary tribunal to deal with deserters and cowards. Another train followed with cavalry in cattle wagons, and even an aeroplane ready to be reassembled. In a conspicuous display of his intention to stay with the troops at the front, Trotsky sent his locomotive back to Moscow.

Just a few days after the loss of Kazan, Trotsky and Vatsetis ordered the 3rd Army to advance along the railway line which ran from Perm towards Ekaterinburg. His headquarters reported back with premature triumph: 'The enemy is blowing up tracks while retreating. Death to the enemies of the proletariat!' The 3rd Army on the North Urals Front was commanded by Reingold Berzin. He had great trouble with the untrained and undisciplined sailors of the 1st Expeditionary Detachment of the Baltic Fleet. From Perm, they had been sent forward to take up a position at Sarga. But the detachment spent most of its time holding protest rallies to complain about the food and the way they were treated. In fact, they were reluctant to leave their train and many of their members had reported sick with venereal disease. They claimed that under threat of attack by the Whites they had asked the neighbouring unit for help. 'But the Velikie Luki detachment said: "We are hungry, we have fought for seven days and no-one gave us support. One cannot go and support anyone with empty hands and we have no ammunition." They started explaining that their commanders had run away taking with them all the documents and money. They said that was clear treason so they would not go and provide support.'

The Baltic sailors held another protest meeting and passed a resolution that they should return to Petrograd for retraining. 'This was reported to the commander of 3rd Army Comrade Berzin, so Berzin assembled all the sailors and tried to persuade them to stay at the front, not as a combat force, but as a blocking unit to stop those attempting to flee from the front. The sailors did not agree to that and told him that they would go for retraining and then return to fight again. Comrade Berzin then said: "I cannot hold you sailors by force, all that is left for me to do is to inform the comrades in Petrograd."'

Keeping Red Army troops and sailors in the front line was not just a problem on the North Ural Front, as Trotsky soon found. Larisa Reisner worshipped Trotsky for his appearance at Sviazhsk like a *deus ex machina*. 'At Trotsky's side,' she wrote, 'we could die fighting with the last cartridge gone, oblivious of our wounds; for Trotsky incarnated the holy demagogy of battle, with words and gestures summoning up the most heroic pages of the French Revolution's history.' The strength of her feelings came not just because of the weapons and supplies which he brought to raise morale, but for his strong leadership and organising genius. 'Strong leadership' meant the execution of commanders and regimental commissars as well as any men caught fleeing the front line.

When Colonel Kappel launched a surprise attack on the rear of their positions, 'panic now seized the Red forces', wrote Victor Serge. Trotsky was appalled that little more than 500 men stayed to fight out of Vatsetis's strength of nearly 10,000. Many of those fleeing tried to board the vessels of the Volga flotilla in their desperation. No less than twenty-seven of the 200 Communist Party volunteers Trotsky had brought were shot for cowardice. Trotsky's execution of Communist cadres was definitely *pour encourager les autres*. He also offered a reward of 50,000 roubles on the head of Colonel Kappel. Reisner in her account, however, made no mention of anything that might undermine her glorious images of those days.

Trotsky now advocated the very measures, including machine guns behind the lines, for which the Bolsheviks had condemned Kornilov during the Kerensky offensive. The 'blocking detachment' made up of Communist cadres to prevent unauthorised retreat would become a standard practice in the Red Army. This harshness, combined with the support of more gunboats reaching Raskolnikov's Volga flotilla, extra artillery and some bombers started to stiffen the resistance of the troops facing Kazan. That did not mean, however, that confidence in the quality of sailors sent to the front had improved. The commander-in-chief of the Baltic Fleet sent a signal to Raskolnikov at the headquarters of the 5th Army. '500 Navy communists from the Mine Division are setting off for Sviazhsk today, on 26 August, at 20.00. Ten officers will also be sent off today, but neither the Commander of the Navy, nor the Kronstadt Navy Commissar can vouch for them. We recommend you keep them under tight control. All that we can order you to do is to shoot at least five officers for each traitor.'

The People's Commissar for War would have been taken aback if he had known more about his cavalry escort. Lieutenant Raczyński had decided in a Cheka prison that 'the way to freedom was through the Bolshevik army' and had volunteered along with other Polish legionnaires. The Soviet authorities had gladly sent these 'conscientious comrades' to join the Red Army's Masovian Uhlan Regiment of Red Poles. Raczyński, an experienced cavalry officer, was soon promoted and had the other secret legionnaires transferred to his troop. They all agreed to go on 'Polish leave' as soon as the opportunity arose to return home. Their new task of escorting Trotsky raised the idea of a reckless plan. 'Trotsky, trying to impress the troops as a "fighting commander-in-chief", often set out with his personal escort on reconnaissance patrols along the front, and even made forays through gaps to the enemy's rear positions.' But on the day the Poles prepared their kidnap, everything went wrong because of an unexpected advance by the Reds. Raczyński just avoided disaster and they managed to cover their tracks. Their chance to take 'Polish leave' came later, and eventually they joined the 1st Kościuszko Regiment.

*

The whole pattern of the civil war across the vast Eurasian land mass tended to swing wildly from one direction to another. Mainly because of the huge distances involved, one side could enjoy a series of advances, over-extend itself, and then suddenly find that it had to retreat. After their astonishing successes in May, June and July, Czech units were now exhausted and demoralised. This was partly because they did not like finding themselves in alliance with reactionary officers. They preferred the Socialist Revolutionaries, but now that the days of the Komuch were clearly numbered, mainly due to lack of support from the peasantry, the Czechs began to think of home again.

At the same time, the solid and unflappable Vatsetis had stabilised his command on the Volga and redeployed his troops. With the 5th Army re-equipped, Trotsky stirred their anger and determination with his rousing speeches demanding revenge. They must drown their enemies in the Volga. 'Forward to Kazan!' On 4 September, as the fighting reached the outskirts of the city, the workers in Kazan's arsenal rebelled against the Whites. Many were massacred. The final attack went in six days later and the remaining Whites fled back down the Volga on steamers.

On 11 September, the day after the Reds recaptured Kazan, Trotsky addressed a huge crowd packed into its largest theatre. Referring to himself in the third person, he was obsessed with the idea that the whole Czech revolt and the rebellions on the Volga had been organised entirely by the British and French. 'The plan of the headquarters of the Allies and those in Kazan was as follows: to kill Lenin and capture Trotsky alive together with his train which was at that time in the station at Sviazhsk. Kappel was sent to kill Lenin. As for Trotsky, Savinkov undertook to fulfil this mission, along with Lebedev.' In fact it was Colonel Kappel, not Savinkov, who had come close to capturing Trotsky in the fighting close by at Tyurlema, when he managed to destroy their ammunition train. Trotsky could not resist linking the failure to kill or capture him with what he saw as the turning point in the civil war.

'At that time comrade Trotsky, without any doubt, would have been likely to die,' Trotsky continued. 'And not only comrade Trotsky . . . It seems to me that if we had been defeated near Tyurlema, then not only the Russian, but the social revolution would have been doomed. Success near Tyurlema would have increased the forces of our enemies ten-fold. They would have gone on from Kazan, captured a number of cities, organized a rebellion in Moscow and Petersburg . . . We lost a lot in Tyurlema, but the White Guards lost everything.'

On the next day, 12 September, Tukhachevsky's 1st Army secured a bridgehead on the eastern back of the Volga at Simbirsk. It had cost many casualties after his men crossed the kilometre-wide bridge there under heavy fire. This opened the advance on Samara down both banks. It was the beginning of the end for the Komuch. Deserters from its People's Army were now starting to cross over to the Red Army en masse.

The see-saw of the fighting on land was also true of river fighting between Red and White flotillas. On 18 September Raskolnikov's reinforced Volga flotilla pushed down past Kazan for 60 kilometres to the confluence of the Volga and Kama Rivers. As a member of the White squadron on the Kama recorded: 'the Bolsheviks' flotilla, which was better armed and better organised, consisted of armoured speed-boats that had been brought from the Baltic, but they had difficulty manoeuvring on small rivers, so they preferred to stay at a distance. They were afraid of the floating mines that we used, as they were always down river from us.'

The White vessels were mostly tugboats, armed with a gun on the foredeck with an improvised shield. The boats were commanded by Tsarist naval officers, with artillery gun-layers on deck while the stokers and engineers down below were locals. Refuelled up the Kama in Perm, they would sail down 'to the front line in order to help our troops and prevent the opponent's Red Fleet to seize the control of Kama'. But they had to admit that they were seldom able to give their own ground troops much assistance because of the lack of communications and the difficulty of even knowing where the front line was each day.

During moments of respite from the battles on the Kama, Larisa Reisner continued to write what would become her best-known book *The Front*. At Chistopol on the lower Kama a landing party of Red sailors from the *Kashin* managed to seize the town, which included a stud farm. The remarkable Reisner, who had learned to ride well, appropriated some of the horses and trained a number of her sailors as a cavalry reconnaissance troop.

For the Reds, the most critical moment of the civil war had passed and they had survived. 'All the most important locations that had been captured by the enemy were taken back by the autumn,' an assessment stated. 'Once the middle reaches of the Volga had been retaken, the

Soviet state breathed out with relief.' Their great advantage lay in their strategic position, and this would also prove to be the case in 1919 when the Whites again appeared triumphant. 'With a good network of railways going from the centre to the periphery, our leaders were able to move troops from one front to another. They used Napoleon's tactic of concentrating all the forces at a certain location, crashing down on the enemy's armies, and preventing them from joining up.'

19

From the Volga to Siberia
Autumn 1918

Just after the Czechs and Kappel's force captured Kazan on 7 August, another anti-Bolshevik rebellion broke out to the northeast in the direction of Perm. To the embarrassment of the Reds, munitions workers in the factories of Izhevsk and Votkinsk rose in revolt. They had been ordered to report for duty with the Red Army but were not allowed to serve together. Mostly Socialist Revolutionaries and Mensheviks, the workers were joined by Tsarist officers in the area. The Bolshevik minority in the two towns fled.

Berzin's 3rd Army north of the River Kama was given the task of crushing the rebellion, but at this time of Red weakness he could do little. A Kama region Komuch came into being with the idea of joining up with the Samara Komuch of the Constituent Assembly. After Vatsetis recaptured Kazan in the second week of September, Berzin was ordered to deal with Izhevsk and its allied munitions town of Votkinsk. Trotsky was determined that the Whites should not gain control of their factories.

Berzin sent a patchwork force of Red Guards, Baltic sailors and Chinese internationalists all commanded by a Latvian, Yuri Aplok. The Red Guards and sailors made a mess of their landing on the northern bank of the Kama and had to be withdrawn having lost many men. Aplok asked for reinforcements. Berzin replied that he would send eighty men immediately and his 350 Chinese the next day. They landed at the village of Babki, a little way upstream from Votkinsk. But even though they were far better disciplined, they found that the rebels had set up machine guns in the bell tower of the church, and the Chinese were forced to escape by boat.

The reinforcement of Red forces beyond the middle Volga made life in the Kama region hard for the Izhevsk and Votkinsk rebels. With insufficient volunteers they had to round up conscripts, many of whom deserted to the Reds. Cut off from key raw materials, their factories could not even produce enough ammunition for their own use. At the beginning of October the Red Army captured the town of Sarapul on the Kama south of Izhevsk. When it came to the key battle on 7 November, the rebels, apparently with bands playing, advanced in review order with unloaded rifles. Some of the Red troops lost their nerve and fled, but the outcome was not in doubt. Izhevsk was taken the next day. The rebels withdrew to Votkinsk and that too fell on 11 November, the day that the guns fell silent across western Europe.

Berzin and other Communist commanders on the Siberian-Volga front still had problems with the naval reinforcements they received. 'Over 300 mobilized sailors have arrived,' ran one report to Moscow. 'The majority of these men are of extremely low quality. It is impossible to allocate them to the detachments. Apart from that, many among them are sick or physically unfit ... Can you give instructions for the commissions at locations to conduct medical examinations before sending them off?' In one batch of forty, no less than twenty-eight had to be sent to hospital.

Communist bureaucrats were interested only in achieving the right numbers of reinforcements, and did little about their quality. Flerovsky, the commander-in-chief of the Baltic Fleet, felt obliged to warn Antonov-Ovseenko in Moscow. 'Over 4,000 mobilized men have arrived, they keep arriving every day. The Black Sea and White Sea Navy produce a particularly bad impression, as well as the armed detachment that was sent from Moscow. It is impossible to send them to the front without political and disciplinary training, and we are now concentrating all of our energy on this work.' Leaving aside the shortcomings in the naval infantry, the Red Army on the Volga Front had achieved a strength of 70,000 men. This included the Latvian regiments, and left the Western Front almost completely stripped of manpower.

For the Socialist Revolutionaries of the Komuch, the loss of Kazan and Simbirsk to the Reds on the middle Volga was a serious blow to morale. The peasants refused to join their People's Army and saw little point in fighting for the Constituent Assembly, and even less in fighting the Germans as the Left Socialist Revolutionaries still insisted. Desertion in the People's Army was a much greater problem than in the Red Army. In fact, the increasingly desperate brutality of its

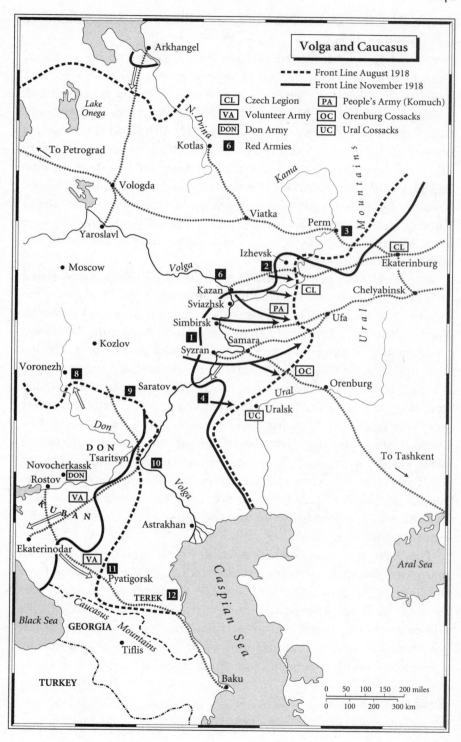

Volga and Caucasus

- - - - Front Line August 1918
———— Front Line November 1918

CL	Czech Legion	PA	People's Army (Komuch)
VA	Volunteer Army	OC	Orenburg Cossacks
DON	Don Army	UC	Ural Cossacks
6	Red Armies		

Arkhangel

Lake Onega

N. Dvina

Kotlas

Kama

Mountains

To Petrograd

Vologda

Viatka

Perm 3

CL

Yaroslavl

Izhevsk 2

Ekaterinburg

Moscow

Volga 6

Kazan

CL

Chelyabinsk

Sviazhsk

PA

Simbirsk

Ufa

Ural

Kozlov

1

Samara

Syzran

OC

Voronezh 8

Saratov

9

Orenburg

4

Ural

To Tashkent

UC Uralsk

Don

DON Tsaritsyn

Novocherkassk

DON

10

Volga

Rostov

VA

Aral Sea

KUBAN

Astrakhan

Ekaterinodar

VA

11

Pyatigorsk

Caspian Sea

TEREK 12

Black Sea

Caucasus Mountains

GEORGIA

Tiflis

TURKEY

Baku

| 0 | 50 | 100 | 150 | 200 miles |
| 0 | | 100 | 200 | 300 km |

officers to round up deserters from the villages provoked a number into outright revolt.

Colonel Kappel struggled to keep up the spirits of his so-called United Corps, which by the end of September was less than a division in strength. 'Valorous Troops! Great Russia is being reborn, albeit amidst great suffering. Your labours and the blood that you are shedding are creating the basis on which History will build the greatness of your Motherland . . . Your success fills with joy and hope the hearts of all the honest citizens of Russia. Our temporary and small-scale bad luck will soon pass.' He avoided mentioning the collapse of the Komuch by hailing the State Conference in Ufa to create a 'united Russian state authority'. The idea of the Ufa gathering was to agree an All-Russia government, bringing together all the anti-Bolshevik adminstrations.

After Tukhachevsky's capture of Simbirsk, the Komuch's days based at Samara had been numbered. On 7 October, the Red Army took the city, causing a flight of Socialist Revolutionaries nearly 500 kilometres eastwards to Ufa. Their only hope was to join this future All-Russia government, alongside the provisional Siberian government and the semi-independent Cossack 'khanates'. But considering how their own Komuch had been infiltrated and taken over by self-promoted reactionaries such as 'General' Galkin, their chances of controlling events were very small. The Socialist Revolutionary Yakov Dvorzhets had no illusions about dealing with 'the brutalised and brazen officers and Black Hundred reaction'.* He even considered staying in Samara with the Reds, rather than leave for Ufa to witness 'the end of the disgraceful adventure'. But since he knew what his fate would be if he did, he left for Ufa, where he 'witnessed the agony of Komuch's shameful bastard child'.

The Ufa State Conference opened on 8 September, although many of its delegates had not yet arrived. A guard of honour from the Samara People's Army and another of Orenburg Cossacks sent by Ataman Dutov greeted some of the trains. The conference in the Siberia Hotel was noisy, with more than 200 delegates from 'various governmental, party, national and public groups that had sprung up on the territory liberated from the Bolsheviks'. There was also a

---

* The Black Hundreds were the reactionary monarchist, nationalistic and anti-Semitic groups of Tsarist times supported by Nicholas II.

delegation from the Czechoslovak corps, even though they were not taking part.

Serebrennikov was all too aware of the tensions which had to be overcome if any agreement could be reached. On the Left there were the Socialist Revolutionaries who had lost Samara and the Volga but had the gold reserves and the support of the Czechs. 'On the right flank were representatives of the Siberian Government and the military governments of seven Cossack armies: Siberian, Ural, Orenburg, Semirechensk, Astrakhan, Enisei and Irkutsk.' They, of course, were supported by the merchants and landowners, who wanted their companies and estates back. 'I will never forget the pair of guards standing to attention with drawn swords in front of the door of General Galkin, commander of the People's Army of Komuch. Evil tongues claimed that the Komuch SRs were as scared of Galkin as the Siberian SRs used to be scared of Grishin-Almazov and that's why they had organized such a close watch.'

General Aleksei Grishin-Almazov was the youngest and most capable of the leaders in the Siberian Provisional Government in Omsk. The Socialist Revolutionaries feared him as a potential military dictator. They also hated him because he had used them as a flag of convenience to achieve his position and then discarded them. So, they turned their powerful supporters, the Czechs, against him. White Russian officers had already started to resent the Czechs, whom they felt were behaving in Siberia as if they had conquered it and were refusing to share out the booty. Like many other White Russians, Grishin-Almazov disliked the Czechs and the western Allies in general because they made them feel patronised.

In Chelyabinsk, after a few too many glasses of wine, Grishin-Almazov made an unwise as well as a wildly inaccurate announcement. 'Russians need the Allies less than the Allies need the Russians, because Russia is currently the only one that can assemble a fresh army which will decide the fate of the war.' He also told the chief Czech representative in Siberia: 'If you Czechs don't like it here, you can leave.' Eventually Czech and Allied pressure, supported by the Socialist Revolutionaries, forced his dismissal, but as so often happened in White Russian military politics, he was replaced by an even more reactionary officer.

The Ufa conference became increasingly split between the opposing poles of Samara and Omsk, which also meant between the ideals of the Constituent Assembly and the instincts of a military dictatorship. It finished on 23 September with an unconvincing compromise of a Directorate of five: two Siberian liberals, Vologodsky and Vinogradov; two Socialist Revolutionaries, Avksentiev and Zenzinov; and General Boldyrev, who was considered a supporter of the SRs. On the surface it was advantageous to the Socialist Revolutionaries, but that would be short-lived.

Vologodsky was tasked with setting up the new Council of Ministers of the All-Russia government. The process went on for almost fifteen days amid endless conflicts and intrigues. Once again, the atmosphere became extremely tense. The Siberians resented the theoretical advantage of the Socialist Revolutionaries. As soon as General Ivanov-Rinov replaced Grishin-Almazov as commander of the Siberian Army, he gave orders to restore officers' shoulder boards without discussing it with the new government. This was followed by more and more orders, 'many of which were not only of military, but also of political significance'.

The restoration of shoulder boards did little to improve the military performance of the White forces. By the first week in November, the Red Army had advanced all the way from Samara to Bolshaya Ustyuba, a village little more than 100 kilometres from Ufa. The retreating Whites were desperate to claim successes however small. When Esaul (captain) Shein's *sotnia* of Orenburg Cossacks raided the rear of the advancing enemy and forced them 'to retreat in haste', they made it sound like a great victory. Even Colonel Kappel was hard pressed to find exploits to celebrate. One was a reconnaissance mission by the 1st Kazan Rifle Regiment which 'captured a Maxim machine gun and five rifles and returned'. The Siberian Army issued a warning to the Reds against the use of improvised dum-dum bullets. 'Soldiers of the Siberian Government are being wounded with explosive bullets and some cartridges with chopped-off ends have been found on Red Army soldiers. All prisoners taken with such cartridges on them will be shot without mercy.' In Siberia, both Reds and Whites strung up the corpses of their victims from the branches of trees either side of the road. A growing population of wolves started to eat their feet.

Far worse horrors of war were to come. The Siberian Cossacks were trained in cruelty from the moment of recruitment, usually with an initiation through slaughter. 'I was taken to serve under Ataman Annenkov in October 1918,' wrote S.A. Zaborsky in testimony nine years later. 'The new recruits were distributed among the *sotnias* . . . Our regiment was sent to the area of Semipalatinsk. A small battle happened while we were on the way to the village Troitskoe. After the battle the detachment commander, Esaul Zotik, ordered us to hack to death absolutely everyone and then set the village on fire, and the order was carried out.'

Ataman Annenkov, who had served in the 1st Siberian Cossack Regiment, started his career during the civil war by organising a small detachment near Omsk. In the autumn of 1918 Annenkov set off towards the south, attacking rebellious villages on the way with great brutality, killing and plundering the population. His approach was very informal. Salutes were little more than a wave, and officers 'addressed each other and the Ataman himself with "ty" rather than "vy".' But Annenkov clearly had delusions of grandeur, creating regiments with dramatic titles – 'the Hussars of Death', the 'Blue Uhlans' and the 'Ataman's Life Guards'. The officers adopted an 'Ataman hairstyle with a fringe reaching down to their eye on one side'.

'Annenkov was a great cavalryman, an excellent shot with rifle and revolver, master of the sword, possessed a great physical strength, slender, young, good-looking, in short, a military man from head to foot,' wrote one of his officers later. 'He always appeared calm and balanced, and the charmed visitor would never guess that the Ataman who listened attentively to his request might immediately order a couple of killers to follow and dispatch him. However, he was not a good strategist.' He should also have added that Annenkov was a terrifying psychopath, as his subsequent conduct would reveal.

Ataman Semenov, he of the huge moustache and suspicious eyes, did not enjoy Annenkov's good looks. He had now established his base in Chita on the Trans-Siberian Railway, nearly 500 kilometres beyond the southern shore of Lake Baikal. Semenov's regime there was one of hedonistic corruption, with apparently limitless Champagne, his own orchestra formed from Austro-Hungarian prisoners of war, and many mistresses. His favourite, Masha, a singer from a Harbin nightclub, was Jewish, which perhaps suggested that he did not share the obsessive anti-Semitism of his close ally, Baron von Ungern-Sternberg.

Refugee women escaping from the Bolsheviks became trapped in Chita. Even wives or daughters of proud Tsarist officers found themselves reduced to prostitution and often a dependency on opium or cocaine. Semenov was basically an old-fashioned bandit, who financed his regime through seizing a portion of all the goods transported along the railway line. Knowing that he would never get away with this on his own, he made an alliance with the Imperial Japanese Army, which would see him through until their defeat in the region in 1945 and his execution by the conquering Red Army.

Siberian Cossacks were reactionary and proud of it. They despised civilians and above all Jews. Ataman Krasilnikov, whom the Socialist Revolutionary Zenzinov described as 'an ignorant and violent person', used to sing 'God Save the Tsar' when drunk at dinners. Allied officers – British, French and Czech – demanded to know how the Directorate, officially committed to the restoration of the Constitutional Assembly, could tolerate such monarchist manifestations.

As the Red Army advanced from the west, the Directorate had been forced to leave Ufa, which risked becoming a front-line city. Ekaterinburg and Omsk were the only two possible bases for the future All-Russian Provisional Government. On 7 October they chose Omsk and two days later the Directorate arrived.

'Its reception was not particularly festive,' Serebrennikov remembered. 'I think some simple arch had been constructed by the station. A small crowd assembled by the railway line where the train was going to stop, and the guard of honour was also there. I officially received the Directorate on behalf of the Siberian Government. The Directorate had to spend some time living in railway cars at the station. Omsk, which found itself an improvised capital, was completely full at that time, and it was extremely hard to find an apartment or even a room. There was a non-stop flow into Omsk of various diplomatic and military missions of the Allies, which demanded vast premises, while refugees were pouring in.'

Plotting and scheming between the factions within the Directorate became destructive. While the Socialist Revolutionaries held their candle for the Constituent Assembly, the Siberians and the military believed that only a dictatorship would work. The name most mentioned for the role of minister of defence was that of Admiral Kolchak, who was on his way from Vladivostok in the train of the Czech leader General Gajda. Boris Savinkov's name was also suggested. The ubiquitous Savinkov happened to be in Omsk but was seen as a 'dangerous man', so the Directorate decided to send him to Europe on a diplomatic errand to the Allies.

Soon after his arrival, Admiral Kolchak decided to introduce himself to the Siberian government, and Serebrennikov received him officially at the Council of Ministers. Kolchak appeared in a civilian suit accompanied by his secretary. He spoke in short, abrupt phrases. Serebrennikov was on the whole impressed. But Valentin Fedulenko, who became the head of Kolchak's bodyguard, suspected that the admiral himself secretly knew he was not made for the grand role being sketched out for him. 'He was a brilliant seaman, a great explorer, a man of rare talents . . . He was [also] very irascible, not very patient, and did not like it when his subordinates did not understand him.'

Kolchak attended the Directorate's next Council of Ministers as an observer. He was thus present when Vologodsky 'declared in a tired voice that all his efforts organizing the new governing authority had not yielded any positive results, that he was feeling completely exhausted from both the physical and the moral point of view, and that he refused to conduct any further negotiations or continue with his mission'. Vologodsky then stood up, passed the chairmanship to Serebrennikov and left the room. 'A sinister silence fell.' The Directorate by then had become something of a joke and was given the nickname 'The Trajectory'.

'Everyone's eyes then turned to Admiral Kolchak,' wrote Serebrennikov, 'as if saying: "Here is the only one who is still persevering. Everything now depends on him." I turned to the admiral and proposed to him on behalf of the entire conference to save the situation by becoming part of the Council of Ministers . . . After a few seconds of tormenting wait, the Admiral finally gave in and accepted. The crisis was resolved.'

During the night of 17–18 November, Cossack patrols appeared in the streets of Omsk, arresting members of what they saw as the far too liberal Directorate. Serebrennikov was also arrested, but then released by the officer of another passing patrol. He was given the password which would allow him to return home unhindered. It was 'Yermak', the first name of the Cossack ataman Timofeyevich who began the conquest of Siberia for Ivan the Terrible in the sixteenth century. Kolchak was appointed 'Supreme Ruler' the next morning. This 'criminal coup' prompted denunciations and threats with a telegram from the ministers of the Komuch, warning that the Allies would be informed.

The Socialist Revolutionaries arrested at gunpoint the night before by Krasilnikov's Cossack officers were furious, but not entirely surprised. 'We felt the reactionary influence of the former Siberian government on the very first day after our arrival in Omsk,' wrote Vladimir Zenzinov. 'It felt as if we were living in a forest of political intrigues and gossip. The military circles in Siberia were clearly anti-democratic, and some were even monarchist.' Two days later, Zenzinov and other Socialist Revolutionaries were taken under Cossack guard by train to the Chinese border, where they were released and told not to return.

The Byzantine politics in Siberia made President Woodrow Wilson extremely cautious. His secretary of war had warned the commander of the American Expeditionary Force, Major General William S. Graves, 'Watch your step. You will be walking on eggs loaded with dynamite, God bless you.' Graves's orders in an aide memoire drafted by the President himself limited him to facilitating the safe exit of the Czech Legion from Russia, guarding the nearly $1 billion worth of American military equipment stored at Vladivostok and Murmansk, and helping the 'democratic' Russians organise their new government.

Graves, who looked like an old-fashioned schoolmaster with his toothbrush moustache and rimless spectacles, reached Vladivostok on 1 September, a month after the first US units. But the end of the war in Europe in November did not mean a homecoming for the American Expeditionary Force in Siberia. Wilson wanted to pursue a 'wait and see' policy until the Paris peace conference concluded, before deciding which of several Russian governments to recognise and whether to withdraw the AEF from Vladivostok.

Apart from the deteriorating military situation, Kolchak's first problem to resolve was the Trans-Siberian Railway and the Czech trains. Kolchak overlooked the fact that workers on the Baikal Railway were on strike, because they had 'not received any pay for four months'. Instead he complained to the senior Allied officer in Siberia, the French General Pierre Janin, as well as to Major General Knox, to Consul-General Harris and to the Japanese that 'organized traffic was harmed by the interference of Czech trains in the operation of the railways. The Czechs have demanded that only their trains should be allowed through . . . If the situation continues, it will lead to the complete

American troops land in Vladivostok.

halt of Russian trains. If this happens I will reserve the right to take extreme measures.' Kolchak may have arrived in Omsk as the guest of the Czech General Gajda on his train, but his quarrels with the Czechs over who controlled the Trans-Siberian Railway would eventually lead to his own betrayal and execution.

Another problem was Ataman Semenov at Chita. 'I cannot recognise Admiral Kolchak as the Supreme Ruler of the state,' Semenov wrote in a telegram to Omsk which arrived on 25 November. 'I propose the following candidates who are all acceptable to me: Generals Denikin, Horvath and Dutov – for this extremely responsible post.' American diplomats, both Ambassador Morris in Tokyo and Consul-General Harris in Irkutsk, guessed who was responsible for this provocation. They were already concerned about the 'excessive Japanese forces in Siberia'. Japan, Morris observed, 'seems generally to be pursuing a policy to prevent the establishment of any kind of united orderly government in Siberia'. General Kouroki, he heard, had advised Semenov and other atamans not to cooperate with Kolchak. And the Japanese were also starting to take control of the Chinese Eastern Railway.

General Knox, the British representative, ordered Major Steveni to go and find out more about Semenov's refusal to recognise Kolchak. Steveni found him 'sitting astride the Trans-Siberian Railway and interfering with the movement of munition trains, then already carrying military stores to Admiral Kolchak's forces operating in western Siberia beyond Omsk'. Semenov, who had been wounded in a bomb attack, had retired to bed with Masha. He promised not to interfere with trains, but Steveni did not believe him. So, he went to visit General Oba, the commander of the 3rd Nagoya Infantry Division who had his headquarters in Chita. They agreed that in future munitions trains would go through with British military personnel as escorts.

Major General Graves (seated centre) meets Ataman Semenov (seated left) whom he abhorred.

Kolchak's fury against Semenov startled Serebrennikov. 'If Ataman Semenov had fallen into his hands now, the Admiral would not have hesitated to have him shot on the spot.' Kolchak's sycophantic entourage fanned his anger, to the point that he issued an order dismissing Semenov from all his positions. With tacit Japanese support, Semenov still refused to obey orders and cut communications with Omsk. This ill-considered démarche served only to undermine Kolchak's authority.

It also became clear that Kolchak, along with all the White military commanders and Cossack warlords in Siberia, did not have any idea of how to deal with their notional Japanese ally or with the Chinese authorities along their southern flank. China was a vital source of food and raw materials for the whole of eastern Siberia – the Transbaikal, Amur and Maritime provinces. White warlords, such as Semenov in Chita, Kalmykov with his Ussuri Cossacks in Khabarovsk, Rozonov in Vladivostok and Ungern-Sternberg on the Mongolian border, provoked a deep resentment among the Chinese of their imperialistic behaviour. Their 'anarchic militarism', which left a 'trail of havoc and devastation', was seen by the Chinese as a return to those Tsarist Russians who had imposed 'unequal treaties' and heaped humiliation on the fragile Qing Empire of the late nineteenth century. The Reds, on the other hand, proved far more intelligent in their overtures to the Chinese authorities, emphasising their anti-imperialist ideology.

The most urgent task facing Kolchak, the Supreme Ruler, was man-power. His chief of staff envisaged an army of 700,000 men. Kolchak's aide Fedulenko noted that the Siberian peasantry was 'enormously rich' yet was deeply reluctant to join the fight against the Bolsheviks. 'I was amazed at their wealth and yet despite all this they were completely passive, as though our fight did not concern them.' Kolchak had to introduce conscription but most of the recruits deserted at the first opportunity.

An unexpected reinforcement arrived in the form of a Polish Legion, which joined the recently promoted Major General Kappel's Integrated Corps. 'Valorous troops, our Polish Brothers!' he greeted them. 'Your arrival at our front was associated with an important military success achieved in five days of hard fighting, in which you have demonstrated your knightly valour and the great strength of your spirit.' The Polish community in Siberia had been invigorated by the proclamation of their country's independence and did not trust the Communist gov-ernment. 'The Bolshevik press spoke of Poles as foreigners with a large dose of sarcasm,' they noted. What soon became called the 'Polish Army in Siberia' demanded transfer back to the home country to defend its new borders.

General Pierre Janin was not impressed by Kolchak's chief of staff, whom he had 'last met as a captain with the Stavka at Mogilev and considered over-promoted then'. Nor did he think much of those around Kolchak. 'Reliable men seem rare to a degree which aston-ishes me despite my experience from so many travels.' And as for the

Supreme Ruler himself, Janin was unconvinced by his 'pretention to military competence in the tactics of ground forces'.

During the night of 22 December, a Bolshevik uprising took place in Omsk. Armed workers, including one unit won over by Bolshevik propaganda, attempted a coup. The rebels seized the prison and released all the prisoners. They also seized the station and the weapons of the railway police. This uprising was suppressed by Cossacks with predictable brutality, and almost all of the rebel workers were killed.

There were many political prisoners among those freed from the jail, not only Bolsheviks, but also some prominent Socialists who had recently refused to accept Kolchak as Supreme Ruler. The garrison commander, General Brzhezovsky, issued the order: 'All those unlawfully freed from the jail are to return there at once; all those that fail to do so will be immediately shot if arrested.' This caused great alarm among those released, many of whom had been working for the Directorate. Some of them begged friends to ask the minister of justice in Kolchak's government what they should do. The advice came back that the safest thing would be to return to the prison, which they did the next day. But that night some drunken officers came to their cells, hauled out twelve of them and took them to the frozen River Irtysh where they were hacked to death with sabres on the ice. Seven of them were Right Socialist Revolutionary members of the Constituent Assembly. The body of one of them, Ivan Fomin, had thirteen sabre slashes, of which five had been inflicted while he was still alive. The leader of the drunken killers was arrested, but then released. He went off to join Ataman Annenkov's Siberian Cossacks.

This horrific incident was deeply embarrassing for Kolchak at a time when he was trying to persuade the British and French of his democratic credentials. General Janin absented himself just afterwards, leaving on a visit to General Gajda in Ekaterinburg, who greeted him at the station with a Czech guard of honour. Janin, a tall man wearing his French general's red and gold *képi* and a huge bearskin coat with a ceremonial sword outside, was not impressed by the squalor he found there. 'Horse manure and goat droppings everywhere,' he noted in his diary, unsurprised to hear of a typhus epidemic developing. He assessed Gajda as surprisingly young, with a prominent nose. He heard that he was a man of difficult moods, but that he also possessed natural military qualities. Gajda, who had taken over the ill-fated Ipatiev House as his headquarters after the capture of Ekaterinburg, held a huge open-square parade in the snow. This took place outside the walls of a monastery on 8 December with bands, colour parties and Maxim machine guns on wheels lined up in front of their ranks. His Czechoslovak troops wore a mixture of uniforms. Most had Russian greatcoats and high Cossack sheepskin *papakhas*, but many still wore their tall képis from the Austro-Hungarian army.

Another commander in Siberia with natural military qualities was the twenty-seven-year-old General Anatoly Pepelyayev. He was the younger brother of Viktor Pepelyayev, who became Kolchak's prime minister and would be executed with him. A lieutenant colonel before the Bolsheviks' October coup, he subsequently raised a large volunteer force in his native city of Tomsk. In the summer he had advanced rapidly to the east from Krasnoyarsk to Chita where he linked up with Ataman Semenov. Then he took his Siberian Corps west to the Ural Front. There they found themselves up against Berzin's 3rd Army, which included a Chinese regiment commanded by Zen Fu-Cheng. Its machine gun detachment was well armed with Maxim, Colt and Lewis guns. There was heavy fighting in deep snow at Nizhnyaya Tura, 250 kilometres north of Ekaterinburg, which changed hands several times. 'We had to save ammunition, so we were firing in short bursts,' one of the machine gunners recorded. 'A Chinese rifle platoon was covering our flanks. Exactly thirty minutes later we loaded the machine guns onto the carts and retreated into the forest. Commander Li Tse-hen said to me: "We don't want to die, we still need to beat the Whites, so I order you to take us through the forest to the village of Aleksandrovka, so that we join up with the 17th Petrograd Regiment."'

Berzin's 3rd Army on the northern flank of the Ural Front was beaten back towards Perm in December, in one of the few White successes on the Eastern Front. The Red forces also suffered from a lack of winter clothing, especially a shortage of *valenki* felt boots. Whole regiments were reduced to little more than 120 men because of 'frostbite and disease'. Even a company of Red Finnish volunteers lost seventy men out of 160. The Red artillery ran out of shells and the retreat became chaotic. The brigade commissar had to force the commander to return to his headquarters and replace him on the spot. He found units retreating in columns down the highway to Perm. Vasily Blyukher, a partisan commander who later became a Marshal of the Soviet Union, took over and ordered the 5th Brigade to withdraw towards Perm to redeploy. It was not ready to move as he had ordered, so he arrested the brigade commander and told the chief of staff to take over.

The Chinese regiment suffered so many casualties in the retreat to Perm that it had to be reinforced with local recruits and was renamed the Chinese Internationalist Battalion. Still the Siberian Corps and Czech units kept advancing. 'The White Guards' artillery was firing at the city streets with shrapnel; enemies of the Revolution from among local dwellers began firing with rifles . . . Some of the former Tsarist officers who were serving with the Reds betrayed us and defected to the enemy's ranks together with their units. The traitors captured the city's arsenal, installed machine guns on the tall buildings, and opened fire on the Reds. Units of the 3rd Army left Perm and the enemy immediately attacked the retreating troops. Losses were great. Hundreds or even thousands of Red warriors died when crossing the river Kama.'

The Siberian Corps captured 20,000 demoralised conscripts from the pitiful remnants of Berzin's 3rd Army. This victory, which shocked the Communist leadership in Moscow, made Pepelyayev a great hero in Omsk at an opportune moment. Kolchak and his administration wanted to divert attention away from the massacre of the Socialist Revolutionary deputies and the loss of Ufa on the southern sector. Meanwhile Pepelyayev wanted to carry his advance on to Vyatka, the over-optimistic objective of the British advancing south from Arkhangel, but the temperature dropped so low that it would have been madness. He knew, like almost everyone else, that the coming year would see the decisive battles for the future of the former Russian empire.

20

The Central Powers Depart
Autumn–Winter 1918

On 11 November 1918, after more than four years of mud and slaughter, a ghostly silence descended along the whole of the Western Front. The armistice terms dictated by the Entente in the forest at Compiègne also forced Germany to renounce the Treaty of Brest-Litovsk, and withdraw all its occupation forces in the east behind Germany's pre-1914 borders. The only exception allowed was in the Baltic provinces, so that Estonia, Latvia and Lithuania would not be over-run by the Bolsheviks. Two days later, the Sovnarkom announced that it too renounced the treaty but also reclaimed authority over the three provinces.

Just the week before, Bruce Lockhart had written to Arthur Balfour, the foreign secretary: 'It is obvious today first, that even if Lenin took money from the German Government, he used it for his own ends and not for German ends, and secondly, that Bolshevism has now gone far beyond the stage of any outside control. It is perhaps no exaggeration to say that Bolshevism is now a far greater danger to Europe than German militarism.'

The Communist leadership saw the Baltic coast as the vital route to link up with the German revolution, spreading it from the High Seas Fleet in Kiel and Wilhelmshaven to Berlin and to Munich. The treaty of Brest-Litovsk had been Germany's greatest triumph in the whole of the First World War. But now, just eight months later, all its hopes of an eastern empire from the Black Sea to the Baltic had collapsed. This was something which Adolf Hitler burned to revive twenty-three years later.

An uneasy inter-regnum began across Ukraine and the Crimea. The first German troops to be withdrawn were pulled back from their easternmost point, the Taman peninsula sticking into the Sea of Azov. 'They disappeared in the night, quietly, as if they had never been there at all,' recorded Maksim Kulik of the White Taman Regiment, which the Germans had been supporting. 'One morning,' wrote Nadezhda Dubakina in the Crimea, 'the maid who brought us the samovar said that the Germans had disappeared. When I went out there was a sinister silence. It was completely calm in Simferopol for two or three days, but then rumours began to spread that the Bolsheviks were getting close and that it was time to leave.' In Odessa the locals joked that the Germans were sure to have swept the floors of their offices before they went, but this was to mask their fear at what came next.

The sudden departure of German forces in the south left many exposed again to the return of Petliura's Ukrainian nationalists, and then to Red forces. Those landowners who had used German troops to avenge themselves on the peasants who had seized their land now faced retaliation. There were a number of cases of White officers taking a group of mounted Cossacks, supposedly on a reconnaissance mission, to exact revenge. One, when asked what he had been up to after a three-day absence, replied: 'Well, we went with the captain to his estate in order to whip the muzhiks for ploughing up his land.' The punishment was exacted in the Tsarist army fashion of flogging with rifle-cleaning rods.

On 14 December, as Petliura's forces approached Kiev, the hetman Skoropadsky escaped, pretending to be a wounded German officer. He settled in Berlin, where he purchased a property on the Wannsee. The villa had plenty of wall space for all the portraits of his hetman ancestors, and he developed a large vegetable garden of which he was very proud. But unlike other White Russian generals sheltered in Germany, he avoided having anything to do with the Nazis. In the spring of 1945, while escaping a second time from advancing Soviet forces, he was mortally wounded in an Allied bombing attack.

The arrival of British and French warships offshore raised great hopes in Odessa, but no troops landed at first. Petliura's forces attacked the city on 18 December. Officers of the Volunteer Army fought back, as did a detachment of the Polish Legion trapped there. The Ukrainian artillery bombarded the Hotel Passage, the city park and the port. The French gave them an ultimatum and by nightfall the battle was over.

The next day, Yelena Lakier went out to view the damage with her grandmother. 'Suddenly we saw a hearse half-filled with corpses,' she wrote in her diary. 'We saw bare legs sticking out. These were Petliura's men on the way to the mortuary.' French forces then landed, sailors in striped shirts and navy blue berets with red pom-poms, Zouaves, and some infantry from the 156th Division. Rumours spread in the city that Ukraine would become a French *département*, with President Poincaré himself coming to inaugurate it.

At first the French did not meddle much in the internal affairs of the Russian administration, but as more troops and headquarters arrived, the French commander General Philippe d'Anselme wanted to enlarge the zone of occupation as much as possible. The Volunteer Army in Odessa was commanded by Grishin Almazov, who had arrived from Omsk. Their relations with the French were embittered by Anselme's intention to negotiate with Petliura's representative. Two battalions of Greek troops also landed.

Globachev, the former head of the Okhrana who was running the Whites' intelligence service, was distinctly uneasy at the effectiveness of Bolshevik propaganda directed at French troops. 'The French occupation forces in Odessa were undisciplined,' he wrote. 'The soldiers spent time drinking with Jews and Jewesses. There were lots of Bolshevik agitators who spoke French. By February there was unrest among the soldiers of the Allies and the sailors who were tired of the war wanted to return home. There were also some who openly took the side of the Bolsheviks, and French counter-intelligence did little to fight Bolshevik propaganda.'

Criminal activity had also reached 'monstrous proportions'. Soaring food prices meant that sugar profiteers became 'the economic dictators of Odessa'. The Volunteer Army decided to take extreme measures. Robbers caught red-handed were shot without mercy, and the police were told to kill known thieves like dogs when they came across them. Mischka Yaponchik, known as 'Mischa the Japanese' (in reality Moisei Vinnitsky), and his enormous gang terrorised the town, while working closely with covert Reds. The Communists gave him command of his own regiment when he helped their takeover later, but the Cheka ambushed and killed him as soon as he was no longer useful.

Further east, the Red Army concentrated forces between Voronezh and Saratov to prevent any chance of Kolchak's forces joining up with Denikin's. Eduard Dune, the young Latvian Red Guard from Moscow, was sent as a commissar to the headquarters of the 9th Army on the southern front in Balashov, due west of Saratov. He was astonished at how unlike a proletarian army it was. 'The headquarters personnel were well-dressed, with no stubble on their cheeks,' he noted. 'They addressed each other by name and patronymic and were emphatically polite to visitors like me. There was no *makhorka* smoke there and no cigarette butts on the parquet floor.'

As he had lunch in the canteen he was told he was being attached to the 1st Nizhny Novgorod Regiment. Late the next day he finally caught up with their convoy of carts and field kitchens. 'The unit was marching as if on parade. The regiment commander introduced me to the battalion commanders.' He also found that 'Red Army soldiers were not talking in a Soviet manner. They addressed the regimental commander as "colonel" and referred to someone else as "our captain". It was clear that military men from the Tsar's army were in charge here, and no familiarity would be possible, even if I wanted it.' The soldiers were peasants who talked only of home or admired the rich soil of the area in which they found themselves. 'Whites or Reds, revolution or counter-revolution, nationalisation or socialisation, all of this was absolute gibberish to them, and about as interesting and intelligible as a sermon from the pulpit. I started feeling very uncomfortable as an outsider. There was nothing I could discuss with the soldiers and even less with the commanders who were former officers.'

Dune soon heard rumours of treason in the 9th Army headquarters which focused on its 15th Division. The commander, a former Guards officer called Gusarsky, was executed on Trotsky's order, yet those who knew him were convinced he was innocent. 'Trotsky found the wrong culprit,' Dune wrote later. He was convinced that the traitor was the 9th Army commander, Knyagnitsky, who 'in the autumn of 1919 abandoned his troops and joined Denikin's army as it advanced'.

In November, during the Volunteer Army's advance into the Donbas after the German withdrawal, General Vladimir Mai-Maevsky was in command of the western flank. Mai-Maevsky was so obese that he could hardly fit into his uniforms. With heavy jowls, a huge 'plum-like nose', shaggy moustache and pince-nez, he looked more like a dissolute circus manager, even though he had commanded the 1st Guards Corps in the Tsarist army just before the Bolshevik takeover. Mai-Maevsky was not just a glutton, but also a dissolute pasha with a travelling brothel. He was also an extraordinarily effective and courageous general in this railway war, during which the station of Konstantinovka changed hands twenty-eight times. Ungainly and sweating profusely, Mai-Maevsky was constantly at the front and he never took cover from the bullets which inexplicably failed to hit such a large and tempting target. His great skill was to use aircraft for reconnaissance and move his far smaller forces rapidly from one spot to another on the Donbas's railway network.

General Vladimir Mai-Maevsky.

Within his command he had the Samur regiment based on the 83rd Infantry Regiment, which consisted almost entirely of Red Army captives who still fought bravely for the Whites. Mai-Maevsky also worked closely with the impudent and cruel Kuban Cossack Andrei Shkuro. He was, however, unconvinced by Shkuro's report on his battle with the Anarchist guerrillas of Nestor Makhno near Hughesovka (later Stalino, and now Donetsk). 'Makhno's men bolted in panic, abandoning their weapons, fur coats and even boots,' Shkuro wrote to him. 'I think Andrei must be exaggerating a bit,' Mai-Maevsky remarked drily to his chief radio officer, Erast Chevdar.

According to one of his orderly officers, a secret Bolshevik called Pavel Makarov, Mai-Maevsky was more afraid of Makhno than of the Red Army. 'Makhno always turned up unexpectedly and interfered with Mai-Maevsky's offensive,' he wrote. 'The general allocated special units, commanded by General Revishin, to fight against Makhno. His headquarters were at the Volnovakha station, and Mai-Maevsky visited them many times. General Mai-Maevsky would smile. "I don't doubt your ability, but it is not likely that you will manage to catch him. I am following his operations closely and I wouldn't mind having such an experienced troop leader on my side."'

Nestor Makhno.

Nestor Makhno was one of the most extraordinary leaders of the civil war. Even though he was very short and looked young for his age, he was known by his men and the peasants of southeastern Ukraine as 'Batko' or 'Father'. Some saw him as an Anarchist ataman, others as a mounted gangster, and many as a Robin Hood of the steppe. He was born to an impoverished peasant family from the large village of Gulyai-Polye in the *guberniya* of Ekaterinoslav (Dnipro). Gulyai-Polye, where he was elected president of the local soviet in 1917, would later become his base of operations against the Whites, Petliura and the Red Army.

The revolt against the German and Austrian looting of the countryside had started in the summer of 1918. Mounted guerrilla bands struck back at the occupiers, and the landlords of the grain producers' association led by the Hetman Skoropadsky. Makhno, who returned from Moscow in July, rapidly proved to be a brilliant and persuasive organiser as he brought the different bands together into a considerable force. He soon became a legendary figure for his reckless bravery and clever tactics. The vicious circle of revenge and repression intensified. Officers, whether German, Austrian or Ukrainian, were killed while ordinary soldiers or members of the Varta militia were disarmed and released if they had not committed acts of cruelty.

In November Makhno's forces took the city of Ekaterinoslav from the Petliurists by one of his ruses. He packed a train with his troops disguised as workers and sent it straight into the main station. His men charged out and seized the city centre. After just three days, Makhno's force pulled out again. He was to use the railways often when moving his men over greater distances. From a station platform, Paustovsky described them passing through. 'I could see the laughing faces of young fellows loaded down with weapons – curved swords, naval cutlasses, silver handled daggers, revolvers, rifles and cartridge pouches made of oilskin. Enormous black and red ribbons flew from every kind of hat and sheepskin cap.'

The Revolutionary Insurrectionary Army of Ukraine was a force to be reckoned with. Many called it the Black Army because of its black Anarchist flags. It could also be called a flying army for its speed across country, with cavalry and their Parthian weapon guarding against pursuit after a raid. This was the *tachanka*, a droshky open carriage pulled by a *troika* of horses, with a heavy machine gun mounted at the back. They used the *tachanka* as the equivalent of an ancient chariot, with a driver, rifleman and machine gunner. Their enemies – whether Red, White or Ukrainian Nationalist – had been warned.

Although an ally of the Reds to start with, Makhno and his followers turned against their dictatorial state Communism later. As the war swung in different directions, both Whites and Reds would send a force to occupy Gulyai-Polye, hoping to catch the legendary rebel, but often they themselves would be taken by surprise in a sudden night attack.

Makhno's wife, Galina Kuzmenko, described one such counter-attack in her diary: 'Red Army soldiers did not protest very much; they surrendered their weapons quickly while their commanders fought to the end, until they were killed on the spot. By the morning almost three quarters of the 6th Regiment were disarmed. Part of the regiment engaged bravely in a fire-fight with us, but when they learned that their comrades had already been disarmed, they surrendered their weapons on their own initiative. Our lads were very cold and tired, but every one of them was rewarded by the realization that even a small group of people, with weak bodies but strong spirit, inspired by one great idea, can achieve great deeds. In several hours, 70 or 75 of our lads had captured over 450–500 of the enemy, killed almost all of their commanders and taken a lot of rifles, cartridges, machine-guns, carts, and horses.'*

A White horse artillery officer, part of the special force assembled to hunt him down, acknowledged that 'the whole population was on Makhno's side'.† He also admitted that he was so scared of being captured by Makhnovists that when he finally reached safety after a lonely ride returning to the battery, 'my legs were so weak that I almost fell from the saddle.'

Once, when they entered a village, he asked a peasant which side he was on. 'Nobody's,' he replied. 'The Whites pillage, the Reds pillage, the Makhnovists pillage. So, who do you think we should support?' This White officer called Mamontov discovered for himself that soldiers did not pillage just to eat. He was once persuaded to go out looting by some comrades to see what it was like. It disgusted him, 'but another bad feeling invaded me little by little. The intoxication of absolute power. These terrified people were at your mercy. You could do with them what you wanted.'

Far to the southeast, Dunsterforce had been withdrawn from the Caucasus and disbanded following the armistice with the Ottoman

---

* Doubts over the authenticity of Kuzmenko's diary have been raised. There are indeed parts added to it which appear dubious, but that does not necessarily mean that all is false.

† The special force consisted of three squadrons of the 2nd Officers Mounted Regiment, two companies of the Drozdovsky Infantry Regiment and the 11th Ingermanland Hussars, the remains of a regular regiment from the Tsarist army.

Empire. But the other two British military missions across the inland sea in Transcaspia (subsequently known as Turkmenistan), found themselves in action against the Red Army. In July, the Socialist Revolutionary organisation in Askhabad had signed a military assistance agreement with Major General Malleson in Meshed. With pretentions to forming a government, the Askhabad Committee was led by Fyodor Funtikov, an engine driver on the Central Asian Railway who, according to Captain Teague-Jones, was unsubtle, verbose (a fault not helped by a stutter) and had a tendency to drink too much (perhaps to get over the stutter). His deputy was another railwayman called Kurilev, a more dramatic character, who never went anywhere without a very large revolver and a leather briefcase. Other members of this improbable Socialist Revolutionary administration included Count Aleksei Iosepovich Dorrer, a multiple bigamist called Dokhov and a mysterious stranger who had just appeared in Askhabad called Semeon Lvovich Drushkin. Funtikov, trusting him to be a fellow Socialist Revolutionary and lawyer, appointed him head of the security police. With no professional expertise, the finances of the Askhabad Committee fell into chaos. Soon there was no fuel and the railway workers were left unpaid.

The commander of Transcaspia's tiny army was 'a fine-looking old Turkman named Oraz Sardar'. Many of his fellow Turkmen wore astrakhan *papakhas* as large as guardsmen's bearskins. Advancing from the north, the far larger Bolshevik force they faced had been greatly strengthened by Magyar prisoners of war from the Austro-Hungarian Army. On 25 August there was fierce fighting at Kaahka, southeast of Askhabad. The Reds attacked but a machine gun platoon of the 19th Punjabis, supporting Oraz Sardar's men, inflicted heavy casualties. The rest of the battalion and a squadron of 28th Lancers were hastening to the scene, all the officers in regulation solar topis under the ferocious sun. The Indian Army sepoys wearing their distinctive khaki turbans were at first a little confused, since many on both sides wore similar goatskin caps. But they gave a very good account of themselves and the Reds pulled back to re-form. A lull in the fighting followed.

At dawn on 15 September, Mikoyan, Shahumyan, Petrov and the other Bolshevik leaders who had fled the fall of Baku in the steamer *Turkmen* arrived off the harbour of Krasnovodsk in Transcaspia, despite having ordered the captain of their steamer to take them to the Red stronghold of Astrakhan. The captain sounded his siren as they approached to alert the guardship, which came alongside. The Bolsheviks on board were forced to surrender. They were all arrested and marched off to the local jail.

The commandant wired the Askhabad Committee to ask for instructions. They in turn contacted their representative in Meshed, the bigamist Dokhov, and told him to ask Major General Malleson if the British could take the prisoners back to India. According to Teague-Jones, Malleson replied on 18 September that he simply did not have the guards or transport to do that. On the other hand, Malleson and the chief of the general staff in Simla believed that the commissars might prove useful as hostages to exchange for any Britons taken prisoner by the Bolsheviks, but Teague-Jones made no mention of that in his diary or in his official report to the Foreign Office later.

That afternoon, Teague-Jones attended a meeting at Count Dorrer's house with Funtikov, the head of the Askhabad administration, Kurilev of the large revolver, and the schoolmaster Zimin, who acted as 'foreign minister'. Teague-Jones, who was on crutches having been wounded in the thigh during the battle at Kaahka, was exhausted. His role of political officer as well as intelligence officer seemed to cover everything in the area, from dealing with the British and Indian wounded to acting as interpreter in the hospital, as well as for all Anglo-Russian dealings. He claimed to have had no more than 'a hazy recollection' of what was said, but admitted that he did not intervene when Funtikov and Kurilev suggested shooting them, while Zimin and Dorrer disagreed. 'I remained strictly neutral and took no active part in the discussion,' he wrote

The next evening, 19 September, Teague-Jones heard from Funtikov that they had decided to shoot the 'twenty-six commissars', as they were soon to become known. He almost certainly could have stopped the executions if he had insisted since the Askhabad Committee depended on the British. The following evening, 20 September, Kurilev had the twenty-six, including Lenin's friend Shahumyan, loaded into a railway truck. Anastas Mikoyan was, inexplicably, not among them. They were taken along the line some 60 kilometres from Krasnovodsk and executed in batches beside the track.

When news of the killings reached Moscow, Bolshevik fury exploded. Trotsky accused Teague-Jones of ordering the murders personally, and Stalin in April 1919 denounced the British as 'cannibals'.

The Baku commissars became Soviet martyrs. Their deaths were commemorated in monuments, postage stamps and other iconography, a poem by Sergei Yesenin, 'The Ballad of the Twenty-Six', and a highly imaginative painting of the execution by Isaak Brodsky, depicting the scene in daylight, with both General Malleson and Teague-Jones looking on. Teague-Jones in fact had been well over 300 kilometres away and Malleson in Meshed in Persia. As recently as 2004, a Russian historian claimed that all the prisoners had been decapitated by a giant Turkman with a huge sabre.

The Royal Navy flotilla on the Caspian, on the other hand, seem to have regarded the killings as an amusing bit of local colour. They heard that the leader of the firing party had complained to Funtikov: 'Your orders have been carried out, but the five spades provided were hardly enough for the work.' From then on they referred to Funtikov as 'the five of spades'.

The Transcaspian front relapsed into inactivity, mainly because the Bolsheviks north of the Central Asian line were convinced that British Indian forces in the area were far larger than was the case. Both sides had an armoured train in action which would play 'tip and run', advancing up the line to a convenient cutting, firing a shell and promptly going into reverse. British troops had received orders not to advance beyond Bairam Ali and certainly not to the line of the River Oxus as the Transcaspians wanted. The conviction in Moscow that the British were secretly planning to occupy all of Transcaspia was very far from the case.

Major General Malleson sat in his headquarters in Meshed and came over the frontier to Askhabad only once that year, for a few days in mid-November. Communications between British Indian headquarters in Baghdad, Meshed and Enzeli had never been good. They had also not improved when the Royal Navy organised its Caspian Sea flotilla to help defend Baku and Transcaspia from the Turks and resist the Red flotilla operating out of Astrakhan and the Volga delta. Commodore David Norris, the commander, brought some 4-inch naval guns by road from Baghdad to mount on Caspian ships. The steamship *Kruger* now became HMS *Kruger*, as his flagship. The flotilla included another five armed merchantmen serving as auxiliary cruisers flying the White Ensign. Later on, a dozen of the Navy's very fast coastal motorboats arrived by train from Batumi on the Black

Sea. After the departure of Turkish forces, the Caspian would soon see three flotillas in action, a Red flotilla, a White one and the Royal Navy, by then based in Baku, defended by the 27th Indian Division.

Events in the Caspian region sometimes had a superficial flavour of operetta, but tragedy and pitiless violence were never far away. The Turkmen, whose historic activity had been raiding Persian frontier regions and then selling their captives, mainly women, as slaves, now feared the future. As Teague-Jones observed, once the British withdrew, they 'had no illusions as to their own fate at the hands of the Reds'.

21

The Baltic and Northern Russia
Autumn–Winter 1918

Southwest of Petrograd, the German withdrawal left General Aleksandr Rodzyanko's small White force, the Northern Corps, exposed in the city of Pskov near the southern end of Lake Peipus. As the Red 7th Army reached the outskirts, Rodzyanko's very mixed force of Tsarist officers and reluctant conscripts, some 5,000 strong, scuttled back across the frontier into Estonia. Rodzyanko, the nephew of the former President of the State Duma, had been a member of the Tsar's Chevalier Guards and an Olympic rider, which were not qualifications to make him popular with the Estonians. He, like most Tsarist officers, regarded their country as an integral part of Russia, but at that moment the Estonians were intensely vulnerable and needed support. The German 405th Infantry Regiment had pulled out, leaving the lightly armed Estonian 4th Infantry facing impossible odds.

On 18 November, the Estonian Provisional Government re-emerged and announced the creation of a national army. Three days later it proclaimed universal mobilisation to resist a Russian invasion. The Estonian Defence League was revived as a militia reserve and delegates were sent to London by sea to beg the British government for military assistance.

On 22 November, Lenin ordered the 7th Army to attack towards the capital Tallinn in support of local Bolshevik groups. Conscious that the Red Army would be seen as a foreign invader, Lenin wanted the force to consist of as many Estonians as possible, but only 2,300 could be found. The plan was first to take Narva, then occupy Estonia, and then capture Riga. This was to be the first stage of an attempt to join up with the revolutionaries in Germany. The Red 6th Rifle Division, including some of the Estonian Bolshevik volunteers, took Narva on 28 November after nearly a week of fighting.

The legality of the Estonian Provisional Government was confirmed by a decisive vote on independence in their parliament, the Maapäev.

Local Bolsheviks loyal to Moscow reacted by calling for a general strike in protest. Although less than 4,000 workers responded, the Kremlin still proceeded to recognise its own creation, an 'Estonian Soviet Republic'. From an Estonian national point of view, however, this was 'tantamount to a declaration of civil war from outside'. When the Bolsheviks in Tallinn proclaimed a Commune on 17 December as the Red 7th Army approached, the Estonian government had no hesitation in crushing their revolt.

After the largely middle-class Estonian government first appealed for volunteers to enlist, students had enrolled en masse but the peasantry proved deeply reluctant. So, on 20 December, a programme of land reform was announced in the Maapäev to almost universal acclaim. The large estates owned by German 'Baltic barons' were to be divided up, with plots of land promised to each soldier for his service. Peasants too now flocked to volunteer.

Despite the anti-German mood, a battalion of what later became the *Baltenregiment* was formed with students from the German minority and other anti-Bolshevik volunteers. A remarkably effective command structure evolved under a liberal Tsarist officer, Colonel Johan Laidoner, who was to prove an exemplary leader. Laidoner, although born the son of a simple farmhand in Livonia, had worked his way up to become the chief of staff of a division through sheer talent and application. Immaculately turned out, with a neat little moustache, he possessed a natural authority. He was the obvious choice to become commander-in-chief of Estonian forces during their war of independence.

Laidoner formed three more regiments, which were equipped from German armouries. Help also arrived from Finland in the form of a shipment of 5,000 rifles and twenty field guns, and volunteers who would later include the Northern Sons of Finland Regiment. Others began to arrive from Denmark, eventually to form a Danish-Baltic company, and from Sweden under Major Carl Axel Mothander, a veteran of the Finnish Civil War.

The War Cabinet in London had refused the Estonians' urgent plea in November for British ground troops. Instead it ordered the Royal Navy's 6th Light Cruiser Squadron to Tallinn, bringing rifles, Lewis guns and field artillery for their fledgling army. The squadron was commanded by Rear-Admiral Edwyn Alexander-Sinclair, a redoubtable Scot whose ship had first sighted the German High Seas Fleet at Jutland. He now promised the Estonians that he would attack the Bolsheviks as far as his guns could reach.

In the latter part of December 1918, word reached Petrograd that a British squadron had appeared off the Estonian capital of Tallinn. None of the Baltic Fleet's submarines were capable of crossing the Gulf of Finland to reconnoitre 'due to their poor technical state'. A squadron which included the battleship *Andrei Pervozvanny*, the cruiser *Oleg* and three destroyers – *Spartak*, *Avtroil* and *Azard* – were sent under the command of Fyodor Raskolnikov, who had left both his Volga flotilla and Larisa Reisner behind. Raskolnikov convinced himself that intercepts of Royal Navy radio signals were simply a ruse by the British to keep the Soviet fleet bottled up in Kronstadt. So, with a large icebreaker opening a route, they set off for the Estonian coast. The *Azard* had to turn back because it had forgotten to take on coal before leaving – 'Such outrageous lack of order was only possible during the chaos of 1918!' Raskolnikov commented.

The two remaining destroyers went on ahead to test the Estonian shore batteries by firing on them to provoke a response, but there was none. Encouraged by this, Raskolnikov in *Spartak* and the *Avtroil* carried on to the port of Tallinn, but as they approached they spotted smoke from ships getting up steam. They turned about to run back to Kronstadt, but the British light cruisers and destroyers were too fast for them. To make matters worse, the *Spartak* ran aground. According to Raskolnikov, the captain kept repeating bitterly: 'Everyone knows this shoal, it is on all the charts. How terribly upsetting!'

A boarding party from the destroyer HMS *Wakeful* took them prisoner and they were soon consuming biscuits and strong tea in its hold. They were brought back up on deck later to witness the capture of the *Avtroil*. This, Raskolnikov protested, was done 'to hurt our revolutionary pride'. The two Soviet warships were then handed over to the Estonians to form the nucleus of their navy, and Raskolnikov was taken back to London as a prisoner to be exchanged later for British officers captured by the Red Army.

There was, however, little that the Royal Navy could achieve against the Red Army's superiority on land. On 22 December, the Red Latvian Rifle Division captured the city of Tartu, the second-largest in Estonia. By New Year's Eve the 7th Army, some 7,000-strong, had occupied the eastern half of the country, yet the Estonians proved a far more determined and effective opponent than the White Northern Corps. In the south of the country Laidoner formed another division out of new regiments and raised a partisan battalion with a death's head cap badge.

Estonian patriotism was symbolised by the blue-black-white cockade. It was about the only standard item of uniform. Students and peasants alike wore a mixture of sheepskin jackets, greatcoats, German helmets, Russian forage caps or lambskin shapkas, riding boots or puttees. Over Christmas and during the last week of the year, the Estonians began to prepare their counter-attack using some rapidly converted armoured trains, and deploying the 3,800 White Finnish volunteers whose language they shared. Encouraged by the Royal Navy's cruiser squadron operating along their coast in open support, the Estonian government outlawed the Soviet in Tallinn as the Red 7th Army approached. On 6 January 1919, the Estonians launched their counter-offensive.

On 1 December 1918, the Latvian Civil War began when the Red Army invaded. Three of the Bolshevik Latvian rifle regiments captured Daugavpils in the south while another three swung round from Pskov through southeast Estonia. As they headed for Riga, Moscow proclaimed the Latvian Soviet Socialist Republic on 17 December. Eighteen days later they entered the city. The Latvian Provisional Government called a national militia into being. Otherwise, their one hope was the German Baltic defence force, the *Baltische Landeswehr*, which was mainly interested in establishing a Teutonic hegemony in the region. Only the western part of the Courland peninsula held out as German and Latvian units prepared a counter-attack.

The Lithuanian Civil War was even more complicated, since it would eventually involve Russian, German and Polish forces. Two Red rifle divisions, which were rapidly reinforced, began the invasion from Belarus on 12 December 1918. By mid-January 1919 the Reds had occupied two thirds of the country, but they too would soon face much greater resistance than they had expected. The Kremlin's insistence that the three countries were still subject to its will proved distinctly premature and the term 'civil war' looked increasingly inaccurate. The Baltic provinces were fighting for their national identities and independence from Moscow.

*

In November General Nikolai Yudenich, who had been the Tsarist commander-in-chief of the Transcaucasian Front, reached Finland. He went to see General Mannerheim, having decided to raise an army with many of the 2,500 Russian officers who had escaped to Finnish territory. He also contacted Admiral Kolchak, who financed him with a million roubles, and he received another 2 million roubles from rich Russians in the Baltic region. Since Kolchak acknowledged Yudenich as the commander-in-chief of the Northwestern Army, and because he held the purse strings, General Rodzyanko, with great reluctance, had to accept him as his superior. Mannerheim was also unimpressed.

General Nikolai Yudenich (holding his cap) is dwarfed by General Aleksandr Rodzyanko, his most reluctant subordinate in the Northwestern Army.

While Estonia hastened to defend itself against German power and Bolshevik incursion, the Baltic suddenly became of pertinent interest to the French as well as the British government, even though the situation was fiendishly complex. German forces in the whole Baltic region provided the most effective barrier to Bolshevik expansion, and under Article XII of the Compiègne Armistice, they were permitted to remain for the moment. There was no guarantee that the Baltic states could defend themselves, yet at the same time the White Russian forces planned to attack Petrograd. But neither the Finns nor the Estonians welcomed these anti-Bolshevik Russian supremacists who refused to acknowledge their independence. A White venture to invade Soviet territory was likely to fail and provoke a Red counter-attack. And to complicate the Baltic imbroglio further, while Yudenich applied to the British and French for military support, there was another White Russian force under Colonel Pavel Bermondt-Avalov financed from Berlin.

On the other side of the lines, Petrograd was still gripped by famine as well as the cold of another winter. Anyone who could leave had done so, and the inhabitants who remained had a foretaste of the horrors which the siege of Leningrad by the Nazis would bring a generation later. The stoves burning books and furniture were insufficient to stop people freezing to death in their own apartments. Many made tents in the middle of the floor with old carpets or tarpaulins, draped over chairs like children's dens. Their days were spent in the desperate search for food. Even a diet based on official rations was totally insufficient, and the paucity of fats meant that wounds failed to heal. People lacked the strength to tow corpses on sledges to the graveyards, so many of the dead remained in their beds until the spring thaw. 'It was so cold outside,' wrote Viktor Shklovsky, 'that it frosted your eyelashes; your nostrils froze up. The cold penetrated under your clothing like water. There was no light anywhere. We sat long hours in the dark.'

The Northern Front was the least volatile theatre of war, largely due to the dense forests and bogs which restricted movement to railway lines or rivers, and the extreme weather of the Arctic circle. Here, the Soviet 6th Army of General Samoilo faced the Allies based at Murmansk and Arkhangel in direct combat with ground units of multi-national forces under British command.

Ever since Trotsky's deliberately confusing policy of neither peace nor war during the Brest-Litovsk negotiations, the local authorities at Murmansk and Arkhangel had sensed that they would never receive any help from their own government. In July the Murmansk Soviet 'threw off allegiance to the Soviet government in Moscow', and on 1 August 'the coup d'état took place at Arkhangel, whereby the North Russian Provincial Government was established'. The bloodless coup could not have succeeded without the support of the guns of the Royal Navy offshore in the White Sea and the bayonets of Royal Marine Light Infantry on land. The moderate Right Socialist Revolutionary Nikolai Chaikovsky was installed as its leader, but under the heavy-handed tutelage of Major General Poole.

The initial landings intended to form a bulwark against German attack had been tacitly accepted by the Bolsheviks, but now the Allied presence aroused deep hostility in Moscow. The optimistic Poole wanted to raise a large army from the region and advance south to Vologda, to link up with the Czech troops in the Urals. He had no idea that Vologda was the headquarters of Samoilo's 6th Army. Vologda also happened to be the city where the Allied ambassadors and missions had been installed after the Bolsheviks abandoned Petrograd. Only on 25 July did the Communist authorities allow the foreign diplomats to leave for Arkhangel, and from there by ship to their home countries.

Allied efforts to revive a front against the Germans in the east could be justified since the Bolsheviks in 1918 were again receiving considerable support from Berlin. This argument was sufficient to convince President Woodrow Wilson to send an American infantry regiment to reinforce the British troops in North Russia, but this could not be maintained after the November armistice. Rather than formulate a clear plan to overthrow the Communist regime, the Allied Supreme War Council at Versailles had been keeping its options open at a complicated time. It was, after all, dealing with the untidy aftermath of the First World War as well as trying to reshape the Europe of 'good' winners and 'bad' losers.

French, Canadian, Polish and Italian reinforcements also arrived, bringing the Allied force in Murmansk up to 6,000-strong and Poole's to nearly 10,000. Poole had already started his advance south the previous month. Part of his force, supported by an armoured train, followed the Vologda railway line, while the River Force took the Northern Dvina, supported by Royal Navy monitors, gunboats and some obsolete seaplanes and RAF bombers.

Although able to float mines down the river against the British vessels, the Reds felt themselves badly outgunned. The 4th Baltic Naval Expeditionary Detachment sent an urgent message back to Kronstadt demanding that 120mm guns, 'of which a sufficient number are available on board the ships', be sent to arm the Red steamships on the river. 'If that is done, according to the delegates, Arkhangelsk is going to be in our hands in two weeks or less.'

Force C of the North Russian Expeditionary Force of brigade

strength included the 2/10th Royal Scots and a Russian detachment. In an engagement at Troitka on 18 August, they managed after a night approach march to surprise a Red battery of guns which they turned on the Red flotilla sailing past.

On Friday 13 September, as they advanced with two American companies along the banks of the Dvina, their luck held better than it might have done on such a date. Their new commander arrived unannounced in a seaplane to inspect the front and everyone opened fire on the aircraft, including the monitor on the Dvina. 'Much to our surprise,' an officer recorded, 'General Finlayson stepped out of the machine and we thanked our lucky stars the gunners had not hit it.' Four days later a much nastier incident took place. Three young soldiers of the Royal Scots taken prisoner 'were murdered in cold blood by the Bolsheviks'.

During the autumn rainy season British troops suffered an epidemic of dysentery, which was treated with castor oil. It was time to start seeking winter quarters. A convent was taken over up the River Vaga, a tributary of the Northern Dvina. On Monday 21 October, Captain William Serby of the Queen's noted in his diary: 'Winter has undoubtedly started. Most of the ground was covered with the first snow and the weather much colder.' Force C received winter clothing in the form of 'fur caps, sheepskin lined coats, and woolly "Shackleton" boots'. The Canadian artillery, which had just arrived to support them, was even better equipped for the temperatures and long nights ahead. By mid-December there was less than four hours of daylight and morale began to suffer. Allied troops and sailors had naturally begun to question what they were doing there. Now that the war was over, they expected to be demobilised and returned home.

'With the defeat of Germany,' Lockhart had written to Balfour for the War Cabinet, 'it is clear that our intervention in Russia has now entered upon a most dangerous phase. Our victories over Germany have removed our original pretext for intervention and have at the same time strengthened the position of the Bolsheviks by raising their hopes for a revolution in Austria and Germany; and by increasing their power in Ukraine, Poland and the other Russian districts at present occupied by Germany.

'Without the active support of foreign troops,' he added in another despatch to Balfour, 'the counter-revolutionary forces in Russia are not strong enough to overcome the Bolsheviks. By financing these organisations, and yet not supporting them actively, we lay ourselves open to the same charges as if we were intervening in force, and at the same time we are only prolonging civil war and unnecessary bloodshed in Russia.'

Lockhart, however, was using the arguments against an arm's-length involvement in the civil war to demand outright intervention with ground troops. 'By restoring order in Russia at once not only are we preventing the spread of Bolshevism as a political danger, but we are also saving for the rest of Europe the rich and fertile grain districts of Ukraine, which in the event of half-measures, or no measures at all will be rendered sterile by anarchy and revolution. As Europe will require after the war all the grain she can get, the question of order in South Russia and in Romania is one of extreme importance.'

Although he was aware of some of the problems, especially the enormous numbers of men needed over several years, Lockhart seemed to under-estimate the very real dangers of civil unrest at home and mutinies among the troops sent. Even Churchill, the new secretary of state for war, was shaken by what Field Marshal Sir Henry Wilson defined as 'a state of general incipient mutiny' in the British Army during January and February 1919.

An uprising by 4,000 British troops in Calais required two infantry divisions to put down. There was also rioting in Glasgow and Liverpool, and an invasion of the War Office itself by large numbers of rebellious troops furious at not being discharged. 'The foundations of British society were more insecure at that time than they have ever been,' Churchill wrote soon afterwards. He was even more determined to defeat Bolshevism, whatever it took.

Part Three

―――――

1919

22

The Fatal Compromise
January–March 1919

The new year of 1919 opened with a strange scene inside the Kremlin walls. The chief of the Cheka, Feliks Dzerzhinsky, usually a man of iron self-control, became hopelessly drunk. He begged Lenin and Kamenev to shoot him. 'I have spilt so much blood,' he told them, 'that I no longer have any right to live.' And yet the class genocide threatened by Lenin and the Cheka had barely begun.

The Communists had already won the internal civil war in the areas they controlled, as Lenin claimed, but following the German armistice, they feared the reactionary forces of the Entente. And yet the Supreme Allied War Council in Paris lacked any cohesion on the subject. A peace conference to end the civil war was proposed to take place on the island of Prinkipo in the Sea of Marmara, less than 20 kilometres from Constantinople. A number of different motives were involved. Woodrow Wilson, who issued the invitations to the Sovnarkom and the various anti-Bolshevik administrations, genuinely hoped to end the conflict. Others thought that going through the motions would allow them to wash their hands of the Russian imbroglio. But Georges Clemenceau, the French prime minister, loathed Bolshevism and longed to crush their power. He even believed that the Soviet government had no business to attend the conference, since its agreement to the Treaty of Brest-Litovsk represented a grave betrayal of the Entente. Winston Churchill, the British secretary of state for war, also hoped Lenin would reject the proposal. That would lend legitimacy to his plans for assisting the White armies.

White Russians saw the Bolsheviks as criminal usurpers, so they greeted the idea of a peace conference with dismay and fury. The Tsar's former foreign minister, Sazonov, asked a British diplomat how the Allies could expect him to sit down with people who had murdered his family. Boris Savinkov did all he could to frustrate the Prinkipo proposal. He suspected that the Allies had a greater interest in Russia's natural resources than concern for its people. 'I recognized the smell of oil' in their plans, he later recalled.

Peace never stood a chance. The Sovnarkom replied that it would attend, but then refused to implement a ceasefire as required. President Wilson was ill and planning to return home, so he more or less abandoned the project. 'Wilson's last words before leaving on Friday,' wrote Churchill with barely suppressed glee, 'were to say that while he was anxious to clear out of Russia altogether, and was willing "to meet the Bolsheviks alone at Prinkipo", if all negotiation failed, he would "do his share with the other Allies in any military measures which they considered necessary".'

On 16 February, the day after the deadline for the conference expired, Churchill wrote to Lloyd George. 'I do not see that we are called upon to show our hand immediately. It will be a more prudent course to set up a Military Commission at once to take stock of the whole situation, to prepare out of the resources which are available a plan of war against the Bolsheviks.'

The three words 'plan of war' stung Lloyd George into an alarmed reaction. 'Following from Prime Minister. Am very alarmed at your telegram about planning war against the Bolsheviks. The Cabinet have never authorized such a proposal . . . If Russia is really anti-Bolshevik, then a supply of equipment would enable it to redeem itself. If Russia is pro-Bolshevik, not merely is it none of our business to interfere with its internal affairs, it would be positively mischievous: it would strengthen and consolidate Bolshevik opinion. An expensive war of aggression against Russia is a way to strengthen Bolshevism in Russia and create it at home . . . The French are not safe guides in this matter. Their opinion is largely biased by the large number of small investors who put their money into Russian loans and who now see no prospect of ever recovering it. There is nothing they would like better than to see us pulling the chestnuts out of the fire for them.'

Lloyd George, like Woodrow Wilson, felt that the old Tsarist order had received its just deserts. The 'Welsh wizard' even said of Churchill that 'His ducal blood revolted against the wholesale elimination of Grand Dukes in Russia.' But Churchill was not wrong when he argued that 'There is no "will to win" behind any of these ventures. At every point we fall short of what is necessary to achieve real success . . . The Allied Powers in Paris have not decided whether they wish to make war upon the Bolsheviks or to make peace with them. They are pausing midway between these two courses with an equal dislike of either.'

This fatal compromise, which even Churchill felt forced to pursue in the hope of an opportunity to strengthen Allied policy into full-blooded intervention, simply protracted the agony. Events in Odessa could have hardly been more revealing. By March French commanders decided to distance themselves from the Volunteer Army and set up a new administration with General Schwarz as commander-in-chief of the Odessa region.

Grishin-Almazov's chief of staff, General Aleksandr Sannikov, had been appointed by General Denikin, so he went to see General Philippe d'Anselme, whom he found wearing a skull-cap and the Legion of Honour around his neck. 'Anselme was very polite, but he could not understand the reason for my presence,' wrote Sannikov. 'As far as he was concerned this city was under French control.' General Grishin-Almazov had done little to improve relations with the French. The writer 'Teffi' who knew him well, described him as a 'little Napoleon'. Flamboyant, energetic and arrogant, with his large entourage and personal guard, Grishin-Almazov failed to persuade the French to help the Volunteer Army by allowing them to introduce conscription and take over the armouries in Odessa and outside. D'Anselme's refusal meant that all the military supplies fell into the hands of the Bolsheviks.

General Henri Berthelot arrived in February and appeared to be more open to the Volunteer Army, but the impression remained that French officers were nervous of supporting the Whites because they feared the Bolshevik sympathies of their own troops and seamen. They had good reason, especially after their army mutinies following the disastrous Nivelle offensive in 1917. After the evacuation of Odessa, mutinies spread in the second half of April among French warships of the Black Sea squadron, including the battleship *Jean Bart*. It began in the Romanian port of Galatz, led by the French Communist André Marty, later an organiser of the International Brigades in the Spanish Civil War. In Sevastopol, the crews of French warships began singing 'The Internationale' and refused to work.

Red forces had recaptured both Kharkov and Kiev in January 1919. Ataman Grigoriev, who had joined them, took Kherson in March, forcing the French and the Greeks to withdraw. The Greeks were said to have fought bravely, but French soldiers, including the Zouaves, did not have their heart in the fight. When it came to the defence of

Voznesensk, even the Zouaves flatly refused to fight. At Berezovka the French troops fled, abandoning five Renault tanks and their field guns. Embarrassed French commanders, stunned by this collapse, asked the Volunteer Army to send its forces to the front, despite having refused them weapons and ammunition a short time before. Grigoriev then took Nikolayev, and at the end of March, the French had to pull out of Mariupol on the Sea of Azov, the furthest extent of their occupation.

The fighting in Ukraine produced anti-Semitic pogroms of unprecedented scale by Grigoriev's horde and Petliura's Ukrainians. The writer Ivan Nazhivin described how Petliura's troops rampaged in Zhitomir and Berdichev and 'organized a professional pogrom, supported not only by machine guns, but also by armoured vehicles and artillery! . . . It was followed by mad plundering in which not only the Jews suffered, but all well-to-do residents. Hundreds of Jews were killed.' He was forcefully reminded of a discussion in Moscow in an editorial office. 'One clever cynic said to us then: "I can tell you a very brief history of our revolution . . . we will continue for a while with this stupid and bloody mess, and then the great Russian revolution will end in a Jewish pogrom of a magnitude yet unknown to history."'

On reaching Odessa, Nazhivin went to visit Ivan Bunin to exchange thoughts and experiences. 'Bunin, who was one of my favourite writers, looked back to the days when they had welcomed any indication that the Tsarist regime might fall without ever imagining the true consequences. "Ivan Fyodorovich," Bunin said, "we used to be so thoughtless! I remember how I heard about Stolypin's assassination when I was in my village. It is hard to believe now but I was running around my terrace screaming with joy!"'

When little more than Odessa and its surrounding area was left in French hands, Clemenceau ordered the garrison to hold on at all costs, even though he was deeply sceptical. On 1 March, Field Marshal Wilson reported after a discussion that Marshal Foch also had 'not much faith in Kolchak or Denikin', and he was 'dissatisfied with the situation at Odessa, as the French division is very weak and the morale of the men not very good and he does not think Greek troops will assist much'. The same day Lloyd George wrote to Churchill to complain about General Franchet d'Espèrey, the French commander-in-chief for the Black Sea region. 'The French are becoming quite intolerable. The third power, in point of strength, they want to create the impression that they are the first in point of authority. We cannot allow our men to be ordered about in the East where prestige is more important to us than in any other quarter of the globe.'

On 20 March, Franchet d'Espèrey reached Odessa by warship from Constantinople to see the situation for himself. Finding the troops there utterly demoralised and the city in a chaotic state without food, he asked for permission to evacuate. Clemenceau gave his consent most reluctantly on 1 April. In the hope of avoiding a stampede to ships in the port, Franchet provided no warning to the civilian population or the Volunteer Army. Because of the shortage of shipping, the bulk of the French and Greek troops set off marching westwards through Bessarabia to Romania. Warships and other vessels began to embark the rest of the Allied forces.

The following day, news of the French withdrawal got out and a colossal exodus began. The passport bureau was swamped as many thousands of people queued for exit visas. Others besieged the banks, but to no avail. The Odessa Soviet of Workers' Deputies had forbidden any money to be taken out. Yelena Lakier and her grandmother, knowing that they could not survive abroad without any money, decided to stay. At five they heard that the Red Army had entered the city.

Bolshevik sailors on the ships taking the refugees away to Constantinople sabotaged the engines and refused to sail, so the ships were stranded outside the harbour for up to a week. People had nervous breakdowns, afraid they would be handed back to the Bolsheviks. Speculators were shameless. A piece of bread cost 200 roubles and a glass of water 300 roubles.

On 6 April, Red Army units also surged through the Perekop Isthmus into the Crimea, causing panic. The next day, on the orders of King George V, the *Iron Duke*-class battleship HMS *Marlborough* anchored off Yalta. Its mission was to rescue the Empress Maria Feodorovna, the mother of the murdered Tsar and sister of Queen Alexandra, along with seventeen Romanov relations.

'Yalta is being evacuated today,' wrote Commander Goldsmith, the captain of the escorting destroyer HMS *Montrose*, 'and with that fairy-land town of Russia goes the last house of her former great ones. The poor old Empress, and that fine fellow the Grand Duke Nicholas embarked on board the *Marlborough* this afternoon. They are lucky, they only lose their country. But what of the others?'

The *Montrose* continued on to Sevastopol. There, Goldsmith watched with great interest as some Bolsheviks under a flag of truce were taken out to the French flagship, the battleship *Jean Bart*. 'The delegates looked a pretty shifty couple of customers. One was a little rat of a man in khaki, the other was a black-eyed little cavalryman in dark blue, a big black astrakhan busby and a silver-mounted scimitar. The French refused to allow the army to enter the town and the Bolsheviks refused to keep out, so at 4pm next day the *Jean Bart* opened a tremendous banging with her 12" and 6" guns which, at any rate, broke all the glass in Sevastopol.' On HMS *Iron Duke*, Lieutenant Webb-Bowen recorded an intense programme of weapon training. 'During the afternoon every seaman in the ship did rifle drill and all the Marine gun crews stripped and fired their Lewis guns.'

Two days later, Webb-Bowen recorded that French warships in the bay, including the dreadnoughts *Jean Bart* and *France*, 'hoisted the red flag at the jackstaff'. 'The men having cheered and generally gone mad, landed and marched in a procession through the town in company with the delightful townsfolk, who of course are mostly Bolshevik too by this time. On reaching the Greek barracks the Greeks turned out and opened fire on this mob, which fled at once back to its ships, and retorted by training their turrets on a little Greek man-of-war lying in the harbour.' Not trusting the mutinous French sailors, the *Iron Duke* had 'two officers on watch all night, 6-inch guns and searchlights manned, and a picket boat patrolling round the ship'.

The family of the writer Vladimir Nabokov was rescued that day. 'A tumultuous evacuation of anti-Bolshevik groups began,' Nabokov recorded. 'Over a glassy sea in the bay of Sevastopol, under wild machine-gun fire from the shore, my family and I set out for Constantinople and Piraeus on a small and shoddy Greek ship, the *Nadezhda* [Hope], carrying a cargo of dried fruit.'

HMS *Montrose*, escorting the *Centaur* and *Emperor of India*, sailed round the Crimea into the Sea of Azov, where the Volunteer Army had retreated to the Kerch peninsula. Goldsmith wrote a letter home. 'I called on Colonel Count Rimsky-Korsakov', who commanded a remnant of the Tsar's Life Guards. 'He asked me to send his compliments to the Colonel of our 1st Life Guards. Poor chaps – no wonder they looked a party of ruffians as they sat in the low cottage living room, the small, dirty window dimly illuminated the filthy table they fed around ... War has made fiends of the illiterate, simple-minded, superstitious Russian peasants, and devils of the reckless, drunken pleasure-loving aristocracy they wish to exterminate ... Both sides are equally barbarous, and the torture applied to prisoners is so inhuman that I cannot write it here. Every man carries a grenade fastened to his tunic button, with which to blow off his own head if captured.'

The start of 1919 was truly a period of mixed fortunes. While the Red Army suddenly pushed back Krasnov's numerically inferior Don Cossacks from Tsaritsyn and advanced rapidly across Ukraine, it suffered its greatest defeat in the Caucasus. Denikin had once again turned the main body of the Volunteer Army south to secure the northern Caucasus as a firm base. In January General Wrangel crushed the isolated 11th Army, already weakened by a typhus epidemic, when it was ordered to march north on Rostov. Ice-cold and calculating, Wrangel was pitiless.

The main battle started near Petrovskoye, when Wrangel deployed the best part of his 8,000 sabres. The Red forces of the 11th Army assumed that they were in an impregnable position along a nearby ridge, until the Cossack regiments mounted the steep incline in silence under an erratic fire which they did not return. This unsettled the defenders even more. The ill-trained Red conscripts fled and were pursued for 18 kilometres by the Kuban Cossacks, who cut them off near the village of Spitzevka. They returned to Petrovskoye with some 5,000 prisoners. 'For the first time since the start of the civil war,' wrote a young officer of horse artillery, 'prisoners were not shot. There were too many of them.'

At a halt, the regiments formed a huge open square. There was a sudden shout of 'Smir-na!'. The Kuban cavalry and horse gunners stood to attention by their mounts. A triumphant Wrangel galloped into the centre on a magnificent charger. He was wearing full Cossack uniform – the cherkesska with cartridge cases sewn diagonally on the chest, the black papakha fur hat which he wore sideways, almost on the back of the head, and a woollen burka cloak. 'Thank you, my eagles!' he shouted. They answered with a deafening 'Urrra!'. One or two claimed that even some of their prisoners were so carried away by the dramatic sight that they cheered too.

Wrangel's victory forced the 12th Army to pull back to Astrakhan, which enabled the Volunteer Army in February to capture all the major towns as far as the mountain range and join up with the Terek

Cossacks. Trotsky was clearly shaken by this disaster inflicted on their Caspian-Caucasus Front by a far smaller force. Red Army conscripts were terrified of the Cossacks.

North of the Caucasus, the Red Army was otherwise holding its own. Soviet troops advancing into Ukraine consisted mainly of the Special Army, some 30,000 strong, and one of their first cavalry regiments. Red forces across southern Russian also included the 8th Army based in Voronezh, the 9th Army at Balashov, and the 10th Army at Tsaritsyn. All told, they were estimated to total 160,000 men, roughly similar in numbers to the Don Cossacks and Volunteer Army combined. Almost 20,000 of them are said to have been Chinese.

One Chinese battalion in the 1st Moscow Workers' Division played a major part in January 1919 during the fighting round Lugansk. This battalion, trapped in the *stanitsa* of Luganskaya, ran out of ammunition, so units of the Volunteer Army managed to capture the survivors. When the Reds retook the place three days later, they found that all of the 200 Chinese prisoners had been executed. Their bodies were hanging from lamp posts and trees, with bellies ripped open, eyes poked out and tongues cut off. This atrocity prompted the Chinese Red Guards, when they entered Odessa in April, to exact a bloodthirsty retribution on officers from the Volunteer Army there.

Filipp Mironov, the Left Socialist Revolutionary Cossack who commanded the 23rd Division, continued to attack the stupidity of the Red Army's brutality in the Don region. On 18 January he sent another telegram on the subject to Trotsky, urging that the Soviet authorities respect the Cossack 'way of life, its beliefs and traditions'. Three days later he issued an order to his men: 'In the name of the Revolution, you are from now on banned from unauthorized requisitions of livestock, horses and other property from the population . . . There is no place in the Red Army for bandits! If this order fails to stop the evil, I will have to take the most drastic measures, and my hand will not shake.'

The Central Committee responded a few days afterwards with its own very different instructions. 'The relentless struggle against the Cossack elite and its complete extermination should be seen as the only correct way of action. No compromise and no half-measures are acceptable.' Cossacks were to be completely disarmed. Weapons were to be issued only to 'reliable elements from among non-Cossacks'. Cossack grain was to be confiscated and their land handed over to poor non-Cossacks.

Trotsky, well aware of the following Mironov had among the Cossacks, summoned him to Serpukhov, 100 kilometres south of Moscow, 'so that Field Headquarters and I get a chance to know him better'.

Within a matter of weeks, Mironov's previous warnings of a reaction to the oppressive measures of 'de-cossackization' came true. On 16 March the Southern Front issued orders to the 8th, 9th and 10th Armies. 'The most drastic measures should be used against the hamlets that are behind the uprising: (a) setting the hamlets on fire; (b) the ruthless shootings of all persons who have taken direct or indirect part in the uprising; (c) the shooting of every fifth or tenth male in the adult population; (d) the mass seizure of hostages from hamlets next to the rebellious ones; (e) spreading word to all Cossack villages and hamlets, that in all those known to be helping the rebels the adult male population will be ruthlessly exterminated and the settlements will be burned down.'

The consequences of such a war were not hard to guess. As Commander Goldsmith noted in a letter home, 'A great famine is predicted this year. The peasants see clearly that whatever they grow will be practically robbed from them by whichever army lies nearest, and are not troubling to sow their land at all.'

Stalin constantly demanded reinforcements for Tsaritsyn, the main objective of the Don Cossacks, because of the need to keep the Volga open down to the Bolshevik stronghold of Astrakhan where the Red flotilla was based. On 10 March, however, a workers' protest began in Astrakhan supported by some soldiers from the 45th Infantry Regiment. Although a perfectly peaceful demonstration, the local Communist authorities ordered it to be crushed without mercy. The 1st Independent Chinese Cheka Detachment, led by Pu Qisan, opened fire with rifles, then with machine guns, and finally hurled grenades into the crowd. 'Dozens of workers were killed, but it was only the beginning. The Chinese were chasing men all day.'

The Revolutionary Committee led by Sergei Kirov signalled Moscow, asking for instructions. On 12 March, Trotsky, presumably infuriated by all the other strikes going on in other cities, including Tula, Briansk and Petrograd, replied: 'Deal with mercilessly.' The prisoners were at first shot, but later, as cartridges were in short supply, the Chinese started drowning them. Witnesses recalled how the prisoners' hands and feet were tied and stones attached to their necks. They were then thrown from barges into the Volga. One of the workers managed to hide in the hold and survive. He said later that around 180 people were thrown off the steamship *Gogol* in just one night. In Astrakhan itself, so many were shot in the Cheka offices that the detachment had trouble transporting all the bodies to the cemetery, where they were thrown into a mass grave on the pretence that they were typhoid victims. Estimates of those killed range from 2,000 to 4,000. During the same month of March, protests at the Putilov works in Petrograd, another Bolshevik bastion, prompted a savage Cheka reaction on Lenin's orders, with 900 arrested and 200 shot.

Vladimir Lenin and Leon Trotsky (saluting) in Red Square 1919.

In the Baltic states, January 1919 saw the start of the fight-back against the Soviet 7th Army, which was some 8,000 strong. During the first week of January, the Estonian commander-in-chief General Laidoner used his new regiments to halt the advance of the Bolshevik forces. Then, on 7 January, the 1st Estonian Division in the north, supported by the Finnish volunteers and the new armoured train units, counter-attacked. Tapa was retaken two days later. Landings on the coast covered by the two captured destroyers surprised the Red forces and on 19 January, they were chased out of Narva by the Finns and student volunteers.

In the south on 14 January, Estonian armoured trains and the Kuperjanov Partisan Battalion forced the Reds to flee from Tartu, while the the 2nd Division launched its counter-offensive, seizing back Tõrva and Valga over the next two weeks. By the middle of February, Estonian territory was clear of Red Army forces.

The Latvian Provisional Government had not ordered general mobilisation until New Year's Eve, so it depended almost entirely on the German *Landeswehr* and 4,000 Freikorps volunteers from the 46th Saxon Division, consisting mainly of officers and soldiers embittered by the Armistice. On 2 January members of the government fled from Riga to the coast of Courland, hoping to find sanctuary on British warships. A counter-attack on 16 January with the 1st Independent Latvian Battalion, the German 'Iron Brigade' Freikorps and a White Russian battalion forced back the Red Latvian Rifle Division. This bought the Latvians time to increase their forces under their commander-in-chief Jānis Balodis.

Alexander-Sinclair's 6th Cruiser Squadron was replaced in the Baltic by Rear Admiral Walter Cowan's 1st Light Cruiser Squadron. One of his destroyers, HMS *Seafire*, was captained by Commander Andrew Cunningham, the outstanding leader of the Royal Navy in the Second World War. Cowan's force soon dominated the coastline, keeping the Red Baltic Fleet bottled up in the Kronstadt naval base and guarding the flank of the anti-Bolshevik forces in the region.

After their recapture of Pskov next to the Soviet-Estonian border, the Reds reported unexpected problems to Petrograd despite a 'thorough cleansing of all counter-revolutionaries and enemies of the people'. They found that engine drivers were 'traitors' and had deliberately sabotaged their locomotives. 'Many of them had to be dragged from under their beds to be forced back to work. The sabotage of the engine drivers was a colossal blow to the Soviet authority, resulting in the loss of a thousand freight cars, either empty or loaded, as well as ninety-eight locomotives.' These railway workers were handed over to the Cheka. 'The black clique of engine drivers knew that communists have no mercy for counter-revolutionaries.'

Even more seriously, they were facing their third revolt in the Luga district as a result of Red Army troops looting the peasants' grain. In June of the year before, 'the cavalry detachment of Balakhovich, known for his drastic solutions, was particularly active in suppressing this uprising. For example Balakhovich and his men hacked to death whole villages with their sabres. Only a few were executed by shooting after a judgement.' The uprising was blamed on 'deserters and suspicious characters' taking advantage of 'the low cultural level of the local peasantry which creates wide opportunities for provocations. And the lack of cultural enlightenment and their complete ignorance of the true policy of the Soviet authority.' Artillery was needed to complete the repression. Perhaps not surprisingly, the Cheka strongly supported the savage reprisals ordered by Balakhovich.* 'The Kulak-White Guard rebellion in the Luga district,' it reported, 'was eliminated thanks to the resolute actions of the independent joint revolutionary detachment commanded by Comrade Balakhovich.'

The chief commissar of the 7th Army was clearly nervous at the peasant anger they faced around the whole of the Gulf of Finland and Lake Ladoga region. He wrote to Yelena Stasova of the Central Committee about the need 'to fight the predatory, bandit-appetites and plots of the bloodthirsty Finnish bourgeoisie which has been egged on by the British and American capitalists. It is necessary to create an atmosphere of hatred and to make the population loyal towards the Soviet Socialist Russia.' The military council of the Karelia Front was also reporting 'many cases of Red Army soldiers murdered by locals'.

Terror begat terror, which in turn led to even greater conspicuous cruelty. Those in Britain and France who were reluctant to abandon their White protégés to their fate could only shrug off the horrors as inevitable in a civil war. Lloyd George, on the other hand, was deeply suspicious of Churchill's enthusiasm for the anti-Bolshevik cause. He wrote to Churchill from the peace conference in Paris: 'I have had a long interview with Chaikovsky† and Paderewski‡ upon the position in Russia and regret that neither of them take your views as to Kolchak

* Stanislaw Bulak-Balachovich (1883–1940) commanded a cavalry guerrilla unit operating behind German lines in the war, joined the Red Army with Trotsky's approval, but very soon switched sides to join the White forces of General Yudenich.
† Nikolai Chaikovsky (1851–1926) had been the Socialist Revolutionary leader in Arkhangel.
‡ Ignacy Paderewski (1860–1941). When Clemenceau at the Versailles Peace Conference asked one of his entourage who he was, he heard that he was the famous pianist Paderewski, but now had become the prime minister of Poland. 'Quelle chute!' ('What a downfall') came the inimitable retort.

and Denikin and their entourage: on the contrary they are genuinely alarmed lest their success should result in the triumph of reaction . . . if our efforts simply ended in establishing a reactionary military regime in Russia, British Democracy would never forgive us.'

23

Siberia
January–May 1919

The almost endless expanse of Siberia from Vladivostok to the Urals contained a far greater variety of Allied troops than anywhere else in the civil war. Japanese ambitions in the Far Eastern Maritime region had led to the largest foreign force distributed between Chita, Harbin, the Amur and Novo Nikolaevsk. This was the only national contingent which did not answer to the French General Pierre Janin, the overall Allied commander appointed by the Supreme Council in Paris.

The largest formation under Janin's command was the Czech Legion, which now became the Czechoslovak Army in Russia. Admiral Kolchak promoted Gajda to the rank of lieutenant general as commander of the Ural Front. There were two British battalions, the 1/9th Battalion of the Hampshire Regiment in Ekaterinburg, and the 25th Battalion of the Middlesex Regiment split between Omsk, Krasnoyarsk and Vladivostok. The Hampshires were unimpressed by what they saw of Kolchak's officers and their many girlfriends. One captain wrote of their 'staff trains, most of which might be briefly described as *bordels ambulants*'. A Canadian battalion and part of a force of 1,600 Italians were also stationed in Vladivostok, while a French colonial battalion was sent to Chelyabinsk and 3,000 Romanians to Irkutsk. There were also General Graves's 8,500 American troops spread between Vladivostok and the Amur district.

Siberia proved an eye-opening experience for the Americans. Captain William S. Barrett of the 27th Infantry Regiment commanded a detachment at Khabarovsk out on the frozen tundra 1,000 kilometres north of Vladivostok. They were grateful for their fur hats, sheepskin coats and gloves in temperatures below minus 30 degrees centigrade. Barrett was surprised to find that the Japanese troops based in the same town had 'brought their *Yoshewara* or public women along with them. Each of their soldiers is given a certain allowance of *Yoshewara* tickets, which they use or trade, or gamble with, as they see fit. I understand that their venereal rate is kept very low by this system. Our venereal rate was very high.'

The local warlord was Colonel Kalmykov, the ataman of the Ussuri Cossacks. He acted like a gangster chieftain, killing any 'luckless citizen who incurs his displeasure' and forcing banks to pay protection money. He had his own Cossack band which played his favourite march as soon as he entered a room, at which point everyone was expected to leap to their feet.

The first American personnel in Siberia, just over 300 railway engineers from the US Army called the Russian Railway Service, had arrived at the beginning of 1918. Woodrow Wilson's administration had offered them to the Kerensky government. Their task had been to reorganise the Trans-Siberian Railway to help maintain supplies for Russian armies in the war against Germany. Now, in the chaos of the civil war, they were more necessary than ever to keep the lines open, but they needed a company of the 31st Infantry Regiment for close protection. The other great contribution from the United States came from the American Red Cross mission to Russia. It worked to improve the appalling state of prisoner-of-war hospitals as well as care for Allied troops, but it also trained up local people as nurses and medical personnel and looked after unaccompanied children sent to Siberia to escape the famine in Petrograd.

An American Red Cross hospital train in eastern Siberia, but probably not part of the 'Great White Train' which treated the victims of typhus.

Tensions between the United States and Japan soon flared up. On 25 February, a Japanese detachment sent out from Khabarovsk was ambushed and cut to pieces. Out of a force of 311 officers and men, 302 were killed and the remaining nine badly wounded. Japanese commanders were outraged that General Graves had refused to send the 27th Infantry to their aid. He justified this on the grounds that 'the Japanese had shot down women and children and also that he did not recognize the Russians against whom the Japanese were sent as the real enemy'.

Franco-American relations in Russia were not much better. They were marked by 'frigidity and dissatisfaction', mainly it seems because French officers felt that their allies had forgotten that France had 'had to bear the heaviest burden of the war on her shoulders'.

The presence of so many foreign detachments and military missions contributed to the optimism in Kolchak's headquarters at Omsk in the early part of 1919, which had already been greatly bolstered by the young General Anatoly Pepelyayev's victory at Perm. Kolchak's chief minister Vologodsky was clearly delighted with the national and international position, although Kolchak himself was still suffering from pneumonia, probably brought on by the 'Spanish' flu pandemic and not helped by his heavy drinking.

'The military are confident that Ufa will be taken back within about three weeks,' Vologodsky told the provincial head of Irkutsk in a telephone call on 23 January. 'The significance of our government on the international stage has grown remarkably. The fact is that Denikin has recognised Admiral Kolchak as the Supreme Ruler of Russia and Sazonov as foreign minister has made a very favourable impression on the Allies. People in Paris, who had been taking their news from interviews given by Avksentiev [one of the forcibly exiled Right Socialist Revolutionaries] to Japanese and American journalists, regarded us as a reactionary government, but clearly this view has changed. It has also been influenced by the fact that we have authorised Boris Savinkov and Chaikovsky together with Prince Lvov to define Russia's needs and present them at the Peace Conference.'

Vologodsky was also relieved that squabbles over the chain of command appeared to have at last been settled. 'What a lot of energy has been expended on defining the relationship between the Supreme Ruler as the supreme commander-in-chief of the Russian Army and

General Janin, whom the Allies have appointed to command the Allied forces. This issue has now been resolved painlessly as you know from the telegrams.' There were soon other encouraging developments as spring approached. In the north, Gajda's army advanced on Kazan and planned to head for Kotlas, in the forlorn hope of meeting up with Allied forces from Arkhangel on the Northern Dvina. But the boots of his men were rotting in the spring thaw and the seasonal mud and rain known as *rasputitsa*. White Russian officers rebelled against Gajda retaining field command after they were beaten back from Kazan, but this failure was partly due to the Red Army's advantage of interior lines and better communications. In addition, the Reds' river flotillas meant that they were not as tied to railway lines as the Whites, so they found it relatively easy to march round and outflank White positions. In any case, Churchill's fanciful dream of threatening Moscow while evacuating the Czechs via Arkhangel had come to nothing.

In the Urals and Siberia, the Whites had 220,000 men in theory, but more than half of them were nowhere near the front. There was also a lack of unity due to the egos of the Cossack atamans. Large numbers of troops were kept in reserve, or were needed to guard the Trans-Siberian Railway from attacks along its length by Red partisan groups, which would grow in size and daring.

These partisans emerged from the forests mainly to burn wooden bridges, sabotage tracks and attack trains. On 20 May, a band of around 400 strong attacked a train and burned down a bridge near Adrianovka, southeast of Chita. They were fought off by Japanese troops with machine guns. More attacks were mounted through the month against the Japanese 14th Division. Its commander, Lieutenant General Kurita, announced that they have 'firmly decided to exterminate the enemy'.

Partisans also terrorised villagers into giving them shelter and food. Melting snow at Belebey revealed a winter massacre from their takeover of the village. The corpses revealed 'fractured skulls, gaping wounds, the traces of torture'. The victims included a sixteen-year-old girl who had allegedly been 'killed for rejecting the love of a commissar'. One group infiltrated the coal mines of Suchan to provoke strikes and threaten the miners. Work halted 'at the majority of gold mines in the Amur region owing to the systematic Bolshevik attacks'.

Semenov's 14,000 men never moved far from Chita, and the ataman himself sheltered in a walled compound guarded by heavy machine guns. Many of his men worked for the counter-intelligence department run by Colonel Sipailov, a sadistic psychopath. In May alone, some 350 prisoners are said to have been massacred in his killing ground next to Adrianovka.

Annenkov's division, with its Afghan, Uighur and Chinese mercenaries, spent more time terrorising the locals than in hunting down Red partisans. Regular White officers were furious at the hatred they created. They also resented the fact that Annenkov, although supposedly commander of the Steppe Front, refused orders to move his men west to fight the Reds. He argued that the Kirghiz and Chinese in his division were 'unwilling to leave the Russian-Chinese border while the Semirechensk Cossacks did not want to leave their *stanitsas* without protection'. The few regiments that he did send to the front were extremely ill-disciplined, including his Black Hussars and Blue Uhlans. They started a bout of such outrageous looting in Petropavlovsk that sixteen of their men were executed on the orders of field courts martial.

On 25 February, Semenov opened a Pan-Mongol Congress in Chita with representatives from Tibet and Mongolia. Semenov longed to create an independent state named Daurskii after a nearby mountain. His pretentions provoked deep suspicion in China. Semenov apparently awarded himself the title of Grand Duke, but the Chinese press called him 'a Caliph for an hour and a toy of the Japanese'. Semenov wanted his own army and a People's Militia. He had originally moved to Chita with Baron von Ungern-Sternberg, who supported his plan of creating a Mongolian-Buryat cavalry division, including Transbaikal Cossacks, Buryats and Mongols. The problem was that many of the Buryats were living across the border in Outer Mongolia, which was under Chinese control. Yet with the establishment of an officer training school they soon had a cavalry brigade of 4,500 sabres.

Counter-intelligence was also a major preoccupation at Kolchak's headquarters in Omsk. Underground Bolshevik cells, in some cases joined by Left Socialist Revolutionaries, were spreading all over the Urals and Siberia. In late March, the White special investigations department carried out 'sweeping arrests of Communists in Chelyabinsk, Ekaterinburg, Kurgan, Petropavlovsk, and Omsk'. On the night of 3 April alone, White counter-intelligence arrested sixty-six Communists in Chelyabinsk. They were brought to Ufa, which had just been recaptured, for brutal interrogation. 'A court martial sentenced 34 of them to death, some were to be hanged and others, to be shot. However, they all died the same death. During the night of 16/17 [April] they were all hacked to death by drunken Cossacks.' This appears to have been part of a general massacre of 670 prisoners, including many Left SRs.

The underground Communist committee in Omsk assumed that their networks had been betrayed by a double agent known as 'Karlovich', alias Stanislav Rogozinsky, who had come to Omsk from Chelyabinsk as a delegate to the Third Siberian Underground Party Conference in March. Once denounced, he was rapidly eliminated, yet 'Karlovich' was innocent of any betrayal. The Whites had caught three Communists carrying out an 'expropriation' unsanctioned by the local Party committee. All three were 'fried', and one of them, Obraztsov, 'gave up the whole organisation, probably forced into it by beatings'.

General Mikhail Khanzin's Western Army had recaptured Ufa on 13 March after crossing the frozen River Belaya and taking Blumberg's 5th Army by surprise. Trotsky in his armoured train only just escaped capture. On 17 April Khanzin captured Buguruslan, but then had to halt while he diverted a division south towards Turkestan to save Ataman Dutov and his Orenburg Cossacks. Tukhachevsky's 1st Army of 14,000 men, which had just taken Orenburg itself, was about to threaten Khanzin's rear. The weakness of Dutov's Orenburg Cossacks on the southernmost part of the Ural front soon developed into a fatal flaw.

Conscripted troops on both sides had already shown an unwillingness to sacrifice themselves unnecessarily. Kolchak's chief of staff in Omsk, Major General Lebedev, was outraged when he heard that 'Some new recruits in operational units, request the district administration to provide them with a document to prove that they had not volunteered for the army, but were conscripted. This is so as not to be persecuted by the Bolsheviks in case of capture. I hereby ORDER that such documents must never be provided. Commanders and officials are to explain that soldiers making such requests are not worthy of the high title of a RUSSIAN WARRIOR, who openly and honourably defends his Motherland.'

Not long afterwards, the Supreme Ruler himself issued another order which revealed a rising panic in Kolchak's headquarters.

'Young, recently conscripted soldiers from our army are surrendering to the enemy or crossing over before the battle. During battles there are cases of hostile action by members of the local population.' All the property and land of families involved were to be confiscated for the benefit of the state. 'In the course of operations, do not take the afore-mentioned traitors prisoner. They should be shot on the spot without a trial.'

The Reds too were finding little sympathy among the civilian population. A Red Army commissar on the Ural Front complained to Stasova of 'Sabotage in almost all institutions'. Locals had such a negative attitude towards the Soviet authority that they hated Party agitators and called them 'alligators'. Not long afterwards forced labour camps were set up for civilians sentenced by revolutionary tribunals.

An even greater vulnerability existed south of Orenburg. The Ural Cossack Army, commanded by its new ataman General Vladimir Tolstov, tried to recapture its capital of Uralsk (now Oral in Kazakhstan). A raid by Vasily Chapayev's 25th Division redeployed from Ufa put the force to flight, but a sudden counter-attack at Lbishchensk caught Chapayev's men off-guard and he was killed.* Most of the Ural Cossacks rushed back to their *stanitsas* to defend their homes and families. On 5 February, Tolstov issued a stand and fight order. 'The army will be reformed. The panic-stricken retreat must stop immediately. Any Cossack who abandons the fight to return to their settlements must return to their unit at the front, otherwise they will be punished in the strictest fashion. The *stanitsas* must assist in returning Cossacks to their units.'

They had lost so many horses that Tolstov ordered that dismounted Cossacks would be transported five to a sledge or cart. All Cossacks over fifty were to enlist in the Holy Cross Militia of the Elder Kabaev. 'Although we are now suffering the disintegration of units, with men leaving of their own accord, officers should remain at their posts even if they are the only ones left. Officers must return to their units in the shortest possible time. Special departments are to be set up to look for deserters and weapons held back in *stanitsas*.' But for General Tolstov, worst of all was the 'shameful phenomenon of Cossacks selling rifles and machine-guns'.

---

* Vasily Chapayev was one of the most famous Red heroes of the civil war. A film was made in 1934 about his life and death.

His dwindling force retreated south in the second week of March to Guryev (Atyrev) on the Caspian. There, to the fury of the local inhabitants, they abandoned their wounded and those sick with typhus, so as to escape northeast to rejoin Kolchak's forces. The calvary that the remnants of the Ural Army suffered in the wastes of Turkestan was one of the lesser-known horrors of the civil war.

Given the lack of reliable communications across vast swathes of the Eurasian land-mass, Allied leaders had little idea of the true situation on the ground, especially when events turned against the Whites. Often their own military missions were reluctant to admit quite how bad things were in their reports. Even though there seemed little hope of an early resolution to the conflict, the Allied Powers in Paris stated at the end of May that they were prepared to continue their assistance to Kolchak's forces 'provided they are satisfied that it will really help the Russian people to liberty, self-government, and peace'. Therefore, their conditions for continued support with munitions, supplies and food included the need for a guarantee that the Whites would 'summon a Constituent Assembly elected by a free, secret and democratic franchise as the Supreme Legislature for Russia', and 'will make no attempt to reintroduce the regime which the revolution has destroyed'.

Other conditions insisted that Admiral Kolchak's declaration honouring Russia's foreign debts should be maintained; and that 'the independence of Finland and Poland be recognised', along with that of the Baltic states and Transcaucasian and Transcaspian countries, with any territorial disagreements to be settled by the League of Nations. The Allied and Associated Powers also 'noted with satisfaction the solemn declaration made by Admiral Kolchak and his associates that they have no intention of restoring the former land system'. This communication was signed by Georges Clemenceau, David Lloyd George, V.E. Orlando for Italy, Woodrow Wilson, and Saionji Kinmochi for Japan.

On 4 June Count Damien de Martel, France's representative in Omsk, passed on the admiral's full assurance that he would call elections for the Constituent Assembly at the first possible moment. Kolchak rather unconvincingly claimed that 'A commission is now at work on direct preparation for them on the basis of universal suffrage.' He then wriggled out of responsibility to recognise the borders and independence of neighbouring states which had broken away from the Tsarist Empire by saying that it would only be democratic if the final decision on territorial frontiers was left to the Constituent Assembly. On 12 June, the leaders of the Allied Powers signalled their satisfaction at Kolchak's full acceptance of their conditions. It does not appear, however, that any Allied representatives with the White forces exerted pressure on their Russian counterparts to honour the obligations which had been agreed.

Churchill was frustrated that the British government refused to recognise Kolchak as the head of 'the Russian Government', but the foreign secretary Lord Curzon warned him that 'There is great suspicion of Kolchak's imperialistic inclination.' He was not prepared to go beyond the 'the more modest formula of the Provisional Government of Siberia'. A bullish Churchill had no inkling of how rapidly things could go wrong.

The Red Army was increasing in strength, and by May it achieved a breakthrough which even Kappel's better-trained forces could not prevent. Khanzin's Western Army was forced to pull back sharply, yet Gajda, determined to resume his advance, refused to do the same. The political situation also deteriorated. On 20 May, the reactionary General Sakharov agreed to become chief of staff of the Western Army on the condition that all Socialist Revolutionaries were suppressed. This of course would play into the hands of the Communists. Three days later, Red forces advanced on Ufa. Dutov's Orenburg Cossacks were defeated near Sterlitamak and pushed further south. Kappel, however, taking advantage of the Reds' lack of cavalry, launched a counter-attack and forced them back. It was no more than a temporary respite. Volkov's cavalry was ordered to dismount to help the infantry to defend Ufa, but it achieved nothing. Ufa was abandoned on 8 June.

24

Don and Ukraine
April–June 1919

The repeated and costly failures of the Don Cossack attacks against Tsaritsyn led to General Krasnov's downfall in February. Denikin's successes in the Caucasus and the promise of British aid now meant that the Don Army had to join the Volunteer Army in a subordinate position. A third formation, an Army of the Caucasus manned mainly with Kuban Cossacks, would also come into being under General Baron Wrangel, the hero of the campaign there. Denikin would be the commander-in-chief of what now became the Armed Forces of Southern Russia and established his headquarters in the Kuban capital of Ekaterinodar.

The relationship between the Volunteers and the Don Cossacks was initially more a marriage of necessity than convenience. The Don Army was in a state of collapse and Krasnov resigned in mid-February. The new ataman of the Don Cossacks was Lieutenant General Bogaevsky, a former Tsarist commander of the 1st Guards Cavalry Corps, who, unlike his predecessor, worked well with the Volunteers. The two armies, however, remained entirely different in outlook. The Volunteer Army still saw itself as part of the Entente and at war with the Central Powers. Its leaders and officers still resented the Don Cossack collaboration with the German occupation and saw Krasnov's hopes of an independent Cossack federation as a separatist defiance of Russian nationalism.

The first priority in the spring of 1919 was to win back Don territory. The partial disintegration of Krasnov's army meant that even Rostov-on-Don was threatened by Red counter-attacks. Rostov, however, was preserved by that strange, obese figure of General Mai-Maevsky, who outmanoeuvred and outfought the Reds in the Donets basin, helped by his terrifying protégé, Andrei Shkuro.

Shkuro was a brave and cunning commander, worshipped by his men, but he was also arrogant and reckless, with absolutely no respect for authority. He shamelessly blackmailed both Denikin and Mai-Maevsky into promoting him to lieutenant general at the age of thirty-two. Many who encountered him would have shuddered at his politics. Shkuro was not merely ferociously anti-Communist, he was an anti-Semite and sadist. He loved to watch a good flogging and revelled in drunken orgies with prostitutes. According to an officer who arrived later with the British military mission, Shkuro was 'highly popular with the troops because he allows them to plunder' and 'very dissolute in his habits, having a harem of ten concubines'.

When the prosperous citizens of Rostov gathered to thank him for their liberation, they presented him with a substantial sum of money as a token of their appreciation. Shkuro simply passed the wad of bank-notes to a member of his Cossack escort. 'Here, go visit the whores,' he told him out loud. He then addressed the bourgeoisie: 'I am shedding blood here to give you a calm life. Do you really think that this kind of money will be sufficient?' He expected them to provide 10 million roubles.

The writer Ivan Nazhivin recounted how Shkuro celebrated his dubious promotion. 'Shkuro's train consisted of several good wagons, with two orchestras: a symphony orchestra and a brass band. There was a whole pack of dolled-up cabaret singers in Shkuro's carriage, and orgies went on day and night.' As the train slowed on the approach to a station in the reconquered mining area of the Donets, a drunken Shkuro at an open window sang his favourite verses:

> With my gang I will loot a hundred cities!
> Flow, flow, my lovely vodka,
> You are my joy!

'A crowd of filthy, dusty miners standing there,' continued Nazhivin, 'had no choice but to listen to the singing of drunken officers, fighters for the united and indivisible Russia. Shkuro raised his glass and shouted: "Workers and peasants! Long live Great Russia! I am drinking to your health, *Urra!*" He drained his glass to the bottom and hurled it down to smash on the platform. The workers remained silent and gloomy while Shkuro's Wolf Sotnia were shouting *"Urra! Urra! Urra!"*.'

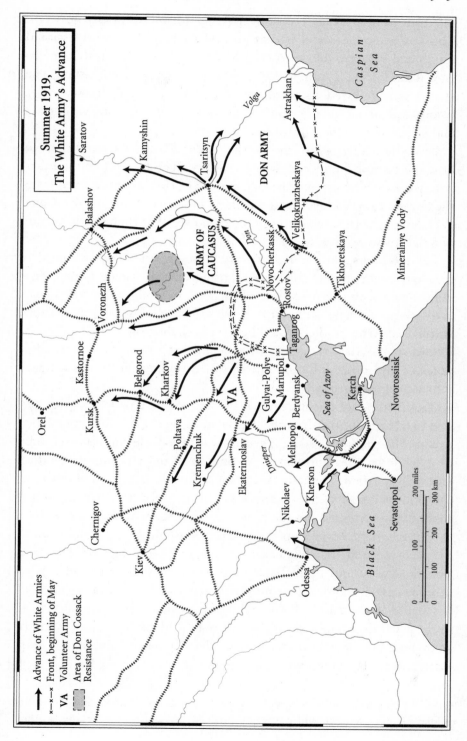

Summer 1919,
The White Army's Advance

In April, Mai-Maevsky's Volunteer Army advanced rapidly north on Kharkov after successful battles around Pavlograd. His professional forces had little trouble scattering Makhno's guerrilla cavalry on the way. After taking Izyum, General Shkuro halted for a short time. The victors were received with a storm of applause, Shkuro's radio officer recorded. 'Girls and ladies pinned flowers to the chests of Volunteers and I soon turned into a walking bouquet.'

It was not long before the Bolshevik citadel of Kharkov began to hear the distant thunder of White artillery. 'The faces of communists who were rushing around the city in their leather jackets looked lost,' the lawyer Valentin Lekhno, a member of the city Duma for the Kadet Party, noted with satisfaction. 'One could see that they would be out of Kharkov in no time at all.'

Lekhno had spent the night before hiding in an overgrown garden to avoid being seized, either as a hostage or for forced labour digging trenches on the south side of the city. By midday, he could hear artillery from the fighting round Merefa, just to the south. Soon afterwards Red Army soldiers could be seen in flight from the Drozdovsky Regiment. 'As they ran, they were abandoning their rifles, cartridge pouches and other military equipment, throwing them over a fence into someone's garden.'

As a member of the city Duma, Lekhno joined a panel to interview and to free innocent citizens held as hostages in the Kholodnogorskaya prison. 'The name of Preobrazhensky was called. He had been arrested as a "counter" [revolutionary]. A young man in semi-military clothes entered the room. His hair was completely white. It turned out that the Bolsheviks shot lots of hostages and counter-revolutionaries the night before. About 2 am the Cheka butcher Saenko, known to everyone in Kharkov, turned up at the jail. As usual, he was dead drunk. He went around the cells calling out names from his list. He took people outside and immediately shot them in the courtyard of the jail. He called two people from Preobrazhensky's cell and then called his name. Very calmly Preobrazhensky replied: "But you shot him yesterday". Everyone else in the cell remained silent. "Aha", Saenko mumbled. Preobrazhensky's cellmates did not betray him, but his hair went completely white during that night.'*

* Saenko, the head of the Kharkov Cheka, was both an alcoholic and a cocaine addict. His pathological sadism was notorious. He enjoyed sticking a knife a short

Lekhno then worked with pathologists on the Duma commission to examine Cheka crimes. He was taken to three large pits filled with the bodies of hostages, which had been found next to the Technological Institute in Tchaikovsky *ulitsa*. 'We examined the scene, it was absolutely horrifying. Everywhere in the multi-storey building we found traces of atrocities committed by the Bolsheviks. Traces of blood were almost all over the place. People had written on the walls, on the window-sills, everywhere where they could write. Many of these martyrs were doing so to inform their families about their death and wrote the addresses. It was clear from these writings that many of the victims were not *burzhuis* at all. The walls of the basement where they had performed executions were covered in blood, pieces of skin and hair, brains. In the room next to this basement we found one intact "glove" skinned from a hand of a person who was still alive, and two torn ones ... When we passed on to the examination of over 300 corpses that were found there, my hair stood on end. Piled on top of each other, there lay bodies, piled together without any distinction of age, sex, social status or nationality, and all of them were victims of the "new regime".' In other pits they found torture victims. 'They were all naked, with shoulder boards cut out of their shoulders, straps on the backs, and stripes on the legs. We were unable to establish who these unfortunate people were.'

General Mai-Maevsky, who had set himself up in style in the Hotel Astoria, took no interest in the life of the city except as a source of revenue. The liberation from Communist controls meant that economic life revived instantly. 'Traders returned to the market bringing goods that were unimaginable only a few days before.' Many merchants, however, petitioned the Volunteer Army for the return of their goods which had been requisitioned by the Reds but were still locked in warehouses. When Valentin Lekhno approached the relevant officer on Mai-Maevsky's staff, he replied: 'Yes, we have saved your property, and this costs money.' Lekhno asked how much, and he came out with 'an eye-popping figure. I had to bargain, and we reached an agreement.'

*

way into flesh, then twisting the blade, as well as scalping prisoners while still alive and giving them 'the glove treatment'. A Left Socialist Revolutionary who survived described him as 'short with shining eyes and a twitching maniacal face'.

The Whites were greatly helped in May when Ataman Grigoriev in Ukraine deserted the Reds to embark on his campaign of anti-Semitic pogroms and looting. Fighting was harder on the eastern flank, where the Cossacks were hoping to take back land beyond the River Don. The 15th Don Cossack Regiment was ordered to send agents across offering rewards for important information. The Red 9th Army was struggling with Cossack revolts in its rear, provoked by attacks on priests and churches as well as the savage 'de-cossackisation' programme to destroy their traditional culture, which Mironov had condemned to Trotsky.* 'Cossacks armed themselves with weapons that they had hidden (for example, in the river, or in coffins in the cemeteries) and attacked the Revolutionary Committee,' the Don Bureau reported on one uprising to the Kremlin. 'Part of the committee was killed, but some members together with small garrisons managed to break through to our troops.'

Lenin, aware of the damage being done by 'de-cossackisation', sent a telegram to the Military Revolutionary Committee of the Southern Front. 'We would like to draw your attention to the importance of being especially cautious concerning the break-up of small aspects of daily life that don't play any role in the general policy but at the same time irritate the population. Hold your course firm on the principal issues and make concessions on the archaic throwbacks that the population is used to.'

Such instructions were ignored by commissars waging a virtually genocidal campaign. Iona Yakir, now on the Military Revolutionary Council of the 8th Army, clearly did not agree. 'We have defeated in open battle the decomposing and stinking monster of Krasnov's troops, and now we tolerate and warm on our chest the serpent of treachery by the Tsar's eternal lackeys, the Cossacks.' But there was also bitterness against another danger. 'Makhno is a dangerous focus of attraction for the unstable units of the 8th and 13th Army,' the commissar of the 12th Army reported. 'Deserters are crossing over to join him.'

---

* On 16 March, Vatsetis, the commander-in-chief of the Red Army, gave Mironov the authorisation to raise a Red Cossack division. The very next day, the Don Bureau informed the Party Central Committee that they had 'made the decision to remove Mironov from the Don oblast' because he was a trouble-maker.

The 14th Division on the left flank of the 9th Army was supposed to join up with the 10th Army based in Tsaritsyn. 'This 10th Army became famous twenty years later,' wrote the commissar Eduard Dune, 'because Josef Djugashvili had been a member of its revolutionary council, but at the time it was famous only because it terrorised the city with mass executions.' At one stage, 'the Headquarters of the 9th Army bolted in a shameful manner.' The whole of the left bank of the Don for 300 kilometres was left bare because 'the 10th Army was scared to venture far from Tsaritsyn'.

The 10th Army's cavalry units consisted mainly of Red Cossacks and still owed much less to the previous year's recruiting campaign of 'Proletarians to Horse!'. A Cossack sergeant from the Tsarist army, Boris Dumenko, had formed the 1st Cavalry Brigade in the 10th Army, with Semyon Budyonny as his second-in-command. Budyonny, who was as famous for his ever-increasing cavalry moustache as for his drinking, peasant cunning and courage, was a non-Cossack – an *inogorodny*. The two men fell out, with Budyonny supported by Stalin and Dumenko by Trotsky. Dumenko's soldiers worshipped him. 'Soldiers talked about him in a reverential voice,' wrote one of them, 'speaking proudly of his valour.' Cut off with his troops by Wrangel's campaign in the Caucasus, Dumenko led them back to rejoin the 10th Army in a heroic march, threatening Rostov on the way, only to find that his wife and daughter had been killed by the Whites in his absence.

Commanding different formations after their clash, Dumenko and Budyonny began to build the Reds' cavalry arm, but Dumenko did not survive in the snake-pit of Communist rivalries. After his cavalry corps took the Don capital of Novocherkassk in January of the next year, he was accused of the murder of a commissar sent to investigate him and he was shot a few months later.

During May, the Red 9th Army broke into small groups along the Millerovo railway line. 'The battered remains of the 14th and 23rd Divisions and the Kamyshin Brigade are retreating to the Cossack village of Ust-Medveditskaya,' the 1st Don Cossack Infantry Division reported. 'Small Red combat units and rear units are holding the area between the Don and the Tsaritsyn railway line.' The division was ordered to continue to 'clear the whole area of the Reds, to mobilise the bulk of the Cossack population aged from 18 to 48 and to arrest anybody who has been working for the Reds'. The Don Cossack uprising in the rear of the 9th Army was developing into a major blow for the Reds. Soldiers, officers and even the commander of the 9th Army deserted to the Whites.

The fortunes of war had suddenly swung in the Whites' favour. Ukraine lay exposed after Grigoriev's desertion of the Reds. To the west of the Don Army, Mai-Maevsky's Volunteers led by Shkuro's cavalry corps, having cleared the Donets and advanced rapidly to Kharkov, then took Poltava and later Ekaterinoslav. Little more than Makhno's guerrilla force remained to carry on the fight. The threat of the Whites cutting off the Crimea prompted the Red forces to retreat precipitately. Meanwhile, on the Ural and Siberian fronts, the White recapture of Ufa and the apparent threat to Kazan from Gajda's army had switched the Kremlin's attention away from the southern front with grave consequences. Some 80,000 reinforcements and the bulk of the supplies left for the Urals.

In the third week of May, General Wrangel's Kuban Cossacks inflicted a severe defeat on the 10th Army southwest of Tsaritsyn. That outspoken thorn in the side of the Red Army, Filipp Mironov, saw the consequences in Tsaritsyn station. 'Moaning Red Army soldiers, abandoned and begging for help, were lying around the station next to

The White armoured train United Russia which helped take the city of Tsaritsyn on the Volga.

fences and in the station itself. I then came across the medical train . . . dead bodies had lain in the wagons for two days, and next to them were sick people. Flies covered the bodies of their dead comrades, then came back to the living ones. I spoke to the senior doctor Dmitrovsky, who pointed out that he had no one to attend to the wounded; but in fact the train was full of personnel, with armbands on their sleeves. Things simply cannot go on like this, otherwise the revolution will drown in the blood of workers.'

A month later Wrangel's troops were at the edge of Tsaritsyn, ready to achieve what Krasnov had failed to do. His Army of the Caucasus had British assistance, and not just in supplies. The Royal Air Force's 47 Squadron, with DH.9 bombers and Sopwith Camel fighters, were based at an improvised landing strip outside Beketovka. The fighters took off early one morning, having been warned that Budyonny's cavalry was preparing to attack. They were told that Wrangel's Kuban Cossacks facing them would make an X formation on the ground to identify themselves. As the Sopwith Camels flew north, they clearly saw part of the White cavalry form an X within an open square. Beyond they could see that the Red cavalry was preparing a trap for the Kuban Cossacks. A small force advanced towards them to provoke a response while their main body was concealed in low ground beyond. The fighter pilots, cocking their twin Vickers machine guns, dived into the attack. Low-level strafing soon put the Red cavalry to flight.

Just before the main attack on Tsaritsyn's defences, the Sopwith Camels reconnoitred the approach and shot down a Red observation balloon, which could have spotted the six British tanks lining up. But when it came to the main assault next day, it was found that there was only sufficient petrol for a single tank. So Major Ewen Cameron-Bruce of the Tank Corps led the attack in a Mark V, despite having lost an arm in the Battle of Messines two years before. This lone iron monster, rolling over barbed-wire entanglements and the first line of trenches, was enough to put the Red defenders to flight. The military booty taken was considerable. As well as Tsaritsyn's munitions factories and large quantities of field artillery and machine guns, the Whites captured armoured trains and many badly needed locomotives and wagons.

Colonel Count Dmitry Heiden reached Tsaritsyn just after its capture. He was struck by how dead the city was. 'The streets were empty,

British armoured cars at Tsaritsyn (later Stalingrad) in August 1919.

the residents had been so intimidated during the Bolshevik rule that they were now afraid of leaving their houses. The market was almost deserted, houses had boarded up windows, stalls were closed, no restaurants were open either at the station or in the city, and the Volga was empty, not a single boat.'

Denikin had told Heiden to study the supply and equipment situation in his different armies. Large quantities of British military materiel, including khaki uniforms, were being landed at the port of Novorossiisk and needed to be allocated. Heiden went straight to report to Wrangel, whom he had not seen since the retreat from the Bukovina in 1917. 'General Wrangel had not changed much in those two years, he still seemed cheerful, vivacious and impulsive, while at the same time he gave an impression of a person made for being in power.' Wrangel's army consisted of I and II Kuban Corps, and IV Cavalry Corps, as well as three independent divisions: the Astrakhan Cossack Division and the 6th and 7th Infantry Divisions. Wrangel warned him to pay close attention to the situation in the Astrakhan Cossack Division. At least food supplies, he explained, were not as bad as they had been thanks to what they captured from the Reds in Tsaritsyn.

Heiden was indeed shocked when he visited the Astrakhan Cossacks in Raigorod fifty kilometres downstream where they were raided from time to time by the Red Volga-Caspian flotilla. 'The troops were looking like absolute paupers. Many were in bare feet or slippers. Less than half of them had high boots, or boots with laces. Many had their shirts and trousers in rags, just like the captured Red Army soldiers.' It suddenly occurred to Heiden that 'during the Civil War, all the previous transactions between the front and the rear were completely turned upside down. In the past, the rear provided the needs of the army. Now the roles were reversed. All transactions were based on whatever could be taken from the enemy, which included men.' It was true. Both sides, for at least part of the war, relied on press-ganging enemy prisoners to make up their own numbers after a battle. If they were unfit due to wounds or sickness, then they took their clothes or boots. Heiden, dejected to see so much 'flesh through holes in their clothing', had only 3,000 sets of British uniforms to distribute among the two infantry divisions.

Commander Goldsmith of HMS *Montrose* had heard that the Whites at Novorossiisk were so 'apathetic and lazy' that the Royal Navy had to use their Turkish prisoners of war to unload the supplies for Denikin's forces. But unloading was only part of the problem. The real drain on supplies was theft and corruption at every stage. Beds and bedclothes delivered for field hospitals disappeared immediately, while the shortage of clothing for the civilian population meant that women refashioned the khaki uniforms for themselves as well as their menfolk.

As Heiden found in their conversations, Wrangel was ferocious in his criticism of Denikin's strategy and reliance on a firm base in the Caucasus. Although his Army of the Caucasus consisted largely of Kuban and Terek Cossacks, Wrangel felt that Denikin's close defence of Cossack regions hampered the one chance they had of winning the war for Russia as a whole. In his view, their only hope lay in linking up with Kolchak's forces. The two men could hardly have been more different both in character and physique. The rotund and avuncular Denikin was of humble origins, while the ramrod-tall Baltic baron, with his sunken yet piercing eyes, possessed an ice-cold determination.

Denikin had given Wrangel the Army of the Caucasus, not to win his support, but purely because he was the outstanding cavalry general on the White side. Yet Denikin, although not exactly a moral coward, still preferred to avoid conflict with fellow senior officers, as his concession to the outrageous Shkuro had shown. His chief of staff,

General Romanovsky, once said to Denikin at a meeting with other generals: 'Anton Ivanovich, in the corps of General Shkuro there is looting, drinking, disobedience, awful excesses! It cannot go on like this!' But Denikin, although embarrassed, would not do anything, even though he knew that Shkuro flouted all his orders against looting and anti-Semitic pogroms.

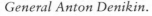
General Anton Denikin.   *General Baron Pyotr Wrangel.*

Denikin had a certain *faiblesse* for victory parades and ceremonies in cities they had conquered. In Poltava, a wildly grateful bourgeoisie bombarded his open automobile with flowers. He murmured to General Mai-Maevsky beside him: 'Vladimir Zenonovich, I am a bit worried that they will throw us a bomb instead of bunches of flowers.' And yet Denikin was received outside the cathedral by the full clergy, greeting him as if he were the Tsar.

On 3 July, the most important victory parade of all took place in Tsaritsyn. Outside the cathedral, Denikin issued his 'Moscow Directive', declaring his intention 'to gain our final goal, the capture of the heart of Russia'. His plan was for his different armies to follow the main railway lines to Moscow. On the western flank, Mai-Maevsky's Volunteer Army would advance north, leaving the great River Dnieper on its left. General Sidorin's Don Army in the centre would continue north from Voronezh, while Wrangel's Army of the Caucasus on the eastern flank was to advance roughly parallel with the Volga as far as Nizhny Novgorod then turn west towards Moscow. Wrangel expressed his doubts about the operation in the strongest terms. There was no concentration of force and too much optimism. He felt it vital to deal with the Red stronghold of Astrakhan first. To leave that in their rear with the Volga-Caspian flotilla intact seemed a grave mistake.

3 July 1919, Denikin announces the 'Moscow Directive' in Tsaritsyn, taken by Wrangel.

In fact, the Royal Navy had the Caspian well in hand with its eight armed merchantmen, twelve coastal motorboats and seaplanes. They were supplying the Ural Cossacks in Guryev on the northeastern shore and bottling up the Red warships in the Volga estuary. They had disarmed the unreliable Centro-Caspian flotilla in March, commanded by 'an ex-cavalry officer and first-class rogue' named Voskerensky. And when the ice in the north finally broke up, they began to attack the Red warships, now based at Fort Aleksandrov in a bay south of Guryev. The Red flotilla included eight destroyers, at least six armed merchant ships, three submarines and a variety of other vessels.

On 20 May, Commodore Norris assembled his ships and the next day, which was at last clear of fog, they sailed past the mouth of the V-shaped harbour to have a look. Remembering Lord St Vincent's maxim that 'Such a moment was not to be lost', Norris in HMS *Kruger* led his squadron of five ships into battle just after midday, 6-inch and 4-inch guns blazing. The Bolshevik shore batteries opened fire at close range but were wildly inaccurate. Only two British ships were hit, and casualties were astonishingly light when compared to the destruction wreaked on the Red ships. 'Nine craft including one large torpedo boat destroyer were sunk or blown up, and we may say that the enemy had a pretty good thumping.' They were particularly pleased to have knocked out the submarine depot ship *Reval*. The Red flotilla abandoned Fort Aleksandrov in the next few days. All surviving craft withdrew into the shallows of the Volga estuary, where the larger British ships could not follow. As the Red Army *Stavka* put it, their Caspian flotilla 'avoided combat collisions in unfavourable conditions'.

On a subsequent visit to the Ural Cossacks at Guryev, Commodore Norris heard that his Bolshevik opposite number, the commander of the Red flotilla, had been executed for their defeat at Fort Aleksandrov. His replacement was Fyodor Raskolnikov, who had brought his Volga flotilla down the river just as Tsaritsyn fell to Wrangel and now commanded the remnants of the Caspian squadron too. British officers also heard that Madame Raskolnikov – Larisa Reisner – had been put in charge of the motor gunboats. Soon afterwards, White Russian officers from Denikin's headquarters in Ekaterinodar began to visit the British, asking for naval gunfire support. They wanted, like General Wrangel, to capture Astrakhan before the great advance north. But since they lacked any charts of the Caspian and knew little of ships and their draught, they could not understand why the Royal Navy could not help in the shallows of the Volga delta. In any case, Norris received orders on 20 July to pull out all personnel via Baku and Batumi, despite Churchill's plea to the Admiralty to keep them there. Their ships were to be handed over to General Denikin's rather unqualified naval forces. The White Ensign had been flown for the last time on the inland sea.

25

Murmansk and Arkhangel
Spring and Summer 1919

In an attempt to raise morale, a group of actors, singers and dancers from the arts organisation ProletKult arrived to entertain the Soviet 6th Army on the Northern Front. Originally the troupe of fifty-one artistes had headed for Perm, but the crushing defeat of the 3rd Army and the capture of the city by the Whites in December put an end to that idea. In January, they were diverted to Vologda and then Plesetskaya. 'There was resentment and protests from the chorus,' the commissar in charge reported angrily to Petrograd. There were 'whining' complaints about being fed on Red Army rations and the lack of hot food. 'Some of the women from the chorus showed that they had come only in order to flirt.'

At Plesetskaya they gave two concerts in the church and complained of the cold, which made it hard for them to sing. 'On the day of a funeral of a comrade who had fallen in battle,' the report continued, 'our glorious ProletKult, in the form of several young ladies from the choir organised an all-night party with dancing. In front of Red Army soldiers they began hanging round the necks of clerks from the headquarters. I in turn started taking very strict measures with them and told them they were disgracing the name of ProletKult, they were corrupt and did not belong there. I promised to send them to Petrograd if they did not reform.' He told them that they were a disgrace to the 'soldiers of the Red Army who are holding back the imperialists of four countries in freezing conditions'.

The imperialists, due to better hygiene, had not suffered as much as the Red Army in the waves of dysentery, cholera, scurvy, typhoid and smallpox, although there had been some 10,000 cases of Spanish influenza in Arkhangel. But the morale of Allied troops was hardly better. The French and American troops at Murmansk mutinied, but not as often as the White Russian troops. 'And we have had four or five unpleasant incidents ourselves,' Churchill informed the prime minister.

With only three or four hours of daylight out of twenty-four, paralysing cold and a lack of hot food, few were convinced by their officers' justification of the mission in North Russia when it seemed that everyone else in their respective armies were going home. It was easy for the Reds to shout across the lines in the frozen stillness, demanding what they were doing in Russia. The same question was posed increasingly in the British press. Most of the troops sent to North Russia to guard the supply depots were of 'low medical category'.

On 19 January, the Red forces launched a series of attacks at Shenkursk on the River Vaga 200 kilometres south of Arkhangel. The American defenders suffered heavy casualties and the town had to be abandoned. On 8 March Churchill, still secretly hoping to use the Allied presence in Murmansk and Arkhangel to link up with Kolchak's forces, managed to persuade the War Cabinet that the demoralised British garrisons should be replaced by two brigade groups of 4,000 men each to cover the eventual withdrawal. They would 'consist of volunteers who have re-engaged'. He was authorised to make any necessary arrangements.

Churchill persisted in his unrealistic dream, badgering Lloyd George for permission to exploit the opportunity if it arose. 'As regards Gajda's move on Viatka and Kotlas,' Field Marshal Wilson reported from Paris, the 'Prime Minister would not go further than to say that if Gajda reaches Viatka and establishes himself there firmly and if he moves up the railway to Kotlas there would be no objection to [Brigadier-General William] Ironside having everything prepared for a blow up the Dvina on Kotlas, but that Cabinet would have to be consulted before such a move were actually carried out.' But as Harris, the American consul general in Irkutsk pointed out, Gajda, 'encouraged by the Entente, wanted to carry on northwest, when in fact he needed to head southwest to protect Khasin's flank. Some accused him of a crazy ambition in his desire to enter Moscow.'

No more than a purely symbolic junction was achieved on the River Pechora, 850 kilometres north of Perm. A small unit from Arkhangel met up with a company-sized group from Gajda's Northern Army. But the vast distances in such hostile terrain made the whole project unrealistic in purely logistic terms. Field Marshal Sir Henry Wilson was a good deal more pragmatic than Churchill. 'In view of the enormous size of the country,' he had written on 24 February, 'the destitution of the inhabitants, the paucity of communications, the deplorable condition of the railways, and the military exhaustion of the Allies, the invasion and occupation of Russia at the present time is not considered to be a practical military proposition.'

Churchill's hopes of creating an effective White Russian army to defeat Bolshevism did not look encouraging in late March and early April. First a battalion of the 3rd North Russian Rifles and then the whole of the 8th Russian Rifle Regiment crossed over to join the Communists. British as well as Russian officers slept with loaded revolvers to hand. It was a relief when Brigadier-General Grogan's brigade group arrived on 26 May and Brigadier-General Sadleir-Jackson's landed on 10 June. The evacuation of the unhappy troops who had suffered the Arctic winter began with the American and French troops leaving on the first ships, along with the two batteries of Canadian artillery. Newly arrived British officers, on the other hand, rather liked the picturesque white churches with green domes and enjoyed snipe and duck shooting around the Dvina estuary.

Red Army attacks came at monthly intervals on the Dvina and Vaga river systems. With the Dvina running north to the Arctic Circle, the upper reaches thawed before the lower, and this meant that the Red flotilla was able to operate while British vessels remained stuck in the ice at Arkhangel until 13 May. The Royal Navy flotilla included four gunboats, *Cockchafer*, *Cicada*, *Cricket* and *Glow-worm*, and two monitors as floating artillery. They all proceeded up-river in the second half of May as soon as the heavy ice had broken. 'Hopes were entertained of assisting the Russians to reach Kotlas and join hands with Kolchak,' wrote Major Lund, repeating the astonishingly persistent fantasy of Winston Churchill.

On 19 June, in a heavy engagement, the British flotilla supported Grogan's brigade at Troitskaya (now Zherlyginskaya). Its monitors provided the opening bombardment while the gunboats fought off the Red flotilla. The next day, the 2nd Battalion of the Hampshire Regiment and the 3rd North Russian Regiment attacked the villages of Rochegda and Tonsa on the right bank of the Dvina. They took 400 prisoners, three field guns and many machine guns, greatly helped by the Royal Navy flotilla and the RAF flying boats working closely together.

Brigadier-General Ironside was given permission by the War Cabinet to attack south to Kotlas, even though by then it was clear that Kolchak's Siberian army would never make it. Ironside, a remarkable linguist with seven languages, was easy to spot in a crowd because of his immense height. This had prompted his ironic school nickname of 'Tiny', which stayed with him for the rest of his life. The new plan was to crush the Red flotilla base at Kotlas so that the Red forces could not follow the Allies down the River Dvina while they were pulling out. Back in London, Lloyd George was still afraid that Ironside might push on south of Kotlas. He wanted Ironside to know that under no circumstances was he to get himself 'embroiled in the south as to necessitate a relief column being sent out from England to extricate [him] as no such troops could or would be sent'. He also had to make sure that his force was in a position so that it could be evacuated 'before the ice set in'.

By the end of June, Ironside had 22,000 Russian troops, including the Slavo-British Legion with British officers and NCOs commanding deserters and prisoners from the Bolshevik side. To call this increase in strength a mixed blessing would be an understatement. On the night of 7 July another mutiny began in White Russian units, including Dyer's Battalion of the Slavo-British Legion consisting of former Red soldiers, and the 4th North Russian Rifles. Three British and four Russian officers were murdered, and others wounded. 'The enemy who was evidently fully conversant with the situation,' wrote Major Lund, 'seized the opportunity to attack.' Red forces came within '1,200 yards of the flotilla anchorage and the seaplane base'.

A detachment of bluejackets and marines landed to secure the position until British reinforcements arrived. Seaplanes also helped with bombing runs while a monitor and HMS *Humber* with its twin 6-inch gun turret forced the Red flotilla to withdraw. But two minesweepers, *Sword Dance* and *Fandango*, were sunk by mines floated down river by the 'Bolos', as the British and Americans called the Bolsheviks. Naval shore parties had to stretch nets across the river to catch more mines later. Some of the mutineers were tried by courts martial and shot, but the ringleaders escaped.

On 19 July, the Italian contingent was withdrawn. Three days later, the Russian regiment near Lake Onega mutinied and opened the front to the Bolsheviks. On the Vologda Railway Front Russian troops also attempted to mutiny, but they were rapidly dealt with by a detachment of the Polish Legion and British troops. Contagion had spread to almost all Russian units and they had to be withdrawn. Once word of a full Allied evacuation had been confirmed by British press reports, the British military authorities could do nothing to prevent Bolshevik propaganda at the front. Russians who had served there in White regiments feared that they might be left to their fate at the hands of the Communists. The British evacuation had been planned for between 15 October and 10 November, just before the Dvina became icebound, but with the state of the Russian forces, it seemed better not to wait.

In August, General Lord Rawlinson took over as commander-in-chief North Russia. With two fresh infantry battalions, some field artillery and five tanks, he was to oversee the withdrawal. A battalion of marines was also sent to Murmansk, which needed to be held for longer so that the river flotilla could be refitted for the voyage back to British waters. The plan was to administer a sharp blow up the Dvina against Red Army forces to push them right back to provide breathing space.

On 10 August, Sadleir-Jackson's brigade made their attack on Red Army positions at Puchega and Borok on the Northern Dvina. An observation balloon floated up from a barge helped correct the range for shellfire. Altogether some 2,000 prisoners and eighteen field guns were captured. This advance enabled the Royal Navy to prepare their mining operation to block the river to the Red flotilla as the withdrawal started. Rawlinson and Ironside tried to persuade the leader of the North Russian Government, General Evgeny Miller, to abandon Arkhangel and concentrate on Murmansk, but he refused, citing an order from Admiral Kolchak 'to hold Arkhangelsk to the last'. At Miller's request, a last attack was made on 29 August on the Vologda Railway line.

On 6 September Red forces counter-attacked but were beaten off by Sadleir-Jackson's troops, who six days later withdrew down river. Ten days later, Rawlinson's military assistant, Major Lund, recorded in his diary: 'Cold and windy weather. Looks like winter starting.' That same day Field Marshal Wilson told Churchill what he had heard from Rawlinson. The Russian General Miller said he intended to defend Arkhangel to the last, but in Rawlinson's view, he 'has really neither the intention nor the pluck to do anything of the kind . . . His soldiers are the limit. Last night a battalion of the 4th [North Russian Regiment] was on its way to the railway front and had to be transferred from the steamer to the train. When the train started all the officers were absent and only 250 men turned up. The officers were all drunk in the town and were rounded up by the Provost Marshal.' Miller then demanded that the British leave him the five remaining tanks, but Rawlinson warned London: 'If I leave him with what he asks, I am, I know, handing it over to the Bolos.' In the end, the White Russians were furious when the British left only two tanks and destroyed the rest to prevent them falling into the hands of the Red Army.

By 23 September almost all British personnel had reached the inner defensive perimeter round Arkhangel. 'The final evacuation on 27 September was conducted in perfect order, the monitors falling back' on the cruiser HMS *Fox*, stationed just off Arkhangel. With embarkation completed, General Ironside and his staff set sail. So did the French cruiser *Condé* in a gesture of Allied support.

Meanwhile, the force at Murmansk began its withdrawal after a successful strike. Brigadier-General Jackson took over from Maynard, who had suffered a heart attack. By 4 October all British troops were north of Kandalaksha. The final evacuation from Murmansk was completed on 12 October. Only 6,535 anti-Bolshevik Russian nationals, many fewer than expected, embarked on British ships for transfer to the Baltic states or South Russia. Total British casualties, including wounded and deaths from disease, amounted to 106 officers, 877 other ranks, with forty-one officers and 286 other ranks killed in action.

Field Marshal Wilson was undoubtedly right when he concluded: 'In no Allied country has there been a sufficient weight of public opinion to justify armed intervention against the Bolsheviks on a decisive scale, with the inevitable result that military operations have lacked cohesion and purpose.'

26

Siberia
June–September 1919

The great surge of optimism at Kolchak's headquarters following the recapture of Ufa in March had soon turned to ashes. The Kremlin's reaction to the threat from the White Siberian armies had transformed the Eastern Front, even if it had weakened the Red Army in southern Russia. Mikhail Frunze of the 4th Army took over command in the southern Urals and started his advance towards Ufa in the second week of April. Frunze, a Bolshevik from 1903, proved to be a highly competent commander. The reinforcements sent by the Kremlin to the Eastern Front included large numbers of Communist cadres to stiffen the resolve of Red Army troops, especially the badly mauled 3rd Army in the north. This gave them numerical superiority, with 81,000 men to 70,500 Whites.

Frunze's forces occupied Ufa on 9 June, despite a suicidally brave defence by Kappel's troops. His Southern Group reported a total 25,500 White prisoners and deserters for the cost of 16,000 Red casualties wounded and killed. Tukhachevsky's 5th Army pushed on towards Chelyabinsk, taking Zlatoust on the way. On 1 July, just two days before Denikin in Tsaritsyn announced his advance on Moscow, Kolchak's ministers heard that Gajda's army in the north was also retreating.

The different armies of Kolchak in Siberia, Denikin in the south and Yudenich in the Baltic had never been able to coordinate their operations. The very few communications between them, which went via Paris, took several weeks to arrive. The great handicap of the Whites was their dispersion around the central core of Communist territory, while the Red Army benefited enormously from interior lines of communication and a more centralised command structure. Yet the Red leadership could also be riven with bitter quarrels.

Battle lines had developed the year before, following Trotsky's withering criticism of Stalin's role at Tsaritsyn and Stalin's attacks on

Trotsky's employment of former Tsarist officers to make the Red Army more professional. That was now followed by a fundamental clash over strategy. Sergei Kamenev, the commander of the Eastern Front, argued strongly that their victories over Kolchak's armies should lead straight on to their total destruction without a pause. Stalin backed Kamenev, even though he was a former Tsarist officer. Vatsetis, the commander-in-chief of the Red Army, supported by Trotsky, insisted that Denikin's armies presented the greatest threat. The Red Army therefore must halt on the Eastern Front and strengthen their forces in the south. Lenin backed Kamenev and Stalin, which provoked Trotsky into offering his resignation as chairman of the Military Revolutionary Committee. Lenin pacified him with the promise that he could issue any order on his own account with his automatic backing. Trotsky relented and agreed to stay, but Stalin managed to get more of his own supporters onto the committee.

Gajda's withdrawal in the north was forced on him by the retreat of Khanzin's Western Army. But the intense resentment of White Russian officers against the Czechs also played a part, as Kolchak's foreign minister Viktor Pepelyayev noted. 'Here they have such a desire to finish off Gajda,' he added, 'that they distort the whole picture of reality. This has to end.' Kolchak himself accused Gajda to his face of 'having democratic tendencies, preferring the Socialist Revolutionaries and surrounding himself in his army and on his staff with men of advanced ideas'.

Gajda replied that it was far more dangerous to have a reactionary view and reminded the admiral of his promises about democracy made to the Allies. Kolchak then accused him of lacking military science. Gajda retorted that the command of three boats in the Black Sea did not permit him to pretend to know anything on the subject. Kolchak threatened him with a court martial and Gajda responded that he was a Czech and did not report to him. Gajda went straight to Janin to ask for his backing as he feared that he might well be arrested, and the French general told him that he could count on his support absolutely. The Czechs resented their role of defending dyed-in-the-wool Tsarists and saw no further reason for staying on in Russia. They wanted to go home.

It was especially bitter for Pepelyayev to hear of the loss of Perm at the beginning of July, the city which his younger brother Anatoly had captured to such acclaim in December. 'The troops abandoned

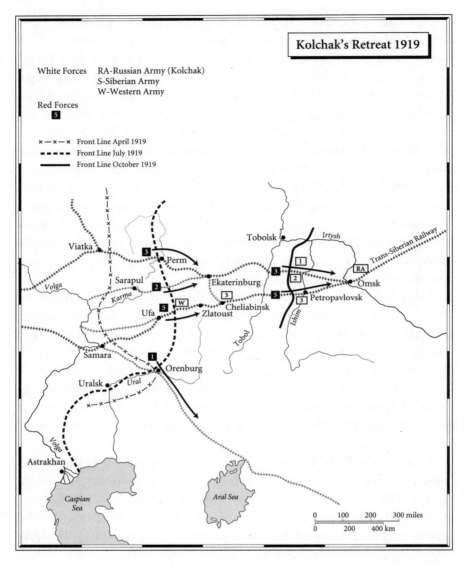

Kolchak's Retreat 1919

White Forces   RA-Russian Army (Kolchak)
                S-Siberian Army
                W-Western Army

Red Forces
    5

× —×—× Front Line April 1919
▪ ▪ ▪ ▪   Front Line July 1919
—————— Front Line October 1919

Perm this evening,' he wrote. 'Our flotilla has been burned. Oil was discharged into the river and set on fire. Twenty-five vessels were destroyed as a result.' The Chinese regiment, which had suffered so much on the retreat through Perm the previous December, was now reformed with Fu I-Cheng as commander and a Comrade Spiridonov as commissar. Their joy at the recapture of Perm was intense.

On 14 July in Omsk, General Janin wrote in his diary: 'The front is disintegrating more and more. A series of symptomatic events – an excessive number of officers murdered [by their own men]. A Colonel tried to stop one of his battalions led by an officer from crossing over to the enemy. And this officer shot him down with his revolver.' In the 1st Infantry Division, three regiments had also crossed over to the enemy.

For Kolchak's government, the 'Czech issue' was paramount, Pepelyayev recorded. 'They are not inclined to fight. Therefore, it has been proposed to invite the Japanese to take on the defence west of [Lake] Baikal.' The idea of bringing the ambitious Japanese into central Russia seemed strange for such a nationalistic administration, which was loath to recognise the independence of Finland and the Baltic states. The Japanese did not even bother to conceal their interests. Their newspaper in Vladivostok, the *Vladivo-Nippo*, when discussing the possible dispatch of Japanese forces to the Ural Front, argued: 'It is much better to send our troops straight to the Urals and thus strengthen the confidence of the All-Russian population. At the same time, we would thus secure our exceptional rights in Siberia and in the Far East.' One American officer was left open-mouthed when a Japanese intelligence officer, a Captain Yamamoto, declared to him: 'The world will be speaking Japanese within ten or fifteen years. It will have to in order to keep abreast of Japanese progress.'

American intelligence estimated that the Japanese had no less than 85,000 men and 14,550 horses in Siberia. They had lost 831 dead and 376 wounded in all their battles and skirmishes, a striking reversal from the usual ratio of three wounded to one dead. In early July Japanese and American troops fought side by side, guarding the mines at Suchan from a Red attack. The Americans were commanded by Colonel Robert L. Eichelberger, who received several decorations from the Japanese including the Order of the Rising Sun. Yet twenty-six years later, it was Eichelberger's Eighth Army which finally defeated the Japanese in the Philippines.

As well as 'the Czech issue', there was also a Polish issue. The Polish 5th Division in Siberia had armed themselves and were guarding a 1,000-kilometre stretch of the railway, but the White Russians were provoked by their refusal to fight at the front. They insisted that their mission was to return to Poland to defend it. Janin found himself having to take their side against the furious criticism of the admiral and his ministers, who accused them of 'all the sins of Israel'. One of Kolchak's advisers told Janin that if the Poles did not go to the front then they should be disarmed. He retorted that they could only fight there if they had an order from their government, which the Whites were reluctant to recognise.

On 9 July, Kolchak arrived back from a visit to the Northern Army. 'The Ruler returned from the front,' Pepelyayev wrote in his diary that evening. 'We listened to his impressions in his railway coach. The situation is desperate.' General Diterikhs warned that 'probably Ekaterinburg and Chelyabinsk will be surrendered'. Pepelyayev also noticed the increasing instability of Kolchak. On 20 July, he wrote: 'Ruler suddenly said "You know what, don't you think that a dictatorship should really be a dictatorship?" He did not elaborate.' Kolchak increasingly suffered from terrifying tantrums, especially when anybody suggested that some enlightened reforms might gain a little support from the civilian population. He also boiled over in constant arguments with the Allied commander General Pierre Janin, mostly about the Czechs whom Kolchak accused of making *'exigences insolentes'*. After a typical row, Janin wrote in his diary: 'It's an exhausting waste of nerves to keep one's sang-froid when trying to reason with a man who is not master of himself.'

The Supreme Ruler, Admiral Kolchak.

The head of the British military mission, Major General Knox, was by then convinced that the White cause in Siberia was irretrievably lost. Field Marshal Wilson echoed Knox's report for the War Cabinet on 23 July. 'The incompetence of the Russian staff and regimental officers, which is only equalled by their vanity and impatience of any foreign advice, has resulted in squandering both men and materiel in premature and ill-considered enterprises, so that practically nothing remains for future use. General Janin, who arrogated to himself responsibility for advising Kolchak as to military operations, has proved to be a mere cipher without the slightest influence on the situation . . . The Russian staff appears to have learned nothing and forgotten nothing.'

Knox was not alone in his assessment. On 25 July, General Anatoly Pepelyayev telephoned his elder brother, the minister of foreign affairs. 'His view,' Viktor recorded, 'is that the situation is almost hopeless unless the "Army", which has to be recreated, will listen to the people and agree to fight. He would like to leave.' That evening Viktor Pepelyayev learned that the Reds had now taken Chelyabinsk. 'Disintegration due to low morale . . . The Supreme Ruler indeed looks burned out.' The disaster at Chelyabinsk came from an ill-thought-out scheme to encircle the Red 5th Army dreamed up by the inexperienced General Sakharov. Both Kolchak and his chief of staff General Lebedev refused to listen to warnings that the manoeuvre was too complicated for the White formations involved. The plan went badly wrong and the Whites lost 15,000 men in prisoners alone, which they could ill afford, as well as the important industrial city of Chelyabinsk. The Red Army was firmly beyond the Urals.

The Communists wasted no time whenever they captured a Siberian city. They issued an order conscripting all 'former White officers up to the age of 50, staff officers up to the age of 55, and generals up to the age of 60, both those from the region, and living there temporarily'. This demonstrated a greater confidence that examples of officers crossing back to the Whites were becoming much rarer.

The low morale in White ranks was partly due to the uselessness of the war ministry in Omsk, which had failed to replace the rotting boots of Gajda's army or improve the conduct of reactionary White officers. Gajda, who was blamed for the loss of Perm, had made himself unpopular by condemning the Tsarist army practices which White officers had reintroduced in Siberia, such as flogging and punching their soldiers in the face when they did anything wrong.

Perhaps most damaging of all was the utter corruption in the rear, which even exceeded the rot behind Denikin's armies. The majority of officers in staff or administrative positions were out for themselves, selling rations, equipment and even guns to compensate for what they had lost in the revolution, or to provide a nest egg in exile. Many had their wives and families with them and made sure that they received preferential treatment, using military transport, rations and supplies. 'There are masses of officers' families in the immediate rear, driving around in army carts, while units are complaining . . . there are no carts available to evacuate the sick and wounded.' An order was issued that no families were allowed further forward 'than the area of Army headquarters'. As the Whites began to retreat, a virulent black market in rail tickets developed.

American cynicism about Kolchak's attempts to impress the Allies increased when they read an announcement in the press that General Kasatkin, the chief of military communications, had been arrested in Omsk. This was after 'rolling stock for the transport of supplies and troops was being issued to private persons at the price of about 25,000 to 50,000 roubles per car. The arrested have been arraigned before a field court martial. They may receive a death sentence.' But two months later, they were not surprised to hear that Kasatkin, far from being executed, had just been appointed chief quartermaster.

Many officers in the rear areas relied on a constant intake of alcohol and drugs to blot out rational thought. (It is surprising that cocaine, apparently consumed so copiously in Omsk, was available in the depths of Siberia.) However, ordinary items of food became scarce in the overcrowded capital of a supposedly free Russia. This caused rampant inflation in a city which somehow did not have the money to pay its workers and railwaymen. Members of the government convinced themselves that the problem must be due to the Allies speculating against the rouble. The only reason the whole economic system had not collapsed was thanks to the gold reserves captured by Kappel's men in Kazan, but Kolchak refused to spend it.

In the rear areas, the Bolsheviks who had gone underground formed more guerrilla groups sabotaging the Trans-Siberian Railway, burning wooden bridges and tearing down telegraph lines. At the same time, the savagery of Cossack detachments on anti-partisan sweeps turned the usually conservative peasantry against the Whites. Ataman Semenov, who had once again declared to Kolchak that he recognised 'the Russian Government headed by Your Excellency and will abide by your orders', naturally proceeded to ignore them all again. It was the *atamanshchina* – the reign of terror and torture by gangster atamans such as Semenov, Ungern-Sternberg, Kalmykov, Krasilnikov and Annenkov, as well as Generals Ivanov-Rinov and Rozonov – that ultimately guaranteed a Red victory in Siberia. Lieutenant General Sergei Rozonov, who commanded the Cis-Amur region, was notorious for his execution of hostages, despite Kolchak's orders to the contrary, and for hanging his victims on telegraph poles along the Trans-Siberian Railway.

As recently as 1 June, Kolchak's chief minister Vologodsky had announced that 'the seat of the Supreme Ruler will soon be moved to Ekaterinburg'. The 1/9th Battalion of the Hampshire Regiment, which had taken over from the Middlesex in Omsk, was moved to Ekaterinburg as the guard force for Kolchak's headquarters even though it remained in Omsk. Churchill had to reassure Lloyd George that their purpose was not to fight, 'but their presence gives a certain moral support to the Omsk government'.

There was also a British training team of officers and NCOs in Ekaterinburg, attempting to create an Anglo-Russian brigade out of 2,500 conscripts, many of them without boots. The young Captain Brian Horrocks was the second-in-command. He spoke some Russian, but the task of training illiterate peasants with very few interpreters proved impossible. General Gajda had promised some of his NCOs, but they never appeared. The greatest resentment was shown by a core of White Russian officers, who clearly objected to any British presence or assistance at all. Then, just as the training started to show results, orders arrived via Major General Knox in Omsk that British personnel were to be withdrawn from Ekaterinburg along with the Hampshire battalion.

Their departure coincided with the rapid advance of the Red 2nd Army on the city, provoking accusations of cowardice from White Russian officers. Even General Janin was shocked. But the British were perhaps doubly fortunate to have escaped in time. They left just before the Whites wreaked an appalling pogrom on the Jewish population five days before the Reds seized the city on 15 July. Some 2,200 people died in this atrocity, largely fired by the vengeance myth of the extreme right that every Jew must be a Bolshevik. The Whites claimed that more than 3,000 inhabitants of Ekaterinburg had been killed after the Reds took over the city, but this may well have been an attempt to conceal the pogrom.

*

On 11 July, just as Ekaterinburg was about to fall, Kolchak had appointed Diterikhs to replace Gajda as commander of the Siberian Army in the north. A further reorganisation followed two weeks later. On 26 July it was divided into the 1st and 2nd Armies commanded by Lieutenant General Anatoly Pepelyayev and Lieutenant General N.A. Lokhvitsky, while the 3rd Army, the former Western Army, was given to General Sakharov. The designation of armies, corps and divisions started to have even less meaning as the desertion rate soared in the retreat, as a local teacher recorded. 'Ordinary soldiers in Kolchak's army who had been conscripted by force did not want to fight the revolutionary troops. One could find them anywhere: in the forest, in marshes, by lakes, in the tall wheat . . . Kolchak organized punitive expeditions in order to find them, but the harsh treatment of local civilians increased the disintegration of the army rather than restrained it.'

Even Kappel's Siberian Rifle regiments started to see self-inflicted injuries to escape the fighting. 'A number of shameful incidents have been registered: avoiding fighting by getting injuries, most notably self-inflicted wounds in the fingers. It is with regret that I have to point out that the greatest numbers of finger injuries took place in those units that are supposed to be setting an example to others, such as the strike units and training teams. The notion of a "Siberian" is incompatible with that of a "finger shooter".' Those reported by doctors were court martialled. The American Captain William Barrett guarding the Trans-Siberian Railway recorded that hospital trains passing through seemed to be full of soldiers with self-inflicted wounds who just wanted to get out of the fighting. 'They shoot themselves through a loaf of bread in order that no powder burns will poison the wound.' They were lucky not to have been executed for such obvious attempts.

There were also fears in the Southern Army that the continued use of Austrian and German prisoners of war was a danger. 'The corrupting effects of such cohabitation and cooperation are clearly facilitating espionage and growth of internationalist ideas.' The Western Army, meanwhile, warned that 'All those voluntarily surrendering to the enemy or defecting will be stripped of all their property as traitors, their land will be taken from them, they will be reduced to poverty. When the region is freed from the Bolsheviks, none of these traitors will be able to live in their home places, they will be handed over to a court martial and executed as persons that have committed the worst possible crime. Let those that might be nurturing criminal or cowardly thoughts about surrendering or treason, think of the consequences, such as irrevocable loss of all their property and the right to land, and inevitable execution.'

By early August, refugees in carts could be seen in increasing numbers in columns interspersed with Kolchak's troops. On 10 August, the admiral's attempt to disguise the gravity of the situation was unconvincing. 'Our armies have been fighting since March,' he announced. 'They need a rest and on my orders they are retreating and do not engage in any large battles with the enemy . . . the Army and I myself are confident of ultimate victory.'

Just before they withdrew, some embittered Whites pretended to be Reds to teach a lesson to secret Bolshevik sympathisers. 'A small group of soldiers appeared on a sunny day on the road to Malo Beloe,' wrote the teacher A. Astafiev. 'Four of them were in a droshky, one was holding a red flag. It was revealed later that they were Kolchak soldiers in disguise . . . Mikhail Ivanov from village Pestereva came out to greet them. "Hello, comrades!" They tied him to a birch tree and tortured him. They pierced his chest with a bayonet and cut off his nose with a sabre, then hacked off his head. They wrote above the unrecognizable body: "Death to Bolsheviks!" The body was found three days later by soldiers of the Red Army.'

Captain Barrett, at Mysovaya on the southern shore of Lake Baikal, found himself faced with a horrible task on 4 August. A train had arrived with 2,200 Bolshevik prisoners captured at the front. 'Most of the prisoners appear to be sick with typhus, and starving. Several dead were removed from the cars. It seems that there are dead to be removed at every station.' Barrett's company had to guard the train on to Chita, where Semenov's men would deal with them. From there they would be taken to Adrianovka, where they would be forced to dig their own graves and remove their boots before being shot.

In August, the retreat from the Urals was matched in the south. Just after Wrangel took Tsaritsyn, he sent Colonel Izergin south to Guryev on the Caspian as a liaison officer with Ataman Tolstov's Ural Cossack army. Izergin, however, found that the Ural Cossacks had set off eastwards into the deserts of Turkestan, hoping to join up with Dutov's Orenburg Cossacks or another formation from Kolchak's forces. Izergin also discovered that Cossack families, fearing the vengeance of the Reds, had ignored Ataman Tolstov's appeal to stay behind. Although many were sick with typhus, they had abandoned their settlements and moved out with their belongings and livestock.

Tolstov's force continued east towards the northern tip of the Aral Sea, where they were soon surrounded by Red forces. Their only escape route to the Trans-Siberian Railway was through a narrow pass which led to the Turgai desert. Camels towed their artillery as well as all the two-wheeled carts taking their dwindling supplies and their sick and wounded. After the summer disappeared, they endured icy winds and dust clouds which lashed their faces with grit. Drivers had to wear goggles in the sandstorms, as Sergei Hitoon, the commander of their motorised column, recorded. 'Horses, camels, livestock and all available food supplies were confiscated from the peasantry of nearby villages.' The villages had emptied in fear of this disease-ridden force as it approached. Short of food and water, they stole and ate the water-melons grown by locals, but this increased the spread of cholera and typhoid fever.

Soon, anything which held them up, including their artillery and the thousands of sick and wounded, had to be abandoned. 'The few motor vehicles struggled in the sand, driven on alcohol as fuel.' It could take as long as an hour to unfreeze the engine to get it going in the morning. Their most reliable vehicle was the hospital truck known as the 'Hotel Benz'. Only a few Cossack detachments were capable of fighting rearguard actions against the pursuing Reds.

On hearing of the accelerating retreat of Kolchak's forces, the Ural Cossacks knew that they would not be able to catch them up in a diag-onal march northeastwards to the Trans-Siberian Railway, so they continued east. With strong Red forces between them and the railway, their only chance now lay in crossing most of central Asia to reach the Chinese border. 'The hasty retreat left behind it a ghastly trail of frozen dead bodies. Camels hopelessly worn out by the over-strenuous work, lay here and there with their humps hanging down.'

In August, a major battle developed between the River Tobol and the city of Petropavlovsk. It began with intense fighting on the sector where the Trans-Siberian Railway crossed the Tobol. Then, towards the end of the month, the Red 5th Army managed to cross the river while the Whites prepared their counter-attack, which was to be commanded by Anatoly Pepelyayev. 'The role of [their spearhead]', the Red Army assessment recorded afterwards, 'was to be entrusted to a corps of Siberian Cossacks numbering up to 7,000 sabres.' While they attacked the flank of the 5th Army, the White 3rd Army was to attack head on. But assembling and deploying the cavalry force took longer than expected and the counter-attack did not begin from Petropavlovsk until 1 September. In the course of another month's fighting, the 5th Army was forced back almost 100 kilometres to behind the Tobol, where the front remained for a time due to exhaustion on both sides. The White losses were greater than they could afford, while the Red Army was receiving constant reinforcements.

On hearing of this counter-attack later, Churchill's hopes surged. He sent a signal to Kolchak via Major General Knox. 'I rejoice beyond words that the supreme effort of Your Excellency's Army has at last been attended with so great a measure of success.' He then went on to explain that the British had concentrated on supporting Denikin's armies in the south because they were more accessible, and that they had expected the United States government to support Admiral Kolchak in Siberia. 'We have pointed out through various channels to the United States that while we are doing our part in the south, we are relying on them to bear the burden in Siberia.' General Graves and his political masters in Washington had no intention of doing so.

Churchill's message of congratulation had arrived too late, for more and more setbacks had obliterated the brief moment of hope. Partisan attacks increased dramatically, encouraged by the Red Army's continuing advance. According to Fedulenko, the commander of Kolchak's escort, 'The Cossack general Ivanov-Rinov promised the Admiral that he would mobilize all the Cossacks and stop the retreat. This never happened.' Diterikhs sacked the boastful Ivanov-Rinov, who then went over to the Bolsheviks. Kolchak's great mistake, and one which would cost him his life, was his refusal to listen to General Diterikhs when he urged him to give up Omsk and retreat all the way to Irkutsk near Lake Baikal.

Even the more rational Viktor Pepelyayev shared the general feeling of outrage against the United States in Kolchak's headquarters. 'America's conduct is outrageous,' he wrote on 22 September. 'It has demanded that we remove Semenov and Kalmykov. General Graves has blocked the weapons which were being sent to us, for which we have already paid in gold.' In fact, the Americans had a far more accurate idea of the horrors perpetrated by the Cossack atamans than

Kolchak's government in Omsk, which preferred to look the other way. General Knox also warned Pepelyayev how angry the Czechs still were at the sacking of Gajda. There were stirrings of revolt against Kolchak in Vladivostok, with an 'attempted coup during the night of 18–19 September'. The Inter-Allied Commission demanded the withdrawal of General Rozonov's troops from Vladivostok but Kolchak and his ministers firmly refused.

Major General Knox had few illusions about Kolchak's forces. He was furious at the way that 80 per cent of the White's conscripts, all clothed and equipped by the British, crossed over to the Reds at the first opportunity. He complained bitterly to General Janin how 200,000 sets of uniform had been wasted. To add insult to injury, Trotsky sent Knox a letter to thank him for his generosity. Knox was not surprised when Tobolsk fell to the Reds in the first week of October. Omsk would follow soon after.

The Red Army was not the only threat advancing in Siberia. Cholera in Harbin had started to spread, while in Vladivostok there was a large outbreak of smallpox as well as cholera. There were rumours of black death – the plague – and in Tomsk there was a typhus pandemic. 'Owing to the congestion,' the American Expeditionary Force reported, 'the epidemic is likely to assume horrible dimensions in the winter. The influx of refugees continues.'

To the bemusement of American officers Russian newspapers seemed more preoccupied by the behaviour of young Russian women, no doubt hoping to escape the coming catastrophe on the arm of a 'doughboy'. Their intelligence section collected clippings which denounced 'Dollar Scrapers', and 'Russian Shame Ladies' consorting with American soldiers. 'At every stop one can see such revolting instances of indecent conduct on the part of Russian women.' 'The cup of humiliation has not yet been drunk to the dregs. The merciless hand of fate is threatening the honour of Russian women.' 'These so-called women see neither the sick and wounded soldiers moving from the front, nor the fugitives driven from behind the Urals by the appalling "pestilence".' In Vladivostok on 6 September, *Dalny Vostok* described scenes in the Zolotoy Yakor [Golden Anchor] restaurant. 'Half clad, drunken women and American gentlemen feel themselves at ease here and arrange orgies, with the windows open and the electric lights burning.' Vladivostok was also seen as a spy city where young women working for the Reds tried to seduce officers, to obtain details on shipments along the Trans-Siberian Railway.

On 6 September, a gunfight nearly broke out at the train station of Iman when one of Ataman Kalmykov's officers accused an American sergeant of misbehaving with a Russian woman. He threatened the American with a pistol, declaring that Cossacks 'could not treat as friends the ravishers of their wives and daughters'. The sergeant drew his Colt and there was a tense stand-off. US troops rushed to release him, and the 'Ataman ordered the Cossacks to throw out a skirmish line, mount a gun and meet force with force'. Kalmykov, who insisted on travelling escorted by two armoured trains, could produce heavy guns in no time so some earnest and firm diplomacy was required.

Russian jealousy and distrust even extended to the American Red Cross. 'When the fighting was going on,' wrote a senior member, 'loads of Russian wounded were brought in in a dreadful state. Not even first aid had been given. The Red Cross wanted to take care of these people but were refused. We have spent millions of good American dollars on these ungrateful people. They regard our gifts with suspicion – they want to know the motive.'

Most American officers thought there was little point in staying since they believed that the country was bound to go Bolshevik anyway. The only time there was a real taste for fighting came after an American detachment was surprised at Romanovka in their tents just before dawn. Nineteen were killed and forty wounded. But when it came to the civil war between Reds and Whites, they were dismayed. 'Kolchak has poor discipline in his army and the men are very young indeed, mere boys. They are given a rifle, clothes, a piece of black bread and salt, and sent to the front line . . . The Americans, however, one and all want to get out as it isn't a man's fight.'

27

Baltic Summer
May–August 1919

Moving the Bolshevik capital to Moscow was bound to reduce the importance of Petrograd, but it did not diminish the strategic significance of its position. The eastern end of the Baltic was now flanked by potentially hostile nations which the Kremlin wanted back under its control, partly as a land-bridge to Germany. The Bolshevik dream of revolution spreading across Europe was remarkably persistent despite the setbacks. After the Spartacist uprising in Berlin was crushed in January and members of the Guards Cavalry Freikorps murdered Rosa Luxemburg and Karl Liebknecht, the Kremlin's revolutionary hopes focused instead on Bavaria and Hungary.

A Soviet Republic in Hungary led by Béla Kun came about in March 1919, in an initially bloodless coup helped by the bitter consequences of defeat and hatred of the old imperial order. Kun, already a committed socialist, had been radicalised in a Russian prisoner-of-war camp, and formed the prototype of the Hungarian Communist Party in Moscow. He fought for the Bolsheviks in the civil war as an internationalist in 1918 and returned to Budapest towards the end of the year with funds provided by Lenin. Kun achieved power by out-manoeuvring the far larger Social Democratic Party.

In early April, a *Räterepublik* – a republic of soviets – came about in Munich following the assassination of Kurt Eisner, the socialist Minister-President of the People's State of Bavaria. Its initial version was mainly a bohemian Anarchist fantasy which lasted barely six days, when a far more hard-line Communist administration took over. As the counter-revolutionary forces, including a Freikorps contingent, advanced on Munich at the end of April, the Communists killed ten hostages of whom one was the Prince von Thurn und Taxis. The White forces, which included a number of future Nazis, used the killings as an excuse to slaughter almost any leftists they captured.

Meanwhile, Hungarian fury at the decision of the Paris peace conference to transfer a large slice of territory to Romania greatly strengthened the hand of Kun and his Communists. When Romanian forces marched into Transylvania, Communist internationalism became the beneficiary of patriotic outrage. Volunteers, including former officers, flocked to join a Hungarian Red Army. The French and British governments became deeply alarmed that the Bolshevik disease could spread to all of central Europe and the Balkans. By June there was economic chaos and a savage Red terror against both bourgeoisie and peasantry. This gave rise to a White movement, headed by Admiral Miklós Horthy. In August Béla Kun's regime fell amid a humanitarian disaster, compounded by collapsing infrastructure and famine. Kun fled to Moscow. The White terror which ensued killed many more people than its Red predecessor, as anti-Bolshevik death squads hunted down their enemies. Admiral Horthy appointed himself 'Regent' and ruled as such until Hitler deposed him in 1944 for not cooperating sufficiently in the 'Final Solution'.

In May, General Yudenich in Helsinki was demanding vast quantities of weapons and even aircraft from the Allies for his army in Estonia. His reluctant subordinate there, General Aleksandr Rodzyanko, the Olympic horseman, launched a joint offensive with the Estonians under General Laidoner. Yet it was the guerrilla cavalry force of Bulak-Balakhovich, who had now abandoned the Reds, which captured Pskov during a raid into Russian territory. Rodzyanko was unable to control Bulak-Balakhovich, who was as savage in his control of the city as he had been suppressing the Luga revolt for the Reds. He launched pogroms against the Jews if they did not hand over their money and hanged suspected Reds from the city's lamp posts.

Laidoner continued the advance towards Petrograd in support of the White Russian Northern Corps and an Ingrian battalion. His plan was to create a buffer zone on Soviet territory, because the Lutheran Ingrians of the region identified themselves far more with Finns and Estonians than they did with Russians. Less than ten years later under Stalin, they were one of the very first ethnic groups in the Soviet Union to face deportation. Laidoner's idea was for the Northwestern Army to establish itself in a buffer zone there rather than remain based in Estonia, where Rodzyanko's reactionary and overbearing officers proclaimed their belief that it should remain part of the Russian Empire.

They did not endear themselves to their long-suffering hosts by singing 'God Save the Tsar' when they had had too much to drink in the restaurants and streets of Tallinn.

General Johan Laidoner, the Estonian commander-in-chief, visits Bulak-Balakhovich (left) in Pskov on 31 May 1919, soon after its capture.

Lenin ordered Stalin to take charge in Petrograd to ensure that the sacred symbol of their revolution should never be captured. After his reign of terror in Tsaritsyn, Stalin had been sent to investigate the loss of Perm to Anatoly Pepelyayev's army in December. His subsequent arrival in Petrograd militarised and terrorised the whole city. Workers were drilled and trained in basic weapon skills while potential enemies were arrested. Stalin demanded Red Army reinforcements, but the real threat to Petrograd that summer came from the sea, despite the immense defences of the Baltic Fleet at Kronstadt.

On 13 May, the 1st Estonian Division and the Northwestern Army attacked east from Narva, supported whenever possible by the 6-inch guns of Cowan's light cruisers. Using the two destroyers captured from Raskolnikov, Estonian marine infantry landed behind the Red Army's front line. The Bolshevik leadership was seized with panic that Petrograd might fall, helped by Whites still hidden in the city. During the night of 12–13 June, Stalin and Yakov Peters of the Cheka, having secretly assembled a force of 15,000 men, carried out mass arrests in Petrograd of former officers and their families, as well as deserters from the Red Army. Several hundred were shot.

Stalin's fear of treachery increased. With the help of a mutiny by some of the defenders, the Ingrian battalion captured the great fortress of Krasnaya Gorka which guarded the southern approaches to the Kronstadt naval base. Most of the garrison were Ingrians recruited locally. On Stalin's orders, the coastal artillery batteries guarding the base began to retaliate in a massive bombardment, as did the two battleships, *Petropavlovsk* and the *Andrei Pervozvanny*, with their 12-inch main armament. Viktor Shklovsky, writing in a dacha in Lakhta on the northern shore of the Narva estuary nearly 30 kilometres away, was distracted by his windows rattling constantly from the dull boom of gunfire across the water.

That day, the Baltic Fleet reported to Petrograd: 'At 8.50 Krasnaya Gorka started responding to our bombardment. Their shells were falling in the Small Harbour [of Kronstadt naval base]. So far they haven't damaged anything. Our spirits are high. *Andrei* and *Petropavlovsk* are constantly covering us.'

The revolt of the Ingrians at Krasnaya Gorka also triggered Stalin into ordering an immediate witch-hunt against officers in the Baltic Fleet. 'We are attaching for your consideration the list of officers from the battleship *Gangut* and the cruiser *Aurora*,' a report to the revolutionary military council stated. 'I would like to inform you that we have received from the commissar of Genmor [naval general staff], comrade Gan, the list of certain members of the ships' leadership who are on the lists of the All-Russia Cheka as members of counter-revolutionary organisations.' Some seventy officers would be executed. The suspects included the commander of the armoured cruiser *Oleg*, which was soon targeted by Lieutenant Augustus Agar, in charge of the Royal Navy's high-speed coastal motorboats, hidden in a bay on the Finnish coast.

On Wednesday 18 June, with a crew of three in a fast coastal motorboat, Agar managed to sink the *Oleg* while it was bombarding Krasnaya Gorka. But their success changed little. The cannonade from the coastal batteries and battleships was so intense that the Ingrian battalion and the mutineers were compelled to abandon the fortress.

Despite the sinking of the *Oleg*, the Whites still complained about the lack of support from British warships. They refused to accept the fact that Admiral Cowan's cruiser squadron in the Gulf of Finland could not penetrate the minefields around Kronstadt. This excuse became Rodzyanko's justification for the failure of his Northern Corps to take Gatchina and advance on to Petrograd. His officers also blamed the lack of success on their British tanks breaking down. They even tried to claim that the six iron monsters had been sabotaged with sand in their engines. This bizarre notion was supposedly caused by British displeasure at the way these Tsarist officers openly proclaimed that Estonia would always be part of the Russian Empire. Whatever the truth, their precipitate retreat from Gatchina earned them the Estonians' contempt.

The 2nd Estonian Division, meanwhile, had been rather more successful by defeating the Red Estonian Rifle Division, and prompting its 1st Rifle Regiment to change sides. But the main threat to Estonia came not just from the Bolsheviks. As soon as the Reds were forced back, the ambitions of German nationalists surged into the open. They believed that their rights to the region went back to the Northern Crusade launched by Pope Innocent III in 1193. The united councils of Livonia, Courland and Estland, representing Baltic Germans, had conceded at the Treaty of Brest-Litovsk that these provinces were independent states. Yet German nationalists still claimed rights to the region that went back to the Northern Crusade. In September 1918, the Kaiser amalgamated the provinces into a United Baltic Duchy. Its freshly minted duke never took office because of the defeat of German forces in the west but its armed force, the *Baltische Landeswehr*, still tried to exert German authority.

At the beginning of February 1919, Generalleutnant Rüdiger von der Goltz, who had played such an important part in the success of the White Finns, had landed in Courland to reorganise the Freikorps as the VI Reserve Corps, now reinforced by the Guards Reserve Division. On 16 April, the Germans overthrew the Latvian government of Kārlis Ulmanis and installed their own puppet administration. After the recapture of Riga from the Reds, the now expanded 'Iron Division' and the *Baltische Landeswehr* advanced northeast into Livonia, in defiance of warnings from the Supreme Allied Council in Paris. There, they came up against the 3rd Estonian Division and a Latvian brigade in June at Cēsis, in sight of the great fortress of the Teutonic Knights. Largely due to General Laidoner's brilliant leadership and the timely intervention of three Estonian armoured trains, the *Baltische Landeswehr* was decisively defeated. The Estonians and the Latvians pushed on towards Riga and, with the full support of the Supreme Allied Council, restored the Ulmanis government. Estonian morale and national pride surged after their victory.

To complicate Baltic relations further at this time, a White Russian 'Western Volunteer Army' was formed under Major General Pavel Bermondt-Avalov in Latvia. His men were mostly Russian soldiers recruited from German prisoner-of-war camps. They were armed and equipped by General von der Goltz, who used this force of less than 10,000 to conceal as many of his own troops as possible, including the Iron Division and the German Legion, which were supposed to have left the Baltic on the orders of the Inter-Allied Commission.

After the German defeat at Cēsis, the *Baltische Landeswehr* was placed under the supervision of Lieutenant Colonel Harold Alexander, an Irish Guardsman later to become another major figure in the Second World War. He ordered all the non-Baltic officers to return to Germany, but many simply joined the German Legion under Bermondt-Avalov. The remnants of the *Landeswehr* became a part of the Latvian Army under General Jānis Balodis. Latvia's independence was thus saved, at least until Stalin, with Hitler's assistance, forced the submission of the Baltic states in June 1940 during the Nazi-Soviet pact.

The unenviable task of establishing some sort of logic and order in the Baltic region had been given to General Hubert Gough in May, when the Supreme Allied Council in Paris appointed him head of its military mission. Gough had been a controversial choice. British politicians distrusted him after his role in the Curragh incident just before the outbreak of the First World War, when army officers resigned en masse rather than accept orders to march against Ulster Unionists. He had also been unfairly blamed for the buckling of the Fifth Army when the Ludendorff offensive smashed into it in March 1918. But Lloyd George could do nothing to prevent his appointment as the decision had been made in Paris. On the other hand, Churchill and General Wilson (a fellow Ulsterman) supported him.

Gough faced impossible contradictions in policy. His role was to keep German troops in the Baltic to halt the Bolsheviks, yet also control and then repatriate them without any Allied ground forces to back him up. To complicate matters further, Lord Curzon, the foreign secretary, had summoned Gough just before his departure. He told him not to let Churchill push him into intervening in the Russian Civil War and to restrain forces backed by Britain from capturing Petrograd.

Gough was most impressed by the Estonian commander-in-chief General Laidoner, who had defeated the *Baltische Landeswehr* and other German forces at the Battle of Cēsis. Laidoner's victory gave the Estonians the confidence to express their intense dislike for their traditional oppressors, the Baltic barons, and also for their unwelcome ally, the Northwestern Army.

In June, General Yudenich, the presumptive commander-in-chief of the Northwestern Army, submitted to Kolchak's headquarters a draft agreement between him and General Mannerheim of Finland. On General Wilson's advice, Churchill had persuaded Yudenich to consult Kolchak on the matter. Churchill longed to create an anti-Bolshevik coalition in the region which could be supported by Cowan's 1st Light Cruiser Squadron. The navy was one thing, but Churchill knew that the overt deployment of ground forces was out of the question. Public opinion at home would not stand for it.

The possible agreement with Finland was debated at a meeting of the Council of Ministers in Omsk. 'The Finns', Viktor Pepelyayev noted, 'demand in exchange for their participation in taking Petrograd that we recognise the complete independence of Karelia and Olonets'. This represented a vast area of northwest Russia adjoining Finland, from Lake Ladoga up to the White Sea. Four days later, Kolchak and his ministers rejected the proposal as 'completely unacceptable', much to Churchill's frustration.

Following their humiliating retreat, Rodzyanko's troops behaved appallingly in their Ingrian buffer zone. Anti-Semitic pogroms, looting, and the mindless brutality with which they treated anyone suspected of Bolshevik sympathies destroyed any illusion that the Northwestern Army came as liberators. Their demoralised soldiers, unpaid and underfed, began deserting to the enemy in greater and greater numbers during the summer, even though the 'white nights' made it difficult to steal away undetected.

Stalin, meanwhile, had managed to increase the strength of the 5th and 7th Armies to a total of around 40,000 men. On 1 August, they attacked and began to push back both the Northwestern Army and the two Estonian divisions, who saw little reason to sacrifice themselves on foreign soil. They withdrew across the border into Estonia and Yamburg fell to the Reds on 5 August. Only Pskov remained in White hands.

General Gough, disgusted with the behaviour of the Whites and carried away in his enthusiasm for all things Estonian, warned Yudenich that the British military mission would cut off supplies if he did not recognise the country's independence. He and his chief of staff, General Marsh, connived with the Estonian formula of a 'Pskov Republic'. This would become the seat of a notional Northwestern Government, responsible for any areas east of the Estonian border taken from the Bolsheviks. Lloyd George and Curzon were outraged at the way Gough had exceeded his brief. The foreign secretary condemned it as a 'Ruritanian experiment', but there was little they could do.

Gough, who was based in Helsinki, was certain that Mannerheim wanted to take Petrograd. He had no illusions about Mannerheim's illiberal views. Lloyd George and Curzon were much more uneasy. Contemplating the capture of Petrograd, they did not know who would cause more problems, Mannerheim or Yudenich. Churchill hoped that Yudenich would, if only because he had been appointed by Kolchak and that would make a White victory more straightforward. He wanted the Allies to recognise Kolchak outright as Russian head of state, even though the Supreme Ruler continued to evade a firm recognition of the independence of border states. Kolchak again used the doubly disingenuous argument that Russia's borders had to be decided by a future Constituent Assembly, while he knew perfectly well that the vast majority of White officers had no intention of allowing such a democratic body to exist.

On 4 July the Cabinet in London, while avoiding any declaration of hostilities, privately acknowledged that a state of war existed between Soviet Russia and Great Britain. General Wilson did not agree with Churchill's hopes for a three-pronged attack on Soviet Russia. 'We should close down our military effort on all fronts except South Russia, with the object of concentrating all our available resources for the assistance of Denikin,' he argued. 'It is in that theatre that we can most easily apply our weight.'

Lloyd George became even more scathing about Churchill's enthusiasm for the White cause. 'Russia does not want to be liberated,' he wrote to members of the Cabinet on 30 August. 'Whatever she may think of the Bolsheviks, she does not think it worthwhile sacrificing any more blood to substitute for them men of the Yudenich type . . . As to the "great opportunities" for capturing Petrograd,' he continued, 'which we are told were "dangling at our fingertips", and which we never grasped, we have heard this so often of other "great opportunities" in Russia which have never materialised in spite of lavish expenditure on their prosecution.' He estimated that they had already spent more than a 100 million pounds that year. 'General Yudenich never had a chance of taking Petrograd . . . He is a notorious reactionary, as much distrusted by the Estonians as by the Russian people. If North Russia were groaning under Bolshevik tyranny and the Estonians and Latvians were eager to join in a war of liberation, there would now have been an army numbering hundreds of thousands sweeping over northwest Russia. The fact that out of a population of several millions the anti-Bolsheviks have only mustered 20,000 or 30,000 men is another indication of the complete misreading of the Russian situation, upon which the military policy has been based.' Lloyd George's logic had important flaws. A civil war was not an election with military overtones, because the vast majority of people wanted to stay out of trouble. Yet his instincts about an unsuccessful outcome were right.

Just when Lloyd George wanted to curtail his country's involvement in the Russian Civil War, the most audacious attack by British forces took place. On 12 August, Rear Admiral Cowan summoned the officers of the Royal Navy's coastal motorboat flotilla on board his flagship. Based just inside Finnish territory at Terijoki, 20 kilometres north of Kronstadt, the coastal motorboat flotilla had been sent to the Baltic under Lieutenant Augustus Agar to ferry British secret agents in and out of Petrograd. Now Cowan wanted to go much further than the sinking of the cruiser *Oleg*. The flotilla had been joined by seven more 'skimmers', as the coastal motorboats were called for their ability to skim over minefields. Mechanics were working through the night to prepare their highly tuned engines.

Cowan was determined to ensure that the Baltic Fleet did not venture out from its heavily defended complex of harbours at Kronstadt to challenge his cruiser squadron. He had five main targets, he told the assembled officers. The most important were the two battleships, the *Andrei Pervozvanny* and the *Petropavlovsk*. The next most important was the depot ship *Pamiat Azova*, which had two submarines moored alongside. Cowan also wanted to neutralise the *Rurik*, a cruiser converted into a minelayer. Unfortunately, she had just received a fresh consignment of 300 mines, so a successful torpedo strike could destroy not just the whole harbour area, but probably all the Royal Navy boats in the attack. The gates of the dry dock were the last objective, apart from the destroyer *Gavriil*, which acted as guardship at the entrance to the three harbours.

The 'skimmers' were capable of 45 knots so certainly had speed on their side, but the noise of their engines could be heard from a great distance. To cover this, Cowan agreed to launch a diversionary air attack just before the skimmers reached the Kronstadt defences. The aircraft, four Short seaplanes and four biplane fighters, included a single Sopwith Camel. They had arrived on board the improvised aircraft carrier, HMS *Vindictive*, an old cruiser given a wooden flat-top deck. The other major problem which faced the flotilla was the restricted area inside the triple harbour. There was a real risk of collision, especially since they needed to reach maximum speed as they fired their torpedo. This was because the torpedo was carried in a bay in the centre of the boat. The launch process required setting its motor running, then activating a ram which pushed it out of the back. As soon as the torpedo hit the water, the boat had to accelerate fast to get out of its way.

With the attack delayed by a storm, the flotilla finally waited for darkness to fall late in the short northern night of Sunday 17 August. The Gulf of Finland was calm as the eight coastal motorboats emerged to take up positions ready for the air attack. As they 'sat bobbing in the water with the engines ticking over, gunners checked ammunition drums and mechanics made last minute adjustments to their notoriously temperamental charges'. Just before midnight a green light flashed, the engines roared into life and Lieutenant Agar set off, leading the flotilla line astern behind him.

Things got off to a bad start, with the column splitting and the larger group taking a different route. The aircraft had trouble taking off so the skimmers, which had sailed past the line of forts without casualties, then had to halt and wait well short of the harbour entrance. To their amazement, no lights showed ahead, not even on the destroyer *Gavriil*. Without any radios, they had no idea what had happened to the air diversion so, unable to wait any longer, the attack began. This took place at the very moment when the aircraft did finally arrive.

Instead of starting with the *Gavriil*, the first motorboat accelerated, with sheets of spray flying on either side like wings, and swung behind the destroyer into the harbour mouth. Heading straight for the *Pamiat Azova* depot ship under machine-gun fire, the crew fired their single torpedo. The explosion, flames and smoke confirmed a direct hit, and the ship began to keel over.

The attack on the *Gavriil* near the harbour mouth had to be aborted because another motorboat raced across its bows on its run into the harbour, and this gave the Soviet destroyer's crew the time to find their target. With searchlights on the wreckage of the fragile craft, they then began to fire at the survivors struggling in the water. The next two boats were more successful, the first hitting the *Andrei Pervozvanny* then the second the *Petropavlovsk*, despite machine-gun fire killing its helmsman.

In the chaos of tracer bullets and explosions, two skimmers collided in the chaos of the inner harbour, sinking one of them. The failure to eliminate the *Gavriil* proved very costly for the British. Her gunnery, aided by the illumination of searchlights and flames from the stricken ships, was impressively accurate. One of the CMBs attempted another attack with suicidal bravery and fired at close range, but the torpedo ran deep and went just under her hull. The forts also were concentrating more on the surface craft than the aircraft overhead. The last attack was Agar's, sending his sole torpedo into a cluster of ships to distract the gun crews in the harbour.

A couple of the boats' crews owed their lives to two of the aircraft pilots, one in a seaplane, the other in the Sopwith Camel, who stayed after the other biplanes had departed. They harried the forts, machine-gunning the searchlights until they ran out of ammunition. The toll remained heavy. Nearly half of those who had set out the night before were missing, eight of them dead and nine taken prisoner. Two Victoria Crosses were awarded among other decorations for what many regarded as a raid of suicidal bravery. Admiral Cowan reported to the Admiralty that the damage inflicted on the Red Baltic Fleet in this action would play a large part in assuring the independence of the Baltic states.

28

The March on Moscow
July–October 1919

On 3 July, the day that General Denikin announced his Moscow directive in Tsaritsyn, Sergei Kamenev (no relation of Lev Kamenev), was
appointed commander-in-chief of the Red Army.* Although a former
Tsarist colonel, Kamenev was nominated by Stalin, who had packed
the Revolutionary War Council with allies to outvote Trotsky, the
chairman.

Five days later, the former commander-in-chief, Vatsetis, who had
been appointed by Trotsky, was arrested on a trumped-up charge
of belonging to a secret 'White Guardist' organisation.† The bitter
dispute had started the year before, when Kamenev had insisted that
the counter-attack against Kolchak's forces should be carried through
without a break.

Vatsetis and Trotsky had wanted to fight Denikin by attacking
through the Donbas, with its population of industrial workers who
supported the Reds. Kamenev and Stalin, on the other hand, argued
for the recapture of Tsaritsyn. Although Stalin's reputation was linked
to that city, he was right to argue that troops could be more easily
transferred to that flank from the victorious Red Army in Siberia.

The Red Army in southern Russia facing Denikin's summer offensive was at an acute disadvantage after Kamenev's insistence on award-
ing priority to the Siberian Front. The 14th Army on the north shore
of the Sea of Azov had been shattered by the Volunteer Army under
Mai-Maevsky in its advance to Kharkov, leaving Ukraine completely
exposed. On the eastern flank, General Wrangel's victory at Tsaritsyn

---

* By a curious coincidence, Sergei Kamenev would die from a heart attack on 25
August 1936, the very day Lev Kamenev was executed at the start of Stalin's purges.
† The accusation against Vatsetis was soon shown to be false and he was released,
but Stalin never forgot a victim as well as an enemy. During the Great Terror, Vatsetis
was again accused of being a secret Fascist and shot in 1938.

had also meant the loss of vast quantities of weapons, supplies and rolling stock. Arms factories in Communist territory were soon incapable of keeping pace with the Red Army's ammunition expenditure, while the Whites were receiving their supplies from the British.

One advantage the Communists enjoyed was an extensive network of spies and underground informants behind White lines who reported to the Party's Don Bureau. One of their number had passed back some details of the situation in Tsaritsyn since its loss: General Wrangel was very pleased with the support provided by the British pilots; and emaciated Red Army prisoners of war were begging for bread. Communist propaganda had scared them by emphasising the brutality of the Cossacks, but they surrendered anyway.

Another report from the underground Don Revolutionary Committee agreed with Mironov's warnings about the dangers of ill-treating Cossacks. 'Our failures on the southern front are not only the result of strategic mistakes but also of our ill-judged policy towards the Cossacks and the confiscations and requisitions as well as shootings that at times turned into an ugly form of sport. This could not have helped give the Cossacks a positive view of Soviet attitudes. Of course, we are not counting on the Cossacks as a reliable support for the Soviet authority, however we think that they need the gingerbread as well as the whip.'

Communist underground networks had started to re-establish themselves in the summer after White counter-intelligence had crushed a number of their groups, particularly their most important cell in Taganrog. Many of their organisers and agents were women. But now they could report that 'the exposure of agents has been halted. We have almost restored the organisation in the Rostov district. In the Novocherkassk district, the exposure was limited to just the city itself. The rest of the organisation is intact.'

Not all of the intelligence passed back to the Don Bureau was welcome. 'We would like to inform you of the following, because probably you do not have a very clear picture of the situation at the local level. Morale among the workers and peasants is very low due to the retreat of our army and the close proximity of Makhno's army. This has compromised the Soviet authority in the eyes of workers and peasants.' Traitors and 'provocateurs' were being assassinated in the region. They also acknowledged receipt of 250,000 roubles smuggled

to them through the lines to help their work, which included infiltrating the White Army, but also Green groups in the northern Caucasus.
The 'Greens' were partisans, mainly deserters from both White and
Red armies, who hated and attacked both sides, a phenomenon which
increased as the war continued.

Denikin's plan for the march on Moscow, which he had announced in
front of Tsaritsyn's cathedral, included four main elements. Wrangel's
Army of the Caucasus was to advance north between the Don and
the Volga, then carry on all the way to Nizhny Novgorod before
swinging west on Moscow. On his right General Sidorin's Don Army
would advance up the Volga to Saratov. In the centre, Mai-Maevsky's
Volunteer Army would attack north, following as its centre line the
railway to Moscow via Kharkov, Kursk, Orel and Tula. It would also
push forces to the west up the line of the River Dnieper, and take Kiev.
And finally, General Dobrovolsky was to advance deep into Ukraine
to seize Kherson and Nikolaev.

General Wrangel was highly critical of Denikin's plan. He considered it far too optimistic and a dangerous dispersal of their forces.
Wrangel was right about the lack of concentration, but once again he
demanded that his army should receive all the reinforcements and supplies. There was no justification for this. Kolchak's battered Siberian
armies were in retreat far from the Volga, so any hope of a conjunction
of forces was well past. Military logic dictated that priority should be
given to the central thrust by the Volunteer Army.

General Mai-Maevsky gave little sign of urgency in his advance on
Moscow. When Heiden arrived in Kharkov to inspect depots he went
to see the commander-in-chief. 'The first unpleasant surprise was the
commander himself, a shapeless rounded mass with puffy eyes and
slurring speech, which must have been a result of the previous wild
night and mad drinking. In the several days that I spent in Kharkov,
there were non-stop lunches, dinners or suppers in this or that restaurant, for the commander with a whole entourage of officers and a military band. The merriest parties took place when the famous General
Shkuro with his Wolf Sotnia was also in the city.'
    Mai-Maevsky's Volunteer Army then consisted of General Kutepov's
I Corps, General Prolitov's II Corps, General Shkuro's III Cavalry

Corps stationed in Prokhorovka* and General Yuzefovich's V Corps in Poltava. Heiden was deeply concerned about the supply situation just before the momentous advance. While inspecting the depots, he found that only half the bread ration was available and there was a complete lack of fats, meat, tea, milk, matches and, perhaps most serious of all, forage. The regions they had conquered and which they were about to cross could not provide what the Volunteer Army needed to keep going.

After the capture of Poltava on 31 July, the remaining Red forces in Ukraine became increasingly nervous as regiments of the Volunteer Army approached. French warships once again anchored off Odessa, while inland a revolt broke out in the German communities, supported by Ukrainian peasants. Yelena Lakier heard that the Cheka was carrying out executions every night. 'They rev the engines of trucks to hide the noise of gunshots.'

On 5 August, when a French monitor came in close to shore to rescue people swimming out to it, the Bolsheviks opened fire on it. There was a terrible shortage of water in the city. It was being sold for fifteen roubles a bucket. Yelena Lakier, who had to queue for it every night, felt so weak from lack of food that she feared she would faint when carrying it. Only after a landing by 2,000 troops of the Volunteer Army and a brief battle on 23 August was Odessa liberated. The following day, Lakier wrote: '*Urrrrraaa!* There is not a single Bolshevik left in Odessa now. At last! Four and a half months under these five pointed star oppressors.' Two days later she noted that all the Jews were in hiding.

Volunteer Army troops advanced out of the Crimea and, swinging west along the coast, had seized Kherson and Nikolaev on 18 August. Shkuro's Kuban and Terek Cossacks, meanwhile, approached Ekaterinoslav and were met by heavy fire as they approached the bridge over the Dnieper. A White cavalry *sotnia* made a sudden charge across the bridge and the Reds pulled back. Any Red Army soldiers or suspected Communists caught in the city were hacked to death by Cossack sabres.

---

* Prokhorovka, according to Soviet propaganda, was the site of the Red Army's great tank victory in the Battle of Kursk in 1943, when in fact it was worse than Phyrric. It has now been shown that the Tiger tanks of the Waffen SS destroyed most of the 5th Guards Tank Army during its ill-planned counter-attack.

*

On 10 August, General Konstantin Mamontov and his IV Don Cavalry Corps, with some 8,000 sabres, had set out to raid the rear areas of the Red Army and unofficially loot a few cities on the way. They could cover huge distances. Unlike conventional Russian cavalry, which rode European-style with the heavy upright trot, the Cossacks, knowing their horses, leaned forward shifting their weight. Cossacks also rode long, with their legs straight. As a result, they could remain in the saddle for far longer than regular cavalry with shorter stirrups and bent knees. Mamontov, despite his old-fashioned Victorian moustaches, was a loose cannon and a freebooter. General Wrangel considered him little short of an outright criminal and later claimed responsibility for his sacking.

Mamontov's cavalry corps made its way through a gap between the 8th and 9th Armies, by-passed Voronezh and took Tambov eight days later. 'The Tambov axis was all the more dangerous,' the Red *Stavka* recorded, 'because the headquarters of the Southern Front was near there in the town of Kozlov.' Kozlov (now Michurinsk) lay just another 50 kilometres to the northwest. The front commander and headquarters personnel fled to Orel on hearing of Mamontov's approach, leaving just odd militia groups to face Mamontov's cavalry corps.

'There was no one left in town to maintain law and order, but it was not necessary,' wrote Antonina Maximova-Kulaev, a surgeon in the hospital. 'Citizens cowered in their homes. The wires were down, and no news was coming through. We were cut off from the rest of the world.'

On 23 August, when she was working in the surgical dressing room, a member of staff rushed in. 'Doctor! Look out of the window! Cossacks!' She saw a mass of horsemen in the square outside in Cossack uniform, their officers wearing gold shoulder boards, something she had not seen since before the February revolution two and a half years before. They were General Mamontov's advance guard.

Fearing a pogrom, two Jewish physicians in the hospital wisely ran to hide in the attic, while Maximova was summoned to report to the head of the Cossack medical detachment. She knew the danger she was in from both sides. The Cossacks could treat her as a Red in a senior position, on the other hand the orderlies were all Bolsheviks, so if she cooperated with the Whites she risked being denounced as a traitor when the Red Army returned. Fortunately, the Cossack doctor was a decent man and did not put her in an impossible position.

Outside, church bells began to peal in celebration. The better-off citizens, who had longed for liberation by the Whites, emerged to hail their saviours. Cossack officers threw open the government warehouses where items confiscated by the Bolsheviks were held. This led to a mad rush which extended into a general looting of other places, especially houses owned by Jewish families. Communist sources state that 101 Jews were killed in the Cossacks' pogrom. Peasants from nearby villages began arriving with carts, determined to seize their share. The supplies of kerosene were carried off, some of it in double milk pails suspended from a yoke. The Red Army *Stavka* later accused Mamontov of 'crude demagogy, that is by distributing stolen property to the population, to bring it over to his side'.

To maintain appearances, Mamontov had issued orders to his troops against looting. 'Rank and file Cossacks are not allowed to send back recaptured booty. Once the troops enter Russian districts, I order requisitions to cease whenever possible.' It appears to have had little effect. Several houses were set on fire in the chaos and a number of suspected Bolsheviks were hanged from gibbets or street lamps in the main square. Mamontov was rather more insistent on being obeyed when he found too many Cossacks travelling with the supply train, which offered a better means of transporting booty. He was even more angry when he found that 'the carts were drawn by excellent horses', which should have been at the front as cavalry chargers.

Drunken officers entered the hospital and began carousing. Nurses continued to work as best they could while fighting off the Cossack officers' advances. Scenes in cubicles became increasingly violent, so Maximova withdrew all the young nurses and hid them in a storeroom at the back of the building. She went to bed that night utterly exhausted. When she awoke late the next morning, the town was eerily quiet. A number of Mamontov's squadrons had ridden off at dawn in their mission of destruction and chaos.

Accounts vary on how long the Cossack occupation continued, but all Mamontov's men had left within a week. A day or two later, according to Maximova, joyful cries could be heard: 'The Cossacks are back!' White sympathisers rushed out into the streets again to welcome them with cries of 'Long live the Cossacks! Long live National Russia!'. But these were Red Cossacks with Budyonny's 1st Cavalry

Army, who promptly shot or sabred them. Commissars with the 1st Cavalry put up posters which warned: 'Any person found in possession of stolen goods will be shot on the spot.' That night sacks of flour were dumped in the streets while kerosene flowed in the gutters, tipped away in terror by the looters.

On the eastern flank of the White advance in southern Russia, General Wrangel, who had annoyed Denikin with his constant demands for reinforcements, suddenly needed every man he could get when Kamenev launched a double counter-attack in mid-August. The 9th and 10th Armies attacked Wrangel's Army of the Caucasus, forcing it back down the Volga from Kamyshin towards Tsaritsyn, until his Kuban Cossacks fought them off. The other attack from the north was less powerful, so the Volunteer Army and the Don Cossacks together crushed it rapidly. Churchill was exultant when he received the news. 'Denikin is doing better and better,' he wrote to Lord Curzon. 'He has heavily repulsed the enemy at Tsaritsyn without the need of bringing troops from other parts of his front. He has completely repulsed the Bolshevik counter-attack on the Donets coal basin. He has enormously extended his gains in the Ukraine.' Churchill thought that the war might well be over by the end of the year, yet at the same time he was deeply concerned at developments further south in the Caucasus.

Like other White generals, Denikin was committed to the integrity of the Russian Empire. This was a self-defeating handicap. It alienated Finland, the Baltic states and Poland. Churchill under-estimated this imperial obsession which prevented the alliances he wanted to defeat the Communists. He had told General Briggs, who had come straight from Denikin, to persuade the Polish leader Józef Piłsudski to join in with Denikin's advance. When Briggs had left, an unconvinced Piłsudski spoke to the British military attaché Brigadier General Adrian Carton de Wiart. He also predicted that 'Denikin would fail to get to Moscow, and worse still, that he would soon be back in the Black Sea'.

Denikin would have been horrified to hear that privately Lloyd George wanted Russia broken up into small independent states, such as Ukraine, a Cossack Republic and various other territories. Churchill was appalled to hear that the prime minister 'considered that we had done enough to reach the equilibrium between the two factions and should now drop Russia and let the best man win. That it was indeed by no means certain which *was* the best man.'

Denikin's Greater Russia obsession was also a problem in the Caucasus, a British sphere of interest. The Menshevik government in Georgia, which had received help from the Germans the year before, clashed with Denikin when his troops occupied the town of Sochi on the Black Sea coast. Minor battles had followed. Denikin was gravely disappointed when the British supported the Georgian claim to Sochi.

The Foreign Office had sent Oliver Wardrop, a passionate pro-Georgian, as Chief Commissioner of Transcaucasia to their capital of Tiflis. Churchill feared that the Georgian government was becoming increasingly pro-Bolshevik in Denikin's rear, and aggressive in its stance towards the Armenians. 'Is there not a great danger,' he wrote to Curzon, 'of Wardrop running their point of view to the exclusion of all others and in direct hostility to Denikin whom we have decided to back. If we are not careful we shall have battles taking place with British officers on both sides, each stirring up their particular game-cock to fight.'

Churchill was already concerned that the Admiralty's decision to withdraw its personnel from the Caspian would enable the Red flotilla to dominate the inland sea, and allow Transcaspia to pass into Bolshevik hands. 'Bolshevism may over-run the whole of those enormous regions from the Caspian to the Indian frontier,' he wrote to Curzon. His imperial nightmare was certainly exaggerated, but the revolts against the Whites which the Georgians stirred up and armed, first in Chechnya and then in Ingushetia and Dagestan, forced Denikin to divert large numbers of troops at the crucial moment during the advance on Moscow.

Denikin's push across Ukraine faced little resistance. On 31 August, Symon Petliura's Ukrainian forces, who had remained hidden in villages to the west of Kiev, emerged just as the Reds pulled out and Denikin's troops were about to enter from the other side. The Ukrainians appeared marching up the main street and ran up their blue and yellow flag on the Municipal Duma. Rumours spread through the city that Denikin was giving Kiev to Petliura while the Whites advanced on Moscow. But then a Volunteer Army cavalry detachment arrived, followed by a regiment of Don Cossacks. Astonished to find Petliura's men, the Cossacks drew their sabres and charged with their wild whooping. The Ukrainians retreated in a rush and abandoned the city.

General Mai-Maevsky was welcomed to Kiev with a production of Gounod's *Faust* at the State Theatre. His appearance in the royal box prompted a standing ovation. The grateful rich of the city began sending bouquets of flowers up to the gilded box. Mai-Maevsky, still standing, shouted to the audience: 'People of Kiev! I greet you and congratulate you on being free of the Red filth!' The singers all bowed to him, just as they used to bow to Nicholas II. When the performance began, Mai-Maevsky paid little attention to the singing. He chatted with General Efimov about the assassination in 1911 of Prime Minister Pyotr Stolypin in the same theatre close to where they were seated. Mai-Maevsky then discussed the atrocities of the Cheka in the city and told Efimov: 'Please pass the information to Osvag for propaganda purposes. Publicise them widely and do not spare the details.'*

Once again, the regional Cheka had carried out a massacre just before a city fell to the Whites. On the night of 28 August, 127 prisoners had been killed in the concrete garage of their headquarters on Sadovaya ulitsa. 'Many of the heads of the corpses appear to have been crushed,' it was reported. 'Another 70 bodies were found at the district Cheka on Elizavetinskaya ulitsa; a similar number at the "Chinese Cheka", and another 51 corpses of railway workers at the Railways Cheka by the main station.' In the so-called 'Chinese Cheka' the commission found one horrifying rumour to be true. A short length of pipe was attached to the stomach of a victim and fastened securely. A rat would be introduced into the pipe, and a fire was lit at the far end, forcing the rat to eat its way into the intestines of the prisoner to escape.

Only a handful of prisoners had survived in the prison. 'They were walking dead, dragging their feet and looking at us with motionless, dull eyes,' General Reberg's commission noted. Over the following days more mass graves were discovered.

*

* Osvag, the acronym of *osvedomitel'noe-agitatsionnoe otdelenie*, was the propaganda arm of the Armed Forces of South Russia and based in Rostov. Since it had little positive news to offer on the political front due to the refusal of the Whites to contemplate any reform, its success was very limited. Paper shortages did not help.

Mai-Maevsky's adjutant Pavel Makarov, in fact a secret Communist, described the moment on 12 September when the general finally made a show to launch the Volunteer Army's advance on Moscow from Khanzhenkovo station. He climbed out of his railway carriage, then discussed details in French with the British officer in charge of the supporting tanks. The British claimed that 'after three engagements it was no longer necessary even to de-train them. The Bolsheviks did not wait to be attacked.' General Shkuro, leading his Wolf Sotnia with their deep cavalry saddles and ostentatious harnesses, could not resist his own moment of drama. 'Valorous Kuban and Terek Cossacks!' he yelled at the top of his voice, 'Forward! Follow me!' as if they were the vanguard. The real spearpoint of the Volunteer Army was Kutepov's I Corps with the elite Kornilov, Markov and Drozdovsky Divisions.

On 20 September, the day that Kutepov took Kursk, Churchill sent a 'Personal and Secret' signal to Major General Herbert Holman, the head of the British military mission in southern Russia. 'I consider it inadvisable that British airmen should be used in present circumstances to bomb Moscow.' He then sent his congratulations to the officers and men of 47 Squadron RAF based near Tsaritsyn. Two days later, an evidently tense Churchill signalled Holman again. 'Wire me your private opinion whether there is any chance of Denikin reaching Moscow this year.' He also asked him whether General Wrangel's artillery needed armour-piercing shells to take on the Red Volga flotilla south of Tsaritsyn. Churchill misled the House of Commons time and again, pretending that the British assistance was limited to providing equipment, weapons and training advisers. The active involvement in the fighting of British pilots, gunners and tank corps personnel was consistently denied.

The Kremlin leadership was already in a nervous state after the loss of so much territory and so many cities in the south. Then, on 25 September, Anarchists in Moscow set off a bomb in a building occupied by senior Communists in Leontiev Lane, killing several of them. Pretending that those responsible for the explosion were 'Whites', not Anarchists, the Cheka set off another wave of reprisals across the country similar to those of a year before, which followed the attack on Lenin and the killing of Uritsky. 'Pale as paper, Dzerzhinsky came to the Cheka straight from the scene of the bombing,' the leading Chekist in Moscow wrote. 'He ordered that all those listed as Kadet party members, police officers, officials of the monarchy, and all sorts of princes and counts imprisoned in Moscow jails and concentration camps were to be executed.'

Mamontov's extraordinary rampage behind Red lines continued. As his Don Cossacks crossed the province of Tambov, peasants greeted them, offering sheaves of wheat. But their welcome did not last long once his men helped themselves to whatever they wanted. The cavalry corps turned to the northwest, but as the force of Reds pursuing them became increasingly threatening, they swung round and headed towards Voronezh in three columns. Progress had slowed because of their vast accumulation of loot, both attached to their saddles and piled in supply carts. On 19 September they broke back through Red lines and joined Shkuro's III Corps of Kuban and Terek Cossacks. This prompted the commander of the Red Army's Southern Front to swear he would end this 'cavalry nightmare'. Yet, to Shkuro's dismay, three quarters of Mamontov's men then proceeded to head home to the Don with their loot. Less than 1,500 out of the original 8,000 sabres remained at the front.

Martin Alp, a young Latvian cavalry officer forcibly recruited by Mamontov's corps, wrote a brief account of his experiences after they nearly shot him as a suspected commissar. 'We caught members of local Soviets unawares in their villages. Commissars and communists were shot straight away or hung on the winding gear of the wells. As for women, their lives were normally spared, but all young ones were raped. The contents of any store-houses were loaded on our carts.' He was fascinated by Shkuro's 'Angels of Death', as his famous 'Wolf Sotnia' were also known. 'I couldn't get enough of a look at them,' he wrote. 'As for them, they never looked at us, or if they did, it was with arrogance. They were very proud of the fact that they never took prisoners and would never agree to be taken prisoner, either.'

During their brief rest period after the raid, Alp was billeted together with several young officers, who kept reproaching him. 'You fought side by side with us, but you don't want to join in when we are having fun.' He replied as carefully as he could: 'I value you as my comrades-in-arms and I am happy to sit at the table with you. But I don't want to drink with you.'

'I was not able to change their behaviour,' Alp explained, 'but I resisted drinking with them and taking part in their orgies with women, especially with the arrested female communists among whom there were some principled, good Russian women, even though they were communists. I felt a great pity for them when they were in the hands of those male dogs. Soon I could no longer stand it.' He managed to transfer to an infantry regiment.

On 30 September, Shkuro led his corps across the Don and took the city of Voronezh several days later. The front remained very unstable, with Red forces raiding right up to the city limits. The radio communications officer, Erast Chevdar, described how Shkuro and his officers were enjoying a performance of Planquette's comic opera *Les cloches de Corneville* when word came of another attack. All the officers present rushed off, causing panic among the audience, but it proved a false alarm. The officers returned to their seats and the performance continued. Afterwards Shkuro invited the whole cast to dinner in the hotel which he had taken over. More than 100 people sat down to much drinking as well as to solo and chorus singing. At one point, Shkuro stood up to make a patriotic speech. He ended it with a rousing toast to the success of the White armies and 'their self-sacrificing struggle for the bright and free future of Russia'.

Some of the best descriptions of the Volunteer Army's advance in early October appear in the diaries of Captain John Kennedy, who became the assistant chief of the general staff in the Second World War. Soon after his arrival, at the beginning of September, he was struck by the sense of almost limitless space. 'A country of great rolling plains, here and there a little village with a quaint domed church, but for the most part the great expanse was unbroken by human habitation. The plain is only partially cultivated – now we saw a stretch of stubble and the wheat stacked in little heaps, now a patch of Indian corn or of melons, and then great stretches of grass as far as the eye could reach. There were few signs of life except for an occasional springless country cart, or a flock of geese, or a herd of cattle or horses.'

Kennedy was unimpressed by fellow officers in the British military mission, many of whom had been transferred there from Salonika. After he arrived at their base in Taganrog on 7 September, he wrote: 'the officers of the Mission we have come across so far are of the lowest type and obviously inefficient'.

His first destination was Kursk, where General Mai-Maevsky, 'who rather reminded me of a toad', was going to celebrate its capture.

Kennedy was scornful of the way White generals indulged themselves with all the trappings of royalty. 'Mai-Maevsky had a special carpet rolled out in the station to cross the platform to reach his richly appointed personal train ... Scores of staff officers and sentries, armed to the teeth, stood on the platform awaiting the great man. What a contrast this scene of luxury formed to the condition of the miserable peasants, huddled up asleep on the platforms and in the waiting rooms.' Even the more junior General Belyaev had a train with wagons attached to carry the 'General's chargers, his luggage cart and the two horses which pulled it, and his bodyguard of twenty or thirty Cossacks'.

Kennedy finally reached the front on 1 October, attaching himself to Kutepov's I Corps. 'All the troops collect in the nearest village at night. In the morning the batteries go out and take up position and are followed by the infantry. The guns blaze off at maximum range into the blue, limber up and go on when the signal to advance is given, followed by the infantry, who don't like to get in front of the artillery.'

'The advance still continues,' he wrote the next day. 'Much colder now, and there is a slight frost at nights. Still hot in the middle of the day.' An artillery officer himself, Kennedy noted that the field guns which the British had supplied were 'out of action owing to careless usage. They never oil the springs. And if anything goes wrong, the Russians expect the British to replace the gun rather than repair it themselves.'

Back at corps headquarters on 6 October, Kennedy saw General Kutepov. He had returned from the front to interview General Brusilov's son, 'who had just been captured having been forced to fight for the Bolsheviks'. Back in liberated Kursk the next day, he attended a collective funeral in the cathedral square for 'some hundred disinterred victims of the Bolsheviks'. A priest infuriated many officers present by saying that 'we must not bear malice against the Bolshevist torturers and murderers, for they were but the explosion of the charge laid by the liberals'.

Three days later, Kennedy was back at the front with an artillery battery which was engaging a squadron of Red cavalry. 'They gallop forward in two lines (which means, they tell me, that the first is of mobilised soldiers, and the second of Communists, who shoot the former if they attempt to retreat). A droshky also appeared, driving across the fields behind the cavalry, and in this, they told me, there was probably the commander or a commissar.' The shells fired by the battery chased off the cavalry. Some Red infantry appeared twenty minutes later, and they disappeared when a 6-inch howitzer battery opened fire. Mid-morning, Kennedy then observed an armoured car advance up the road towards the enemy followed by a troop of thirty Kornilovsky cavalrymen with lances and pennons waving. 'These, in turn, are followed by an officer company of the 2nd Kornilovsky Regiment, marching along in fine style, with fixed bayonets, and singing their deep-chested war song.'

Prisoners and Red Army deserters swarmed back unguarded. Kennedy considered their soldiers to be pitifully clothed and armed. Their strength lay only in numbers. He was also impressed and surprised at how well the White infantry and the artillery were now working together.

Optimism swelled in the War Office back in London. 'The Bolsheviks are falling and perhaps the end is not distant,' Churchill wrote to Curzon. 'Not only their system but their regime is doomed. Their military effort is collapsing at almost every point on the whole immense circle of their front.' But Churchill was gravely ill informed. He claimed that the anti-Bolshevik forces now mustered 630,000 men against a Red Army of 450,000 men, when Communist forces, at least in theory, outnumbered the Whites more than two to one. Figures on both sides were never reliable because of the proportion of deserters, especially when things were not going well.

On 12 October General Dragomirov's forces attacking north from Kiev reached Chernigov on the edge of Belarus. That same day the commander of the Kornilovsky Regiment told Kennedy that they would take Orel within two days. At this moment, the Tsarist rouble rose on currency exchanges to sixty times the value of the Soviet rouble. After all they had suffered from Bolshevik pillaging, the peasant welcome for the Volunteer Army struck him as quite genuine. They recounted how the Bolsheviks had smashed their icons and stolen the last of their grain. Within a day or two, Kennedy was driven to complain that he had never eaten so much goose in his life.

As the Kornilovsky commander had predicted, the Whites entered Orel two days later on 14 October. Kennedy heard that the Communists had shot 120 hostages before abandoning the city, yet the Kornilovsky had captured 10,000 prisoners. They shot all their leaders, including the commander of the 13th Division, took the overcoats and weapons of the men and then released them. Kutepov held a curious victory parade. 'The proceedings commenced by a tank walking over and demolishing the wooden tribunal of the Bolsheviks in the central square, amid the half-frightened cheers from the crowd.'

The White press claimed that the population of Orel had come out with icons to meet the Volunteer Army and knelt down to sing 'Christ is risen!'. In Vladivostok the newspaper *Volya* suggested that the Bolsheviks were about to propose peace terms on the basis of 'the abolition of the Soviet government, the cessation of the Terror, the cessation of executions and the free passage of Bolshevik leaders to South America'. Even some of the foreign press was carried away. Swedish newspapers stated that the Bolsheviks were evacuating Moscow and moving to Vyatka.

Beyond Orel lay Tula, and beyond Tula, Moscow. 'Orel to the Eagles!' Mai-Maevsky exclaimed on hearing the news, since Orel meant eagle. But in private he was less exuberant. 'So far we have only grabbed the Eagle's tail,' he muttered.

29

Baltic Surprise
Autumn 1919

In the late summer of 1919, after the Northwestern Army had retreated from Gatchina all the way back into Estonia, it was reorganised into what were called two 'rifle corps'. This was very optimistic. Together they totalled less than 15,000 men, with a cavalry detachment of 150 chasseurs and forty 3-inch field guns. Denikin's successes in the south of Russia were now of far greater concern to the Kremlin, yet Lenin decided that it would still be wise to remove the threat to Petrograd by diplomatic means.

On 31 August, just as the Whites were about to lose Pskov, the Soviet foreign minister, Georgy Chicherin, proposed talks with the Estonian government. Field Marshal Wilson warned Churchill that on their side the Estonians were likely 'to try to make some arrangement with the Bolsheviks'. The Estonians, as Yudenich should have realised before he so rudely dismissed their claims to independence, were in quite a strong position. They could offer the dissolution of the Northwestern Government and a refusal to help his White army as a bargaining counter for the Kremlin to recognise their independence. Yudenich was outraged by what he saw as Estonian betrayal, but he also knew that he could not count much longer on British support.

Churchill was deeply frustrated that the 'great opportunities' of capturing Petrograd in the summer with the help of the Finns had not been grasped. The fault lay with Kolchak and Yudenich, who both still refused to guarantee Finnish independence. Churchill frequently demanded to know why the British were not better at putting together anti-Bolshevik coalitions, yet he never acknowledged that the Whites had always been their own worst enemy when it came to dealing with possible allies. The British representative in Estonia reported that White leaders of the Northwestern Army had even boasted that 'after Petrograd they would capture Reval [Tallinn]'.

Churchill's hopes that the Poles might attack the Red Army to help Denikin were also dashed. Denikin refused any compromise over Russia's future borders with Poland, so the Polish head of state Józef Piłsudski was hardly encouraged to help him. This allowed the Red Army to bring its remaining troops in the west, including the Latvian Rifle Division, across to face Denikin. Churchill, meanwhile, continued to justify British support to Yudenich, because he was 'aiding Denikin's advance and keeping pressure off us during our dangerous withdrawal from Archangel'. Lloyd George was unimpressed. He suspected that Churchill's anti-Bolshevik obsession had led him to be less than straight when reporting to the Cabinet.

Faced with the prospect of losing a secure base in Estonia as winter approached, Yudenich felt obliged to attempt a final, wild gamble to take Petrograd. To increase his minuscule army, he attempted to make an alliance with General von der Goltz and his force of Freikorps thugs. Many of them later became early members of the Nazi Party and its paramilitary organisations. This so-called 'Army of Western Russia' was closely linked with the largely German formation of the bejewelled and perfumed Prince Pavel Bermondt-Avalov. Both continued to rampage in the Baltic in defiance of General Gough's orders to disband and return to Germany. But to Yudenich's disappointment both Goltz and Bermondt-Avalov's troops attacked Riga instead, forcing Admiral Cowan and his cruiser squadron to come to its aid.

The irresponsibility of Yudenich's whole enterprise was all too evident. In the unlikely event of success, the Northwestern Army would be incapable of controlling, let alone feeding, the starved population of Petrograd. Yudenich blithely assumed that the Allies, particularly the British, would be forced to take over the task.

'The besieged city had only cabbage to eat,' the writer Viktor Shklovsky recorded. 'I kept alive by buying nails in Petersburg and taking them to the country to exchange for bread.' One old man, greatly weakened by famine, took his last item of value, a gold watch, out into the countryside to exchange it for a small sack of flour. 'On his way home, he met an apparently nice young *moujik* who offered to carry his sack for him, seeing that he was exhausted and that they were both going the same way. When the parting of their ways came, and the old man asked for his sack back, the *moujik* took off his cap, laughing as he said: "Many thanks, Uncle. It's a long time since any flour has fallen into my hands so miraculously." And with that he took to his heels with the precious bag. The poor old gentleman arrived home empty-handed, and not long after he succumbed to starvation.' Even those who had secretly held on to their Russian Orthodox faith were reduced to catching and eating pigeon, which supposedly represented the Holy Ghost.

Yudenich took pride in his contempt for the 'government' which General Gough had forced him to create. He was in theory its minister of war, but he never attended any session or bothered to inform fellow ministers of anything. On 23 September, the minister of the interior informed his colleagues that Yudenich had ordered mobilisation 'due to the difficult situation of the army'. They demanded an explanation but received no reply. They also had no idea that Yudenich intended to dissolve the government 'the moment his troops entered Petrograd'.

On 26 September, the Kremlin transferred some of the best units of the 7th Army to face Denikin's advance from the south. An attack by the Northwestern Army from Estonian soil seemed unthinkable so soon after Chicherin's peace overture. Two days later, Rodzyanko began the campaign to take Petrograd with a feint attack on the southern flank below Lake Peipus against the 15th Army, secretly assisted in his plans by the 7th Army's chief of staff. The Petrograd Cheka had been surprisingly slow to break up the National Centre and the Union for the Regeneration of Russia, the underground White organisations in the city. Only the shock of the mutiny at Krasnaya Gorka in May had stirred them into action, with constant round-ups and searches of apartments.

Yudenich, although officially commander-in-chief of the Northwestern Army, had curiously little influence on Rodzyanko's plan and direction of operations. Rodzyanko, 'a jolly man, a carefree nobleman', could joke with his soldiers, but all he had to recommend him as a military leader was his fine seat on a horse. The motives of some his senior officers were shamelessly cynical. 'I have already accumulated 300,000 roubles,' the commander of the 2nd Division boasted, probably when drunk. 'I want to keep going until I have made a million, and that's it. With money, I will have respect, women will love me, I will have everything I need.' The 4th Division was commanded by Prince Dolgoruky, 'who thought himself brighter and more capable than anyone else in the army, and therefore did not bother to follow orders'. As for Yudenich, the Northwestern Army 'did not recognize the authority of the commander-in-chief whom they didn't know, of whom they had seen very little, and for whom they had no respect'. The round and flabby Yudenich, with his preposterous cavalry moustaches reaching down either side to his shoulders, stayed cocooned by his staff in his headquarters throughout the campaign.

Clearly unaware of what was afoot, Churchill asked the directorate of military operations in London to consider what could be done with the Northwestern Army if the Baltic states were to make peace with Moscow. 'Is it not possible for them to be moved southwards into the Polish sector and so gradually make their way to Denikin's left flank?'

On 10 October, General Rodzyanko launched the main thrust of Operation White Sword from Narva. It took both the 7th and 15th Armies by surprise, and nearly three quarters of the barely trained Red Army conscripts surrendered or deserted. The former Semyonovsky Guard Regiment crossed over to the Whites en masse. Despite their corrupt and incompetent leaders, Rodzyanko's men fought well. In six days they took Gatchina. Four days after that they reached Tsarkoe Selo just 25 kilometres from the centre of Petrograd. On hearing of five British tanks in Yudenich's vanguard, Red Army conscripts fled in panic. As for the White generals, the surprising ease of their advance went to their heads. The commander of Rodzyanko's 3rd Division ignored his orders to cut the main Moscow–Petrograd line at a key railway junction. Instead, he wanted his force to be the first to enter the city. According to Russian military tradition dating back to Marshal Suvorov, this would give him special privileges as commandant.

The dull boom of artillery fire could be heard across the Gulf of Finland. Viktor Shklovsky on the north shore observed the Peter and Paul fortress wreathed in smoke from its guns, which made it look like a great ship in a naval battle. The 'shell bursts hung in the air like clouds in the sky', he wrote. Fear that the Finns would take the opportunity to attack from the north across the isthmus spread, as did the possibility of another mutiny like that of the Ingrians in the fortress of Krasnaya Gorka five months before. Grigory Zinoviev, the Communist leader in Petrograd, suffered a nervous collapse.

In an extraordinary statement never revealed until after the collapse of the Soviet Union, Lenin declared: 'If the offensive has started, isn't it possible to mobilise 20,000 Petrograd workers plus 10,000 bourgeois, place artillery behind them, shoot several hundred and achieve a real mass impact on Yudenich?' As the Red forces disintegrated, Lenin then considered abandoning Petrograd to the enemy (as Stalin was to do twenty-two years later during the German onslaught). Trotsky seized the opportunity. The 'cradle of the Revolution' had to be defended at all costs, he argued. Lenin conceded, and Trotsky ordered up his armoured train once again for the journey to Petrograd.

Trotsky's arrival in the former capital on 17 October was predictably dramatic. Deploying his considerable oratorical ability, he roused a fatalistic population with the prediction that they would turn the granite city into a killing ground: 'a stone labyrinth'. He combined his promise to double the food ration with a stark warning of what treatment they could expect at the hands of the Whites. Trotsky was in his element, stirring large audiences with his revolutionary rhetoric. He mounted a charger at one point to rally retreating troops. Whatever scepticism one might have about the 'great man theory of history', there can be little doubt that Trotsky managed to convert mass panic into mass courage.

To reduce the tank fright of his troops, he claimed that the British tanks were just boxes made of painted wood. He also called on Putilov metalworkers to fabricate a few vehicles to look like their own tanks for the sake of morale. The gravity of the situation convinced Lenin to divert experienced troops from the front against Denikin to save Petrograd. Kamenev called them their 'Queen of Spades' trump card. They managed to get through thanks to the egotism of that White divisional commander who failed to block the railway line in his impatience to enter Petrograd first. This senior officer had even refused the offer of some field glasses to observe the centre of the city from the Pulkovo Heights. He replied that he did not need them because he would be strolling down the Nevsky Prospekt the next evening.

On the same day Trotsky reached Petrograd, Churchill sent a message to Yudenich via the mission in Helsinki to congratulate him 'on the very remarkable measure of success which has attended the opening of your offensive'. He promised to send a further consignment, including 'rifles, clothing and equipment for 20,000 men', twenty 18-pounders with 3,000 rounds per gun; twelve 4.5-inch howitzers with 2,000 rounds per gun; and four 6-inch howitzers with 1,000 rounds per gun, 'as well as some aeroplanes and a few more tanks', and also 400 Russian officers trained in Britain.

Four days later, Churchill, once again behind events because of slow communications, assured Curzon that 'our officers here continue to be confident that the overthrow of the Bolsheviks is certain, taking the situation as a whole.' He had sent General Haking 'to be at Yudenich's side in the event of his entry into Petrograd'. The reason for this was that 'we may otherwise be held to have done nothing to prevent lamentable reprisals following the fall of the city'.

Late that same day, Rodzyanko's advance came to an abrupt halt. Trotsky counter-attacked with the reinforcements from Moscow who had reached Petrograd by train. The Northwestern Army was forced to abandon Pulkovo and then Gatchina six days later. Rodzyanko's men fought desperately, but they were heavily outnumbered and beginning to succumb to a typhus epidemic. On 31 October, Churchill signalled General Haking, asking for an appreciation of the state of the Yudenich army. 'Ice may form in [the] Gulf of Finland any time after 12th November, and [the] Cabinet have decided that [the] British Fleet should quit Finnish waters as soon as ice forms.'

In the first week of November the Red Army forced the remnants of Yudenich's forces all the way back to Narva. They recaptured Luga and Yamburg on 7 November, the anniversary of the Bolshevik coup. The retreat became pitiful. Thousands of civilian refugees, who had hoped to return to Petrograd in the baggage train of the White army, had attached themselves to the troops, and hampered their every movement. They also suffered from typhoid and many who made it back to the Estonian frontier were placed in quarantine camps. The situation of those still trapped on the eastern side of the frontier became even bleaker as the weather worsened. When a report reached General Yudenich describing their appalling state, he refused to provide any funds on the grounds that his budget could be spent only on the needs of the army.

Some of Rodzyanko's officers did not miss the chance of looting before they pulled back. Members of the 1st Rifle Corps headquarters 'took two or three railway wagons of palace property, among which there was silver and other porcelain tableware with the royal insignia as well as other valuables'. The Estonian department of counter-intelligence soon identified where most of the items had been hidden.

The Estonians, well aware of Trotsky's threat if they harboured Yudenich's forces again, allowed military personnel into the country providing they surrendered their weapons. While part of the Northwestern Army held on to a strip of Russian territory, its 'government' tried to negotiate with their former hosts. Yudenich, as minister

of war, had not bothered to attend any session since September. General
Kondyrev, his deputy war minister, reported: 'the Estonians clearly
desire to disarm our army, which they do not want to regard as an ally
and which they do not want to keep on their territory'.

Yudenich continued to exasperate his fellow ministers by ignoring
them and 'carrying out a policy completely different to that of the
government'. When at last he had to face them, the minister of agriculture Bogdanov exploded. 'Either General Yudenich reports to the
government, in which case he must join the commission to negotiate
with the Estonian government and cannot conduct a separate policy,
or General Yudenich does not report and the government must chose
another strategy. It is time to put an end to the deception.'

The deception did not last. In November, the town commandant
of the Estonian army in Tallinn wrote to remind 'the former Army of
the Northwest' that 'according to international law, the military personnel of another country do not have the right to wear their uniform,
and above all that of an army which has completely ceased to exist'.
On 13 December Estonia signed an armistice with Soviet Russia, this
was followed by the Treaty of Tartu on 2 February 1920, recognising
the country's independence. Latvia, Lithuania and Finland followed
soon afterwards, signing similar agreements with Moscow.

Churchill's hopes for a great anti-Bolshevik alliance in the Baltic
were at an end. So was the White dream of restoring 'Russia One and
Indivisible'. Food shortages meant that Yudenich's troops had nothing
to eat but lampreys, which they thoroughly disliked. Worse was to
come. Until their transfer to Poland, the Estonian government refused
to feed them unless they worked. They were sent logging in the forests to provide firewood for the winter. The humiliation for Greater
Russian imperialism was complete.

30

Siberian Retreat
September–December 1919

On 17 September, Churchill wrote an urgent message to the chief of the air staff. He feared that the collapse of Kolchak's southern front had 'opened the road to Turkestan' and the Bolsheviks' sweeping advance would encourage the Afghans to attack British India. 'The Prime Minister gave me most explicit directions yesterday,' he continued, 'to take steps to make sure that the Indian aviation was in the highest state of efficiency and that it possesses machines capable of striking at the cities of Afghanistan, including Kabul, within a few hours of an outbreak of hostilities . . . We ought to have our best machines out in India without delay, including the best bombing machines.'

While Churchill was concerned with the threat to the British Raj, Russians, Chinese and Americans were worried by Japanese ambitions in eastern Siberia. The Japanese showed special interest in the island of Sakhalin, having sent expeditions there to study its natural resources and oil deposits. 'Some Japanese openly express the supposition that the island will soon belong to them,' the American consul general in Irkutsk reported. The Japanese were also surveying the bays and gulfs of the Pacific coast and the mouth of the mighty River Amur. There were strong suspicions that the Japanese military wanted to occupy Manchuria along with the Amur and Maritime provinces, including Vladivostok. Colonel William J. Donovan, commander of the 165th Infantry, and better known as 'Wild Bill' Donovan, the founder of the Office of Strategic Services, was quoted as saying: 'It is generally known that Kalmykov and Semenov are nothing more than Japanese agents. Japan dreams of establishing a militaristic authority, as well as of erecting economic barriers over northern Manchuria and Siberia.'

Japanese army reinforcements kept arriving, even though the Americans and Japanese had originally agreed to limit their forces to no more than 7,000 men each. General Tanaka admitted that a total of 145,000 had been sent but emphasised that many of those were simply replacements for others brought home. Yet the *Yamato Shimbun* newspaper was said to have declared: 'Japan has no other way out, save that of sending her surplus population to Manchuria and Siberia,' and this was why there was no question of withdrawing her troops. Japan rejected the American proposal that both countries should withdraw their troops at the same time.

Ataman Semenov continued to hold up trains passing through Chita. On 24 October, his men halted one taking 68,000 rifles to Irkutsk. Semenov demanded 15,000 of them as his share. Lieutenant Ryan who commanded the platoon escorting the train insisted on delivering the full complement as he had been ordered. Semenov's Cossacks surrounded the train. But Colonel Morrow sent a message to Semenov: 'Release Lieutenant Ryan's train immediately or I will move on your forces with my regiment at once.' Semenov knew he was not bluffing and allowed Ryan's train to depart.

Ataman Annenkov's so-called Semirechensk Independent Army, meanwhile, continued to crush the rebellions its looting had provoked. In October his men suppressed revolts by twelve Russian peasant villages in the Lepsinsk district. It took three attempts to crush them. Once they captured Cherkasskoe, Annenkov's men massacred 2,000 peasants, another 700 people in Kolpakovka, and 200 in Podgornoe. The village of Antonovka was burned to the ground, while in the small town of Kara-Bulak, all the men were killed. Another group of Greens called the Mountain Eagles, in the Urdzharsk region, were also crushed by Annenkov's men. The methods were typical for Annenkov: 'on one day, the White detachment raided Kyryk-Orshak, made up of forty houses. They rounded up everyone in a great yurt. They hacked them to death with sabres.' Only a three-year old girl, whom they failed to see, survived.

After the short-lived success of their counter-attack in September, Kolchak's troops were again forced back along the Trans-Siberian Railway. On 30 October, General Knox gave a dinner party on his train for his fiftieth birthday. The Supreme Ruler attended with his much younger lover, the twenty-six-year-old Anna Timieryova, a poet and painter whom he would later describe as 'an acquaintance of mine of long standing who has volunteered to share my fate'. Knox's celebration was dampened by news that day that the Red Army had just captured Petropavlovsk and thus had a foothold across the River Ilmen.

Admiral Kolchak and his lover, the poet Anna Timieryova, surrounded by British officers. Major General Knox, with pipe, stands behind them.

General Diterikhs again warned the Supreme Ruler that he should abandon Omsk and withdraw to Irkutsk at the southern end of Lake Baikal. Some Cossack regiments were reduced to less than 100 men. Kolchak refused. 'If we lose Omsk, we lose all!' he insisted angrily. By 4 November the Reds had two bridgeheads across the River Ilmen. Although the enemy were now less than 200 kilometres from Omsk, Kolchak still refused to abandon what he saw as his capital. He clung to the idea that the fortunes of war might change, following newspaper reports the month before of the successes of Denikin and Yudenich, and that the Soviet government 'was living out its last days'.

Consul General Harris reported that relations between the Czechs and Admiral Kolchak had deteriorated even further. Czech leaders with their troops in Siberia protested to the Allies that their army was being forced to defend the Trans-Siberian Railway 'against its own conscience to support and uphold the authorities which act wilfully and illegally. Under the protection of Czechoslovak bayonets, local Russian military institutions commit acts which horrify the whole civilized world. The burning of villages, the killing of peaceful Russian citizens in hundreds, the shooting without trial of democratic people, only on suspicion of political disloyalty.' They demanded to be allowed home and released from responsibility of being implicated in such crimes.

Kolchak exploded in rage to Generals Janin and Knox, claiming that 'the overt sympathies of the Czech Representatives' were with those elements 'which are practically indistinguishable from the Bolsheviki', by which he meant the Socialist Revolutionaries. He regarded such attitudes 'during the days of great trial when the Russian Army experienced misfortunes' as nothing less than an attempt by the Czech representatives 'with all their power to undermine the Government's authority and the prestige of Russia's National work'.

On 5 November Kolchak again insisted that Omsk would not be surrendered. No man below the age of thirty-five was allowed to leave. Panic broke out in the city. Its population had quadrupled to half a million with White refugees who had managed to get there, imagining the city to be a safe haven. Instead they found misery and squalor, with nowhere to shelter. The streets were almost impassable with freezing mud, there was virtually no food to be had. 'Soldiers and their families begged from house to house for bread. Officers' wives turned into prostitutes to stave off hunger. Thousands who had money spent it in drunken debauches in the cafés. Mothers and their babies froze to death upon the sidewalks. Children were separated from their parents and orphans died by the score in the vain search for food and warmth.' Even the richer refugees found themselves virtually penniless if they had changed their money into Siberian denominations. The value of the White rouble had collapsed, following the announcement by the Chinese Eastern Railway in Harbin that it would no longer accept it.

General Knox and his staff left for Vladivostok on 7 November, the second anniversary of the Bolshevik coup, referred to by the Whites as 'the Day of the People's Grief', or 'the Day of Penitence'. With black humour, Knox remarked that he had been retreating ever since the Battle of Tannenberg in 1914, when he had been attached to the staff of the ill-fated General Samsonov. Horrocks left a few days later with the British railway mission. Captain Hodges and Lieutenant Moss, attached to General Dutov's Orenburg Cossacks, could not reach Omsk station in time. It took them three months to ride to safety across the Chinese border of Sinkiang province. The other military missions left Omsk two days after Knox.

Before leaving, General Janin went to see Kolchak. He described him as 'thin, with a haggard look and in an extreme state of nerves. At one moment he stopped talking, his neck jerked backwards twisting a little and he went rigid with his eyes closed. Are the rumours of his addiction to morphine true? In any case he has been very agitated for days. I was told that on Sunday he had smashed four glasses at table.'

On 8 November the frost was so hard that rivers, including the Irtysh which flowed through Omsk, began to ice over. Soon, this would leave no further natural barriers to the Red advance. Two days later, the headquarters of the Supreme Ruler announced: 'The evacuation of Omsk is being carried out splendidly, according to a logical plan. Order and peace reign in the city. The iron will as well as the inexhaustible energy of Admiral Kolchak produces a favourable effect on the soldiers and population. Admiral Kolchak has solemnly declared that he will defend Omsk to the last. He will personally participate in the fighting.'

On 10 November, Kolchak's ministers left Omsk for Irkutsk, nearly 2,500 kilometres further to the east. They had to bribe officials and railwaymen, who had not received their pay for months, to let them leave. The Supreme Ruler failed to fight to the end as had been promised. He departed two days later, with the gold reserves seized by Kappel's troops in Kazan attached to his train. The delay in his departure would cost him dearly. The bottleneck ahead on the Trans-Siberian Railway and the determination of the Czechs to thwart his progress would eventually lead to his capture.

A couple of premature attempts at revolt by workers and Chinese were crushed by Cossacks, but the Red Army entered the city next day virtually unopposed. Its *Stavka* boasted that its 5th Army had 'covered 600 kilometres in 30 days'. The Reds took possession of three armoured trains, 4,000 railway wagons, 38,000 prisoners, 100 field guns, half a million artillery shells, 1,000 machine guns and 200,000 British army uniforms which had still not been issued to the threadbare White troops.

The capture of the city was marked by relatively few acts of revenge and very little looting, except for seizing fur coats off people in the streets. Commissars were perfectly happy to allow refugees and other civilians to carry on to the east. A senior railway official who arrived for work, unaware that the city had changed hands, found a strange man in his office. 'The stranger then introduced himself as a commissar and expressed his surprise about the official's shoulder boards. He pulled a pen knife from his pocket and cut off the shoulder boards, then removed the insignia from the cap that was lying there. When he heard that the official would like to leave Omsk to follow his family, the commissar gave him the necessary pass.'

When it came to the military prisoners, they rounded up the young officers and offered them the chance of joining the Red Army. 'Half of the officers refused and were imprisoned,' another White report stated, 'however, after three days' arrest they accepted the Bolshevik offer and were released. According to our information, the seized and recruited officers are being sent by the Reds to the Denikin Front, with the necessary paperwork.' The disintegration of Kolchak's armies with the loss of Omsk allowed the *Stavka* to leave just the 5th Army to follow the remnants and transfer a large proportion of its forces to the Southern Front.

Just after the fall of Omsk, a revolt against Kolchak began in Vladivostok, 6,275 kilometres by rail to the east. The city was notorious for its lawlessness. Allied officers were 'advised never to go out alone after dark and always to carry a loaded stick and a revolver'. Above all they should avoid the red-light area known as the 'Bucket of Blood', which averaged at least one murder a night.

On Sunday 16 November Czech troops, supporting the sacked General Gajda, issued a proclamation that Kolchak's regime was intolerable. They demanded immediate repatriation, or the 'freedom and power to act in Siberia to prevent lawlessness and crime'. Gajda was particularly bitter that Kolchak had stripped him of his rank of lieutenant general and believed this was an insult to his military honour. The next morning, Gajda and a group of Right Socialist Revolutionaries called for an armed uprising, with I.A. Yakushev as leader and Gajda as military commander. (The Left SRs and Mensheviks later insisted that they had never supported Gajda.) By the afternoon heavy firing had broken out around the main railway station which resulted in six dead and twenty wounded, with Gajda's supporters in control of the station and marshalling yards. The Japanese responded by establishing a heavily armed cordon and General Rozonov's artillery began to bombard the station. American and British troops remained strictly neutral. Other Czechs were warned to keep clear or they would be treated as deserters. The revolt collapsed rapidly. Gajda, who had been lightly wounded and captured in the fighting, was forced to leave Russia, but it should have been a clear warning to Kolchak of things to come.

According to Captain William Barrett, who had just arrived in Vladivostok, the whole affair cost just over 1,000 dead. This figure appears much too high if restricted to the fighting around the railway station, and yet there was another aspect to the disorders. Ataman Kalmykov had sent his ill-disciplined Cossacks into the city in defiance of Allied orders. According to US military sources, the American provost marshal rapidly assembled a large multi-national force of 4,000 men. 'Major Johnson ordered that every robber and murderer caught at the scene of crime be shot without trial. Thanks to these precautionary measures, no robberies occurred.' The number of summary executions was not given, but those shot would almost certainly have been Cossacks.

After Omsk the Bolsheviks continued their advance towards the east, following the railway. Making use of the captured locomotives and wagons, they averaged an advance of 25 kilometres each day. The retreating White trains were averaging 40 kilometres a day, until a blockage caused chaos at Novo-Nikolaevsk. Matters were made far worse by constant Red partisan attacks along the Trans-Siberian Railway. The lawlessness extended even to supposedly White groups. General Janin heard that at Kansk, 150 kilometres east of Krasnoyarsk, Krasilnikov's Cossacks were pillaging everything, 'down to women's clothing which they resell in markets. The exasperated peasants, whose sole idea is to stay quiet and not fight, have become bolshevised as a result.'

Tensions soon increased between White Russians, Poles and Czechs. On 29 November, the Polish commander Colonel Czuma sent a message to the chief of the Polish military mission. 'Please clarify with General Janin and the Staff of the Czech forces, why they are not letting our provisions, hospital and administrative trains even as far as Tayga. We must have that order changed if we are to avoid a catastrophe.'

The Polish Legion had been raised from the many communities in Siberia descended from all those exiled after the great Warsaw uprising of 1863 against Tsarist oppression. Orenburg alone had been home to 15,000 of them. The 'Polish Army in Siberia' was commanded by General Wojciechowski. He had asked Polish representatives in Paris to make urgent representations to the Supreme War Council to provide 60,000 tons of shipping for its repatriation from Vladivostok.

A logjam of trains at Novo-Nikolaevsk produced furious altercations, as the *sauve-qui-peut* battle intensified. White Russians blamed detachments of the Polish 5th Division which took control of the station. Instead of twenty trains leaving each day, they claimed that only six departed. The Polish military mission retorted that the Kolchak government's communications department had collapsed in chaos and Red troops were approaching. The Czechs, who had far more control over the railwaymen than the Poles, took revenge on Kolchak by pushing his six trains onto sidings at every opportunity to make sure that their troops and others had priority.

On 14 December, the Reds caught up with the tail of the railway logjam and took Novo-Nikolaevsk, along with numerous trains still blocked there. The city itself had not been evacuated. It was in the grip of a typhus epidemic, and many of the refugees were trapped there. Worse lay ahead, with some 30,000 cases in Krasnoyarsk. All horses, carts and sledges available had already been taken. Kolchak's troops, now commanded by the widely despised General Sakharov, showed barely any resistance during the retreat. The only exception was General Kappel's force, despite being hampered by 23,000 refugees who had clung to them. General Diterikhs told Janin that the admiral had sent him a signal offering him the role of commander-in-chief, so he replied demanding the absolute condition that Kolchak himself should leave immediately to join Denikin's army. The whole command structure, Janin wrote, suffered from a '*paralysie générale*'. Kolchak could only yell and curse, even at those offering help.

'A mass retreat is one of the saddest and most despairing sights in the world,' Captain Horrocks wrote. 'The sick just fell down and died in the snow.' He was horrified by the squalid condition of the refugees packed into cattle wagons. If they were lucky they were in a *teplushka*, a box-car with wooden bunks on either side and a stove in the middle, but most wagons lacked any heating as temperatures dropped to minus thirty. 'The thing which impressed me most was the fortitude with which the women, many of them reared in luxury, were facing their hopeless future. The menfolk were much more given to self-pity.'

'The Czechs treated the Poles as the Poles treated the Russians,' an American consular official reported. They allowed 'no trains to pass through until the complete evacuation of Czech troops was accomplished. In this manner Admiral Kolchak's train was being detained by the Czechs at Krasnoyarsk as well as all other Russian trains between Tayga and Krasnoyarsk.'

At Tayga, beyond Novo-Nikolaevsk, real fighting over trains broke out on 20 December between Czechs, Poles and Russians. The Poles wanted to ensure that no Russian train left until all their men were through, but this was simply not possible. 'On 22 December 1919, a blood-red sun set over Tayga,' as part of the Polish 5th Division marched back along the railway track towards the west to hold off the Red 27th and 30th Rifle Divisions from the 5th Army. Captain Werobej, together with Captain Dojan, commander of 'Dojan's Ptichki',* joined up with a large detachment of General Kappel's army at Yashkino station. They fought all the next day. The Poles alone lost 100 killed and several hundred wounded, but it meant that they had won a crucial breathing space.

Amid the chaos of national rivalries, British officers were amused to receive a message from Vladivostok telling them: 'If the situation seems to warrant it, do not hesitate to take complete control.' Sometimes they were progressing less than five kilometres a day. Janin heard from the Czech commander that between Mariinsk and Krasnoyarsk almost all the railway workers had deserted. The few who remained were carrying out acts of sabotage by dousing the fire in a locomotive, so the pipes froze solid. At Bogotol, thirty locomotives had been left to freeze and there was a foot of ice on the rails. There was no coal available because the miners had not been paid for three months. The Supreme Ruler had refused to touch the gold reserves as a point of honour. Janin also heard that the officers in Kolchak's entourage were drinking themselves into oblivion.

Trapped on his train in Krasnoyarsk, Kolchak sent a message to Allied representatives to complain. 'The Czechs have actually stopped all the supplies for our Armies, have held up the evacuation of the wounded, the sick and the families of officers and volunteers from the front, dooming them to certain destruction. I as Supreme Ruler and commander-in-chief have received a series of insults and threats. Kolchak.'

---

* 'Ptichki' – Russian for 'birdies' – was what the Bolsheviks called the Polish eagle badge on the caps of Captain Dojan's men.

The situation ahead was little better. The chairman of Kolchak's Council of Ministers was informed that only two weeks' worth of grain remained in Irkutsk. Even if they purchased more in Manchuria, there was no guarantee that Ataman Semenov in Chita would let it through. There was no coal left, so neither the waterworks nor the electricity generating station were working. 'The main reason for the shortage of coal is the shortage of workers. The workers are running away. They can only be persuaded to stay if there are better provisions and items of vital necessity. Have sent prisoners to work in the Cheremkhovo coalmines while the mines are guarded by Japanese troops.' The litany of disaster continued, with a report that 'the Bolshevik uprising in the north of the Irkutsk province is growing. The rebels have already taken Verkholensk and are continuing to advance.'

A Socialist Revolutionary revolt in Krasnoyarsk took over the city for two days, until Kappel marched in with his troops and expelled them after a brief battle. Viktor Pepelyayev, who had taken over as chairman of the Council of Ministers soon after the fall of Omsk, then heard that the Verkholensk revolt had spread and was now within 100 kilometres of Irkutsk. They had also lost the coalmines. 'A revolt happened in Cheremkhovo the day before yesterday. The garrison of four hundred men changed sides to the rebels, who are led by local officials. I am negotiating with Czech commanders so that they take all measures to assure the unimpeded passage of trains, those of the Supreme Ruler and yours . . . In Irkutsk the atmosphere is nervous.'

This was hardly surprising when Pepelyayev issued a very ill-chosen call to arms. He tried to invoke Russian pride and Siberian nationalism, which infuriated Kolchak's officers who detested any form of separatism. 'Russian women! Do you want to serve the lust of the Commissars and Red Guards? . . . Let the white-green banner [of Siberia] unite all in a single desire to save and defend the country from devastation, famine and ruin.'

While the commanders argued bitterly over priority for their troop trains, conditions for the starving and frozen refugees became fatal for all too many. 'At the bigger stations bodies were being unloaded from trains in tens, and hundreds, and even by carloads, dead from frost, hunger and disease. For instance, in the station of Barabinsk there arrived a train with six hundred patients of which only 200 were alive.

At every point where trains stopped bodies were taken from car roofs, from passageways and platforms of cars . . . These bodies were stacked up at the stations like so much cordwood. Those who remained alive never talked, never thought of anything save how they might escape death and get farther and farther away from the Bolsheviks.'

31

The Turning Point
September–November 1919

General Denikin had trouble with ill-disciplined subordinates, such as Wrangel, Shkuro and Mamontov, but rather more surprisingly, so did the Reds. On 23 August, Kamenev, the Red Army commander-in-chief, received an urgent and secret signal. At Saransk, halfway between Tambov and Kazan, their own Don Cossack corps commander, the outspoken Left Socialist Revolutionary Filipp Mironov, had just addressed a large rally. 'His Cossacks closed off the place and arrested the Communists (about 100 of them) who were declared hostages. The situation is grave. We expect him at any minute to start advancing. We have no armed men except for 100 railway guards.'

Mironov was not just furious with the Communists for their brutal crushing of the Don Cossacks. He genuinely wanted to take the fight to Denikin, but all his attempts to form his new cavalry corps were being sabotaged by Cossack-haters. Just two days before, one of Mironov's officers, the commander of the 1st Don Cavalry Division, had written to that other Red cavalry commander, Semyon Budyonny. He tried to explain Mironov's position, after 'he had been sent from the Don to the Western Front as a deputy army commander and was called back to the Don urgently to save the situation there' with the new cavalry corps. Mironov was in disgrace because he had written to Lenin and Trotsky that 'the only way to proceed with the construction of a socialist society is with the active participation of the people themselves. He advised them to set up a people's representation in order to save the revolution, rather than a one-party system.'

'Comrade Mironov is sending his greetings to you and to all the commanders. Not only is he a great strategist and troop leader; he is also a great prophet. I will be sincere with you. He is in disgrace because he loves truth and fights for it, dislikes opportunism and hates communists who have caused the Don uprising by their criminal behaviour.'

Mironov himself wrote the same day to the headquarters of the 9th Army: 'Can you please pass the message to the Southern Front, that I can no longer stay inactive, seeing the ruin of the revolution and open sabotage regarding the setting up of the corps . . . I am setting off with the forces that I have to fight against Denikin and the bourgeoisie.'

That afternoon, Kamenev wasted no time issuing orders for the commander of the Reserve Army. 'Immediately send a detachment of internationalists to eliminate the uprising at Mironov's Cossack Corps.' Evidently, he believed it was safer to send non-Russians on this task. They were to be supported by field guns from the Red Army artillery officers' school and similar machine-gun detachments.

Sergei Gusev, one of Stalin's supporters on the Military Revolutionary Committee, told Ivar Smilga, the commissar of the Southern Front: 'I have declared Mironov a traitor and a rebel, I am sending out troops against him.' He added that Mamontov's units had reached Ryazhsk, just 310 kilometres from Moscow. 'They are probably headed for Tula.' This appeared to rule out any fear that Mironov might be involved in a plot to join up with Mamontov. 'Mironov is busy making sentimental speeches. I have informed him that if he surrenders, his life and freedom will be granted.' But next morning Smilga immediately accused Mironov of attempting 'to join up with the troops of Mamontov and Denikin . . . Rebel Mironov is to be brought to the headquarters of the Soviet troops dead or alive.'

Mironov responded to Smilga by saying: 'The first shot can only be fired by you, so it will be you who will shed the first blood.' Smilga issued another warning to Mironov's troops. 'Mironov is a rebel, strong detachments are being sent to fight against him. He will be treated as an outlaw . . . anyone who dares take up arms against the Soviet authority will be wiped off the face of the earth.' He then claimed that Mironov had stolen 5 million roubles and food destined for the peasants. Next, Smilga claimed that a letter to Denikin had been intercepted. 'Red Eagles of the 9th Army! The Military Revolutionary Committee is sure that not a single Red soldier, not a single Red Cossack will support the traitor and kin-slayer . . . The blood of brothers is being shed in the rear. Those guilty of this unheard-of crime will be wiped off the face of the earth. Death to traitor Mironov! Long live the revolution! Long live the Soviet power!' Smilga had to admit to Kamenev that Mironov, accompanied by 500 sabres, had broken through the reserve army cordon. He blamed Goldberg for trying to catch cavalry with infantry, who clearly could not keep up. An uneasy Goldberg tried to claim that he had surrounded and defeated one of Mironov's columns, but then on 4 September, the Saratov Cheka reported that Mironov did not have just 500 sabres, he had 2,000 men with him and had 'slipped through to Balashov', between Saratov and Voronezh.[*] Lenin had meanwhile sent in the 21st Division in an attempt to catch Mamontov, but it had as little luck as Goldberg.

On 12 September, Trotsky issued another order to the 9th Army on leaflets and posters run off on the mobile printing press in his armoured train. 'Mironov has been proclaimed an outlaw and a traitor. Every honest citizen who crosses paths with him ought to shoot him as a mad dog.' Extraordinary measures were taken on Kamenev's orders to deal with this eccentric demonstration. 'Units were taken from the Eastern Front's 1st and 4th Armies, and units from the reserve army in Kazan' and the Samara fortified area to eliminate Mironov's uprising. However, there was no need of their assistance. Mironov's detachment ran into Budyonny's cavalry corps and was scattered.

Mironov himself was captured on 14 September by Budyonny's 4th Cavalry Division. The order came through to bring him to Saratov, 'with an escort of absolutely loyal people, keeping constant watch day and night, to the Revolutionary Military Tribunal. The commander of the escort is responsible for him with his own head.' Budyonny, who loathed Mironov for his politics, hated him even more as a rival cavalry commander. One of the strangest parts of the story is that a Cheka report claimed that, four days after Mironov's capture, '810 Kuban Cossacks arrived in Saransk' saying that they had come to 'take revenge for Mironov'. The Cheka said that they could be 'characterised as bandit partisans', yet the only Kuban Cossacks in the whole region were either with Shkuro or Wrangel. This was more likely to have been another invention to blacken Mironov's name as a traitor.

The next stage of the story was even more bizarre. The show trial, for which the public received tickets, was organised by Trotsky and took place on 7 October. Smilga was the chief prosecutor. 'Mironov and ten others have been sentenced to death,' Smilga recounted in a telephone call immediately afterwards. 'The scene at the court reminded one of

---

* The official Red Army account, on the other hand, states that Mironov had '5,000 men (of these, only 2,000 were armed and 1,000 with horses).'

the trials of the great [French] revolution. The accused shouted with their last words: "Long live the Soviet authority and Communists!".'

Yet three days later Trotsky sent Smilga a telegram marked 'top secret'. He first informed him that the Politburo of the Central Committee would discuss 'changing the policy towards the Don Cossacks. We will give the Don and Kuban complete "autonomy". Our troops will stay clear of the Don. The Cossacks will make a complete break with Denikin. Respective guarantees are needed. Mironov and his comrades can act as intermediaries . . . Second. Caution is needed, Mironov should not be released immediately; he should be sent to Moscow under gentle but vigilant control. Here in Moscow his fate can be decided upon while it is linked to the aforementioned plan.'

It is impossible to tell how much Trotsky's plan contributed to undermining Cossack support to Denikin over the next few months. An even more astonishing reversal of policy was Trotsky's telegram in August of the following year about the man he had ordered to be shot down 'like a mad dog'. He wrote to the military revolutionary committee of the Southern Front: 'I suggest that comrade Mironov is considered as a candidate for the position of the commander of 2nd Cavalry Army. Trotsky, Chairman of the Military Revolutionary Council.' But that was no guarantee. A free spirit like Mironov was bound to face an unhappy end.

In the first week of October, General Shkuro in Voronezh became aware that the Reds had been developing their cavalry arm more swiftly than the Whites had realised. A large enemy force commanded by Budyonny was assembling at Gryazi, a little over 100 kilometres to the north. The Southern Front had issued the order to Budyonny: 'Mamontov and Shkuro have linked up in Voronezh – seek them out and destroy them.' He sensed, as General Wrangel had feared from the start, that Denikin's Armed Forces of South Russia were over-extended. Many were already well aware of other fundamental flaws.

Soon after he took over, the head of the British military mission, Major General Holman, had warned Churchill in July: 'Unless [Denikin] can offer to the wretched inhabitants of the liberated districts, which now number some sixty million souls, conditions of existence better than those which they suffered under the Bolshevik regime, he will in the course of time be faced with revolt and hostility

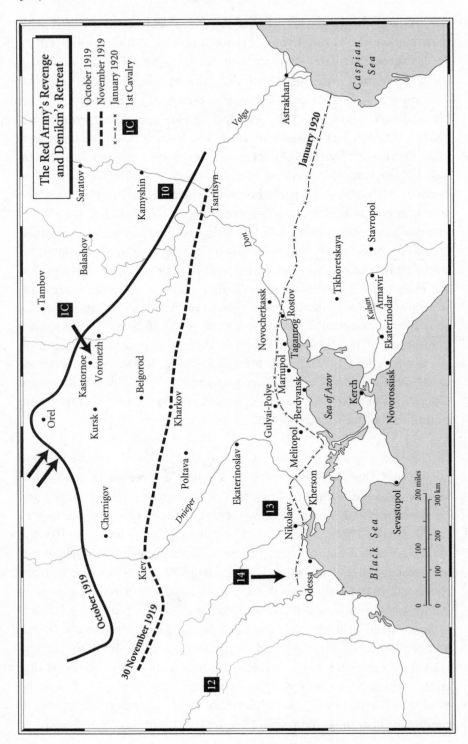

The Red Army's Revenge
and Denikin's Retreat

October 1919
November 1919
January 1920
1st Cavalry   1C

in his rear just at the time when the Bolsheviks will be concentrating large numbers of troops for a counter-offensive on his front.'

With Tsarist officers appointed to run the police and what passed for a civil administration, revolt and hostility in the rear could not be avoided. Konstantin Globachev, the former head of the Okhrana, was not wrong in some of his assessments. 'When the Volunteer Army entered a town, the church bells rang, people rushed up with tears in their eyes to kiss the stirrups of the cavalry, but before two weeks were out they hated the Volunteers as much as they hated the Bolsheviks. Many officers were just as brutal as the Reds.'

Although Globachev's views reflected the extreme right-wing critique of Denikin and his 'government', he did not soften his bitter observations at the White cause as a whole. 'The disinterested fulfilment of one's duty and serving one's country became a rare phenomenon. The majority thought only of their own personal advantage. It was not much better at the front. Some of the army officers regarded the civil war as an opportunity to get rich. Some right up to army commanders were also tainted in the same way. There were cases of generals sending back whole wagons of state property. The government took some steps to stop this but encountered unbelievable resistance. Once they got rich at the front, they preferred to go to the rear to Rostov or Ekaterinodar, where they partied on the back of their booty.'

The lack of security and infrastructure in White areas soon proved disastrous, as General Holman had warned. Mikhail Rodzyanko, the former chairman of the Duma, kept writing to Denikin about the threat from Makhno and the hopeless preparations to deal with it. The governor of the city and province of Ekaterinoslav, General Shchetinin, revealed himself 'as a typical old-style governor, scared of any contact with the public and afraid to inform the government on the true situation in the region that he was entrusted with'. Internal security depended on a Civil Guard which 'mostly consisted of militiamen who previously had served the Bolsheviks'. They were commanded by army officers who, 'completely unfamiliar with the nature of police work, committed a number of major mistakes that had disastrous consequences'.

'Local counter-intelligence played a serious role in the disaster. Its head was a young man, almost an adolescent, Esaul Shcherbakov. This gentleman was openly living with the actress Leskova, who, according to rumours, had previously been close to one of Bolshevik commissars. He drove around the city with her in an open car that bore the insignia of the Volunteer Army. Madame Leskova stunned the locals with the glamour of her outfits and the dazzling brilliance of her jewels. There was a special table in every big restaurant, with a sign: "Table of the Chief of Counter-Intelligence", and the dinners to which Shcherbakov treated the lady of his heart were extremely expensive, costing from eighteen to twenty-two thousand roubles. Rumours began to spread that any man who had been arrested could buy his freedom with the help of Mme Leskova, who had large sums in her account in the State Bank.'

'General Revishin commanded the troops operating in the province against Makhno's troops. There were two reserve battalions of conscripted soldiers in Ekaterinoslav. One of these was sent to fight against Makhno and, according to rumours, the officers were soon killed by their own soldiers who defected to Makhno. The other battalion remained in Ekaterinoslav, and [General] Korvin-Krukovsky told me that he was afraid to arm them as they were all supporters of Makhno.'

A total lack of communication between the civil administration, the Civil Guard and the army enabled Makhno to take them all by surprise. On 4 October, a group of his men seized a railway station leading to the city. 'Evil tongues said that the State Guard had quite simply been asleep in its positions, but one can also suspect an agreement between part of the Guard and Makhno's men, as all that had happened was completely insane . . . No attempts were made to take back the station. An armoured train did sometimes appear. It would fire a few shots, and retreat, soon becoming a subject for jokes in Makhno's army . . . And all the time while when Makhno was preparing for the final onslaught, the commanders in Ekaterinoslav kept worrying about their ranks and positions and settling scores with one another.'

The governor and commanders continued to reassure the citizens that they were in no danger. But on the evening of 12 October, rumours began to spread that Makhno's men had brought machine guns concealed under hay and vegetables on carts and hid them with their supporters in the Ekaterinoslav suburb of Chegilevka. On the morning of 14 October, Rodzyanko attended a meeting demanded by leading citizens. 'However hard we tried, the leadership remained completely calm, and, in fact, made several mocking remarks about us spreading panic . . . When I [Rodzyanko] demanded categorically, who exactly was the overall commander, both Shchetinin and Korvin-Krukovsky pointed to one another.'

Two hours later, firing started and 'unbelievable panic' ensued. 'The Governor with a detachment of the Guard (150 men with machine guns) galloped to the railway station and then towards the bridge across the Dnieper.' A sudden order was given to evacuate the city, and half an hour afterwards Makhno's forces entered Ekaterinoslav virtually unopposed. Rodzyanko joined an artillery battery that was retreating across the Dnieper.

Makhno's forces were striking all over eastern Ukraine. According to the Red Army *Stavka*, he had 28,000 infantry and cavalry with fifty field guns and 200 machine guns. Early in October, one of his large detachments took Berdyansk and destroyed an artillery park containing 60,000 shells provided by the British for Denikin's advance on Moscow. And as well as the occupation of Ekaterinoslav 'for an entire month', Makhno attacked Taganrog, which held both Denikin's advance headquarters and the base of the British military mission. His forces also took Berdyansk and Mariupol on the north coast of the Sea of Azov. The Red Army acknowledged later that Makhno 'did much to split the Volunteer Army into two completely isolated groups'.

The middle of October marked 'the culminating point' for Denikin's forces – the moment when an army has over-extended itself and has lost both momentum and the initiative. Tula, between Orel and Moscow, with its arms factories, was the second-greatest objective for the Whites after the capital. Trotsky feared that the loss of the arms industry there could be even more disastrous than the loss of Moscow.

The Communists had prepared Tula for defence with typical 'backs-to-the-wall' excess. Martial law was declared because of worker unrest in the factories due to severe food shortages. These had prompted the slogan 'Down with the Commissars!'. Lenin, well aware that they could not rely on proletarian support, sent Dzerzhinsky down with Cheka detachments. Many thousands of the population, peasants and *burzhui* alike, were conscripted into forced labour companies to dig trenches. The Red Army had reinforced its defences at Tula with the

21st Division from the Eastern Front when Mamontov approached.[*]
Yet the key battle was still around Orel, the most northerly point of
the main advance. Kamenev ordered in the regime's praetorian guard,
the Latvian Rifle Division, Pavlov's infantry brigade and Primakov's
cavalry brigade. They were to be reinforced by an 'Estonian' division,
but how many were genuinely from Estonia is unknown. This counter-
attack was planned as 'a double envelopment', but the real strength
was on the western flank.

Their assault, on the left flank of General Kutepov's I Corps of the
Volunteer Army, seemed to come out of nowhere. Kutepov reported
that the Kornilov division 'withstood seven bayonet attacks of the
Reds during the day. New units have arrived, mostly Latvians and
Chinese.[†] It has not been possible to establish their numbers. Our
losses are reaching 80% . . . Only 200 men are left in some regiments
of the Kornilov and Drozdovsky divisions.' Although they had inflicted
almost as many casualties on the Latvian Rifle Division, Kutepov's
men had to withdraw during the night of 20 October. 'The streets of
Orel were deserted,' wrote Aleksandr Gubarev. 'Only in some windows there were scared, anxious faces. The people that received us
with such joy a few days ago now feared for their lives. We quickly
passed through the city and got to the main road.'

Like Shkuro, Kutepov and others were shaken by the overwhelming
numbers of the enemy they were suddenly facing. Subsequent reports
from the British military mission alarmed and baffled Churchill
back in London, who could not believe the changing fortunes of
war. 'During September and October,' he signalled back to General
Holman, 'Denikin's armies advanced on broad fronts, taking Orel,
Yeletz, Voronezh and threatening Tula and Moscow. If the Bolsheviks
had all these reinforcements available, why did they allow these advances
to take place with so little opposition? Were they preparing all this time
to strike this blow, or have they in their need thrown in all available
reserves? Do you think their offensive is a desperate effort which cannot
last long, or is it evidence of really superior power on their side?'

---

[*] Altogether, the Red Army *Stavka* had transferred 60,000 men from the Eastern
Front since May, making a total of 171,600 Red troops facing 151,900 Whites,
many of whom were guarding against uprisings in the rear.
[†] There is no indication from Red Army sources that Chinese units were engaged in
this battle.

The answer lay in a combination of that transfer of forces from the Siberian front, now that Kolchak's armies had collapsed, and the return of deserters to whom the Communist regime had offered an amnesty. Peasants, who had seen the White advance as a threat that the old landowners might seize back their land, were now far less reluctant to serve in the Red Army. The front-line strength of the Reds was now more than double that of the White Army, because of desertion and the increasing numbers of their troops recalled to defend the rear.

On 19 October, it was the turn of Budyonny's I Cavalry Corps to advance towards Voronezh, as Shkuro had feared. Immediately following Makhno's capture of Ekaterinoslav, which he combined with an attack on Taganrog, Denikin had ordered Shkuro to send the Terek Cossack Division from his corps back to deal with these threats to the rear. Shkuro ordered Erast Chevdar to send his reply by radio. 'To General Denikin, My duty as a soldier and citizen forces me to report to your High Excellency that I am not able to resist Budyonny's cavalry corps. This corps is concentrated in the area of Gryazi and numbers some 15,000 sabres. It is now advancing on our forces. I have only about 600 sabres of the Caucasian division, which is short of horses. The 1,500 sabres remaining from Mamontov's corps are very unreliable. They all want to go back to the Don. All that remains of my corps is the Terek Division, about 1,800 sabres with good horses. But this division is now being taken away from me on your orders. It is currently boarding a train to be sent to Taganrog to fight Makhno's gangs there. Due to the above, I am giving the order to abandon Voronezh. Signed Shkuro.'

'I could not sleep at all that night,' Chevdar wrote after sending it, 'because of the great disaster in store for us. Townspeople were horrified to hear that we were leaving.' A mass of refugees began to abandon the city carrying bundles with their vital belongings. The lucky ones were in carts which hindered the movement of troops. Refugee peasants and workers cursed the Whites: 'If you cannot hold a city, you should never have taken it in the first place.' It was an 'insane tragedy', Chevdar acknowledged, reflecting on the great gamble with insufficient troops. By 24 October, Budyonny's Red cavalry had occupied a half-empty city.

Makhonin, a former battery commander in the Tsarist army, was bitterly bemused to find himself in charge of a press gang. 'In advancing on Moscow,' he wrote, 'nothing was done to mobilize all the men up to forty to complete our army, and only when we were obliged to retreat, did the order come to collect all the available men in the towns and villages which we had to abandon.' They raided houses by night, hauling victims from their beds. The women begged them in vain not to take their husbands or sons. 'The poor creatures were sent as they were, half-dressed to the rear of the army. The result was, as could have been foreseen, that none of these men gave us any help and for the most part disappeared at the first opportunity.'

Shkuro somehow managed with his severely reduced corps to hold off further advances for nearly three weeks while the remnants of Kutepov's battered corps retreated to Kursk. Budyonny's former commander and hated rival, Boris Dumenko, who had set up the cavalry corps in September, 'scored a brilliant victory in the battles near the *stanitsa* Alekseevskaya on 2 November', the commander of the 9th Army informed Lenin in a telegram.

On the same day, Denikin summoned a conference in Kharkov with Mai-Maevsky and Sidorin, the commander of the Don Army, to discuss the situation. The meeting began badly with an embarrassing hunt for a map. It rapidly became clear that Mai-Maevsky's headquarters had no idea of where its own units were or the whereabouts of the enemy. Denikin became exasperated. The last reserves, 700 conscripts, had been sent off that morning. 'He also spoke with great indignation about Shchetinin, the Governor of Ekaterinoslav,' who had failed to fight off Makhno's attack. Mai-Maevsky explained that he had already removed Shchetinin.

Another crisis was even more serious. Denikin, increasingly angered by separatist tendencies in the Kuban, was outraged to discover that a delegation of the Kuban Rada had signed a treaty of friendship with the Chechen and the Ingush who, with Georgian encouragement, had been attacking the Volunteer Army in the Caucasus. Five days after the conference in Kharkov, Denikin gave orders for the arrest of those who had signed the document and their court martial for high treason. Wrangel was afraid of the effect it might have on the majority of Kuban Cossacks in his army. At Denikin's insistence, martial law was declared. General Pokrovsky, that staunch friend of the Volunteer Army from the Ice March of the First Kuban Campaign, ordered his troops to surround the Rada. The leader of the delegation which had signed the document, A.I. Kalabukhov, was court martialled and hanged the next day from a lamp post in the centre of Ekaterinodar. His corpse was left there with a placard declaring him to be a traitor. The rest were exiled from the Kuban. Denikin's firmness on this occasion, for once surpassing that of Wrangel, brought events rapidly back under control, but it was a hammer blow to the fighting spirit of the Kuban Cossacks.

On 7 November, Kennedy recorded: 'Better news. Red cavalry attack beaten off by the Kornilovsky who were very pleased with the horses they captured as a result.' They were supported by some fresh battalions sent out with an armoured train. Winter had arrived in earnest. 'Freezing hard,' Kennedy noted, 'the snow is powdery and sparkles in the sun.'

The Kornilovsky success was short-lived. On 15 November, Budyonny's Red Cavalry charged out of a snowstorm to seize the small but vital railway junction of Kastornoe, halfway between Voronezh and Kursk. This split the Don Army from the Volunteer Army, and Kursk fell two days later. The bitterness of defeat provoked much cruelty. Sergeant Berry reported later to the British military mission what he had seen in Belgorod. 'Men and women accused of being pro-Bolshevik [were] hanged in the town square. They were not given a drop but were simply strung up and drunken Cossacks hewed their arms and legs off with their swords while the wretched people were still alive.' In Kiev, even the extreme reactionary Vasily Shulgin was shocked by the behaviour of Volunteer officers. 'In one house they hung a "commissar" by the arms, made a fire underneath and slowly fried him. The drunken gang of "monarchists" around him was howling: "God save the Tsar!".'

Kharkov became the next major city threatened with capture. The main railway station was besieged by panic-stricken crowds. Some wounded Volunteer Army officers, knowing their likely fate at the hands of Red troops, were seen literally crawling on hands and knees from the hospital in the hope of finding a place on a train.

Retreat from the major cities in the south brought out the worst in the Whites, as the terrible massacre of 2,000 Jews in Ekaterinburg had shown earlier in the year. But the Whites were not the only perpetrators. It is estimated that there were some 1,300 anti-Semitic pogroms in Ukraine during the civil war, with some 50,000 to 60,000 Jews killed

by both sides. There were pogroms in Belarus as well, but they were
not nearly as murderous as those in Ukraine. In total, a Soviet report
of 1920 mentions 150,000 dead and as many again badly injured.

Petliura's Ukrainian nationalists had led the way. 'It had been quiet
for a little while after the terrible *Gajdamak* pogroms,' Konstantin
Paustovsky wrote of Kiev in 1919. 'And it stayed quiet for a while after
Denikin took over. For the present they were not touching the Jews.
Occasionally, but only at some distance from the busier streets, a few
Junkers with drug-crazed eyes, prancing on their horses, would sing
their favourite song:

> *Black Hussars!*
> *Save our Russia, beat the Jews.*
> *For they are the commissars!*

But after the Soviet forces had retaken Orel and begun to drive
southwards, the mood of the Whites changed. Pogroms started in the
little towns and villages of the Ukraine.' Outside their own territory,
Cossacks acted all too often as if they were in an enemy country where
anything was permitted.

Churchill was well aware of the effect of anti-Semitic pogroms
on public opinion in the West and had already written to General
Holman. 'It is of the very highest consequence that General Denikin
should not only do everything in his power to prevent massacres of the
Jews in the liberated districts but should issue a proclamation against
anti-Semitism. Considering that anti-Semitism is so much more pro-
nounced among Petliura's men than in the Volunteer Army, it ought
to be possible to make a strong distinction between the methods of
the two forces. The Jews are very powerful in England and if it could
be shown that Denikin was protecting them as his armies advanced it
would make my task easier.'

Churchill then wrote to Denikin himself. 'I know the efforts you
have already made and the difficulty of restraining anti-Semitic feeling.
But I beg you as a sincere well-wisher, to redouble those efforts and
place me in a strong position to vindicate the honour of the Volunteer
Army.' Denikin had issued a number of edicts against pogroms, but
since some of his most successful generals refused to comply or even
encouraged them, he did nothing more. Churchill may have finally
realised that General Dragomirov, the governor of Kiev, was 'the kind

of military martinet who is particularly unfitted for civil administration', yet he still seemed unaware that Dragomirov had allowed one of the worst anti-Semitic pogroms of the war to continue in Kiev for six days.

The *Times* correspondent in South Russia, a New Zealander and extraordinary linguist called Dr Harold Williams, wrote to the Foreign Office and Churchill: 'You can have no idea of the bitterness against the Jews right through Russia. Bolshevism is identified in everybody's eyes with Jewish rule.' Williams found that although Volunteer Army officers hated Jews, they were not the ones who started pogroms. 'The Cossacks are bad and it is hard to restrain them. They are great robbers and they have a most violent antipathy to Jews.' This was especially true of Ukrainian atamans, such as Grigoriev, but there are conflicting versions about Makhno's followers, who included quite a number of Jews. Budyonny's cavalrymen were also guilty. 'The curious thing,' Williams concluded, 'although it is not curious if you understand the popular feeling – is that the Red soldiers pogrom when they get a chance. In Gomel they massacred about half the Jews in town (a tenth probably because the Jews and everyone else exaggerate the figures frightfully). And they often chalk up on their troop trains "Beat the Jews and Save Russia".'

32

Retreat in the South
November–December 1919

On the last day of November, a curious diplomatic ceremony took place at the British military mission in Taganrog. Captain Kennedy recorded the event in his diary. General Holman, who had the 'extraordinary habit of turning up the whites of his eyes and blinking at you while he talks', invested General Shkuro with the Order of the Bath. 'In his ranting speech of acceptance, [Shkuro] began swearing that he would slay Bolsheviks and "build up a new Russia on their stinking corpses". Shkuro then went on to say: "I hear there are some dirty dogs of Socialists in England and if they rise up against her, I would like to bring my corps to England just to show the English people what Cossacks can do".'

No doubt Holman felt obliged to flatter White generals since they had just heard of Lloyd George's speech at the Mansion House dinner and felt betrayed. Great Britain was abandoning them. There would be no further deliveries of military equipment and the mission would be withdrawn. The announcement signalled to everyone that the White cause was doomed. The Denikin rouble plunged in value as those with any money left sought to change what they had into sterling, dollars or francs. Churchill wondered if the Whites could at least make terms so that Denikin could hang on to the territory that he still held, but Lenin and Trotsky would never release the death-grip they now had on the White armies. Churchill could not imagine the extent of the collapse in morale, compounded by the desertion of Cossacks returning home.

'In a time of disaster, everyone blames everyone else,' wrote Chevdar, 'Cossacks blamed the Volunteers and our men blamed the Cossacks.' Wrangel once again tried to blame Denikin for everything that had gone wrong as he reorganised his forces. Denikin summoned Mai-Maevsky back to Taganrog as his drinking now rendered him incapable of command. He greeted him in a friendly way. 'This was a hard decision . . . You will take some rest now and you will return to work later.' Mai-Maevsky asked to be allowed to retire to Sevastopol where he wanted to settle, still drinking heavily but also reading a lot of Dickens.

With Mai-Maevsky's departure Kutepov would take over the remnants of the Volunteer Army, but he would report to Wrangel, who would also command all the cavalry. But according to the White war correspondent Grigory Rakovsky, 'It turned out that Wrangel had already informed the front Kuban units that they would be reorganized. Shkuro was away at the time. Wrangel's order had a great effect on the Kuban Cossacks, who were tired, disappointed, and laden with loot. They immediately started leaving the front . . . Some said: "We are going back to Kuban, we have orders." Others claimed: "We are going to chase the rear rats back to the front." Yet others said: "We've done enough fighting. Let the *burzhuis* fight now."'

Wrangel's promotion did not prove a success. He made every conceivable difficulty, and the two generals again disagreed over strategy. Denikin wanted to base their defence on Tsaritsyn in the east and Kiev in the west, but they were pushed further back in the course of the next week. Wrangel, on the other hand, did not want to withdraw into the Caucasus, where Denikin still believed that their alliance with the Cossacks was vital. He was more attracted to the Crimean peninsula because it was much easier to defend until they rebuilt their forces. This raised the suspicions of General Sidorin and the Don Army that Wrangel would betray them. At the same time, Wrangel considered the Cossacks to be politically unreliable, even suspecting them of moving to the Left.

On 9 December Sidorin went to see Denikin. He wanted both armies to stay together to reconquer and defend Don territory. According to Sidorin, Denikin replied: 'I too can see this, and I share your opinion about the current situation. I am so worried that I have ordered staff to report to me on every new order given by Wrangel, so that I can personally check on them.' Denikin advised Sidorin to arrange a meeting with Wrangel and clarify their respective positions.

Two days later, the trains of the two army commanders pulled up alongside each other in the station of Yasinovataya. Wrangel's first words on entering Sidorin's saloon carriage were: 'Well, Vladimir Ilich, we should honestly admit that our cause is lost. We should think about the future.' Sidorin disagreed. Wrangel insisted: 'It is obvious to me that further resistance is pointless.'

Wrangel then spoke about the state of the Volunteer Army. According to him, there were no more than 3,000 to 4,000 men really fighting at the front, while the majority were skulking in the rear, 'corrupted to the last degree. It was enough to say that some regiments had up to 200 freight cars full of various property. The units, including the majority of officers and even the most senior commanders, were actively involved in profiteering.' Wrangel believed that Mai-Maevsky, at the pinnacle of all misdeeds, should be court martialled. Sidorin insisted that the state of the Don Army was completely different from that of the Volunteer Army. There were still 40,000 bayonets and sabres on the Don Front, with a reserve of 15,000 well-trained reinforcements. Wrangel then changed the subject to demand that Denikin should resign. There appeared to be a curious contradiction in the way that Wrangel argued that they were finished, while revealing that he still wanted to replace Denikin as commander-in-chief.

After a thaw, hard frosts returned in mid-December. 'Moustache freezes,' Kennedy noted, 'horse's sweat becomes hoar frost.' Despite Lloyd George's declaration of British withdrawal, more officers were still arriving to join the military mission. Captain Lever of the Royal Engineers headed to Taganrog as instructed with revolver, rifle and 150 rounds. A British major he met in Rostov told him, 'whilst delving into a tin of bully-beef with a hefty jack-knife', what it had been like on the last train out of Kharkov, with refugees clinging to the roof and outside of every carriage. A number died of hypothermia and rolled off by the side of the track, frozen into a ball.

In Taganrog, Lever found the place swarming with those refugees who had survived so far. 'Every corridor, alley-way, waiting room, restaurant and veranda is packed with sleeping or resting forms – men, women and children bundled together indiscriminately – full-length on the floors.' The value of the 'Bell', the Denikin rouble, had halved again in ten days, down to 2,500 to the pound.*

The remnants of Shkuro and Mamontov's cavalry, still retreating from Voronezh, moved 'in great zigzags' in an attempt to avoid Budyonny's forces pursuing them. Conditions included temperatures of minus 20

---

* 'Denikin roubles' were called 'Bells' because they bore the image of the huge Tsar Bell in the Moscow Kremlin.

degrees centigrade and lower. When they halted, they slept in the snow wrapped in their cloaks. Both men and horses were exhausted and famished. Erast Chevdar, the radio officer, was in their midst, with his equipment escorted by three Cossacks. 'Along the way we encountered animals, sometimes wolves, sometimes white hares, who seemed to have lost any fear because of the cold. Once I saw a marmot sitting in the middle of the road and it did not move. The cavalry horses instinctively stepped round it.'

At one point when riding the length of a *balka*, a natural ravine in the steppe, one of his escorts rode up beside him and murmured: 'Mr Captain, just look up and to your left.' Chevdar saw a dense body of horsemen also moving south. 'It was easy to guess that it was Budyonny's cavalry. They had certainly spotted us, but probably mistook us for one of their own detachments. We were dressed similarly with our cavalry cloaks. One could only tell Whites and Reds apart when up close.'

Shkuro was not with them because he was ill, so Mamontov was now their commander. As dark was falling, he summoned all officers for a council of war to discuss their options now that they were almost entirely surrounded. Everybody present rejected any idea of surrender, even though they risked very heavy casualties from artillery fire if they tried to break out. 'Mamontov, stroking his huge moustaches, as he listened to their opinions,' then came to a decision. They would break out across country, not following any roads. The cavalry would form up in a single column with horse artillery and the radio station in the middle. Speaking and smoking were forbidden, and they set off led by two old Cossacks who knew the area.

Their way was lit by the moon, and the snow crunched under their horses' hooves. When they came close to a village, they could see the smoke rising straight up from chimneys in the freezing air. As the front of the column entered the village, they knew they had been sighted. Artillery shells began exploding all around. The thatch of whitewashed cottages caught fire, and inhabitants rushed out in panic. There was blood on the snow from both horses and troopers. Riderless mounts galloped past, bucking with fear. Mamontov did not need to give any orders. They charged forward and broke through the encirclement.

Some time later they joined a force of about 4,000 cavalry and 3,000 infantry near Valuyki, 100 kilometres east of Kharkov. Valuyki was the town where Denikin had wanted to concentrate his cavalry forces since the conference in Kharkov. Churchill, having heard of this plan, had come to expect an 'important decisive battle' there with six cavalry divisions, but he was to be disappointed. When Mamontov's drastically reduced command clashed with Budyonny's renamed 1st Cavalry Army, the *Konarmia*, a Red victory was virtually inevitable.

While the bulk of his forces were pushed back south towards the Sea of Azov, Denikin had meanwhile received an unexpected reinforcement on his extreme left flank. A formation of 15,000 Galicians with 130 field guns had agreed to join the Whites rather than the Poles, whom they feared wanted to incorporate their territory into Poland. Churchill was alarmed to hear that Denikin proposed simply to 'absorb them into his existing units', which would be the last thing the Galicians wanted. Denikin felt that this solution was less likely to antagonise the Poles, for whose help he was desperate. Yet, as the Foreign Office confirmed, the Poles were still strongly opposed to an alliance. They suspected, with justification, that White generals wanted to restore Russia back to its old Tsarist borders, including much of Poland.

Churchill's dream of a borderlands alliance against the Bolsheviks was still frustrated by their suspicion of Denikin and White imperialism. He had heard that General Mannerheim was going to Warsaw to 'encourage the Poles to join in a concerted movement against the Bolsheviks before next spring'. Churchill wanted Brigadier General Carton de Wiart of the British military mission to Poland to 'keep us informed about General Mannerheim's activities'. Carton de Wiart, who got on well with both Mannerheim and Piłsudski, met the Finnish leader just after he arrived and signalled Churchill. 'He came to find out if the Poles meant business in their fight with the Bolsheviks, and if there was a chance of a combined offensive in the spring. I assured him on my part that the Poles were to be relied on to fight the Bolsheviks and he is quite agreed with me on that point.'

Mannerheim and Piłsudski met on 13 December. Carton de Wiart initially reported that evening that Mannerheim said the meeting was 'most satisfactory' because Piłsudski 'was very much in favour of a combined offensive'. But Mannerheim became uneasy about the Baltic states making peace with the Bolsheviks and doubted whether Denikin could survive until the spring. Mannerheim and Piłsudski 'are both agreed that this offensive cannot take place unless England backs it strongly'. Churchill must have cursed in frustration, knowing only too well that Lloyd George would flatly refuse.

Mannerheim left Warsaw with nothing agreed. 'The inactivity of the Poles has enabled the Bolsheviks to concentrate against Denikin,' Churchill raged. 'The destruction of Denikin will then enable them, if they choose, to concentrate against the Poles . . . The Bolsheviks are now within measurable distance of complete military triumph on all fronts where they are active.'

The Red Army could hardly believe its luck that Makhno's guerrilla campaign from Ekaterinoslav to Taganrog had forced the retreating Volunteer Army to split up. Shkuro's former chief of staff, Major General Yakov Slashchov, commanded a mixed force of 3,500 infantry and cavalry, with 32 field guns. Unable, or unwilling, to rejoin the main bulk of the army, he pulled back via Melitopol towards the Crimea and secured its entry point, the Perekop Isthmus. Both Denikin and the Red Army high command suspected that this was part of Wrangel's 'secret aims' to become commander-in-chief himself and secure the Crimea. Soon afterwards, White counter-intelligence identified an 'officers' group hostile to the commander-in-chief', General Denikin, which was suspected to be 'connected to the headquarters of Lieutenant General Baron Wrangel'. Slashchov was definitely identified as a member. Denikin said soon afterwards that he wanted to court martial and hang him.

The *Stavka* blamed itself for underestimating the longer-term significance of Slashchov's comparatively small force and the route of its withdrawal. 'It enabled Slashchov's detachment to hold out in the Crimean isthmus,' Kamenev and his colleagues wrote soon afterwards, 'and to transform the Crimea into a new base for the southern counter-revolution.'

Denikin's Armed Forces of Southern Russia were in fact now split into three. The main body remained on the lower Don at the entrance to the Caucasus. Slashchov's force was acting as the cork in the neck of the Crimea, while in the west Major General Nikolai Shilling withdrew with his small force to Odessa. The Red Army command redeployed accordingly. Unaware of Piłsudski's reluctance to help Denikin, it sent the 12th Army to face west and 'in the event of difficulties with the Poles to be ready to go over to the offensive'. The 14th Army would deal with Odessa. The 13th Army was to attack the Crimea, and the redesignated Caucasus Front was to cross the Don to take on the bulk of the enemy forces there. The 10th Army, having now retaken Tsaritsyn, was to advance southwest following the railway to seize the vital junction of Tikhoretskaya and cut them off from behind.

On Christmas Eve, British officers in Taganrog heard that their military mission was being pulled back to the port of Novorossiisk. 'A retreat to the Caucasus is impossible,' Kennedy wrote in his diary, 'for the people of Daghestan and Georgia are hostile, and the mountains are impassable in winter.'

Gubarev, the officer in Kutepov's corps who had retreated all the way from Orel, arrived in Rostov on Christmas Eve with his comrades. They found themselves unusually fortunate in their billet. 'The crew of my field gun are all former students. We happened to stay at the house of a Jewish intellectual. We have just had a good bath, which was an enormous delight. We scalded our lice-infested underwear with boiling water. We are now sitting clumsily on soft comfortable armchairs in the sitting room, we are too shy to put our boots on the fluffy carpet. The daughters of our host are sweet young lady students. For the first time during this eventful year we are discussing literature and philosophy. Not a word is mentioned about the war . . . My God! What a special feeling, to be clean, to sit in a warm place, and to think about nothing, nothing at all. All of a sudden, there is banging at the door. The soldier on duty runs in and looks in surprise at the unusual scene. He bends down to speak to me and whispers quickly: "The front has been breached. Get ready at once. We set off in an hour".'

Outside in the street, the contrast with the calm they had just left was confusing. The chaos was considerable, as carts of refugees from the north impeded troops rushing out to defend the city. 'Orderlies gallop past. Passing cavalry units trot past noisily. It is dark and foggy. The air is cold, and one's soul is gloomy. We march.' Out in the steppe, with the lights of Rostov far behind, the artillery faced their first obstacle. 'Infantry and carts pass easily over a frozen shallow and narrow river, but the very first field gun falls through the ice and gets stuck. We add horses from another gun and manage to pull it back, with a lot of difficulty. Retreating units keep marching past, they are in a hurry to reach the new, reduced front line. Another battery stops behind us. We wait. The drizzle becomes stronger. Our greatcoats become wet and heavy. We moved on and took our position under gunfire. Before we can fire a single shell, an orderly gallops over with the order to retreat at once.' They learned later that the enemy had unexpectedly crossed the Don at night. They had taken the large *stanitsa* of Olginskaya 17 kilometres to the southeast, and destroyed the Markov Division that was stationed there.

One cavalry detachment from Budyonny's army, crossing the frozen Don fell through the ice. Desperate refugees took the same route despite the danger. It was a time of heartlessness. 'As for the refugee carts which went through the ice,' an officer admitted, 'nobody paid much attention.' Cossacks were determined not to leave good horses to the enemy. One group herded 200 purebreds from the stud farms of Proval and Streletsk across the ice without loss. Also, during the retreat, an old Cossack wanted to give the Don Cossack officer Mitrofan Moiseev his magnificent chestnut stallion, but he could not take it, so the old man shot it rather than let it fall into the hands of the Reds. Later Moiseev heard that the old man had shot himself. He had lost all four of his sons in the war and his wife had died of typhus.

On that night before Christmas, it suddenly became clear to the White command that Novocherkassk was more at risk than Rostov itself. Dumenko's cavalry corps was advancing more rapidly than Budyonny's, but Mamontov had decided to strike at Budyonny's *Konarmia* first. Don Cossack morale had been high at this moment after several successful engagements. The next morning, Budyonny's cavalry army surrounded and captured most of a brigade of Terek Cossacks, while Dumenko closed on the Don capital.

'The crucial battle,' wrote Rakovsky, 'started in the morning on Christmas Day, on the approaches to Novocherkassk. The snow-covered subdued city was lit by the bright sun. It was clear that the critical moment had come. Men on horseback and on foot started rushing around. Artillery fire was now heard close to the city. Supply carts were driving fast through the streets. Escort *sotnias* were urgently falling in line in front of the Ataman's Palace. Regular units were passing through Novocherkassk in exemplary order, at times even singing. Something incomprehensible, inexplicable was happening . . . It seemed that the forces were more than sufficient. The mood had been terrific. But all of a sudden, Don Cossacks were leaving the Don capital, cradle of the Volunteer Army, the city of Novocherkassk, without any stubborn, bloody and ruthless fighting . . . Shrapnel was already exploding over the city.'

Kennedy heard similar news from two British officers who had just returned from the front. 'They say the whole army is running and not fighting at all. Wrangel is hanging people all over the place and for the slightest offences.' He even arrested a colonel 'who was loading a train with machine gun stores and armoured cars [and] allowed some furniture to be put on board. He was immediately hanged.' When the Russians failed to find any trains to evacuate the British military mission from Taganrog, the senior British officer present warned that if they did not immediately provide the trains, then the support from 47 Squadron RAF would be withdrawn. 'Complete capitulation on the part of the Russians,' noted Captain Lever, 'as our air force is the only reliable deterrent against a wholesale bolshy advance.'

'Wrangel's train drew into the railway station in the evening,' Kennedy wrote on 30 December just before they left Taganrog. 'A long line of luxurious coaches drawn by two powerful engines. The roofs of the coaches were covered with snow and bearded with icicles.' The rumour was that Wrangel was about to have it out with Denikin and set 'himself up in his place'. Wrangel, 'a great tall slender figure in Cossack uniform, with a white hood draped over his shoulders', came over to talk to Kennedy and Colonel Barne. He spoke excellent French. 'His plans were to leave for Rostov either tonight or tomorrow morning, and that he would like us to come with him. He was on his way to see Romanovsky, the chief of staff, and said that he hoped to receive decisions on certain matters, after which he would tell us definitely what he was going to do. He said that possibly he would go to the Kuban to form a new army, as the Volunteer Army was now so reduced that it was to be formed into an army corps with Kutepov in command. He impressed one immensely by his commanding presence and his decisive manner. He has fine features – a thin rather pale face and an eagle eye.' The temperature that night, Kennedy noted, fell to 40 degrees below zero both in Fahrenheit and centigrade, the only point on which the two systems coincided.

Erast Chevdar, the radio officer, found himself caught up in Rostov in the general flight. 'A mass of carts, field kitchens and field guns heads towards the bridge over the Don. Tired and embittered people give way to their despair in the most foul and coarse swearing. Everybody is desperate to break free of the city and the pincer movement of the enemy. You cannot get any information from anyone. Everyone is only thinking about themselves. I left my two-wheeled carts in the street and walked to the station hoping to find some officials there. In the evening mist I see a figure which seemed to be rocking in the wind. With snow in my eyes I could not see clearly. In front of me, with the points of his shoes almost touching the gutter, hands blueish, a dreadful corpse with the tongue stuck out has been hanged from the lower branch of a tree. On his chest is a piece of cardboard with a sign saying "Looter".' General Kutepov had been ordering executions of deserters and suspected Bolsheviks as well.

'South of Rostov,' Chevdar added, 'I saw General Denikin moving slowly in a sledge. I was shocked by his expression of concentration and deep grief. I started to feel sorry for him. Corpses of horses mark the route of our retreat. People at least obtained some food from the settlements through which we passed. There was no hay for the horses. A peasant woman in one of the villages expressed her indignation. "We are feeding you so that you can continue fighting. We should stop feeding you and then you will stop fighting. There is no life left here because of your war. Sometimes the Reds raid us, sometimes the Whites. And all they can say is *"davai! davai!"* and what can we give if we have nothing to live on ourselves?"'

'There seems to be very little doubt of the complete victory of the Bolsheviks in the near future,' Churchill wrote gloomily to Field Marshal Wilson the next day, which was New Year's Eve. He asked him for his forecast of the military situation over the next few months. What would be the position of Poland, the Caucasus and Transcaspia, Persia and Turkestan? They should withdraw the British brigade in Batumi as soon as Denikin's fate was settled. The navy should prepare for the evacuation of the British military mission. 'I am convinced,' Churchill concluded, 'that very great evils will come upon the world, and particularly upon Great Britain, as a consequence of the neglect and divided policies of this year on the part of the Allies and of ourselves.'

The withdrawal of Slashchov's force to the Crimea at the end of December saved the peninsula for the Whites, with its defence of the Perekop isthmus. Like his mentor Shkuro, Slashchov was a dissipated looter and a cruel anti-Semite. Unlike Shkuro, he had the air of an over-grown and corrupt cherub. It is said that the main character in Mikhail Bulgakov's play *Flight* (in many ways a sequel to *The Days of the Turbins*) was based on him.

General Yakov Slashchov.

The famous singer Aleksandr Vertinsky left a memorable description of Slashchov after he was summoned by the young general's military aides one evening. 'There were ten or twelve people at the table in the huge, brightly lit Pullman railway car. There were dirty plates, bottles and flowers. Everything was already crumpled, stained with wine, scattered around. Slashchov, long and trim, noisily got up from the table. A huge hand was stretched towards me.'

Vertinsky was both repelled and fascinated by his face, 'which was a long, white, deadly white mask with a cherry-red swollen mouth, greenish-grey clouded eyes and greenish-black rotten teeth. His face was powdered. Sweat was pouring down from his forehead in murky milky streamlets.'

'Thank you for coming,' Slashchov said. 'I am a great fan of yours. You sing about many things that torment all of us. Would you like some cocaine?' Vertinsky refused, eyeing the 'big round tobacco box in the middle of the table, which was full of cocaine. Those seated around the table had small goose feathers. They picked up the white powder and sniffed, putting it in one nostril then in the other one.' Slashchov insisted on introducing him to Lida, his lover, 'who shared his warrior life, participated in all battles and twice saved his life! She was thin and straight, with crazy grey eyes, she chain-smoked nervously.'

In the end, Slashchov's fearlessness and warlike skills as the commander of the Crimean-Azov Corps would not be enough to make General Wrangel overlook his insubordination and mental instability. Among many bizarre examples of his behaviour, Slashchov rode into battle with a pet crow in a cage attached to his saddle. Wrangel considered that he had 'crossed that fragile boundary that separates eccentricity from madness'.

Nearly 300 kilometres further west, the extreme right-wing writer Shulgin, who had set up Azbuka, the White counter-intelligence service, spent New Year's Eve in Odessa with General Dragomirov. 'The two of us were sitting in his carriage,' Shulgin wrote. 'The train was in the port of Odessa and one could see the sea from the windows when it was light. The train now had nowhere to go. Dragomirov said: "I still think that resistance will start. Once nothing is left but a choice between death in battle or death by drowning, an outburst of energy will suddenly be produced . . . At the moment, the mass of people just want to get away, but what will happen when they have nowhere to go? What do you think?"'

Part Four

1920

33

The Great Siberian Ice March
December 1919–February 1920

The immobile queue of trains beyond Novo-Nikolaevsk caused many to abandon the railway, constantly attacked from both sides by groups of partisans. Refugees resorted to purchasing horse-drawn sledges from the peasants. Many officers simply seized them at gunpoint. Everything depended on the shaggy little Siberian ponies. They had to descend steep banks down to the ice of frozen rivers. 'Our horses slid without even moving their feet,' Vice-Consul Hansen reported, 'and this we think only the Siberian horse could do.' Along the track they passed overturned sleighs and dead ponies. Either side, the snow-laden trees in the virgin forest of the taiga formed almost impenetrable barriers.

Villages along the way were packed at night, when the temperature dropped below minus thirty-five. 'There were so many people going through and so few houses that only half of them could get under a roof at night.' At night, soldiers and refugees invaded peasant log houses to warm up, before braving the cold again. Every floor was packed with sleeping soldiers and refugees, which enabled typhus-bearing lice to spread infection. Lice bred in such quantities in the Siberian winter that the old trick of sprinkling tobacco in your clothes had little effect. Outside, camp-fires blazed in the street lit by those who could not find shelter and would otherwise freeze to death.

Those who remained on the trains could not just sit and wait for them to move. 'Siberia was completely wrecked,' a Polish officer wrote. 'Waterworks had been damaged or frozen. The locomotives had to be supplied with water which meant bringing constant sacks or buckets filled with snow.' And if the fire in the locomotive was allowed to go out, then all the pipes would freeze solid, so passengers had to spend much of the day searching for firewood in the forest.

Few of those blocked along the railway knew then that Viktor Pepelyayev, Kolchak's prime minister, and his brother Anatoly had arrested the disastrous commander-in-chief General Sakharov and appointed General Kappel instead. Admiral Kolchak himself, still blocked in his train by the Czechs, had little choice but to acquiesce. He did not know that most of his ministers, who had left Omsk just two days before him, were safely on their way to Vladivostok, which they reached on 7 January. General Sakharov was released and allowed his own train, but this did him little good as it was soon caught in the massive jam. This hold-up was not caused by the Czechs. Units of the 1st Army sent ahead to Krasnoyarsk had been won over by the Socialist Revolutionaries, who were coming round to the idea that they would have to make some sort of deal with the triumphant Red Army.

On the southern side of the Trans-Siberian Railway Konstantin Semchevsky, a young cavalry officer and former member of the Tsar's imperial convoy, was fretting impatiently. He had just heard that the central column of the Red 5th Army had suddenly advanced on the northern flank along the railway. He guessed that the Reds stood a good chance of encircling the bulk of Kolchak's army, right up to Krasnoyarsk. Semchevsky knew that his wife had a berth on General Sakharov's train, and thus would be trapped in the queue. He decided that he had to save her from the imminent disaster.

Although aged only twenty-five, he was now just about the most senior officer left with the remnants of the 1st Cavalry Division, since the divisional commander and his staff had already abandoned them. He promised his comrades that he would be back within three days, ordered his men to harness three good horses to a *troika* and took a trusted veteran with him called Mishka Popov.

The two of them drove north on forest tracks to the Trans-Siberian Railway. 'The further we went, the louder became the sound of firing,' he wrote. They arrived at a tributary of the Yenisei. A barge loaded with small barrels was frozen into the river. Popov immediately guessed that they contained butter. Once they were across the ice, Popov jumped off the sledge, climbed on to the barge and brought one back in triumph. 'We moved on listening to the gunfire.' On reaching the edge of the forest, they halted, transfixed at the sight ahead. 'Black dots made up of horsemen, sledges and men on foot were moving feverishly in all directions on the low hills. It was like a huge, disturbed anthill. Lots of riderless horses were charging around. There were many carts and sledges abandoned. Under heavy artillery fire, everyone in the Krasnoyarsk encirclement was trying to escape.'

Semchevsky started to despair. The area was enormous, and he wondered how he would ever find his wife. 'The snow was not deep, but soon our horses began to tire. The day was drawing to an end. If I did not manage to find her by dusk, I might never find her.' Just as he was starting to lose hope, he spotted a woman's blouse in the snow which looked like one of his wife's. They pulled up alongside a large covered sledge, whose driver was throwing baggage out to lighten the load. Inside it he spotted General Sakharov. Semchevsky's wife was in the back.

The General's driver had already thrown away his wife's small suit-case, which included a few of his own memorabilia, 'including altar wafers which the Metropolitan of Moscow had blessed in the Uspensky Cathedral for the 300th anniversary of the Romanov dynasty, which the sovereign had given to me, his page-boy, as a souvenir. There was also a large porcelain egg with the monograph of the Empress Aleksandra Feodorovna which she had given to me at Easter 1913.'

Sakharov's horse clearly lacked the strength to pull the large sledge, so Semchevesky's wife moved to the *troika*. Popov threw out the barrel of butter with a sad expression but did not hesitate. Semchevsky invited Sakharov to join them. 'It will make the *troika* too heavy,' he replied. 'I will stay here. If the worst comes to the worst, I have a revolver.' Semchevsky insisted and Sakharov joined them. The general's driver unharnessed their exhausted horse and rode it away slowly. It was already twilight.

Semchevsky decided to break out of the encirclement to the northeast rather than forge ahead as most people seemed to be doing. They then would swing round north of Krasnoyarsk. 'We reached the Yenisei in almost complete darkness. The bank turned out to be steep. Everyone got out to search for the best place to descend onto the ice. My wife fortunately found the right spot. The expert, Mishka Popov, thought it over, and said, "I'll make the horses go fast and with any luck we'll manage." He whipped them up. The troika flew through the air onto the ice and the horses managed to keep their footing.'

Finally, they saw the lights of Esaulskoe, a large settlement ahead, and heard the sound of church bells. It was only then that they remembered that it was Orthodox Christmas Eve and people were going to church. Next day, 6 January, would be Christmas, and the day when the 5th Army occupied Krasnoyarsk. Semchevsky and his companions had been unbelievably lucky. The Reds captured 20,000 prisoners in the Krasnoyarsk pocket and lacked the provisions to feed them properly. 'Only small remnants continued their journey to the Trans-Baikal under the command of General Kappel,' the Red Army *Stavka* reported.

Consul-General Harris reported on the chaos in Krasnoyarsk just before the Red Army moved in. 'Every Russian was panic stricken . . . The Czechs were the recognized masters of the situation and did just as they pleased.' Word spread that the Czechs had handed over White Russian officers to Red partisans. General Janin, the Czechs' champion, apparently even gave orders that the Czechs were to take over as guards on the train with the Russian gold reserves. White officers were outraged, but the disintegration of their forces left them helpless.

The triangular quarrels between Czechs, White Russians and Poles dominated the chaos of the retreat. 'Polish troops became disgruntled with having to form the rearguard of the Czech retreat,' a White Russian report stated. General Janin never wavered in his favouritism towards the Czechs.* The Polish liaison officer with Kolchak's headquarters protested: 'To be the rear guard over a distance of thousands of kilometres may be an honour to the Poles, but it is too heavy a burden to be borne all the time by one and the same Polish division.' Janin's reply was dry and firm. 'The fact that the Polish Division will serve as rearguard for the majority of our way East has not escaped me, but under the circumstances, we could not have done otherwise. By moving the Division up, we would have delayed the general traffic by at least three weeks.'

The commander of the Czech 3rd Division refused to offer any help as the Poles fought off the Red 27th Division. Polish headquarters informed both General Janin and the commander of all the Czech forces, General Syrový, of their men's 'extreme exhaustion, losses in hundreds of killed and its current catastrophic situation'. Janin never replied, while Syrový's answer was curt to say the least. 'To Commander of the Polish Army Colonel Czuma. I am surprised at the tone of your correspondence. According to Gen. Janin's orders, you

* As well as Czechs and Poles, there were also a Romanian Legion, a Slovakian Regiment and a Croat detachment, which all came under his Allied command. Janin, to the deep suspicion of Russian officers, favoured the creation of individual national units, including Ukrainians and other groups who had been part of the Tsarist Empire.

are to come last. I cannot permit even one Polish transport to move East, until the last Czech transport leaves Klukviennaya station. There shall be no more negotiations or requests regarding this issue, for the matter is closed.'

As a last resort to escape their Red Army pursuers, the Poles abandoned their blocked trains and set out on foot, but it was too late. 'On the night of 9 January, they arrested their commanding officer and demanded that they surrender to the Bolsheviks on the condition that if they handed over their arms they would be allowed home to Poland intact through European Russia.'

The next day, the capitulation of the Polish 5th Division to the Red Army produced bitter emotions, especially among its officers. 'Grief over our losses,' wrote one of them, 'the lack of opportunity to show the outstanding combat abilities of Polish soldiers and the failure to complete our objective of reaching Poland with weapon in hand, pushed some into the arms of death. For it was clear from the start that the surrender agreement would remain a dead letter. Our fears proved true. We were stripped of everything, even the smallest provisions.' They would be left half starved in prisoner-of-war camps until the end of the Polish-Soviet war in 1921.

A British officer captured in Krasnoyarsk was struck by how meekly White officers surrendered. Their ripped-off epaulettes lay on the ground 'like fallen leaves in autumn'. He was also surprised at how polite Red Army officers were. Civilian Communists, on the other hand, who had been joined by a large number of former German prisoners of war, were the fanatics.

Families were separated in the chaos of retreat. A parent who had to go off to forage for food might well return to find the train had gone, or that their wagon had been attached to another one. Young women and girls separated from their families were especially vulnerable in a time of utter lawlessness and defeat. Stations had scrawled messages pinned up everywhere as relatives tried to find each other.

American Red Cross personnel, who had left their train earlier, caught up on foot with the last Czech echelon further down the line. On 10 January, Colonel Blunt and seven American officers of the Railway Service Corps were captured by the Bolsheviks. American and British contingents managed to avoid the typhus epidemic mainly through basic precautions. In almost all trains, at least one wagon was filled with typhus victims. One train carried nothing but typhus patients, and naked bodies were thrown out into the snow at every halt, 'with as little ceremony as the stoker threw out ashes', as a British officer observed. Roland Morris, the American ambassador to Japan, was furious to discover that a million dollars' worth of medicines and equipment given to the Whites to control the epidemics had been sold off along the Trans-Siberian Railway.

The greatest fear of catching typhus was to be taken to one of the so-called hospitals, where conditions were unspeakable. 'Everyone moaned and raved,' wrote a rare survivor, 'memories of home shattered the feverish minds; a tiny lamp was dying in a corner. After a few hours, one of the patients rose up, reeled and fell on top of me, never to rise again. It felt like being in a grave. I literally had no strength to free myself of him but mustered the remainder of the energy that did still flicker within me and pushed him off.'

Although typhus created a fear akin to that of a medieval plague, all the clothes were stripped from the bodies of victims by people who were so desperate that they took the suicidal risk of catching the disease. According to US Army reports, the refugees were not just dying of typhus, but also from smallpox and diphtheria. In Krasnoyarsk, people were shocked by the sight of children playing around the frozen mounds of naked corpses. There was no question of burial in the permafrost of winter. Whole warehouses were filled in some of the larger towns. Estimates of those who died from typhus by the end of the winter ranged up to 60,000 people in Novo-Nikolaevsk alone.

In Krasnoyarsk, some 5,000 cavalry chargers and transport horses abandoned by the White forces wandered around hopelessly, left to starve. Many of them had been confiscated by the Whites from Siberian farmers, but nobody dared to take them in case they were accused of stealing Soviet government property. The 5th Army contingent in the city had no cavalry who could have used them, yet their transport section had no forage to spare. When they died their carcasses provided some meat, but the remains had to be dragged out of the town and left to rot in the snowfields.

Pity was in short supply everywhere. Women refugees trapped in the icicle-covered cattle wagons gave birth, but had no milk for their babies and they had to watch their small children dying from starvation. Their menfolk, 'covered with dirty furs, unshaven, wild-eyed, and desperate', would collapse in self-pity. Those who had access to vodka and became careless in the extreme cold faced frostbite and then possibly gangrene. On the night of 10 January, a temperature of minus 68 degrees centigrade was recorded further east at Chita, where on other nights it was down to minus 40. American soldiers who became drunk and passed out on the way back to camp often lost fingers toes or even feet to frostbite.

All this time, even worse scenes had been taking place in the great city of Irkutsk, 1,000 kilometres beyond Krasnoyarsk. On 23 December 800 Russians of the White 53rd Infantry Regiment, trained by the British, had seized the rail station of Irkutsk. They did this right under the eyes of Czech troops manning their armoured train, the Orlik. The Czechs clearly acquiesced in or even supported the action, which had been inspired by the Left Socialist Revolutionaries. The 54th Regiment also joined the mutiny.

The rebels then destroyed the bridge over the River Angara, causing panic in the city. The commander of the 53rd begged Ataman Semenov to send troops to restore order, but Semenov was hardly the best candidate to deal with the mayhem of murder, looting and rape. A force of his Cossacks and an armoured train soon arrived from Chita, but Allied representatives demanded that they stayed outside. The rebels attempted to storm the citadel until they were driven back across the River Ushakovka by troops under General Sychev. The Japanese also sent troops ready to ensure the evacuation of their citizens from Irkutsk.

Viktor Pepelyayev, still the minister of the interior as well as prime minister, declared his intention to negotiate with the Socialist Revolutionaries in Irkutsk: 'seeing that the present Government, with public opinion ill-disposed towards it, and with no authority within the country, and without support from outside, could not bank upon any success'. But Pepelyayev's overtures were firmly rejected by the Left SRs and Mensheviks. They claimed control on forming an administration on 4 January, which they called the Political Centre. They dismissed Kolchak, who resigned on hearing the news, and declared that General Denikin was now the Supreme Ruler. The Americans, among others, were none too pleased when they heard that Kolchak had appointed Ataman Semenov to replace him as commander-in-chief in Transbaikalia. He may well have thought that Semenov might be his last hope of rescue, but that was an illusion. Semenov, now confirmed as the most powerful of the Siberian Cossack brigands, immediately ordered 'that all freights be subject to taxation; the money to be used for the army of the ataman of the Far Eastern Cossack troops. A part of the goods passing through the Trans-Baikal is to be confiscated for the relief of the local population.'

The situation in Irkutsk 'is each day becoming more and more appalling', a newspaper reported. Starvation was a real threat since supplies had dried up. American troops heard that Bolsheviks were taking over from the Socialist Revolutionaries and throwing White patients out of the windows of the Red Cross hospital to freeze to death in the snow, but that might well have been an exaggeration or invention.

Ever since mid-December, the Czech commander General Syrový refused to admit that Admiral Kolchak was being held back deliberately by his troops. The Allied commissioners wanted him moved out of danger, but General Janin ignored their instructions. Janin had promised Kolchak safe passage to the British military mission, but on 15 January the 6th Czech Regiment handed over three railway carriages containing the former Supreme Ruler, his chairman of the Council of Ministers and the gold reserves to the Left Socialist Revolutionaries in Irkutsk. Six days later, a Communist Military Revolutionary Committee took over, but included Left SRs and Mensheviks.

Consul-General Harris in Irkutsk was consumed with rage in his reports to Washington. 'The Czechs have intentionally and wilfully adopted an entirely different policy than that laid down by the Allies . . . They have committed many acts of perfidy by surrendering Kolchak and the gold to the Bolsheviks and now openly and shamelessly acknowledge the same to the whole world.' Harris argued that 'their last dishonourable acts in Irkutsk prove that they would have no difficulty in easily arranging with the Bolsheviks for a safe and rapid transit through European Russia.' So why should they respect their 'insistence upon returning home by sea' and provide them with 'a pleasure ride'?

The Military Revolutionary Committee interrogated Kolchak and Pepelyayev for just over two weeks. Meanwhile General Kappel's force, which had escaped the encirclement at Krasnoyarsk, marched in their direction through hundreds of kilometres of wilderness, often along the ice of frozen rivers, to Lake Baikal. Kappel, leading his charger on foot, fell through the ice. Although he managed to extract himself having held on to his horse's reins, he suffered such frostbite that his toes turned gangrenous. They were amputated without anaesthetic, and on 26 January, Kappel died from double pneumonia.

Four days later, his loyal force of 1,100 'Kappelevtsy', now commanded by General Voitsekhovsky, came up against a Red force near Zima, 240 kilometres north of Irkutsk. The Reds did not stand a chance against Kappel's veterans and retreated rapidly, yet Voitsekhovsky had to acknowledge that his men did not have the strength to take Irkutsk on their own. To bypass the city, he led them across the frozen surface of Lake Baikal on their seemingly endless Siberian ice march.

Throughout the interminable sessions of his interrogation Kolchak never lost his train of thought or his temper, in the way he had so often in Omsk. He was uncharacteristically calm, knowing well what the outcome would be. He asked to be reunited with his young lover Anna Timiryova, who had 'wanted to share' his fate, but she was imprisoned separately and badly treated. At four in the morning on 7 February 1920, both Kolchak and Pepelyayev were shot at the confluence of the Angara and Ushakovka, and their corpses pushed through a hole in the ice.

34

The Fall of Odessa
January 1920

Odessa, that most cosmopolitan of cities, had suffered every time it changed hands. Soviet rule had ended once again on 23 August 1919, with the landing of the Volunteer Army detachment of 2,000 men. Coinciding with the heady emotions of the March on Moscow, this had created the greatest excitement among all anti-Bolsheviks.

Just over a month later, General Denikin made a grand entrance aboard the White cruiser *Kagul*, flying the 'Andreevsky' ensign – Peter the Great's pale blue Saint Andrew's cross on a white background. 'British and Italian warships fired salutes,' Yelena Lakier recorded. 'The city was decorated with flags and carpets hanging from the balconies.' But just three months later, General Shilling had been forced to pull back towards Odessa in December when Denikin's march on Moscow collapsed.

Even during the previous period of Communist rule, the writer Ivan Bunin had lived quietly in his spacious apartment, 'tastefully furnished with many antiques'. An 'elegantly dressed maid' greeted visitors at the door and ushered them into 'lordly rooms' with polished parquet floors and high ceilings. Bunin had dared to wear that symbol of gentry in hot weather: a panama hat. His charmed existence, if not almost inexplicable, had been totally unrepresentative of the population at large. And yet Bunin did not isolate himself in an ivory tower. He was a fascinated observer of street life, constantly jotting vignettes in his notebook. Now, with the advance of the Red 14th Army, he knew that his last days in Russia were approaching. 'Everything has turned unpleasant in this world,' he remarked to Paustovsky. 'Even the sea smells of rusty iron now.'

Odessa reeked of corruption, having attracted so many gamblers, speculators and confidence tricksters. Men hunched over tables in cafés were selling diamonds said to come from the imperial crown jewels. Even as Odessa was about to fall, Royal Navy officers were still going ashore to pick up bargains from those ruined by the collapse of the Denikin rouble, the 'Bell'. 'The most valuable furs etc. are going at absurdly cheap prices,' Commander Webb-Bowen wrote in his diary.

The nights were sinister. 'Sometimes out of the dark, out of the city, came the sounds of rifle shots,' Paustovsky wrote. 'Dogs would bark for a long time after each shot, then gradually fall silent.' Shulgin found that 'masses of people were moving around in this spooky semi-darkness.' There were 'lots of cocaine prostitutes and half-drunk officers'.

The threat to the city increased. The Red Cross decided to move from Odessa as the Communist regime now classified it as a counter-revolutionary organisation. Yelena Lakier, working for the Red Cross, left for Sevastopol on the British transport ship *Hanover* taking the wounded. With the temperature at minus thirty, she slept in a fur coat and her boots, yet still was sobbing from the cold.

General Shilling warned Denikin that his small force was incapable of defending Odessa. An evacuation to the Crimea must be organised. Denikin replied, supposedly under heavy pressure from British and French officers, that Odessa must be held at all costs. Globachev, the former head of the Okhrana, now in his role of head of counter-intelligence, knew that 'nobody wanted to fight', while Shulgin was convinced that Baron Stempel, the city's governor, regarded his position as nothing more than 'a reward for his previous service'.

In the third week of January 1920, Shilling's headquarters began secretly preparing for evacuation. They did not even tell Globachev, although he was well aware of the two Red divisions advancing on the city. The Volunteer Army in Odessa suppressed the news, claiming that all the Red attacks had been beaten off. They did not want a mass exodus when there were so few ships left, which they wanted to keep for themselves. On 23 January, Globachev arrived at the headquarters for work, but found the place abandoned. Shilling and his staff had prepared their departure on the SS *Vladimir*, yet remained down by the port.

During the evening of 24 January, Shulgin felt that any minute 'the situation could change. I dressed and we went out. In the street there were trains of carts and parts of artillery that entered the town. Mountains of suitcases and boxes were growing in the Ekaterininskaya Square, cars were making their way among them.' Anybody who feared what the future held under the Soviet regime faced a fundamental choice, whether to leave or to stay. 'Decisions in those days had to be quick ones,' wrote Paustovsky, even though he had chosen to remain under Lenin's regime. 'One moment of indecision could ruin a life or save it.'

'Shilling was still ashore,' Shulgin wrote. 'He seemed to get angry when someone spoke to him about evacuation and promised to hold on for at least another 10 days. However, everything was packed, down to the last crate.' But as soon as a French cruiser in the road-stead began firing its main armament, with shells screaming over the rooftops to explode outside in the countryside, the whole city suffered 'evacuation fever'. White troops began surging back through the town towards the port. Members of so-called 'Death battalions' wore the skull and crossbones insignia on their sleeves, yet appeared to be most reluctant to live up to their regimental names. There was no sign of what Shulgin called the 'coffee-shop army' of thousands of officers who had done little but hang around the Odessa bars. Rumours spread of Bolshevik infiltration everywhere and of generals already hiding on board ships in the harbour. Crowds besieged banks and consulates trying to get visas.

Young *junker* cadets, co-opted as military police, could not prevent the rush to the harbour. The roads to the port were packed, and people were crushed. 'Bulging suitcases, packages and baskets slithered along under the legs of the people like some horrible living creatures. The contents poured out of them, getting tangled in people's legs.'

Shilling and his staff had now boarded the *Vladimir*, where Globachev joined them. The crew refused to set sail until they had been paid. A general from the headquarters ordered Globachev to go to the offices of the State Bank to take out 2 million *kerenky* roubles, as the sailors refused to accept 'Bells'. 'It was extremely dangerous to go into the town and the steamship was due to leave at one p.m. The treasurer and two armed officers from my department accompanied me in the automobile. As we approached the bank, we saw a chaotic crowd of civilians packed round the entrance, waiting for it to open to withdraw their money. The treasurer and I forced our way into the bank. We obtained the money quickly from the manager.' He asked if they could take him and his sister with them and Globachev agreed. The manager took them out to a rear entrance, but they found that all the exits were blocked by the former police who were now siding with the Bolsheviks. 'Finally, we discovered why. It was because they had not received their pay. They were afraid that the manager would take away all the money and they would be left without any.' As soon as a large amount of money was handed over to the police, they were able to escape. Firing in the city had started. Nobody knew whether it was a rising of underground groups or it signified the arrival of the 41st Division. Globachev and his companions ran back to the port. The *Vladimir* was still alongside the mole, but the gangway had already been pulled up to prevent the ship being stormed. Ropes were thrown and Globachev, the bank manager and his sister were hauled up to the deck.

Shulgin, like several prominent individuals, had formed his own defence detachment. They were down by the port when gunmen opened fire from the Aleksandrovsky Park above them. People rushed to hide behind the stone warehouses at the entrance to the harbour. 'Bolsheviks were not good marksmen,' Shulgin noted. 'Not many people were wounded.' Then, he remembered his New Year's Eve conversation with General Dragomirov. 'It was at this moment that the impulse of resistance was finally born. Suddenly several people rushed forward – not officers, but rank and file dragoons. They started shouting, making wild gestures: "So what, gentlemen? Are you going to stay like this for much longer? Where are we to go, there is only the sea around us! Are we going to just die here? Let's go and beat them, the fuckers, never mind their machine guns. Fuck them! Let's go!"

'On the way my men caught a lad of around twenty who claimed not to be a "Yid", but when ordered to cross himself did it incorrectly.* One of them was convinced that this was a Bolshevik who had got rid of his rifle just after firing at us. I had to threaten them to let him go ... We came across other groups. Everyone was terribly thirsty. Some ladies were giving us water but with great caution. They were scared of Bolsheviks taking revenge on them.'

Shulgin, hearing that it was time to leave, went down to the port. He had been warned that if they did not make it in time, they would have to escape on foot to the Romanian border. 'I reached our own barge and was terrified. The barge was supposed to be pulled by our

---

* This was the way that anti-Semitic gangs tested somebody they suspected of being Jewish.

"own" steamer. It was evident, when seeing both the steamer and the barge, that they could not possibly get out of the port, and if they could they were certainly doomed. Both were stuffed full of people, among them many of my close friends and family.' He decided to join Colonel Stessel, who set off for the long march through snow and across the ice of the lagoon. No welcome awaited them when they eventually reached the frontier post. The Romanian army stripped them of everything worth having, including their boots, for which they received birch-bark *lapti* in exchange.

On that day, 7 February 1920, Paustovsky watched 'the Homeric flight' from an old pavilion. He wrote about 'the blindness of fear when people can see only one thing – the rickety gangway of a ship with its steps broken under the weight of human bodies, soldiers' rifle butts over people's heads, children held up in their mothers' arms over the mad stampede of hurrying men, their desperate crying, a woman trampled underfoot and still wriggling, screaming on the pavement. People literally destroyed each other, not letting even those save themselves who could manage to crawl up the gangways and grab a railing of a ship . . . Captains, afraid their ship was becoming swamped, gave orders to pull away, leaving gangways to fall into the sea with those still on them doomed to drown. We could see men on the ships chopping through the mooring lines and the ships pulled away from the docks without even raising their gangplanks . . . Almost all of these grimy boats, the black paint peeling off their sides, pulled out of the port with a heavy list, loaded down.

'A mounted detachment of Soviet cavalry slowly rode down one of the streets leading to the port, filled with broken suitcases and trunks, and lined with the bodies of people who had been crushed to death. The soldiers were riding with their heads lowered, as if they were thinking, and they stopped next to the bodies, leaning over from their saddles.' They continued on to the end of the breakwater and gazed out to sea at the ships passing the Vorontsovsky lighthouse.

With a lyrical sadness that was unmistakably Russian, Paustovsky watched the departure of the ships and thought of their imminent exile. 'One of the ships emitted a ball of steam into the grey sky and blew a long, shuddering whistle. All the other ships followed it with whistles in all keys and degrees of loudness. These were the parting salutes of the dying – of men who were quitting their native land, abandoning

their own people, the Russian fields and forests, spring-times and winters, their sufferings and their joys, breaking away from the past and
the present, from the radiant genius of Pushkin and Tolstoy, from the
great filial love for every blade of grass, for every drop of water from a
well somewhere in our simple and beautiful land.'

The Last Hurrah of the White Cavalry
January–March 1920

On New Year's Eve it had looked inevitable that the Red Army was going to capture Novocherkassk and encircle the remnants of the White Army. Then the weather changed and the *coup de grâce* did not happen. A sudden thaw rendered the marshlands around the lower Don impassable. The 1st Cavalry Army lacked any bridging equipment and the Don did not freeze again until 15 January. For Kamenev and the *Stavka*, news of the 10th Army's recapture of Tsaritsyn on 2 January, Budyonny's seizure of Taganrog on 6 January and then Rostov two days later seemed to pale beside this lost opportunity to snatch total victory. Red cavalrymen set the hospital in Rostov ablaze, supposedly with wounded White officers trapped in their beds.

The White withdrawal was chaotic, and the British were little better when it came to evacuating Taganrog. In General Holman's constant absence, nobody could take a decision. Kennedy was not the only officer to become exasperated with Holman. 'He should be at headquarters now to settle the numerous important questions,' he wrote. Instead, Holman was as excited as a schoolboy, flying as a bombardier in RAF aircraft, which was hardly the job of a major general. Kennedy heard on 2 January that Holman had 'bombed, with his own hand, one of Denikin's batteries, thinking they were enemy cavalry'. Later, Kennedy discovered that Holman did not just harbour an obsessive hatred for the Bolsheviks. 'Cragg saw Holman this morning,' he noted in his diary, 'and says that the latter is obsessed by the idea of wiping out the Jews everywhere and can talk about little else.'

Unable to ship out the large quantities of equipment stored in Taganrog, Captain Lever and others simply blew it up. The last trains were getting up steam. The British military mission made sure that there was always an officer in the cab of its locomotive with a loaded revolver, to ensure that the engine driver did not desert his post. Expecting an attack at any moment, the other members of the mission slept cradling a rifle. They passed soldiers in 'greatcoats frozen stiff like planks' and terrified refugees trudging on to Rostov and the great bridge over the Don. With 'the masses pouring through', Lever noted unsympathetically, 'each and every halt has become an indescribable cesspool, like a festering sore on the face of the earth. Small wonder at the amount of typhus, cholera and small-pox that raged.'

The Whites were lucky. Vasily Shorin, the Red commander-in-chief of the newly formed Caucasus Front, had a plan that would make things far worse for his forces and give the Whites the breathing space they desperately needed. Budyonny saw the dangers in Shorin's unimaginative head-on attack across the river against the Volunteer Corps in Bataisk. He suggested instead that his army of 9,000 sabres and 5,000 bayonets should follow a wide envelopment by crossing much further to the east, and then swing round behind the Volunteers. The obdurate Shorin rejected any change to his plan.

On 17 January, Budyonny's attack supported by the 8th Army failed, and a renewed attempt the next day also petered out with heavy casualties. To Budyonny's disbelief and fury, they were ordered to try a third time. He pointed out 'the completely unsuitable terrain, consisting of continuous bogs, and the limited space for deploying cavalry'. Bitter reproaches followed. Shorin tried to blame Budyonny's lack of follow-through at the start of the month, saying that he had given the Whites the chance to reorganise their defence. The accompanying 8th Army then accused Budyonny's men of 'manifesting an extreme lack of combat resilience'.

The danger of defeat forced the components of the White alliance to discuss strategy, as well as their considerable political differences. On 18 January a meeting of the Supreme Krug was held in Ekaterinodar. While the Cossacks debated, Denikin worked hard to hammer out a new programme. The dramatic reduction in the size of the Volunteer Army had reduced the grip of monarchist reactionaries, forcing concessions to the Cossack majority which were anathema to Wrangel. Working with politicians from the centre and even the centre left, Denikin recognised the past mistakes of failing to offer land reform to the peasants or guarantee a commitment to the Constituent Assembly. He even included the veteran socialist Nikolai Chaikovsky, the leader from Arkhangel, in his new government. This was not just a case of too little too late. It revealed the White movement's inability to function effectively either as a dictatorship or as a quasi-democratic coalition. The only issue its factions could agree on was a negative: their hatred of Bolshevism. The Reds, on the other hand, had all the necessary characteristics for winning a civil war in the world's largest country: an utterly centralist and ruthlessly authoritarian structure. This enabled them to survive even disastrous incompetence.

Shorin insisted on repeating the attacks on Bataisk on 20 and 21 January. The *Stavka* described the operation as a 'knowingly impossible offensive' yet did not intervene until 24 January to change the plan of attack. They ordered the 9th Army, and also the 10th Army advancing southwest from Tsaritsyn, to join the fray. Budyonny was finally allowed to put his plan into action – crossing further to the east to outflank the Volunteer position at Bataisk. But he must have been irritated when the corps of his detested rival, Dumenko, was given a free hand and not placed under his command. Their manoeuvres led to major cavalry clashes at the end of the month.

On 28 January, Budyonny's *Konarmia* put a large group of White cavalry to flight, capturing a dozen field guns and thirty machine guns. The very next day Mamontov's Don Cossacks counter-attacked and battered Budyonny's 11th Cavalry Division, leading to more furious arguments on the Red side. Stalin's crony Voroshilov predictably backed Budyonny. He blamed Dumenko for charging ahead and crossing the River Manych without waiting for the 1st Cavalry Army.

The White success was short-lived. Mamontov fell sick with typhus and died shortly afterwards. The mud was so deep that the Whites had to abandon many of their field guns. On one occasion General Sidorin was nearly captured when his aircraft was stuck in the mud and he could not take off. Just in time, a *sotnia* of Kalmyks appeared. Seeing what was needed, they leaped from their horses, pulled the aircraft out by hand and carried it over to a dry track. Worst of all, instead of blocking the 10th Army on the northeastern flank, the Army of the Caucasus, now renamed the Kuban Corps, started to disintegrate. Its Kuban Cossacks had come to hate Denikin and the Whites. His crackdown on their Rada in November had imposed an artificial calm for a time, but now the relationship was becoming deeply embittered. Kuban Cossacks, individually and in groups, were heading home with their booty. With ill-judged optimism they thought that if they severed their alliance with the Whites, the Soviet government would allow them some sort of independence. This was not an encouraging moment for an American fact-finding mission, led by Vice Admiral Newton McCully, to visit the front and report back to Washington.

Budyonny argued repeatedly for the concentration of Red cavalry under his command, partly for egotistical reasons but also because it offered the best way to destroy the mounted backbone of the White armies. As the *Stavka* put it, 'the strength of the enemy's defence lay in the active manoeuvre of his cavalry units, which were being brought in from various sectors of the front and from the reserve'. When relations between Budyonny and his Front commander Shorin broke down completely, Budyonny appealed over his head to Kamenev and the *Stavka*. Kamenev accepted his arguments and Shorin was replaced by Tukhachevsky, who halted operations until he could reorganise the front and its armies.

Tukhachevsky, a professional officer from an impoverished noble family did not lack self-confidence or ambition. On joining the Semenyovsky Guards at the outbreak of the First World War, he had announced his intention of becoming a general before the age of thirty or die in the attempt. He was captured and escaped four times from prison camps, but the story that he shared a cell in one of them with Captain Charles de Gaulle is unconvincing. What is much more likely is that once the foreign press described him as a 'Red Napoleon' following his victories in Siberia, he simply considered high command to be his due.

Tukhachevsky wanted to prepare a knock-out blow in the northern Caucasus by creating a strike force, with the 1st Cavalry Army and the 9th and 10th Armies. They would attack from the River Manych towards the key junction of Tikhoretskaya and thus threaten the rear of the Volunteer Corps and the Don Army. The breakthrough would happen at the point of 'the least political and operational resistance', which meant the junction between the Kuban Cossacks and the Don Army. Budyonny's 1st Cavalry Army was to play 'the role of a surgical knife, which was to forever separate the Kuban and Don counter-revolutions from each other'. The 10th Army was also given the task of preventing the Whites from withdrawing deeper into the Caucasus via Armavir.

The Whites ordered the IV Don Cavalry Corps under the command of General Pavlov to concentrate at Torgovaya, ready to counter the massing of Red cavalry. 'In the grey dawn,' wrote Rakovsky, 'the cavalry regiments produced a great impression. One had to look closer to see how much these people had suffered . . . Worn-out boots, torn greatcoats, shabby saddles, or, in many cases, just filthy horsecloths with stirrups made of rope . . . And the tormenting, terrifying question in the tired faces: "What is going to happen?"'

The last hurrah of the White cavalry took place on 17 February. A poignant letter home, from the brother of the twenty-two-year-old Prince Aleksei Cherkassy, described his death.

> My dear, beloved Papa! It was the Lord's will to send us the hardest ordeal. I beg you to accept it with the same strength and firmness as I have done. Our darling Alesha was killed in a cavalry battle around 3 to 4 p.m. on 17 February near Stanitsa Egorlinskaya. He died like a true hero. In that terrible battle, our integrated guards-cavalry regiment lost 11 officers, and around 380 soldiers, killed or wounded. General Barbovich was ordered to be in the first line attacking Budyonny's cavalry. At ten, almost a division of Cossacks were supposed to follow in his steps, with another Cossack division a verst behind them. However, one of these divisions only arrived an hour after the battle finished, and the other one never appeared at all. Our regiment was fighting on the left flank. It attacked, broke up the cavalry charge of the Reds and started chasing them. It continued the chase across two streams. After that the regiment attacked the enemy's reserve and caused great confusion. Alesha chased the Red's *tachanka*, but it managed to get away, so he attacked a Red battery. His horse was killed but he bravely continued on foot, firing his Browning pistol . . . Alesha was seen for the last time reloading his pistol, after which he was attacked by a group of Reds. Mikhailsky rushed to his rescue, but neither of them was seen after that. The Reds had a great numerical advantage and all of them were armed with revolvers, so it was almost impossible to fight against them with just our sabres . . . At that time General Pavlov had a reserve of nearly 30 cavalry regiments! Damn these bloody Cossacks that have let us down so badly!

The bulk of Pavlov's cavalry had in fact attacked two divisions of the 10th Army successfully that morning, which was not part of the plan. This was why they turned up too late to help General Barbovich's force and were repulsed in their turn.

An even greater disaster awaited Pavlov's regiments the next day as they fell back. A sudden blizzard caught them in the open and Pavlov 'lost half of his horses which froze in the steppe', the Red Army *Stavka* noted. Their human losses were far graver. 'We left behind in the steppe thousands of men frozen to death,' a Cossack officer told Rakovsky, 'and the blizzard buried them. The surviving ones were huddling against their horses. You stand still for 5–10 minutes, you start feeling that you are dozing off, and falling . . . A few more minutes, and you might fall asleep forever.' Pavlov, who had ignored warnings of the change in the weather, suffered severe frostbite himself.

On 20 February the Volunteer Corps launched an attack which managed to retake Rostov, but the weakened state of Pavlov's forces and an attack on the Terek Cossack Division forced them to pull back again. The advance of the 10th Army to the northeast and their capture of Armavir made Denikin move his headquarters from the rail junction of Tikhoretskaya back to Ekaterinodar. Then on 1 March, the Red Army entered Stavropol. The remnants of the Volunteer Corps and the Don Cossack cavalry had to withdraw rapidly to escape being cut off and create a fresh defence line along the Kuban river. They had little rest, pulling back 20 to 30 kilometres a day, but at last, after all the mud, the going was firmer.

'The dry, compact ground allowed them to ride in a wide front, also using open fields,' wrote Rakovsky. 'This mass was like a sea flooding the Kuban steppe. Colossal numbers of carts, their drivers terrified of getting encircled, stormed towards the south, ten carts in a row. And horses, horses everywhere you looked. The equestrian Don was pouring into the Kuban. One did not see a single person on foot. Late in the evening, almost three cavalry corps stopped for the night in Stanitsa Korenovskaya.'

Next day, he described a desperate battle after some Red cavalrymen managed to slip ahead unobserved with a machine gun, and set it up covering a vital bridge just 15 kilometres short of Ekaterinodar. 'There was mad shouting. General Kucherov, his head bare, was galloping around between Kalmyks and Bolsheviks, yelling something unintelligible. He was trying to save the crossing and those still caught on the wrong side. The Kalmyks, their teeth clenched, were firing desperately with their rifles. I will never forget the furious resolve, the hatred in the faces of these normally peaceful and calm steppe people, whom the Bolsheviks had robbed and slaughtered. A Kalmyk officer was rushing around in front of the troops, on horseback. He was pointing his whip at the Bolshevik machine-gunner . . . Only the Kalmyks were still fighting; and thanks to them the situation was saved.'

An atmosphere of death and dissension hung over the Whites when they reached Ekaterinodar. They felt betrayed both by the Kuban Cossacks and by the British. General Mamontov's funeral took place in the five-domed St Catherine's Cathedral of Ekaterinodar with Allied officers attending. British jaws clenched and upper lips stiffened when Archbishop Antony in his address referred to the Allies as 'dubious friends'.

Communist funerals were very different to the rather gloomy fare-well of Russian Orthodox rites. The writer Isaac Babel, serving with Budyonny's *Konarmia*, described how dead heroes were hailed at the graveside for 'pounding the anvil of future centuries with the hammer of history'.

The White war correspondent Rakovsky wrote that 'Ekaterinodar in those days reminded one of Rostov shortly before its fall. It was as if the city had started agonizing. There was drinking, plundering, rapes, executions without trial, reckless spending.' The commander of the Don Army imposed martial law on the Kuban capital, already overflowing with dispirited troops and refugees.

Ekaterinodar had to be abandoned as the Reds advanced from the northeast. The port of Novorossiisk, with its bitter winds, offered the only possible escape. Many soldiers were tempted to desert to the Green partisan groups in the mountains who were already ambush-ing the retreating columns and removing sections of track to derail trains. 'Soldiers and civilians, women and children, Russians and Kalmyks, on countless carts of all shapes and types were all mixed up in one continuous flow,' wrote Chevdar. 'There was a huge jam leading to the bridge over the Kuban river. The air was thick with shouts and swearing.' He was exasperated when his second-in-command suffered a nervous collapse. The young lieutenant became terrified of being left alone and started holding on to his greatcoat. 'Shame on you Ivan Petrovich, what sort of a Cossack are you, chasing after me like small child after his Nanny. Are you really afraid that I will abandon you?' The boy admitted that he just could not control himself.

Many could not forget the scenes of panic on the bridge which carried both road and rail traffic. A number, including a nurse, were crushed under the wheels of trains. Their bodies were rolled into the river below. A Kalmyk in despair stabbed his children and wife to death, then killed himself. Rakovsky watched people's different reactions to disaster with fascination. 'A girl was rushing around helplessly in the whirlpool of people and horses. A general passing by shouted to her: "What are you up to? You are going to get crushed!" The girl ran to him: "I took part in the Kuban campaign. I cannot stay in the city. For God's sake, help me!" "Quick, get on my horse!" She climbs on the horse with help from Cossacks and hugs the general's back with both arms.'

South of the River Kuban, the mass of humanity on foot followed the railway track. They had to work their way round carriages pushed over sideways and carts abandoned along the road. Suddenly, at one point much further down the road, the wind brought the first whiff of the sea.

After the departure of the Whites from Ekaterinodar, a painter called Yakob Glasse recorded the scene in his remarkable diary. 'It is a gloomy grey day. Everywhere there is a sea of mud. The city's pavements have been completely destroyed by the carts of the retreating army and cavalry detachments.' The only people who had not departed were about 6,000 Kalmyks – old people, women and children who had followed the retreat of Denikin's armies from the Stavropol steppe, where they had been persecuted by the Reds. These families just sat in the muddy streets with their camels and carts.

Glasse, who fortunately for him was of humble origins, awaited the arrival of the Red Army and the Communists. Having no idea how much more killing there was to go, he mistakenly thought he was witnessing the final drama of the Russian Civil War. 'At dusk there is all of a sudden an unbelievable chaos of noises, shouts, and howling, the inhuman howling of women and children and, finally, sobbing. The Red Army broke into the city. The harmless unarmed Kalmyks were attacked with great brutality that has no obvious reason and slaughtered to the last child. Twenty minutes was enough. The silence that came after was especially sinister, one couldn't even hear any moans from the wounded people. It feels as if the city's population is

also dead, all gates and doors are locked. Everywhere there are detachments of drunken cavalrymen. What will the night bring?'*

'More Red detachments are arriving,' he wrote next day. 'There are
mounted patrols everywhere . . . The Red cavalry horses are decorated
with officers' epaulettes and medals, generals' ribbons are flying from
the bridle. One horse has an archbishop's hat. They are just missing
some human heads . . . Two women from the dregs of society point
a cavalryman to a man in civilian clothes. "That's an officer" they
whisper. Immediately the man's skull is split with one blow of a sabre.
He turns out to be a book-keeper from the post office.'

On the following day, a neighbour warned him not to leave his
house as the Reds were forcing townsfolk to carry away the corpses
of the Kalmyks. Glasse still decided to go. 'An acquaintance whom
I ran into stopped me and advised me to take off my starched collar
and tie, "otherwise they will knock the hell out of you thinking you
are a *burzhui*. And stain your hands with some engine oil and dirt.
Don't shave. Take off your glasses so you don't look intellectual."'
He followed his advice before venturing forth again. 'In the streets I
saw thousands of townsfolk wandering in liquid mud and pulling out
corpses of Kalmyks. Camels, walking solemnly through the streets,
transported on carts the bodies of their owners. The creaking of these
araba carts was heard until late at night.'

On 22 March, he writes: 'In the main square the orchestra has been
playing "The Internationale" since the early morning. Columns of
workers and soldiers are passing with red flags. A rally. A speaker
thanks the Red Army on behalf of the proletariat for liberating the city
from "mercenaries of world capital" and expresses his conviction that
the brave Red Guards will liberate the entire world from the "capitalist
yoke". The order is given after the short rally: "Comrades, everyone is
to go to the station to greet the new administration!" The crowd moves
towards the station, accompanied by the orchestra. The locomotive
that has brought the new masters of the city and the whole region is
decorated with red flags and the bodies of officers from Denikin's army
hanging on it. The guard of honour takes its place on the platform.
What is this? The forces of hell that broke into the age of locomotives?

---

* Red forces in the civil war were carrying out a policy close to genocide against the
Kalmyks. This, no doubt, was the reason why so many Kalmyks collaborated with
the German Wehrmacht in the autumn and winter of 1942.

I leave the station shaken.' One of the very first announcements next day is that Ekaterinodar, named in honour of the Empress Catherine the Great, was henceforth to be the Red city – 'Krasnodar'.

Most of the British military mission had moved straight to Novorossiisk in January after the fall of Taganrog. Their new headquarters was the cement works on the eastern quay. They were angered by a letter from General Holman addressed to all officers, criticising them for dereliction of duty when he had been 'spending the whole of his time sculling about in an aeroplane at the front doing spectacular stunts in the way of bomb-dropping'. By the middle of the month, the mission area was defended by barbed wire and sand-bagged defence positions with Lewis guns, ready to deal with any disturbances.

Refugee trains began to fill Novorossiisk's sidings. The cattle trucks packed with the misery of humanity began, in Lever's phrase, 'breeding a moral and physical pestilence'. But just as Horrocks had observed in Siberia, Lever had to acknowledge that 'The women appear to be outstandingly the finer sex, the great majority of such example, of fortitude, still-existent culture, and finer instincts . . . The men with few exceptions are seemingly reduced to a deadly apathy from which nothing but primal instincts will rouse them.' Almost all had brought the deadly lice with them and a typhus epidemic raged through the town, as it had through the countryside. Vladimir Purishkevich, Yusupov's fellow assassin in the killing of Rasputin, died from it in Novorossiisk on 1 February.

The conditions in the improvised hospital were unspeakable, with two, sometimes three patients to a single bunk, and nobody to remove the dead. Dmitry Shvetzoff, a former officer of the Tsar's Horse Guards Regiment, wrote: 'I had to spend the whole night with these corpses next to me, and lice do not stay on dead people, so they all migrated to me. There were so many lice that during the night when it was quiet and the medic would walk, the sound of lice being squashed by his boots resembled the sounds of someone walking on sugar which had been spilt on the floor.'

Novorossiisk was soon suffering the dread northeasterly gales, which overturned railway carriages and washed several tanks off the breakwater and into the sea. The wind was so powerful that at times people in the streets had to crouch on to their hands and knees. Temperatures fell to minus 30 degrees centigrade, freezing warships at anchor, 'whose foredecks, lifeboats, and forrard guns are solidly encased in ice with festoons of huge icicles'. It was said in the region that if the wind swung round from the south to a northeasterly, the thermometer could drop 40 to 50 degrees in a couple of hours. On the night of 8 February, 177 refugees froze to death in Novorossiisk railway station alone.

On 14 February, the military mission heard that 'two British officers (Cootch and poor old Frecheville)', captured in Rostov, had been paraded naked in the streets, 'their arms having been broken, and that they were then cut to pieces and mutilated'. With the *sang-froid* which British officers had been forced to assume in the trenches of the Western Front, they said no more about it. They returned, when the weather permitted, to shooting woodcock and hare on the foothills beyond the town and tufted duck in the harbour, both for sport and to provide an alternative to bully beef.

When the military mission first heard that Halford Mackinder, the High Commissioner sent out from London, had guaranteed the complete evacuation of 'Russian wounded, wives and families of soldiers, and all those wishing to get away', officers shook their heads in disbelief. But by the end of February, the evacuation of civilians was 'well under way'. Merchant steamships chartered by the British government had started a ferry service to Constantinople and the Prinkipo Islands in the Sea of Marmora.

On the orders of General Milne, a battalion of Royal Scots Fusiliers arrived from Constantinople to man perimeter defences. But first the battalion was marched through the town on 17 March with both pipes and drums in a show of force, augmented by bluejackets in shore-fighting kit, with light field guns, and a Royal Marine band. The idea was to impress Communist agents and sympathisers of the Greens who, ten days before, had raided the prison to release captives. Kennedy thought that the show 'created an enormous impression amongst the inhabitants who, I fancy, have never heard the pipes before. It is splendid to see a fine disciplined body of troops after Denikin's robber bands and rabbles.'

Royal Navy destroyers in the harbour used their searchlights to illuminate the port area. 'The accepted rule is "Shoot first – enquire afterwards",' Captain Lever recorded. There would be many night-time bugle calls ordering a 'stand-to', but almost all proved to be false alarms.

*

On 24 March, the battleship HMS *Benbow* dropped anchor beyond the breakwater. On an earlier visit in January, the captain of the *Benbow*, no doubt keen to give his crew some action, had steamed south along the coast towards Sochi to bombard a village which had been identified as a base for Green attacks. It opened up with its main armament of ten 13½-inch guns, leaving 'a large hole there'. This time the *Benbow* had come from Constantinople with Admiral Seymour and General Milne, the commander-in-chief of the Black Sea region. They held a conference with Denikin on board and promised to do what they could to help with the evacuation. The Whites' own fleet and merchant ships were still unavailable due to lack of coal and spare parts.

Seymour estimated that the Royal Navy could take some 6,000 troops, but they warned that if they were to accommodate any more, they would need the White Army to hold back the Reds so that they could not bombard the harbour with their artillery. The problem would be to find any men willing to form a rearguard which would have to be sacrificed. The Volunteers were the only troops left with a modicum of discipline, and even they refused to see why they should be sacrificed again. In any case, Denikin wanted every one of them to defend the Crimea.

The next day, 25 March, a Mark V tank was used to crush thirteen aeroplanes. Even so, a huge amount of undamaged materiel, including field guns, was left to the Reds, as well as all the trucks from which only the magnetos had been removed. Around the British headquarters at the cement works, the Royal Scots Fusiliers withdrew to the inner perimeter.

Novorossiisk provided a depressing sight for soldiers and refugees who reached it as the end approached. Teenage *junkers* from military academies under the command of two officers tried to act as military police. They were supposed to stop the flood of troops still trying to enter the city, where there was already scarcely room to move. Thousands of hungry horses wandered in search of food. Some soldiers selected the best ones and rode off to join the Greens. Many Cossacks had taken their saddles and bridles and shot their horses, which just lay there in the streets.

At night the Allied warships, in the port and at anchor outside, played their searchlights on the hills. In the atmosphere of confusion and fear, men sick with typhus were trying to drag themselves towards the docks. Those already down there refused to leave their positions. One of the *junkers* observed that carts were on the edge of the water with Kalmyk families in them. 'These people had fled the Stavropol steppe trying to save their only wealth, their livestock, and here they were sitting by the water without any help whatsoever. For them there was no hope that anyone would rescue them. They would either be killed or die of hunger.'

On the morning of 26 March, two days after Denikin's conference with Admiral Seymour, General Kutepov warned that it was now impossible to defend Novorossiisk. The Red Army had established artillery positions in the hills above and could descend on the port by nightfall. British destroyers expertly laid alongside the quay were swamped by Russian troops until not a square foot of desk space was left, and then ferried them out to other warships. Denikin and his staff were welcomed aboard the HMS *Emperor of India*, another *Iron Duke* class battleship, before a mass of Cossacks swarmed aboard. The captain later told Kennedy ruefully that 'he thought he would never get his quarterdeck clean again. When bully beef was served out to the Cossacks, they would place the tins on the deck and cut them in two with their swords!'

Barges were also towed back and forth, taking troops out to other ships at anchor. They included the *Benbow*, the cruiser HMS *Calypso*, several Royal Navy destroyers and also the American cruiser USS *Galveston*. The Volunteers controlled much of the embarkation. Some warships took the wounded. Others took only members of the Volunteer Corps, to the fury of the Don Cossacks who accused Denikin of betrayal. Most refused civilians. Some men decided to try to walk down the coast to Sochi. Many fled to the mountains having lost hope that they would ever obtain a berth, or even standing room on deck.

Erast Chevdar was dismayed to find that the gangways to the transport ships in the harbour were closely guarded by officers and soldiers with rifles and fixed bayonets. Although he too was a member of the Volunteer Corps, he found they would only allow those from their own units to board. Some of the decks were packed with luggage and bundles and even carts, not with human beings. 'Many of the guards are clearly drunk and take pleasure in threatening people with their bayonets,' Chevdar observed angrily. 'I would never have thought it possible among us, the Volunteers. I sat down on the nearest bollard with a sense of total hopelessness.'

By late afternoon, it was clear to the crowds packed in the harbour area that their last chance had passed. Red artillery had set a number of buildings alight in the town. Many officers tore off the shoulder boards sewn on to the tunics. Even some from the Volunteer Corps never managed to get through the mass of humanity to the dockside. 'I saw a captain of the Drozdovsky Regiment near me with his wife and two children aged three and five,' wrote the Don Cossack Mitrofan Moiseev. 'He took one child and shot him in the ear, then took the other and did the same, each time making the sign of the cross. He made the sign of the cross over his wife. They kissed each other in tears. The body of the wife collapsed when he shot her. The last bullet he used on himself.'

When the Red artillery began ranging on the ships, the French heavy cruiser *Waldeck-Rousseau* added her broadsides to that of the British warships firing at the mountains behind Novorossiisk. Lever described the scene as 'a veritable masterpiece of British seascape'. And while others muttered something about the fortunes of war, he consoled himself with the notion: 'Ah well! We are at least going out with flags a-flying and tails well up, leaving a sting behind that is likely to be remembered.' But after the firing in the darkness died away, he could not help wondering uneasily about 'the fate of those Russian nurses who at the end refused to leave'.

As gangplanks were drawn up men hurled themselves at them in a forlorn attempt to grab hold. Others dived into the harbour hoping that someone might throw them a line. Even some Cossack horses are said to have jumped in to swim after the ship on which they thought their master was departing.

Next morning, 27 March, the 22,000 soldiers and officers left behind were forced back into the town by Red troops. Some officers tried to disguise themselves by tying on a red handkerchief, but this enraged the guards who shot them straight off. A few were betrayed by their own soldiers. One orderly denounced his colonel, whom the Reds shot, but they then shot the orderly for his disloyalty.

Don Cossacks on the deck of the HMS Emperor of India after their evacuation from Novorossiisk.

A confused old woman started offering water to the prisoners from a bucket. When she announced how much she hated the Whites one of the guards explained to her that she was giving water to Whites. She became angry, thinking they had somehow tricked her. She said she would like to shoot a couple, so the amused guard handed her his rifle. She fired, but did not hold the butt properly against her shoulder, so the recoil knocked her over. The infuriated prisoners jumped up and started kicking her to death. One of them grabbed the rifle as she went down and fired at the guards. 'They then started shooting into the crowd with a machine-gun.'

The odd prisoner benefited from the incompetence of executions. On the following night a group of about thirty Don Cossack officers, including Moiseev, were identified and rounded up. 'They led us away to be finished off. I felt completely apathetic. Nothing could be done. Some out of complete despair threw themselves on the guards with bare hands and were shot immediately. Others were crying and shouting like children, and fell to the ground but they were beaten and dragged along. We didn't go far. We were ordered to stand in a line lit by kerosene lanterns. There was shouting and swearing on both sides, suddenly a pause, they levelled their rifles, then a voice gave a command, and like in a photographic instant, they fired a volley.

Everyone fell to the ground. I am still unable to analyse my feelings at that moment. I wasn't even wounded, yet I fell down with everybody else, sure that I had been killed, and was already in another world. Some nightmare thoughts were passing through my head. I did not move my hands or my feet. For some reason I thought this would be a sin. Finally, I started shivering with cold and came to my senses. A miracle had happened. I was alive. It was God's will. It was not yet my time. The Reds left without checking that everyone was dead.'

36

Wrangel Takes Command and the
Poles Take Kiev
Spring and Summer 1920

On 23 January, as Slashchov's detachment withdrew a little into the Crimea, the Red 46th Division advanced on the Perekop isthmus. This was a trap. Slashchov suddenly counter-attacked when they least expected it. Unable to manoeuvre in the narrow neck of land, the Reds fell back in disorder. The Red Army then found itself in a similar position to that of the Whites two months before, as Makhno's forces began to attack them from behind.

A politically naïve Captain Orlov, whom Slashchov ordered to Simferopol to raise more troops, started a mutiny, without thinking it through. The fact that Slashchov had to send troops against him three times revealed quite how unfocused White authority was in the rear areas. It all ended with a bloody clash in Simferopol towards the end of March, and Orlov disappearing into the Crimean mountains to join the Greens.

With the Red Army concentrating on the final defeat of White forces in the northern Caucasus, little happened in the Crimea until General Denikin himself arrived from Novorossiisk on 27 March, exhausted and crushed. Denikin, an honourable and honest man, was not up to dealing with the back-stabbing of the White rear areas and Wrangel's constant attacks. Wrangel's vanity led to him publicise their every disagreement, which damaged morale. He was supported by many generals and prominent civilians who regarded Denikin as far too liberal.

Wrangel had moved to the Crimea on 10 February during the Orlov mutiny, when General Shilling was in overall command. Shilling had arrived straight from the disastrous evacuation of Odessa, for which he was roundly blamed. Denikin considered this unfair and supported Shilling, which was a mistake. Wrangel's supporters demanded that he should replace Shilling as the commander in the Crimea. General Holman, appalled by the destructive effects of the bad blood between Denikin and Wrangel, tried to arrange a meeting between the two men, but Wrangel refused. Holman then worked with Denikin on a letter to ask Wrangel to leave the Crimea for the sake of the White cause.

Before departing for Constantinople, Wrangel wrote a vitriolic letter to Denikin, accusing him of jealousy, liberalism, favouritism to the Cossacks and disastrous leadership, while boasting of his own victories. He even claimed that Denikin had not strengthened the Tsaritsyn Front the previous summer because he wanted Kolchak to fail so that he, Denikin, would be the unchallenged leader of the White cause. Wrangel sent copies of his letter in all directions and inevitably the text soon appeared in the press. Even Wrangel sensed that he had gone far too far. Denikin responded rationally to Wrangel's attacks, but his confidence was too badly shaken for him to continue as commander-in-chief. He felt that even Kutepov had turned against him.

On reaching the Crimea and establishing his headquarters at Feodosia, Denikin assessed the situation before making his final decision. The British ships had brought about 25,000 Volunteers and 10,000 Don Cossacks from Novorossiisk, while Slashchov had nearly 5,000 men. That represented a sufficient force to hold the Crimea, which was slightly larger than Wales, while the Red Army was preoccupied with the Poles and tied up in the Caucasus and Caspian.

The Red Army *Stavka* made no bones about its role in enforcing Communist rule in the southern Caucasus. It described them as 'the political results of the final rout of the Armed Forces of South Russia'. Remnants of the Kuban Army and Terek Cossacks were pushed up against the frontier of Georgia on the Black Sea coast and forced to surrender to the Red 9th Army near Sochi. The British had managed to evacuate some of them to the Crimea, while extracting their own forces from Batumi as part of a general withdrawal.

On 2 May the Azerbaijani Democratic Republic, which had existed since May 1918, was swallowed up in a Soviet coup 'supported by the 11th Army', which 'brought this country, along with its oil riches', into the Soviet Union. Menshevik Georgia was spared for the time being, having agreed to expel British troops, but the country would be taken over in February of the following year, once the Kremlin was confident that the Allies were safely out of the region.

Commodore Norris and the Royal Navy's Caspian personnel had left their armed merchantmen to the Whites, but their ill-trained and reluctant crews stood little chance against Raskolnikov's Volga-Caspian flotilla. On 10 April, Raskolnikov trumpeted his success in a signal to Trotsky and Lenin, copied to Kamenev and the Red Army *Stavka* for good measure. 'The destroyer *Karl Liebknecht*, under my flag, set off and at 17.00 approached Fort Aleksandrovsk and engaged the enemy cruisers *Milyutin* and *Opyt*. After a stubborn battle, *Milyutin*'s stern was hit and both cruisers turned away and fled. Due to the fall of darkness it was not possible to pursue them. The successful battle determined the result of the operation: Fort Aleksandrovsk was taken by our sailors at dawn on 6 April. Generals Tolstov and Borodin were captured and brought to Astrakhan, as well as 70 officers and 1,096 Cossacks. The last remains of the Uralsk [Cossack] Group have been eliminated . . . A great deal of booty has been taken, including 80 poods of silver and about 100 million in banknotes, as well as rifles and machine guns. I would like to suggest that *Karl Liebknecht* is decorated with the banner of honour.'

On 16 May, Raskolnikov was in Baku having tea with Sergo Ordjonikidze, Stalin's confederate, and N.N Narimanov, chairman of the Sovnarkom of the Azerbaijan Soviet Republic. He looked at the clock and announced that he must rejoin his ship. The *Karl Liebknecht* was lying alongside the harbour wall. 'The steam-winches hissed, the bell of the engine telegraph rang, the heavy iron links of the anchor-chain crashed down, and the destroyer began, smoothly and slowly, to move off from the stone sea-wall. We sailed slowly past the flickering beacon light on Nargen Island, and out into the pitch-black darkness of the Caspian night.' His wife Larisa Reisner described how she went with him, but she is not mentioned in his version.

The other destroyers took up position in line ahead, while the tanker which carried their landing party was protected by two gunboats. They were heading for Enzeli, the Whites' only remaining base which they had taken over from the Royal Navy on the southern shore in Persian territory. Raskolnikov's colourful account claims that they arrived at dawn and, finding the shore battery unmanned, decided to wake the British garrison with a few shells fired at the barracks. It is hard to take his version too literally when he writes of 'swarthy Gurkhas in their snow-white turbans' rushing down to the beach, and then fleeing under fire. In fact the 1,500 Soviet sailors in the landing party were opposed by the 1st/2nd Gurkha Rifles and the bombardment lasted for an hour and a half.

The British force was taken totally by surprise. Their commander, Brigadier-General H.F. Bateman-Champain, asked Raskolnikov by radio telegraph what he wanted, as they were on Persian territory. He answered that their 'purpose was to recover the ships and military equipment stolen by Denikin's men from Soviet Azerbaijan and Soviet Russia'. Bateman-Champain agreed to his demands to hand over all the vessels and military equipment, including British seaplanes, and to evacuate Enzeli. Commodore Norris and the Royal Navy cannot have been impressed after their mastery of the Caspian. Not surprisingly, Bateman-Champain was relieved of his command. Communist agents in the southern Caucasus were instructed to investigate the morale of troops from the Indian Army and discover whether they really were to be withdrawn from Persia.

On 29 March, Denikin reduced the size of his headquarters in Feodosia and put an end to the liberal government, which he had formed as a result of his speech in Ekaterinodar. On 2 April, he asked his chief of staff to call a meeting of the military council in Sevastopol to elect a new commander-in-chief. Denikin admitted that he felt spiritually broken and physically ill. The army had lost its faith in him and he had to leave. The key generals met next day. Slashchov was one of those who objected to the idea of electing a successor, as if they were Bolsheviks. Yet Denikin did not want to nominate his successor as there was only one obvious candidate, General Wrangel, whom he could not forgive. The following day, 4 April, the council chose Wrangel and Denikin concurred. He left for Constantinople that evening on a British ship accompanied by Major-General Holman and General Romanovsky. Holman's departure was not regretted by his officers, according to Kennedy. 'General Holman,' wrote Kennedy, 'has been superseded by [Major General Sir Jocelyn] Percy, who is a much finer soldier, and a gentleman, which Holman was not.'

Members of the British military mission were now based in the Grand Hotel in Sevastopol. Some of them, who had been rerouted via Constantinople, did not land until 10 April. They were greeted by the ominous sound of gunfire ashore, only to discover that it was a salute to Easter Sunday. With an exchange rate of 10,000 roubles to the pound they enjoyed many advantages, but they knew what it meant for those White refugees whose money was now worthless, especially the women. 'Prevailing conditions have swollen to flood proportions the streams of courtesans,' Lever recorded in the Crimea. 'What else remains to these women, deserted or left the sole representatives of one time happy and thriving families, destitute and friendless. What else remains? Undeniable starvation.'

Most British officers had seen or heard of similar situations. 'At Batum before the evacuation,' Captain Kennedy wrote in his diary, 'a Russian girl, the daughter of a Colonel, came to a British officer and asked him to consider marrying her. "I am of good family and will make you a good wife. I do not love you, but I like you very much. Probably you do not love me. For me it will mean freedom. If I do not go with you, I will have to go on the streets."'

General Wrangel wasted no time in answering the summons to take up the command he had always believed was his by right. He appears to have been pleased to hear that the Bolsheviks had now nicknamed him the 'Crimean Khan'. Vasily Shulgin, having finally reached the Crimean peninsula after his escape from Odessa across the ice to Romania, went to pay homage and interview him as a journalist.

Wrangel greeted him with congratulations on his survival. 'You know, we had already buried you,' he joked. Shulgin had last seen him in Tsaritsyn a year before, when he was recovering from typhus, and his eyes had looked even more sunken. But now he found him rejuvenated. In answer to his questions, Wrangel played down any expectations. 'If this is the end, then at least it should happen without shame,' he said. 'It was hopeless when I took over command. But I at least wanted to stop this disgrace, this outrage, to go honourably and save what still could be saved. I have to say that I don't make big plans. I think I need to gain time.' He certainly appeared to have learned the lessons of the Whites' previous mistakes. 'I understand perfectly well that nothing can be done without help from the Russian people. One has to give up the politics of conquering Russia. We used to feel as if we were in a conquered land. It should not be like this. One cannot fight against the whole world, one has to find support somewhere . . . To hold on to a territory, one has to find men right there, and grain.

'What am I fighting for? I am fighting to make life possible at least on this small patch of land, in the Crimea. To show to the rest of Russia, so to speak: well, what you've got is hunger and the Cheka, while here there is a land reform in progress, regional authorities are being elected, order is being established, and there is freedom. No one is suffocating you, no one tortures you, you can just live.' He then outlined his determination to deal harshly with looting. 'I just want to win time, to start the chapter: to show that one can live in the Crimea. Then we will be able to move forward, not like we did with Denikin, but slowly, securing what we have won. And then the regions that we capture from the Bolsheviks will become the source of our strength, not a weakness like it was before.'

General Dragomirov was making his own attempt to improve relations with the peasants. Now commanding the 9th Cavalry Division in Stary Krym, just to the west of Feodosia, Dragomirov would order tables to be laid in the town square. Barrels of wine and spirits were rolled out, lambs were cooked on spits and a wild drinking party would begin, with endless toasts. Dragomirov would shout: 'Soldiers and officers! We have understood our mistakes. Units advancing on the road to Moscow engaged in looting, and treated the population badly. This was a good lesson for us! This will not happen again! I am firmly convinced that the day will soon come when we will hear the bells of Moscow. We will liberate Holy Russia from the Bolshevik force that is bringing only destruction and ruin. I raise my glass to it!'

Despite the fine words, some things did not change. On 3 May, Wrangel appointed Globachev director of the police department. The former head of the Okhrana encountered 'rampant corruption and the theft of funds'. One colonel ran off to Paris with £3,000. Currency speculation was a major activity, even within the police. The Crimea also seemed to be overrun by dubious agents of different intelligence services, all trying to make money by selling information. According to Globachev, a Russian poet in Constantinople had written: 'And forty-three counter-intelligence services have created a new Babylon.' Communist agents reported back to the Don Bureau that in Kerch alone 'there are five branches of counter-intelligence, that of General Pokrovsky, of the Stavka, of the army headquarters, of the garrison and of the fortress. Despite all of that there have been just two round-ups in all. Our members have been operating successfully.'

At times Kennedy's diary of the Crimea reads like an Edwardian traveller's, as he describes the lilac at Livadia, the cypresses on the hillsides and the sound of nightingales. Yet while fellow British officers were visiting the battlefields of Balaklava and Inkerman with a copy of Kinglake, he was impatient to see the situation at the front for himself. He set off to visit northern Crimea and the Perekop Isthmus, encountering German settlements going back to the time of Catherine the Great. 'The cottages are scrupulously clean, and orchards and gardens well filled and well kept.' He also came across 'occasional Tartar villages with mosques and slender minarets'. He spotted a bustard on the rolling grassland of the steppe and listened to larks.

At the headquarters of II Corps, Kennedy encountered Slashchov's famous 'lady orderly' and bodyguard. 'She was in breeches and boots and spurs and rode well.' As for the general himself, 'He is a fine-looking tall man, with an attractive face – richly dressed in fur-trimmed cap and doublet – about 33 years of age. Barne says he is a good man gone wrong – drinks, dopes and keeps two women on his train, but he appears to be popular with the troops.' Yet when the energetic Wrangel appeared, striding around on a tour of inspection, Slashchov 'found the exercise too strenuous and slept during these inspections covering himself with his cloak'.

Kennedy was dismayed to find that for the 4.5-inch howitzers, there was hardly a round in the whole Crimea. The only artillery in the north was on an armoured train, which was fighting a 'shoot and scoot' battle, a sort of gunner's tennis match with a Red train across the water. The only real warfare in the region was taking place some 500 kilometres to the northwest. On 8 May, a vanguard of Polish Hussars clattered into Kiev.

The Polish-Soviet conflict had started with a 'scuffle' between irregulars on both sides in February 1919, following the German withdrawal which left a power vacuum between them. There was no clear frontier or even national identity in the central European borderlands, which had all been under Tsarist or Austro-Hungarian domination. Poland awaited the decision of the Supreme Allied Council in Paris, yet at the same time feared Bolshevik encroachment from the east as they tried to create a land-bridge westwards for their road to world revolution. Their concerns were justified.

Ever since those first clashes, fighting had surged or died down. Piłsudski ensured that the Poles seized his birthplace of Wilno

(Vilnius) on 20 April of that year, and Minsk on 8 August.* They had then advanced to the line of the River Berezina and halted there. To Churchill's frustration Piłsudski wisely resisted the temptation to march on Moscow, as Denikin advanced from the south. Apart from Denikin's reluctance to recognise Polish independence, the country had been ravaged and impoverished after being fought over for most of the First World War. The Polish Army had reached its limits, at least for the time being. As a newly reborn state its armed forces represented a strange mixture of different military cultures and weaponry, coming from German, Austro-Hungarian, Russian and French origins. Above all Piłsudski knew that, if he attempted such a gamble, he would receive little help from the Allies in Paris, mainly due to Lloyd George's disapproval.

Peace negotiations between Moscow and Warsaw began on 11 October 1919, three days before Kutepov's corps took Orel. Piłsudski's assurance that he would not attack the Red Army in the flank while they dealt with Denikin allowed the Kremlin to redeploy 40,000 men from their Western Front against the Volunteer Army. Piłsudski, however, played for time and delayed a final agreement. Talks collapsed in December.

In January 1920, Lenin approved plans for a major double offensive in the west as soon as the Caucasus Front had finished with Denikin's forces. On 27 February he issued the watchword 'prepare for war with Poland' and ordered 'lightning transfers' of troops from Siberia and the Urals. The Red Army increased its forces fivefold on the Western Front in the first four months of the year. It was also able to deploy weaponry, including British tanks and aircraft, captured from Yudenich and Denikin's armies. On 5 March, the Polish 9th Infantry Division under the future leader, General Władysław Sikorski, seized Mozyr on the Pripet river in the centre. This was the preparatory part of Piłsudski's plan to split operations between a northern front and a southern front.

---

* Vilnius – its current and original name – was the ancient Lithuanian capital, founded by the Grand Dukes of Lithuania in the thirteenth century. Many distinguished Poles, including their national poet Mickiewicz, came from there. Piłsudski captured it during this counter-attack against the Reds and refused to return it to the newly independent Lithuania. The Lithuanians had to shift their capital to Kaunas. The Soviet Union under Stalin gave it back to the Lithuanians, but many Poles still believe in their hearts that it belongs to them.

Polish confidence increased at this time with the arrival from France of General Józef Haller's 'Blue Army', so-called because of their blue-grey French uniforms. Haller's force even came with a regiment of seventy Renault tanks. Having started in December 1918 with just on 9,000 men, the Polish armed forces reached a strength of 900,000 by July 1920. Piłsudski also built up a small but effective air force, thanks to those who had learned to fly in their original armies during the war in the West. They were joined by American volunteers in the Kościuszko Squadron commanded by Major Cedric E. Fauntleroy, with Captain Merian C. Cooper, who later achieved fame as director of *King Kong*.

Polish 'legions', formed secretly in many different places including Kiev, Murmansk, Vladivostok and Orenburg, had made their way back to the motherland to join the army of 'The Commandant', as Piłsudski was known.* The most unfortunate of all were the 5th Siberian Division, abandoned by the Czechs and General Janin at Krasnoyarsk. 'All colonels and high-ranking officers were imprisoned; all officers and soldiers of the storm battalion and all those who had been involved in action against the Bolsheviks, were on Cheka orders executed by firing squad. Due to malnutrition, almost all imprisoned officers came down with epidemic typhus. Bolshevik authorities provided no medical help.' The bulk of the survivors were forced into labour brigades, as miners or loggers in the forests of the Yenisei. Only a few hundred of the former 5th Division lived to reach Poland.

In mid-April the Polish Army carried out a covert mobilisation, while Piłsudski suddenly made an alliance with the 'Head Ataman' of Ukraine, Symon Petliura. The Soviet reaction was predictably scathing. 'This agreement, which would actually have made Ukraine a colony of bourgeois-aristocratic Poland, was necessary for Piłsudski as a political pretext for justifying the invasion of Ukraine by Polish legions.'

On 23 April, the Red Army *Stavka* heard that two Galician brigades of the 12th Army had rebelled. 'Take decisive measures,' the Southern Front ordered, 'to wipe out the rebellious Galician brigades and resist the advance of White Poles to the last soldier. According to the order of the Military Revolutionary Council, all the leaders and instigators

---

* The legion formed in Vladivostok included Poles who had been former soldiers of the German garrison in Kiao-Chau, captured by the Japanese back in 1914.

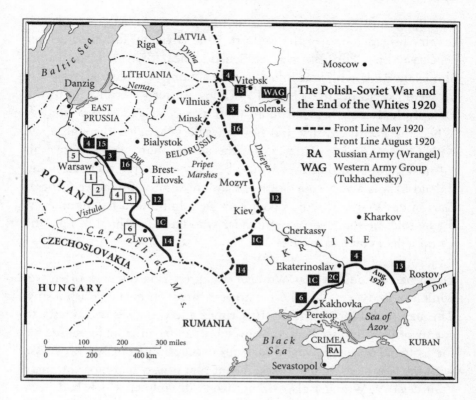

The Polish-Soviet War and
the End of the Whites 1920

- - - - Front Line May 1920
———— Front Line August 1920
RA   Russian Army (Wrangel)
WAG Western Army Group
        (Tukhachevsky)

of the uprising are to be shot on the spot.' The Reds then found to their dismay that Makhno's forces, which they called a 'mutinous kulak movement', now close to 50,000 strong, were launching another series of attacks in their rear. They destroyed bridges around Kiev, which gave the Reds the wrong idea that Makhno was working closely with both the Whites and the Poles. Commissars gloomily reported back to Moscow that 'Makhno is popular'. Some uneducated soldiers 'refer to him as a Lieutenant General'.

On the western side of the Dnieper, Red forces suffered guerrilla raids by groups supporting Petliura. 'The entire rear of the 12th and 14th Armies was crawling with large and small bands which carried out raids on transport and railroad stations, while disorganizing the supply and feeding of these armies.'

On 25 April, Piłsudski's offensive began in earnest with nine Polish divisions and one Ukrainian. The Third Army commanded by General Eduard Śmigly-Rydz reached Zhitomir the next day. The day after that, Berdichev fell. The Red 12th and 14th Armies collapsed in disorder, managing only a very few rearguard actions. At Malin, a Polish cavalry brigade charged the Red 7th Rifle Division, inflicting 40 per cent casualties. Piłsudski was saddened to hear that his former aide, Stanisław Radziwill, was killed in that action, yet Polish losses over-all were extraordinarily light. To occupy western Ukraine up to the Dnieper had cost them no more than 150 dead and 300 wounded. When the Polish cavalry and horse artillery paraded through Kiev, with General Śmigly-Rydz taking the salute, many Poles, above all Piłsudski, doubted that they would be allowed to stay there for long. 'Piłsudski was a very superstitious man,' recounted Brigadier-General Carton de Wiart. 'Having taken Kiev he admitted to feeling uneasy, for he told me that every commander who had attempted to take the Ukraine had come to grief.'

Lenin had no doubts that Wrangel was preparing his own offensive, while the Red Army faced a far greater threat from the Polish Army. Through mobilisation within the Crimea and promises of amnesty to enemy officers and soldiers, the new commander-in-chief increased his forces to 70,000 men. The disastrous evacuation from Novorossiisk, with the loss of so many horses, meant that it now had more infantry than cavalry. Wrangel also strengthened discipline, which had been Denikin's greatest weakness. 'Wrangel has thoroughly reorganised the army which was a mere rabble when he took command,' wrote Petr Struve, the foreign minister in the new administration. 'His discipline is stern and he hangs officers and men convicted of disorderly conduct.'

The main purpose of Wrangel's offensive was to take advantage of the Polish-Soviet conflict to achieve a bridgehead on the mainland. More immediate needs included grain to feed the army and the swollen population of the Crimea, and also horses to remount the cavalry. Wrangel was warned by the British foreign secretary Lord Curzon that if he advanced out of the Crimea, he would receive no more help from the British either by land or by sea. Churchill was horrified and so were most senior officers, but Lloyd George was adamant.

On 6 June, making use of the greatly improved and refuelled White Navy, General Slashchov landed his troops at Kirillovka on a promontory south of Melitopol. He completely surprised the 13th Army by appearing in their rear. At the same time, General Kutepov sent forward his corps with the Drozdovsky, Markov and Kornilov Divisions to burst out of the Perekop Isthmus, while the Don Corps attacked along the railway bridge on the Salkovo Isthmus 70 kilometres to the east. Wrangel did not miss the opportunity to ride at the head of his troops when they advanced onto the mainland of the Tauride province. His tall figure in black Cossack uniform, erect in the saddle riding his magnificent black charger, provided an inspiring sight for his soldiers: as he knew it would.

Poles in the West, Wrangel in the South
June–September 1920

On 5 June, General Slashchov's II Corps was embarked on twenty-eight ships in Feodosia. It consisted of the 13th and 34th Infantry Divisions and a brigade of Terek and Astrakhan Cossacks. After the corps had paraded through Feodosia to the harbour with bands playing, secrecy was hard to achieve. Fortunately for General Wrangel's plan, the Don Bureau's agents did not have the means to communicate the information rapidly. A deception operation, with White radio transmitters suggesting that Odessa was the target, may also have played a part.

The invasion fleet departed at dusk to sail east and then north through the narrow strait at Kerch, into the Sea of Azov. The ships started disembarking at 10.00 on the Kirillovka promontory south of Melitopol. Their first objective was Melitopol itself, which would cut the supply road to the rear of the 13th Army. On that morning of 6 June, while Kutepov's corps attacked at Perekop supported by a troop of tanks and the Don corps advanced up the Salkovo isthmus, the 13th Army deployed its reserves and ordered counter-attacks. But as the Red *Stavka* admitted afterwards, the 13th Army's main formations had been 'morally broken down'. This was due to a policy of holding them on high alert for far too long, during which time they had not been allowed any chance to rest and refit.

The Red 1st Cavalry Corps was ordered in from near Ekaterinoslav, where it had been fighting Makhno's Insurgent Army, which the *Stavka* insisted was a '*kulak* counter-revolution'. The cavalry corps was now commanded by the former coalminer Dmitry Zhloba, who took over in January after the arrest in the Kuban of Boris Dumenko. The campaign of harassment against Dumenko had been a murky affair, with strong echoes of the one against Mironov. According to one of Dumenko's officers, a group of Budyonny's men arrived late at night, 'with orders to shoot Dumenko and disband his headquarters'. The same officer insisted that this was all part of a 'plot by Stalin,

Voroshilov and Budyonny'. 'During the time the Corps was in the Caucasian Front,' the Cheka reported, 'we received a lot of information proving anti-Soviet propaganda at the Corps under the slogan: "Beat the Yids, commissars, and communists who have stayed in the rear!" There are reasons to suggest the presence of a counter-revolutionary organisation.' Dumenko was accused of strangling a commissar to death in his bed, tried for murder in Rostov and sentenced to death.

On the orders of 13th Army, Zhloba sent most of his two cavalry Divisions together with rifle units to form a defence line in front of Melitopol. This was broken over the next few days by Slashchov's two divisions and the Cossack brigade. The fiercest fighting took place on the Perekop axis. The Red 3rd Division and the formidable Latvian Rifle Division were forced back by Kutepov's corps when he launched his reserve, the Drozdovsky Division and the Mark V tanks.

By 10 June, the day that Slashchov's divisions captured Melitopol on the eastern flank, the *Stavka* admitted that 'the weakened 52nd and Latvian Divisions were almost incapable of active operations' on the western axis. A sudden charge the same day by the Blinov 2nd Cavalry Division gave the Kuban Cossacks a nasty shock, when they lost a battery of guns and an unspecified number of prisoners. The official Red Army account tried hard to brush over the defeat of the 13th Army, yet it had to acknowledge that 'The seizure of Melitopol led to the final disruption of the army's command and control. The units' operational cooperation became impossible.' Within two days, Wrangel's forces were right up to the lower Dnieper, having chased the Latvian and 52nd Divisions across to the other bank. They now held the mainland Tauride, along with most of the grain and the horses they needed.

Piłsudski had been right to fear that the occupation of Kiev might prove a step too far. The fact that he intended to install a Ukrainian government was not well known, so it appeared to many to have been an act of territorial greed. The international reaction against Poland was strong, with the Communist regime winning support at home and sympathy abroad. In any case, the precipitate retreat of the Red 12th and 14th Armies back beyond the Dnieper saved them from destruction, which had been Piłsudski's main objective.

Budyonny's 1st Cavalry Army arrived from the Caucasus with 16,700 sabres, a large number of *tachankas* mounted with machine guns, forty-five field guns, five armoured trains, eight armoured cars and twelve aircraft. The Tsaritsyn triumvirate was back together: Budyonny and his commissar Voroshilov joined Stalin, who was Commissar for the Southwestern Front. Budyonny had always believed in massing his cavalry like a Mongol horde to terrify his enemies and punch a hole in their line. It was an unsubtle tactic which usually worked, but had failed at Tsaritsyn when the RAF fighters from 47 Squadron had broken up his formations with relentless strafing. Budyonny had since then insisted on acquiring his own Nieuport fighters, but his aircrew were no match for the Polish pilots. This time, however, he planned to infiltrate the Polish defence line south of Kiev, rather than attempt to smash through it.

Red Army men in the invasion of Poland with a British Mark V tank captured on the Southern Front from Denikin's forces.

A week after the Polish occupation of Kiev, the twenty-seven-year-old Tukhachevsky, now commander-in-chief of the Western Front, launched his offensive on the Berezina sector north of the Pripet marshes. The Polish First and Fourth Armies were taken by surprise and pushed back, but then, with a reserve army put together in great haste, they counter-attacked on 31 May. This forced Tukhachevsky's Western Front to retreat. Morale collapsed to such a degree in some formations that a whole cavalry brigade surrendered to a single troop from Colonel Władysław Anders's 15th Lancers.

Although, as the Red *Stavka* admitted, 'the enemy managed to completely restore his position along the Berezina River' by 8 June, Piłsudski would not allow the two armies to pursue the retreating Reds. They were ordered to stand firm where they were, while some of their formations were diverted to the Kiev sector south of the Pripet. There Yegorov's Southwestern Front, reinforced by Budyonny's 1st Cavalry Army, was preparing a counter-offensive.

On 26 May, the Red 12th Army attacked the Third Army of Śmigly-Rydz around Kiev, while further south, Budyonny's cavalry prepared to strike the main blow against the Sixth Army in the direction of Zhitomir. After numerous attempts, Budyonny achieved his break-through on 5 June. The Polish 1st Cavalry Division, breasting a ridge near Volodarka, sighted the massed squadrons in the valley below. Their commander, in one of those coincidences of civil war, had promoted Budyonny to the rank of corporal when in the same regiment of imperial dragoons. The Red cavalry, blinded by the setting sun just above the western horizon, could not see that the Polish force was only a sixth of their size.

One of the 1st Krechowiecki Lancers described the sensations of the charge against the Reds. 'We moved off at a gallop, arched low in the saddle, lances at the horse's ear . . . A man who has not been through the emotions of a cavalry engagement can never know the exhilaration and frenzy experienced by the charging horseman. Nerves are stretched to breaking-point, the fear one might have felt vanishes, while the horse, warmed by the passion of the rider, carries him at a wild gallop, frenzied and ready to trample or bite.' This, however, was a rare success for the Poles, who found themselves under considerable pressure from the much larger Red forces.

The Red attacks either side of Kiev had surrounded part of the Third Army. 'The situation is remarkably interesting and dangerous,' wrote Władysław Broniewski, a Polish poet serving as an officer in the 1st Legionary Infantry. 'Budyonny and his cavalry have broken through our right and left flanks, captured Zhitomir and while they have been gallivanting behind our lines, we are closing our little circle around Kiev. Incredibly fierce and bloody fighting goes on continuously.'

A fellow officer in the same regiment, Mieczysław Lepecki, described their withdrawal. 'At first, we thought that Malin would be the last stage of our retreat . . . But we were ordered to march again at around 9 or 10 in the evening. There must have been a battle on the road near Malin; I could tell by the carcasses of horses, abandoned rifles, smashed wagons, in a word – the unmistakable signs of recent action. When we got on the road again, we didn't think we could keep marching for more than a few kilometres, that it was physically impossible, but we carried on for several more long days, and still no end to our torment was in sight. The continued retreat surprised us. We did not expect our army's situation to have been so dire that we should have to withdraw all the way to Volhynia.' They were marching 50 kilometres a day and their boots were falling to pieces.

On 14 June, Broniewski was able to catch up after another march. 'For the first time in five days, I am in a relatively safe place, the village of Korosten . . . For five days, I haven't eaten anything substantial (even now, as I write this, I am hungry), haven't slept, haven't undressed – in a word, in spite of my assignment to the staff, I feel like an average front-line soldier, maybe even worse. We fought our way out of the Bolshevik pocket at Borodzianka. The fierce battle lasted two days. Heavy losses, but not Napoleonic. Our retreat was a sort of "masterpiece" of the art of war: a completely surrounded army, burdened with an enormous supply train, fights off the enemy and manages to keep almost all of its equipment.

'The most difficult element of the operation was to bring out our supplies . . . the baggage train stretching for tens of kilometres. It is a terrible Polish habit, always bringing along all the rubbish; and a whole hen party of all kinds of officers' wives besides. It was for that "army treasure" that the 1st Brigade shed so much blood at the front line. This time, the Bolsheviks threw at us some better, more valiant troops, and in large numbers.'

'The atmosphere was anything but cheerful,' Lepecki wrote. Armies usually withdraw along roads, but Budyonny moved in a wide line, across fields and pastures . . . In every village, we found unmistakable signs that his troops had recently stopped there. Smashed and burned fences, thatch torn off roofs for litter for his horses, looted food and fodder stores and the lament of girls – everything clearly testified to the passage of Budyonny's "grand" cavalry.' A former White officer captured at Novorossiisk and forced into the Red Army found himself commanding a cavalry squadron of '120 assorted proletarians who were the most incorrigible bandits' and he could not stop them when they went out looting 'for pigs, chickens or girls'.

Polish women soon found they had even more to lament. 'A terrible truth – all the soldiers have syphilis,' wrote Isaac Babel, with Budyonny's 6th Cavalry Division. 'All Galicia is infected.' He posed the question: 'What sort of person is our Cossack? Many-layered: looting, reckless daring, professionalism, revolutionary spirit, bestial cruelty. The population await their saviours, the Jews look for liberation – and in ride the Kuban Cossacks.'

There were, it appears, women fighting in Cossack ranks, not just nurses. 'A whole volume could be written on women in the Red Army,' a sex-obsessed Babel wrote in his diary. 'The squadrons go into battle, dust, din, bared sabres, furious cursing, and they gallop forward with their skirts tucked up, covered in dust, with their big breasts, all whores, but comrades, whores because they are comrades, that's what matters, they're there to serve everybody, in any way they can, heroines, and at the same time despised.'

Whether infantry or cavalry, Polish officers were extremely conscious of their heritage from 1812, when Prince Poniatowski's lancers invaded Russia with the *Grande Armée*. A strikingly Napoleonic scene took place when one of the 1st Legionary's officers called Holinkowski led half a battalion of the regiment to reconnoitre a village. 'It was only when they were approaching the village that Holinkowski noticed a great commotion,' his fellow officer Lepicki wrote. 'Expecting only a small force, he gave the command for extended battle order and advanced. He was in for a dreadful surprise. Once they reached a distance of no more than a hundred paces from it, the innocent-looking village exploded with a murderous artillery barrage.' Shortly afterwards, 'a great mass of cavalry appeared behind the unfortunate battalion. The men, in a field of tall grain, would have immediately succumbed to the cavalry charge, so Holinkowski tried to gather them on the road and form a square . . . Holinkowski was wounded a second time. To avoid captivity or becoming a burden to his men, he ended his own life on the battlefield, blowing himself up with a hand grenade.'

The June battles as the Poles retreated westwards from Kiev towards Lublin were chaotic on both sides, due to bad communications. Budyonny, encouraged by Stalin, had preferred to ignore Kamenev's orders to destroy the Third Army of Śmigly-Rydz and charge around instead capturing Zhitomir and Berdichev. He succeeded in terrifying the population by slaughtering the garrison at Zhitomir and burning down the hospital in Berdichev with 600 Polish wounded and the nurses trapped inside.

A new Polish defence line was established further back, but on 26 June Budyonny managed to punch his way through that. Soon afterwards, Tukhachevsky made another successful attack north of the Pripet. Tukhachevsky was under pressure to capture Warsaw before the middle of August so his group of armies, nearly 100,000 strong, were bombarded with propaganda. On 3 July, the eve of a major assault, they were read a proclamation. 'The time of reckoning has come. In the blood of the defeated Polish Army we will drown the criminal government of Piłsudski . . . The fate of World Revolution is being decided. Over the corpse of White Poland lies the road to World Conflagration. On our bayonets we will bring happiness and peace to the toiling masses of mankind.'

On Tukhachevsky's right flank, nearest to the border of Lithuania, was the III Cavalry Corps of Gaia Bzhishkian, an Armenian known as Gai. Polish officers called his forces the 'Golden Horde of Gai-Khan'. Gai's task was to outflank the Polish line at the first opportunity and the tactic succeeded time and again. In a matter of days Polish troops abandoned Minsk and were in full retreat. On 11 July, Rabbi Yechezkel Abramsky wrote: 'Miserable, I walk through the ruined streets, without the strength to keep my head up, buried under the burden of destruction, freshly spilled blood and cries of orphans . . . theft and murder in every section of the city and in every neighbourhood touched by the Polish Army.' As with Denikin's forces, anti-Semitic pogroms by Polish forces were carried out not when they advanced, but in bitterness when they were forced to retreat. Their suspicions that Jews supported the Bolsheviks in many cases often became a self-fulfilling prophecy, yet even the poorest Jewish traders and artisans soon found themselves treated as *burzhui* and exploiters.

On 13 July, Broniewski wrote: 'The Bolsheviks have broken through the front also in the north – always the cavalry.' Gai's cavalry corps in the north had outflanked the Polish line and advanced 40 kilometres on the first day. 'So, the situation is grave. Our armies, exhausted by the uneven fight, continue to retreat. The Soviets have flexed all their muscles against Poland; hordes of Great-Russians and half-savage

Bashkirs, Chinamen, storm at us, with the battle cry of "Death to Poland".* In the past, [under the Tsars], it was "Death to rebellious Poland". Today I read in one Bolshevik handbill: "Death to lordly Poland"! The content has not changed at all. It is a struggle between two nations – between fire and water – a war between the idea of nation-states and political rapacity.' For Broniewski, the only encouraging news was the surge in patriotic emotions, and a *'levée en masse'* to defend the country.

The Poles were ordered to fall back 100 kilometres, prompting Tukhachevsky to think that he had achieved a far greater victory than was the case. He thus missed the opportunity of destroying the First and Fourth Armies. The momentum of their retreat, however, was hard to break. Each time they formed a new defence line, Gai's cavalry would break it. Wilno, Grodno, Baranowicze and Pińsk. Piłsudski's handling of the campaign faced furious criticism and a new Government of National Defence was formed.

The retreat continued into August, 'moving closer and closer to the heart of Poland', wrote Lepicki with the 1st Legionary Regiment, as they reached Lublin. 'The news is wretched: Brest-Litovsk and Białystok are said to have been given up . . . Today, we are supposed to keep retreating – all the way to the Bug. Reports from other sectors of the front, especially from the north, told us that elsewhere things were worse, even much worse. The papers spoke of trains packed to impossibility with refugees, of rapid retreats of entire divisions and groups, of the Country being in danger.' And then they heard that the Reds had cut the line between Warsaw and Lublin. Nobody could be in any doubt that Tukhachevsky intended to capture the capital itself. 'Warsaw is on the eve of an occupation by the Bolsheviks,' wrote the Russian symbolist poet Zinaida Hippius, and left the city rapidly.

In the northern Tauride, Wrangel's forces had secured a flattened triangle of territory from the mouth of the Dnieper in the west to Nikopol at the top and Berdyansk on the Sea of Azov in the east. The battered 13th Army was preparing a counter-attack. Zhloba received specific orders in code for his I Cavalry Corps to advance at 04.00 on 3 July. They were to attack Slashchov's corps northeast of Melitopol.

---

* The 'Chinamen' were part of Iona Yakir's force of two divisions on the left wing of the Red 12th Army commanded by Sergei Mezheninov.

Boyarchikov, who decoded the message, recorded the events leading to disaster. 'At the indicated time, all three divisions of I Cavalry Corps crashed down on the enemy breaching the first lines of their defence. Following the order, a division of our corps turned towards the north-west in order to meet up with the rifle units. Mounted reconnaissance sent ahead reported to our commanders that there was no advance whatsoever of our rifle units in the northwest, and that our cavalry corps was now inside a closed enemy ring. Indeed, soon field guns, machine guns and even planes started pouring fire from all directions on our cavalry. We were being executed point-blank. It seemed as if we had been betrayed, lured into a trap. We knew by midday that none of the other units of the 13th Army had advanced. Rifle units which we were supposed to join were firing at us because they had mistaken us for the enemy.'

A torrential downpour eventually enabled them to break out, but their casualties had been devastating. The exultant Whites claimed to have captured 3,000 badly needed horses, which was no doubt a con-siderable exaggeration, but the action was a great boost to their morale. Zhloba was accused of wrecking the offensive by attacking two hours too early, and thereby permitting the defeat of the 1st Cavalry Corps. Kamenev later tried to pretend that Zhloba, entirely on his own initia-tive, had decided 'to carry out a night raid'. A commission was sent down from Moscow to try him. He was sentenced to expulsion from the Red Army even though his division commanders and commissars testified on his behalf. 'Many people were of the opinion that this was the revenge for Zhloba's closeness to Dumenko,' Boyarchikov wrote. Zhloba departed, but they heard later that he was brought back to the Caucasus to command a cavalry division there.

Curzon's threat to Wrangel about the end of British assistance meant the end of the British military mission. The final evacuation of officers was fixed for 29 June. Captain Lever wrote about his very mixed feelings. 'Two Guards officers from our mess refused to desert the Russians, threw up their commissions and joined the White Army . . . I shall never free my mind from the knowledge that we did desert the Whites, but I have no illusions about the amount of help I could have rendered had I stayed.

'On the boat just before departure,' he continued, 'the sense of desertion is profound. Only two Russian officers are aboard to bid farewell to those who have worked with them personally. In the background of the saloon I watch them, glasses in hand, bidding good-bye to their friends. Tense feelings of emotion are kept in check with an iron will; the raised glasses, the sharp-cut phrases, the ill-concealed tears of the Russians; the crash of glass as, the drinks dispatched, the containers are hurled to the ground and smashed to smithereens. I steal away to my cabin to brood.'

In spite of his distrust of the Cossacks, Wrangel decided to raise the Kuban in revolt and perhaps even the Don, where there had been an uprising in May. He knew that the Polish-Soviet War would not last for ever and then the full force of the Red Army would be concentrated on the Crimea. He even sent emissaries to Nestor Makhno, to sound out any possibility of an alliance against the Reds. Makhno's forces had just attacked Ekaterinoslav, now the headquarters of a 2nd Cavalry Army. After Zhloba's arrest, this was being formed under a useless and short-lived commander, using the remnants of the battered I Cavalry Corps. The next leader would be none other than the Left SR Cossack Filipp Mironov, rehabilitated by Trotsky after his death sentence.

Makhno's men 'burst into the city on *tachankas* which were camouflaged as carts carrying hay', wrote Boyarchikov. 'They opened fire, wreaked panic and attacked Soviet institutions. Guards did not let them near the army headquarters. On the following day, military patrols found ten killed Red Army soldiers on the outskirts of the city, their bellies ripped open and grain stuffed into them, with notes left on their bodies: "This is for the *razverstka*" [the seizure of grain]. The corpses were brought to the army headquarters, and a rally was organized; a representative of the political department of the army spoke from the balcony of the headquarters' building.'

Wrangel's overture to Makhno, however, was not just rejected. According to the Red *Stavka*, he 'even hanged the delegates'. Wrangel may well have set up some units with former Makhnovists, yet Kamenev's claim that he called them 'Batko Makhno detachments' is hard to believe.

Before attempting to raise the Kuban in rebellion, Wrangel first attempted landings on the Donets coast of the Sea of Azov. Encouraged by Don Cossack revolts, a force some 800-strong under the command of Colonel Nazarov landed between Mariupol and Taganrog on 9

August. White sources claim that Nazarov soon doubled the size of his force, while the Red *Stavka* claimed that it never stood a chance due to 'the completely passive attitude of the Don Cossacks'. In any case, it was destroyed by the Red Army near Konstantinovskaya.

The Kuban offered greater potential, even after the bad blood between the Whites and the Kuban Cossacks. Those who had dreamed in the winter that abandoning Denikin's forces would persuade the Reds to leave them in peace received a nasty shock when the reality of Communist rule hit them. Wrangel's foreign minister Struve pointed out that the peace terms signed in March at Tuapse by Ataman Bukretov for the Kuban Cossacks stated that only those convicted of criminal actions would be persecuted. 'When asked to define criminal offences, the Bolsheviks said, "killing commissars and other bolshevists and looting the civil population". As nearly every Kuban Cossack who ever campaigned committed both these offences wherever he had the opportunity, the margin for clemency was evidently very small. Bukretov signed the treaty and then wisely retired to Tiflis.'

In Krasnodar, the renamed Ekaterinodar, the painter Yakob Glasse had kept a secret account of events since the arrival of the Red Army and their massacre of the Kalmyk families. On 24 March, he wrote that the Cheka had taken over a big hotel. 'Their black work started. My encounters with victims, on whose legs the Bolsheviks had cut red stripes and shoulder boards on their shoulders, were still fresh in my memory, and now they were at work close by. Basement windows were being boarded up with two rows of planks of wood in the Cheka building, with sand in between so that not a sound would escape.'

'Krasnodar is "ruled" by marine infantry,' he recorded on 28 March. 'Everyone is talking about their violence, especially to women.' Two days later, he wrote: 'The streets are empty. Scared, we peer out into the street through slits in the doors. Many arrests are taking place today. Chekists are leading crowds of merchants through the city to the Cheka, priests, teachers, engineers, officials from the post, banks, and other institutions. Registration of officers and military officials has been announced. It is taking place at the theatre. For those that don't show up, execution. Those that do walk into the theatre don't come out.'

On 4 April, he recorded: 'Today a crowd of arrested "*burzhui* women" was sent to the typhoid hospitals of which there are six. They will wash floors there, wash clothes, etc. No measures can slow the epidemics. Sick people lie on the floor in these so-called hospitals, on straw as there are no mattresses. There are cases when people who were not yet quite dead were sent off to the cemetery to create space for new patients. I have seen a grave that had a thin layer of earth on top and I could see hands of the buried corpses. The director of the cemetery told me that he had seen these hands move.'

'All day searches are in progress in the houses that are more or less rich,' Glasse wrote on 17 April. 'They are sawing the legs off furniture, digging up the floor in cellars, as well as gardens.* Among those conducting searches are well-known thieves and other town riff-raff. They have been released from jails and are now working for the Cheka with great zeal. The requisitioned gold is supposed to be deposited in the bank, but a great deal gets appropriated . . . A book seller who is well known in town demanded a receipt from the Cheka men who took his gold. He was then arrested as a counter-revolutionary and shot on the way to the Cheka, allegedly for trying to escape. The following day his belongings were confiscated, and his wife and two young children found themselves in the street. Robbing and settling personal scores is being covered up by accusations of counter-revolution. The sentence, invariably, is execution.'

A few days later, Glasse found that his father had been arrested. 'His apartment is completely ransacked. Everywhere there are splinters of wood, the legs of furniture have been sawn off [in the search for gold]. The wallpaper torn off, sofas ripped open, the spines of books torn off, the bottoms of suitcases broken open, some of the floorboards taken up. The piano and icon had been chopped to pieces with an axe. They had been through the album of family photographs. Luckily our family are people of the plough, pure bred proletarians. These albums are often used as evidence to reveal the social background of an individual. The most unfortunate are those who have hung on to photographs of officers or those dressed as *burzhuis*. One post official lost his life the other day. A metal button with a double-headed eagle was found in a sewing box in his home. It was from his uniform and it was enough for him to be executed.'

Next day Glasse wrote that his father had been released. 'He was saved by the son of his janitor whom he unexpectedly found among

---

* Search parties sawed the legs off furniture because hollow legs were a favourite place for hiding gold coins.

the Chekists. My father had paid for his education at school and university.' When Glasse's father was about to be released, he was held for a time in a room with a clear view of the courtyard. 'A person with his hands bound was placed by the entrance to the basement. He was shot in the back of the head and fell straight into the basement. The Chinese enjoyed themselves the most. One of them managed to kill more than one person with a single rifle bullet by placing people in a line.'

Glasse dwelled on the question of what turned people into killers. 'A court investigator once told me: "You don't know human nature. You idealise humans. We who work in the lawcourts are all too familiar with the depths of the human soul. Have you ever tried in a zoo to find any emotions in the eyes of a wolf, tiger or panther? Aren't you struck by the terrifying detachment of these beasts? It is the same detachment that we see in the eyes of hardened murderers. They don't understand punishment. When they are released, they immediately look for a victim. Are these not beasts?" I remembered this conversation today when a group of Red Army soldiers broke into the museum. They were noisy at first, but then they stopped and became quiet in front of the big antique mirror above the mantelpiece. They contemplated their faces in silence. One of them took off his bandolier of ammunition, put it on the mantelpiece, assumed a Napoleonic pose, kept frowning for a long time, then smiled, then frowned again. It was a proper group portrait in the mirror. In the mirror facial features become sharper. The murders are imprinted in them. Among them were Russian city boys together with Chinese drifters, marine infantry, *frontoviks* who lost their home in 1914 and wandered wherever they were blown by the wind. The Communists are using them, getting rid of the last traces of humanity in them.'

'My friends and acquaintances continue disappearing,' he wrote on 4 May. 'Each day I wait anxiously to see whether it is my turn today.'

'The searches continue,' he added next day. 'My wife has advised me to start painting a portrait of Lenin. "Let it hang in the apartment and maybe it will save us." I fastened a sheet on the stretcher and I sketched an outline of Lenin in charcoal.' The tactic worked far better than he imagined.

On 8 May, just three days later, a requisitioning and housing committee arrived. 'The "visitors" have dropped in to see us after searching and taking belongings from my neighbour's apartment. They took a look at the room, saw Lenin's portrait, Marx's *Capital*, Soviet newspapers and the sketch of a poster declaring "*Death to burzhuis!*". They asked for some tea and unbuttoned their coats and settled down to relax. When leaving they said rather shyly, "And we keep looking for gold". My wife replied "Yes, the state really needs the gold now." "Well, goodbye, your place is rather cramped."' They were saved. He was classified as an 'art-worker' and their little apartment defined as a workplace.

Both in and outside the city, fear and anger were growing at the way the Cheka and food detachments paid no attention to any law or Soviet decree. 'The Cheka is executing people without any court hearing, and in the Cossack villages the punitive detachments are acting on their own judgement, executing people and burning their houses with all their belongings. I went to Pashkovskaya in order to try and buy a little bit of flour. I walked eight kilometres keeping to the bush as there were roadblocks everywhere. I saw a lot of burned houses in the village. I did not find my friends alive. They are dead. I came home with an empty sack.'

'The food situation in the city had been bearable until the arrival of the Red Army,' he added five days later. 'Now, because punitive detachments are operating in the Cossack villages, no food supplies are arriving. There is food fever in the city. Apart from that the region is now full of detachments that are taking supplies to starving Moscow. These armed food detachments are now robbing peasants of their last grain supplies. The word sabotage has become popular. It provides the pretext for the execution of peasants who do not give up their grain. Therefore, it is not surprising that there are small-scale riots and there are now some partisans. People refer to them as the Greens because they live in the forests. Legends are circulating about their bravery.'

As well as Greens, there were also many White partisan groups throughout the Caucasus, most of whom had failed to get away on a ship from Novorossiisk in March. 'In the area of Kislovodsk, many officers are hiding in the mountains as well as Cossacks,' a Don Bureau agent reported to the Red 10th Army. 'They are organising *sotnias* in the mountains with White generals and colonels. There are rumours that they have artillery . . . and that Cossacks between the ages of sixteen and fifty will be called up.' By the summer, 15,000 partisans were thought to be active in the foothills of the Caucasus. The Red

Stavka called them 'White-Green detachments'. The largest group operated southeast of Krasnodar, around Maikop. 'Having united into the so-called "Army of Russian Rebirth" (General Fostikov), by the first half of August they had reached an overall strength of about 6,000–7,000 infantry and cavalry.'

Wrangel's plan was to seize Krasnodar, rally the rebel groups to join his forces, and spread out across the Kuban. On 14 August, while the main force under General Ulagai landed at Primorsko-Akhtarsk, north of Krasnodar on the Sea of Azov, diversionary beachheads were also seized on the Taman peninsula and between Anapa and Novorossiisk to confuse the Red command. According to Wrangel, the total of these three auxiliary forces amounted to no more than 5,000 men. The Red *Stavka*, on the other hand, estimated that when including those who joined them in the Kuban, Ulagai had around 8,000 men with him, half infantry, half cavalry. The mass of camp-followers did not help clarify numbers.

Ulagai was a highly respected Kuban Cossack leader, but not a very imaginative tactician or a good organiser. He assembled an unnecessarily large staff of hangers-on wanting to return home, and even allowed many families to accompany them on the ships. Security, not surprisingly, was non-existent. The plan became common knowledge in the Crimea, in fact Communist agents reported on it to the Don Bureau on 30 July, and yet Kamenev implied that the *Stavka* was caught unawares.

When Ulagai's main force landed at Primorsko-Akhtarsk, the Red commander Atarbekov is said have shot some 1,600 people. It is impossible to tell whether this was done out of panic, as was claimed, or whether it was a deliberate attempt to deter the Kuban Cossacks from joining the invading force because he knew the plan was to create a snowball effect as it advanced on Krasnodar.

Ulagai advanced rapidly to within 50 kilometres of Krasnodar, seized his first objective, the station of Timoshevskaya, and halted. Instead of seizing the Kuban capital when he had a chance and joining up with General Fostikov's force, he decided to return to his base at Primorsko-Akhtarsk where he had left all their supplies. He would await volunteers there. This gave the Red 9th Army the chance to bring in large reinforcements, and Trotsky once again rushed to a threatened front in his armoured train. Ulagai, having allowed himself to become trapped on a peninsula, had no alternative but to evacuate his force back to the Crimea on 7 September. This wasted venture left Wrangel with little choice except to try to expand out of the Northern Tauride, while the dust settled from the clash of giants taking place on the Vistula.

38

The Miracle on the Vistula
August–September 1920

Each morning at the Second Congress of the Communist International in the Kremlin, a huge map of Europe was updated to show little red flags moving closer to the Polish capital. 'The delegates stood with breathless interest before this map,' wrote Zinoviev. 'The best representatives of the international proletariat followed every advance of our armies with palpitating hearts.'

Victor Serge described the arrival of the Soviet leader. 'Lenin, jacketed, briefcase under arm, delegates and typists all around him, was giving his views on the march of Tukhachevsky's army on Warsaw. Lenin was in excellent spirits and confident of victory. Karl Radek, thin, monkey-like, sardonic and droll, hitched up his over-sized trousers and added, "We shall be ripping up the Versailles Treaty with our bayonets!".' Serge was unconvinced by their bravado. He considered that they had made a 'psychological error by including Dzerzhinsky, the man of the Terror', to lead the Polish Revolutionary Committee that was to govern the country after their victory. The dictator-in-waiting was already installed as Tukhachevsky's army group commissar in Białystok.

In Poland there was dismay at the relentless advance of the Red Army, an ill-disciplined, famished and unkempt mass with hardly an item of uniform between them. The only exception was the odd pixie-pointed *budenovka* cap with its large red star, which prompted Polish soldiers to call them 'peak-headed dogs'. Their clothes were in rags. Many wore bast shoes or were even barefoot, yet they somehow managed to outflank or penetrate every defence line and force another retreat. The advance of the 1st Cavalry Army through Volhynia, raising huge clouds of dust along the way, stopped only for brief nights in villages to demand milk and bread, chase hens and pigs, decapitate geese with their sabres, and sleep on a pile of hay.

The loss of Piłsudski's birthplace Wilno on 14 July had been enough of a shock, made worse when the Kremlin offered it to Lithuania. Yet the collapse of the defence of Brest (Brześć) with its famous fortress on 2 August was a crueller blow to Polish confidence. Local Communists had helped the attackers by increasing confusion among the defenders. The Red Army was across the River Bug, the last line of defence before Warsaw and a marker of the Curzon line – the theoretical Eastern Frontier of Poland recommended by Britain's foreign secretary. Piłsudski complained of a 'kaleidescope of chaos'.

Budyonny's 1st Cavalry Army, or Konarmiya, with one of them wearing the pointed budenovka *cloth cap, supposedly based on the helmet of a medieval Bogatyr knight-errant.*

Piłsudski's hope of destroying Budyonny's 1st Cavalry Army was snatched away at the last moment. Close to Brody, some 70 kilometres east of Lwów, Budyonny had created his own trap. He had failed to break the Polish line, which bent and folded around his forces. Then, on 3 August, just as two Polish cavalry divisions were about to cut the *Konarmia* off, Piłsudski had to call them back to defend the capital after the disaster at Brest. The 1st Cavalry Army was able to escape. 'A few days ago,' wrote Broniewski, 'I realised that "morale" has broken

down quite badly. The men believe they should defend their own homes.
I have had quite a few deserting – especially after the last battle.'

While confidence in a Soviet victory over Poland swelled in Moscow,
Polish intercepts of Red Army radio traffic suggested that their enemy
might be reaching a 'culminating point': that is the moment when an
army, over-extended and tired after a triumphant advance, loses both
momentum and the initiative.

'The exhaustion and demoralization of the Bolshevik troops increases
from one day to the next,' the Polish Army's II Bureau reported on 31
July. 'More and more enemy troops defect to our side . . . The mal-
nourished, but most of all, exhausted, troops are continually pushed
forward and are on their last legs. The enemy interprets the Polish
retreat as a trick to pull the Soviet forces into a trap. According to the
POWs, on 29 July one of the Soviet brigades refused to obey orders due
to exhaustion and losses.'

In the south, Budyonny, with the encouragement of both Stalin
and Yegorov, the front commander, was ignoring Kamenev's order to
support Tukhachevsky, whose operation against Warsaw had priority.
Tukhachevsky was concerned that his left flank was vulnerable, yet out
of moral cowardice when dealing with Stalin, Kamenev prevaricated
and failed to insist that his orders were obeyed. Budyonny, meanwhile, continued to head further away to the southwest towards the
industrial city of Lwów, to ensure his own triumph. There were wildly
optimistic illusions of striking into Romania, Hungary and even Italy.
Babel wrote in his diary on 8 August, 'We shall advance into Europe
and conquer the world.' Lenin was quite serious in his planning for a
'Union of Soviet Republics of Europe and Asia' run from Moscow. He
became furious with Stalin and accused him of chauvinism when he
argued that the Germans would never accept that.

Stalin had warned against a war with Poland while Wrangel
remained a threat in their rear. He had also urged Lenin not to under-
estimate Polish patriotism, but now also Stalin found himself carried
away with a premature intoxication of victory, convinced that the
Polish armies were collapsing. Based in Kharkov for most of the time,
Stalin had not been close enough to the fighting to assess it clearly. In
the north, meanwhile, Gai's cavalry corps had by-passed Warsaw and
was now much closer to Berlin than to its start-line on the Berezina,
but it had outrun its supply services. Trotsky ordered the Comintern to

prepare propaganda leaflets in German for the Red Army to distribute as soon as it crossed the frontier.

On 13 August, as Tukhachevsky's armies advanced on Warsaw, the diplomatic corps departed for Poznań. Only Italian diplomats remained, along with the Inter-Allied Commission of mainly French officers led by General Weygand and including a young Major Charles de Gaulle. 'Poles thrive on crises,' remarked the British military representative in Warsaw, Brigadier General Carton de Wiart, who had only just managed to escape from the fortress of Brest-Litovsk when the Reds stormed in.

This proved to be one of Poland's finest moments. The war ministry, led by General Kazimierz Sosnkowski, rose to the occasion. Morale was boosted by a programme of re-equipping infantry regiments with new boots, to replace all those which had come to pieces in the long retreats. Volunteers with a wide range of political opinions had appeared in their thousands to join militia units to defend the capital. Many were socialists, rebellious students and freethinkers, not just the faithful of Catholic Poland turning out to do battle with the anti-Christ. Altogether 164,615 young men and women came forward to be brigaded and deployed by General Haller. Most were less than twenty years old.

On 14 August, more bad news arrived as the 1st Legionary Regiment tried to get across Lublin. The Reds had cut the railway line to Warsaw, yet morale was high. 'The city,' wrote Lepicki, 'was filled with marching infantry, horse-artillery and cavalry and most of all, supply trains without number, making it impossible to push through. All those endless masses of men, horses, motor-vehicles and wagons were headed towards the front. They were the clearest evidence that our Supreme Command was undertaking an enormous offensive which would bring our country either death or victory. Our division, now again magnificently equipped, proud of its experience and confident, carried itself with excellence, generating enthusiasm among the crowds surrounding the cars. I will never forget the sight of an old woman kneeling at the edge of the pavement and blessing our column with a cross she held in her hand.'

What the Legionaries were witnessing in Lublin was part of a massive redeployment by their supreme commander, Marshal Piłsudski, which he had finalised on the morning of 6 August. The gruff old warhorse had dismissed the advice of General Weygand and his own chief of the general staff, who both wanted him to stick to a solid line of defence in front of Warsaw and counter-attack later. Piłsudski had instead decided to prepare a strike force further south on the River Wieprz, a tributary of the Vistula, by withdrawing the Fourth Army from the Bug. He would then attack Tukhachevsky's southern flank and rear, just as the Reds assaulted Warsaw head-on. In fact, Tukhachevsky had decided against a head-on attack. It would hit heavy defences and the bulk of the Polish troops defending Warsaw, so he was planning to swing round just north of the city and attack via Modlin.

Marshal Józef Piłsudski.

On 12 August, the day that Tukhachevsky had been told to take the Polish capital, the Battle for Warsaw started when the Red 1st Army began probing the city's defences on its northeast side. General Haller ordered Sikorski's weak Fifth Army northwest of Modlin to attack two days later to relieve the pressure. A series of disasters ensued, with troops arriving either completely exhausted after a long march or without their ammunition train. Several formations panicked and ran, and terrifying rumours of collapse ran through Warsaw. Volunteer groups prepared to defend the capital, fighting street to street, and women armed with rifles and some machine guns took their positions.

Priests came forward, leading processions to bless troops and pray for deliverance from the heathen Bolsheviks. One is said to have died leading a counter-attack with crucifix held high, and word spread of a vision of the Virgin Mary seen in the clouds above the battlefield.

Tukhachevsky, obsessed with destroying Sikorski's Fifth Army, had no idea of the threat developing on his own southern flank. 'The morning of 16 August was fresh and lovely,' wrote Lepicki in the 1st Legionary. 'Our marching orders came before the sun had the time to absorb the abundant summer dew . . . We were moving forward. The final test.' Unable to wait any longer with the critical battles around the north of Warsaw, Piłsudski launched his strike force of five divisions from the line of the River Wieprz. They mustered 52,500 bayonets and 3,800 sabres. Everything depended on speed for shock effect and maintaining the momentum, so that Tukhachevsky's armies never had a moment to recover.

The Poles also needed to cause maximum confusion. Their head of radio intelligence first had to raise the choice they faced. 'Should we allow the Bolsheviks to communicate via the radio [to keep track of their movements], or would it be better to wreak chaos in their ranks by stopping their radio communications? Our staff decided to block Bolshevik radio communications for 48 hours from the start of our offensive.' Being Catholic Poland, religion again played its part. 'We transmitted over the enemy's morse dots and dashes to create a thoroughly garbled babble. Radio operators at the Citadel station took turns and continued broadcasting without pause during the most crucial hours of the Battle of Warsaw. One needed to find a text that was long enough for the radio operators of the next shift to be able to continue: it was the Bible.' This tactic is thought to have delayed the Red 4th Army's attempt to escape from the corridor between Warsaw and East Prussia by a crucial twenty-four hours, which enabled its destruction.

On the first day of the great counter-attack, Piłsudski was in a state of nervous anxiety. Although he did not want to be slowed by a major battle at the outset, he was perplexed to hear that his five divisions had encountered no more than a few small detachments of the enemy. Air reconnaissance and cavalry patrols provided no explanation. The five divisions tramped on the next day, still heading north towards the frontier of East Prussia, with just the 3rd Legionary on the right aiming for Brest and the great bend in the River Bug. Only when Piłsudski was preparing for bed on the second night of the advance did he start to hear the rumble of guns like distant thunder. His left flank formation, the 14th Poznań Division, was finally in action against the Red 16th Army southeast of Warsaw. He immediately decided to bring the 15th Division in from its defensive position on the Vistula, to strengthen his left flank.

On the following day, 18 August, Sollohub's Red 16th Army found itself attacked from two directions and disintegrated rapidly. As they retreated further eastwards they were hit in the flank by one strike formation after another. Polish lancers charged the headquarters of Sollohub's 8th Division and killed its commander. Piłsudski, reassured that his plan was working well, returned to Warsaw. Few people there had any idea that the defeat they feared from Gai's cavalry corps to the north was turning into a crushing triumph from the south. Major de Gaulle was one person who truly admired Piłsudski's achievement. 'Our Poles have grown wings,' he wrote. 'The soldiers who were physically and morally exhausted only a week ago are now racing forward in leaps of forty kilometres a day. Yes, it is Victory! Complete, triumphant Victory!'

'First we hit an empty space, covering fifty versts every day in a forced march,' wrote Broniewski with the 1st Legionary Division. 'It wasn't until we reached Drohiczyn that we ran into Bolshevik supply trains on their flight from Warsaw.' Heading for Białystok, they even found the bridge over the Bug to be unguarded. 'Bolshevik supply trains are still scampering off to Wołkowysk. Idiots. We take them and leave it behind, pressing on . . . We find all kinds of loot on captured carts: coats, violins, women's shoes, ammunition, machine guns.' In the 13th Infantry Regiment the teenage volunteers, some as young as fourteen, who had 'broken down, sobbing' when writing farewell letters to their parents before the battle, now 'marched in full formation, battalion after battalion, using the main tracks. The Poles marched during the day and the Bolsheviks fled at night.'

Largely due to the Polish radio-jamming operation, Tukhachevsky at the Western Front headquarters in Minsk still had no idea of the disaster afflicting his armies 550 kilometres to the west. When he finally heard of the attack from the south, he assumed it was a diversion to help the hard-pressed Polish forces around Modlin. He never knew that Sollohub's 16th Army was fleeing to Białystok.

Gai only heard about Piłsudski's offensive and the Soviet withdrawal on 20 August. He turned back to the east and broke through one line of Polish infantry. The Reds could be as savage in defeat as the White Russians, and Gai's cavalry corps was famous for its cruelty. On 23 August, part of the Siberian Brigade advanced on Chorzele, 100 kilometres north of Warsaw, without realising that Gai's troops were there. 'The battlefield was an appalling sight,' wrote General Żeligowski afterwards. 'It was strewn with a great number of corpses. A vast majority of them were our soldiers, not wounded or killed in action, but killed after the battle. Long lines of bodies dressed only in their undergarments and without boots, lay along fences and in nearby underbrush. They were stabbed with sabres and bayonets, their faces mangled, eyes gouged out.'

The next day, Gai's cavalry found itself blocked up against the East Prussian border by the 14th Poznań Division. The infantry with him surrendered their weapons and crossed into German territory. Gai made another attempt to break out, but his men and their horses were too exhausted. Afraid to surrender after the atrocities they had committed, they too saved themselves by crossing into East Prussia. Escorted by German uhlans, they managed, nevertheless, to muster the strength to sing 'The Internationale'.

The 1st Legionary Division had meanwhile reached Białystok on 22 August, hard on the heels of the fleeing 16th Army. The poet Broniewski would receive the Order of Virtuti Militari for his bravery in that extraordinary advance. 'The loveliest thing of all,' he wrote, 'is the unfeigned joy which meets us everywhere. Marching, marching without end . . . We go on and on – rain, horrid damp weather.'

Soon after they entered the city, Lepicki's company came under fire. 'Right next to a small bridge, by the roadside, I saw the body of a good friend, Lieutenant Soja. Death had come to him quickly, an enemy bullet struck him in the head. He lay there with an open mouth, filled with ruby-red blood, which trickled down, giving him a strangely doleful appearance. He lay there as if asleep, his fingers still tightly clasped around his inseparable companion, a knobbed cane. I had no time to take prisoners, we had to head for the station right away. Meanwhile, throughout the city resounding with machine gun fire and battle cries, white-and-red signs of Polish freedom appeared in the windows. The more affected ladies began to spill out into the streets, where bullets were still whistling and shrapnel still played its terrible music, weeping and sobbing in line with the feminine rule that one must cry in sorrow and in joy.'

Lepicki, hearing the whistle of a train about to depart, rushed with his men to the Białystok marshalling yard. It seemed to take an age to set up their machine gun, yet the train took even longer to get moving. 'That brief moment was enough for our machine guns to rake the train which was literally bedaubed with Bolsheviks clinging to its every part. Those that were hit, fell to the rails and the wheels of the slowly moving carriages crushed their heads, arms, legs and bodies. It was a horrifying sight – those piles of massacred corpses . . . "That's for Soja," I thought, and walked over to the station building where a small group of desperate communists were fiercely resisting the Poles. Some fifteen more minutes of struggle and no enemy was left in front of my company.'

While Tukhachevsky's troops fled east back to the River Niemen, or escaped north into East Prussia, Budyonny had found the conquest of Lwów far harder than he had expected. As early as 6 August, Yegorov, the front commander, had ignored orders from the Red *Stavka* to divert his forces all the way northwest to Lublin ready to support Tukhachevsky. Kamenev had been weak and slow in his follow-up, but the pretence by Yegorov, Stalin and Budyonny that they had never received their instructions, or never in full, was shameless. The 1st Cavalry Army did not reach the outskirts of Lwów until 19 August, where it found itself engaged in bitter fighting with young Polish volunteers and strafing attacks from the air force. Budyonny could no longer brush aside orders from Tukhachevsky, Kamenev and even a telegram from Trotsky. Dispirited by the failure at Lwów and the change in orders, the 1st Cavalry Army pulled back across the Bug.

Budyonny still had only the vaguest idea of the disaster which had befallen Tukhachevsky's Western Front, when he received a formal order from Kamenev, the commander-in-chief of the Red Army, that he was still expected to advance on Lublin. The plan made no sense. It was a futile gesture which Kamenev, perhaps trying to make up for his earlier weakness, insisted was a necessary diversion. This time, the Cavalry Army clique felt obliged to obey to make up for their earlier refusals. Slowly, due to the exhaustion of both men and horses, Budyonny's *Konarmiya* set off towards Lublin. The Polish victory in the north now allowed Piłsudski to redirect Sikorski and part of his Fifth Army south to join up with the Third Army, to hunt down the hated Red Cavalry Army. They found that on 29 August they had it trapped, quite by chance, outside the walls of Zamość, half-way between Lwów and Lublin.

This beautiful Renaissance city, named in 1580 after its founder, Jan Zamoyski, was built to attract the greatest craftsmen from all over Europe, most of whom were Jewish.* Budyonny was not too concerned until he discovered from prisoners the extent of Tukhachevsky's defeat. His army was advancing, quite isolated, into the heart of victorious Poland.

On 31 August 1920, the last great cavalry engagement in Napoleonic style took place east of Zamość as the *Konarmiya* tried to break towards the River Bug. The battle centred on and around some high ground defined as Hill 255. It became a day-long melee of Lancers against Red Cossack regiments, charging, turning, and charging again with lance, sabre and revolver. Thanks partly to the heavy rain and bad visibility, Budyonny and his staff managed to extricate themselves with many of his men. This had been the last major action of the *Konarmiya*. 'Beginning of the end for the 1st Cavalry Army,' Babel wrote of its broken spirit. Utterly demoralised, they retreated, venting their rancour on any Polish village or Jewish *shtetl* in their path.

Stalin had returned to Moscow. He felt that the best method of defence in front of the Politburo was attack. He poured scorn on the whole handling of the Warsaw campaign, implicitly blaming Kamenev and Trotsky. He refused to accept any blame for the disaster in the north, which could be justified since the *Konarmiya* could not have arrived in time to make a difference, but his flouting of orders was hard to forgive. Stalin resigned from the Revolutionary Military Committee with ill grace and never forgave Trotsky. Lenin, on the other hand, at least demonstrated some humility. He acknowledged that the whole project for the 'Sovietisation of Poland' had been disastrous.

Tukhachevsky, meanwhile, tried to form a defence line along the River Niemen, but Piłsudski pushed on. International pressure for an armistice was building. Both sides wanted to stake as large a claim as possible to those borderlands, but the Red Army had lost any stomach

---

* With grotesque bad taste, Himmler so loved the place that he had it renamed Himmlerstadt during the German occupation.

for the fight. By mid-October, the Poles had retaken Wilno and Minsk and were back on the Berezina. General Wrangel, watching events from the Crimea, was resigned to the bitter paradox. Polish victory meant the end of that war, the redeployment of the Red Army towards the south, and the end of the White cause on Russian soil.

39

The Riviera of Hades
September–December 1920

Even during the worst moments of the Red Army's chaotic retreat from Poland, the Kremlin leadership did not forget General Wrangel in the Crimea, although the Whites never presented a serious threat to the Red Army's rear. Wrangel's army simply did not have the strength to launch a major break out from the shallow triangle of the northern Tauride.

Piłsudski never encouraged him. In his view, Wrangel was no better than that All-Russia imperialist Denikin, and he was certainly not going to gamble any Polish lives or political capital helping what he knew to be a lost cause. Wrangel himself had never suffered any illusions, from the moment he took over as commander-in-chief. It was just a question of whether they could survive the winter.

On 21 September Mikhail Frunze was appointed commander of a reorganised Southern Front. Six days later he arrived at the headquarters in Kharkov. The Kremlin needed Frunze's confidence and competence after the disastrous vacillations of Kamenev in the Polish war. Along with the 13th Army, the Front included Vasily Blyukher's 51st Division and the recently formed 2nd Cavalry Army, still only 2,770 strong. At Trotsky's insistence, it was now led by Filipp Mironov, to the rage of Stalin's clique, partly because Budyonny's 1st Cavalry Army was also to join the assault on the Crimea as soon as it had recovered from the Polish campaign.

There was another wild card in the Southern Front's order of battle. In August, the Reds had come to an agreement with Makhno's Insurgent Army that it would provide troops equivalent to a brigade to fight against Wrangel. The *Stavka* was mainly interested in preventing any more attacks on its rear areas and saw Makhno himself as nothing more than a 'temporary ally'. Relations between Makhno and the Communists had been extremely tense. Just before the agreement the Cheka had tried to recruit assassins to kill him, meanwhile 'Makhno

broke into Konstantinograd and hacked to death 84 Red Army soldiers in the course of two days.' Makhno himself stayed in Gulyai-Pole
while his forces set off for the northern Tauride.

Frunze concentrated his artillery and his strongest force, 'the right
bank group' on the northwestern side of the lower Dnieper opposite Kakhovka, where Slashchov's corps was based. In mid-August,
Wrangel had been forced to relieve Slashchov of his command after his
corps had failed to crush Red forces crossing the Dnieper. On visiting
his headquarters, Wrangel had found him prostrate from drugs and
alcohol in a gold-trimmed Turkish robe and surrounded by his collection of birds. The brilliant and cruel young commander had definitely
crossed the boundary between eccentricity and madness.

General Barbovich's cavalry corps, which had been held back in the
middle of the northern Tauride ready to counter any breakthrough, also
suffered heavy losses in the fighting round Kakhovka. Kamenev said
that the reckless cavalry counter-attacks, without artillery support,
against the barbed wire of the Red positions in the bridgehead was
nothing less than 'daring insanity'. The trouble was that the Whites
were down to less than twenty shells a day to fire from their field guns
and could not count on receiving any more from either the British or
the French. Wrangel and his commanders could see the importance
of Kakhovka from just a glance at the map. The road from there ran
straight to the Perekop Isthmus just 80 kilometres away. As the Red
Stavka put it, Wrangel was deprived of 'operational freedom'.

The main reason for not playing safe with a withdrawal back into
the Crimea was due to the failure of General Ulagai's Kuban expedition. They now needed to extract as much grain as possible from
the northern Tauride to feed the swollen population of the Crimea
throughout the coming winter. Yet with the Polish-Soviet negotiations
heading for an agreement, Wrangel suspected that they would probably not be able to hold out beyond the autumn.

On 8 September, Frunze renamed the 'right bank group' the 6th
Army. The subsequent arrival of the 4th Army would give him a
crushing superiority with 133,000 men to 37,000 Whites. An intense
recruiting campaign had been launched in factories. Loyal proletarians
and Communist Party members had been called forth as volunteers to
put an end to the White presence polluting Soviet soil.

Frunze's other advantage was that the Don Bureau's network of
spies had increased greatly as the victory of the Reds became certain.

This extended even to areas recaptured by the Reds – the Donets, the Don, the Kuban and the Caucasus. Red commanders desperately needed intelligence on both Green and White partisan groups and their uprisings. Agents deep in the Caucasus reported that General Shkuro had established his headquarters in Terekli (Khemtob in Dagestan). A network of Cossack women acted as messengers between his staff and the other cavalry guerrilla units, one of which was 5,000-strong. They were recovering stockpiles of ammunition which had been buried by Denikin's troops before their departure. 'The headquarters communicate with Wrangel via Sukhumi and Kazbek. The headquarters is to conduct propaganda and start an uprising in the Terek and Kuban regions. The local population supports these gangs.' Red agents also had orders to provide hard evidence of the way the Menshevik Georgian government was secretly sending White officers who had been interned in Tiflis across to the Crimea because Wrangel had 'sent emissaries to negotiate their release'.

An agent with the codename 'Perets' [pepper], reported on shortages of shells and coal in the Crimea. 'I managed to make friends with an artillery officer and some sailors. I learned from them that there have been no deliveries of shells and uniforms for the last two months. There has been an order to conserve ammunition. The sailors say that the reserves are small.' Coal was in such short supply that the harbour at Sevastopol was packed with merchantmen unable to refuel. There had been an uprising which General Kutepov had brutally suppressed. The White authorities had then placed students on most of the ships to watch the sailors and report any problems to the counter-intelligence department. Communist agents also sent back reports of conditions, attitudes and conversations within the coastal cities of the Crimea. They claimed that officers were even trying to spread a rumour to boost White morale that Makhno was secretly working to help the Whites.

A junior officer's pay of 9,000 roubles a month, assuming he received it on time, might just cover the cost of accommodation for his wife or family in the Crimea but not their food. Refugees too were starving. They mostly survived on anchovies, because a pound of bread cost 500 roubles. People were forced to sell almost all their belongings, including overcoats, as winter approached. 'We are dying of hunger,' one army wife wrote to her husband in despair. 'We have sold everything we had. I have only my body left to sell.'

All eye-witnesses of this displaced society tended to focus on the desperation of the majority and cynical corruption of the minority, such as those hunched over café tables doing currency deals or selling passages to safety abroad. One account regarded the impoverishment of 'former people' with a noticeable measure of *schadenfreude* at their approaching fate. 'Noble ladies and maidens, former ladies-in-waiting, tall and now skinny as rakes, sell their family jewels in the mornings at the black market. Their lips tremble and tears never dry in their eyes. Profiteers paid them in Denikin "bell" banknotes, which nobody wants to accept now. During the day they crowd in the corridors of consulates, in the hope that something will turn up, as well as in institutions where the trade in passes is in full swing, and where one can buy the passport of any nation for a decent amount of money . . . At night, in restaurants and cabarets where some very dubious looking women wait on the tables, drunken white officers spend their loot on drink, shoot at the ceiling with revolvers, and sing "God save the Tsar", forcing the audience to stand up.'

On 8 October, Wrangel launched a counter-attack against the Reds' Kakhovka bridgehead and crossed the Dnieper opposite Aleksandrovsk to swing west against Nikopol. The main objective was to reduce the threat of a sudden strike from Kakhovka towards the Perekop Isthmus. Within twenty-four hours, Kamenev acknowledged that the Markov Division 'had occupied a bridgehead along the right bank of the Dnieper 25 kilometres deep'. The next day, just as the Soviet government and the Poles signed an armistice in Riga, the Whites fought their way into Nikopol.

Frunze rapidly increased his counter-attack against the Whites on the northwest bank of the lower Dnieper. On 14 October the 2nd Cavalry Army, 'concentrating a powerful mounted fist in the area of the village of Shelokhov, routed the enemy's cavalry group, consisting of three divisions'. The Southern Front's military revolutionary committee reported to Trotsky that the 2nd Cavalry 'started a decisive advance with support from infantry, and after a seven-hour stubborn battle pushed back three cavalry and two infantry divisions of the enemy to Nikopol. Under pressure from the Red Cavalry, their chaotic retreat turned into a panic-stricken flight. The enemy units fled, abandoning weapons, supply carts, armoured vehicles and ammunition . . . According to numerous statements from prisoners, General Babiev was killed and Barbovich heavily injured. The Red warriors have displayed astonishing heroism.' Mironov, who led the 2nd Cavalry charge in person, had his horse shot from under him. This day, 14 October, they proclaimed, was the day that 'marked the beginning of Wrangel's defeat'. Budyonny and Stalin cannot have been pleased at this account of Mironov's success.

Knowing that the time had come, Wrangel conducted his withdrawal back into the Crimean peninsula via the Perekop Isthmus. His men fought so bitterly against the overwhelming odds that Frunze reported back to Moscow on his amazement at their resistance, when both starving and frozen in their tattered uniforms with temperatures already below minus 15 degrees centigrade. 'The autumn of 1920 was very cold,' Boyarchikov, with the 2nd Cavalry headquarters, recorded. 'Frost started early.' Although the bulk of the White troops escaped capture, the stockpiles of grain from the northern Tauride were captured by Frunze's forces.

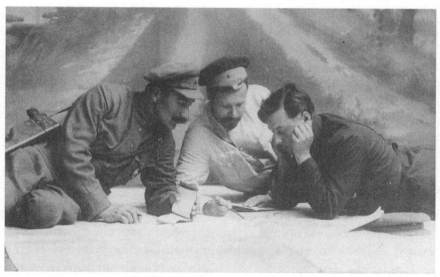

A very posed photograph of the victors Budyonny, Frunze and Voroshilov, Crimea, 1920.

Blyukher's full strength 51st Rifle Division, accompanied by Mironov's cavalry, approached the Perekop Isthmus ready to deliver a frontal attack on the ancient defences of the 'Turkish wall', which had been refortified by Kutepov's veterans. The bulk of the Whites' artillery, machine guns and remaining armoured vehicles were concentrated there, with their remaining armoured trains on a railway line behind. Yet as things turned out, that was not where the breakthrough would come.

Wrangel, determined not to make the mistakes of the chaotic evacuation from Novorossiisk, ensured that panic did not break out. He reassured the civilian population and the refugees that the Crimea was virtually impregnable, and strolled out of the Hotel Kist, his new headquarters in Sevastopol, to talk to anxious people in the streets. All the while he was quietly organising the evacuation of all those who would need to leave. He contacted the Royal Navy, the commander of the US Navy in Turkish Waters and the French Navy to ask for their assistance while also ensuring that all the White vessels were ready for sea. He had a great advantage over Denikin. He had five ports to use for his evacuation, not just one. It would also prove fortunate that the Red Army's pursuit would be so sluggish.

It was just as well that Wrangel had not wasted any time. During the night of 7 November, the third anniversary of the Bolshevik coup in Petrograd, Frunze's assault on the Crimea started from an unexpected direction. The 4th Army, supported by part of the 2nd Cavalry Army, began to cross the shallow Syvash salt lake. A secular miracle had occurred favouring the unbeliever. A raging northwesterly had uncovered the mudflats beneath, and large parts were frozen hard. This allowed two divisions of the 4th Army, supported by the 7th Cavalry Division and Makhno's Insurgent Army, to cross the six kilometres to the Litovsky peninsula. The three-hour journey was not without hardship. 'The impassable mud was sucking in men and horses,' one participant recorded. 'Frost struck, wet clothes were freezing on the soldiers.' And when the wind dropped, the salt water surged back, drowning a number of men. Despite these losses, the Reds took the demoralised Kuban cavalry brigade unawares. By the time the main attack on the Turkish Wall took place the next day at 13.00 hours, Kutepov had already had to divert men to strengthen the Kuban Cossacks as well as face the Red 6th Army head-on. His troops managed to repel the first two attacks, inflicting heavy losses, but the third wave broke through.

As Kutepov's regiments fought in retreat, Barbovich's White cavalry managed to attack the rear of Blyukher's 51st Division, but they in return were attacked by Mironov leading part of his 2nd Cavalry Army. This turned into the last mounted engagement of the war, 'sabres gleaming'. Mironov's tactic was to charge, but then at the last moment his squadrons swerved outwards, allowing their *tachankas* to rush through 'firing their 250 machine guns'. 'The first cavalry lines of the enemy were immediately swept away. Others tried to flee, but very few survived.'

The 1st Cavalry Army's progress into the Crimean peninsula was slower, but that was probably because of the revenge it was taking on the way. The nurse Anna Ivanovna Egorova rejoined her colleagues from a field hospital in Dzhankoy, behind the front, which had been taken by Budyonny's troopers. 'They had been robbed, stripped of all their clothes,' she wrote, 'the nurses had been raped, their faces were red from being beaten up. It was done by Budyonny's cavalry . . . The doctors were crying. "And they killed Lida, the pharmacist's wife. They cut her in two halves, as well as the baby that she was expecting." I did not go to look at Lida . . . All the nurses' clothes were in rags. Their faces were red, they had cried while they were being raped. And the men hit them in the face and demanded that they laugh . . . Doctors and nurses were telling Doctor Gruber what they had been through. All the doctors turned away when the nurses were being raped. A man from Budyonny's cavalry approached a doctor who had turned away and slapped his face. "You should be happy to see us here. Do you have any idea of who Budyonny is?"'

News of the Red Army's breakthrough into the Crimean peninsula produced a rapid reaction. On 11 November, Wrangel ordered all White ships to their designated ports: from west to east they were Eupatoria, Sevastopol, Yalta, Feodosia and Kerch. The staff-work was impressive. Every formation in the army received instructions on which port they were to head for. The Allied navies also reacted quickly, despite one report of a Red submarine off the Crimean coast. Admiral McCully issued orders to all American naval vessels in the region. He said that 'Wrangel's forces could not hold out more than a few days longer,' and he refused to have 'these people left behind knowing that they would be murdered by the Bolshevists'.

On the same day, Thursday, 11 November, when news came through that Red forces had broken the White line of defence across the Perekop isthmus, the US Navy warships in Turkish Waters redeployed immediately. The brand-new destroyer USS *Humphreys* was sent from Batumi to Theodosia, the USS *John D. Edwards* on its way to Varna was diverted to Sevastopol, the USS *Whipple* made full speed to Constanza to fill up with oil before heading to the Crimea and the USS *Fox* was ordered to make ready. The next day, with confirmation that the situation was deteriorating fast, the cruiser USS *St Louis* received an urgent 'P signal in cypher', ordering it to coal and then sail.

The American Red Cross in the SS *Faraby* made for Feodosia, which they reached on 13 November to find the streets shuttered and dark as the remnants of the Don Cavalry Corps entered the town. 'It was rumoured that the Bolshevists were about 15 miles out.' The next day, the *Faraby* loaded wounded in Sevastopol, along with the USS *Whipple* and *Overton*, two British destroyers, and the USS *Humphreys*, which took on 113 stretcher cases. The wounded and sick were kept on deck while each ship's doctor worked flat out on their wounds. 'Stringent orders were issued to prevent the crew from coming into contact with lice-infection,' an officer recorded. But he acknowledged that the crew still did what they could for them. 'Cigarettes and candy were passed round freely.'

An exile on one of the other ships watched as 'Cossacks with grim faces and their eyes full of tears they could not hide, strained to see their beloved friends among the thousands of horses who stood on the quay . . . The tie between the Cossack and his horse was proverbial. I think something must have died in the hearts of the Cossacks that day.' The evacuation in Sevastopol was accomplished on Sunday 14 November. Wrangel, once satisfied that he had done all he could, then proceeded to Yalta during the night in the White cruiser *General Kornilov*, formerly the *Kagul*.

The USS *St Louis* reached Sevastopol accompanied by several destroyers, but since they sighted no further troops to collect, they headed on round to Yalta, where they found HMS *Benbow* and the French cruiser *Waldeck-Rousseau*. The *St Louis* was captained by William D. Leahy, later Fleet Admiral and close adviser to President Roosevelt at the Yalta conference. It was a sunny afternoon and the Black Sea was calm. Officers on board gazed at the cypresses around the 'glowing white façades of mansions' on the hillsides below the Crimean mountain range. Leahy had no inkling that he would return there a quarter of a century later when the world was carved up again with an even greater advantage to the Communist cause.

Canvas awnings were strung above the decks as shelter for the refugees being ferried out to the warships. Suddenly somebody on the *St Louis* shouted. 'The hills! Look at the hills!' 'On the heights above the western extremes of Yalta, on a ledge or open roadway, a marching group of brown figures broke file and ran irregularly down the hillside. As the figures scurried, puffs of whiteish smoke rose against the darker background, followed by the sound of rifle-fire, with other hillsides bouncing the echoes. The French cruiser, as soon as it was under way, opened fire with its secondary armament in a futile gesture.'

The evacuation at Yalta had been quiet and orderly until the final moments. As the last civilian steamers left, they could hear 'intermittent rifle fire in the town'. There was also a huge explosion as an ammunition dump was blown up. General Wrangel on the *Kornilov* saluted each ship as it passed, receiving cheers in return. 'He was trying to inspire us with a little hope for the dark future that awaited us,' wrote one exile. 'We all cheered him as we passed, he who had never failed us.'

Feodosia and Kerch were not cleared until the following day, 16 November. The *Waldeck-Rousseau* fired a farewell salute of twenty-one guns to Wrangel in the *Kornilov* – 'the last salute to the Russian flag in Russian territorial waters'. Altogether some 126 ships of varying sizes managed to evacuate a total of 145,693 civilians and soldiers, of whom 83,000 were refugees. They landed them either in Constantinople, where there were already 35,000 Russians, or on the Prinkipo Islands in the Sea of Marmara.

'On 16 November 1920 the Red Army's forces occupied the entire territory of the Crimea,' the Red *Stavka* declared. For the Reds this marked the end of the war. 'When our cavalry entered Simferopol and Sevastopol, the streets of these cities were filled with abandoned carts that were loaded with ammunition, foodstuffs and uniforms. Horses were tangled in their harnesses, trying to break free. The streets were jammed and it was hard for our squadrons to get through. Windows in the houses were boarded up, which created an impression that they were empty, while, in fact, a majority of residents of these towns never went away. I am not talking about the rich people but about the townspeople, craftsmen, and traders. An exotic scene met our eyes when we rode down to the harbour of Sevastopol. The horizon was filled with ships taking away for ever Russian *burzhuis* and the remains of the defeated White Army.'

*

The impression given in Wrangel's own account, as well as in those of many survivors, was that the evacuation had allowed everyone who had wanted to leave to escape. That is hard to reconcile with the waves of executions which followed immediately after the departure of the ships. The Red Army *Stavka* pointed out that many rear units and 'a large number of refugees were not embarked'. Reliable figures suggest that 15,000 wounded were left behind, as well as 2,009 officers and 52, 687 soldiers of Wrangel's Russian Army.

'From now on exile and pitiful intrigues would become the lot of those who sought to halt the course of history,' wrote Kamenev of the departed. The Red *Stavka* made no mention of the 'full pardon for all delinquencies connected with the civil struggle' which Frunze had promised to all those who surrendered their weapons. Lenin was clearly displeased by such generosity and ordered that it should not be repeated under any circumstances. Victory meant vengeance both at home and abroad.

Pavel Makarov, the secret Communist and General Mai-Maevsky's adjutant, joined up with Red Army troops. He described how eighty-three Whites had ripped off their shoulder boards just before capture and pretended to be Greens. The cavalry regiment wasted no time and 'sent them to Kolchak', the new joke euphemism for execution. When he reached Feodosia, just after Makhno's Insurgent Army, he went to one of the highest points in the town to look around with binoculars. He saw 'a lava-like mass of cavalry' descending a hillside. Like most of the Red Army, they were no doubt impatient to teach any remaining officers and the pampered *burzhuis* of the Crimea a lesson.

Lenin told Dzerzhinsky not to keep the surviving White prisoners from the Crimea in southern Russia and the Caucasus as he proposed. It would be more convenient, he told him 'to concentrate them some-where in the north'. This meant the concentration camps around the White Sea. Very few emerged alive. Most prisoners, however, were saved from this extended death by a far more rapid one. The man in charge of the Crimean Red terror, almost certainly the most concen-trated in all Soviet territory, turned out not to be Dzerzhinsky, but the Hungarian Communist Béla Kun, assisted by Rozalia Zalkind, a woman commissar known as Zemlyachka. Béla Kun seemed to imply that he was acting under orders. 'Comrade Trotsky told us that he would not visit the Crimea as long as the very last counter-revolutionary remains there. The Crimea is a bottle that none of the counter-revolutionaries will be able to escape.'

Prisoners were supposedly sent for 'screening' to the Chekists in the Special Department of each Red Army formation.* Posters ordered all uncaptured officers to register, and because of Frunze's promise, many went along only to find themselves arrested immediately. In Simferopol, a young officer called Demidov begged his mother from prison to bring him some warm socks, which she did. On her next visit, she was told he had been transferred elsewhere, but then she heard that all the prisoners had been executed. Relatives of other victims told her the most likely site. She went there with them and in the dirt spotted one of her son's socks which she had darned. She found a piece of paper in the sock which turned out to be a note from him. He had written to say that it looked as if they were all going to be shot that night. The family has held on to that piece of paper ever since.

The killing began on the very first night. Estimates of the total number of victims range from 15,000 up to many more than 100,000. When figures from individual locations are added together, they point to the higher end.

The worst massacres took place in Sevastopol itself and outside at Balaklava where a total of 29,000 died. More than 8,000 of them were killed in the first week. At least 5,500 were killed on the Krimtaev estate next to Simferopol. In a deliberately conspicuous display of vengeance, many were also hanged from lamp posts in Sevastopol wearing their uniforms with shoulder boards. Non-combatants with even the most tenuous connection to the Volunteer Army were not spared. Members of Wrangel's army who had been too wounded or sick to board the ships were dragged from the hospitals in Yalta, Alupka and Sevastopol and killed. Apparently seventeen Sisters of Charity nurses tending them were also killed. Even dockers who had continued to work during the evacuation were executed for assisting the Whites.

---

* The counter-intelligence 'Special Department', or OO (Osobyi otdel), was set up the year before by Feliks Dzerzhinsky on Lenin's order to ensure that the Cheka retained control over the Red Army's political discipline. This continued under the Cheka's successor organisations until April 1943 when the NKVD special departments were hived off under Viktor Abakumov to form SMERSh: *Smert shpionam*, or 'Death to spies'.

The victims did not consist solely of officers and soldiers. Family members, including wives, children and the elderly, were also killed. Many were not shot but hacked to death with sabres. In Kerch they were taken out to sea and drowned, which was called 'landings in Kuban'. On land, the prisoners were marched out during the day to dig the mass graves which they would fill that night. Killers worked in shifts, often dealing with up to sixty victims at a time. Using machine guns quickened the pace. A.V. Osokin testified for a trial in Lausanne that 'the slaughter continued for months . . . Machine guns could be heard every night until dawn . . . The residents of the nearest homes moved out. They could not stand the horror of mental torture. It was dangerous too. The wounded crawled up to the houses and begged for help. Some were executed for harbouring survivors.'

In 1918, the Communist leadership had justified the use of terror as a necessary weapon to achieve power in the civil war, yet its worst manifestation followed the hour of absolute victory. In a foretaste of SS Einsatzgruppen practices during the invasion of the Soviet Union twenty years later, some victims were forced not only to dig mass graves, but then undress and lie in the pit to be shot. The next batch would be forced to lie on the dead to be killed in their turn. Some were not dead when the pit was covered over with earth. When it came to the Nazi invasion of the Soviet Union two decades later, Himmler's SS and Gestapo appear to have learned a great deal from the methods of the Cheka.

40

The Death of Hope
1920–1921

Announcements of Red triumph in November 1920 failed to conceal the nervousness of the victors. They faced resistance in even larger parts of the country than during the civil war itself. Chekas almost everywhere uncovered 'conspiracies', not just White and Cossack, but also Green, Left Socialist Revolutionary, Right Socialist Revolutionary, Makhnovist, Petlyurist and Menshevik, even Tolstoyan. Yet most of the revolts were not political, but peasant anger at the seizure of their grain and animals by Communist food detachments from the cities. The killing of Soviet officials prompted massive reprisals and the vicious cycle of repression and revolt continued right across the Caucasus, southern Russia and Ukraine as well as Belarus, the Tambov and Volga regions and western Siberia. 'The vengeful hand of the Soviet Government will ruthlessly eradicate all its enemies,' proclaimed the Cheka in the north Caucasus and Don.

The Reds wasted no time in turning on their 'temporary ally', the Makhnovist Insurgent Army, which was ordered to disarm and become part of the Red 4th Army. Semeon Karetnik, who had commanded their detachment in the invasion of the Crimea, was summoned to Frunze's headquarters. On the way there, he and his staff were captured by Red Army troops near Melitopol and executed. Both Budyonny's 1st Cavalry Army and the 2nd Cavalry Army were ordered into action against the remnants of the Insurgent Army. By the summer of 1921, just Makhno, his wife Galina and seventy-seven followers were left. 'Our group reached the Romanian border,' one of them stated under interrogation, 'and we swam our horses across [the River Dniester] in the area of Kamenka. During the last five to six days we had ridden only at night, avoiding clashes with the Reds, and we crossed the frontier on 28 August 1921.'

The 2nd Cavalry, downgraded to a corps, was sent back to the Caucasus once the Makhnovist movement was almost entirely crushed. The Special Department of the Caucasian Front then revived suspicions about its Left SR commander, Filipp Mironov. 'There are reasons to suggest the presence of a counter-revolutionary organisation,' it reported. On 17 January 1921, Mironov was informed: 'You have been relieved from your position . . . You are to hand over your command.' His known associates were all arrested too. 'Everyone confessed when interrogated,' the Cheka reported. On the basis of secret informer reports and interrogations, Mironov was arrested because of an alleged connection to a revolt led by another Cossack officer in December. He was sent under escort to the Butyrka prison in Moscow, where, on 21 April, he was shot dead while exercising in the prison yard.

The renewed repression of the Don and Kuban Cossacks produced many more revolts. All were crushed, yet it was the Bolsheviks' war on the peasantry which produced the most disastrous consequences. They claimed that they were attacking only the kulaks, the better-off peasantry, yet often made little distinction between them. 'The Tula Food Detachment set about working actively,' wrote Georgy Borel. 'Immediately they summoned meetings where some threatening resolutions were made. The peasants turned up, but there was no discussion. They were then forced into the unheated church in which village reunions normally took place and kept there for 8 days with no food or water. They [the Reds] also went for the kulaks. All their property was confiscated, many were shot while others were sent to labour camps. Unbelievable atrocities were committed towards these unfortunate people: they were whipped till they bled, then water was poured over the wounds and they were put outside to freeze . . . All the grain had been confiscated, there was none left even for sowing.' Famine was inevitable. To make matters far worse, the winter of 1920–21 was terrible. 'It was so cold,' wrote Boyarchikov, 'that birds froze in flight and fell to the ground like stones.'

In comparison to 1917, only a quarter of the land was sown in the *guberniya* of Tula, yet the demand of the Food Commission came to six times more than the total of the harvest. The detachments grabbed what they could, yet widespread reports indicated massive waste. The expropriated grain was left to rot while the confiscated livestock died from neglect. On top of the brutal incompetence came the outrageous looting carried out by the Communist requisitioning squads. By 1920, more than 8,000 members of the squads had been murdered by peasants. 'Cities were sending detachments to the villages,' wrote a participant in the Tambov rebellion, 'and the detachments whipped, shot peasants, raped women and robbed peasants of their grain. The hatred of peasants towards the cities played a major role. It was the reason for the peasants' brutal treatment of any Bolsheviks they caught.'

Starvation in western Siberia in the region of Chelyabinsk.

After western Siberia, where the Red Army faced some 60,000 rebels, the largest and longest peasant rebellion provoked by food requisitions had started in the Tambov region in August 1920. Led by the Left Socialist Revolutionary Aleksandr Antonov, the revolt spread to large parts of the neighbouring regions of Voronezh, Samara and Penza. Antonov deployed his forces most skilfully, attacking, dispersing and reappearing elsewhere. They were often joined by deserters still in hiding from the civil war and thus had experienced soldiers to train them. Captured officials and members of food squads were treated with savage cruelty. The Communist Party, in rebel eyes, had betrayed the 1917 revolution in the countryside and made their lives far worse than under the Tsar. Collective farms were attacked, and their tools and grain shared out.

After initial successes for the peasants, the Red Army would return in strength, as the Tula region discovered. 'Units sent against the uprising included Budyonny's cavalry as well as Latvian and Chinese infantry. They had a total of about 6,000 men. We could not resist this force and began retreating.' Artillery was brought up to bombard villages and even poison gas shells were used to clear forests on the orders of Tukhachevsky and Antonov-Ovseenko.

From the start, Red reprisals were conspicuously cruel. Wives and children were taken as hostages, with some 50,000 held in concentration camps in the Tambov region. An unknown number were executed or sent to labour camps in the frozen north, a probable death sentence in itself when winter came. In the region of Tomsk in western Siberia, 5,000 peasants were slaughtered. A similar revolt in the region of Ufa produced an even more savage response, with estimates of 10,000 to 25,000 dead. In Belarus countless villages were burned to the ground, just as the Germans would do a generation later in response to partisan attacks. The survivors were shipped off to Vologda, 400 kilometres north of Moscow, or to areas of famine. Squads smashed the fingers of their victims between doors and their frames. In winter, they saved bullets by using the 'ice statue' method of killing, which meant stripping the victim naked and pouring water over them until they froze solid. 'Following its "pacification", the Tambov Province was left with no teachers or medics. Part of this village intelligentsia was killed in the battles, others were shot in the basements of Tambov's Cheka. By 1922, there were many villages whose population consisted entirely of women and children.'

Suffering in the cities was different and in some ways even worse, with the slow death of starvation. Glasse, the painter and diarist, had returned from the Caucasus to his old neighbourhood in Petrograd. This was because his apartment in Krasnodar with all his belongings and books had been confiscated by the local Communist Party boss for his own use.

Glasse was appalled by what he saw in the former capital. 'Silent people with tired eyes, emaciated or bloated. The deserted Nevsky Prospekt. On Vasilievsky island there are patches of wasteland. The wooden houses and dachas there had been stripped to the ground for firewood. In 1919 when the city was literally dying of hunger, they burned anything combustible, antique furniture, libraries, archives and paintings. It was with trepidation in my heart that I approached the house which I left in the autumn of 1917. The family of the writer Z— had all starved to death in 1919. Only the maid was still alive. She told me that they had hidden the corpses of dead family members under sofas or beds in order to use their ration cards until they began to smell.'

With many of the cities on strike and large parts of Soviet territory in open rebellion, Lenin and the Communist leadership felt under siege. On 8 March 1921, Lenin confessed to the Tenth Party Congress that the peasant rebellions were 'far more dangerous than all the Denikins, Yudeniches and Kolchaks put together'. Yet even this admission was disingenuous since it came in the middle of a far greater threat: the regime's battle to crush a major uprising of the Baltic Fleet at Kronstadt.

The catastrophic food situation in that savage winter had been made far worse by the Communists' ideological obstinacy and ruthlessness. All of their repressive measures, with food detachments demanding impossible requisitions, and all their attempts to prevent any form of free trade or barter had become utterly counter-productive as well as inhumane. Horses could be rated as more valuable than people. 'A paradox of Soviet life,' a former law professor in Petrograd pointed out. 'While people are starving here, horses are being fed with . . . spaghetti! Eighteen poods [295 kilos] of spaghetti were issued for one institution to feed its horses.' Anger at Communist methods led to a massive loss of support even among their supposedly loyal supporters in the factories and the Baltic Fleet.

Widespread strikes began in Moscow and on 23 February 1921, Communist authorities declared martial law. The protests spread rapidly to Petrograd, where workers demanded the right to obtain food from the countryside without it being confiscated on their return. 'In the dead factories,' wrote Victor Serge, 'the workers spent their time making pen-knives out of bits of machinery or shoe-soles out of the conveyor-belts, to barter them on the underground market.'

The protest became increasingly political. Left Socialist Revolutionaries, Mensheviks and Anarchists objected to the dictatorship of the Communist Party now that the civil war against the Whites was over. They wanted freedom of speech and a return to the original ideals of the February revolution, with power flowing upwards from freely elected Soviets rather than imposed top-down by Lenin's Sovnarkom. This was an existential challenge which prompted Lenin and Trotsky to resort to unlimited force as the mood in Petrograd became strikingly similar to that against the Tsarist regime in February 1917, exactly four years before.

The sailors of the Baltic Fleet at Kronstadt had always shown a strong Anarchist streak. On 26 February the crew of the battleship *Petropavlovsk* sent a fact-finding mission into Petrograd to learn more about the strikes. They soon discovered the reality of famished workers. Two days later the whole crew of the battleship voted a resolution demanding freedom of speech, freedom of assembly and secret voting. At a mass meeting on Anchor Square, the *Petropavlovsk* programme demanding reforms was adopted by an overwhelming majority of the Kronstadt base. The President of the All-Russia Central Executive Committee (in fact the Soviet head of state), Mikhail Kalinin, had come to call the sailors back to Party loyalty, so this rejection was seen as a declaration of war. 'Grandpa' Kalinin, supposedly a bluff character of peasant birth, was furious.

That night, Victor Serge, still working for the Comintern in Petrograd, was awoken in his room in the Hotel Astoria by the telephone ringing. The caller was Zinoviev's brother-in-law. 'Kronstadt is in the hands of the Whites. We are all under orders.' Serge was shaken to the core. How could the defeated Whites have suddenly seized Kronstadt? 'What Whites?' Serge demanded. 'Where did they come from? It's incredible.'

'A General Kozlovsky.'

'But our sailors? The Soviet? The Cheka? The workers at the Arsenal?'

'That's all I know.' The great lie had started, perhaps invented by Kalinin on his return.

On 2 March, the naval base set up its own revolutionary committee. The sailors were convinced that support for their cause would spread and the regime would have to become more answerable to the masses. Trotsky had described the sailors of Kronstadt as 'the pride and glory of the Russian Revolution'. Now the Communist regime needed to explain why they faced war with their own heroes. Resorting to that outright lie, they claimed that the mutiny was led by General Kozlovsky, a 'White' general, sent in by the French capitalist government in a plot to overthrow the regime. In fact, Kozlovsky was simply a former Tsarist artillery officer who, like so many others, had volunteered to serve the Red Army. He had been sent to Kronstadt by Trotsky himself to reorganise the coastal batteries protecting the approaches to Petrograd, and was now accused of being the leader of a rebellion he had nothing to do with. His ten-year-old daughter living in Petrograd was seized as a hostage.

Serge was even more shocked when he learned that the 'White Guardist plot' was a complete invention. 'The truth seeped out little by little, past the smokescreen put out by the Press, which was positively berserk with lies. And this was our own Press, and hence the first incorruptible and unbiased Press in the world!'

A delegation of Kronstadt sailors sent to Petrograd to parley were seized by the Cheka and never seen again. The American Anarchists Emma Goldman and Alexander Berkman tried to persuade Zinoviev to negotiate but he instead tried to send them off in a special train on a tour to understand the country. The Communist leadership did not want foreign witnesses because it had every intention of crushing the revolt with unrestricted violence.

On 5 March, Trotsky arrived in Petrograd and issued an ultimatum to the mutineers that if they did not surrender immediately they would be 'shot like partridges', a threat which would have sounded convincing on the lips of a White general. Trotsky then ordered that the sailors' families in Petrograd should be seized as hostages. The defeated Whites in exile felt a surge of hope on hearing of the revolt. Longing to believe the preposterous story that this naval mutiny was led by a White general, they played into the hands of the Communist propagandists by starting to organise supplies and financial aid. Proletarian support for the uprising was immediately undermined.

In Petrograd itself, 'the numbers of arrested people are growing', the former professor of law at St Petersburg university recorded. 'As prisons are overfilled, some of the prisoners are sent to Vologda, on average, up to 800 people a day. They are removing activist elements, not just those of today, but potential ones, including families, children . . . They are now really being brutal.' One of the last cries of protest by the rebel sailors had been: 'All of Soviet Russia has been turned into an all-Russia penal colony.'

Military preparations went ahead with great speed under Trotsky's preferred commander, Tukhachevsky. Concerned that Russian troops might sympathise with the rebels, Tukhachevsky brought in the

Bashkir Brigade as one the main formations for the assault, as well as the completely reliable Special Regiment for counter-insurgency. He had the 27th Rifle Division with four brigades ready for the occupation of Kronstadt.

The fortress and batteries would have to be attacked across the ice from the Karelian Isthmus to the north, and Oranienbaum on the southern shoreline. A command centre in the Winter Palace was desperate to find 2,000 white medical coats to use as snow camouflage for the assault troops. In a 'very urgent and secret' telephone call they found that there were only old and dirty ones available. 'Well, it's not very nice that they are torn and with blood stains,' the commissar, acknowledged, but they would have to do. The defenders meanwhile longed for a sudden thaw so that the ice would crack under their attackers, but instead the temperature dropped with a blizzard.

On the evening of 7 March, Tukhachevsky's bombardment began with Red Army artillery, followed by the coastal batteries of the fortress of Krasnaya Gorka. Next day, the 12-inch guns of the battleship *Petropavlovsk* replied, severely damaging Krasnaya Gorka 'with heavy fire'. Attacks that day across the ice from both north and south failed. Snow capes improvised from sheets and the doctors' white coats did not conceal Tukhachevsky's men sufficiently, even though they had advanced in extended order to avoid putting too much weight on the ice. Machine guns swept the Gulf of Finland and shells fired towards the southern shore smashed the ice to drown a number of soldiers.

Military commanders, unsure of the reliability of their men, had demanded Communist Party members stiffen their political will. 'We received 77 Communists,' a commander called Avrov complained. 'Ten of them are reliable, the rest are mere boys. Against these Kronstadt people we need cutthroats, not boys. Yesterday I sent a coded telephonogram to Zinoviev, asking for 200 good men who will fight. A Red commander from Kronstadt defected to us yesterday. He told us about trainees who surrendered in Kronstadt, having been lured by the rebels. A company of the 561st Regiment refused to advance; also men from another battalion. They are purging those units today.'

On 9 March, the propaganda lie was developed further. 'At the regular session of the Petrograd Soviet Executive Committee, Zinoviev informed the Committee that, according to their information, Tsarist officers were making their way from Finland.' Further failed offensives made Tukhachevsky's troops even more reluctant to attack former comrades, especially at a time when the civil war was supposed to have finished. With large numbers of reinforcements, they outnumbered the 16,000 rebel sailors three to one. Aircraft bombed the Kronstadt defences on Kotlin Island, to little effect. Peter the Great's fortress was proving a far tougher objective than the Communist leadership had imagined. At the same time, the rebels were dejected at the lack of support they were receiving from the rest of the working class. Famished and physically weakened, they proved susceptible to Soviet promises of increased rations and market liberalisation.

In the early hours of 17 March, Red forces set off across the ice in a milky mist that began to disperse as they closed with the line of forts stretching out from Kotlin Island. They suffered fearful casualties, with hundreds dead and several thousand wounded, yet by midnight they had secured most of the island and gun batteries. The next day, 18 March, happened to coincide with a failed Communist revolt in Berlin and the fiftieth anniversary of the Paris Commune. Tukhachevsky's headquarters signalled 'Kronstadt has been taken by our units. Rebels fled to Finland, part of them scattered around Kotlin Island'. Four brigades were to secure the area. The Special Regiment was to take over the iced-in battleships *Petropavlovsk* and *Sevastopol*. 'Revolutionary discipline must be re-established.'

Altogether some 9,000 sailors and their supporters fled north over the ice to Finnish territory. An unidentified report in the Soviet navy archives describes the situation there. 'Within a few hours, the coast, especially Terijoki, turned into a veritable refugee camp. The Finnish administration and military tackled an impossible task. Patrols were sent to the coast to direct refugees on to Terijoki, where they were disarmed, split into groups and mostly accommodated in empty dachas. Refugees kept arriving all day on 18 March. As well as Red Army soldiers and sailors, there were civilians, women and children. There were a few men with light wounds.' Quite a number had fled over the ice barefoot. All were famished and the American Red Cross rushed in provisions. One of the refugees was General Kozlovsky, who was interrogated by the Finnish 'central security police'.

Communist authorities felt compelled to perpetuate the lie of White involvement in the uprising. 'Part of the Kronstadt rebels have left for Finland,' the 7th Army was informed in an order. 'It cannot be ruled out that they will attempt, together with White Guard formations in

Finland, to undertake an attack on the Kronstadt Fortress to take it.

'On the morning of 18 March refugees stated that around 3,000 sailors who stayed in the Kronstadt forts, will fight up to the last round, which they will use to shoot themselves.' Later arrivals reported that 'executions are being carried out on the ice in front of the fort.' Burning with anger, the rebel sailors faced the firing squads. They shouted out 'Long live the Communist International!' 'Long live the World Revolution!'

The Revolution devours its own. Tukhachesky's troops crushing the Kronstadt uprising.

CONCLUSION

The Devil's Apprentice

The Whites lost the civil war largely because of their inflexibility, including their refusal to contemplate land reform until it was far too late or to allow any autonomy to the nationalities of the Tsarist Empire. Their civil administration was so useless that it barely existed. Paradoxically, they also lost for reasons very similar to the way the left-wing side lost the Spanish Civil War less than two decades later. In Spain, the fractious anti-fascist alliance of the Republic could not hope to prevail against Franco's disciplined and militarised regime. In Russia, an utterly incompatible alliance of Socialist Revolutionaries and reactionary monarchists stood little chance against a single-minded Communist dictatorship.

Extremes fed on each other in both cases, and the vicious circle of rhetoric and violence was a major factor leading to the rise of Hitler and the Second World War itself. For far too long we have made the mistake of talking about wars as a single entity, when they are often a conglomeration of different conflicts, mixing national resentments, ethnic hatreds and class warfare. And when it comes to civil wars, there is also a clash of centralism against regionalism and authoritarianism against libertarianism. The idea of a purely 'Russian' civil war is another misleading simplification. It prompted one historian recently to describe it instead as 'a world war condensed'.

A number of historians have rightly emphasised the point that the February revolution in 1917 did not provoke a counter-revolution. The overthrow of the Tsarist regime prompted a wide variety of reactions among the former ruling class: a resignation to events, a bitterness at the incompetence and obstinacy of the imperial court, yet also an initial optimism among its more liberal and idealistic members. Most of the nobility and bourgeoisie supported the Provisional Government in the hope that it would at least restrain the worst excesses and keep the country together. The initial absence of any attempt to fight back illustrated not so much apathy, as the feeling that there was little of the *ancien regime* left that was worth defending. A determination to resist only began to develop during the summer, when the Bolshevik programme polarised opinion. The question is important when it comes to the origins of the civil war itself, which led to the deaths of up to 12 million people, the utter impoverishment of the whole country and suffering on an unimaginable scale.

Konstantin Paustovsky lamented the lost opportunity for democratic change. 'The idyllic aspect of the first days of the Revolution was disappearing. Whole worlds were shaking and falling to the ground. Most of the intelligentsia lost its head, that great humanist Russian intelligentsia which had been the child of Pushkin and Herzen, of Tolstoy and Chekhov. It had known how to create high spiritual values, but with only a few exceptions it proved helpless at creating the organisation of a state.'

Spiritual values never stood a chance against a fanatical determination to destroy all those of the past, both good and bad. No country can escape the ghosts of its past, least of all Russia. The writer and critic Viktor Shklovsky compared the Bolsheviks to the devil's apprentice who, in an old Russian folk tale, boasted that he knew how to rejuvenate an old man. To restore his youth, he first needed to burn him up. So, the apprentice set him on fire, but then found that he could not revive him.

Fratricidal wars are bound to be cruel because of their lack of definable front lines, because of their instant extension into civilian life, and because of the terrible hatreds and suspicions which they engender. The fighting right across the Eurasian land-mass was violent beyond belief, especially the unspeakable cruelty of Cossack atamans in Siberia. Even that arch-conservative politician V.V. Shulgin believed that one of the major reasons for the failure of the Whites was a 'moral collapse' – that they behaved as badly as their Bolshevik enemy. There was, nevertheless, one subtle yet important difference. All too often Whites represented the worst examples of humanity. For ruthless inhumanity, however, the Bolsheviks were unbeatable.

Glossary

Anarchist   The left-libertarian anti-statist ideology of Anarchism
            flourished in Russia and Spain in the latter part of the
            nineteenth century and was almost as strongly opposed
            to Marxism and Bolshevism as it was to Tsarism and
            capitalism.

Bolshevik   See RSDLP.

burzhui   The revolutionary term for a member of the bourgeoisie
            who were presumed to be counter-revolutionaries.

Cheka   The acronym for the *Vserossiiskaya chrezvychainaya
            komissiya po borbe s kontrrevolyutsiei i sabotazhem.*
            This was the All-Russia Extraordinary Commission for
            combatting counter-revolution, profiteering and sabotage
            founded by Feliks Dzerzhinsky which later evolved into
            the OGPU, the NKVD and the KGB.

Chokha   Cossack or Caucasian tunic with cartridge holders
            angled on breast.

Esaul   A captain of Cossack cavalry commanding a squadron
            or *sotnia*, in theory of a hundred men.

Greens   Partisan groups of deserters and those who had avoided
            conscription by Reds or Whites. They were called Greens
            because most of them lived in forests.

isba   Russian peasant house or log cabin.

junkers   Officer cadets generally between the ages of 12 and
            17 from military schools who rallied in support of the
            Provisional Government against the Bolsheviks from just
            before the October Revolution.

Kadets   The Kadets or KDs were members of the conservative
            Konstitutsionno-demokraticheskaya partiya, a centre
            right party.

Krug   The assembly of Don Cossacks which proclaimed an
            independent Don Republic in May 1918 on expelling the
            Soviet administration and its Red Guard supporters.

Menshevik See RSDLP.

OSVAG   The acronym for *OSVedomitelnoe Agentsvo*, the
           information agency or propaganda arm of the Volunteer
           Army and then the Armed Forces of Southern Russia.

RSFSR   The Russian Soviet Federative Socialist Republic was
           proclaimed by the Fifth All-Russian Congress of Soviets
           in July 1918. In January 1924 it became the Union of
           Soviet Socialist Republics.

RSDLP   In 1903, the the Russian Social Democratic Labour Party
           split between the so-called Menshevik (minority) faction
           led by Julius Martov and the Bolshevik (majority) faction
           led by Vladimir Lenin.

sotnia   A military group, or squadron, of a hundred Cossacks,
           but the term was also used in *chornaya sotnia* – the
           'black hundreds', the anti-Semitic reactionaries, sup-
           ported by Tsar Nicholas II.

Soviet   A committee, originally of revolutionary worker or sol-
           dier delegates. The Bolsheviks, having achieved control
           of the key Soviets in the autumn of 1917, then turned
           them into administrative organs carrying out the orders
           of their government, the Sovnarkom.

Sovnarkom The acronym for Sovet Narodnykh Komissarov, the
           Council of People's Commissars, which was essentially
           the Bolshevik cabinet, with Lenin as chairman.

SRs   The mainly rural-based Socialist Revolutionary Party
           divided into Left SRs and Right SRs during the autumn
           of 1917, with the Left Socialist Revolutionaries support-
           ing the Bolsheviks in the hope that Lenin would follow
           their agrarian reforms all the way through. When they
           found that they had been tricked, they rebelled without
           success the following year.

stanitsa   A Cossack settlement, varying in size from a village up
           to a town.

tachanka   A fast, four-wheeled cart or droshky with a machine
           gun mounted on it and used rather like a Roman chariot
           hauled by two or three horses. The crew usually con-
           sisted of a driver and gunner, but sometimes held up to
           four fighters.

ACKNOWLEDGEMENTS

A project of this scope has naturally depended on a great deal of help from many people in a number of countries and I am deeply grateful to them all. In Poland Anastazja Pindor was once again of great assistance in the archives and libraries. Michael Hödl collected material in Vienna and in Ukraine Aleksei Statsenko and Oleksii Ivashyn delved in the Kyiv archives. Oleksii, at the time of writing, is now a rifleman/medic with the 10th Independent Rifle Battalion of Territorial Defence. At Stanford I was helped by Sarah Patton at the Hoover Institution Archives, as well as advised on sources by Professor Norman Naimark and Anatol Shmelev, the Robert Conquest curator for Russia. I am also very grateful to Allen Packwood and his staff at the Churchill Archives Centre in Cambridge as well as the Liddell Hart Centre for Military Archives at King's College London.

The greatest and most essential contribution of all came from my friend and partner in history, Dr Lyubov Vinogradova, with whom I first worked twenty-eight years ago when we began researching *Stalingrad*. This book, which is dedicated to her, would never have been possible without her work in so many archives over the last five years and her inspired selection of material.

I am also indebted to a number of others for their assistance on sources, including Anne Applebaum, Sebastian Cox, Angelica von Hase, Sir Max Hastings, James Holland, Sue Lucas, Hugo Vickers and Antony Wynn. Orlando Figes, Sir Rodric Braithwaite and Dr Vinogradova were all kind enough to have read the first draft and corrected mistakes. Any which remain are of course entirely my fault.

I have been most fortunate in my editors at Weidenfeld & Nicolson, especially Alan Samson who made possible my longing to tackle a subject which I had reluctantly abandoned just over thirty years ago. Maddy Price has been the ideal hands-on editor and made excellent suggestions for the ending of the book, while Clarissa Sutherland guided the whole process through the system in exemplary fashion. In the United States, I am very lucky to have Brian Tart and Terezia Cicel looking after me at Viking and of course Robin Straus as my New York agent. Andrew Nurnberg, my friend and literary agent of just on forty years, has been a brilliant and enjoyable companion in the world of books, but of course most important of all, my greatest thanks are for Artemis, ever my adviser and editor of first resort.

Canterbury
April 2022

ABBREVIATIONS

AFSB-RB	Arkhiv Upravleniia Federal'noi sluzhby bezopastnosti po Respublike Buryatiya, Archive of the Directorate of the Federal Security Service in the Buryat Republic, Ulan Ude, Buryatia
ASF-ARLM	Archives of the Solzhenitsyn Foundation, All-Russia Library Memoirs, Moscow
BA-CU	Bakhmeteff Archive, Columbia University, New York
CAC	Churchill Archives, Churchill College, Cambridge
CAW-WBH	Centralne Archiwum Wojskowe – Wojskowe Biuro Historyczne (Central Military Archives), Warsaw
DASBU	Derzhavnyi arkhiv sluzhby bezpechny Ukrainy, Department Archive of the Security Service of Ukraine, Kyiv
GAI	Gosudarstvennyi arkhiv Irbit, State Archive Irbit
GAIO	Gosudarstvennyi arkhiv Irkutskoi oblasti, State Archive of Irkutsk oblast
GAKK	Gosudarstvennyi arkhiv Krasnoyarskogo Kraya, State Archive of Krasnoyarsk Region
GARF	Gosudarstvennyi arkhiv Rossiiskoi federatsii (State Archive of the Russian Federation)
GARO	Gosudarstvenny arkhivi Rostovskoi oblasti, State Archive of the Rostov Oblast, Roston-on-Don
GASO	Gosudarstvennyi arkhiv Sverdlovskoi oblasti, State Archive of Administrative Organs of Sverdlovsk Oblast, Yekaterinburg
HIA	Hoover Institution Archives, Stanford, CA
IHR	Institute of Historical Research, London
IWM	Imperial War Museum
JSMS	Journal of Slavic Military Studies
KA-KM	Kriegsarchiv Kriegsministerium, Vienna
KCF	Karta Centre Foundation, Fundacja Ośrodka KARTA, Warsaw

KCLMA	Kings College London, Liddell Hart Military Archive
LCW	Lenin, V.I., Collected Works, 45 vols., Moscow 1960–70
NAM	National Army Museum, London
NZh	*Novaya Zhizn (New Life)*, Maksim Gorky, *Untimely Thoughts: Essays on Revolution, Culture and the Bolsheviks, 1917–1918*, New York, 1968
Oe-StA-KA	Österreichisches Staatsarchiv – Kriegsarchiv, Austrian State Archives – War Archives, Vienna
OGAChO	Obedinennyi gosudarstvennyi arkhiv Chelyabinskoi oblasti, Consolidated State Archive of Chelyabinsk Oblast, Chelyabinsk
OR-RGB	Otdel rukopisei – Rossiisskaya gosudarstnennaya biblioteka, Department of Manuscripts Russian State Library, formerly Lenin State Library, Moscow
PIA	Piłsudski Institute Archives, New York
RACO	Red Army Combat Operations. Bubnov, A.S.; Kamenev, S.S.; Tukhachevskii, M.N.; Eideman, R.P. (eds.); *The Russian Civil War 1918–1921 – An Operational-Strategic Sketch of the Red Army's Combat Operations*, Havertown, PA, 2020
RGALI	Rossiiskii Gosudarstvennyi Arkhiv Literatury i Iskusstva, Russian State Archive of Literature and Art, Moscow
RGASPI	Rossiiskii Gosudarstvennyi Arkhiv Sotsialno-Politicheskoi Istorii, Russian State Archive of Social and Political History, Moscow
RGAVMF	Rossiiskii Gosudarstvennyi Arkhiv Voenno-Morskogo flota, Russian State Archive of the Navy, St Petersburg
RGVA	Rossiiskii Gosudarstvevennyi Voennyi Arkhiv, Russian State Military Archive, Moscow
RGVIA	Rossiiskii Gosudarstvennyi Voennyo-Istorischeskii Arkhiv, Russian State Military History Archive, Moscow
THRR	Trotsky, Leon, *History of the Russian Revolution*, London, 2017
TNA,	The National Archives, Kew

TsA FSB	Tsentralnyi arkhiv Federalnoy Sluzhby Bezopasnosti, Central archive of the FSB, Moscow
TsDNITO	Tsentr dokumentatsii noveishei istorii Tambovskoi oblasti, Centre for Documentation of Modern History of Tambov Oblast
TsGAORSS	Gosudarstvennyi Arkhiv Oktyabrskoi Revolyutsii i Sotsialisticheskogo Stroitelstva, Central State Archive of October Revolution and Soviet Construction, Moscow
TsGASO	Tsentralnyi Gosudarstvennyi Arkhiv Samarskoi Oblasti, Central State Archive of the Samara Oblast
TsNANANB	Tsentralnyi Nauchnyi Arkhiv Natsionalnoi Akademii Nauk Belarusi, Central Scientific Archives of the National Academy of Sciences of Belarus, Minsk
VIZh	*Voenno-istoricheskii zhurnal*
WiR	*Wavell in Russia*, ed. Owen Humphrys, privately printed, 2017

NB In the case of most Russian archives the format indicates the reference given, for example GARF 4949/1/3/174, stands for State Archive of the Russian Federation, fond 4949, opis 1, delo 3, and page 174.

NOTES

Foreword

1   'nice and amiable . . .', CAC-CHAR 1/3/20–21

1   'Supper was served . . .', ibid.

1   'We are two hundred years . . .' Consuelo Vanderbilt Balsan, *The Glitter and the Gold*, p. 125

1   'The Grand Duke Vladimir . . .', CAC-CHAR 1/3/20–21

2   'An example of the . . .', WiR, p. 13

2   'But people will not . . .', ibid., p. 11

2   'as bureaucratic oppressors . . .', ibid., p. 4

2   'Russia swung . . .', 'Teffi' (Nadezhda Lokhvitskaya), *Rasputin and Other Ironies*, p. 75

2   'Our peasantry lives . . .', NZ-UT, No. 35, 30/5/1917

3   'It is deplorable . . .', Second Army, RGVIA 7789/2/28

3   'Russian revolt . . .', *The Captain's Daughter*, p. 203

3   'the devastating effect . . .', quoted Charlotte Hobson (ed), M.E. Saltykov-Shchedrin, *The History of a Town*, p. xiii

3   Count Dmitry Sheremetev, Douglas Smith, *Former People*, p. 35

4   'There are no sewage . . .', NZ-UT, No. 35, 30/5/1917

Part One: 1912–1917

Chapter 1: The Suicide of Europe

7   'The Suicide of Europe!', Maksim Gorky, NZ-UT, No. 4, 22/4/1917

7   Mobilisation and the July crisis: for an excellent account, see Dominic Lieven's *Towards the Flame*, pp. 313–42

8   'the German stranglehold', Allan K. Wildman, *The End of the Russian Imperial Army*, Vol. 1, p. 113

8   'Having dug . . .', NZ-UT No. 4 22/4/1917

8   'The most recent technological . . .', V.P. Kravkov, 14/5/1916, *Velikaya voina bez retushi: Zapiski korpusnogo vracha*, p. 222

9   'Corpses are still lying . . .', RGVIA 2067/1/2932/228

9   'We collected the bodies . . .', RGVIA, 2067/1/2931/465

9   'The ordinary soldier. . .', RGVIA 2031/2/533/38

9   'It was very simple . . .', Kravkov, pp. 202–3

9   Odessa students, RGVIA 12067/1/ 2935/348–9

10   'Please write to me . . .', ibid.
10   'Commander of the *sotnia* . . .', RGVIA 2007/1/26/170
10   'Another delivery . . .', Kravkov, 14/5/16, p. 243
10   'Dr Tolchenov, whom I had dispatched . . .', Kravkov, 11/10/16, p. 268
10   'We received reinforcements . . .', Kravkov, p. 272
11   'And here we are . . .', V.V. Shulgin, *Days of the Russian Revolution – Memoirs from the Right*, p. 51
11   'chatter about treason', ibid., pp. 53–4
11   'occult forces fighting . . .', Sean McMeekin, *The Russian Revolution*, pp. 78–9
11   'Everyone knows that . . .', RGVIA 2067/1/2937/172
11   'the handsomest and most impressive . . .', WiR, 47
11   'Autocracy without an autocrat . . .', Shulgin, p. 69
12   'General Dolgov's chief-of-staff . . .', Kravkov, p. 204
12   'The Adventures of Grishka', V. B. Shklovsky, *Sentimental Journey*, pp. 8–9
12   'Two Guards officers . . .', V.V. Fedulenko, HIA 2001C59
13   'Whatever the outcome . . .', Kravkov, p. 277

Chapter 2: The February Revolution

14   'The current situation . . .', D.N. Tikhobrazov, BA-CU 4078150
14   300,000 workers in Petrograd, K.I. Globachev, BA-CU 4077547
14   'Most of them were former . . .', M.F. Skorodumov, in Michael Blinov collection, HIA 2003C39 9/12
14   *praporshchiki*, Peter Kenez, 'A Profile of the Pre-Revolutionary Officer Corps', *California Slavic Studies*, Vol. 7, 1973, 147; Allan K. Wildman, *The End of the Russian Imperial Army*, Vol. 1, pp. 100–2
14   'To finish we drank . . .', Maurice Paléologue, *Le crépuscule des Tsars*, p. 556
15   'On the contrary . . .', ibid., p. 557
15   'I am listening', ibid., pp. 562–3
15   'to break down the barrier that separates you . . .', George Buchanan, *My Mission to Russia*, Vol. 2, p. 44
15   'Adieu, Monsieur l'ambassadeur', Paléologue, p. 563
16   'warn your Majesty . . .', ibid, p. 47
16   'Every evening . . .', ibid., p. 564
16   'Queues began . . .', Shultz, ASF-ARLM 1/R-145, p. 129
16   57,000 wagons, Paléologue, p. 586
16   'We never faced . . .', Globachev, BA-CU 4077547, p. 16
17   'I am certain that . . .', ibid.
17   'the dull despair and resentment . . .', Shklovsky, p. 7–9
19   International Women's Day, see Ruthchild, Rochelle Goldberg. 'Women and Gender in 1917', *Slavic Review*, Fall 2017, Vol. 76, No. 3, pp. 694–702
19   'Are you going to whip . . .', Anonymous, ASF-ARLM E-100, 1/1/310/ 3

20   'There was a certain accumulation ...', Sergei Prokofiev, *Dnevnik*, 24/2/1917

20   'German Woman', quoted Richard Pipes, *The Russian Revolution*, p. 275

20   'They are very picturesque ...', Louis de Robien, *Journal d'un diplomate en Russie, 1917–1918*, p. 10

20   'very chic ...', ibid.

20   'The charge was carried ...', ibid., p. 12

21   Pavlovsky mutiny, Globachev, BA-CU 4077547

21   'The army is loyal ...', Robien, p. 11

21   'Cossacks were riding ...', Vladimir Zenzinov. '*Iz zhizni revolyutsionera*' (*From a Life of a Revolutionary*), p. 11

21   'I saw my first ...', Vladimir Nabokov, *Speak Memory*, p. 71

21   Protopopov and Rasputin, Paléologue, p. 587

23   'lugubrious ...', Robien, p. 13

23   'The snow deadened ...', ibid., p. 14

23   'We won't shoot!' Wildman, *The End of the Russian Imperial Army*, Vol. 1, p. 143

23   'Sa Majesté Impériale ...', Tikhobrazov, BA-CU 4078150

23   'That fat fellow ...', quoted Pipes, *Russian Revolution*, p. 282

24   'Asiatic savagery', Brian Moynahan, *Comrades 1917*, p. 95

24   'incarnation of spiritual ...', ibid., p. 201

24   'Gorky was tall ...', Shklovsky, p. 188

25   'to my great sadness ...', Buisson (ed.), *Journal intime de Nicholas II*, p. 57

25   'Cavalry patrols allowed ...', Globachev, BA-CU 4077547

25   'finally understood ...', ibid.

26   'to crush the revolt ...', Tikhobrazov, BA-CU 4078150

Chapter 3 The Fall of the Double-Headed Eagle

27   'Streets were filled ...', Prokofiev, *Dnevnik*, 28/2/1917

27   'Wealthier looking people ...', Eduard E Dune, BA-CU 4077481

27   'saw a big bonfire ...', Prokofiev, *Dnevnik*, 28/2/1917

27   *Stavka* questionnaire, Wildman, *The End of the Russian Imperial Army*, Vol. 1, pp. 153–4

28   'What a disgrace! ...', Buisson (ed.), p. 58

29   'Yes, we've come ...', Shulgin, p. 129

29   'Hatred for the dynasty ...', Tikhobrazov, BA-CU 4078150

30   'I am certain ...', ibid.

30   'Not wanting to be separated ...', ibid.

30   'absolutely impossible', Diary of Grand Duke Andrei Vladimirovich, GARF 650/1/55/83–154

31   'I left Pskov ...', Buisson (ed.), p. 59

31   'Instead of the enthusiastic...', Raskolnikov, *Kronstadt and Petrograd in 1917*, i.,1

32   'We by God's mercy . . .', quoted Donald Crawford, 'The Last Tsar', in Brenton (ed.), *Historically Inevitable? Turning points of the Russians Revolution*, p. 88; also Pipes, *Russian Revolution*, p. 319–20

33   'It seems that Micha . . .', Buisson (ed.), p. 59

Chapter 4: From Autocracy to Chaos

34   'They were filled to the brim . . .', Prokofiev, *Dnevnik*, 1/3/1917

34   'thirty or forty policemen . . .', quoted Helen Rappaport, *Caught in the Revolution*, p. 99

35   'Beat the constable!' A.I. Boyarchikov, *Memoirs*, p. 39

35   'The people's hatred . . .', Gd Duke Andrei Vladimirovich, GARF 650/1/55/83–154

35   'Only one man could . . .', Shulgin, p. 135

35   'Inside, the palace . . .', Zenzinov, p. 39

36   'We, the women, demand . . .', Anonymous, ASF-ARLM E-100, 1/1/310/12

37   'an actor to the marrow', Shulgin, p. 119

37   'The Duma sheds no blood!', quoted Pipes, *Russian Revolution*, p. 303; Globachev, BA-CU 4077547

37   Litovsky Castle, Evguénia Iaroslavskaïa-Markon, *Revoltée*, p. 28

38   'Tell me, is life going to get better?', Y.I. Lakier diary, BA-CU 4077740

38   'I slept badly . . .', Kravkov, p. 295

38   'News of the Sovereign's . . .', Gd Duke Andrei Vladimirovich, GARF 650/1/55/83–154

38   'Everyone seemed depressed . . .', Tikhobrazov, BA-CU 4078150

40   'the incarnation of the . . .', Konstantin Paustovsky, *The Story of a Life*, p. 464

40   'Lots of rumours . . .', Aleksei Oreshnikov, *Dnevnik*, 1/3/1917, p. 108

40   'Go off and feed . . .', Paustovsky, p. 489

41   'the beloved Czar', Cdr Oliver Locker-Lampson, RNAS Armoured Car Division, CAC-CHAR 2/95/2–36

42   'military aristocracy cannot . . .', Kravkov, p. 297

42   'babushka's underwear', quoted Wildman, Vol. 1, p. 242

42   'Dossier of the Revolution', Tikhobrazov, BA-CU 4078150

42   Desertion rate following *prikaz* No. 1, WiR, 14; see also Wildman, Vol. 1, p. 368, n64

43   'The mass of soldiers . . .', Maksim Kulik, *Kubansky Sbornik*, No. 6, 22/9/2015, ASF-ARML

43   'A crowd was standing all around . . .', Maj Gen V.N. v. Dreier, BA-CU 4077478, pp. 317–18

43   'How could the infantry . . .', Locker-Lampson, CAC-CHAR 2/95/2–36

43   'lifted on bayonets', Wildman, Vol. 1, p. 211

43   'In Kronstadt . . .', Locker-Lampson, CAC-CHAR 2/95/2–36

44   'wharf-rats', Evan Mawdsley, *The Russian Revolution and the Baltic Fleet*, p. 16

44   'Mutiny in the *Andrei* ...', Mawdsley, p. 1
44   'the reputation of ...', Raskolnikov, *Kronstadt and Petrograd in 1917*, Vol. 2, p. 1
45   'All of the navy ...', Lakier, BA-CU 4077740
45   'It was not you who ...', Makhonin, BA-CU 4077787

Chapter 5: The Pregnant Widow

46   'The death of the ...', Herzen, *From the Other Shore*, London, 1956, p. 124
46   'at the same time ...', Isaiah Berlin, introduction to *From the Other Shore*, p. xv
48   'a little light-haired ...', Ransome, *Autobiography*, p. 275
48   'In six months ...', quoted Victor Sebestyen, *Lenin the Dictator*, p. 273
49   'predatory imperialist ...', LCW, Vol. 24, p. 19–26; *Pravda* 7 April 1917
49   'Lenin's programme ...', Robert Service, *Lenin*, p. 264
50   'in most of ...', LCW, Vol. 24, pp. 19–26
50   'As an orator ...', 'Teffi', *Rasputin*, pp. 105–7
51   'the soldiers only wanted ...', A.A. Brusilov, quoted Orlando Figes, *A People's Tragedy*, pp. 379–80
51   'Desertion in the army ...', Kravkov, p. 316
51   'Everyone here ...', RGVIA 2031/1/1181/330
51   'Will we be better off ...', quoted Orlando Figes, *Peasant Russia Civil War*, pp. 41–2
51   Mtsensk rampage, Douglas Smith, *Former People*, 94
52   The death of Boris Vyazemsky, Douglas Smith, pp. 105–7; for another less reliable version, G.A Rimsky-Korsakov, *Rossiya 1917 v ego-doku-mentakh*, p. 121
52   'I implore you, don't destroy ...', website of Natalia Mikhailova 'Family Archive' www.domarchive.ru
53   'The countess, who was currently ...', I.F. Nazhivin, *Zapiski o revolyut-sii*, p. 238
53   'In those turbulent times ...', Paustovsky, p. 485
54   'To insist, as Milyukov does ...', Kravkov, p. 312
54   'The foul ruthlessness ...', Shklovsky, p. 60
57   'In the name of ...', quoted N.N. Sukhanov, *The Russian Revolution 1917*, p. 361
57   'The scores of robberies and murder ...', Kravkov, p. 329
57   'On the whole ...', ibid.
58   Transfer of divisions, Wildman, Vol. 1, p. 358, n44
58   'return home soon', Rudolf Rothkegel, Bundestiftung zur Aufarbeitung der SED-Diktatur, Berlin
58   'The men had fraternized ...', Shklovsky, p. 34
58   'The 45th and 46th ...', Kravkov, p. 329
59   'Commissar Savinkov ...', ibid.
59   'My greetings to you ...', M.F. Skorodumov, HIA 2003C39 9/12

59   'He would throw . . .', Paustovsky, pp. 484–5
59   'I am full of joy . . .', Lakier, BA-CU 4077740

Chapter 6: The Kerensky Offensive and July Days

61   'The nearer we approached . . .', CAC-CHAR 2/95/2–36
61   'fervent appeal . . .', ibid.
62   'I don't think that even . . .', Shklovsky, p. 29
62   'The officers are . . .', RGVIA 2067/1/3868/244
62   'ready at any moment . . .', Sukhanov, p. 380
65   'to encourage . . .', etc., Locker-Lampson, CAC-CHAR 2/95/2–36
65   'magnificent dash . . .', ibid.
65   'distraught beyond belief', ibid.
65   'Mr Kerensky . . .', ibid.
66   'There was noise . . .', Prokoviev, *Dnevnik*, 1/7/1917
66   'Our soldiers were scratching . . .', Shklovsky, p. 44
66   'While going through . . .', ibid. p. 48
66   Kalush and 23rd Division, Wildman, vol. 2, p. 99
67   'Those who had doubts . . .', Maksim Kulik, *Kubansky Sbornik*, No. 6
      22/9/2015, ASF-ARML
67   'Without it . . .', Locker-Lampson, CAC-CHAR 2/95/2–36
68   Colonel Nikitin, see McMeekin, pp. 165–9
68   'We never called . . .', Sukhanov, p. 429
69   'Arrest the Executive Committee. . .,' ibid., 431
69   Inflation in 1917, S.A. Smith, *Russia in Revolution – An Empire in Crisis*,
      p. 143
69   'The prices are crazy . . .', Prokofiev, *Dnevnik*, 1/7/1917
70   'apparently under Anarchist . . .', etc., Raskolnikov, VII.1
70   'the Party always kept . . .', ibid.
70   'Kronstadt as a symbol . . .', Raskolnikov VII.2
71   'The sailors formed up . . .', ibid.
71   'The frightening sortie . . .', NZ-UT, No. 74, 14/7/1917
71   'The Kronstadters have . . .', Raskolnikov, VII.2
72   forged ten-rouble notes, Globachev, 5/7/1917, BA-CU 4077547; Pipes,
      Russian Revolution, p. 412
72   Lenin in Alliluev apartment, Service, *Lenin*, p. 282–3

Chapter 7: Kornilov

80   'Alexander IV', Aleksandr Vertinsky, '*Dorogoi dlinnoyu*' (The Long
      Road), p. 27
80   'utterly crushed . . .', Shklovsky, p. 62
81   'assist them by placing . . .', Buchanan *My Mission*, Vol. 2, p. 173
82   Moscow State conference, see Figes, *People's Tragedy*, pp. 448–9; Pipes,
      Russian Revolution, pp. 444, 446–7
83   'upstarts on the . . .', Sukhanov, p. 495
83   'Who was the . . .', 'Now do you see . . .', ibid., p. 497

84 'no less than . . .', Wildman, Vol 2, pp. 134–6
86 'The Corps will . . .', quoted Gen Alekseev in letter to Milyukov, 12/9/1917, Borel Collection, BA-CU 4078202
86 'Russian citizens! . . .', RGAVMF R-21/1/25/37
86 'His staff subsequently . . .', Locker-Lampson to First Ld Admiralty, 5/12/17, CAC-CHAR 2/95/73–81
87 'Mannerheim reacted . . .', Dreier, BA-CU 4077478
87 'evasiveness', Alekseev diary, Borel Collection, BA-CU 4078202
87 'Minister Kerensky . . .', RGAVMF R-21/1/25–26/36
87 'Urgent. To Naval . . .', RGAVMF R-21/1/25/26
87 Kerensky and Tsentrobalt, RGAVMF R-21/1/25–26/36
87 'the 2nd Baltic Guards . . .', Tsentroflot to Kerensky, 29/8/1917, RGAVMF R-21/1/25–26/41
87 'would rather die than . . .', 30/8/1917, RGAVMF R-21/1/25/59
88 'to occupy and hold . . .', RGAVMF R-21/1/25/15
88 'for the sake of . . .', RGAVMF R-21/1/25/23
88 'railway tracks have been . . .', RGVAMF R-21/1/25–26/36
88 'seven trains of Don Cossacks . . .', RGVAMF R-21/1/25–26/49
88 'The agitated crowd . . .', Maksim Kulik, *Kubansky Sbornik*, No. 6, ASF-ARML
89 'spree of violence', RGAVMF R-21/1/24/10
89 'to be at the disposal . . .', 31/8/1917, RGAVMF R-21/1/24
89 'Generals Kornilov, Lukomsky . . .', Chairman of Tsentroflot, Magnitsky, RGVAMF R-21/1/25–26
89 'The last card . . .', quoted W. Bruce Lincoln, *Passage Through Armageddon*, p. 423
89 'Greatly respected . . .', Borel Collection, BA-CU 4078202
89 'The corps commander . . .', Abramov of Tsentroflot, RGVAMF R-21/1/25/40
90 'The prisoners were brought . . .', Lieutenant Il'in, ASF-ARLM E-27 1/1/109, p. 24
90 Wrangel to Crimea, Dreier, BA-CU 4077478
91 'about the unacceptability . . .', RGVAMF R-21/1/23/7
91 'All the objective conditions . . .', LCW, Vol. 26, 25

Chapter 8: The October Coup

92 'His thin pointed face . . .', John Reed, *Ten Days that Shook the World*, p. 59
92 'intellectual, pseudo-aristocratic . . .', THRR, p. 749
93 'The Bolsheviks were a lot . . .', I.I. Serebrennikov, HIA 51004
93 'They repeated slogans . . .', G.A. Rimsky-Korsakov, *Rossiya 1917 v ego-dokumentakh*, p. 124
94 'can and *must* . . .', etc., LCW, Vol. 26, p. 19
94 'Distrust of the Bolshevik . . .', THRR, p. 681
94 'ready to fight . . .', THRR, p. 752
94 'no longer a militia . . .', THRR, p. 754

94   'It was clear ...', Dmitry Heiden papers, HIA 75009
95   'Boxes with the Hermitage ...', Aleksei Oreshnikov, *Dnevnik*, 1/10/17
95   'the openly prepared ...', *Rabochii put'*, No. 33, 1917, cited in Pipes, *Russian Revolution*, p. 479
95   'Although an insurrection ...', THRR, pp. 769–70
96   'With this same purpose ...', THRR, p. 685
97   'I only wish ...', Buchanan, Vol. 2, p. 201
97   'Rumours are more ...', NZ-UT, No. 156, 18/10/1917
97   Historical Museum, Aleksei Oreshnikov, *Dnevnik*, 16/10/1917
97   'None of us went ...', Yelena Ivanovna, 20/10/1917, BA-CU 4077740
98   'cold and raw Baltic winds', THRR, p. 706
98   'Guards officers still ...', THRR, p. 765
99   Ivanovsky Military Academy, Steveni papers, KCLMA
100 'Latvians and *junkers* ...', Boyarchikov, p. 42–3
101 Fyodor Dan and Lenin, Service, *Lenin*, pp. 306–7
101 'To the Citizens of Russia!', 'The Provisional Government ...', LCW, Vol. 26, p. 236
102 'When evening came ...', Antonov-Ovseenko, *Zapiski o grazhdanskoi voine*, pp. 19–20, quoted Lincoln, *Armageddon*, p. 452
102 'As far as could be ...', Knox, *With the Russian Army*, Vol. 2, p. 714
102 'One party after another ...', Zenzinov, p. 59
103 'the inevitable hunger ...', 'frightened petty ...', THRR, p. 784
103 'You are miserable ...', S.A. Smith, p. 150
103 'The working class should ...', NZ-UT, No. 174, 7/11/1917

Chapter 9: The Boys' Crusade – Revolt of the *Junkers*

104 'We shall now proceed ...', Reed, p. 105
104 'But we hope', ibid.
105 'Lenin ordered him ...', N.I. Podvoisky, *God 1917*, p. 169, quoted Wildman, Vol. 2, p. 304
105 Volynsky Guards, Belov G.A. (et al. eds.), *Doneseniya komissarov Petrogradskogo Voenno-Revolyutsionnogo komiteta*, p. 93
107 'Before dawn a group ...', Belov G.A. (et al. eds.), p. 154
107 'Suddenly a boy officer ...', Bessie Beatty, *Red Heart of Russia*, p. 226, quoted Pitcher, *Witnesses*, p. 225
107 'Officers supporting ...', Belov, p. 154
108 'While the firing ...', Knox, Vol. 2, p. 717
108 'The *junkers* capitulated ...', M. Philips Price, *My Reminiscences of the Russian Revolution*, p. 154
108 'Editorial offices ...', Aleksei Oreshnikov, *Dnevnik*, 26/10/1917
109 'firewood, furniture ...', Eduard E Dune, BA-CU 4077481
109 'The shots keep ...', ibid.
109 'There were very many artillery rounds ...', Ivan Bunin. Collected Edition vol viii, *Okayannye dni (Cursed Days)*. Memoirs. Articles and Speeches. 1918–1953. Moscow, 2000

110 'Lenin and company . . .', Aleksei Oreshnikov, *Dnevnik*, 1/11/1917
110 'We had been told . . .', Eduard E Dune, BA-CU 407748
110 'The *junkers* were standing . . .', Paustovsky, pp. 504–5
110 Dutov, GARF 127/1/3/28
111 'He was lean, shabby . . .', quoted Kuzmin, S. (ed.), *Baron Ungern v do-kumentakh i materialakh*, p. 270
112 'His only serious . . .', RGASPI 71/33/2209/1
112 'Deputy Naval Commissar . . .', L.Tamarov, *Nash Put*, No. 10, 14 January 1934
112 'Cossacks, especially the front . . .', *Protokoly zasedaniy Soveta narod-nykh komissarov RSFSR, Noyabr 1917–Mart 1918*, p. 56
113 *Junkers* in Taganrog, Figes, *A People's Tragedy*, p. 526
113 'Due to Kaledin's uprising . . .', RGAVMF R-22/1/5/1
113 Finlandsky at Novgorod, Belov G.A. (et al. eds.), pp. 96–100
114 Value of the rouble, Pipes *Russian Revolution*, p. 505
114 'And so the Bolsheviks . . .', M. A. Krol, *Pages of My Life*, pp. 187–190
114 'I saw a small . . .', Serebrennikov, HIA 51004, p. 40
114 'had not counted . . .', ibid., p. 61
114 'The victors guaranteed . . .', Krol, p. 191
115 'a control post for . . .', Serebrennikov, HIA 51004, p. 46
115 'Something mad is going on . . .', Lakier, BA-CU 4077740
115 'Local women set it . . .', Federovsky, GAI R-1020/1/2/1–10
115 'a nice, quiet capable . . .', WiR, p. 30
116 'lifted him on their bayonets', N. Dubakina, BA-CU 4077480
116 'Generals Kaledin, Kornilov . . .', 28/11/1917, GARF 127/1/1/34
116 'the misty romanticism . . .', Paustovsky, p. 507
116 'You suckling babes!', ibid., p. 511

Chapter 10: The Infanticide of Democracy

117 'The army of . . .', Paustovsky, p. 513
117 'civil war is the sharpest . . .', LCW, Vol. 26, pp. 28–42
118 'class enemies', 'enemies of the people', Council of People's Commissars Decree, 28 November, 1917
118 'Far more than . . .', Nicolas Werth, 'Crimes and Mass Violence of the Russian Civil Wars, 1918–1921', Sciences Po, 2008
118 'I am the new Minister . . .', Bunyan & Fisher, *Bolshevik Revolution*, p. 225
118 'All of those refusing . . .', N.K. Nikolaev, 4/12/1917, BA-CU 4077869
119 'You know . . .', A. Borman, 'In the Enemy Camp', GARF 5881/1/81/13
119 'intelligentsia pessimism', NZ-UT, xxii
119 'If you took the most . . .', quoted Daniel Guerin, *Anarchism: From Theory to Practice*, pp. 25–6
120 'He was sitting . . .', RGVA 1304/1/483/86-7; GARO 4071/2/10/21
120 'Many people, even . . .', Lakier 17/11/1917, BA-CU 4077740
121 'Almost nobody . . .', Globachev, BA-CU 4077547, p. 132

121 'They have started making . . .', Lakier 11/12/1917, BA-CU 4077740

122 'The bourgeoisie are prepared to commit . . .', LCW, Vol. 26, p. 374

122 'lice', 'fleas', etc., LCW, Vol. 26, pp. 404–15

122 'Feliks would not spare . . .', GARF 5881/1/81/13

123 'There is no greater joy . . .', by Aleksandr Eiduk, in Valerii Shambov, *Gosudarstvo i revolutsii*, p. 17, quoted Rayfield,.*Stalin and his Hangmen*, p. 76

123 'burning heart . . .', Mitrokhin (ed.), *Chekisms – A KGB Anthology*, xxiii

124 'Lenin made the Revolution . . .', J. Scholmer, *Die Toten kehren zurück*, p. 128

124 Jews in Smolensk, see Hickey, Michael C., 'Smolensk's Jews in War, Revolution and Civil War', in Badcock, Sarah; Novikova, Liudmila G.; and Retish, Aaron B., *Russia's Home Front in War and Revolution, 1914–22*, Vol. 1, *Russia's Revolution in Regional Perspective*, pp. 185–97

124 'Soviet authorities tacitly . . .', ibid.

124 'spontaneity of the masses', For Left Socialist Revolutionaries in Sovnarkom, see Lara Douds, '"The dictatorship of the democracy"? The Council of People's Commissars as Bolshevik-Left Socialist Revolutionary coalition government, December 1917–March 1918'

125 'humiliated and demoralized', ibid.

125 Left SRs joining Cheka, TsAFSB 1/10/52/5–6, Rabinowitch, p. 88

126 Generals escaping from Bykhov in disguise, Figes, *A People's Tragedy*, p. 558

126 'Near Baku, I saw . . .', Shklovsky, *Sentimental Journey*, p. 74

126 'I arrived . . .', ibid.

127 'None of these tribes . . .', Shklovsky, p. 80

127 'In the army committee . . .', ibid., p. 87

127 'Men I knew . . .', ibid., 100–1

127 'I kept seeing . . .', ibid., p. 102

127 'A rifle, especially . . .', ibid., p. 110

128 Theodosia, Gorky, NZh, 16 /3/1918

128 'Khatchikov eventually . . .', Shklovsky, p. 104

129 For Dunsterforce, see Lionel Dunsterville, *The Adventures of Dunsterforce*; Teague-Jones, Reginald, *The Spy who Disappeared – Diary of a Secret Mission to Russian Central Asia in 1918*; Richard H. Ullman *Anglo-Soviet Relations 1917–21. Vol. I. Intervention and the War*; William Leith-Ross papers, NAM 1983-12-71-333; TNA FO 371 8204/8205/9357

Part Two: 1918

Chapter 11: Breaking the Mould

133 'Anyone who took part . . .', Zenzinov, p. 97
134 'Gusev assembled . . .', Anon. ASF-ARML C-15/3/4
134 'The night session . . .', Zenzinov, p. 99
134 'whistling, rattling and shouting . . .', Anon. ASF-ARML C-15/3/4
135 Escape of Vladimir D. Nabokov, V.V. Nabokov, pp. 186–7
136 For reintroduction of the death penalty, see Melgunov, *Red Terror in Russia, 1918–1923*, pp. 36–8
136 'They were inventing . . .', G.K. Borel, Borel Collection, BA-CU 4078202
137 'a sailor with high . . .', Paustovsky, p. 515
137 Death of General Abaleshev, Lt Gen M.A. Svechin, BA-CU 4078130, 17
137 'An arrested officer . . .', Lakier, BA-CU 4077740
137 'indescribable horror . . .', Bunin, p. 38
137 'The most senior . . .', Melgunov, pp. 89–90
138 The pier at Yalta, Nabokov, p. 189
138 'up to 20,000 workers . . .', Peters, *Izvestiya* 29/8/1919, Melgunov, p. 155
138 'Everyone treated people . . .', Paustovsky, p. 615
139 'Inhabitants of the capital . . .', M. K. Borel, Borel Collection, BA-CU 4078202; see also Globachev, BA-CU 4077547
139 'selling themselves for . . .', Goldman, *My Disillusionment*, p. 39; quoted Figes, *Tragedy*, p. 605
139 'In the very centre . . .', Lakier, BA-CU 4077740
139 'On Tverskaya . . .', Bunin, p. 39
140 'were given a spade . . .', Globachev, BA-CU 4077547
141 'The same circus . . .', Heiden, HIA 75009
141 'the history-themed . . .', Nazhivin, p. 193
142 'Kiev's situation . . .', Mogilyansky, N.M., *Kiev 1918*, pp. 36–7
142 'started dragging . . .', ibid.
142 looting, murder and rape in Kiev, Anon, ASF-ARLM A-94
142 'Machine gun belts . . .', Mogilyansky, p. 39
142 Mass executions . . .', ibid.
143 'The anatomy theatre . . .', Heiden, BA-CU 75009
143 'At night it is dark . . .', Gubarev, BA-CU 4077582

Chapter 12: Brest-Litovsk

144 Recruitment of Stashkov, I.G. Fokke, 'Na stsene i sa kulisami brestsakoi tragikomedii', in *Arkhiv russkoi revoluiutsii*, I.V. Hessen (ed.), Vol. 20, 15–17, Wheeler-Bennett, *Brest-Litovsk*, pp. 86–7
145 'a Jew recently . . .', quoted Wheeler-Bennett, p. 113
146 'Which is the stronger . . .', ibid., p. 114
148 'The bourgeoisie has to be . . .', RGASPI 17/1/405/1–13
148 'inciting the German troops . . .', Wheeler-Bennett, p. 221

149 'the Germans will be unable . . .', quoted ibid., pp. 185–6
150 'It is the most . . .', Hoffmann, Vol. 1, pp. 206–7
151 'Great Russian chauvinism . . .', LCW, Vol. 24, pp. 135–9
153 'somewhat embarrassing', Steveni, KCLMA
153 'In accordance with the request . . .', quoted Steinberg, 18/4/1918, HIA XX692
154 'from the Red Terror', Goltz, p. 48
154 'both my head . . .', ibid.
155 'There was no pretence . . .', Mawdsley, *Baltic Fleet*, p. 150
155 'The Brest Treaty has been . . .', RGAVMF R-96/1/6/118
155 'Shchastny, acting heroically . . .', 'a bloody comedy . . .', Melgunov, *Red Terror*, p. 38
156 'The execution of Shchastny . . .', RGAVMF R-96/1/6/124
156 'Ration cards . . .', Memoir of Ambroży Kowalenko, KCF AW II/1993
156 'We live in a dead . . .', quoted, Teffi, *Memories*, p. 15
157 'they put up ugly . . .', Borel Collection, BA-CU 4078202
158 'prehistoric gloom', Serge, *Conquered City*, p. 30
158 'Bandits get in . . .', ibid., p. 32

Chapter 13: The Volunteer Army's Ice March

159 'No, thank you . . .', Lt Gen M.A. Svechin, BA-CU 4078130, p. 2
161 'many workers had scores . . .', Dune, BA-CU 4077481, p. 77
163 'It was the first time . . .', Dune, BA-CU 4077481, p. 86
163 'Would they have treated . . .', Dune, BA-CU 4077481, p. 92
163 'Of course, we felt . . .', ibid.
163 Taganrog killings, Melgunov, *Red Terror*, pp. 88–9
165 'the complete unwillingness . . .', Alekseev Papers, Borel collection, BA-CU 4078202
165 'The ground is wobbly . . .', Mironov, RGVA, 192/6/1/2
165 'There's been enough talking', Svechin, BA-CU 4078130
165 'I congratulated him . . .', etc., ibid.
166 'The enemy was nowhere . . .', Dune, BA-CU 4077481, 91
166 'Stand up when . . .', Svechin, BA-CU 4078130, 26
167 'My dear, beloved Nyuta . . .', Alekseev Papers, Borel Collection, BA-CU 4078202
168 Breakdown by rank of Volunteer Army, Kenez i, *Red Attack*, p. 100
171 'I act in complete concordance . . .', 2/5/1918, Alekseev Papers, Borel Collection, BA-CU 4078202
171 'The half-destroyed army . . .', Pavel Konstantinov, GARF 5881/1/106/1–14
172 'Neither side took . . .', Makhonin, Box 33, BA-CU 4077787
172 'The Bolsheviks are burying . . .', Lakier, BA-CU 4077740
172 'On the other side . . .', Nazhivin, p. 199
172 'A civil war is always . . .', Alekseev Papers, Borel collection, BA-CU 4078202

173 'I told them . . .', Makhonin, BA-CU 4077787, p. 26
173 'There was great joy in the city . . .', Svechin, BA-CU 4078130, p. 34

Chapter 14: The Germans March In

175 'We haven't slept . . .', Lakier, BA-CU 4077740
175 'They came down the steps', ibid.
176 'the well-organized . . .', Heiden, BA-CU 75009, p. 19
176 'The Bolsheviks vanished . . .', Nabokov, p. 190
176 'As soon as the train . . .', Dreier, BA-CU 4077478, p. 350
177 'a wonderful and unprecedented . . .', Teffi, *Memories*, p. 124
177 'In those days . . .', Paustovsky, p. 567
177 'gathered in front of . . .', Mogilyansky, p. 77
177 'This whole comedy . . .', Heiden, HIA 75009
178 'little Pavel . . .', Heiden, HIA 75009
178 'Most Illustrious Hetman', Svechin, BA-CU 40781309
178 'I can see they are guarding . . .', ibid.
179 'Ukraine interests . . .', quoted Mark R. Baker, 'War and Revolution in Ukraine', in Badcock (et al. eds), iii, 1, p. 137
179 'There were many cases . . .', Mogilyansky, p. 83
180 'Your Imperial and Royal Excellency . . .', 27/7/1918, M.V. Rodzyanko, HIA 27003, Box 1
180 'To the Ataman of the Great Don . . .', ibid.
181 'To the Citizen . . .', ibid.
181 'Like most of the well-to-do . . .', Bruce Lockhart, TNA FO 371/3332/9748
181 'because they rejected . . .', Svechin, BA-CU 40781309, p. 55
181 'All the Red Army . . .', Dune, BA-CU 4077481, p. 95
181 'Our eternal enemies . . .', Mironov, RGVA 192/6/1/11
182 'I need to know . . .', Mironov to SKVO (North Caucasus Military District) Tsaritsyn, RGVA 1304/1/489/108
183 'They are going . . .', GARF 5881/1/81/24
183 'completely new class . . .', GARF 5881/1/81/14
184 'the pervasive corruption . . .', quoted Pipes, *Russian Revolution*, p. 617
184 'They had come to . . .', GARF 5881/1/81/14
184 'The tables were . . .', GARF 5881/1/81/51
184 'to Kursk in order . . .', GARF 5881/1/81/16
185 'Finally, Stalin . . .', GARF 5881/1/81/18
185 'On the very first day . . .', GARF 5881/1/81/25
186 'What permission do . . .', GARF 5881/1/81/29

Chapter 15: Enemies on the Periphery

187 'hunger and the ignorance . . .', 29/6/1918, RGASPI 67/1/96/29
188 'Once a military force . . .', Lund Collection KCLMA
188 'If we receive no help . . .', 19/7/1918, RGASPI 67/1/96/34
190 'principles of discipline . . .', LCW xxii, 378

190 'interests of the working masses', quoted Karsten Brüggemann, 'National and Social Revolution in the Empire's West', Badcock (et al. eds.), iii, 1, p. 150

191 'It is absolutely necessary . . .', Ernest Lloyd Harris, HIA XX072 Box 1

191 'not wanting to cooperate . . .', Pierre Janin Diary, 18/9/18, HIA YY239

192 'Transport German prisoners . . .', Harris, HIA XX072 Box 1

192 'He is a great sportsman . . .', Lt Col Blackwood to Maj Gen Poole, 14/2/1919, Poole, KCLMA

193 'the brutal five-day battle . . .', Pavel Konstantinov, GARF 5881/1/106/1

194 'This time the Army . . .', GARF 5881/1/106/3

194 'Everything was mixed up . . .', ibid.

195 'He would take five . . .', Nazhivin, 200

197 Krasnovodsk etc., Teague-Jones report, 'The Russian Revolution in Transcaspia', TNA WO 106/61; Sinclair Papers, IWM, 67/329/1

197 'The poor native people . . .', Harris, HIA XX 072 – 9.23 Box 5

197 'to deny sea-power . . .', 'The Royal Navy on the Caspian, 1918–1919', *Naval Review*, 8(1), p. 89

199 'They preferred . . .', William Leith-Ross, NAM 1983-12-71-333

199 'The town is a queer . . .', 'The Royal Navy on the Caspian', p. 93

199 'A British General on the . . .', Teague-Jones, *The Spy who Disappeared*, p. 99

200 'that unless the Armenians . . .', 'The Royal Navy on the Caspian', p. 95

200 'The Turks and Tatars . . .', Teague-Jones, *The Spy who Disappeared*, p. 101

Chapter 16: The Czechs and Left Social Revolutionaries Revolt

202 'All Soviets . . .', Harris, HIA XX072 Box 1

203 'We split into groups . . .', Lenkov, BA-CU 4077747

203 'News of the Czech . . .', Yakov S.Dvorzhets, GARF 127/1/3/15

203 'The German government . . .', to Sec of State from Alfred R. Thomson, 16/8/19, HIA XX 072–9.23 Box 2

204 'I opened the door . . .', GARF 127/1/3/17

204 'A crowd of officers . . .', ibid.

204 'On the very day . . .', Dvorzhets, GARF 127/1/3/21

205 'The People's Army headquarters . . .', Dvorzhets, GARF 127/1/3/28

206 Diterikhs, Steveni, KCLMA

206 'the Czechs stormed . . .', S. Lubodziecki, 'Polacy na Syberji w latach 1917–1920. Wspomnienia', *Sybirak*, 2/1934, 42

206 'Its presence . . .', Serebrennikov, HIA 51004, 69

207 'The Irkutsk Bolsheviks were . . .', ibid.

207 'Factory whistles sounded . . .', to Sec of State, Harris, 29/7/1918, HIA XX072 Box 1

207 'consisting chiefly of . . .', ibid.

208 Yaroslavl rebellion, Shultz, ASF-ARML R-145

208 '[Savinkov] bases his hopes . . .', Bruce Lockhart, 28/5/1918, TNA FO 371/3332/9748

209 Colonel Aleksandr Perkhurov, RGVA 39458/1/9/11
210 'sometimes pushing . . .', Paustovsky, p. 540
211 'Long live the rebellion . . .', ibid.
211 'as *agents provocateurs* . . .', Steinberg, HIA XX692
211 'all questions of peace . . .', ibid.
212 'Lenin did not turn pale . . .', quoted Pipes, *Russian Revolution*, p. 640
212 'Long live the revolt!', Paustovsky, p. 538
212 'eight artillery guns . . .', quoted Pipes, p. 641
212 'Comrade, will we hold. . .,' Steinberg, HIA XX692
213 Siege of the Pokrovsky barracks, ibid.
213 'to make use of . . .', quoted Mawdsley, *The Russian Civil War*, p. 76
213 'It was reported that Muraviev . . .', ibid.
214 'Isn't it a shame . . .', Svechin, BA-CU 40781309, p. 55
214 'It is certainly . . .', Buisson (ed.), p. 204
215 'assaulted and raped . . .', Helen Rappaport, *Ekaterinburg*, p. 36
215 'we received two letters . . .', Buisson (ed.), p. 210
215 'The counter-revolution is . . .', Ural exhibition, ASF-ARLM
215 'Alexis has had his first . . .', Buisson (ed.), p. 212
216 'the sanctity of human life', Figes, *Tragedy*, p. 641

Chapter 17: Red Terror

218 Fanya Kaplan and attempt on Lenin, Vasily Mitrokhin, [ed], *'Chekisms'
     – A KGB Anthology*, pp. 65–9
219 'We need to take . . .', 9/9/1918, RGASPI 67/1/95/134
219 Uritsky's funeral, Globachev, BA-CU 4077547
219 'Thousands of your . . .', Melgunov, *Red Terror*, pp. 40–1
220 Party newspapers, RGASPI 67/1/95/ 31
220 500 hostages, *Cheka Weekly* 20 October (No.5), quoted Melgunov, p.
     21
220 'Dzerzhinsky only works . . .', Grigory Aronson, *Na zare krasnogo ter-
     rora*, p. 46
220 'The district's population . . .', Cossack Department of VTsIK Danilov,
     GARF. 1235/83/8/43–52
221 'Sometimes they shot 50–60 people a day . . .', TsA FSB RF S/d N-217.
     T.D S. pp. 149–153
221 'In Kursk, the population . . .', Mitrokhin (ed.), *Chekisms*, p. 72
222 'When interrogating . . .', quoted Rayfield, p. 71; *Pravda* 25/12/1918
223 'Markets were banned . . .', Borel Collection, BA-CU 4078202

Chapter 18: Fighting on the Volga and the Red Army

225 'At 08.00 after . . .', GARF 127/1/8/1–2
225 'warrior Diana', letter from Raskolnikov to Reisner, quoted Cathy
     Porter, *Larissa Reisner*, p. 54
225 'an Olympian goddess . . .', quoted Bruce Lincoln, *Red Victory*, p. 188
225 'The town isn't taken . . .', ibid., p. 59

226 'Suddenly the rumour spread . . .', Zenzinov, *Iz zhizni revolyutsionera*, p. 134

226 'the Serbian International . . .', RACO, p. 52

226 'Our leading units . . .', RGVA 39458/1/7/2

227 'Komuch's evil genius . . .', GARF 127/1/3/66

227 'to visit some . . .'; 'I asked him if . . .', Prokofiev, *Dnevnik* 26/11/1918,

228 'Tukhachevsky, with whom . . .', WiR, p. 72

229 'protection document', Ural exhibition, ASF-ARLM

229 'Proletarians to Horse!', Boyarchikov, *Vospominaniya*, p. 50

229 Red uniforms, Olga Khoroshilova, 'Red Revolutionary Breeches', *Rodina*, No. 10, 2017

230 'A moral "quarantine" . . .', Oe-StA-KA FA AOK OpAbt Akten, Heimkehrergruppe 1918 K358 130078

230 'In the [Khabarovsk] camp . . .', Maj F. Reder Ritter von Schellmann, Oe-StA-KA NL F Reder, 763 (B,C) B763

230 'propaganda is being . . .', Oe-StA-KA FA AOK OpAbt Akten, Heimkehrergruppe 1918 K358 130055

230 Tsaritsyn death rate, Oe-StA-KA, 10 7/7–862, quoted Wurzer, Georg, *Die Kriegsgefangenen der Mittelmächte in Russland im Ersten Weltkrieg*, Vienna, 2005, p. 465

231 Conditions in Russian prisoners-of-war camps, Wurzer, p. 111

231 'foreign invasion', Jansen, Marc, 'International Class Solidarity or Foreign Intervention? Internationalists and Latvian Rifles in the Russian Revolution and the Civil War', *International Review of Social History*, 31(1) (1986), p. 79

231 'internationalist occupation', I.Bernshtam, 'Storony v grazhdanskoi voine, 1917–1922 gg', in *Vestnik Russkogo Kristianskogo Dvizheniia*, 128 (1979), p. 332.

231 Recruitment of Chinese labour during the war, Alexander Lukin, *The Bear Watches the Dragon*, p. 60

231 'Soviet authority . . .', GAKK R-53/1/3/41

232 'not only reliable . . .', Nikolai Karpenko, *Kitaiskii legion: uchastie kitaitsev v revoliutsionnykh sobytiiakh na territorii Ukrainy, 1917–1921 gg. (The Chinese Legion: Participation of the Chinese in the Revolutionary Events in the Territory of Ukraine, 1917–1921)*, p. 323

232 'I feared capture . . .', Shipitsyn, Fyodor, in *V Boyakh i Pokhodakh (In Battles and on the March)*, 1959, p. 504

232 Chinese in Red Army and Cheka, Aleksandr Larin, 'Red and White, Red Army from the Middle Kingdom', *Rodina*, 7 (2000)

232 'In the area controlled . . .', ibid.

232 'The Chinese were very serious . . .', Karpenko, *Kitaiskii legion*, p. 323

233 'the enemy is blowing up tracks . . .', telegram 10/8/1918, Ural exhibition, ASF-ARLM

234 'But the Velikie Luki . . .', Head of Political Department of Commander of North-Eastern Sector 13/8/1918, RGAVMF R-96/1/6/92–9

234 'This was reported . . .', RGAVMF R-96/1/6/97
234 'At Trotsky's side . . .', Reisner, *Letters from the Front*, Moscow, 1918, quoted Serge, *Year One*, p. 334
234 'panic now seized . . .', Serge, *Year One*, p. 335
235 50,000 roubles for Kappel, Andrei Svertsev, 'Tragedy of a Russian Bonaparte', 16/4/2013, *Russkiy Mir*
235 '500 Navy Communists . . .', RGAVMF R-96/1/6/70
235 'the way to freedom. . .', Col. Jan Skorobohaty-Jakubowski, 'Jak legjoniści sybiracy zamierzali porwać Trockiego?', *Sybirak*, 2(10) (1936), pp. 56–60
236 'The plan of the headquarters . . .', RGVA 39458/1/8/1; see also *Izvestiya*, No. 41, 22/2/1919
237 'the Bolsheviks' flotilla . . .', Shultz, ASF-ARML R-145
237 'to the front line . . .', ibid.
237 'All the most important locations . . .', RGVA 39458/1/8/2

Chapter 19: From the Volga to Siberia

240 'Over 300 mobilized sailors . . .', To People's Military Commissar Sklyansky, RGAVMF R-96/1/13/234
240 'Over 4,000 mobilized . . .', RGAVMF R-96/1/13/285
242 'Valorous Troops! . . .', 28/9/1918, RGVA 39458/1/5/36
242 'the brutalised and brazen . . .', GARF 127/1/3/77
242 'witnessed the agony . . .', GARF 127/1/3/78
242 'various governmental . . .', Serebrennikov, HIA 51004,125
243 'On the right flank . . .', Serebrennikov, HIA 51004,130
243 'Russians need . . .', Serebrennikov, HIA 51004,113
244 'many of which . . .', Serebrennikov, HIA 51004,117
244 'to retreat in haste', RGVA 39458/1/5/33
244 'captured a Maxim machine gun . . .', ibid.
244 'Soldiers of the Siberian . . .', Ural exhibition, ASF-ARLM
244 'I was taken to serve . . .', S.A. Zaborsky, 19/8/1927, OR RGB 320/18/1/27
244 'addressed each other . . .', OR RGB 320/18/1/26
244 'Annenkov was a great . . .', ibid.
246 'an ignorant . . .', Zenzinov, *Iz zhizni revolyutsionera*, p. 143
246 'Its reception . . .', Serebrennikov, HIA 51004, p. 154
246 'dangerous man', ibid.
247 'He was a brilliant seaman . . .', Fedulenko, HIA 2001C59
247 'declared in a tired voice . . .', Serebrennikov, p. 162
247 'criminal coup', Telegram from Komuch ministers 18/11/1918, GARF 193/1/1/18
248 'We felt the reactionary . . .', Zenzinov, p. 154
248 'Watch your step . . .', Lyon papers, US Red Cross, HIA 74096
248 AEF American Expeditionary Force, HIA XX546
248 'not received any pay . . .', GARF 193/1/6/19
248 'organized traffic . . .', Kolchak, 24/11/1918, GARF 195/1/18/1

248 'I cannot recognise . . .', GARF 193/1/3/19

248 'excessive Japanese forces . . .', telegram Morris to Harris, 23/12/1918, Harris, HIA XX072-9.23 Box 5

248 'sitting astride the . . .', Steveni, KCLMA

250 'If Ataman Semenov had fallen . . .', Serebrennikov, HIA 51004, p. 173

251 'anarchic militarism', Yuexin Rachel Lin, 'White Water, Red Tide: Sino-Russian Conflict on the Amur, 1917-20'

251 'enormously rich . . .', Fedulenko, HIA 2001C59

251 'Valorous troops . . .', 13/12/1918, RGVA 39458/1/5/38

251 'The Bolshevik press . . .', S. Lubodziecki, 'Polacy na Syberji w latach 1917–1920. Wspomnienia II', *Sybirak*, 3–4 (1934), pp. 5–18

251 The Polish Army in Siberia, Situation report by Józef Targowski, High Commissioner of the Republic of Poland in Siberia, PIA 701-002-024-337

251 'last met as a captain . . .', Janin Diary, HIA YY239

252 'All those unlawfully . . .', Serebrennikov, p. 183

252 'Horse manure and goat . . .', Janin diary, 26–31/12/1918, HIA YY239

253 'A Chinese rifle platoon . . .', Fyodor Shipitsyn, 'V Odnom Stroyu', pp. 498–513

253 'frostbite and disease', Military commissar of the 5th Brigade Zonov, RGASPI 67/1/99/44

254 'The White Guards' artillery . . .', Fyodor Shipitsyn, 'V Odnom Stroyu', p. 513

Chapter 20: The Central Powers Depart

255 'It is obvious today . . .', 7/11/1918, TNA FO 371/3337/9829

255 'They disappeared in the night . . .', Kulik, *Kubansky Sbornik*, 6 (22/9/2015), ASF-ARML

256 'One morning . . .', N. Dubakina, BA-CU 4077480

256 'Well, we went with the captain . . .', Maksim Kulik, *Kubansky sbornik*, 6 (22/9/2015)

256 Skoropadsky, Svechin, BA-CU 4078130/63

256 'Suddenly we saw . . .', Lakier, BA-CU 4077740

257 Grishin Almazov in Odessa, Globachev, BA-CU 4077547/149

257 'The French occupation . . .', ibid., p. 150

257 'monstrous proportions', 'the economic dictators . . .', ibid.

258 'The headquarters personnel . . .', Dune, BA-CU 4077481/101

258 'The unit was marching . . .', ibid., p. 103

258 'Trotsky found . . .', ibid., p. 107

258 'plum-like nose', Erast Chevdar, BA-CU 4077432

259 'Makhno's men bolted . . .', ibid.

260 'Makhno always turned up . . .', Makarov, Pavel, *Adjutant generala Mai-Maevskogo (Aide-de-Camp of General Mai-Maevsky)*, p. 28

260 'I could see the laughing . . .', Paustovsky, p. 640

262 'Red Army soldiers . . .', DASBU 6/68112/FP

262 'the whole population . . .', S.I. Mamontov, BA-CU 4077797

262 'Nobody's . . .', ibid.

263 'a fine-looking . . . ', Teague-Jones, p. 104

264 'a hazy recollection', ibid., p. 120

264 'I remained strictly . . .', ibid., p. 121

264 For Teague-Jones and executions, see Taline Ter Minassian, *Reginald Teague-Jones: Au service secret de l'empire britannique*; Teague-Jones, pp. 204–216; Richard H. Ullman *Anglo-Soviet Relations 1917–21*, Vol 1., *Intervention and the War* Princeton, p. 324; TNA FO 371 8204/8205/9357

265 'Your orders have been . . .', *The Naval Review*, 8, p. 219

265 'tip and run', Teague-Jones, p. 195

266 'had no illusions . . .', ibid., p. 200

Chapter 21: The Baltic and Northern Russia

268 'tantamount to a declaration . . .', Brüggemann, 'National and Social Revolution in the Empire's West', in Badcock (et al. eds), p. 155

269 'due to their poor . . .', Raskolnikov, *Rasskazy Michmana Ilina (Stories by Midshipman Ilin)*, p. 14

269 'Such outrageous lack of order . . .', ibid.

269 'Everyone knows . . .', Raskolnikov, *Ilin*, p. 18

269 'to hurt our . . .', ibid.

272 'It was so cold . . .', Shklovsky, p. 195

272 'threw off allegiance . . .', CIGS to Cabinet, 23/7/1919, CAC-CHAR 16/19/38

273 'of which a sufficient . . .', RGAVMF R-96/1/13/195

274 'Much to our surprise . . .', Captain William Serby Diary, KCLMA

274 'With the defeat of Germany . . .', Sir Robert Hamilton Bruce Lockhart, 1/11/1918, TNA FO 371/3332/9748

274 'Without the active support . . .', TNA FO 371/3337/9829

275 'By restoring . . .', ibid.

275 'a state of general . . .', CAC-CHAR 16/11/4

275 'The foundations of British society . . .', CAC-CHAR 2/106/178–9

Part Three: 1919

Chapter 22: The Fatal Compromise

279 'I have spilt . . .', quoted George Leggett, *The Cheka: Lenin's Political Police*, p. 252

280 'I recognized the smell . . .', Vladimir Alexandrov, *To Break Russia's Chains*, p. 535

280 'Wilson's last words . . .', WSC to DLG, CAC-CHAR 16/20/7

280 'I do not see . . .', WSC in Paris to DLG, ibid.

280 'Following from Prime Minister . . .', DLG to WSC, CAC-CHAR 16/20/19–20

280 'His ducal blood . . .', quoted Macmillan, *Peacemakers*, p. 75
280 'There is no "will to win" . . .', 27/2/1919, WSC to DLG, CAC-CHAR 16/21/34–5
281 'Anselme was very polite . . .', Sannikov, BA-CU 4078022
281 'little Napoleon', Teffi, *Memories*, p. 161
282 'organized a professional pogrom . . .', Nazhivin, Ivan, *Zapiski o revolyutsii, 1917–1921*, pp. 216–17
282 'Bunin, who was one . . .', ibid., p. 223
282 'not much faith . . .', CAC-CHAR 16/5/7
282 'The French are becoming . . .', CAC-CHAR 16/5/5
283 'Yalta is being evacuated . . .', Commander M.L. Goldsmith, KCLMA
284 'The delegates looked . . .', ibid.
284 'During the afternoon . . .', Webb-Bowen, KCLMA
284 'hoisted the red flag . . .', ibid.
284 'A tumultuous evacuation . . .', Nabokov, p. 194
284 'I called on . . .', Goldsmith, KCLMA
285 'For the first time . . .', Sergei Mamontov, BA-CU 4077797
285 'Thank you, my eagles!', ibid.
286 Special Army, CAC-CHAR 16/19/12
286 'way of life . . .', RGVA 33987/1/142/149
286 'In the name of the Revolution . . .', RGVA 192/6/1/13
286 'The relentless struggle . . .', RGASPI 17/4/7/5
287 'so that Field Headquarters and I . . .', RGVA 33987/1/ 174/5
287 'The most drastic . . .', RGVA 100/3/100/17–18
287 'A great famine . . .', Goldsmith, KCLMA
287 'Dozens of workers . . .', V. Tikhomirov, *Istoricheskaya Pravda*, http://www.istpravda.ru/research/5598/; see also Nicolas Werth, 'Crimes and Mass Violence of the Russian Civil Wars, 1918–1921', Sciences Po; and Melgunov, *Red Terror*, pp. 58–60
287 'Deal with mercilessly,' Melgunov, pp. 58–60
289 'thorough cleansing of all . . .', 17/12/1917, RGASPI 67/1/78/114
289 'the cavalry detachment . . .', 15/2/1919, RGASPI 67/1/100/25
290 'The Kulak-White Guard . . .', RGASPI 67/1/50/247
290 'to fight the predatory . . .', Voskov to Comrade Stasova, 1/2/1919, RGASPI 67/1/99/80
290 'many cases of Red Army . . .', 19/2/1919, RGASPI 67/1/99/81
290 'I have had a long . . .', DLG to WSC, 6/5/1919, CAC-CHAR 16/7

Chapter 23: Siberia

292 Gajda and Czechoslovak Army, Harris, HIA XX072 Box 1
292 'staff trains . . .', McCullagh, *Prisoner of the Reds*, p. 108
292 'brought their *Yoshewara*. . .', Captain William S. Barrett, HIA YY029
293 'luckless citizen who . . .', ibid.
294 'the Japanese had shot down . . .', US Army AEF, HIA XX546–9.13
294 'frigidity and dissatisfaction', 7/6/1919, US Army AEF, HIA XX546–9.13

294 'The military are now confident . . .', transcript of telephone conversation on 23/1/1919, Vologodsky to Yakovlev, GARF 193/1/6/45

294 'What a lot of energy . . .', GARF 193/1/6/43

295 'firmly decided . . .', US Army AEF, HIA XX546–9.13

295 'fractured skulls . . .', ibid.

296 Adrianovka killing ground, Captain William S. Barrett, HIA YY029

296 'unwilling to leave . . .', Viktor Pepelyayev diary, GARF 195/1/27/25

296 Semenov and independent state, Kuras, L.V., 'Ataman Semenov and the National Military Formations of Buriat', in *The Journal of Slavic Military Studies*, x, December 1997, No.4, 83, AFSB-RB d.85273, l.185

296 'a Caliph for an hour . . .', Intelligence section AEF, Siberia 2/6/1919 US Army AEF, HIA XX546–9.13

296 'sweeping arrests . . .', Cheremnykh, HIA 92068, 6

297 Massacre of prisoners in Ufa, see Werth, 'Crimes and Mass Violence of the Russian Civil Wars, 1918-1921', Sciences Po

297 'Karlovich', RGASPI 70/3/669

297 'fried', Cheremnykh, HIA 92068, 7–8

297 Khanzin, Harris, HIA XX072 Box 1

297 'Some new recruits . . .', 21/2/1919, RGVA 39458/1/5/42

297 'Young, recently . . .', 14/5/1919, RGVA 5182/1/10/22

298 'Sabotage in almost all . . .', letter of 10/2/1919, RGASPI 67/1/96/186

298 forced labour camps, April 1919, RGVA 39458/1/6

298 'The army will be reformed . . .', RGVA 5182/1/11/4

298 'Although we are now suffering . . .', RGVA 5182/1/11/5

299 Retreat to Guryev, 10/3/1919, RGVA 5182/1/11/108

299 'provided they are satisfied . . .', Kolchak correspondence 1919, HIA YY268

299 'A commission is now at work . . .', ibid.

300 'the Russian Government', Curzon to WSC, 2/5/1919, CAC-CHAR 2/105/73–4

Chapter 24: Don and Ukraine

302 'highly popular with the troops . . .', Kennedy Diary, 2/2, KCLMA

302 'Here, go visit the whores!', Makarov, 127

302 'Shkuro's train . . .', Nazhivin, Ivan, *Zapiski o revolyutsii, 1917–1921*

304 'Girls and ladies pinned . . .', Chevdar, BA-CU 4077432, 13

304 'The faces of Communists . . .', V.I. Lekhno, BA-CU, 4077745

304 'The name of Preobrazhensky . . .', ibid.

304 Saenko, Melgunov, *Red Terror*, pp. 121–3

305 'We examined the scene . . .', Lekhno, BA-CU, 4077745

305 'Traders returned . . .', ibid.

306 15th Don Cossack Regiment, GARF 4919/1/3/25

306 'Cossacks armed . . .', RGASPI 17/6/83/1–10

306 'We would like to draw . . .', TsA FSB RF S/d N-217 T.D S. 135

306 'We have defeated . . .', RGVA, 24380/7/168/213

306 'Makhno is a dangerous . . .', S.I. Syrtsov, 12th Army commissar, RGASPI 2/1/23678/1-4
306 Vatsetis, TsA FSB RF S/d N-217. T.8. S. 127
306 'made the decision . . .', RGASPI 17/6/81/18
307 'This 10th Army . . .', Dune, BA-CU 4077481/113
307 'the Headquarters of the 9th Army . . .', TsA FSB RF S/d N-217, T.4, S. 80-4
307 'the 10th Army was scared . . .', Dune, BA-CU 4077481/113
307 'Soldiers talked about him . . .', Boyarchikov, p. 52
307 'The battered remains . . .', GARF 4919/1/3/49
308 'Moaning Red Army soldiers . . .', TsA FSB RF S/d N-217, T.4, S. 80-4
309 'The streets were empty . . .', Heiden, HIA 75009, 6-9
310 'General Wrangel had not . . .', ibid.
310 'The troops were looking . . .', ibid.
311 'apathetic and lazy', Goldsmith, KCLMA
312 'Anton Ivanovich . . .', Makarov, Pavel, *Aide de Camp*, p. 129
312 'Vladimir Zenonovich . . .', ibid.
312 'to gain our final goal . . .', Peter Kenez, *Red Advance, White Defeat*, p. 39
313 For the Red Army *Stavka* assessment of the Moscow Directive, see RACO, p. 196-8
314 'Such a moment . . .', *Naval Review*, 8, p. 220
314 'Nine craft . . .', ibid.
314 'avoided combat . . .', RACO, p. 115
315 Churchill plea to Admiralty, CAC-CHAR 16/12/41-2

Chapter 25: Murmansk and Arkhangel

316 'There was resentment . . .', RGASPI 67/1/99/27
316 'And we have had . . .', WSC to DLG, 6/4/1919, CAC-CHAR 16/6
317 'consist of volunteers . . .', CAC-CHAR 16/5/32
317 'As regards Gajda's move . . .', Wilson to WSC, 2/5/1919, CAC-CHAR 16/10/4
317 'encouraged by the Entente . . .', Harris, HIA XX072 Box 1
317 Junction on River Pechora, Lund, KCLMA
317 'In view of the . . .', CIGS, British Government, *The Evacuation of North Russia 1919*, Blue Book, HMSO, 1920, 24/2/1919, CAC-CHAR 16/19/24
318 'hopes were entertained . . .', Lund, KCLMA
319 'embroiled in the south . . .', Wilson to Ironside, 16/6/1919, CAC-CHAR 16/8
319 'The enemy who was . . .', Lund, KCLMA
320 Evacuation plans, *The Evacuation of North Russia 1919*
320 'to hold Arkhangelsk . . .', Lund, KCLMA
320 'Cold and windy . . .', Lund, KCLMA
320 'he has really neither . . .', CAC-CHAR 16/11/87-8
320 'In no Allied country . . .', *The Evacuation of North Russia 1919*

Chapter 26: Siberia

322 Numerical superiority, RACO, 165

322 Southern Group's figures, RACO, 164

323 'Here they have such a desire . . .', Viktor Pepelyayev diaries, GARF 195/1/27/25

323 'having democratic . . .', Janin diary, 12/7/1919, HIA YY239

323 'The troops abandoned . . .', Viktor Pepelyayev diaries, GARF 195/1/27/25

324 Chinese regiment, Shipitsyn, Fyodor, 'V Odnom Stroyu', in *V Boyakh I Pokhodakh*, p. 504

324 'The front is disintegrating . . .', Janin diary, HIA YY239

325 'Czech issue', Viktor Pepelyayev diaries, GARF 195/1/27/25

325 'It is much better . . .', quoted US Army AEF, 1/7/1919, HIA XX546–9.13

325 Japanese strength, US Army AEF, HIA XX546–9.13

325 Polish 5th Division, Col. Jan Skorobohaty-Jakubowski, 'Kapitulacja V-ej Syberyjskiej dywizji w świetle prawdy historycznej', *Sybirak*, 1(13) (1937), 3–8

325 'all the sins of Israel', Janin diary, HIA YY239

326 'The Ruler . . .', ibid.

326 'It's an exhausting waste . . .', ibid.

326 'The incompetence . . .', CAC-CHAR 16/19/40

327 Red 5th Army Chelyabinsk, RACO, 169

327 'former White officers . . .', Ural exhibition, 22/8/1919, ASF-ARLM

328 'There are masses . . .', RGVA 39458/1/2/2

328 'rolling stock for . . .', US Army AEF, HIA XX546–9.13

328 'the Russian Government headed . . .', US Army AEF, 27/5/1919, HIA XX546–9.13

329 Rozonov and hostages, GARF 193/1/11/8

329 'the seat of the Supreme Ruler . . .', US Army AEF, HIA XX546–9.13

329 'but their presence . . .', WSC to DLG, 21/5/1919, CAC-CHAR 16/7

330 'Ordinary soldiers . . .', A. Astafiev, *Zapiski izgoya (Notes of an Exile)*, Omsk, 1998, p. 61

330 'A number of shameful . . .', Kappel Papers, 9/6/1919, RGVA 39548/1/1/9

330 'They shoot themselves . . .', Captain William S. Barrett, 4/9/1919, HIA YY029

330 'The corrupting effects . . .', 27/5/1919, RGVA 39458/1/2/1

330 'All those voluntarily . . .', 16/5/1919, RGVA 39458/1/9/11

331 'Our armies have been . . .', US Army AEF, HIA XX546–9.13

331 'A small group of soldiers . . .', Astafiev, p. 61

331 'Most of the prisoners . . .', Captain William S. Barrett, 4/8/1919, HIA YY029

332 'Horses, camels, livestock . . .', 'Civil war in Central Asia', Hitoon, HIA ZZ070

332 'The hasty retreat . . .', ibid.

332 'The role of . . .', RACO, p. 175

333 Tobol and Petropavlovsk operations, RACO, 174–7
333 'I rejoice beyond words . . .', WSC to Knox, 5/10/1919, CAC-CHAR 16/18A–B/153
333 'The Cossack general . . .', V.V. Fedulenko, HIA 2001C59
333 'America's conduct . . .', Viktor Pepelyayev Diary GARF 195/1/27/25
334 Knox complaint to Janin, 29/7/1919, HIA YY239
334 'Owing to the congestion . . .', US Army AEF, HIA XX546–9.13
334 'Dollar Scrapers', etc., ibid.
335 'could not treat as friends . . .', ibid.
335 'When the fighting . . .', Lyon papers, US Red Cross, HIA 74096
335 'Kolchak has poor discipline . . .', ibid.

Chapter 27: Baltic Summer

338 'God Save the Tsar', Karsten Brüggemann, in Badcock (et al. eds), iii, 1, p. 161
338 Stalin and Peters in Petrograd, Rayfield, p. 70
339 Shklovsky in Lakhta, Shklovsky, p. 186
339 'At 8.50 Krasnaya . . .', Polozov, RGAVMF R-34/2/53/80
339 'We are attaching for . . .', RGAVMF R-34/2/53/82
342 'The Finns . . . demand . . .', Viktor Pepelyayev diaries, GARF 195/1/27/25
342 'completely unacceptable', Wilson to WSC, 2/5/1919, CAC-CHAR 16/7
343 'Ruritanian experiment', quoted Lincoln, *Red Victory*, p. 293
343 Gough on Mannerheim, Wilson to WSC, 14/6/1919, CAC-CHAR 16/8
343 Lloyd George on Petrograd, DLG to WSC, 6/5/1919, CAC-CHAR 16/7
343 'We should close down our . . .', CIGS to WSC, 23/7/1919, ibid.
343 'Russia does not want . . .', DLG to Cabinet 30/8/1919, re WSC's memorandum on Northwestern Russian position 24/8/1919, CAC-CHAR 16/10/133
344 'skimmers', by far the best account is in Ferguson, *Operation Kronstadt*, 229–56
345 'sat bobbing . . .', ibid., 239–40

Chapter 28: The March on Moscow

348 Information to Don Bureau from Tsaritsyn, RGVIA 7789/2/30
348 'Our failures on . . .', Documents of the Don Bureau, RGASPI 554/1/3/86
348 'the exposure of agents . . .', signed Blokhin and Ikonnikov, 17/8/1919, RGASPI 554/1/3/41, and GARO R-97/1/123/482-483
348 'We would like . . .', ibid.
349 'The first unpleasant surprise . . .', Heiden, BA-CU 75009
350 'They rev the engines . . .', Lakier, 22/7/1919, BA-CU 4077740
350 '*Urrrrraaa!* There is not . . .', ibid.
351 Southern Front headquarters, ROCA, p. 211
351 'There was no one . . .', A.A. Maksimova-Kulaev, HIA YY323

352   101 Jews killed, Landis, Eric-C, 'A Civil War Episode – General Mamon-tov in Tambov, August 1919', in Carl Beck Papers, Russian and East European Studies

352   'crude demagogy . . .', RACO, p. 208

352   'Rank and file Cossacks . . .', GARF 4919/1/3/61

352   'The Cossacks are back!', Maksimova-Kulaev, HIA YY323

353   'Denikin is doing better . . .', 17/9/1919, CAC-CHAR 16/11/113

353   'Denikin would fail . . .', Carton de Wiart, p. 118

353   'considered that we had . . .', Lt Gen Tom Bridges to WSC, 30/9/1919 CAC-CHAR 16/12/34

354   'Is there not a great danger . . .', WSC to Curzon 10/9/1919, CAC-CHAR 16/11/80

354   'Bolshevism may over-run . . .', 10/9/1919, CAC-CHAR 16/11/81

355   'People of Kiev . . .', Makarov, p. 39

355   'Many of the heads . . .', General Reberg's commission, quoted Melgu-nov, pp. 125–6

356   'after three engagements . . .', CAC-CHAR 16/19/30

356   'Valorous Kuban and Terek . . .', Makarov, p. 43

356   'I consider it inadvisable . . .', CAC-CHAR 16/18A-B/103

356   'Wire me your . . .', 22/9/1919, CAC-CHAR 16/18A-B/116

356   'Pale as paper . . .', Zakharov, quoted Melgunov, p. 28

357   'cavalry nightmare', ROCA, p. 216

357   'We caught members . . .', M.Alp, ASF-ARLM E-100, 1/1/7 (A-63), p. 9

357   'You fought side by side . . .', ibid.

357   'I was not able to change . . .', ibid.

358   'their self-sacrificing struggle . . .', Chevdar, BA-CU 4077432

358   'A country of great rolling plains . . .', Kennedy diary, 6/9/1919, KCLMA

358   'the officers of the Mission . . .', Kennedy diary, 7/9/1919, KCLMA

358   'who rather reminded me . . .', Kennedy diary, 21/9/1919, KCLMA

359   'Mai-Maevsky had a special . . .', ibid.

359   'All the troops . . .', ibid.

359   'out of action . . .', ibid.

359   'some hundred disinterred . . .', ibid.

359   'They gallop forward . . .', Kennedy Diary, 10/10/1919, KCLMA

360   'The Bolsheviks are falling . . .', WSC to Curzon, 5/10/1919, CAC-CHAR 16/12/34

361   'The proceedings commenced . . .', Kennedy Diary, 14/10/1919, KCLMA

361   'the abolition of the . . .', *Volya* 16/10/1919; and Swedish press, *Voenny viestik*, US Army AEF, 18/10/1919, HIA XX546–9.13 Box 2

361   'Orel to the Eagles!', Makarov, p. 162

Chapter 29: Baltic Surprise

362   'to try to make . . .', 1/9/1919, CAC-CHAR 16/11/15

362   'after Petrograd they would . . .', Col Tallents to WSC, CAC-CHAR 16/14/68

363   'The besieged city . . .', Shklovsky, p. 187

363   'On his way home . . .', Makhonin, BA-CU 4077787/23

364   Eating pigeon in Petrograd, Makhonin, BA-CU 4077787/20

364   'due to the difficult . . .', GARF 6385/2/3/17

364   'the moment his troops . . .', GARF 6381/2/1/14/3–4

364   'a jolly man . . .', etc., 'Situation of the North-Western Army by the Start of the Autumn Advance on Petrograd', Grimm, HIA 77002, Box 3

365   'Is it not . . .', 2/10/1919, CAC-CHAR 16/18A–B/145

365   'shell bursts hung . . .', Shklovsky, p. 187

365   'If the offensive . . .', quoted Service, *Lenin*, p. 395

366   'stone labyrinth', quoted Mawdsley, p. 276

366   'on the very remarkable . . .', 17/10/1919, CAC-CHAR 16/18A-B/293

366   'our officers here . . .', WSC to Curzon, 21/10/1919, CAC-CHAR 16/12/202

367   'Ice may form . . .', CAC-CHAR 16/18A–B/258

367   Yudenich's refusal of funds for refugees, GARF 6385/2/3/77

367   'took two or three railway wagons . . .', GARF 6381/2/1/14/14

367   Yudenich's government attendance, GARF 6385/2/3/66

368   'the Estonians clearly desire . . .', GARF 6385/2/3/68

368   'carrying out a policy . . .', 'Either General Yudenich . . .', GARF 6381/2/1/14/8

368   'the former Army . . .', Yudenich, HIA XX048 Box 4

368   Treaty of Tartu and 'Russia One and Indivisible', Karsten Brüggemann, Badcock (et al. eds.), iii, 1, 143–74

Chapter 30: Siberian Retreat

369   'opened the road to Turkestan . . .', WSC to CAS, 17/9/1919, CAC-CHAR 16/18A–B/74–5

369   'Some Japanese openly . . .', Harris, HIA XX072 Box 1

369   Japanese interest in eastern Siberia, *Volya*, US Army AEF, 18/10/1919, HIA XX546–9.13

369   'It is generally known . . .', *Golos Rodini*, US Army AEF, 20/11/1919, HIA XX546–9.13

370   'Japan has no other . . .', *Dalnevostochnoe Obozrenie*, US Army AEF, 19/10/1919, HIA XX546–9.13

370   'Release Lieutenant Ryan's . . .', Captain William S. Barrett, HIA YY029

370   Annenkov, National archives of Kazakhstan, Arkhiv.kvo.kz

370   'an acquaintance of mine . . .', Steveni Papers, KCLMA

371   'If we lose Omsk, we lose all!' Fedulenko, HIA 2001C59, p. 27

371   'was living out . . .', ibid.

371   'against its own conscience . . .', B. Pavlu and Dr Girsa, 13/11/1919, Harris, HIA XX072 Box 1; and Janin Diary, HIA YY239

372   'the overt sympathies . . .', ibid.

372   'Soldiers and their families . . .', quoted Pipes, *Russia under the Bolshevik Regime*, p. 114

372 'the Day of the People's . . .', *Dalnevostochnoe Obozrenie*, 8/11/1919

372 Knox and military mission, Steveni, KCLMA

372 'thin, with a haggard look . . .', Janin Diary, HIA YY239

373 'The evacuation of Omsk . . .', Fedulenko, HIA 2001C59

373 Fall of Omsk, Kappel Papers, RGVA, 39458/1/8/4

373 'covered 600 kilometres . . .', RACO, p. 177

373 'The stranger then . . .', RGVA 39458/1/8/4

374 'Half the officers refused . . .', RGVA 39458/1/8/5

374 5th Army and transfer of forces to Southern Front, RACO, p. 177–8

374 'advised never to go . . .', Horrocks, *Full Life*, p. 39

374 'freedom and power . . .', Fedulenko, HIA 2001C59

374 For Vladivostok uprising, see J.R. Ullman, *Anglo-Soviet Relations,
     1917–1921*, Vol. 2, 242–51

375 Casualties in Vladivostok, Capt William S. Barrett, HIA YY029

375 'Major Johnson ordered . . .', US Army AEF, HIA XX546–9.13

375 'down to women's . . .', Janin Diary, HIA YY239

375 'Please clarify . . .', Col. Jan Skorobohaty-Jakubowski, 'Kapitulacja
     V-ej Syberyjskiej dywizji w świetle prawdy historycznej', *Sybirak*, 1(13)
     (1937), pp. 3–8

376 Poles at Novo-Nikolaevsk, RGVA 39458/1/8/5

376 'Polish Army in Siberia', Situation report by Józef Targowski, High Com-
     missioner of the Republic of Poland in Siberia, PIA 701-002-024-337

376 Poles in Orenburg, A. Zab.,'Orenburg – złe miasto', *Sybirak*, 1(5) (1935),
     pp. 47–52

376 Repatriation of Polish troops, 5/10/1919, PIA 701-002-005-416

376 Czech–Polish railway dispute, US Army AEF, HIA XX546–9.13 Box 2

376 Polish 5th Division in Novo-Nikolaevsk, Col. Jan Skorobohaty-
     Jakubowski, 'Kapitulacja V-ej Syberyjskiej dywizji w świetle prawdy
     historycznej', *Sybirak*, 1 (13)/1937, pp. 3–8

376 *'paralysie générale,'* Janin Diary, HIA YY 239

376 'A mass retreat. . .', Horrocks, *A Full Life*, p. 37

376 'The Czechs treated the Poles. . .,' Vice Consul Trygve R. Hansen, Harris,
     HIA XX072 Box 2

377 'On 22 December 1919 . . .', Col. Jan Skorobohaty-Jakubowski, 'Cie-
     niom towarzyszy broni pod Tajgą', *Sybirak*, 4(8) (1935), pp. 53–5

377 'If the situation seems to warrant it', Horrocks, p. 52

377 'The Czechs have . . .', Harris, HIA, XX072, Box 1

378 'The main reason for the shortage of coal . . .', GARF 195/1/27/12

378 'A revolt happened . . .', 23/12/1919, GARF 195/1/27/25

378 'Russian women! Do you want . . .', *Dalny Vostok*, 4/12/1919, Harris,
     HIA XX072 Box 2

378 'at the bigger stations . . .', Lt JRJ Mesheraups, ibid.

Chapter 31: The Turning Point

380 'His Cossacks closed . . .', RGVA 6/10/131/12

380 Saransk, RACO, p. 212
380 'he had been sent . . .', Bulatkin to Budyonny, 21/8/1919, TsA FSB RF S/d N-217, T. 8, S. 158
381 'Can you please . . .', RGVA 24406/3/1/28
381 'Immediately send . . .', Kamenev to Goldberg, 23/8/1919, RGVA 6/10/131/14–15
381 'I have declared . . .', RGVA 24406/3/1/28
381 'to join up with . . .', RGVA 33987/3/25/1–2
381 'The first shot . . .', TsA FSB RF S/d N-217. T.8. S.99
381 'Mironov is a rebel . . .', RGVA 246/6/1/1
381 'Red Eagles . . .', RGVA 192/6/5/130–1
382 Saratov Cheka Special Department, 7/9/1919, TsA FSB RF 1/4/478/3
382 'Mironov has been proclaimed . . .', 12/9/1919, RGVA 33987/2/3/69
382 'Units were taken . . .', RACO, p. 212
382 'with an escort . . .', RGVA 245/3/99/64
382 '810 Kuban Cossacks', Kuznetsov, TsA FSB RF S/d N-217. T. 8. S. 262
382 Smilga to Trifonov, 7/10/1919, RGVA 246/6/1/38
382 '5,000 men . . .', ROCA, p. 212
383 'changing the policy . . .', RGVA 33988/2/44/277
383 'I suggest that . . .', RGVA 33987/3/52/469
383 'Mamontov and Shkuro . . .', RACO, p. 216
383 'Unless [Denikin] . . .', 8/7/1919, CAC-CHAR 19/19/40
385 'When the Volunteer Army . . .', Globachev, BA-CU 4077547/159 ff.
385 'The disinterested fulfilment . . .', ibid.
385 'as a typical . . .', M.V. Rodzyanko, HIA 27003, Box 1
385 'Local counter-intelligence . . .', ibid.
386 'General Revishin commanded the troops . . .', ibid.
386 'Evil tongues . . .', ibid.
387 'However hard we tried . . .', ibid.
387 'The Governor with . . .', ibid.
387 Makhno's forces in October, RACO, p. 229
387 'for an entire month', ibid., p. 218
387 'did much to split the Volunteer Army . . .', ibid., p. 231
387 'Down with the Commissars!', for Tula, see Figes, *A People's Tragedy*, pp. 666–8
388 21st Division, ROCA, p. 210
388 'double envelopment', RACO, p. 216
388 'withstood seven bayonet . . .', Makarov, *Aide-de-Camp*, p. 156
388 'The streets of Orel . . .', Gubarev, BA-CU 4077582
388 'During September and October . . .', 19/11/1919, CAC-CHAR 16/18A–B/211
388 Units at Orel, RACO, pp. 220–3
389 'To General Denikin, My duty . . .', Erast Chevdar, BA-CU 4077432/33
389 'I could not sleep . . .', ibid.
389 'In advancing on Moscow . . .', Makhonin papers, BA-CU 4077787/41–2

390 'scored a brilliant . . .', Boyarchikov, *Vospominaniya*, p. 53

390 Kharkov conference, Rakovsky, *V stane belykh*, http://www.dk1868.ru/history/rakovskiy_plan.htm

390 'He also spoke . . .', ibid.

391 Better news . . .', Kennedy Diaries, KCLMA

391 'Men and women accused . . .', Kennedy Diary 29/12/1919, KCLMA

391 'In one house . . .', Shulgin, p. 147

391 50,000 to 60,000 Jews killed, Ian Kershaw, *To Hell and Back, Europe 1914–1949*, p. 106

392 Pogroms in Belarus, see Elissa Bemporod, *Becoming Soviet Jews*, p. 30

392 Soviet report of 1920, Figes, *A People's Tragedy*, p. 679

392 'It had been quiet . . .', Paustovsky, p. 623

392 'It is of the very highest . . .', 18/9/1919, CAC-CHAR 16/18A–B/83

392 'I know the efforts you have already made . . .', CAC-CHAR 9/10/1919, 16/18A–B/175

392 'the kind of military . . .', CAC-CHAR 16/18A–B/210

393 'You can have no idea . . .', Williams to Leeper and WSC, CAC-CHAR 16/12/126

Chapter 32: Retreat in the South

394 'extraordinary habit . . .', Kennedy Diary, KCLMA

394 'In his ranting speech . . .', ibid.

394 'In a time of disaster . . .', Chevdar, BA-CU 4077432

394 'This was a hard decision . . .', Makarov, 68–74

395 'It turned out that . . .', Rakovsky, http://www.dk1868.ru/history/rakovskiy_plan.htm

395 'I too can see this . . .', ibid.

395 'Well, Vladimir Ilich . . .', ibid.

396 'corrupted to the . . .', ibid.

396 'Moustache freezes . . .', Kennedy Diary, KCLMA

396 'whilst delving . . .', G.H. Lever, KCLMA

397 'Along the way . . .', Chevdar, BA-CU 4077432/35

397 'Mamontov, stroking his . . .', ibid.

397 'important decisive battle', 11/12/1919, CAC-CHAR 16/18A-B/179

398 'absorb them . . .', 5/12/1919, CAC-CHAR 16/14/23

398 'encourage the Poles to join . . .', 29/11/1919, CAC-CHAR 16/13/130

398 'keep us informed', ibid.

398 'most satisfactory . . .', Carton de Wiart, 13/12/1919, CAC-CHAR 16/14/66

399 'the inactivity of the Poles . . .', 15/12/1919, CAC-CHAR 16/19/88

399 'secret aims', RACO, p. 233

399 'officers' group hostile . . .', 27/1/1920, GARF 6396/1/7/7

399 'It enabled Slashchov's . . .', RACO, p. 235

399 'in the event of . . .', ibid.

400 'A retreat to the Caucasus . . .', Kennedy Diary, 26/12/1919, KCLMA

400 'The crew of my . . .', Gubarev, BA-CU 4077582
400 'Orderlies gallop past . . .', ibid.
401 'As for the refugee carts . . .', Moiseev, BA-CU 4077851/12
401 'The crucial battle . . .', Rakovsky, http://www.dk1868.ru/history/rak-ovskiy_plan.htm
402 'They say the whole army . . .', Kennedy Diary, 29/12/1919, KCLMA
402 'Complete capitulation . . .', Lever, 28/12/1919, IV/1, 114 KCLMA
402 'Wrangel's train . . .', Kennedy Diary,30/12/1919, KCLMA
402 'A mass of carts . . .', Chevdar, BA-CU 4077432/35
403 'South of Rostov . . .', ibid.
403 'There seems to be . . .', WSC to CIGS, 31/12/1919, CAC-CHAR 16/19/110
404 'There were ten or twelve . . .', Vertinsky, *Dorogoi dlinnoyu*, p. 147
405 'Thank you for coming . . .', ibid.
405 'crossed that fragile boundary . . .', Lincoln, *Red Victory*, p. 436
405 'The two of us were sitting . . .', Shulgin, p. 168

Part Four: 1920

Chapter 33: The Great Siberian Ice March

409 'Our horses slid . . .', Harris, HIA XX 072-9.23 Box 5
409 'There were so many . . .', ibid.
409 'Siberia was completely wrecked . . .', Piotr Paweł Tyszka, 'Z tragicznych przeżyć w V-ej Syberyjskiej Dywizji i w niewoli (1918–1921)', *Sybirak*, 4(12) (1936), p. 21
410 Encirclement battle of Krasnoyarsk, RACO, pp. 177–8
411 'The snow was not . . .', ibid.
412 'Only small remnants . . .', RACO, p. 178
412 'Every Russian was . . .', Harris, HIA XX072 Box 2
412 'Polish troops became disgruntled . . .', GARF 195/1/27/28
412 'To be the rearguard . . .', Col. Jan Skorobohaty-Jakubowski, 'Kapitulacja V-ej Syberyjskiej dywizji w świetle prawdy historycznej', *Sybirak*, 1(13) (1937), pp. 3–8
412 'extreme exhaustion . . .', GARF 195/1/27/28.
412 'To Commander of . . .', Skorobohaty-Jakubowski, pp. 3–8
412 National minorities under Janin, Lt Comte Kapnist, HIA YY252
413 'On the night of 9 January . . .', GARF 195/1/27/28
413 'Grief over our losses . . .', Piotr Paweł Tyszka, *Sybirak*, 4(12) (1936), p. 21
413 'like fallen leaves . . .', McCullagh, p. 22
414 'with as little ceremony . . .', McCullagh, p. 31
414 Ambassador Morris, *Dalnevostochnoe Obozrenie*, 24/2/1920
414 'Everyone moaned and raved . . .', Tyszka, *Sybirak*, 4(12) (1936), p. 22
414 Smallpox and diptheria, *Voennyi vestnik*, 5/1/1920; US Army AEF, HIA XX546-9.13 Box 2

415 'covered with dirty furs . . .', McCullagh, p. 21

415 Chita and frostbite, Capt William S. Barrett, HIA YY029

415 'seeing that the present . . .', GARF 195/1/27/25; *Golos Rodini*, 2/1/1919, US Army AEF HIA XX546–9.13 Box 2

416 'that all freights . . .', US Army AEF, HIA XX546–9.13 Box 2

416 'is each day becoming . . .', *Dalny Vostok*, 5/1/1920

416 Patients thrown from hospital windows, Barrett, HIA YY029

416 'The Czechs have intentionally . . .', Reports of 21 and 22/2/1920, Harris, HIA XX072 Box 1

417 Kappel's death, Andrei Svertsev, 'Tragedy of a Russian Bonaparte', 16/4/2013, *Russkiy Mir*

417 Engagement near Zima, US Army AEF, HIA XX546–9.13 Box 2

417 'wanted to share', Steveni, KCLMA

Chapter 34: The Fall of Odessa

418 'British and Italian warships . . .', Lakier, BA-CU 4077740

418 'tastefully furnished . . .', Vera Muromtseva-Bunina, letter, 4/12/1918, in Bunin, *Cursed Days*, p. 10

418 'lordly rooms', Valentin Kataev, quoted Thomas Gaiton Marullo, *Cursed Days*, p. 11

418 'Everything has turned unpleasant . . .', Paustovsky, p. 657

419 'The most valuable furs . . .', Webb-Bowen diary, 26/1/1920, KCLMA

419 'nobody wanted to fight', Globachev, BA-CU 4077547/170

419 'a reward for . . .', Shulgin, p. 169

419 British and French pressure on Denikin to hold Odessa, see Kenez, *Red Advance, White Defeat*, p. 237

419 'the situation could . . .', Shulgin, p. 170

420 'Decisions in those days . . .', Paustovsky, p. 659

420 'Shilling was still ashore . . .', Shulgin, p. 170

420 'Bulging suitcases . . .', Paustovsky, p. 660

420 'It was extremely dangerous . . .', Globachev, BA-CU 4077547/173

421 'Bolsheviks were not good . . .', Shulgin, p. 172

422 'the Homeric flight', Paustovsky, pp. 659–60

422 'A mounted detachment . . .', Paustovsky, p. 661

422 'One of the ships . . .', ibid.

Chapter 35: The Last Hurrah of the White Cavalry

424 'He should be at headquarters . . .', Kennedy Diary, 1/1/20, KCLMA

424 'bombed. With his own hand . . .', Kennedy Diary, 2/1/20, KCLMA

424 'Cragg saw Holman . . .', Kennedy Diary, 14/2/20, KCLMA

424 'greatcoats frozen stiff . . .', Chevdar, BA-CU 4077432/16

424 Blowing up equipment, Captain G.H. Lever RE, KCLMA IV/1, p. 129

425 'the completely unsuitable terrain . . .', RACO, p. 238

425 'manifesting an extreme lack . . .', ibid.

426 Voroshilov, Budyonny and Dumenko, RACO, pp. 238–9

427 'the strength of the enemy's . . .', RACO, p. 242

427 'the least political . . .', RACO, p. 243

427 'the role of a . . .', RACO, p. 244

427 'In the grey dawn . . .', Rakovsky, http://www.dk1868.ru/history/rakovskiy_plan.htm

428 'My dear, beloved . . .', 26/2/1920, Cherkassky, HIA 75105

429 'lost half of his horses . . .', RACO, p. 245

429 'We left behind . . .', Rakovsky, http://www.dk1868.ru/history/rakovskiy_plan.htm

429 'The dry, compact ground . . .', ibid.

429 'There was mad shouting . . .', ibid.

430 'dubious friends', Chevdar, BA-CU 407743/48

430 'pounding the anvil . . .', Babel, *Red Cavalry*, p. 133

430 'Ekaterinodar in those days . . .', Rakovsky, G.N., http://www.dk1868.ru/history/rakovskiy_plan.htm

430 'Soldiers and civilians . . .', Chevdar, BA-CU 4077432/48

431 'A girl was rushing . . .', Rakovsky, http://www.dk1868.ru/history/rakovskiy_plan.htm

431 'It is a gloomy . . .', Glasse, 19/3/1920, BA-CU 4077552

431 'The last of Denikin's trains . . .', ibid.

431 'At dusk there is . . .', ibid.

432 'More Red detachments . . .', ibid.

432 'An acquaintance . . .', ibid.

432 'In the main square . . .', ibid.

433 'spending the whole of his time . . .', Lever, 16/1/1920, Lever IV/1, 154, KCLMA

433 'breeding a moral . . .', Lever IV/1, 162, KCLMA

433 'I had to spend . . .', Shvetzoff, HIA 72039–10.

434 'whose foredecks . . .', Lever IV/1, 156, KCLMA

434 177 refugees freezing to death, Lt Col F. Hamilton-Lister, KCLMA

434 'two British officers . . .', Kennedy, 14/2/20, KCLMA

434 'Russian wounded . . .', Lever IV/1, 178, KCLMA

434 'created an enormous . . .', Kennedy, 17/2/1920, KCLMA

434 'The accepted rule . . .', ibid.

435 'a large hole there', Lever IV/1, 160, KCLMA

436 'These people had fled . . .', A.P. Kapustiansky, HIA 2010C21

436 'he thought he would . . .', Kennedy Diary, 1/4/1920, KCLMA

436 'Many of the guards . . .', Chevdar, BA-CU 4077432/54

437 'I saw a captain . . .', Moiseev BA-CU, 4077851/15

437 'a veritable masterpiece . . .', Lever, 191–3, KCLMA

437 22,000 prisoners in Novorossiisk, RACO, p. 248

438 'They then started shooting . . .', Moiseev, BA-CU 4077851/16

438 'They led us away . . .', Moiseev, BA-CU 4077851

Chapter 36: Wrangel Takes Command and the Poles Take Kiev

441 'the political results . . .', RACO, p. 249

442 'The destroyer *Karl Liebknecht* . . .', RGAVMF R-1/2/25/99–100

442 'The steam-winches. . .,' Raskolnikov, *Ilyin*, https://www.marxists.org/
     history/ussr/government/red-army/1918/raskolnikov/ilyin/cho5.htm

442 'swarthy Gurkhas . . .', ibid.

443 'purpose was to recover . . .', ibid.

443 'General Holman has been . . .', Kennedy Diary, 2/4/1920, KCLMA

444 'Prevailing conditions . . .', Lever IV/1, 229, KCLMA

444 'At Batum before . . .', Kennedy Diary, 18/9/20, KCLMA

444 'You know, we had already . . .', Shulgin, p. 187

445 'Soldiers and officers! . . .', Makarov, p. 183

445 'rampant corruption . . .', ibid.

445 'And forty-three . . .', Globachev, BA-CU 4077547

445 'There are five branches . . .', RGASPI 554/1/8/26

446 'The cottages are . . .', Kennedy Diary 19/4/1920, KCLMA

446 'occasional Tartar villages . . .', Kennedy Diary, 25/4/20, KCLMA

446 'lady orderly', ibid.

446 'scuffle', Norman Davies, *White Eagle, Red Star*, p. 22

447 Piłsudski negotiations with Lenin, Adam Zamoyski, *Warsaw 1920*,
     p. 11

447 Lenin and plans, ibid., pp. 32–3

447 'Prepare for war with Poland', quoted Davies, p. 95

448 Haller's 'Blue Army', Halik Kochanski, *The Eagle Unbowed*, p. 16

448 Kościuszko Squadron, Zamoyski, p. 23

448 'The Commandant', Lt. Col. Włodzimierz Scholtze-Srokowski, 'Geneza
     Wojska Polskiego na Syberji', *Sybirak*, 1(9) (1936), pp. 6–13

448 'All colonels . . .', 'Losy byłej 5 Dywizji WP po poddaniu się pod Krasno-
     jarskiem 2 stycznia 1920 r.' – in Teofil Lachowicz (ed.), *Echa z nieludzkiej
     ziemi*, Warsaw, 2011, pp. 15–19

448 For the fate of the 5th Division surrendered in Siberia, see Lt. Col.
     Włodzimierz Scholtze-Srokowski, 'Geneza Wojska Polskiego na Syberji',
     Sybirak, 1(9) (1936), pp. 6–13; Piotr Paweł Tyszka, 'Z tragicznych prze-
     żyć w V-ej Syberyjskiej Dywizji i w niewoli (1918–1921)', *Sybirak*, 4(12)
     (1936), pp. 15–31

448 'This agreement . . .', RACO, p. 269

448 'Take decisive . . .', quoted, Nikolai Karpenko, *Kitaiskii legion: uchastie
     kitaitsev v revoliutsionnykh sobytiiakh na territorii Ukrainy, 1917–1921*,
     p. 143

448 Vladivostok legion, S. Lubodziecki, 'Polacy na Syberji w latach 1917–
     1920. Wspomnienia III', *Sybirak*, 1(5) (1935), p. 44

449 'mutinous kulak movement', etc., RACO, p. 273

449 'Makhno is popular . . .', RGASPI 554/1/8/17

449 'The entire rear of . . .', RACO, p. 274

450 Malin and Polish casualties, Davies, pp. 108–110

450 'Piłsudski was a very . . .', Carton de Wiart, p. 96
450 'Wrangel has thoroughly . . .', Petr B. Struve, HIA 79083, p. 17

Chapter 37: Poles in the West, Wrangel in the South

452 Parade through Feodosia, Capt Istomin ASF-ARML E-127
452 'morally broken down', RACO, p. 397
452 '*kulak* counter-revolution', RACO, p. 275
452 'with orders to shoot . . .', Boyarchikov, p. 56
453 'During the time . . .', TsA FSB RF S/d N-217. T.2. S.27
453 'the weakened 52nd . . .', RACO, p. 401
453 'The seizure of . . .', RACO, p. 402
453 Budyonny's 1st Cavalry Army, RACO, p. 289
454 Battle of the Berezina, Zamoyski, pp. 40–2
455 'the enemy managed . . .', RACO, p. 287
455 'We moved off . . .', J. Fudakowski, quoted Zamoyski, 46
455 'The situation is . . .', 9/6/1920, Broniewski, Władysław, *Pamiętnik*, p. 260
455 'At first, we thought . . .', Mieczysław Lepecki, *W blaskach wojny. Wspomnienia z wojny polsko-bolszewickiej*, p. 143–4
456 'For the first time . . .', Broniewski, p. 264
456 'The atmosphere was . . .', Lepicki, p. 145
456 '120 assorted proletarians . . .', Moiseev, BA-CU 4077851/36
457 'A terrible truth . . .', Isaac Babel, *1920 Diary*, p. 41
457 'What sort of person . . .', ibid., p. 28
457 'A whole volume . . .', ibid., 18/8/1920, *1920 Diary*, p. 69
457 'It was only . . .', Lepicki, 150–1
458 Hospital in Berdichev, Davies, 125
458 'The time of reckoning . . .', *Direktivy*, No. 643, quoted Zamoyski, p. 53
458 'Golden horde . . .', Davies, p. 144
458 'Miserable, I walk through . . .', TsNANANB 72/1/4/67, quoted Elissa Bemporad, *Becoming Soviet Jews*, p. 28
458 'The Bolsheviks have broken . . .', Broniewski, p. 271
459 'moving closer and closer . . .', Lepicki, p. 173
459 'Warsaw is on the eve . . .', Zinaida Hippius, *Between Paris and St Petersburg*, p. 181
460 'At the indicated time . . .', Boyarchikov, pp. 63–4
460 'to carry out a night raid', RACO, p. 405
460 'Many people were . . .', Boyarchikov, p. 65
460 'Two Guards officers from . . .', KCLMA Lever IV/1, p. 244
461 'burst into the city . . .', Boyarchikov, p. 68
461 'even hanged the delegates', RACO, p. 408
462 'the completely passive . . .', ibid.; see also report to Don Bureau by E. Minayev, 20/7/1920, RGASPI 554/1/8/13
462 Konstantinovskaya, Moieseev BA-CU 4077851

462 'When asked to define . . .', Struve, HIA 79083/17
462 'Their black work started . . .', Glasse, 24/3/1920, BA-CU 4077552
463 'His apartment is . . .', Glasse, 21/4/1920, BA-CU 4077552
464 'A person with his hands bound . . .', Glasse, 22/4/2019, BA-CU 4077552
464 'A court investigator . . .', Glasse, 3/5/1920, BA-CU 4077552
465 'The Cheka is executing . . .', Glasse, 19/4/1920, BA-CU 4077552
465 'The food situation . . .', Glasse, 24/4/2019, BA-CU 4077552
465 'In the area . . .', 26/6/1920, RGASPI 554/1/10/3
466 'White-Green detachments . . .', RACO, p. 418
466 Communist agents report to Don Bureau, RGASPI 554/1/10/53
466 Atarbekov, Moiseev, BA-CU 4077851

Chapter 38: The Miracle on the Vistula

467 'The delegates stood . . .', quoted Carr, *The Bolshevik Revolution 1917–1923*, Vol. 3, p. 192
468 'Lenin, jacketed . . .', Serge, *Memoirs of a Revolutionary*, pp. 108–9
468 'peak-headed dogs', Lepicki, p. 181
469 'kaleidescope of chaos', quoted Davies, p. 149
469 'A few days ago . . .', Broniewski, p. 287
470 'The exhaustion . . .', 31/07/1920, II Bureau, CAW-WBH, I.301.8.402
470 'We shall advance into . . .', Babel, *Diary 1920*, p. 60
470 'Union of Soviet Republics . . .', Robert Service, *Stalin*, p. 189
471 'Poles thrive . . .', Carton de Wiart, p. 99
471 164,615 volunteers, Zamoyski, pp. 74–5
471 'The city . . .', Lepicki, p. 176
473 'The morning . . .', Lepicki, p. 177
473 'Should we allow . . .', J. Kowalewski, 'Szyfry kluczem zwycięstwa w 1920 r.', *Na Tropie*, 1969, Issue XXII/7–8, reprinted in *Komunikat*, 2001
473 'We transmitted over . . .', Nowik, Grzegorz, *Zanim złamano „Enigmę"… Rozszyfrowano rewolucję. Polski radiowywiad podczas wojny z bolszewicką Rosją 1918–1920*, Vol. 2, p. 899
473 For Piłsudski's counter-attack, the best account is Zamoyski, pp. 97–102
474 'Our Poles have . . .', De Gaulle, 'Carnet d'un officier français en Pologne', *La Revue de Paris*, November 1920, pp. 49–50, quoted Zamoyski, p. 101
474 'First we hit . . .', Broniewski, p. 290
474 'broken down . . .', Władysław Kocot, *Pamiętniki i korespondencja z lat 1920, 1939–1945*, p. 98
475 'The battlefield . . .', quoted Lucjan Żeligowski, *Wojna 1920 roku. Wspomnienia i rozważania*, p. 186
475 'The loveliest thing . . .', Broniewski, p. 291
476 'That brief moment . . .', Lepicki, p. 184
477 'Right next to . . .', Lepicki, pp. 181–2
477 'Beginning of the end . . .', Babel, *Diary 1920*, 1/9/1920, p. 90
477 'Sovietization of Poland', Service, *Stalin*, p. 193

Chapter 39: The Riviera of Hades

479 2nd Cavalry Army, RACO, p. 411; Boyarchikov, p. 71
479 Makhno and agreement with Reds, SBU 6/75131FP/Zadov
479 'temporary ally', RACO, p. 431
479 'Makhno broke into . . .', SBU 6/68112/FP
480 'daring insanity', RACO, p. 417
480 'operational freedom', RACO, p. 421
481 'The headquarters communicate with Wrangel . . .', 28/10/1920, RGASPI 554/1/8/74
481 'sent emissaries . . .', RGASPI 554/1/10/53
481 'I managed to make friends . . .', 29/6/1920, RGASPI 554/1/5/10–11
481 'We are dying of hunger . . .', quoted Lincoln, p. 442
482 'Noble ladies and maidens . . .', Vertinsky, p. 153
482 'had occupied a bridgehead . . .', RACO, p. 425
482 'concentrating a powerful . . .', ibid., pp. 426–7
482 'started a decisive . . .', RGVA 33987/2/139/295–6
483 'marked the beginning . . .', ibid.
483 'The autumn of 1920 . . .', Boyarchikov, p. 73
484 'The impassable . . .', ibid.
484 'sabres gleaming', ibid.
485 'They had been robbed . . .', Recollections of Nurse Anna Ivanovna Egorova, *Russky put* (Russian Way) project. http://www.rp-net.ru/book/archival_materials/egorova.php
485 'Wrangel's forces could not .. .', B.T. Pash, HIA 72033 Box 4
486 'P signal in cypher', Clayton I Stafford, HIA 77018
486 'It was rumoured . . .', Pash, HIA 72033 Box 4
486 'Cossacks with grim . . .', ibid.
486 'glowing white façades . . .', Stafford, HIA 77018
487 'The hills! Look . . .', ibid.
487 'He was trying . . .', ibid.
487 'the last salute . . .', quoted Mungo Melvin, *Sevastopol's Wars*, p. 418
487 'When our cavalry . . .', Boyarchikov, p. 75
488 'a large number . . .', RACO, p. 455
488 Figures on those left behind, Melvin, p. 427
488 'From now on . . .', ibid.
488 'full pardon . . .', quoted ibid., p. 415
488 'a lava-like mass of cavalry . . .', Makarov, p. 112
488 'to concentrate them . . .', Pipes, *Russia under the Bolshevik Regime*, p. 386
488 'Comrade Trotsky . . .', Melgunov, *Red Terror*, p. 66
489 Demidov, Ignaty Voevoda, HIA 200C84
489 Estimates and Sevastopol, Melgunov, p. 68
490 'landings in Kuban', ibid., p. 67
490 'the slaughter continued . . .', quoted ibid., pp. 66–7

Chapter 40: The Death of Hope

491 'The vengeful hand . . .', Melgunov, *Red Terror*, p. 71
491 'Our group reached . . .', Lev Zadov interrogation files, DASBU 6/75131FP/48
492 'There are reasons . . .', TsA FSB S/d N-217 T.2. S. 121
492 'You have been . . .', Chief of General Staff Pugachev, TsA FSB RF S/d N-217. T.2. S.29
492 'Everyone confessed . . .', TsA FSB RF S/d N-217. T. 2. S. 452
492 'The Tula Food Detachment . . .', Georgy Borel, Borel Collection, BA-CU 4078202, 20–1
492 'It was so cold . . .', Boyarchikov, p. 76
493 'Cities were sending . . .', Lidin, BA-CU 4077753
493 Western Siberia and Tambov, Figes, *A People's Tragedy*, pp. 753–7
494 'Units sent against . . .', Georgy Borel, BA-CU 4078202/20–1
494 Tomsk and Ufa, Melgunov, p. 85
494 Belarus, ibid., p. 101
494 'Following its "pacification" . . .', Lidin, BA-CU 4077753
494 'Silent people . . .', Glasse Diary, BA-CU 4077552
495 'far more dangerous than . . .', quoted Figes, *A People's Tragedy*, p. 758
495 'A paradox of Soviet life . . .', David Grimm, HIA 77002 Box 4
495 'In the dead factories . . .', Serge, *Memoirs of a Revolutionary*, pp. 115–16
496 'Kronstadt is in the . . .', ibid., pp. 124–5
497 'The truth seeped out . . .', ibid., p. 126
497 'the numbers of arrested . . .', Grimm, HIA 77002 Box 4
497 'All of Soviet Russia . . .', quoted Lincoln, *Red Victory*, p. 511
498 Bashkir Brigade etc., RGAVMF R-52/1/58/1
498 'Well, it's not very nice . . .', RGAVMF R-52/1/87/10
498 'with heavy fire', RGAVMF R-52/1/87/2
498 'We received 77 Communists . . .', RGAVMF R-52/1/87/9
498 'At the regular session . . .', RGAVMF R-52/1/87/14
499 'Kronstadt has been taken . . .', RGAVMF R52/1/58/1
499 'Within a few hours . . .', RGAVMF R-52/1/87/14
499 'Part of the Kronstadt rebels . . .', Order for the units of 7th Army, RGAVMF R52/1/58/14
500 'On the morning of 18 March . . .', RGAVMF R-52/1/87/14
500 'executions are being carried out . . .', Melgunov, p. 76

Conclusion: The Devil's Apprentice

501 'a world war condensed', Jonathan Smele, *The 'Russian' Civil Wars,*
     1916–1926, London, 2016, p. 3
502 'The idyllic aspect . . .', Paustovsky, p. 487
502 'moral collapse', Shulgin, p. xviii

BIBLIOGRAPHY

Acton, Edward, *Rethinking the Russian Revolution*, London, 1990

Acton, E., Cherniaev, V.I. and Rosenberg, W.G. (eds), *Critical Companion to the Russian Revolution 1914–1921*, Bloomington and Indianapolis, IN, 1997

Alexander, Grand Duke, *Collected Works*, London, 2016

Alexandrov, Vladimir, *To Break Russia's Chains: Boris Savinkov and his Wars Against the Tsar and the Bolsheviks*, New York, 2021

Alioshin, Dmitri, *Asian Odyssey*, London, 1941

Allen, W.E.D. and Muratoff, P., *Caucasian Battlefields*, Cambridge, 1953

Anet, Claude, *La révolution russe, Chroniques, 1917–1920*, Paris, 2007

Anon., *V Boyakh i Pokhodakh (In Battles and on the March)*, Sverdlovsk, 1959

Antonov-Ovseenko, Vladimir, *Zapiski o grazhdanskoi voine (Notes on the Civil War)*, Moscow, 1921

Aronson, Grigory, *Na zare krasnogo terrora 1917–1921 (At the Dawn of the Red Terror)*, Berlin, 1929

Arshinov, Petr, *History of the Makhnovist Movement, 1918–1921*, Chicago, 1974

Astafiev, A., *Zapiski izgoya (Notes of an Exile)*, Omsk, 1998

Astashov, A., Simmons P. (eds), *Pisma s voiny 1914–1917 (Letters from the War, 1914–1917)*, Moscow, 2015

Avrich, Paul, *The Anarchists in the Russian Revolution*, London, 1973

Babel, Isaac, *1920 Diary*, New Haven, CT and London 1995

Badcock, Sarah, Novikova, Liudmila G. and Retish, Aaron B., *Russia's Home Front in War and Revolution, 1914–22*, Vol. 1, *Russia's Revolution in Regional Perspective*, Bloomington, IN, 2015

—— *Russia's Home Front in War and Revolution, 1914–22*, Vol. 2, *The Experience of War and Revolution*, Bloomington, IN, 2016

Beatty, Bessie, *Red Heart of Russia*, New York, 1918

Bechhofer-Roberts, C.E., *In Denikin's Russia and the Caucasus, 1919–1920*, London, 1921

Belov G.A. et al. (eds), *Doneseniya komissarov Petrogradskogo Voenno-Revolyutsionnogo komiteta (Commission Reports Petrograd Military Revolutionary Committee)*, Moscow, 1957

Bemporad, Elissa, *Becoming Soviet Jews: The Bolshevik Experiment in Minsk*, Bloomington, IN, 2013

Bisher, Jamie, *White Terror, Cossack Warlords of the Trans-Siberian*, London, 2007

Bodger, A., *Russia and the End of the Ottoman Empire*, London, 1979

Boltowsky, Toomas and Thomas, Nigel, *Armies of the Baltic Independence Wars, 1918–20*, London, 2019

Bowyer, C., *RAF Operations 1918–1938*, London, 1988

Boyarchikov, A.I., *Vospominaniya (Memoirs)*, Moscow, 2003

Boyd, Alexander, *The Soviet Air Force since 1918*, London, 1977

Brenton, Tony (ed.), *Historically Inevitable? Turning Points of the Russian Revolution*, London, 2016

Brinkley, George F., *The Volunteer Army and Allied Intervention in South Russia*, Notre Dame, IN, 1966

British Army Personnel in the Russian Civil War, London, 2010

British Government, *The Evacuation of North Russia 1919*, Blue Book, HMSO, 1920

Broniewski, Władysław, *Pamiętnik (Diary)*, Warsaw, 2013

Brook-Shepherd, Gordon, *Iron Maze, The Western Secret Services and the Bolsheviks*, London, 1998

Brovkin, Vladimir N., *Behind the Front Lines of the Civil War*, Princeton, NJ, 1994

Brovkin, Vladimir N. (ed.), *The Bolsheviks in Russian Society*, New Haven, CT and London, 1997

Bruce Lockhart, Robert, ed. Kenneth Young, *The Diaries of Sir Robert Bruce Lockhart*, London, 1973

Bubnov, A.S., Kamenev, S.S., Tukhachevskii, M.N. and Eideman, R.P. (eds), *The Russian Civil War 1918–1921: An Operational-Strategic Sketch of the Red Army's Combat Operations*, Havertown, PA, 2020

Buchanan, George, *My Mission to Russia and Other Diplomatic Memories*, 2 vols, London, 1923

Budberg, Baron, *Dnevnik (Diary)*, Moscow, 2003

Buisson, Jean-Cristophe (ed.), *Journal intime de Nicholas II*, Paris, 2018

Bunyan, James and Fisher, H.H., *The Bolshevik Revolution 1917–1918, Documents and Materials*, Stanford, CA, 1961

Callwell, C.E., *Field-Marshal Sir Henry Wilson: His Life and Diaries*, 2 vols, London, 1927

Carley, M.J., *Revolution and Intervention: The French Government and the Russian Civil War 1917–1919*, Montreal, 1983

Carlton, David, *Churchill and the Soviet Union*, London, 2000

Carton de Wiart, A., *Happy Odyssey*, London, 1950

Carr, E.H., *The Bolshevik Revolution, 1917–1923*, 3 vols, London, 1956

Chamberlain, Lesley, *The Philosophy Steamer: Lenin and the Exile of of the Intelligentsia*, London, 2006

Chamberlin, William, *Russian Revolution 1917–1921*, New York, 1935

Chernov, V., et al. (eds), *CheKa: Materialy po deyatelnosti chrez-vychainykh komissii (CheKa: Materials on the Operation of the Extraordinary Commissions)*, Berlin, 1922, Moscow, 2017

Churchill, Winston S., *World Crisis: The Aftermath*, London, 1929

Cockfield, Jamie H., *With Snow on their Boots: The Tragic Odyssey of the Russian Expeditionary Force in France during World War I*, Basingstoke, 1998

Courtois, Stéphane, et al. (eds), *Le livre noir du communisme*, Paris, 1997

Danilova, V. and Shanina, T. (eds), *Filipp Mironov, Tikhiy Don v 1917–1921, Dokumenty i materialy (Filipp Mironov, The Quiet Don in 1917–1921, Documents and Materials)*, Moscow, 1997

Dallas, Gregor, *1918*, London, 2000

Davies, Norman, *White Eagle Red Star: The Polish-Soviet War 1919–1920*, London, 1972

Denikin, Anton, *Russian Turmoil: Memoirs*, London, 1922

Douds, Lara, '"The Dictatorship of the Democracy"? The Council of People's Commissars as Bolshevik-Left Socialist Revolutionary coalition government, December 1917–March 1918', University of York, IHR, 2017

Dubrovskaia, Elena, 'The Russian Military in Finland and the Russian Revolution', in Badcock, Sarah, Novikova, Liudmila G. and Retish, Aaron B., *Russia's Home Front in War and Revolution, 1914–22*, Vol. 1, *Russia's Revolution in Regional Perspective*, Bloomington, IN, 2015

Dune, Edward M., *Notes of a Red Guard*, Chicago, IL, 1993

Dunsterville, L.C., *The Adventures of Dunsterforce*, London, 1920

Dwinger, Edwin Erich, *Entre les Rouges et les Blancs, 1919–1920*, Paris, 1931

Efremov, Vasily Nikolaevich, *Krakh beloi mechty v Sin-Tsiane (Ruin of the White Dream in Tsin-Tsian)*, St Petersburg, 2016

Ferguson, Harry, *Operation Kronstadt*, London, 2008

Figes, Orlando, *Peasant Russia Civil War: The Volga Countryside in Revolution 1917–1921*, London, 2001

—— *A People's Tragedy*, London, 2017

Foglesong, David S., *America's Secret War against Bolshevism: U.S. Intervention in the Russian Civil War 1917–1920*, Chapel Hill, NC, 1995.

Footman, David, 'B.V. Savinkov', St. Antony's College, Oxford, 1956

Freund, Gerald, *Unholy Alliance: Russian-German Relations from the Treaty of Brest-Litovsk to the Treaty of Berlin*, London, 1957

Germarth, Robert, *The Vanquished: Why the First World War Failed to End, 1917–1923*, London, 2016

Gilbert, Martin, *World in Torment, Winston Churchill 1917–1922*, London, 1975

Gillard, David, *The Struggle for Asia: A Study in British and Russian Imperialism*, London, 1977

Gilley, Christopher, 'Fighters for Ukrainian Independence? Imposture and Identity among Ukrainian Warlords, 1917–1922', IHR, 2017

Gilmour, David, *Curzon*, London, 1994

Goltz, Rüdiger Graf von der, *Meine Sendung in Finnland und im Baltikum (My Mission in Finland and the Baltic)*, Leipzig, 1920

Golubintsev A.V., *The Russian Vendée: Essays of the Civil War on the Don, 1917–1920*, Munich, 1959; reprint, Oryol, 1995

Gorky, Maksim, *Untimely Thoughts: Essays on Revolution, Culture and the Bolsheviks, 1917–1918*, New York, 1968

Gorn, P., *Civil War in Northwestern Russia*, Leningrad, 1927

Graves, William S., *America's Siberian Adventure, 1918–1920*, New York, 1921

Guerin, Daniel, *Anarchism: From Theory to Practice*, New York, 1970

Harris, John (ed.), *Farewell to the Don: The Journal of Brigadier H.N.H. Williamson*, London, 1970

Hasegawa, Tsuyoshi, *The February Revolution: Petrograd 1917*, New York, 1981

Henderson, Robert, *The Spark that Lit the Revolution*, London, 2020

Herzen, Aleksandr, *From the Other Shore*, London, 1956

Hickey, Michael C., 'Smolensk's Jews in War, Revolution and Civil War', in Badcock, Sarah, Novikova, Liudmila G. and Retish, Aaron B., *Russia's Home Front in War and Revolution, 1914–22*, Vol. 1, *Russia's Revolution in Regional Perspective*, Bloomington, IN, 2015

Hippius, Zinaida Nikolaevna, *Between Paris and St Petersburg*, Chicago, 1975

Hodgson, John, *With Denikin's Armies*, London, 1932

Horrocks, Brian, *A Full Life*, London, 1960

Hosking, Geoffrey, *Russia and the Russians*, London, 2001

Hudson, Miles, *Intervention in Russia 1918–20, A Cautionary Tale*, London, 2004

Hughes, Michael, *Inside the Enigma: British Officials in Russia 1900–1939*, Cambridge, 1997

Iaroslavskaïa-Markon, Evguénia, *Revoltée*, Paris, 2017

Janin, Pierre Maurice, *Ma mission en Sibérie*, Paris, 1933

Janke, Arthur E., 'Don Cossacks and the February Revolution', *Canadian Slavonic Papers*, 10(2) (Summer 1968), pp. 148–165

Jansen, Marc, 'International Class Solidarity or Foreign Intervention? Internationalists and Latvian Rifles in the Russian Revolution and the Civil War', *International Review of Social History*, 31(1) (1986), Cambridge

Jevahoff, Alexandre, *Les Russes blancs*, Paris, 2007

Jones, H.A., *Over the Balkans & South Russia, Being the Story of No. 47 Squadron RAF*, London, 1923

Karmann, Rudolf, *Der Freiheitskampf der Kosaken: Die weisse Armee in der Russischen Revolution 1917–1920* (*The Cossacks' Fight for Freedom: The White Army in the Russian Revolution 1917–1920*), Puchheim, 1985

Karpenko, Nikolai, *Kitaiskii legion: uchastie kitaitsev v revoliutsionnykh sobytiiakh na territorii Ukrainy, 1917–1921* (*Chinese Legion: Participation of Chinese in the Revolutionary Events on the Ukrainian Territory*), Lugansk, 2007

Kawczak, Stanisław, *Milknące echa* (*Fading Echoes*), Warsaw, 2010

Kazemzadeh, Firuz, *The Struggle for Transcaucasia*, Oxford, 1951

Kellogg, Michael, *The Russian Roots of Nazism: White Emigrés and the Making of National Socialism 1917–1945*, Cambridge, 2005

Kenez, Peter, *Civil War in South Russia, 1918: The First Year of the Volunteer Army*, Berkeley, CA, 1971; reprint, *Red Attack White Resistance*, 2004

—— *Civil War in South Russia, 1919–1920: The Defeat of the Whites*, Berkeley, CA, 1977; reprint, *Red Advance White Defeat, 1919–1920*, 2004

—— 'A Profile of the Pre-Revolutionary Officer Corps', *California Slavic Studies*, 7 (1973), pp. 121–158

—— 'The Western Historiography of the Russian Civil War', *Essays in Russian and East European History*, Festschrift in Honor of Edward C. Thaden, New York, 1995

Kershaw, Ian, *To Hell and Back: Europe 1914–1949*, London, 2015

Khoroshilova, Olga, 'Red Revolutionary Breeches', *Rodina*, 10(2017)

Kinvig, Clifford, *Churchill's Crusade: The British Invasion of Russia 1918–1920*, London, 2006

Kirdetsov Georgy, *U vorot Petrograda (1919–1920)* (*At the Gates of Petrograd*), Moscow, 2016

Klußmann, Uwe, 'Kriegsgefangene für Lenin', *Der Spiegel*, 29/11/2016

Knox, Alfred W.F., *With the Russian Army 1914–1917*, 2 vols, London, 1921

Kochanski, Halik, *The Eagle Unbowed*, London, 2012

Kocot, Władysław, *Pamiętniki i korespondencja z lat 1920, 1939–1945* (*Diaries and Letters from 1920, 1939–1945*), Pułtusk, 2009

Kort, Michael, *The Soviet Colossus: History and Aftermath*, New York, 2001

Kownacki, Andrzej, *Czy było warto?: Wspomnienia (Was it Worth It?: A Memoir)*, Lublin, 2000

Kravkov, Vasily Pavlovich, *Velikaya voina bez retushi: Zapiski korpusnogo vracha (The Great War: Notes of an Army Corps Doctor)*, Moscow, 2014

Krol, Moisei Aaronovich, *Stranicy moej zhizni (Pages of My Life)*, Moscow, 1971

Kvakin A. (ed.) *Za spinoi Kolchaka (Behind Kolchak's Back)*, Moscow, 2005

Kuras, L.V., 'Ataman Semenov and the National Military Formations of Buriat', in *The Journal of Slavic Military Studies*, 10(4) (December 1997)

Kuzmin, S. (ed.), *Baron Ungern v dokumentakh i materialakh (Baron Ungern: Documents and Materials)*, Moscow, 2004

Landis, Eric-C., 'A Civil War Episode – General Mamontov in Tambov, August 1919', in Carl Beck Papers in Russian and East European Studies, Pittsburgh, 2002

Legras J., *Mémoires de Russie*, Paris, 1921

Leggett, George, *Cheka*, Oxford, 1981

Lehovich, Dimitry, *White Against Red: The Life of Gen. Anton Denikin*, New York, 1974

Leidinger, Hannes, 'Habsburgs ferner Spiegel', *Zeit Österreich*, 46/2017 (9 Nov 2017)

Lenin, V.I., *Collected Works*, 45 vols, Moscow, 1960–70

Lepecki, Mieczysław, *W blaskach wojny. Wspomnienia z wojny polsko-bolszewickiej (The Glory of War: A Memoir from the Polish-Bolshevik War)*, Łomianki, 2017

Levshin, Konstantin, *Dezertirstvo v krasnoi armii v gody grazh-danskoi voiny (Desertion from the Red Army during the Civil War)*, Moscow, 2016

Lieven, Dominic, *Towards the Flame: Empire, War and the end of Tsarist Russia*, London 2015

Lin, Yuexin Rachel, 'White Water, Red Tide: Sino-Russian Conflict on the Amur, 1917–20', Oxford, IHR, 2017

Lincoln, W. Bruce, *Red Victory: A History of the Russian Civil War*, New York, 1989

—— *Passage through Armageddon: The Russians in War and Revolution*, Oxford, 1994

Lindenmeyr, Adele, Read, Christopher and Waldron, Peter (eds), *Russia's Home Front in War and Revolution, 1914–22*, Vol. 2, *The Experience of War and Revolution*, Bloomington, IN, 2016

Lockart, R.H. Bruce, *Memoirs of a British Agent*, London, 1932

Lokhvitskaya, Nadezhda (see Teffi)

Luckett, Richard, *The White Generals: An Account of the White Movement and the Russian Civil War*, New York, 1971

Lukin, Alexander, *The Bear Watches the Dragon*, New York, 2003

Lukomskii (Lukomsky), A.S., *Memoirs of the Russian Revolution*, London, 1922

Maciejewski, Jerzyf Konrad, *Zawadiaka: Dzienniki frontowe 1914–1920 (The Daredevil: A Journal from the Front 1914–1920)*, Warsaw, 2015

Macmillan, Margaret, *Peacemakers: The Paris Conference of 1919 and Its Attempt to End War*, London, 2001

Makarov, Pavel, *Adjutant generala Mai-Maevskogo (Aide-de-Camp of General Mai-Maevsky)*, Leningrad, 1929

Malet, M., *Nestor Makhno in the Russian Civil War*, London, 1982

Marie, Jean-Jacques, *La Guerre des Russes blancs*, Paris, 2017

Markovitch, Marylie (Amélie Néry), *La Révolution russe vue par une Française*, Paris, 2017

Mawdsley, Evan, *The Russian Revolution and the Baltic Fleet: War and Politics, February 1917–April 1918*, London, 1978

—— *The Russian Civil War*, London, 1987

Maximoff, Gregory Petrovich, *The Guillotine at Work*, Chicago, IL, 1940

Mayer, A.J., *Politics and Diplomacy of Peacemaking: Containment and Counter-revolution at Versailles 1918–1919*, London, 1963

McCullagh, Francis, *A Prisoner of the Reds*, London, 1921

McMeekin, Sean, *The Russian Revolution*, London, 2018

Melgunov, Sergei P., *Red Terror in Russia, 1918–1923*, London, 1925

Melvin, Mungo, *Sevastopol's Wars*, Oxford, 2017

Merridale, Catherine, *Lenin on the Train*, London, 2016

Mitrokhin, Vasily (ed.), *'Chekisms': A KGB Anthology*, London, 2008

Mogilyansky, Nikolai, in Syrtsov, B. (ed), *Kiev 1918*, Moscow, 2001

Moynahan, Brian, *Comrades: 1917 – Russia in Revolution*, London, 1992

Nabokov, Vladimir, *Speak, Memory: An Autobiography Revisited*, London, 1969

Naval Review, 'The Royal Navy on the Caspian', 8(1) (February 1920)

Nazhivin, Ivan, *Zapiski o revolyutsii (Notes on the Revolution)*, Moscow, 2016

Norris, D., 'Caspian Naval Expedition 1918–1919', *Journal of the Central Asian Society*, 10(1923), pp. 216–40

Nowik, Grzegorz, *Zanim złamano „Enigmę"; Rozszyfrowano rewolucję. Polski radiowywiad podczas wojny z bolszewicką Rosją 1918–1920 (Before the Enigma was Solved, the Revolution was Decoded: Polish Radio Intelligence During the War against Bolshevik Russia)*, Vol. 2, Warsaw, 2010

O niepodległą i granice. Komunikaty Oddziału III Naczelnego Dowództwa Wojska Polskiego 1919–1921 (Communications of the III Bureau Supreme Command Polish Army), Warsaw-Pułtusk, 1999

Official History: *Operations in Persia 1914–1919*, London, 1987

Oreshnikov, Aleksei, *Dvevnik, 1915–1933 (Diaries 1915–1933)*, Moscow, 2010

Palij, Michael, *The Anarchism of Nestor Machno 1918–1920*, Seattle, WA, 1976

Palmer, James, *The Bloody White Baron*, London, 2008

Pares, Bernard, *My Russian Memoirs*, London, 1931

Paustovsky, Konstantin, *The Story of a Life*, New York, 1964

Philips Price, Morgan, *My Reminiscences of the Russian Revolution*, London 1921

Picher, Harvey (ed.), *Witnesses of the Russian Revolution*, London, 2001

Pipes, Richard, *The Formation of the Soviet Union – Communism and Nationalism, 1917–1923*, Cambridge, MA, 1964

—— *The Russian Revolution 1899–1919*, London, 1990

—— *Russia under the Old Regime*, London, 1995

—— *Russia under the Bolshevik Regime*, New York, 1995

Pisarenko Dmitry, *Terskoe kazachestvo. Tri goda revolyutsii i borby 1917–1920 (The Terek Cossacks, Three Years of Revolution and Struggle)*, Moscow, 2016

Polonsky, Rachel, *Molotov's Magic Lantern: A Journey in Russian*

History, London, 2010

Polovtsov, Pyotr, *Dni zatmeniya (Days of the Eclipse)*, Moscow, 2016

—— *Russia Under the Bolshevik Regime 1919–1924*, London, 1994

Porter, Cathy, *Larissa Reisner*, London, 1988

Posadsky, A., *Ot Tsaritsyna do Syzrani (From Tsaritsyn to Syzran)*, Moscow, 2010

Posadsky, A. (ed.), *Krestyansky front, 1918–1922 (The Peasant Front 1918–1922)*, Moscow, 2013

Prishvin, Mikhail, *Dnevniki*, St Petersburg, 2008

Prokoviev, Sergei, *Dnevnik*, Moscow, 2002

Protokoly zasedaniy Soveta narodnykh komissarov RSFSR, Noyabr 1917–Mart 1918, Moscow, 2006

Puchenkov, A.S. *Ukraina i Krym v 1918–nachale 1919 goda (Ukraine and Crimea in 1918 and early 1919)*, St Petersburg, 2013

Rabinowitch, Alexander, *The Bolsheviks Come to Power, The Revolution of 1917 in Petrograd*, New York, 2004

Rakovsky, G.N., *V stane belykh (In the White Camp)*, Constantinople, 1920, http://www.dk1868.ru/history/rakovs-kiy_plan.htm

Raleigh, Donald J. (ed.), *A Russian Civil War Diary, Alexis Babine in Saratov, 1917–1922*, Durham, NC, 1988

Ransome, Arthur, *The Autobiography of Arthur Ransome*, London, 1976

Rapoport, Vitaly and Alexeev, Yuri, *High Treason, Essays on the History of the Red Army 1918–1938*, Durham, NC, 1985

Rappaport, Helen, *Caught in the Revolution*, London, 2016

—— *Ekaterinburg*, London, 2009

Raskolnikov, Fyodor, *Rasskazy Michmana Ilina (Stories by Midshipman Ilin)*, Moscow, 1934

—— *Kronshtadt i Piter v 1917 godu*, Moscow, 2017 (*Kronstadt and Petrograd in 1917*), London, 1982

Rayfield, Donald, *Stalin and his Hangmen*, London 2004

Read, Anthony, *The World on Fire: 1919 and the Battle with Bolshevism*, London, 2008

Reed, John, *Ten Days that Shook the World*, New York, 1919

Retish, Aaron B., 'Breaking Free from the Prison Walls: Penal Reforms and Prison Life in Revolutionary Russia', Wayne State University, IHR, 2017

Rigby, T.H., *Lenin's Government: Sovnarkom, 1917–1922*, Cambridge, 1979

Rimsky-Korsakov, G.A., *Rossiya 1917 v ego-dokumentakh* (*1917: Russia in Personal Documents*), Moscow, 2015

Robien, Comte Louis de, *Journal d'un diplomate en Russie 1917–1918*, Paris, 1967

Robinson, Paul, *The White Russian Army in Exile, 1920–1941*, Oxford, 2002

Rolland, Jacques-Francis, *L'homme qui défia Lénine: Boris Savinkov*, Paris, 1989

Ross, Nicolas, *La Crimée blanche du général Wrangel*, Geneva, 2010

Ruthchild, Rochelle Goldberg, 'Women and Gender in 1917', *Slavic Review*, 76(3) (Fall 2017), pp. 694–702

Savchenko Ilya *V krasnom stane. Zelyonaya Kuban. 1919* (*In the Red Camp. In the Green Kuban*), Moscow, 2016

Schmid, A.P., *Churchills privater Krieg, Intervention und Konterrevolution im russischen Bürgerkrieg 1918–1920* (*Churchill's Private War, Intervention and Counter-revolution in the Russian Civil War*), Freiburg, 1974

Schneer, Jonathan, *The Lockhart Plot*, Oxford, 2020

Seaton, A. and Seaton, J., *The Soviet Army: 1918 to the Present*, New York, 1987

Sebestyen, Victor, *Lenin the Dictator*, London, 2017

Semyonov, Ataman Grigory, *O sebe: vospominaniya, mysli i vyvody* (*About Myself: Memoirs, Thoughts and Conclusions, 1904–1921*), Moscow, 2002

Serge, Victor, *Memoirs of a Revolutionary*, New York, 2012
—— *Year One of the Russian Revolution*, Chicago, 2015

Seruga, J., *Udział radiostacji warszawskiej w bitwie o Warszawę w 1920 r.* (*The Role of the Warsaw Radio Station in the Battle of Warsaw in 1920*) , Vol. 17, Part 1, Warsaw, 1925

Service, Robert, *Lenin: A Biography*, London, 2000
—— *Stalin: A Biography*, London, 2004

Shaiditsky, V.I., 'Serving the Motherland', in Kuzmin, S. (ed.), *Baron Ungern v dokumentakh i materialakh* (*Baron Ungern: Documents and Materials*), Moscow, 2004

Shipitsyn, Fyodor, 'V Odnom Stroyu' ('In the Same Ranks'), in *V*

Boyakh I Pokhodakh (*In Battles and on the March*), Sverdlovsk, 1959

Shklovsky, Viktor, *A Sentimental Journey: Memoirs 1917–1922*, Ithaca, NY, 1984

Shmelev, Anatol, 'The Revolution Turns Eighty: New Literature on the Russian Revolution and its Aftermath', *Contemporary European History*, 8(1) (1999), Cambridge

—— 'The Allies in Russia 1917–20: Intervention as Seen by the Whites', in *Revolutionary Russia*, 16(1) (June 2003), pp. 87–107

—— *Vneshnyaya politika pravitelstva Admirala Kolchaka, 1918–1919* (*The Foreign Policy of the Government of Admiral Kolchak, 1918–1919*), Saint Petersburg, 2017

Shukman, Harold, *The Russian Revolution*, Stroud, 1998

Shulgin, V.V., *Days of the Russian Revolution: Memoirs from the Right, 1905–1917*, Gulf Breeze, FL, 1990

—— *1920 god*, Moscow, 2016

Slyusarenko, Vladimir, *Na mirovoi voine, v Dobrovolcheskoi armii i emigratsii* (*In the World War: In the Volunteer Army and Emigration*), Moscow, 2016

Smele, Jonathan, *The 'Russian' Civil Wars 1916–1926: Ten Years that Shook the World*, London, 2016

—— *Civil War in Siberia: The anti-Bolshevik Government of Admiral Kolchak, 1918–1920*, Cambridge, 1997

Smith, Douglas, *Former People: The Last Days of the Russian Aristocracy*, New York, 2012

Smith, S.A., *Russia in Revolution: An Empire in Crisis*, Oxford, 2017

Sollohub, Edith, *The Russian Countess*, Exeter, 2009

Somin, Ilya, *Stillborn Crusade: The Tragic Failure of Western Intervention in the Russian Civil War, 1918–20*, New York 1996

Stefanovich, P., 'The First Victims of the Bolshevik Mass Terror', in Syrtsov (ed.), *Kiev, 1918*, Moscow, 2001

Steinberg, Mark D., *Voices of Revolution 1917*, New Haven, CT and London, 2001

Stewart, George, *The White Armies of Russia*, New York, 1933

Stoff, Lurie S., Heywood, Anthony J., Kolonitskii, Boris I. and Steinberg, John W. (eds), *Military Affairs in Russia's Great War and Revolution, 1914–1922*, Bloomington, IN, 2019

Stone, David R., *The Russian Army in the Great War: The Eastern Front 1914–1917*, Lawrence, KS, 2015

Stone, Norman, *The Eastern Front, 1914–1917*, London, 1975

Sukhanov, N.N., *The Russian Revolution 1917: A Personal Record*, Oxford, 1953

Sunderland, Willard, *The Baron's Cloak: A History of the Russian Empire in War and Revolution*, Ithaca, NY, 2014

Suny, Ronald G., *The Baku Commune: 1917–1918: Class and Nationality in the Russian Revolution*, Princeton, NJ, 1972.

Surzhikova, N.V., et al. (eds), *Rossiya, 1917 v ego-dokumentakh* (*Russia 1917: Personal Accounts*), Moscow, 2015

Syrtsov, B. (ed), *Kiev 1918*, Moscow, 2001

Svertsev, Andrei, 'Tragedy of a Russian Bonaparte', *Russkiy Mir*, 16/4/2013

Tarasov, Konstantin, *Soldatskii bolshevism* (*Soldiers' Bolshevism*), St Petersburg, 2017

Teague-Jones, Reginald, *The Spy who Disappeared: Diary of a Secret Mission to Russian Central Asia in 1918*, London, 1990

Teffi (Nadezhda Lokhvitskaya), *Memories: From Moscow to the Black Sea*, London, 2016

—— *Rasputin and Other Ironies*, London, 2016

Ter Minassian, Taline, *Reginald Teague-Jones: Au service secret de l'empire britannique*, Paris, 2014

Trotsky, Leon, *History of the Russian Revolution*, London, 2017

Trushnovich, Aleksandr, *Vospominaniya Kornilovtsa 1914–1934* (*Memoirs of a Kornilov Man*), Moscow and Frankfurt, 2004

Tsvetaeva, Marina, *Earthly Signs: Moscow Diaries 1917–1922*, New Haven, CT and London, 2002

Ulanovskaya, Nadezhda and Ulanovskaya, Maya, *Istoriya odnoi sem'i* (*One Family's History*), St Petersburg, 2003

Ullman, Richard H., *Anglo-Soviet Relations 1917–21*, 3 vols, Princeton, N.J., 1961–1973

Ustinov, S.M., *Zapiski nachĕal'nika kontr-razveĕdki: 1915–1920 g.* (*Notes of a Counter-Intelligence Chief, 1915–1920*), Rostov, 1990

Vanderbilt Balsan, Consuelo, *The Glitter and the Gold*, Maidstone, 1973

Verkhovsky, Aleksandr, *Rossiya na Golgofe* (*Russia on Golgotha*), Moscow, 2014

Vertinsky, Aleksandr, *Dorogoi dlinnoyu* (*The Long Road*), Moscow, 2012

Von Hagen, Mark, *Soldiers in the Proletarian Dictatorship*, Ithaca, NY, 1990

Ward, John, *With the Die-Hards in Siberia*, London, 1920

Wędziagolski, Karol, *Boris Savinkov: Portrait of a Terrorist*, Twickenham, 1988

Werth, Nicholas, 'Crimes and Mass Violence of the Russian Civil Wars, 1918–1921', Sciences Po, Paris, 2008

Wheeler-Bennett, J.W., *Brest-Litovsk, The Forgotten Peace, March 1918*, London, 1966

Wildman, Allan K., *The End of the Russian Imperial Army, The Old Army and the Soldiers' Revolt (March–April 1917)*, Vol. 1, Princeton, NJ, 1980

—— *The End of the Russian Imperial Army, The Road to Soviet Power and Peace*, Vol. 2, Princeton, NJ, 1987

Woodward, E.L. and Butler, R., *Documents on British Foreign Policy 1919–1939*, First Series, Vol. 2, London, 1949

Wrangel, Baron Peter, *Always with Honour*, New York, 1957

Wurzer, Georg, *Die Kriegsgefangenen der Mittelmächte in Russland im Ersten Weltkrieg* (*The Prisoners of War from the Central Powers in Russia during the First World War*), Vienna, 2005

Youssoupoff, Prince Félix, *L'homme qui tua Raspoutine*, Monaco, 2005

Youzefovitch, Leonide, *Le Baron Ungern, khan des steppes*, Paris, 2001

Żeligowski, Lucjan, *Wojna 1920 roku. Wspomnienia i rozważania* (*The War of 1920: Memoirs and Reflections*), Warsaw, 1990

Zenzinov, Vladimir, *Iz zhizni revolyutsionera* (*From the Life of a Revolutionary*), Paris, 1919

Zürrer, Werner, *Kaukasien 1918–1921, Der Kampf der Grossmächte um die Landbrücke zwischen Schwarzem und Kaspischem Meer* (*The Caucasus 1918–1921: War between the Great Powers in the Land Bridge between the Black Sea and Caspian*), Düsseldorf, 1978

FICTION

Ageyev, M., *Novel with Cocaine*, London, 1999

Babel, Isaac, *Red Cavalry*, London, 2014

Bulgakov, Mikhail, *White Guard*, London, 2016

Grey, Marina, *La Campagne de Glace*, Paris, 1978

Harris, John, *Light Cavalry Action*, London, 1967

Krasnov, P., *From the Double-Headed Eagle to the Red Banner*, 2
    vols, New York, 1926

Pasternak, Boris, *Doctor Zhivago*, London, 1958

Serge, Victor, *Conquered City*, London, 1976

—— *Birth of our Power*, New York, 1967

—— *Midnight in the Century*, London, 1982

Sholokov, Mikhail, *Quiet Don*, London, 2017

Solzhenitsyn, Aleksandr, *Lenin in Zurich,* New York, 1977

Yourcenar, Marguerite, *Le Coup de Grâce*, Paris, 1939

INDEX

Page numbers in italics refer to illustrations